D0988959

The Gilled Mushrooms (Agaricaceae) of Michigan and the Great Lakes Region

ELIAS MAGNUS FRIES

The Gilled Mushrooms (Agaricaceae) of Michigan and the Great Lakes Region

C. H. KAUFFMAN

IN TWO VOLUMES

VOLUME ONE

DOVER PUBLICATIONS, INC.

NEW YORK

Published in Canada by General Publishing Company, Ltd.,
30 Lesmill Road, Don Mills, Toronto, Ontario.
Published in the United Kingdom by Constable and Company,
Ltd., 10 Orange Street, London WC 2.

This Dover edition, first published in 1971, is an unabridged
republication of the work originally published in 1918 by the
Wynkoop Hallenbeck Crawford Company for the Michigan
Geological and Biological Survey as Publication 26 of Biological
Series 5 under the title *The Agaricaceae of Michigan*.
In the original edition, the first volume contained the complete
text and the second volume contained all 172 plates; in the
present reprint, each volume contains approximately half of the
text together with the corresponding plates.
The publisher gratefully acknowledges the cooperation of The
Milton S. Eisenhower Library of The Johns Hopkins University,
which supplied a copy of this work for the purpose of
reproduction.

International Standard Book Number: 0-486-22396-5
Library of Congress Catalog Card Number: 74-142877

Manufactured in the United States of America
Dover Publications, Inc.
180 Varick Street
New York, N. Y. 10014

LETTERS OF TRANSMITTAL.

To the Honorable the Board of Geological and Biological Survey of the State of Michigan:

Gov. Albert E. Sleeper.
Hon. Frank L. Cody.
Hon. Fred L. Keeler.

Gentlemen:—I have the honor to transmit herewith the manuscript and illustrations of a treatise on the Agaricaceae of Michigan by Dr. C. H. Kauffman with the recommendation that it be printed and bound as Publication 26, Biological Series 5, in two volumes.

Respectfully yours,

R. C. ALLEN,

Lansing, Michigan, February 10, 1918.   *Director.*

Ann Arbor, Michigan,

Sir:—I submit herewith a monographic report on the Agaricaceae of Michigan by Dr. C. H. Kauffman. This monograph is the result of field and laboratory studies made by Dr. Kauffman during the past ten years, and its object is to summarize what is known of the occurrence and characteristics of the species which have been found in the State. It should be of service to students and teachers of botany, to mycologists, and to persons interested in fungi as food. The report is to be considered as an addition to the series of monographs on Michigan plants and animals which the Survey is having prepared.

Very respectfully,

ALEXANDER G. RUTHVEN,

Chief Naturalist.

R. C. ALLEN, Director,
Michigan Geological and Biological Survey.

PREFACE

This report is the result of a series of surveys initiated in the summer of 1906. During that season the shore of Lake Superior was visited at six points: Sault Ste. Marie, Munising, Marquette, Huron Mountain, Houghton and Isle Royale at Washington Island. In the summer of 1905 the region around Bay View in Emmet County was well covered in an independent study and these results are also incorporated. During 1907, 1908 and 1909, the flora of Ann Arbor, Jackson, Detroit and neighboring regions was studied. In 1910, 1911, 1912 and 1913, portions of the summers were spent at New Richmond, Allegan County. Brief trips were made to other points in the State; to Negaunee, Alpena, South Haven, etc, but due to dryness or to the time of year, comparatively little material was obtained. At all these places a considerable area was covered so as to include all possible habitats.

The purpose of the report is primarily to afford the people of Michigan a comprehensive account of the Agaric flora of the State. The extended study necessary to determine the material soon showed the need of critical notes for many species. Hence the report has developed into a manual of considerable size since it seemed worth while to include a large amount of general as well as scientific information, such as is widely scattered in books and journals and is not accessible to most readers. There resulted a two-fold arrangement of the commentary under the different species: first, an effort to simplify the identification of a species through suggestive comparisons and data of interest not given in the formal descriptions; second, critical discussions, from a more purely scientific standpoint, intended for advanced students and mycologists. Many species, especially those of small size and for which a microscope is essential for identification, have been discussed in the notes solely for the specialist. But every effort has been made to clarify the descriptions of the larger mushrooms to the advantage of the beginner.

All descriptions of species not in quotation marks were drawn from fresh plants collected in most cases by myself or sent to me immediately after picking. *The reported spore-measurements of all such,* except a few where noted, *have been made by me* and all errors are therefore to be laid at my door; the same is true of the other microscopical details. Outside of the list of species reported by Longyear, nearly all of which I have collected also, few Mich-igan species which I have not seen in fresh condition have been included. It seemed safer not to rely on oral information as to the occurrence of a particular species. All available literature was used in the final determinations and the fresh specimens were com-pared carefully with the original descriptions of Peck and with those discussed in the works of Fries and many other mycologists. Most of the important works were taken along wherever collecting was done away from Ann Arbor, and besides this full descriptions and notes were written on the day on which the specimens were found. Usually sketches or colored drawings were also made of the fresh plants. In many cases photographs were obtained al-though this was not always feasible. The microscope was con-stantly at hand and spore-measurements were made on the day of collecting.

The descriptions of many authors are often very incomplete. Spore-size, presence or absence of cystidia, odor, taste, width or closeness of gills, and many other characters are often lacking. An attempt has been made to complete all descriptions so that the student may have a means to make full comparisons between species of a genus. I have found it very discouraging at times to find the one decisive character in a description lacking; in such cases it often becomes necessary to look through many books for the in-formation wanted. No one can be more fully aware than I of the pitfalls lurking in such an attempt to emend the traditional descriptions. It seemed to me, however, that the errors which may have resulted from a wrong interpretation of some species were far outweighed by the information added to the many others. The principal claim for the descriptions is that they are relatively com-plete and accurate for the plants found in Michigan and that they were drawn from fresh material.

The work on the genus Coprinus has been done by Dr. L. H. Pennington for which I make grateful acknowledgment. That this difficult genus has been properly represented is entirely due to his efforts. Many of the species were cultivated by him in the laboratory and are strikingly shown in his photographs. The work was started while Dr. Pennington was still at the University of Michigan.

The genus Cortinarius has been included in the form of a pre-liminary monograph of the species of the eastern United States.

Experience has shown that it is scarcely wise at present to refer more than a few to synonomy because of the large number of species. Hence I have included the descriptions of those American species which I have not yet seen, placing them in quotations. The species found in the State can be easily separated by the locality given.

Throughout the work on this report I have been indebted to many individuals for help in identification, for specimens and for sympathy and encouragement. From Dr. Charles H. Peck who has so long held out a helping hand to beginner and specialist alike, I have received abundant and unstinted help. To Professor Geo. F. Atkinson I owe the foundation which has made the work possible. For their many favors I am deeply grateful. For material and suggestions I am also indebted to Dr. W. G. Farlow, Dr. R. A. Harper, Dr. C. E. Bessey, Dr. L. H. Pennington, Dr. L. L. Hubbard, Lars Romell and a number of others. To Dr. O. E. Fischer and Mrs. T. A. Cahn of the Detroit Institute of Science I am much indebted for abundant and excellent specimens, and especially to Dr. Fischer for the use of some photographs and for the chapter on Toxicology. Miss Rose Taylor made many collections at Negaunee.

I also wish to thank here those of my colleagues of the various departments of the University for their sympathy and interest and especially those officials who have so generously supplied the University library with the necessary books and plates for the special purpose of furthering this study; and also the staff of the Geological and Biological Survey, especially Dr. A. G. Ruthven, for their patience and encouragement during the long drawn out progress of the work. Grateful recognition is due to my wife for a helping hand in much of the detail work in caring for material, assistance in collecting and in the reading of the manuscript.

The photographs were taken and prepared throughout by myself except those obtained from Dr. Fischer. An effort was made to illustrate as many as possible of the plants not before illustrated. For all other plants full sets of references will provide the student with the means of comparison.

Cryptogamic Herbarium, University of Michigan, April 1, 1915.

TABLE OF CONTENTS

[Vol. I contains pages 1-442; Vol. II contains pages 442-924.]

TABLE OF CONTENTS xxiii

LIST OF ILLUSTRATIONS

FIGURES

PLATES

[Vol. I contains Plates I-XC; Vol. II contains Plates XCI-CLXII.]

THE AGARICACEAE OF MICHIGAN

C. H. KAUFFMAN

GENERAL INTRODUCTION

An Agaric is a plant which, considered morphologically and physiologically, is composed of two portions: the vegetative, called the *mycelium*; the reproductive, called the *fruit-body* or *carpophore*.

The Mycelium

When a spore, derived from the gills of a fruit-body, germinates it forms a protuberance on one or more sides; this elongates into the form of a filament, always growing at the apex and usually branching abundantly, so that finally a weft or mass of such becomes visible, even to the naked eye. The filaments thus formed are referred to as *hyphae,* or collectively as *mycelium*. In diameter they vary from 3 to 6 thousandths of a millimetre and singly can be seen only with the microscope. Cross-partitions are numerous and the separate divisions are the ultimate units of structure, i. e., the cells. Such mycelium is widely distributed in the soil, humus, decaying wood, etc., and once established is doubtless perennial, so that new supplies from spores are probably less common than ordinarily supposed. It absorbs its food directly through the delicate cell-walls and the interior of each cell is thoroughly saturated with water. It appears capable of withstanding considerable drying, perhaps for long periods, reviving and renewing its growth after receiving a new supply of moisture. In some cases the mycelium twines itself into strands which become dark colored and tough and which are spoken of as *rhizomorphs*; or minute tuber-like masses may be formed, termed *sclerotia*. These evidently also serve as a resting stage during dry weather. The mycelium is usually hyaline under the microscope, but massed together appears whitish to the eye; it may also have other colors, green, blue, red, yellow, etc., but these are not very common. When growing luxuriantly in artificial beds of manure it becomes the "spawn" of commercial mushroom growers. Methods are now in use in laboratories, by which many kinds of spores are germinated and the mycelium grown in pure cultures; the "spawn" obtained in this way is called "pure culture spawn."

The distribution of the mycelium in an undisturbed soil, as for example, in a park, lawn, fallow field, roadside or in woods, may be considerable, extending underground for rods, so that the size of the plant in the vegetative stage, in a linear sense, is quite large. Under such permanent conditions, quite a number of species form "fairy rings" when they fruit. The mycelium is started at one point and if the soil is favorably homogeneous in every direction, growth continues radially from the original point and at the circumference of this patch of mycelium, where growth activity is greatest, the fruit-bodies appear each year. In one case a "ring" with a diameter of 65 feet was observed by MacQuan in Africa. (Grevillea, 1880-1881.) The appearance of the fruit-bodies of some species "in troops" is usually due to the fact that only one arc of the circle is left. In the forest, obstacles are too numerous so that the "ring" does not remain perfect and the fruit-bodies appear scattered promiscuously. Observations made in a clean forest in Europe for a period of ten years showed that the "ring" of some forest species traveled radially for several rods but the periphery at length became obscure. The mycelium of many species doubtless is more affected by irregularities in the food supply and hence grows in an unequal manner, or produces such few fruit-bodies that the radial growth does not show. Doubtless also where there are scores of different kinds growing in a small area they intertwine or interfere with each other. During continued wet weather the compressed masses of fallen leaves in frondose woods are often found to harbor patches or sheets of mycelium of many species, which are easily observed by removing the top layers of leaves and which are a forerunner of a good crop of fruit-bodies if the humidity is maintained. Curious sheets of mycelium, of the appearance of sheets of paper, are sometimes found between planks or other piled up lumber, but these usually belong to the Polypore group of fungi.

The Fruit Body

The fruit-body, or carpophore, is the portion popularly referred to as *the mushroom*, but it must be remembered that it is only a temporary product of the plant as a whole, just as is the apple of the tree which bears it. It is usually composed of the *pileus* or cap, *lamellae* or gills, and a *stipe* or stem; in the genera Amanita, Amanitopsis and Volvaria there is present in addition a *universal veil* which breaks away and forms a volva on the stem. In Amanita, Lepiota, Armillaria, Pholiota, Cortinarius, Stropharia, Chamaeota and slightly in a few other genera, there is found a *partial veil,* which on breaking away may form an *annulus* in some of these. For details see the introduction to these genera. The essential parts are the *gills* and *pileus* and these are present in every species described in this book; the stem, however, is also usually present and such a fruit-body is a typical Agaric. The tissue of the fruit-body is primarily an aggregation of hyphae, and hence merely an extension of the mycelium, compacted to form a specialized structure. When a portion of the pileus is cut radially, or of the stem longitudinally, and magnified with the microscope, it is seen that these are merely masses of parallel or interwoven hyphae composed of cells, very similar to those of the mycelium. Some of it is specialized to be sure, as is the cuticle of the pileus or stem; sometimes portions are gelatinous, others hardened or encrusted, but this is more evident in the mature plant. The tiny beginnings of the mushroom are composed of much the same kind of hyphae throughout.

The Pileus

The pileus is essential in that it bears the gills. There are only a few known species in which the gills radiate out from the top of the stem minus any cap, and these constitute the rare genus Montagnites, none of which are known in our state. The principal parts of the pileus are the surface layer, the margin, and the flesh or *trama*. For the many variations of the structure and form of these it is necessary to consult the glossary. (See also Fig. 1.) The trama may however, be briefly considered: in the young, fresh or actively developing fruit-body the hyphae of the trama are usually compact and appear like actual filaments, but as it approaches maturity the hyphae varies. In some, e. g., Coprini, the cells of the hyphae quickly loosen from each other and become rounded, and the whole pileus, if not quickly dried by the wind, collapses. Others are less evanescent and in these the tramal hyphae, although loosened considerably, support the pileus for some days. Many of the larger forms, e. g., Tricholomas, retain their compact form for a long time, and in tough species like Lentinus the hyphae of the trama appear to retain their close-lying position unchanged. The trama of the Lactariae is unique and is described under that group. Many of the smaller Agarics like Mycenas and Galeras have comparatively few layers of hyphae, often of very large cells.

Figure 1.—Structure of Agarics: (1) Gills free; (2) Gills adnate; (3) Gills decurrent; (4) Gills adnexed; (5) Gills seceding; (6) Gills emarginate and uncinate; (7) Pileus convex; (8) Pileus conical; (9) Pileus campanulate.

The Gills

Underneath the pileus the gills are attached in the form of knife-blades collectively called the *hymenophore*. Gravity appears to be responsible for their position on the lower side. Rarely one finds an outgrowth of an abnormal character on the top of the pileus, sometimes in the form of a second mushroom of the same kind with or without a stem, sometimes with the gills growing upward from a small area of the main cap. The latter case has never been satisfactorily explained. The gills are of course attached all along their thicker edge to the pileus. They may be attached to the stem at their inner end, also called the posterior end or base; or they may be free, i. e., not reaching the stem or at least not attached. The manner of attachment is shown in Fig. 1, 1-6, as adnexed, adnate or decurrent. These are important characters for the separation of genera. In some cases all the gills extend from the margin of the pileus to the stem, in many, however, they are dimidiate or with very short gills at the margin of the pileus. The spacing of the gills is quite important, but considerable variation occurs in the same species; only relative terms seem usable: crowded, close, subdistant and distant. The same may be said of their width.

It is very important to understand their structure. Here a microscope is necessary. A section cut tangentially across the pileus and gills will show a good view of the appearance of the trama, etc., of each lamella. The interior is again composed of hyphae and in such a section they lie either parallel, converging along the median axis, diverging, or interwoven irregularly. In all cases this is the gill-trama and is bordered by the hymenium.

The Hymenium   (See Fig. 2, 1.)

The border which extends over the whole surface on both sides of the gills is the hymenium. While the hyphae may lie in a general way parallel to the axis of our section, the large club-shaped cells which form the border extend outward at right angles to this axis and form a sort of nap like that of a Brussel's carpet. These large cells are the *basidia*, (singular, *basidium*), and at its apex, as seen in the figure, each basidium bears typically four *spores;* rarely it may develop only two spores or even three. Each spore is attached by a minute stalk called the *sterigma*, (plural, *sterigmata*). The basidia are in turn continuations of the hyphal filaments which compose the trama of the gills. Often there is a slight specialization

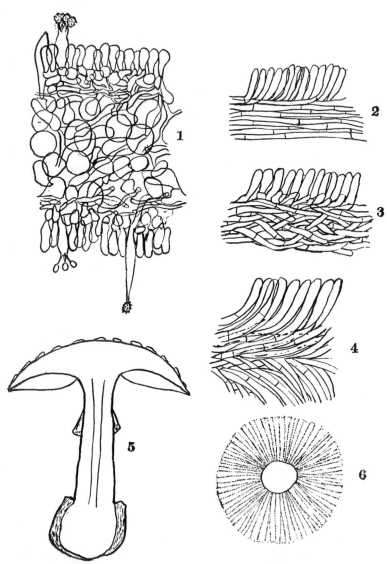

Figure 2.—Structure of Agarics: (1) Vesicular trama of a section through a gill of a Russula, showing also the hymenium, basidia, and a cystidium (adapted from Fayod); (2) Parallel gill-trama-diagramatic;   (3) Interwoven gill-trama diagramatic;   (4) Divergent gill-trama diagramatic;   (5)Section of Amanita, showing volva, annullus and scales on the pileus.

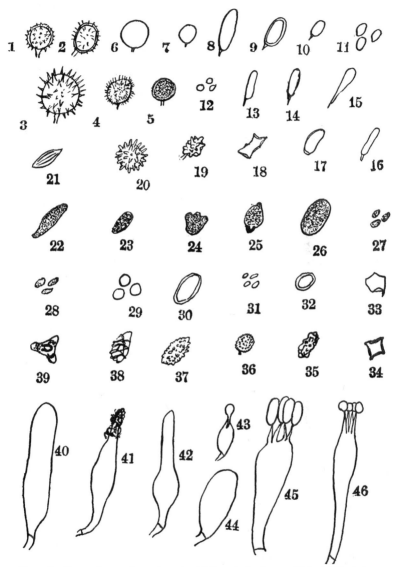

Figure 3.—Types of spores drawn to scale: (1) Russula decolorans; (2) Lactarius nigricans; (3) Lactarius tortilis; (4) Inocybe galliardi; (5) Coprinus sp.; (6) Amanita porphyria; (7) Trichloma laterarium; (8) Amanita peckianium; (9) Lepiota procera; (10) Lepiota naucina; (11) Tricholoma equestre; (12) Tricholoma nobile; (13) Cantherellus clavatus; (14) Hygrophorus subborealis; (15) Marasmius sicus; (16) Inocybe infelix; (17) Inocybe caesariata; (18) Inocybe decipientoides; (19) Inocybe leptophylla; (20) Inocybe calospora; (21) Clitopilus prunulus; (22) Gomphidius maculatus; (23) Coprinus atramentarius; (24) Coprinus boudieri; (25) Hypholoma rugocephalum; (26) Coprinus sterquillinus; (27) Hypholoma hydrophilum; (28) Psalliota arvensis; (29) Cropidotus putrigenus; (30) Pluteolus coprophilus; (31) Pholiota flammans; (32) Plueteus cervinus; (33) Entoloma clypeatum; (34) Entoloma cuspicatum; (35) Noleana dystales; (36) Cortinarius annulatus; (37) Cortinarius atkinsonianus; (38) type of reticulated spore; (39) Heliomyces nigripes; (40-44) Cystidia; (45-46) Basidia.

of the hyphae just inside the hymenial layer termed the *sub-hymenium*.

The hymenium may include, along with the basidia, cells of other shapes or functions; the *cystidia* (singular, *cystidium*), (see Fig. 3, 40-44) are elongated, cells fusiform, lanceolate or have various shapes according to the species, and project at maturity above the basidia. Their function apparently is to aid in the exudation of water from the plants. (F. Knoll, Jahrb. Vol. 50, p. 453.) The presence or absence of *cystidia* is much used to identify certain species. The observations must be carefully made, however, since they quickly collapse at maturity in some cases, and in others do not elongate until full maturity of the mushroom. They occur more or less scattered over the surface of the gills and are often tipped with oxalate of lime crystals. Also, they may occur on the edge of the gills and give this a minutely flocculose or fimbriate appearance. More frequently the edge is provided with elongated *sterile cells* of various shapes which produce the same effect as cystidia. In this work these are the only "sterile cells" referred to in the descriptions.

The spores vary in size, shape, color, structure of surface, etc.. and are fully discussed under each group. (See Fig. 3, 1-34.)

The *stem, volva* and *annulus* are also described under each genus possessing them.

HABITAT AND GROWTH CONDITIONS OF THE AGARICS

The Agarics, like all fungi, are either saprophytic or parasitic. They are dependent on organic matter for a large part of their food; this is due to the absence of chlorophyll which makes them incapable of manufacturing carbon-compounds from the air. As saprophytes they occur on a great variety of substrata; soil, humus, dung, wood, fallen leaves, bank, straw, dead animal remains, decaying fungi and forest debris of all sorts. They can even be cultivated in the laboratory on gelatine and agar with proper addition of sugars, etc. As parasites they are found on living trees or shrubs, rarely on herbs. They are often attached to the rootlets of trees and shrubs on which they cause formation of *mycrohiza*; some consider this relation a parasitic one.

The fleshy fungi are most abundant in woods and forests and hence are largely dependent upon the character of the forest. When the woods are cleaned or the forest cut down, there is often quite a change in the flora of such a place after a few years. In addition to the proper food supply for their growth, moisture and temperature are the two most important factors for the rapid development of the fungi. The fruit-bodies of mushrooms contain a very high proportion of water, varying between 70 and 95 per cent according to species, weather conditions, age of plant, etc. The mycelium is also composed of much water which fills the vacuoles not occupied by the protoplasm. In spite of this fact, a far greater number of species occur in the upland forest than in wet swamps or marshes. It appears as if either some unfavorable soil content of a poisonous nature or too great an abundance of water prevents the mycelium of many species from growing in low wet places or at least prevents them from fruiting. Only certain kinds grow in marsh soil; although where there is an abundance of brush, logs or debris which can be used for support the moist surroundings are very favorable to forms which prefer such substrata. The largest number of species are found in forest hillsides, ravines, etc., where there is a clay sub-soil or where the forest floor is covered with sufficient humus, dead leaves, thick moss or other debris to hold the moisture. With the moisture content neither too large nor too small in such situations and where severe drying out is prevented, it would appear that the mycelium can vegetate luxuriantly, and after rains, especially long continued rains, the fruit-bodies or "mushrooms" form abundantly.

The temperature must also be favorable for each species. Warm or "muggy" weather, continued for several weeks with accompanying rains, usually causes the woods and fields to bring forth a good crop of mushrooms during July and August. Later, in September and October, an entirely different group of species appears, often in relatively cool weather; and some species often appear after the first frosts, always provided that the soil has been previously moist enough for the mycelium to vegetate sufficiently. Romell (Hymen of Lapland), reports that Agarics were abundant near the tree-line, and even in the region along the tree limit right up to the line of perpetual snow. This would indicate that for some species temperature is not so important as moisture, although growers of mushrooms in artificial beds in cellars, etc., find the temperature a very critical factor.

It must be remembered that time is also an element. After a drought it may take several weeks of steady rains before the fruit-bodies appear above ground. Rotten wood and logs retain the moisture and a single rain is often sufficient to induce growth. A single heavy rain or even a number of scattered showers, if too far apart, are not sufficient to produce a crop outdoors. The exact combination of temperature, time and moisture necessary is hard to calculate with certainty even after much experience. The mycelium must be sufficiently well developed before it has enough energy to produce fruit-bodies and this development is often slow for reasons not clear to the collector. Every field student of mushrooms knows that there are "good" collecting grounds and poor collecting places. The conditions mentioned above are probably responsible in large part and yet very similar fields or woods may be exceedingly unlike in the number and abundance of forms which are found in them. Just why this is so is not understood.

The species which grow on living trees are many. The most prominent are here given:

Armillaria mellea. (On roots of living trees.)
Armillaria corticatus. (Hickory, maple.)
Collybia velutipes. (Willow, birch, oak, alder, elm, poplar, etc.)
Pholiota adiposa. (Maple, oak, ash, etc.)
Pholiota albocrenulata. (Maple, birch and hemlock.)
Pholiota destruens. (Yellow birch, willow.)
Pholiota spectabilis. (Birch, oak, etc.)
Pholiota squarrusoides. (Maple, birch, beech.)
Pholiota squarrosa. (Birch, beech, willow, poplar, alder, etc., in
     Europe.)
Pleurotus applicatus. (Maple, poplar, birch, etc.)
Pleurotus atrocuerulius. (Mountain ash, sorbus, etc.)
Pleurotus ostreatus. (Willow, birch, basswood, beech, oak, walnut, locust, etc.)
Pleurotus sapidus. (Similar to *ostreatus.*)
Pleurotus subareolatus. (Maple, basswood.)
Pleurotus ulmarius. (Maple, elm, basswood, hickory, etc.)
Volvaria bombycina. (Maple, beech, elm, horse-chestnut, etc.)

These species are probably all capable of some degree of parasitism, i. e., can affect living tissue. Direct evidence as to the extent of this power in each species is hard to get. The spores probably effect an entrance at a wound, the plant first growing on the dead tissue at the wound, then pushing through the heartwood which becomes rotten as a result and finally affecting the sapwood and cambium and so injuring the vitality of the tree. Even if not killed by the fungus, the decayed interior is a source of mechanical weakness and the tree is eventually blown down by storms.

The rotting of cut or structural timber by the mycelium of some Agarics is perhaps equally important. Bridge timbers, railroad ties and even house timbers may be attacked. *Pholiota aeruginosa* is perhaps a much greater enemy of railroad ties than the rare occurrence of its fruit-body would indicate. *Lentinus lepideus* has long been known as a destructive agent to all sorts of timber. Firewood left in the woods in moist situations, even if piled up, may be attacked by a great variety of the smaller Agarics. There can be no doubt that fungi of all sorts, including Agarics, are extensive agents of decay and are much more effective than bacteria in bringing about the disintegration of dead vegetable matter and thus returning it to the soil; it is only in the later stages of decay that the bacteria play the greater role.

Agarics may show a decided preference for a certain substratum, e. g., kind of wood, kind of dung, kind of leaves, etc., on which they grow. Some are sharply limited to coniferous wood and are never found on wood of broad-leaved trees. Others seem to thrive well on a great variety of substrata. A few are parasitic on other mushrooms. (See Nyctalis.) The field mushroom *Psalliota arvensis* and the common mushroom *Psalliota campestris* are scarcely ever found in the woods, just as *Cortinarius armillatus* is never found in the field. Some consider that the soil is here the controlling factor. It must be remembered, however, that it is decaying vegetable food, which is the foundation of the subsistance of the mushroom, and the presence of barnyard manure or the fact that sheep have pastured in a field is after all more effective than the mineral content. This question is not yet settled and French mycologists lay quite a little stress on the mineral content of the soil, insisting that calcareous soil and clay soil are the homes of different species. With regard to Michigan species, the data are not sufficiently clear.

THE DISTRIBUTION OF AGARICS IN MICHIGAN

Any attempt to give a definite account at the present time of the distribution of species in the state is fraught with difficulties. Many localities have not been visited, and only a prolonged study of a locality reveals an approximation of the species occurring there. The very fascination of the search for fungi consists in their sporadic appearance. The species appearing one season may be absent the next. Some species fruit apparently only at long intervals; others only under special weather conditions.

The principal points in the state around which sufficient collect-

ing has been done to be of any use in such a summary are shown
on the accompanying map.   By far the largest part of the material
of this report has been collected by myself, assisted at Ann Arbor
by some of my students.   Entire seasons have been spent at Ann

Figure 4.—Map of Michigan showing centers of principal collecting areas.

Arbor, New Richmond, Bay View and along the shore of Lake
Superior and the flora of these regions is now partly known.
The activity of members of the Detroit Mycological Club has re-
sulted in a good survey of the region around Detroit.   Between the
years 1896-1903, Longyear and his co-workers studied the flora of
East Lansing, and also obtained material from Greenville, Chatham

and other points. A few species have been received from isolated points but usually such are common and of wide distribution. The main central portion of the Southern Peninsula north of latitude 43° has not been touched; and from the iron-bearing regions of the northern Peninsula there are no records. Isle Royale was visited in a dry season and there were few important finds. Houghton, Marquette, Munising and Sault Ste. Marie were the centers of one season's extensive collecting and we have a fair idea of their summer flora; concerning the many autumn species which assuredly grow in the coniferous regions of the northern half of the state, we have little information, as most students and collectors must return to their school duties before October.

The principal species of field and lawn seem to be equally distributed throughout the state; here may be mentioned *Psalliota campestris* and *Psalliota arvensis, Marasmius oreades, Psilocybe foenesicii, Lepiota naucina* and the Coprini. It appears that *Lapiota Morgani* begins to disappear in the latitude of Lansing; that *Amanita caesarea* scarcely enters our southern border. The species which grow only on distinctly sandy soil are apparently distributed throughout the sandy regions of the state although in many cases the records are not complete; for example, *Amanita russuloides* and *Amanita spreta* have been found only at New Richmond whereas *Russula delica* is abundant in sand under copses and groves all along the Great Lakes, but less abundant in the interior of the state. Many species doubtless prefer a clay soil and are distributed accordingly. By far the larger number of species are, however, dependent for their distribution on the character of the forest. This is most sharply illustrated by the difference between the flora of the coniferous regions north of latitude 44° and along the eastern and western border of the state where conifers have existed in the past, and of the hardwood forests and woodlots of the southern portion. The genus Cortinarius is composed of seven large subgenera. Of these, the subgenera Bulbopodium and Phlegmacium have a large number of representatives in the hardwood region, but are poorly represented in the north; on the other hand, the subgenera Telamonia and Hydrocybe occur in large quantities in the coniferous regions. Whatever factors, therefore, influence distribution of conifers doubtless affect also the distribution of certain Agarics. It is much to be regretted that we have so little data concerning the original mushroom flora of the 15,000 square miles of the central portion of the Southern Peninsula once covered by white pine forests. The nearest approach to original conditions, recorded in this report, was found by the exploration of the white pine lands around New Richmond. None of the virgin pine forest is left at this place, but second growth groves still yield characteristic fungus forms. Many of the sand plains at New Richmond remain uncultivated and are covered with scrub oak; here, however, the pine flora is no longer in evidence except as isolated species. Alternating with the sand plains are clay lands originally covered by hemlock and hardwoods. In the ravines bordering the river bottoms, there are still remnants of these forests and these yield a flora which is comparable with that of Bay View, Marquette, and wherever such forests exist. The flora of the tamarack bogs seems to be very similar throughout the state. In the tamarack bogs around Ann Arbor, we find the same species which are found in the northern bogs.

It is still an open question to what extent the formation of mycohiza may influence the distribution. If certain species can thrive only within reach of the roots of the beech tree for example, then those species are to be looked for only in beech woods. Evidence, however, is at hand to show that some species can form mycorhiza on a number of hosts. Every collector has experienced the feeling that many species growing on the ground in the woods are always to be looked for in the neighborhood of certain tree species. Perhaps collectors exaggerate this impression but in any case the subject needs clearing up. With regard to species found regularly occurring on wood, there is no doubt that they follow more or less the distribution of their specific substrata. In some cases, to be sure, a species may have a wide selection of material on which it can grow, and hence its distribution is not limited in such a manner. The species which have a parasitic tendency, like *Pleurotus ulmarius,* must have their distribution controlled to a large extent by the presence of the foster plant, although no Agaric which requires a living host at all times seems to be known with certainty.

COLLECTING AND PRESERVING AGARICS

For the Table

A basket, clean white tissue paper cut a foot square, a large pocket knife, a knowledge of mushrooms, favorable weather and the right place—these are the essentials. Of these the possession of accurate information is most important, since ignorance may mean sickness or death. If inexperienced and dependent on others for guidance, proceed cautiously and do not become over-confident. Collect first in meadows, pastures and open grounds away from thickets and woods. Always take every part of a mushroom of which you wish to make a study. As soon as you have advanced sufficiently to be able to recognize different kinds always wrap up the species separately. If you are learning how to identify by means of this book, it will be well to run down and compare the description after every collecting trip so as to become versed in the meaning of terms and also as a check on the correctness of your own or others' opinions.

Avoid the genus Amanita. Also at the first avoid anything that appears to belong to the genera Entoloma, Tricholoma, Hebeloma and Inocybe. Avoid all which are no longer fresh and firm, or which have small burrows due to grubs. Avoid the large, colored forms until you are well advanced in the subject. All except Amanitas may be tasted without swallowing with entire safety; avoid all that have a powerful peppery or nauseous taste. Dr. Peck states that he has always found those with a taste of fresh meal (farinaceus) to be edible. Avoid the green-gilled Lepiota. Avoid those with a milky juice until you know a great deal about them.

Try the large white forms which grow on tree-trunks, *Pleurotus ostreatus, sapidus* and *ulmarius*. Try the meadow, field and street mushrooms: *Psalliota campestris, arvensis* and *rodmani*. Try the inky caps, *Coprinus micaceus, atramentarius* and *comatus*. From the woods, always after a thorough study, try *Russula virescens, Hygrophorus russula, Tricholoma personatum* and *nudum*. *Hygrophorus sordidus* and *Tricholoma resplendens* are two white mushrooms of excellent flavor, but beware of mixing them with the white Amanita. If you live among evergreen woods try *Cortinarius violaceus*, if in southern Michigan *Cortinarius michiganensis*. After a start is made, others, one at a time, should be thoroughly studied until finally every trip will yield a meal.

My advice to all beginners and amateurs is: *Collect and study the deadly Amanitas first.* I have found many people who had known and eaten a few kinds for a long time, who were entirely ignorant of any Amanita; such people are always in danger in spite of and often because of their self-confidence. Fatal poisoning does not infrequently occur to just such people.

The specimens should in all cases be carefully gone over again before cooking. An excess supply can be kept on ice for a day only. Samples from the basket can be laid overnight with gills down on white paper and covered, so that the spore print may be used next day to check any error before cooking.

For the Herbarium

The fleshy Agarics may be placed in alcohol but if the container is much handled the specimen soon becomes mushy or crushed; if, however, it is carefully mounted and fastened on a glass plate and immersed in a stationary glass jar it may retain its shape a long time. The alcohol will dissolve the color and extract it. The best way to make a herbarium of these plants is to dry them on a square piece of wire-netting suspended over a kerosene or other flame. In this way the mushroom gradually dries without cooking or scorching. The color may or may not change and this fact itself is useful to distinguish between species. The dried specimens are very fragile and should be transferred for a day to a moist atmosphere where they will absorb moisture enough to become pliant. They can then be straightened or gently flattened but should not be pressed. Placed in a box with a proper label and a handful of naphthalene or moth balls they will last indefinitely. If beetles attack them they must be fumigated in a closed box with carbon-bisulphide; but if the naphthalene is constantly kept with the specimen the beetles seldom find their way thither. The use of boxes of varying size is much to be preferred to the method of pressing and mounting on sheets practiced by the older herbarium men. In either case, if specimens are very valuable beetles can be kept away with greater certainty by Peck's method of the use of strychnine. This is dissolved in warm water and sufficient alcohol added to enable one to spread the mixture easily.

Sulphate of strychnia ....¼ oz.
Warm water .... 5 oz.
Alcohol ....about 2 oz.

Notes for the herbarium. Specimens dried and prepared as above are of little value unless they were correctly identified when fresh by a mycologist, or, in case they remain unidentified, they be accompanied by full notes of the characters in the fresh condition. The taking of good notes is in itself a sign of a trained mycologist. But amateurs can, by care and patience, sufficiently describe a plant so that the specialist can identify it. It is advisable that they follow an outline, of which many have been published. The better way is to write a formal description, but if this is too difficult for the amateur the following outline may be used:

(If you wish the best attention from the specialist, do this part well. See glossary.)

LOCALITY.

DATE.

FINDER.

WEATHER.

HABITAT: ground, leaves, humus, woods, open grove, field, lawn, wood (kind), tree (kind), moss, dung (kind), etc.

HABIT: solitary, gregarious, cæspitose, subcæspitose, scattered, etc.

ODOR: farinaceous, pungent, nauseous, amygdaline, nitrous, earthy, mild or slight, etc.

TASTE: bitter, acrid, peppery, farinaceous, agreeable, mild or slight, etc.

PILEUS: *size. Shape when young;* conical, campanulate, acorn-shaped, cylindrical, convex, etc.
Shape when expanded: plane, convex, obtuse, umbonate, umbilicate, depressed, etc.
Surface: viscid, dry, hygrophanous, moist, glabrous, silky, fibrillose, virgate, floccose, tomentose, scaly (kind of scales as: loose, innate, erect, squarrose, pointed, fibrillose, large, superficial, appressed, etc.), even, rough, wrinkled, rugose, striate, furrowed, etc.
Margin: (when young), incurved, straight, inrolled, glabrous (when older), regular, irregular, wavy, tomentose, hairy, striate, rimose, etc.
Color: (when fresh and moist) (after lying a while). *Important.*

GILLS: *attachment:* adnate, adnexed, decurrent, uncinate, free, remote.
Width, relative to thickness of pileus, relative to species you know, or in millimeters.
Shape, linear, equal width throughout, ventricose, attenuated in front or behind, broadest in front, etc.

    Spacing, (relative) crowded, close, subdistant, distinct, few.

    Texture, waxy, deliquescent, dissolving, dry, arid, fleshy.

    Variations, forked, crisped, veined, intervenose, anastomosing, dimidiate.

    Edge, acute, obtuse and thick, serrate, eroded, entire, fimbriate, flocculose, wavy, etc.

COLOR: very important to give the color of the gills in the young plant, (e. g., Cortinarius, etc.), also when mature, after bruising or touching.

STEM: *size,* length, thickness above and below.

    Shape, cylindrical, tapering up or down, bulb (clavate, rounded, marginate, or abruptly depressed, large or small), flexuous, straight, equal, ventricose, rooting.

    Texture, fleshy, cartilaginous, tough, flaccid, brittle, flexible, fragile, spongy, fibrous, rigid, etc.

    Interior, hollow, tubular, cavernous, stuffed by pith, solid, spongy, etc.

    Surface, (see *Pileus.*)

    Color, difference at base and apex, within and without after handling, etc.

FLESH OF PILEUS: *consistency:* rigid, compact, spongy, soft, brittle, etc.

    Color: when moist, under cuticle.

    Juice: taste and color, abundance, changing after exposure to air.

MYCELIUM: color, abundance.

UNIVERSAL VEIL in young specimens, method of rupturing.

VOLVA: size, texture, color, present, absent.

PARTIAL VEIL: in young specimens.

ANNULUS: texture, color, present, absent, fugacious, persistent, ample, slight, etc.

SPORES: color of spore print, drawing of spores, size.

CYSTIDIA: shape, abundance, present, absent.

SKETCH: a good sketch or diagram of plant or its parts.

REMARKS.

PHOTOGRAPHING AGARICS

Use a basket to collect for this purpose. It is well to have tin boxes, e. g., cocoa boxes, so that each specimen can be kept unharmed, wrapped separately in tissue paper and placed upright in the box. Amanitas especially become deformed or lose some of their surface tissue if not properly protected. The specimens can be set upright on decapitated pins in a row as in the photographs in this report. Natural size photographs are by far the best since comparisons are then easily made. For identification purposes such photographs are much more useful than those taken in the natural surroundings and reduced in size; the latter may be good pictures but are rarely helpful. Every part and every character used in a description that can be shown in a photograph ought to be brought out; to this end the specimens must be properly arranged and the details emphasized. Besides its value in this respect the photographing of Agarics yields much pleasure and entertainment.

THE CULTIVATION OF MUSHROOMS

The history of this business and the methods in use, whether on a commercial scale or for home use, have been so often described that the reader is referred to those works. The best and most complete account is to be found in Bulletin No. 85, Bureau of Plant Industry, U. S. Dept. of Agriculture, entitled: *The Principles of Mushroom Growing and Mushroom Spawn Making,* by Dr. B. M. Duggar. For other papers see Bibliography, part (d), and the mushroom books of Atkinson, Hard, McIlvaine, etc.

THE CLASSIFICATION OF AGARICS

The plant kingdom consists of two large groups; the seed-bearing plants or Phanerogams and the spore-forming plants or Cryptogams. The latter are sometimes referred to as "the lower plants" although they include also the large, tree-like ferns. The Cryptogams include the green plants like the Algae, Mosses and Ferns; they also include an enormous number of plants which do not possess the ordinary green color and these are the FUNGI. In the following outline of the fungi the grouping is given in a scientific manner, since this is the only arrangement sufficiently accurate. For the terms which are strange to the beginner, reference must be made to the glossary. Consistent perseverance and the use of elementary books on botany are the only self-helps that can be advised when one is first plunged into the subject. The best way to begin the study is by the help of a teacher or of a companion who is already somewhat informed and is enthusiastic enough to help others. Mycological clubs are of great value in this respect. This work treats only of a single one of the many families of Fungi, and for others the student is referred to the books dealing with the other groups.

The Keys

The arrangement of the species of each genus in the form of keys or synopses is entirely artificial and arbitrary; hence these keys are merely guide-boards to point the student in the right direction by the use of selected characteristics of each species. A specimen is not to be considered identified when it is "run down" in the key, but the name so obtained should be referred to in the text and the description of the plant carefully applied to the specimen in hand. Such keys cannot be constructed so as to be perfect since plants of this class are quite variable and one often finds specimens not at all typical and hence they do not fit into the key at the right place. An amateur should use the glossary constantly at first until the meanings of the terms become fixed. Many of these keys were tried out for years on fresh plants and continually revised and it is hoped they will seldom mislead very far. The keys are mostly dichotomous; starting on the left, the plant must agree, for example

with either (a) or (aa). This leads to (b) and (bb) or to the
name of the plant. Sometimes the letters are tripled, etc., as
(aaa), (aaaa). In that case there are three or more possibilities
to choose from.

Arrangement of Species in the Text

The student will find, besides the keys, another means of
identification. This is an arrangement in the text, by which
the species which are the most closely related are grouped side by
side. This is called a "natural classification" and is supposed to
represent a relation according to the laws of evolution. Authorities differ on many points involved in such an arrangement, and
hence it was necessary to follow, according to my best judgment,
the order which appeared to be at the present time most acceptable.
Our knowledge of many species is still too imperfect to expect any
final arrangement. Furthermore, the number of species of such a
small area of the world's surface as Michigan, is not representative
of a like arrangement if applied to all the species of Agarics the
world over. In view of this fact it seemed useless to try to be entirely consistent throughout the work. The genera are therefore
subdivided in the way best adapted for each, although a general uniformity is approximated. The genera may be divided into subgenera
and sections, and sometimes the sections are subdivided. In this
way the most closely allied species are usually found together under
the last subdivision.

Nomenclature

The rules of the International Botanical Congress held at Brussels in 1910, have been used (see Authorities and Abbreviations).
Synonyms have been purposely omitted except in so far as they are
mentioned in the commentaries. The study of synonymies is apt
to become a "wild goose chase" and often offers nothing of importance for those who wish to become acquainted with the living
plants; it is well adapted for those who prefer to make their mycological studies in the herbarium and library. There is little doubt
that in the course of time, some of our American plants which were
supposed to be different and were given names, will be found to be
synonyms of European species. But there is no need of passing
judgment on such till the evidence is all in. Undue haste in considering species identical has often brought about more error than
existed in the first place. The field mycologist is constantly finding
species which he had given up as hopeless synonyms, and much col-

lecting will make a mycologist cautious. A keen observer, like Dr. Peck, will often be quite certain of the distinctness of two species but fails in the description to make the distinction clear or strong enough to others. In such a case herbarium material may not show the facts and only the finding of fresh plants can settle the question.

The making of new species in haste is equally unfortunate. In the preparation of this work, scores of unidentified species accumulated, and many still remain unidentified. In many cases, however, the repeated finding of the same thing, often in better condition, perhaps with the necessary young stage, and further and better study on each occasion, resulted finally in its determination. Except in a few genera where I had made more extensive collections and a more exhaustive study, for example in Russula and Cortinarius, I felt it unwise to describe as new more than a few striking species. In spite of the accumulation of synonyms and the great possibility that more American species will end as synonyms, I believe that there are still quite a few Agarics in the United States which are unnamed. But it is hoped that such an expression of my view will not cause every amateur to give names to those he is unable to identify. In the recent German work of Ricken (Die Blätterpilze) over 1500 species of Agarics are given for Germany, Austria and Switzerland alone, and very few new species are included. This is a good example of conservatism with reference to the making of new species.

Credit has been given to Fries wherever possible in the use of names of European species, even where the species is reported under Agaricus in the Systema Mycologia. In certain genera only, where sufficient critical work has been done, e. g., Inocybe, has this procedure been varied. If inconsistencies occur it is because the methods of mycologists past and present have been inconsistent. Outside of possible errors each case has been treated with regard to the Brussels Rules on the one hand and the latest facts obtainable on the other. An attempt is made under many of the species to present as much material as possible for the further study of the species.

I. Mycelium lacking.   *Bacteria.*
                                                         Mycetozoa.
                                                         Chytrids.

I. Mycelium forming the vegetative part of the plant. II.
II. Mycelium non-septate, (i. e., without cross-walls).
                                                      Phycomycetes.

II. Mycelium septate, (i. e., composed of many cells). III.
III. Spores not borne on a differentiated hymenium, not in asci
     nor on basidia.   *Fungi Imperfecti.*
III. Spores usually borne on a differentiated hymenium. IV.
IV. Spores borne in asci, usually eight in an ascus.
                                                    Ascomycetes.

IV. Spores borne on basidia, usually four on a basidium
                                                  Basidiomycetes.

The Basidiomycetes

(1) Basidia not forming a hymenium; spores borne on a four-
    celled basidium arising from resting-spores; parasites.
                                               Smuts and Rusts.

(1) Basidia arranged so as to form a hymenium............(2)
(2) Hymenium not in a special fruit-body but developed directly
    from the vegetative hyphae in the host.   *Exobasidii.*
(2) Hymenium on or within a special fruit-body............(3)
(3) Hymenium concealed within the fruit-body till spores are ma-
    ture. (See 10th Rep. Mich. Acad. of Sci., p. 63.)
                                               Gasteromycetes.
(3) Hymenium exposed ....(*Hymenomycetes.*) (4)
(4) Basidia forked or divided into four cells; plants usually gela-
    tinous, horny when dry.   *Tremellales.*
(4) Basidia clavate or subcylindrical.   *Agaricales.*

Key to the Families of Agaricales

(1) Hymenophore* not differentiated; basidia scattered on a loose
    subiculum of hyphae.   *Hypochnaceae.*
(1) Hymenophore even, not forming special branches, tubes, gills,
    etc.   *Thelephoraceae.*
(1) Hymenophore in the form of wrinkles, warts, spines or tooth-
    like plates, usually on the under side of fruit-body.
                                                  Hydnaceae.

---

*The term "hymenophore" is here used to designate that part of the fruit-body which bears
the hymenium, e. g., gills, tubes, spines, etc.

(1)   Hymenophore in the form of erect branches or an erect, simple, club.   *Clavariaceae.*

(1)   Hymenophore in the form of tubes or reticulations, usually on the lower side of the fruit-body.   *Polyporaceae.*

(1)   Hymenophore in the form of knife-blades (gills) ; mostly fleshy plants.   *Agaricaceae.*

KEY TO THE GENERA OF THE AGARICACEAE OF MICHIGAN

(a)   Spores mostly white in mass (ochraceous-colored in some species of Russula and Lactarius)............. (1)

(a)   Spores ochraceous, cinnamon or rusty-yellow in mass.... (21)

(a)   Spores flesh-color to roseate or salmon-color in mass.... (32)

(a)   Spores purple-brown in mass ....(39)

(a)   Spores black in mass ....(43)

White-Spored Agarics

1.   Gills of waxy consistency: *Hygrophorus.*

1.   Gills not truly waxy .... (2)

2.   Fruit-body, soft and fleshy, decaying.................. (3)

2.   Fruit-body toughish, corky or woody; thin plants shrivel on drying, revive when moistened ....(15)

3.   Gills thick on edge .... (4)

3.   Gills thin .... (5)

4.   Gills decurrent and forked dichotomously: *Cantherellus.*

4.   Gills not decurrent; plants parasitic on other mushrooms:
                                                                Nyctalis.

5.   Trama of fruit-body of two kinds of tissue, i. e., of globular and filamentous cells; spores globose, echinulate..... (6)

5.   Trama filamentous throughout .... (7)

6.   With milky juice: *Lactarius.*

6.   Not with milky juice: *Russula.*

7.   Stem eccentric, lateral or wanting: *Pleurotus.*

7.   Stem central .... (8)

8.   Gills free .... (9)

8.   Gills adnexed ....(10)

9.   Volva and annulus present: *Amanita.*

9   Volva only present: *Amanitopsis.*

9.   Annulus only present: *Lepiota.*

10.   With annulus only: *Armillaria.*

10.   Neither annulus nor volva present ....(11)

11. Stem fleshy or fibrous, sometimes outer rind subcartilaginous ....(12)
11. Stem cartilaginous, mostly throughout ....(13)
12. Gills decurrent or broadly adnate, not sinuate at stem:
                                                    Clitocybe.
12. Gills at length sinuate or emarginate on stem; mostly large plants on the ground: *Tricholoma.*
13. Gills decurrent, pileus umbilicate: *Omphalia.*
13. Gills not decurrent ....(14)
14. Fruit-body small; pileus thin, tending to remain unexpanded and bell-shaped: *Mycena.*
14. Fruit-body small, medium or large; pileus usually expanded when mature, somewhat fleshy: *Collybia.*
15. Fruit-body usually small, toughish, thin, not woody......(16)
15. Fruit-body larger; stem central, eccentric lateral or wanting ....(17)
16. Trama of pileus gelatinous: *Heliomyces.*
16. Trama fleshy-membranous; pileus usually small, not woody: *Marasmius.*
17. Plant woody or corky: (*Lenzites*).
17. Plant fleshy-leathery ....(18)
18. Gills of the usual kind ....(19)
18. Gills longitudinally grooved or split on edge ....(20)
19. Edge of gills serrate-torn: *Lentinus.*
19. Edge of gills entire: *Panus.*
20. Edge of gills split lengthwise: *Schizophyllum.*
20. Edge of gills obtuse, crisped: *Trogia.*

Ochre-Spored Agarics

21. Gills easily separable from the trama of the pileus; margin of pileus involute: *Paxillus.*
21. Gills not separating easily from the pileus..............(22)
22. Trama of pileus vesiculose; spores globose and echinulate.
                              (See *Russula* and *Lactarius.*)
22. Trama more or less filamentous ....(23)
23. Inner veil cobweb-like (cortinate): gills at length dusted dark cinnamon or rusty; terrestrial: *Cortinarius.*
23. Inner veil membranous, fibrous or floccose ....(24)
24. Annulus present: *Pholiota.*
24. Annulus lacking ....(25)
25. Stem lateral or wanting: *Crepidotus.*

25. Stem central .... (26)
26. Stem fleshy or fleshy-fibrous .... (27)
26. Stem cartilaginous or fragile .... (29)
27. Gills at length yellow, yellow-rusty, etc.; lignicolous:
Flammula.
27. Gills alutaceus to sordid brown; terrestrial.............. (28)
28. Pileus fibrillose, silky or innately scaly; spores often
angular; cystidia often present: *Inocybe.*
28. Pileus more or less viscid when moist, smooth: *Hebeloma.*
29. Gills decurrent: *Tubaria.*
29. Gills not decurrent .... (30)
30. Pileus convex or plane, margin at first incurved; stem
rather short: *Naucoria.*
30. Pileus bell-shaped or conical; stem slender.............. (31)
31. Pileus subviscid or viscid; plant very fragile:
Bolbitius and *Pluteolus.*
31. Pileus not viscid: *Galera.*

Pink-Spored Agarics

32. Stem lateral or lacking; on wood: *Claudopus.*
32. Stem central .... (33)
33. Volva present only: *Volvaria.*
33. Annulus present only: *Chamaeota.*
33. Volva and annulus lacking .... (34)
34. Gills free: *Pluteus.*
34. Gills adnexed, adnate or decurrent .... (35)
35. Stem fleshy or fleshy-fibrous .... (36)
35. Stem cartilaginous, slender .... (37)
36. Gills at length sinuate: *Entoloma.*
36. Gills decurrent or broadly adnate: *Clitopilus.*
37. Gills decurrent; pileus umbilicate: *Eccilia.*
37. Gills not decurrent .... (38)
38. Pileus convex, margin at first incurved: *Leptonia.*
38. Pileus bell-shaped to conical, margin at first straight: *Nolanea.*

Purple-Brown-Spored Agarics

39. Annulus present; veil distinct .... (40)
39. Annulus and volva lacking .... (41)
40. Gills free: *Psalliota.*
40. Gills attached to stem: *Stropharia.*

41. Veil present, remaining attached to margin of pileus, rarely forming an annulus: *Hypholoma.*
41. Veil, if at first present, quickly evanescent or none at all; slender-stemmed ....(42)
42. Margin of pileus at first straight; hygrophanous: *Psathyra.*
42. Margin of pileus at first incurved; gills adnexed to adnate-subdecurrent: *Psilocybe.*

Black-Spored Agarics

43. Gills delinquescing into a black mass when mature: *Coprinus.*
43. Gills not delinquescing ....(44)
44. Spores elongate-fusiform; gills decurrent; soft-waxy; pileus viscid: *Gomphidius.*
44. Spores globose to elliptical ....(45)
45. Pileus with striate or sulcate margin, fragile: *Psathyrella.*
45. Pileus not striate, rather fleshy, exceeding the gills; gills variegated-dotted by the spores: *Panoeolus.*

CANTHERELLEAE

Fruit-body fleshy or submembranous. Stem central or lateral. Gills thick, obtuse on edge, fold-like or ridge-form, usually forked, narrow. Veil none.

By the inclusion of Trogia and several tropical or subtropical genera, the group is extended by some authors to include sessile and reviving or arid plants. As limited above the group approaches the Thelepharaceae on the one side, the genera Clitocybe and Hygrophorus on the other. The genus Dictyolus Quel. belongs here, but no species have been found within the state. It is characterized by plants having a lateral stem arising from the larger mosses, and by vein-like, forked gills. *D. retirugus* is probably a native of the state. The group includes Cantherellus, Dictyolus and Nyctalis.

Nyctalis Fr.

(From the Greek, *nyx,* night, referring to the black color of the host-mushroom.)

White-spored; *chlamydo-spores abundant;* gills thick, distinct, obtuse on edge; stem central; *parasitic on other Agarics;* veil none.

Fleshy, putrescent, not large-sized mushrooms, developing on the pileus and stem of the fruit-bodies of Russula, Lactarius, Cantherellus, etc., after the latter have become well developed or are partially decayed. The gills and basidiospores in our species are often dwarfed or entirely undeveloped. The propagation of the plant is, instead, dependent on the presence of secondary spores which are formed in abundance over large parts of the surface of the plants. These spores are elliptical, brownish, long-spiny, 12-18 micr. in diameter. They are formed from the loosened hyphae of the surface of the pileus, etc., which break up into chains of spores, and because of this method of formation, are called *chlamydospores.*

1. Nyctalis asterophora Fr.

Epicrisis, 1836-38.

Illustrations: Cooke, Ill., Pl. 1132, B.
  Gillet, Champignons de France, No. 49.7.
  Michael, Führer f. Pilzfreunde, Vol. II, No. 81 (as *N. lycoperdioides*).
  Ricken, Blätterpilze, Pl. 2, Fig. 6.
  Murrill, Mycologia, Vol. 6, Pl. 129.
  Hard, Mushrooms, p. 204, Fig. 162.
  Plate I of this Report.

PILEUS 1-2 cm. broad, at first subglobose then hemispherical, *whitish*, floccose, *at length dingy brownish and pulverulent*. FLESH pallid, moist, rather thick. GILLS adnate, distant, *rather narrow and thick*, obtuse, sometimes forked, whitish or dingy, *frequently not developed*. STEM 2-3 cm. long, 3-8 mm. thick, relatively stout, stuffed then hollow, pruinose or silky, whitish then brownish, often curved. SPORES often lacking by reason of the undeveloped hymenium, elliptical, smooth, 6 x4 micr., white. CHLAMYDO-SPORES on surface of pileus, etc., abundant, brownish, spiny, 12-18 micr., globose. ODOR and TASTE farinaceous.

Parasitic: on *Russula nigricans*, Bay View. August-September. Infrequent or local.

An interesting case of a parasitic mushroom; it has an entirely different structure from that of the host mushroom on which it grows. For other instances of parasitic mushrooms see *Stropharia epimyces, Volvaria Loveana, Boletus parasiticus,* etc.

Cantherellus Fr.

(From the Greek *kántharos,* a vase or cup, referring to the shape of the mature pileus.)

Spore-mass white or yellowish-tinged; Gills *forked, fold-like* or *almost ridge-form* (except *C. aurantiacus*), obtuse on edge; stem central, confluent with the pileus; veil none.

Fleshy, putrescent, terrestrial mushrooms, with a more or less turbinate, or vase-shaped pileus, in some species almost membranous, on whose outer side the reduced gills run down the stem in the form of fold-like, thick ridges or elevations, sometimes markedly dichotomously forked, sometimes almost entire. They approach

Craterellus, a genus of the Thelephoraceae, whose hymenial surface is merely wrinkled and not gill-like. The fleshy species are much sought after for the table, and all of them are *edible*. Fries, in Epicrisis, included species whose stems are lateral or lacking; these have been segregated under other genera.

The PILEUS may be dull yellow, orange, red, cinereous or lilac-tinged. Sometimes it is deeply infundibuliform, as in the mature *C. floccosus,* or it may remain obtuse as in *C. cinnabarinus.* In the ashy or ashy-brown species the FLESH is thin and almost membranaceus and these approach species of Craterellus; in the others the flesh is thick. The GILLS afford the best means of recognizing the genus. In *C. aurantiacus,* however, the gills are thin, and, except for their marked dichotomous character, this species might be placed in the genus Clitocybe. The STEM is moderately stout in most species. In the fleshy forms it is solid, while in the cinereous-colored, thinner species it tends to become hollow, and in *C. infundibuliformis* the pileus is perforated so as to form an open tube down through the stem. The SPORES are usually elliptical or elongated, smooth, mostly white or whitish, but in some species tinged with yellow or ochraceous in mass. The BASIDIA are unusually elongated and approach those of Hygrophorus in this respect; they are said to be sometimes six or eight-spored. The ODOR and TASTE of our species is mild and agreeable.

Key to the Species

(a) Plant cinnamon-red, fading, medium size. 5. *C. cinnabarinus* Schw.
(aa) Plant not red.
  (b) Pileus and gills some shade of yellow or orange.
    (c) Gills orange, thin, crowded. 9. *C. aurantiacus* Fr.
    (cc) Gills not crowded, ridge-form.
      (d) Stem solid, firm.
        (e) Plant markedly vase-shaped; pileus deeply funnel-form, firm, rufous-orange. 3. *floccosus* Schw.
        (ee) Plant somewhat top-shaped, entirely chrome-yellow or flavus. 4. *C. cibarius* Fr.
      (dd) Stem hollow, pileus thin, funnel-form. 6. *C. infundibuliformis* Fr. 7. *C. tubaeformis* Fr.
  (bb) Pileus and gills not both yellow.
    (c) Gills flesh-color to purplish-lilaceus, ridge-form; stem solid. 2. *C. clavatus* Fr.
    (cc) Gills not flesh-color.
      (d) Pileus infundibuliform, cinereous or brownish cinereous.
        (e) Pileus perforated in center, stem hollow. 6. *C. infundibuliformis* Fr.
        (ee) Pileus not perforated; stem stuffed or solid. 7. *C. tubaeformis* Fr.
      (dd) Pileus obtuse, or depressed; subumbonate, brownish-gray. 8. *C. umbonatus* Fr.

Gills in form of thick ridges, rather distant.

2. Cantherellus clavatus Fr. (EDIBLE)

Syst. Myc., 1821.

Illustrations: Fries, Sverig. Atl. Svamp, Pl. 91.
Michael, Führer f. Pilzfreunde, Vol. II, No. 19 (as Craterellus).
Bresadola, I, Fungh. Mang. e. vel., Pl. 82.
Ricken, Blätterpilze, Pl. 1, Fig. 1.
Patouillard, Tab. Analyt., No. 434 (as *C. neurophyllus*).
Plate II of this Report.

PILEUS 3-5 cm. broad, turbinate to truncate-obclavate, depressed to *concave-cyathiform,* often irregular and lobed, narrowed into the stem, at first purplish-flesh color, *soon* greenish-yellow, surface floccose or slightly scaly. FLESH *thick behind,* white, *compact at first,* at length toughish. GILLS in form of *thick, dichotomous, narrow but distinct ridges, connected by cross-ridges,* anastomosing below, long decurrent from the elevated margin of the pileus, rather distant, *flesh-color to pale purplish umber.* STEM expanding into the pileus, *solid, short,* rather firm, *fleshy,* at first incarnate-purplish, then pallid, below densely white-floccose, 4-8 mm. thick, usually tapering downward. Whole plant 4-9 cm. tall. SPORES subcylindrical or narrow elliptcal, 10-12 x 4-5 micr., smooth, pale ochraceus in mass. ODOR and TASTE mild.

Gregarious, on the ground in hemlock forests of northern Michigan. Bay View, Marquette. July-August. Infrequent.

Well marked by its color and shape. In his later works Fries referred it to the Thelophoroceae under Craterellus. Its thick flesh and the well-marked ridges of the Cantherellus-type, seem to be sufficient reason to refer it back to Cantherellus.

3. Cantherellus floccosus Schw. (EDIBLE)

Trans. Amer. Phil. Soc. II, 4, 1832.

Illustrations: Peck, N. Y. State Mus. Mem. 4, Pl. 55, Fig. 9-13.
Peck, N. Y. State Mus. Rep. 33, Pl. 1, Fig. 18-20.
Hard, Mushrooms, Pl. 23, Fig. 160, p. 201, 1908.
White, Conn. State Geol. & Nat. Hist. Surv. Bull., No. 15, Pl. 19.

PILEUS 5-10 cm. broad (rarely broader), vase-shaped or trumpet-shaped, truncate when young, at length *deeply excavate-funnel-form,* firm, superficially floccose or subscaly, yellow at first, *at length rufescent to orange,* margin becoming undulate at times. FLESH rather thick, confluent with the stem, white. GILLS deeply decurrent, *ridge-form,* close to subdistant, *dichotomously forked, anastomosing throughout,* ochraceus to rufous-yellowish, sometimes darker. STEM short, whole plant 6-15 cm. high (rarely 20 cm.), 1-2.5 cm. thick, *solid,* glabrous, pallid-ochraceus, whitish at base, firm, sometimes abruptly short-attenuate at base, often deep in the ground. SPORES elliptical, "12-15 x 7-7.2 micr.", smooth, ochraceous in mass. ODOR and TASTE mild and pleasant.

On the ground in hemlock forests of northern Michigan, Marquette, Huron Mountains. July-August. Infrequent.

A most striking plant when in full luxuriance, forming a large vase with considerable capacity to its deep interior. It occurs gregariously but sometimes several arise at one place or apparently from the same stem. I have not seen it in the portion of the state where hemlock and pine are unknown. Like the preceding, it is scarcely possible to confuse it with any other species.

4. Cantherellus cibarius Fr. (EDIBLE)

Syst. Myc., 1821.

Illustrations: Fries, Sverig. ätl. Svamp., Pl. 7.
Cooke, Ill., Pl. 1103.
Gillet, Champignons de France, No. 88.
Ricken, Blätterpilze, Pl. 1, Fig. 2.
Michael, Führer f. Pilzfreunde, Vol. 1, No. 26.
Swanton, Fungi, Pl. 15, Fig. 3-5.
Atkinson, Mushrooms, Fig. 123, p. 128, 1900.
Hard, Mushrooms, Pl. 22, Fig. 128, p. 199.
Gibson, Edible Toadstools & Mushrooms, Pl. 19, p. 175, 1903.
Peck, N. Y. State Mus. Rep. 48, Pl. 32.
Plate III of this Report.

PILEUS 3-8 cm. broad, firm convex then expanded, soon depressed in center or margin elevated, often irregular, sometimes top-shaped, infundibuliform or one-sided, margin thick and at first involute, *chrome-yellow or pale egg yellow,* glabrous, not striate. FLESH compact, thick, white or yellowish toward surface. GILLS long, decurrent, thick, dichotomously forked or anastomosing, narrow, *rather distant, chrome-yellow,* edge blunt. STEM 3-6 cm. long, stout, 6-12 mm. thick, narrower downwards, solid, fleshy, glabrous, *chrome-yellow to pale yellow,* often tunneled by larvae. SPORES elliptical, 7-9 x 4-5 micr., smooth, faintly ochraceous-tinged. "BASIDIA 50-75x7-8 micr., 4-spored, sometimes 5-6 spored." ODOR and TASTE mild and pleasant.

Gregarious or subcaespitose, often scattered. On the ground in frondose or conifer forests . Throughout the state, from the southern border to Isle Royale. July-September (rarely earlier or later). Frequent only in certain seasons.

This is the famous *"Chantarelle"* of Europe, where it is highly prized, both on account of its flavor and from the fact that its flesh is free from larvae. In Michigan, and probably elsewhere in the eastern part of the United States, the fastidious lovers of mushroom meat are, alas, not so fortunate as their European brethren. During many years of collecting, I have rarely found this mushroom free from larvae and I have a large number of records. Occasionally, immediately after its rapid development due to favorable weather, I have found unattacked specimens. The color is often much paler yellow than that mentioned above and a white form is sometimes found. It is not easily confused with *C. aurantiacus,* which has thin and crowded gills and different shades of yellow.

5.   Cantherellus cinnabarinus Schw.   (EDIBLE)

Trans. Amer. Phil. Soc. II, 4, 1832.

Illustrations: Peck, N. Y. State Mus. Mem. 4, Pl. 55, Fig. 1-8.
   Murrill, Mycologia, Vol. 5, Pl. 92, Fig. 3.
   Hard, Mushrooms, Fig. 161, p. 202, 1908.
   Plate II of this Report.

PILEUS 1.5-3 cm. broad (rarely up to 7 cm.), firm, *convex and obtuse or expanded-depressed,* often *irregular, glabrous, cinnabar-red,* often faded, entirely faded in dried specimens. FLESH rather thin, whitish or tinged reddish toward surface. GILLS long-decurrent, dichotomously forked, *rather distant,* narrow and ridge-form, intervenose, *cinnabar-red,* yellowish or pinkish. STEM 2-4 cm. long, 4-6 mm. thick, *solid* or subcavernous, terete or compressed at apex, equal or tapering downward, tough-fleshy, glabrous, even, cinnabar-red or paler. SPORES oblong-elliptical, 8-10 x 4-5.5 micr., smooth, white or faintly pink in mass. BASIDIA long and narrow, 4-spored. ODOR and TASTE mild.

Gregarious, on the ground in open frondose woods or on bare soil along woodroads. Ann Arbor, Detroit, New Richmond, at least throughout the Southern Peninsula. July-October. Frequent.

Easily known by its color and size. When fresh the color is cinnabar-red but after exposure to wind and sun the color may be lost. Often the stem is diluted and compressed toward the apex, in which case it is found to be somewhat hollow. Typically the stem is solid. Some think *C. friesii* Quel. is the same, but that species is said to have a velvety-flocculose cap, different colors and probably smaller spores. Both fade, and the dried specimens probably look much alike. Our plant seems to be a distinct American form.

6. Cantherellus infundibuliformis Fr. (EDIBLE)

Epicrisis, 1836-38.

Illustrations: Cooke, Ill., Pl. 1109.
Ricken, Blätterpilze, Pl. 1, Fig. 4.
Michael, Führer f. Pilzfreunde, Vol. II, No. 41.
White, Conn. State Geol. & Nat. Hist. Surv. Bull. No. 3, Pl. 15, op. p. 35.
Peck, N. Y. State Mus. Mem. 4, Pl. 56, Fig. 9-16.

PILEUS 2-5 cm. broad, umbilicate to infundibuliform, *margin undulate or lobed,* pruinose-flocculose, glabrescent, cinereus-yellowish to watery-brown, paler when dry. FLESH *thin,* concolor. GILLS decurrent, narrow, ridge-form, dichotomously or irregularly forked, *pruinose, distant,* cinereous. STEM 3-9 cm. long, 3-7 mm. thick, *slender,* equal or subequal, glabrous, *hollow, terete or compressed, yellow.* SPORES globose- elliptical. 9-11x7-9 micr., smooth, pale yellowish in mass. ODOR and TASTE none.

Gregarious on the ground in wet swampy places, especially in conifer woods. Marquette, Houghton, New Richmond. August-October.

Distinguished from all the preceding by its thinner somewhat pliant pileus and darker colors; it often has a sooty or ashy shade. The center of the cap is usually perforated so as to expose the hollow cavity of the stem from above. Its spores are quite characteristic and set it off from its near relatives, which Murrill (N. A. Flora, Vol. 9, p. 168) has seen fit to include in this single species.

7. Cantherellus tubæformis Fr. (EDIBLE)

Syst. Myc., 1821.

Illustrations: Michael, Führer f. Pilzfreunde, Vol. II, No. 41.
(?) Cooke, Ill., Pl. 1108.

PILEUS 2-5 cm. broad, convex and obtuse, at length depressed
and margin irregular and recurved, sometimes subinfundibuliform,
not perforated in center, brownish-yellow to yellowish ochraceus,
silky-tomentulose, even, scarcely fading. FLESH *thin* at least toward margin, whitish-ochraceus. GILLS arcuate-decurrent, moderately thick, narrow and ridge-form, dichotomously forked, intervenose, *rather distant, not pruinose,* flesh-gray to yellowish-
ochraceus, often slightly deeper in color than pileus and stem.
STEM 3-6 cm. long, 3-6 mm. thick (sometimes thicker), fulvous-
yellow to ochraceous, concolor within, *terete or canaliculate,*
sometimes compressed, subequal, *solid or stuffed at first,* sometimes
at length hollow, glabrous, often curved, white at the very base.
SPORES broadly elliptical, 7-9.5x5-6 micr. punctate-granular, pale
creamy-white in mass. BASIDIA 60-65x6-8 micr. long, slender, attenuate downward. ODOR and TASTE none.

On the ground or debris of frondose woods of southern Michigan.
Ann Arbor and surrounding region. July-August. Infrequent.

Characterized primarily by its spores and its stuffed stem. It
differs from the preceding also in its rather constant colors. Most
of our plants were entirely yellowish-ochraceous when fresh and the
stem was not hollow. The thin structure of the cap separates it
from other yellowish species. Its name is misleading, since in its
near relative, *C. infundibuliformis,* the tube is continuous from the
stem to the surface of the pileus, while here the cap is not perforated, and the stem usually not hollow except in age. My observations agree with those of Ricken in these respects. *Cantherellus lutescens* is a related species, with an orange-yellow stem, blackish-brown, floccose-scaly cap and orange gills. Its spores are said
to measure 10-12x7-8 micr.

**Gills approaching the form of those of true Agarics, close or crowded.*

8. Cantherellus umbonatus Fr. (Edible)

Syst. Myc., 1821.

Illustrations: Cooke, Ill., Pl. 1106.
  Gillet, Champignons de France, No. 94.
  Ricken, Blätterpilze, Pl. 2, Fig. 1.
  Michael, Führer f. Pilzfreunde, Vol. III, No. 51.
  Peck, N. Y. State Mus. Bull. 67, Pl. 84, Fig. 8-21 (as *C. dichotomous* Pk.).

PILEUS 2-4 cm. broad, top-shaped, convex to plane and depressed, *brownish-gray to blackish or smoky-gray, with or without a slight umbo,* pruinose or flocculose, dry, pliant, margin regular or wavy. FLESH *thin,* white, becoming reddish with age or some time after picking. GILLS decurrent, rather narrow, thick, dichotomously branched, *not ridge-form,* close, white, then *stained yellowish or reddish,* even on edge. STEM 3-8 cm. long, 4-7 mm. thick, equal or attenuated up or down, elastic, pallid or pale gray, sometimes smoky above, appressed-silky, stuffed, soft fleshy-fibrous within. SPORES narrow, subfusiform-elliptical, 9-11x3-4.5 micr., smooth, white in mass.

Gregarious, attached to moss, especially Polytrichum, around peat-bogs or in swampy woods.

Houghton, Ann Arbor, probably in lake districts throughout the state. July-October. Frequent in fall till frosts or later.

Distinguished from the preceding two by the more highly developed gills, the slight umbo and the tendency for the flesh and gills to assume reddish stains after being collected. In many cases it is attached directly by its mycelium to the stems and leaves of living mosses. There is no doubt that *C. dichotomous* Pk. is the same species, since the descriptions of *C. umbonatus* with which Peck compared his plant were incomplete, as Saccardo omitted the fact that the gills are dichotomously forked.

9. Cantherellus aurantiacus Fr. (EDIBLE)

Syst. Myc., 1821.

Illustrations: Fries, Sverig. ätl. Svamp, Pl. 79.
  Cooke, Ill., Pl. 1104.
  Gillet, Champignons de France, No. 86.
  Michael, Führer f. Pilzfreunde, Vol. 1, No. 27.
  Ricken, Blätterpilze, Pl. 2, Fig. 2.
  Atkinson, Mushrooms, Pl. 37, Fig. 124-125, p. 129, 1900.
  Hard, Mushrooms, Fig. 159, p. 200, 1908.

PILEUS 2-6 cm. broad (rarely 7) pliant, convex-plane, depressed, at length often concave-subinfundibuliform with elevated margin, margin at first involute at length undulate, *orange-ochraceus to brownish-orange,* sometimes pale, *subtomentose* or subsquamulose on disk, even. FLESH *soft,* somewhat thick, thin on margin, pallid or tinged ochraceous. GILLS arcuate-decurrent, *thin,* edge blunt, dichotomously forked, *crowded,* rather narrow, *not ridge-form,* bright orange or tinged with salmon-color. STEM 3-5 cm. long, 4-10 mm. (or more) thick, *spongy,* thickened downwards, or subequal, *stuffed* sometimes hollow, minutely tomentose, *pale orange* varying brownish or pallid-yellowish. SPORES elliptical, 5-7 x 3-4 micr., smooth, whitish in mass. ODOR and TASTE mild.

Gregarious, on the ground, much decayed logs or wood, among debris, in conifer and frondose woods, more abundant northward. Throughout the state. July-October. Frequent.

Distinguished from *C. cibarius* by its thin, crowded gills and orange colors. A form occurs with pale yellowish-white cap and stem; this I have seen in Sweden where it is more common than with us. Fries says a white form also appears. It is marked poisonous or suspected by many European authors, although Peck, McIlvaine and others have eaten it without bad results, but the flavor is said to be poor. It occurs mainly in conifer woods but also in low frondose woods, perhaps where tamarack once grew.

MARASMIEAE

Fruit-body reviving in moist weather, becoming shriveled when dry; fleshy-leathery, tough or toughish, persistent, normally not putrescent. Stem when present, confluent with the pileus. Partial veil or universal veil lacking.

The species of this subfamily are well-marked by their ability to cease growing and to shrivel up in dry weather, and by their rejuvenescence and further development when they become wet again. The gills are never corky or woody and only slightly fleshy, usually arid and toughish. It is possible, however, to find forms which approach Collybia, Mycena and Pleurotus and which represent connecting links between those genera and Marasmius. The following genera are included: Trogia, Schizophyllum, Panus, Lentinus, Marasmius, and Heliomyces.

Trogia Fr.

(After *Trog,* a Swiss botanist.)

White-spored. Flesh toughish, arid, reviving in wet weather. Gills arid, fold-like, obtuse. Pileus sessile, or resupinate-reflexed.

Small, lignicolous, reviving plants, usually attached to dead branches of frondose trees. Related to Cantherellus by the plicate, i. e., fold-like gills, but tougher and reviving, as in Schizophyllum. The genus is placed under the Canthereleae by some authors but the persistent, reviving and arid characters ally it equally close to the Marasmieae. The pileus is either attached at a more or less eccentric point or resupinate for some distance and the gills are exposed in moist weather, but the dried pileus usually infolds on the margin so as to hide the gills which are mostly irregular or crisped.

10.   Trogia crispa Fr.

Monographia, 1833.

Illustrations: Cooke, Ill., Pl. 1114.
      Gillet, Champignons de France, No. 708.
      Patouillard, Tab. Analyt., No. 14.
      Ricken, Blätterpilze, Pl. 2, Fig. 5.
      Atkinson, Mushrooms, Pl. 39, Fig. 131, op. p. 137, 1900.

PILEUS 1-2 cm. broad, tough, *sessile,* sometimes couchate or shelving, often resupinate when moist, sometimes subimbricate, persistent, *reviving* when moist, irregularly incurved when dry, surface tinged reddish-yellow with whitish hairs, *becoming tan or buff-brownish when dry, margin lobed.* FLESH thin, fleshy-membranaceous. GILLS very narrow, irregularly vein-like, interrupted or entire, often forked, crisped, white or bluish-grey. SPORES cylindrical, smooth, 3-4 x 1-1.5 micr., white.

Scattered, gregarious, often closely crowded on limbs or bark of frondose trees, especially beech, birch and cherry. Throughout the state. Frequent.

When dry the plants roll up irregularly and almost hide the gills, the white color of which when fresh is rather sharply contrasted in most cases with the color of the pileus. It has been placed in the genus Plicatura by some authors.

11. Trogia alni Pk.

N. Y. State Mus. Rep. 24, 1872 (as *Plicatura alni*).

"PILEUS 1.5-2.5 cm. broad, coriaceous, *resupinate-reflexed,* generally imbricated, silky-tomentulose, *brownish-tawny,* the margin sterile. GILLS narrow, irregular, interrupted wavy or crisped, angular, white, becoming inconspicuous on drying."

"On alder, etc."

This species has not been reported in the state, but is included for the sake of comparison. Some consider it identical with *Merulius niveus* Fr., but that species is said to be pure white.

Schizophyllum Fr.

(From the Greek, *schizo,* to split and *phyllon,* a leaf, referring to the split edge of the gills.)

White-spored. Leathery-tough, arid, reviving in wet weather. Gills split halfway from the edge inwards. Trama of pileus thin. Veil none.

Only one species is known in our region, but this is very common. It grows on wood, on dead branches and trunks of standing trees or more rarely on fallen limbs. The gills are very characteristic, differing markedly from those of other genera by being split and the halves recurved, and the structure of the two layers is continued upwards almost through the pileus so that a thin pellicle covers the surface.

12. Schizophyllum commune Fr.

Syst. Myc., 1821.

Illustrations: Cooke, Ill., Pl. 1114 B.
    Gillet, Champignons de France, No. 641.
    Atkinson, Mushrooms, Fig. 130, p. 136, 1900.
    Hard, Mushrooms, Fig. 187, p. 233, 1908.

PILEUS 1-3 cm. broad, thin, tough, pliant, *sessile* by the narrowed base, from which it extends in a fan-shaped manner, often suborbicular and lobed on the incurved margin, tinged with brownish-gray when moist, *whitish when dry*, very hairy or tomentose, reviving. GILLS radiating from the point of attachment of the pileus, leathery-tough, split on edge, white or gray, sometimes with other tints, tomentose, on the inner side of the split. SPORES minute, cylindrical, 3-4 x 1-1.5 micr.

Scattered or gregarious on dead branches or trunks of frondose trees, especially of hickory; also on carpinus, walnut, elm, maple, sycamore, locust, apple and probably others. Throughout the state. Very common.

This is a pretty fungus when growing in luxuriance and can not be easily mistaken for anything else. Some species of Pleurotus have a similar habit, but are different in texture and especially in the structure of the gills.

Panus Fr.

(From the Latin, *panus,* a tumor. Fries says the name was used by Pliny for a tree-inhabiting fungus.)

White-spored. *Fleshy leathery, reviving,* tough, persistent; the texture fibrous, radiating into the hymenium. Stem eccentric, lateral or lacking, confluent with the pileus. Gills at length coriaceous, *edge entire.*

Not putrescent, but arid and tough as in the genera Lentinus, Marasmius, etc. They approach Pleurotus and some species have been described under that genus. They are wood-inhabiting. *P. stipticus* has *poisonous* properties, the others are harmless.

The PILEUS is eccentric, lateral or at first resupinate; none of the last section has been distinguished in the state. The erect forms often have very irregular and crowded and depressed pilei which are somewhat thick. Their surface is usually strigose, villose or slightly scaly. The color is various. The FLESH varies from quite tough in some species to somewhat fleshy in others; the latter may become more tough with age so that several species are easily confused with Pleurotus in the young stage. It is advisable to compare specimens with both genera where the texture is in doubt. The GILLS have an entire edge which distinguishes them from those of the genus Lentinus which have lacerate, serrate, thin edges. They become tough with age and are thickish. Intermediate forms occur, especially among typical species, so that some authors combine Panus with Lentinus. In our plants, however, the character of the edge of the gills is the best means of separation. The STEM is short, as a rule, sometimes continuous with the pileus, so that the pileus is not marginate behind. It is usually hairy or scaly. The SPORES vary in shape and size; they are smooth and white. CYS-TIDIA are present in *P. rudis* and *P. angustatus*.

Several of the species are very common, growing on stumps, de-cayed branches, etc., in the cities, or on any sort of dead timber in the woods and fields. The harmless species are rather tough for the table, but can be used, according to McIlvaine, to flavor soups and gravies.

The genus is divided into three sections, of which the following include the species described below:

   I. Conchati.
  II. Stiptici.

Key to the Species

(A) Pileus sessile or prolonged laterally into a stem-like base.
  (a) Pileus with a gelatinous layer, whitish or yellowish, spathulate to fan-shaped. 16. *P. angustatus* Berk. (Syn. *Pleurotus stratosus* Atk.)
  (aa) Pileus without a gelatinous layer.
    (b) Gills when young covered by a fugaceous veil; pileus about 1 cm., cupulate, rufous. On alder bushes. *P. operculatus* B. & C.
  (bb) Without a cortina.
    (c) Pileus hygrophanous, small, pinkish-gray; gills dark fer-ruginous; on willows. 17. *P. salicinus* Pk.
    (cc) Pileus not hygrophanous, small, heaped in clusters, pale brownish; taste very disagreeable, astringent. 15. *P. stip-ticus* Fr.
(AA) Pileus with an eccentric stem; i. e. pileus marginate behind.
  (a) Pileus white or creamy-white when fresh, becoming yellowish when drying.
    (b) Pileus often very large, densely strigose-hairy; whole plant be-comes dull yellow when dried. 12a. *P. strigosus* B. & C.
    (bb) Pileus up to 6 cm. broad, surface with long, delicate hairs, margin reticulated. *P. laevis* B. & C.
  (aa) Pileus reddish-brown to alutaceous-tan, medium size, margin at first inrolled.
    (b) Pileus rough with tufted hairs, tawny-alutaceous, etc., gills

crowded and narrow. 13. *P. rudis* Fr. (Syn. *P. strigosus* Schw.)
(bb) Pileus glabrous or obscurely fibrillose-scaly.
  (c) Gills crowded and narrow. 14. *P. torulosus* var. *conchatus* Fr.
  (cc) Gills close to subdistant. 14. *P. torulosus* Fr.

(Other species have been described by Peck, *P. betulinus* on birch, from Newfoundland, with a dimidiate, grayish-brown pileus; *P. nigrifolius* from Alabama, with distant, dark-brown gills. *P. dealbatus* Berk. was described from Ohio; it has an umber color throughout, with the shape of *P. angustatus*. *P. albotomentosus* Cke. & Massee, reported by McIlvaine, is probably the same as *Pleurotus albolanatus* Pk. of this report. *P. dorsalis* Bosc. is the same as *Claudopus nidulans*.)

Section I. Conchati. Stem eccentric; pileus irregular or conchate.

12a. Panus strigosus B. & C. (EDIBLE)

North American Fungi, No. 99.

Illustration: Plate IV of this Report.

PILEUS *large,* varying from 10 to 40 cm. broad, *subcentral, strongly eccentric or lateral,* marginate behind, fleshy-fibrous to subcoriaceous, convex, subexpanded, *reniform, covered with a dense, thick, strigose-villose nap* composed of hairs up to 2 mm. long in large specimens, *creamy-white* when fresh, *becoming yellow on drying.* FLESH firm, somewhat tough, up to 2 cm. thick, tapering to the very thin margin, yellowish when fresh, white when dry. GILLS subdecurrent, *broad,* close to subdistant, heterophyllous, thick, white, changing to yellow on drying, *edge entire.* STEM short or long, *stout,* 2-15 cm. long, 2-4 cm. thick, *strigose-villose,* eccentric or almost lateral, whitish to yellowish, sometimes tinged cinereous. SPORES elongated-oblong, 11-13 x 3½-4½ micr., smooth white in mass. CYSTIDIA none. ODOR stronger in age, rather agreeable.

(Dried: Strigosity and cuticle are dull golden-yellow, flesh whitish, gills ferruginous.)

Solitary or caespitose, subimbricate, growing from the wounds of maple and yellow birch; also on apple trees and other deciduous trees. Probably throughout the state; Houghton, New Richmond. August-September. Infrequent or rare. Edible when young.

This is the largest Panus we have; the pileus is often a foot and more in diameter and the stem very stout. The descriptions in the books are very meagre, and no mention is made of the change of color on drying. The dried specimens are elegant. Its flesh is not very tough and it is easily mistaken for a Pleurotus. The gills are very broad in large specimens, not truly distant, and are usually distinct on the stem or anastomose only in an obscure manner if at all. Some specimens are almost lateral, growing in a somewhat ascending-subhorizontal position, but with a marginate pileus; others have a subcentral stem. This is not *Lentinus strigosus* Schw., a species which seems to be synonymous with *Panus rudis*. Some consider *P. laevis* B. & C. to be the same as *P. strigosus*.

<h3 style="text-align:center">13. Panus rudis Fr. (EDIBLE)</h3>

Epicrisis, 1836-38.

Illustrations: Hard, Mushrooms, Fig. 179, p. 224, 1908.
    Ricken, Blätterpilze, Pl. 26, Fig. 4.
    Patouillard, Tab. Analyt., No. 637.
    Plate V of this Report.

PILEUS 2-7 cm. broad, irregular, eccentric or sublateral, ascending, depressed or vase shaped, sometimes infundibuliform, cuneate-rounded when young, *tough, villose-velvety or strigose,* alutaceous to reddish brown, *margin often lobed,* incurved. GILLS *narrow,* crowded, decurrent, pallid or tinged with the color of pileus, pubescent, *edge entire.* STEM *short,* eccentric, sometimes almost lacking, *villose, concolor.* SPORES elliptical-oval, 5-6 x 2-3 micr., smooth, white. TASTE slightly bitter at times. ODOR none.

Caespitose-crowded. Everywhere in town and country, on stumps, logs, dead branches, trunks, etc., of frondose trees. Throughout the state. May to November. *Very common.*

This is *Lentinus lecomtei* of many American notices, not the true *L. lecomtei* Schw. which has serrate gills. Our plant has entire gills. Schweinitz described the true *L. lecomtei* from a specimen sent from Georgia by Lecomte. (See Lloyd, Myc. Notes, Vol. I, p. 60.) It is also *Lentinus strigosus* Schw. to which Peck refers his specimens. Peck says it was found in one case on a balsam fir trunk, while ordinarily it is limited to deciduous trees. Patouillard says the gills of *P. rudis* are serrate, which is a rather remarkable statement. It can be used for flavoring gravies and dries well for winter use, but is readily attacked by beetles.

14. Panus torulosus Fr. (EDIBLE)

Syst. Myc., 1821. (As *Pleurotus torulosus.*) Epicrisis, 1836-38.

Illustrations: Hard, Mushrooms, Fig. 180, p. 225, 1908.
  Gillet, Champignons de France, No. 511.
  Cooke, Ill., Plate 1149.

PILEUS 5-10 .cm. broad, or broader, fleshy-pliant at first then tough, from plane to infundibuliform, eccentric or almost lateral, marginate behind, *livid flesh color or tinged violet or reddish,* surface when young and fresh with a delicate, detersile tomentum, soon *glabrous,* sometimes slightly scaly in the center of the cup., even on the margin, sometimes wavy. FLESH pallid, thickish, becoming thinner when full-grown. GILLS decurrent, *close to subdistant,* narrow, simple, occasionally forked, sometimes anastomosing on the stem, pallid to violet rufescent then alutaceous, *edge even.* STEM short, 2-3 cm. long, 1-3 cm. thick, stout, solid, tough, eccentric or lateral, *covered with a violaceous or gray tomentum.* SPORES elliptical, 6 x 3 micr., smooth, white.

Caespitose, on decaying stumps, logs, trunks, etc., of frondose trees. Ann Arbor. September. Infrequent.

Var. *conchatus* Fr. Pileus thinner, alutaceous and not with violet tints; gills closer. On beech log, Bay View. Infrequent. Becoming quite large, up to 15 cm. broad.

The species of Fries, *Panus conchatus,* does not seem to me specifically distinct, as the characters which he emphasizes occur also in *P. torulosus.* Specimens of the latter can be found whose pileus becomes minutely scaly at length, and whose gills vary forked and anastomosing, although never markedly so. The closeness of the gills depends somewhat on the expansion of the pileus and this varies not a little. Under certain weather conditions, the violet and reddish tints of *P. torulosus* are lacking, and then the plant could be referred to the other species. The spores of the two species, if I have interpreted correctly, are exactly alike, and unless structural differences can be shown it were better to make *P. conchatus* a synonym of *P. torulosus* as was done by Quelet. (Euchiridion Fungorum.) If collected in dry weather, they may be confused with infundibuliform species of Clitocybe.

Section II. Stiptici. Pileus sessile or prolonged behind into a stem-like base.

15. Panus stipticus Fr. (Poisonous)

Syst. Mycol., 1821. (As *Pleurotus stipticus.*) Epicrisis, 1836-38.

Illustrations: Hard, Mushrooms, Fig. 178, p. 222.
  Ricken, Blätterpilze, Pl. 26, Fig. 3.
  Michael, Führer f. Pilzfreunde, Vol. 3, No. 66.
  Gillet, Champignons de France, No. 510.

PILEUS 1-3 cm. broad, *very tough,* pale cinnamon, fading to whitish, convex, subreniform, depressed and abruptly narrowed behind, surface breaking up into minute, furfuraceous scales, even. GILLS thin, *determinate,* i. e., abrupt behind, venose-connected, crowded, *cinnamon.* STEM lateral, short, distinct below, solid often compressed, pruinose, paler than gills. SPORES minute, narrowly oblong, 4-5 x 2 micr., smooth, white. TASTE *very astringent.* CYSTIDIA none on sides of gills.

Caespitose. On wood; stumps, logs, trunks, etc. Throughout the state. May to October. Common.

This little Panus is not edible, because of its toughness and its very disagreeable taste. It is said to be a violent purgative. When fresh it is slightly phosphorescent in a dark room. On the under side it appears to have a very definite stem, ending abruptly at the gills; above, the stem is not distinguishable. It revives when moistened, so that a cluster may be seen in place during the whole season.

16. Panus angustatus Berk.

Lea's Catalogue of Plants, 1849.
See also *Pleurotus stratosus* Atk.=syn, Jour. of Mycol., Vol. 8, 1902.

PILEUS 2-5 cm. broad, *obovate to broadly cuneate,* sessile or prolonged into a stem-like base, convex or depressed, sordid white to pale tawny, *trama composed, under the microscope, of four layers* (a) the surface layer of erect hyphae which form a minute tomentum; beneath this (b) a thin, compact layer; (c) a gelatinous layer of open, slender, distant, palisade threads; (d) a compact, floccose-interwoven layer, about half the thickness of the pileus; margin crenate-wavy. FLESH thin, tough, soft. GILLS converging, very narrow, crowded, white or yellowish. SPORES minute, spheroid-oval, 3 micr. diam., smooth, white in mass. CYSTIDIA numerous, fusoid or lanceolate, 45-60 x 10-14 micr. BASIDIA 4-spored.

Caespitose, often imbricate, sometimes solitary, on very rotten wood of birch, hemlock, etc., of northern Michigan. Bay View, Houghton, Negaunee. July-August. Infrequent. Probably edible.

This species has much the appearance of *Pleurotus petaloides* and *Pleurotus albolanatus*. When fresh it is hard to tell whether it ought to be referred to Panus or Pleurotus. I have found it only in the region of conifer or mixed woods.

17. Panus salicinus Pk.

N. Y. State Mus. Rep. 24, 1872.

"PILEUS 8-12 mm. broad, firm, thin, convex, deflexed or subpendant, *hygrophanous*, minutely farinaceus-tomentose, pinkish-gray. GILLS moderately broad and close, converging to an eccentric point, *dark ferruginous*. STEM very short below or obsolete, obliquely attached to the vertex of the pileus."

"Gregarious. Trunks of dead willows."

This was reported by Longyear in 4th Report Michigan Academy of Science. I have given Peck's description.

Lentinus Fr.

(From the Latin, *lentus,* tough.)

White-spored. *Fleshy-leathery, tough,* reviving, persistent, *often becoming hard when old.* Stem eccentric, lateral or none, confluent with pileus. Gills concrete with pileus, *thin,* membranous, *edge becoming serrate or lacerate.*

Tough, even somewhat woody in age, lignicolous and polymorphous. They approach the fleshy Pleuroti on one side, and the woody Lenzites on the other. From Panus the thin, lacerate edge of the gills alone distinguishes them. They are very abundant in the tropics but there are relatively few species with us.

The PILEUS varies in size, being quite large in *L. lepideus* and *L. vulpinus,* or only about a centimeter broad in our small forms. It is often scaly spotted, by the breaking up of the cuticle. The GILLS are thin as compared with our species of Panus, and become lacerated-serrate on the edge. Their texture is homogeneous with the trama of the pileus and not at all separable from it, as is the case with the section Paxilloideae of the genus Clitocybe. They are white but often become dingy and arid with age, and are usually decurrent or become so at maturity. The STEM is tough, often hard and woody at the base where it is inserted, i. e., instititious, on the ligneous substratum. Although normally eccentric or lateral in our species, it may become central, especially when growing on top of the substratum. Some species have adapted themselves to the debris or humus on the ground, so as to appear terrestrial. In one section there is often a definite *veil,* as in *L. lepideus* and *L. tigrinus* but it soon disappears or only rarely remains on the stem or on the margin of the young pileus as shreds or fibrils. The SPORES vary in shape, in our species mostly elongated-oblong or elliptical. Fries in characterizing the genus (Hymen. Europ.), as well as Quelet (Enchiridion) and Patouillard- (Les Hymen. d'Europe), say the spores are subglobose. This is not at all the case with all of our species, although it may apply to the majority of tropical ones. Massee (Agaricaceae, Eur. Fung. Flora) records comparatively few spore-measurements, so that the statement of the above authors seems remarkable. The spores are white, smooth and often no longer present in old specimens. CYSTIDIA are lacking.

This is a troublesome genus because of the fact that the nature of the context, determines largely its place in the classification. Hence various species have been referred here by mycologists only to be later removed to genera with fleshy or fibrous context. Originally the genus Panus was included and some authors still include it. *Panus rudis* is commonly called *Lentinus Lecomtei,* the latter being a species we do not have with us. *Lentinus strigosus* Schw. is also *Panus rudis. Collybia lacunosa* Pk. is often mistaken for a Lentinus, and was erroneously referred to *L. chrysopeplos* B. & C. in the 8th Rep. Mich. Acad. Sci., p. 34. Others have referred *Omphalia umbellifera* var. *scabriuscula* Pk. to *L. chrysopeplos.* (See White's 2nd Rep. on Hymeniales of Conn., p. 22.) Certain species of Clitocybe, like *C. piceina* are often quite tough, but differ in the gills being discrete from pileus. Again, species of Paxillus might be confused with this genus. It is well for the amateur to compare the prominent characters of these different genera before deciding on a determination. None are reported poisonous; their toughness yields only to thorough cooking. They are hardly to be considered delicacies, but according to McIlvaine may be used to flavor soups. The large *L. lepideus* is often common on railroad ties and cut timber, and doubtless is an important agent in the decay of wood thus attacked.

The key will include also such species as may be looked for in the state. The genus is represented by two sections:

I. Mesopodes.

II. Pleuroti.

Key to the Species

(A) Pileus subentire; stem distinct.
  (a) Pileus more or less scaly.
  (b) Pileus umbilicate, with blackish-brown scales in the umbilicus; often deformed with aborted gills. 18. *L. tigrinus* Fr.
    (bb) Pileus convex, or plane and obtuse.
    (c) Pileus commonly rather large, 5-15 cm. broad.
      (d) Gills anastomosing on the stem; spores 12-15 x 5-6 micr.; pileus large, at first glabrous. *L. underwoodii* Pk.
      (dd) Gills not anastomosing.
        (e) Pileus with spot-like, brownish scales, gills sinuate; spores 11-13 x 4-6 micr. 19. *L. lepideus* Fr.
        (ee) Pileus rimose-scaly; gills not sinuate; spores 8-10 x 4-5 micr. *L. spretus* Pk.
    (cc) Pileus 5 cm. or less in width.
      (d) Pileus thin, rufous-tinged, sulcate on margin, 1-2 cm. broad. *L. sulcatus* Berk.
      (dd) Pileus thick, obconic, not sulcate; gills long-decurrent. *L. obconicus* Pk.
  (aa) Pileus glabrous, not large.
    (b) Caespitose, rarely solitary; pileus subinfundibuliform.
    (c) Stem furrowed, confluent-caespitose. 23. *L. cochleatus* Fr.
    (cc) Stem not furrowed; on the ground. *L. americana* Pk.
    (bb) Not caespitose or rarely so; pileus plane, or slightly depressed to umbilicate.
    (c) Pileus hygrophanous, umbilicate; stem central or eccentric. 20. *L. umbilicatus* Pk.
    (cc) Pileus not hygrophanous.
      (d) Pileus reddish-brown; stem whitish; spores minute, globose, 3-4 micr. 22. *L. microsperma* Pk.
      (dd) Pileus ochraceous to cream-color; stem short, blood-red to reddish; spores oblong. 21. *L. haematopus* Berk.
(AA) Pileus dimidiate, sessile.
  (a) Pileus large, 5-15 cm. broad, imbricate, coarsely hairy and rough-ribbed, flesh-color. 24. *L.vulpinus* Fr.
  (aa) Pileus less than 5 cm.
    (b) Taste peppery; pileus thick, whitish, becoming reddish-brown, hairy. 25. *L. ursinus* Fr.
    (bb) Taste pleasant; pileus thin, whitish or yellowish *L. suavissimus* Pk.

Section I. Mesopodes: Pileus subentire, stem distinct.

Pileus scaly. Provided when young with a veil.

18. Lentinus tigrinus Fr.

Syst. Myc., 1821. (As *Omphalia tigrina*.) Epicrisis, 1836-38.

Illustrations: Patouillard, Tab. Analyt., No. 406.
  Ricken, Blätterpilze, Pl. 26, Fig. 2.
  Gillet, Champignons de France, No. 406.
  Cooke, Ill., Plate 1138 and 1139.
  Lyman, G. R. Proc. Boston. Soc. Nat. Hist., Vol. 33, Plate

23 et al.   (Illustrating the abnormal form, *Lentodium squamulosum.*)

PILEUS 2-5 cm. broad, fleshy-leathery, at first orbicular, convex then plane and *umbilicate,* white but covered, especially at the center, with *blackish-brown,* hairy scales, margin at length wavy and often split. FLESH white, *thin.* GILLS *decurrent,* somewhat narrow, close, white, edge eroded-serrate. STEM 1-3 cm. long, slender, tapering downward, *solid,* minutely scaly, whitish, white within, often darker at base. At first with a delicate *veil,* which may form an evanescent annulus. SPORES elliptical-oblong, 6-7 x 3-3½ micr., smooth, white in mass, often copious.

Gregarious. On dead wood, which is usually hard. Ann Arbor, New Richmond. September. Infrequent.

The umbilicate, thin, pileus, different scales, and much shorter spores, distinguish it from *L. lepideus.* It is at first soft, but becomes coriaceous in dry weather. Ricken gives the spore-length almost twice that of the American plants.

A monstrous form occurs, which is often more common than the normal form or may be the only one found. This was placed by Morgan in a new genus, *Lentodium squamulosum.* Prof. Lyman raised this form in the laboratory from spores and considered it definitely distinct from *L. tigrinus,* as indeed his results strongly indicate. (See reference above to Lyman's paper.) Peck, however (N. Y. State Mus. Bull. 131), points out that the monstrosity and *L. tigrinus* itself appear on the same log and considers this to show that they are one and the same. Lyman never obtained the normal form from his cultures of spores from basidia of Lentodium.

The collection which I made at New Richmond was observed for several weeks, and all stages were seen on the same pieces of wood lying on the ground, both the perfect form with regular gills, and the deformed form. The latter has the gills obliterated by an overgrowth of mycelium, so that the under side of the pileus presents an even surface, much as in one form of *Nyctalis asterophora.* In the light of Lyman's researches, this form must be considered as a regular variation of this mushroom, whose tramal hyphae may produce basidia and spores without the development of true gills. The monstrosity often becomes quite hard and woody in dry weather and is unique among our fungi.

19. Lentinus lepideus Fr. (EDIBLE)

Syst. Myc., 1821. (As *Omphalia lepidea.*) Epicrisis, 1836-38.

Illustrations: Hard, Mushrooms, Fig. 182, p. 228, 1908.
Marshall, Mushroom Book, p. 56, 1905.
Freeman, Minn. Plant Diseases, Fig. 116, p. 237. 1905.
Cooke, Ill., Plate 1140.
Gillet, Champignons de France, No. 405.
Plate VI of this Report.

PILEUS 5-15 cm. or more broad, *compact and firm,* toughish, regular or irregular, *convex or obtuse,* at length plane, buff to pale ochraceous, variegated with subconcentric, brownish, adpressed, *spot-like scales,* even or sometimes areolate-cracked. FLESH white, pliant when fresh, hard when dry. GILLS decurrent, *sinuate behind,* broad, subdistant behind, close in front, white, often ferruginous-stained, transversely rivulose or striate, serrately-eroded, *covered when young by a membranous white* VEIL. STEM short, 2-5 cm. or longer, 1-2½ cm. thick, stout, solid, *hard,* pointed at base, *scaly,* irregular in cross-section, at first ringed at apex by the veil. SPORES elongated-oblong, 10-13 x 4-5½ micr., smooth, white. ODOR pleasant, rather faint.

Solitary or somewhat caespitose. On old timbers of bridges, side walks, railroad ties, fence posts, or on sun-exposed logs, stumps, etc., in woods, preferably on wood of conifers, hemlock, pine, tamarack, but also on oak, etc.

Throughout the state. May-October. Common. Edible when young.

A species has been segregated from this one by Peck, who has described a new form with gills which are decurrent but not sinuate and which has spores 7½-10 x 4-5 micr., under the name *Lentinus spretus.* It has a more slender habit, thinner pileus, and smaller scales. This doubtless occurs also with us. *Lentinus lepideus,* in the happy phrase of McIlvaine, "is a sort of commercial traveler." It is found everywhere on railway ties, whose decay it accelerates. Its ability to grow in rather dry situations makes it a dangerous enemy of exposed timbers, especially of coniferous wood. Specimens found on old tamarack logs measured 20 cm. across the pileus, and had a well developed veil which formed a membranous ring at the apex.

**Pileus glabrous; veil lacking.*

20. Lentinus umbilicatus Pk.

N. Y. State Mus. Rep. 28, 1876.

Illustration: Ibid, Plate I, Fig. 15-19.

PILEUS 1-2 cm. broad, tough, convex, *with a deep umbilicus hygrophanous,* water-brown, (moist), fading, glabrous, even. FLESH thin. GILLS adnate or slightly decurrent, close, broadest behind, narrower in front, whitish, edge serrate. STEM 1-2½ cm. long, 2-3 mm. thick, equal or tapering upward, glabrous, *stuffed or hollow,* tough, *slightly wrinkled or lacunose,* central or eccentric, concolor or paler. SPORES broadly elliptical, 6 x 3.5-4 micr., smooth, white. ODOR none. TASTE tardily acrid.

Gregarious. On the ground, among leaves, in mixed woods of pine, beech, etc. New Richmond. September. Rare.

This little Lentinus has the habit of a Clitocybe. Our specimens had a central stem and grew from the ground. It is, however, said to grow on wood, where it has an eccentric stem. Its serrate gills and tough texture separate it from Clitocybe. It is close to *L. omphalodes* Fr. and may be its American form.

21. Lentinus haematopus Berk.

Grevillea, 1872.

PILEUS 2-5 cm. broad, orbicular or wider than long, sometimes lobed, *umbilicate or depressed,* pale or sordid yellow, glabrous, even. FLESH tough, whitish, tinged yellow, *thin.* GILLS decurrent, narrow, subdistant, white to dull yellowish, edge toothed to nearly entire. STEM short, 4-6 mm. long, 2-4 mm. thick, *eccentric to sublateral,* firm, glabrous *blood-red* or *reddish.* SPORES oblong-elliptical, inequilateral, 7-9 x 3 micr., smooth, white. CYSTIDIA none. ODOR aromatic-pleasant. TASTE bitterish.

Solitary. On wood. Ishpeming. August. Rare.

The specimen from which most of the above description was made, was sent to Peck who identified it as this species. It was first sent to Berkeley from an unknown locality in North America. Peck reports it twice from New York. In our plant the pileus is laterally extended on the short sublateral stem, and the gills and flesh have a distinct dull yellow tinge. It was found in mixed woods in the Northern Peninsula.

22. Lentinus microsperma Pk.

Torr. Bot. Club. Bull. 33, 1906.

PILEUS 3-5 cm. broad, thin, convex, *obtuse,* soft-pliant, glabrous, even, *brownish-tan,* darker on disk, margin spreading. FLESH white, thin. GILLS adnexed-emarginate, rather narrow, attenuate in front, close, white, becoming dingy creamy-yellowish, *edge lacerate-crenulate.* STEM 3-6 cm. long, 4-10 mm. thick, varying slender or rather stout, *hollow,* terete or compressed, eccentric, sometimes grooved, glabrous, equal, whitish. SPORES minute, globose, 3-4.5 micr., smooth, white. CYSTIDIA none. BASIDIA clavate, about 25 x 5 micr. TASTE bitterish.

Caespitose. On decayed wood. New Richmond.' September. Rare.

This species was first sent to Peck from Missouri. It seems to be quite distinct although rare. I have collected it but once.

23. Lentinus cochleatus Fr. (EDIBLE)

Syst. Myc., 1821. (As *Omphalia cochleata.*) Epicrisis, 1836-38.

Illustrations: Gillet, Champignons de France, No. 403.
　　　　Ricken, Blätterpilze, Pl. 26, Fig. 1.
　　　　Patouillard, Tab. Analyt., No. 126.
　　　　Cooke, Ill., Plate 1142.
　　　　Hard, Mushrooms, Fig. 183, p. 229, 1908.

PILEUS 2-5 cm. broad, tough, flaccid, *irregularly-compressed or lobed,* variable in shape, *depressed to infundibuliform,* glabrous, pale reddish ochraceous to brownish-isabelline. FLESH thin, whitish. GILLS decurrent, rather broad, close, whitish tinged flesh-color, edge serrate. STEM 3-7 cm. long, 3-7 mm. thick, glabrous, central, eccentric or sublateral, *confluent at base, deeply sulcate,* solid, variously and irregularly thickened, concolor. SPORES minute, subglobose, 4-5 micr. diam., smooth, white in mass. ODOR somewhat aromatic.

Confluent-caespitose, in dense tufts. On stumps, decaying wood of birch, ash, chestnut, etc., sometimes on wood buried in the ground, in mixed and frondose woods. Throughout the state. July to September. Common locally.

The densely tufted furrowed stems and irregular one-sided vase-shaped pilei distinguish this at once. Often there are many short undeveloped pilei around the base of large tufts. The plant is rare in some localities, and in others it may be very plentiful.

Section II.   Pleuroti.   Stem lateral or none.   Pileus dimidiate.

24.   Lentinus vulpinus Fr.

Epicrisis, 1836.

Illustrations: Atkinson, Mushrooms, Figs. 128, 129, p. 134-5, 1900.
    Hard, Mushrooms, Plate 26, Fig. 181, p. 227, 1908.
    Fries, Icones, Plate 176.

PILEUS 5-15 cm. broad, sessile, multiple-imbricated, conchate-reniform, joined at their bases, *coarsely hairy or scrupose, radiately rough ribbed,* flesh color to alutaceous, margin strongly incurved. FLESH rather thin, tough-fleshy, whitish. GILLS decurrent, broad toward front, *narrowed, to the base of the pileus,* crowded, simple, white or tinged flesh color, edge coarsely serrate. SPORES subglobose, 3-4 x 2-3 micr., very minute, smooth, white in mass, copiously shed on the pilei. ODOR and TASTE rather strong, pungent.

Densely connate-imbricate. On decaying logs, stumps and trunks of various deciduous trees. Ann Arbor, Detroit, New Richmond, Houghton, Marquette. Records from July 25-Oct. 19. Infrequent.

It reappears on the same log in successive years. The very rough and peculiarly colored pileus is not easily mistaken. It grows in shelving masses of many individuals, almost equalling *Pleurotus ostreatus* in this respect, and is by far the largest of the dimidiate species of the genus.

25.   Lentinus ursinus Fr.—Bres.

Syst. Myc., 1821. (As Pleurotus.))

Illustration: Bresadola, Fung. Trid., Vol. 1, Pl. 66.

PILEUS 1-4 cm. broad, *sessile,* ascending, subimbricate, subreniform, convex, *pale reddish-brown,* varying glabrous to sub-tomentose, even, fading. FLESH thickish, very thin on margin, toughish. GILLS subdecurrent or radiating from the stem-like base, *rather broad,* close, dingy white to whitish-alutaceous, *edge lacerate-dentate.* SPORES *spheroid,* 5.5 x 4 micr., almost smooth, white.

CYSTIDIA none. ODOR mild. TASTE none or slightly disagreeable.

On prostrate trunks in woods of beech and hemlock. New Richmond. September. Infrequent.

Known by the sessile, rufous-brown pileus, which is somewhat tomentose or at least pruinose behind. Fries (Monographia) gives the size of the pileus as about 7 cm. broad; our plants agree better with Bresadola's description, averaging even smaller. Peck (N. Y. State Bull. 131) reports the larger-sized plant but says the taste is acrid and the margin of the pileus costate-corrugate.

Marasmius Fr.

(From the Greek, *maraino,* to wither or shrivel.)

White-spored. Flesh tough, arid, shriveling in dry weather, *reviving again in wet weather.* Stem central, confluent with the pileus, but of different texture, often horny. Veil none. Gills arid.

Terrestrial or lignicolous, frequently on midribs or veins of fallen leaves, on grass, etc. Except in the texture of the pileus, it is similar and closely related to the genera Collybia and Mycena, and with the same habit. A few are highly prized for the table. *M. oreades,* is one of our best-flavored mushrooms, especially delicious when used in gravy or soups. *M. scorodonius,* because of its garlic flavor, is used to season various dishes, although *M. alliaceus* which has the same odor is mentioned as not edible. The latter has not been found with us so far. Several are reported as poisonous, e. g., *M. urens* and *M. peronatus.* It is worth while to become acquainted with *M. oreades,* even if one goes no further. The genus is a large one, comprising over four hundred and fifty species, of which the larger part occur in the tropics.

The PILEUS is not putrescent, as it is in Collybia and Mycena, but is composed of a toughish substance which revives in wet weather and this is a fundamental character by which this genus along with Panus, Lentinus and Schizophyllum is to be separated from the Agarics with a putrescent pileus. The size is similar to that of the species of Mycena. It is usually soon expanded as in Collybia and may be depressed or umbilicate. The two main groups correspond, with regard to the position of the margin in the young plant, to Collybia and Mycena respectively, and have the same name. The GILLS are arid, flexible, almost leathery at times, often crisped on drying, the edge entire. They are sometimes joined behind in

the form of a collar which loosens (secedes) from the stem. Often
they are almost free, or, when adnate or adnexed they have a
tendency to secede. It is often confusing to find that authors use
the term "free" or "becoming free," when they mean that the gills
become loosened from the stem after they have been attached. It
is better to use the term "secede" and retain "free" for the usual
purpose of indicating that they never were attached to the stem.
In the smaller species the gills are often few and therefore
very distant. The width is often quite reliable to separate species,
although in some it varies. The STEM is cartilaginous or horny;
in a few, e. g., *M. oreades* it is merely tough-fibrous or with a subcartilaginous cuticle. The nature and presence or absence of the
villose, tomentose, etc., covering of the stem is used to distinguish
some of the sections. The mode of attachment to the substratum,
whether rooting or institutious, also helps to separate the subdi-
visions. Many of the smaller species have a black stem, and usually
the color of the stem in most species is darker below and paler or
white at the apex. With the exception of a small number of our
species, like *C. oreades, C. urens, C. peronatus* and *C. subnudus,* the
stem is hollow or slightly stuffed at first. In the small species the
stem is almost bristleform and inserted by the attenuated base. The
SPORES are white in mass, hyaline under the microscope, varying
in shape from subspheriod to lanceolate. The majority have a sim-
ilarity in form which is rather striking: round-enlarged at one
end and tapering to a pointed apiculus at the attached end. The
reviving ability of the gills explains the variability in size which is
found at different times in separate plants of the same species.
One must be cautious in taking the spore-measurements as in some
cases it is clear that the spores continue to grow after the plant is
revived by rains. CYSTIDIA are rarely present. In *M. cohoerens*
they occur in great abundance in the form of relatively large brown
spicules of the same kind as occur on the surface of the pileus and
stem. In *M. delectans* they are colorless. The ODOR is strong and
often like garlic as in *M. scorodonius, M. prasiosmus, M. polyphyllus*
and *M. calopus.* In *M. foetidus* it is very disagreeable, but not of
garlic. The TASTE is acrid or bitter in a few species, otherwise not
important.

The arrangement of species is that of Fries. Until the development is carefully studied for each species, any new arrangement is
likely to be unsatisfactory. The genus is divided into two subgenera: Collybia and Mycena with the following sections:

I. COLLYBIA

  (1) Scortei
  (2) Tergini
  (3) Calopodes

II. MYCENA

  (4) Chordales
  (5) Rotulae

Key to the Species

(A) Stem velvety, tomentose, floccose, pruinose or minutely pubescent, at least downwards. [See (AA).]
  (a) Gills arcuate-decurrent; plant glandular-pubescent, white. 41. *M. resinosus* Pk.
  (aa) Gills not decurrent, sometimes uncinate.
    (b) Stem rooting or attached by a floccose or strigose base.
      (c) Plants with a strong odor.
        (d) Odor like garlic.
          (e) Pileus 3-5 cm. broad; gills very crowded; spores 5-6 x 3-4 micr. 37. *M. polyphyllus* Pk.
          (ee) Pileus 1-2.5 cm. broad; gills not crowded; spores 12-15 x 3-4 micr. 36. *M. prasiosmus* Fr.
        (dd) Odor very disagreeable, not of garlic. Pileus umbilicate, plicate-striate. 43 *M. foetidus* Fr.
      (cc) Plants not ill-smelling.
        (d) Taste acrid or bitterish; pileus 2-5 cm. broad, brownish-red to alutaceus.
          (e) Stem clothed everywhere by a whitish or grayish pubescence.
            (f) Taste bitter; spores 10 x 4.5 micr. 29. *M. subnudus* (Ellis) Pk.
            (ff) Taste acrid; spores 7-8.5 x 3.28. *M. urens* Fr.
          (ee) Stem with yellow strigose hairs towards base; taste acrid. 27. *M. peronatus* Fr.
        (dd) Taste not acrid nor bitter.
          (e) Stem solid; plants growing in rings in grassy places, dull reddish-brown to dull yellowish. 26. *M. oreades* Fr.
          (ee) Stem stuffed or hollow.
            (f) Stem dark blood-red within; gills very crowded and narrow; pileus red-brown. 38. *M. varicosus* Fr.
            (ff) Stem not with blood-red flesh.
              (g) Gills soon reddish-brown from abundant dark-colored cystidia; stem horny, bay brown, subvelvety. 46. *M. cohaerens* Fr.
              (gg) Gills without brown cystidia.
                (h) Pubescence or tomentosity of stem dark-colored, brown, reddish, tawny or blackish, especially downward.
                (i) Pileus subzonate, umbilicate, tawny-hairy like the stem. (828. *Collybia zonata*.)
                (ii) Pileus not zonate, glabrous.
                  (k) Growing on bark of grape-vines; pileus 2-3 cm. broad, sulcate-striate. 30. *M. viticola* B. & C.
                  (kk) Growing among fallen leaves in woods.
                  (l) Stem spongy-thickened at base; gills broad; pileus fuscous-pallid. 32. *M. spongiosus* B. & C.
                  (ll) Stem equal.

(m) Stem minutely pruinose, horny, almost black below; pileus dark rose-madder. 39. *M. erythropus* Fr. var.

(mm) Stem densely tomentose.

(n) Stem dark reddish-brown throughout, 2-8 cm. long, 35. *M. semihirtipes* Pk.

(nn) Stem brown or fawn color, 5-12 cm. long. 47. *M. elongatipes* Pk.

(hh) Pubescence etc. of stem grayish or whitish, at least when dry.

(i) Growing on tree-trunks, bark, stumps, logs, etc.

(k) Slender; pileus 1-1.5 cm. broad, papillate, dull pinkish-white; on mossy logs. 48. *M. papillatus* Pk.

(kk) Short-stemmed; pileus 1-3 cm. broad, fulvous-alutaceus; caespitose-gregarious. 31. *M. fagineus* Morg.

(ii) Among fallen leaves, etc., in woods; stem 5-12 cm. long.

(k) Stem 2-5 mm. thick, reddish under the dense whitish pubescence; gills very narrow and crowded. (See 827 *Collybia confluens* Fr.)

(kk) Stem 1-2 mm. thick; covered with grayish pruinosity or tomentose.

(1) Gills very narrow and crowded, whitish or grayish. 40. *M. velutipes* B. & C.·

(ll) Gills distant, at length reddish-spotted. 47. *M. chordalis* Fr.

(bb) Stem inserted at the base, instititious, short; plants small.

(c) Gills attached to a collar, distant; pileus rufescent; stem white. 44. *M. olneyi* B. & C.

(cc) Gills attached to stem.

(d) Pileus glabrous, rarely subpruinose.

(e) Pileus milk-white, not sulcate nor plicate; gills distant; stem reddish-brown. 54. *M. epiphyllus* Fr.

(ee) Pileus rufescent, striate when dry; stem brownish to blackish-brown. 50. *M. felix* Morg.

(dd) Pileus pruinose, chalk-white, stem black, white pruinose on surface; spores angular. (See 56. *Heliomyces nigripes* (Schw.) Morg.)

(ddd) Pileus hairy or strigose-hairy.

(e) On cedar twigs; pileus conic, papillate, dark tawny. (See 830 *Collybia campanella* Pk.)

(ee) On twigs, chips, acorns etc; pileus umbilicate; whitish to dark grayish. (See 829 *Collybia stipitaria* Fr.)

(AA) Stem glabrous (except sometimes at the very base).

(a) Stem villose-rooting or attached by a floccose tubercle.

(b) Gills soon reddish-brown from the dark-colored cystidia; stems usually coherent, bay-brown, densely white-hairy at base. 46 *M. cohaerens* (Fr.) Bres.

(bb) Gills white or slightly tinged.

(c) Stem 4-8 cm. long; pileus sulcate, ochraceus-red; spores large. 49. *M. siccus* Schw.=(*M. campanulatus* Pk.)

(cc) Stem 2-5 cm. long.

(d) Pileus, gills and apex of stem white, stem dark-brown below, attached by a spreading mycelium. 34. *M. delectans* Morg.

(dd) Pileus not white.

(e) Stem reddish-brown to chestnut downwards; pileus dingy ochraceus. 33. *M. glabellus* Pk.

(ee) Stem wine-purple or pink upwards; pileus tawny-brown to purplish or pink. 33. *M. bellipes* Morg.

(aa) Stem inserted at the naked base, very slender; **on twigs, leaves**
etc.
 (b) Odor more or less strong, of garlic; pileus rufous to whitish.
  (c) Gills adnate, narrow; stem attenuated at the blackish base.
Odor strong. 42. *M. scorodonius* Fr.
  (cc) Gills adnexed, rather broad; odor faint; stronger as plant
dries. 42. *M. calopus* Fr.
 (bb) Odor not of garlic.
  (c) Gills attached to a free collar.
   (d) Pileus umbilicate, plicate on sticks, wood, etc., filiform.
    (e) Umbilicus white, elsewhere cap is darker; stem black. 55.
M. capillaris Morg.
    (ee) Umbilicus darker, cap white; stem black. 51. *M. rotula*
Fr.
   (dd) Pileus umbonate, sulcate, pale rufous; stem black, on grass.
52. *M. graminum* Libert.
  (cc) Gills adnate or adnexed.
   (d) Plant entirely white; pileus obtuse, 4-8 mm. broad, stem
very short. 45. *M. caricicola* Kauff.
   (dd) Pileus reddish-brown-purplish, umbilicate; stem black. 53.
M. androsaceus Fr.
   (ddd) Pileus fuscous-cinereous; stem short; on bark of living
tree-trunks. (See 845. *Mycena corticola*.)

SUBGENUS COLLYBIA. Margin of pileus at first incurved; stem somewhat cartilaginous; pileus fleshy-pliant, at length tough and sulcate or wrinkled.

Section I. Scortei. Stem *solid or fibrous stuffed,* externally covered by a *detersile villosity,* i. e., an easily removable villosity.

*Stem not strigose at the base.

26. Marasmius oreades Fr. (EDIBLE)

Syst. Myc., 1821.

Illustrations: Cooke, Ill., Pl. 1118.
Gillet, Champignons de France, No. 444.
Patouillard, Tab. Analyt., No. 328.
Hard, Mushrooms, Figs. 101 and 102; p. 136, 1908.
Gibson, Our Edible Toadstools and Mushrooms, Pl. 8, p. 105,
1903.
Swanton, Fungi, Pl. 9, Fig. 3.
Murrill, Mycologia, Vol. 2, Pl. 19, Fig. 3.
White, Conn. State Geol. & Nat. Hist. Bull. 15, Pl. 4, 1910.
Peck, N. Y. State Mus. Rep. 48, Pl. 33, Fig. 7-12, 1896.

PILEUS 2-5 cm. broad, *thickish,* pliant, campanulate-convex, obtuse or broadly umbonate, dull brick-red when young or moist, fading to yellowish-flesh-color, or yellowish-buff when dry, glabrous, even or substriate when moist. FLESH rather thick on disk, pallid.

GILLS rounded behind or almost free, *broad,* rather distant, whitish or tinged yellowish, interspaces often venose. STEM 3-7 cm. long, 3-5 mm. thick, equal, *solid,* even, tough, whitish, covered with a fine, interwoven, dense, detersile, villosity. SPORES ovate-fusiform, 7-9 x 4-5 micr., smooth, white. ODOR somewhat fragrant, agreeable. TASTE pleasant.

Gregarious, usually growing in rings or arcs, in grassy places, lawns, roadsides, pastures, etc., attached to grass, or roots of other plants. Throughout the state, more abundant in sandy regions. June-October. Common.

One of our best edible mushrooms, and very plentiful in some localities during a wet season. Its flavor is delicious and it can be used for this reason to add character to other dishes. Its toughness disappears by long cooking, a reversal of what happens in the case of many other species. When dry from sun or wind, its pale-honey-yellowish color and reviving ability are good marks of recognition; its tendency to form circles of close-growing individuals and its preference for grassy ground aid one to recognize it. Its gills are scarcely as arid as in other species of Marasmius, and this character, along with its fleshy cap indicate a close relationship with Collybia. The "fairy rings" caused by this and other mushrooms are due to the regularity of radial growth which the underground mycelium makes from year to year, starting from a central infection. It is believed by some that this mycelium excretes a substance which injures the grass so that the interior of the circle shows a poor growth of grass, but on the other hand some favorable influence from the actively growing portion along the "ring" causes the grass of this portion to grow better.

**Stem with a woolly or strigose base.

27. Marasmius peronatus Fr. (Poisonous)

Syst. Myc., 1821.

Illustrations: Ricken, Blätterpilze, Pl. 25, Fig. 1.
　　　　Cooke, Ill., Pl. 1117 (var.).
　　　　Gillet, Champignons de France, No. 445.
　　　　Berkeley, Outlines, Pl. 14, Fig. 4.
　　　　Patouillard, Tab. Analyt., No. 411.
　　　　Gibson, Our Edible Toadstools and Mushrooms, Pl. 9, p. 111, 1903.
　　　　Hard, Mushrooms, Fig. 112, p. 149, 1908.

"PILEUS 2-6 cm. broad, convex-plane, obtuse. opaque, pliant, pale reddish-brick color fading to alutaceus, at length lacunose, *margin striate at first,* wrinkled when old. FLESH thin, leathery-membranaceus. GILLS adnexed-seceding, rather thin, at first whitish then rufescent, close to subdistant. STEM 5-8 cm. long, 2-4 mm. thick, fibrous-stuffed, subequal, sometimes compressed, with a villose covering, yellowish then rufescent, *toward base with yellow strigose hairs.* SPORES oval, 6-8 x 3-5 micr., smooth, white. ODOR none. TASTE *acrid."*

Gregarious on the ground among leaves and sticks in frondose and coniferous woods. Probably throughout the state. July-October. Infrequent.

The description is adapted from Saccardo. This species seems less common with us than *M. urens.* Its acrid taste, habit, and the yellow hairs on the lower part or base of stem are good characters for its indentification. Its size corresponds to that of *Collybia dryophila.* The stem is said sometimes to become hollow. It is said to be poisonous.

28. Marasmius urens Fr. (POISONOUS)

Epicrisis, 1836-38.

Illustrations: Cooke, Ill., Pl. 1116.
  Gillet, Champignons de France, No. 448.
  Berkeley, Outlines, Pl. 14, Fig. 3.
  Gibson, Pl. 9, p. 111.
  Plate VII of this Report.

PILEUS 2-5 cm. broad, at first convex, then almost plane, obtuse or subumbonate, reddish-brown to alutaceus, darker on center, *at first even,* at length wrinkled, glabrous, opaque, pliant, margin at first incurved. FLESH thin, toughish-membranaceus. GILLS becoming free, at length remote, joined behind in places, thickish, subintervenose, *close,* at first crowded, narrow, whitish or pallid then tinged reddish. STEM 4-8 cm. long, 1-3 mm. thick, equal, *solid, terete,* pale reddish-brown, paler above, almost blackish at base, *covered throughout by a close, white pubescence,* composed of cohering minute hairs, whitish within, attached by an oblique sub-strigose base. SPORES oblong-lanceolate, slightly curved, 7-8.5 x 3 micr. CYSTIDIA none. ODOR none. TASTE *acrid; poisonous.*

Gregarious or scattered, on the ground in frondose woods, among leaves, debris and grass. Ann Arbor. July-October.

This species is considered identical with the preceding by Ricken, Massee and Romell. Even Fries was loath to separate it, and considered it a var. of *M. peronatus*. (See note under *M. urens*. Epicrisis, p. 373.) According to McIlvaine, *M. peronatus* is edible, while *M. urens* is marked poisonous. If the two are identical this can hardly be true. There is a remote possibility that *Collybia hariolorum* has been confused with *M. peronatus* while testing its edibility. In any case one needs to be careful. *M. urens* if distinct, seems more abundant locally than *M. peronatus*. The latter alone seems to have been differentiated by Peck, who does not report the first. Moffatt (Nat. Hist. Surv. Chicago) reports only. *M. urens* and says it is frequent. Morgan (Myc. Flora. Miam.) reports both.

29. Marasmius subnudus (Ellis) Pk.

N .Y. State Mus. Rep. 51.

"PILEUS 2-5 cm. broad, convex or *nearly plane,* glabrous, tough, flexible, often somewhat irregularly uneven, *dull brownish red or dingy bay,* more or less striate on margin. FLESH thin. GILLS rounded behind, nearly free, narrow, *subdistant, whitish or creamy-yellow,* becoming darker on drying. STEM 4-8 cm. long, 2-4 mm. thick, slender, equal, tough, *inserted, solid,* reddish-brown above, blackish-brown below, everywhere clothed with a *grayish* down or tomentum, which is commonly a little more dense near the base. SPORES 10 x 4.5 micr. (Pennington.) TASTE of dry plant bitter."

On the ground in mixed woods. New Richmond, Ann Arbor. August-September.

This is apparently a variety of the preceding, if that species is distinct, and not of *M. peronatus* as Ellis considered it. It is probable that all three run into each other. The description is that of Peck. Our plants had a bitter taste when fresh, otherwise not very different from *M. urens* Fr. Glatfelter (Trans. Acad. Sci. St. Louis, Vol. 16) gives spores 6-8 x 4-5 micr. which agree with those of *M. urens.*

30. Marasmius viticola B. & C.

Ann. & Mag. N. H., 1859.

PILEUS 1-3 cm. broad, convex-expanded, at length depressed, *sulcate-striate,* pale rufous to alutaceus-brownish, glabrous. FLESH thin, subcoriaceus. GILLS slightly adnate, not broad, ventricose, *subdistant,* pallid or tinged alutaceus. STEM 2-4 cm. long, 1-2 mm. thick, equal, tough, *pruinose-furfuraceus,* stuffed, *dark brown,* slightly enlarged and curved at very base. SPORES ovate-lanceolate, 8-9 x 3-4 micr., smooth, white. ODOR none. TASTE mild.

Gregarious or scattered, on rotten wood, debris, etc. Infrequent.

This is referred here with some hesitancy, although it is clearly distinct from the following, which differs in its subcaespitose habit, its short stem and long spores. It was named by Berkeley from material sent him by Curtis who collected it from grape-vines in **Alabama.**

31. Marasmius fagineus Morg.

Cinn. Soc. Nat. Hist. Jour., Vol. VI., 1883.

PILEUS 1-3 cm. broad, at first convex-campanulate, then plane, obtuse, pliant, striatulate when moist, radiately rugose when dry, *at length repand, pale fulvous-alutaceus,* appressed-silky, sometimes scaly-lacerate, margin at first incurved. FLESH thin, submembranaceus. GILLS narrowly adnate, seceding, rounded and subjoined behind, close, not broad, attenuate in front, crisped, whitish at first, *becoming brown—spotted or stained reddish,* edge subentire. STEM *short,* 1-2 cm. long, 1-2 mm. thick, *curved,* sometimes straight, subequal, *apex enlarged,* with a narrow stuffed axis, terete when fresh, compressed when dry, rufous or chestnut-alutaceus, fading to fuscous-alutaceus, apex paler, *covered by a whitish, villose tomentosity when dry,* strigose brownish-hairy where attached. SPORES subcylindrical, narrow, with curved apiculus, 9-12 (rarely 13) x 3.5-4 micr., with many immature of all sizes, smooth, white. CYSTIDIA none. ODOR and TASTE none.

Gregariously caespitose, usually abundant, on bark near base of living elm, beech and maple, or on stumps, etc., sometimes ascending the trunk five to six feet or more. Ann Arbor. July-August. Not infrequent.

Known by its caespitose, crowded habit, short stems, relatively broad pileus and spores. This may be the true *M. viticola,* but that species is poorly known.

32. Marasmius spongiosus B. & C.

Jour. Botany, 1849.

"PILEUS 1-2 cm. broad, plane, obtuse, *whitish-fuscous,* darker on center. GILLS slightly adnate, *broad,* close, whitish. STEM

3.5 cm. long, *thickened at the base* where it is spongy and fulvous-hairy, elsewhere furfuraceus-pulverulent." SPORES 7-9 x 3-4 micr. (Morgan) ; 4-5x3 micr. (Glatfelter).

Reported by Longyear, as under oak trees among grass. Also said to grow among fallen leaves, and around stumps in rich soil. I have not seen it.

Section II.   Tergini.   STEM tubular, rooting, cartilaginous. Pileus *hygrophanous.*   Gills seceding.

*Stem glabrous except the mycelioid-hairy base.

33.   Marasmius glabellus Pk.

N. Y. State Mus. Rep. 26, 1874.

PILEUS 1-2 cm. broad, convex-expanded, obtuse, often distantly striate, *dingy ochraceous,* uneven on disk.   FLESH membranaceus. GILLS adnate-seceding, *broad, distant,* ventricose, white or whitish, intervenose.   STEM 2-5 cm. long, 0.6-1 mm. thick, slender, equal, horny, tubular, *glabrous,* shining, whitish at apex, *reddish-brown or chestnut* elsewhere, mycelioid-thickened at base.   SPORES (10x4.5 micr., from one of Peck's collections).

Var. *bellipes*=(*M. bellipes* Morg.) Jour. of Myc., Vol. XI, 1905.

PILEUS *pale tawny-brown to pink-purplish,* distantly sulcate or plicate, subpapillate, glabrous or minutely velvety.   STEM with dilated apex, *varying above from whitish to bright wine-purple or pink.*   SPORES elliptical oval, curved-apiculate, 10-12x4-5.5 micr., smooth, white.   BASIDIA 30-42 x 6 micr., slender.   ODOR and TASTE none.   (Otherwise like *M. glabellus.*)

Gregarious or scattered, among fallen leaves on the ground in frondose woods.   Ann Arbor.   August-September.   Infrequent.

As no authentic spore-measurements are published, it is impossible to say whether *M. bellipes* is entirely distinct.   The latter, however, seems to be the form that occurs in our region.   Inasmuch as the plant, as it occurs here, varies considerably in color, it would not be surprising if Peck's species had the colors mentioned for both.   The variety is a beautiful plant when in the fresh state, due to the highly colored stem.   *M. pulcherripes* Pk. differs from the latter apparently only in its narrow gills and very filiform stem; the spore-size is not given.

34. Marasmius delectans Morg.

Jour. of Myc., Vol. XI, 1905.

Illustration: Hard, Mushrooms, Fig. 114, p. 151, 1908.

PILEUS 1-2 cm. broad, pliant, convex-expanded, depressed or
subumbonate, glabrous, *white or whitish*, pale tan in age, rugulose-
striate. FLESH subcoriaceous. GILLS adnexed, unequal, moderately broad, *subdistant, white,* intervenose. STEM, 3-5 cm. long,
1-1.5 mm. thick, *slender,* equal, even, hollow, cartilaginous-tough,
glabrous, shining, pure white above, darker downwards, to dark
brown below, *mycelioid at base,* mycelium forming wide, white mats
over the fallen leaves· where it grows. SPORES narrow elliptical,
7-9x3-4 micr., smooth, acuminate-apiculate, white. CYSTIDIA
rather abundant on sides, especially on edge of gills, slender, spine-
like, 36-45x3-5 micr. ODOR and TASTE mild.

Among fallen leaves in mixed and frondose woods. Ann Arbor,
New Richmond. August-September.

Easily known by the white, mycelioid mats which it forms among
the leafy covering of the ground in woods, by the white color of the
cap and gills and apex of stem, and by its shining stem. It is quite
frequent during continued rainy weather.

**Stem glabrous at apex only.

35. Marasmius semihirtipes Pk.

N. Y. State Mus. Rep. 25, 1873.

Illustration: Conn. State Geol. & Nat. Hist. Surv., Bull. 15, Pl. 6.

PILEUS 2-3 cm. broad, pliant, tough, convex, soon plane, or depressed, glabrous, hygrophanous, even or rugulose, *reddish-brown
when moist,* fading to pale alutaceus, disk darker. FLESH thin,
submembranaceus. GILLS adnexed-seceding, rather narrow, close
to subdistant, whitish, somewhat intervenose, edge subfimbriate.
STEM 2-8 cm. long, 1-1.5 mm. thick, *tough,* subequal, *tubular,* sometimes compressed, substrate, *dark reddish-brown throughout,* glabrous at apex, *densely* velvety-tomentose nearly to apex, tomentum
of same color. SPORES ovate, curved-apiculate, 8-9x4-5 micr.,
smooth, white. ODOR and TASTE mild.

On the ground in frondose or mixed woods among leaves and

debris. Ann Arbor, New Richmond, etc. Probably throughout the state. June-September. Frequent.

Known by the reddish covering of the stem. Hard says the plants are very small, which is scarcely correct. The name is deceptive, since the tomentose covering of the stem more often extends nearly or quite the whole length of the stem and the species could with equal propriety be referred to the next division.

36. Marasmius prasiosmus Fr.

Epicrisis, 1836-38.

Illustrations: Cooke, Ill., Pl. 1120.
        Gillet, Champignons de France, No. 447.

PILEUS 2-2.5 cm. broad, convex then expanded or depressed, obtuse, *pale brown with tinge of flesh color,* to pale isabelline, rugose-sulcate, glabrous. FLESH submembranaceus, toughish. GILLS adnate, seceding, sometimes with tooth, rather narrow, close to subdistant, *concolor* or paler than pileus, thick somewhat crisped. STEM 5-7 cm. long, 2-3 mm. thick, equal, *hollow,* horny-tough, dilated at apex, *dark rufous-brown downwards,* white and glabrous above, *clothed by a whitish or pallid villosity* which is denser below, attached by incurved or straight base to veins of oak leaves. SPORES narrowly lanceolate, curved, accuminate at one end, 12-15 x 3-4 micr., smooth, white. ODOR *strong, of garlic.*

On midribs of fallen oak leaves, in rich woods. Ann Arbor. September. Infrequent.

This differs from *M. scorodonius* in the villose coating of the stem, and from *M. alliaceus* by its habitat on leaves and by the spores; both of those have a garlic odor. Cooke (Ill.) gives the width of spores as 8 micr., and this appears to have been copied by most authors who give the spore size. Ricken departs from this in assigning to it minute spores, 7 x 4 micr. This last discrepancy points to a different species, and may represent *M. polyphyllus* Pk. in Europe.

37. Marasmius polyphyllus Pk.

N. Y. State Mus. Rep. 51, 1898.

"PILEUS 3-5 cm. broad, convex or nearly plane, even, *whitish to pale reddish,* often reddish brown on disk. FLESH thin. GILLS adnexed or almost free, *very numerous, narrow, crowded,* pure white. STEM 3-7.5 cm. long, 2-6 mm. thick, equal, *hollow, reddish-brown* clothed below and upwards by *a whitish down or tomentum,* denser at base, sometimes absent at apex. SPORES minute, elliptical, 5-6x3-4 micr. ODOR and TASTE *of garlic,* persistent in the mouth.

"On damp shaded ground. July."

Reported by Longyear. It is evidently related to *M. prasiosmus,* from which it differs markedly in the size of the spores and the crowded, narrow, pure white gills. It approaches Richen's idea of *M. prasiosmus* more closely than the preceding. I have not seen it.

38. Marasmius varicosus Fr.

Epicrisis, 1836-38.

Illustration: Cooke, Ill., Pl. 1121.

PILEUS 1-2.5 cm. broad, pliant, campanulate then plane, obtuse, sometimes with shallow umbilicus, *at first dark reddish-brown, almost purplish,* opaque, somewhat paler in age, radiately rugulose-striatulate, innately silky. FLESH concolor, slightly fleshy. GILLS adnate-seceding, sometimes sinuate-subdecurrent, *very crowded, very narrow,* whitish at the very first, *soon stained dilute reddish,* finally darker, scarcely reaching margin of pileus. STEM 3-5 cm. long, 1-3 mm. thick, stuffed *soon tubular,* equal above, somewhat spongy-thickened at base, glabrous above or with slight grayish pubescence, *towards base covered by spreading or strigose rusty-fulvous hairs, dark blood-red within,* attached by rooting hairs. SPORES minute, narrowly ovate, 6-8x2.5-3 micr., smooth, white. ODOR none. TASTE slightly acrid or mild.

Gregarious or solitary among fallen leaves and debris in frondose woods. Ann Arbor. September. Infrequent.

Characterized by the dark reddish-umber to purplish pileus, the crowded and narrow gills and the ferruginous covering of the stem. When wet the hairs at the base of stem are almost black. By removing the tomentum of the stem the dark red flesh is revealed beneath. Ricken combines this species with *M. fuscopurpurea* Fr., but our plants certainly fit the old conception of *M. varicosus.* It must not be confused with the black species of Collybia: *C. atrata* has broad gills; *C. plexipes* var. lacks the hairy covering on the stem; *C. expallens* has a farinaceus taste. The interior of the stem of *M. varicosus* seems to secrete a dark-red juice, but it is quite different from *Mycena haematopoda.*

**Stem, at least when dry, everywhere pruinose-velvety.*

39.   Marasmius erythropus Fr. var.

Syst. Myc., 1821.

Illustrations: Cooke, Ill., Pl. 1123.
    Gillet, Champignons de France, No. 441.
    Patouillard, Tab. Analyt., No. 577.
    Patouillard, Tab. Analyt., No. 125 (as *M. calopus*).

PILEUS 1-2.5 cm. broad, hemispheric-campanulate, then plane, obtuse or subumbonate, pruinate, *dark rose-madder,* darker on disk, rugulose when dry, margin at first incurved.   FLESH *white,* thin. GILLS narrowly adnate, seceding, *subdistant,* ventricose, *rather broad,* white or tinged ochraceus, scarcely intervenose, edge very entire.   STEM 4-5 cm. long, 1-1.5 mm. thick, equal, horny, stuffed then hollow, *dark reddish-brown to blackish below,* tough, flexuous, pallid at apex, *minutely pruinose,* with an enlarged mycelioid base. SPORES elliptical-lanceolate, curved-apiculate, 7-9x3-3.5 micr. CYSTIDIA none.   ODOR and TASTE mild.

On decaying leaves and twigs, on the ground in frondose woods, especially of beech.   Ann Arbor.   July-September.   Rare.

This approaches *M. glabellus* and *M. calopus* Fr.; from the former it is separated by its different spores and gills, from the latter by its pruinose stem.   Some specimens seem to have an entirely glabrous stem, thus being close to *M. calopus.*   The color of pileus does not change.   The pileus is not sulcate as in *M. siccus.*   It departs from the descriptions of European authors in the spore-size and the less distant gills.

40.   Marasmius velutipes B. & C.

Ann. & Mag. N. H., 1859 (N. Y. State Mus. Rep. 23, Peck).

Illustration: Hard, Mushrooms, Fig. 105, p. 140, 1908.

"PILEUS 1.5-3.5 cm. broad convex or expanded, glabrous, grayish-rufous when moist, cinereus when dry.   FLESH thin, submembranaceus.   GILLS *very narrow, crowded,* whitish or gray.   STEM

7-12 cm. long, slender, equal, hollow, *clothed with a dense grayish, velvety tomentum throughout.*"

Peck's description, given above, differs from Berkley's in Saccardo, in that the cap does not have an umbilicus, and in the much longer and slender stem. No spore-measurements are published.

Among fallen leaves in woods, on the ground. Ann Arbor.

Our specimens were verified by Peck. The spores measure 6-7x4 micr., oval to ovate, smooth.

41. Marasmius resinosus (Pk.) Sacc.

N. Y. State Mus. Rep. 24, 1872 (as *M. decúrrens* Pk.).
N. Y. State Mus. Bull. 67, 1903 (as var. *niveus* Pk.).
Sylloge Fungorum, Sacc., Vol. V., p. 522.

PILEUS 5-12 mm. broad, convex, then expanded and depressed, pliant, tough, *dull white,* rarely grayish or tawny, sometimes umbilicate or subinfundibuliform, *even or subrugulose, glandular-pubescent.* FLESH thin, submembranaceus. GILLS *arcuate-decurrent,* close to subdistant, *narrow,* white or whitish, often veined or forked, edge flocculose. STEM 2-5 cm. long, 0.5-1 mm. thick, slender, equal, tough, cartilaginous, *glandular-pruinose,* tubular, not striate, white then pallid, *attached by floccose base,* rarely confluent. SPORES oval-lanceolate, 6-7x3-4 micr., smooth, white. STERILE CELLS on edge of gills numerous, narrowly clavate, obtuse, 30x6-7 micr. ODOR and TASTE mild.

Gregarious or subcaespitose, attached to grass, sticks, leaves, etc., in frondose woods. Ann Arbor. July-September. Frequent locally after heavy rains.

The pubescence of cap and stem is due to minute, short hairs which are often glandular-tipped as seen under the microscope. When rubbed between the fingers the fresh plant feels resinous. The decurrent gills suggest an Omphalia, but the reviving and tough substance of the plant are characteristics which place it here. It was first named *M. decurrens* by Peck, who happened on specimens which were not at all typical as to the color of the cap. Saccardo changed the specific name to *resinosus,* because *decurrens* was preoccupied. Later, Peck named the common form var. *niveus,* which still later he changed to var. *candidisimus.* All these names should be dropped, since the plant is practically always white.

Section III.   Calopodes. Stem *instititious,* (i. e., inserted, the mycelium hidden), short, not rooting.

*Stem entirely glabrous.

42. Marasmius scorodonius Fr.

Syst. Myc., 1821.

Illustrations: Cooke, Ill., Pl. 1125.
   Ricken, Blätterpílze, Pl. 24, Fig. 6.
   Hard, Mushrooms, Fig. 109, p. 144.
   Michael, Führer f. Pilzfreunde, Vol. II, No. 44 (as *M. alliatus*).

PILEUS 5-12 mm. broad, pliant, convex then plane, margin at length elevated, rufous-tinged at first, *then whitish, glabrous,* wrinkled in age, crisped on margin. FLESH thin, membranaceus. GILLS *adnate, narrow,* close to subdistant, whitish, crisped, edge minutely flocculose. STEM 2-3 cm. long, 1-2 mm. thick, tapering downward, horny, tubular, terete or compressed, reddish, apex whitish, glabrous, *inserted by the naked, blackish base, somewhat shining.* SPORES narrowly oval-lanceolate, pointed-apiculate, 6-8x3-4 micr., smooth, white. ODOR, when bruised, *strong of garlic.*

Attached to base of grass, herbs and rootlets in fields, roadsides, grassy places in or near woods. Ann Arbor, New Richmond, etc. Probably throughout the state. June-September. Infrequent, but abundant locally.

Var. calopus (M. calopus Fr.).

Syst. Myc., 1821.

Illustration: Plate VIII of this Report.

PILEUS 5-10 mm.. GILLS *adnexed, rather broad,* emarginate, subdistant. STEM 2-3 cm. long, 1 mm. thick, reddish-bay color below, pallid-brownish above. ODOR *faint or none,* more noticeable when drying. (Spores, etc., same as *M. scorodonius.*)

Attached to grass stalks, etc., in woods. Ann Arbor.

M. scorodonius is known by its glabrous, tapering stem, narrow gills and strong odor when the plant is crushed. *M. calopus* is considered identical by some, but its slight odor, and different gills show it to be at least a variety. Hard's figure scarcely represents either plant as it occurs here. This species has long been used in

Europe as a seasoning for mutton-roasts, for other mushrooms and gravies.

**Stem minutely velvety or pruinose.

43. Marasmius foetidus Fr.

Syst. Myc., 1821.

Illustrations: Cooke, Ill., Pl. 1134.
Gillet, Champignons de France, No. 442.
Hard, Mushrooms, Fig. 104, p. 139, 1908.

"Pileus 1-3 cm. broad, pliant, convex then expanded and *umbilicate*, fulvous-bay color or rufescent, *plicate-striate*, pallid alutaceus when dry, margin incurved. FLESH submembranaceus. GILLS adnexed, joined in a collar behind, distant, rufescent or yellowish, somewhat subdecurrent. STEM 2-3 cm. long, 1-2 mm. thick, tubular, chestnut-brown or paler, *velvety-pruinose,* inserted by the floccose base on wood. ODOR *very disagreeable,* but not of garlic similar to *M. performs."* Spores 7-8x3.5-4 micr. (Pennington).

I have not seen this species within the borders of the state, but do not doubt that it occurs. It is not *Heliomyces foetans* Pat., as some think. It occurs on wood, fallen branches, etc. The description is adapted from Ricken.

44. Marasmius olneyi B. & C.

Ann. & Mag. N. H., 1859.

PILEUS 1-1.5 cm. broad, pliant, convex, soon expanded-plane and depressed, glabrous, *rufescent,* striate when moist, at length radiately rugose, dull luster. FLESH membranous, concolor. GILLS *attached to a collar which secedes from stem,* subdistant, narrow, *white,* arid, edge somewhat crenulate. STEM 2-4 cm. long, 1 mm. thick, dilated at apex, tubular, even, *white to pallid,* minutely pubescent-floccose, *attenuated downward* and inserted at base. SPORES narrowly elliptic-lanceolate, pointed at one end, 9-11x4-5 micr., smooth, white. ODOR none.

On fallen leaves and twigs, in frondose woods of beech, maple, etc. New Richmond. September.

This and *M. leptopus* Pk. seem closely related, the latter differing.

according to the description, by its glabrous stem and the spores which measure 7-9x3-4 micr.

45. Marasmius caricicola Kauff.

N. A. F., Vol. IX, p. 277, 1915.

PILEUS 4-8 mm. broad, *convex-expanded, obtuse,* radiately and broadly sulcate or alveolate, *pure white,* toughish, pliant, reviving, *pruinose.* FLESH very thin, membranaceus. GILLS adnate, thick, *very distant,* rather broad, pure white. STEM *very short,* about 2 mm. long, 0-7 mm. thick, terete, equal, central, subglabrous, *pure white,* horizontal or ascending, *inserted by a naked base.* SPORES elliptical-ovate, narrowed toward apiculus, obtusely rounded at opposite end, 15-18x6-6.5 micr. when mature, smooth, white. BASIDIA 2 or 4-spored, about 45x7 micr., elongated-clavate. STERIGMATA stout, awl-shaped, 7-8 micr. long. ODOR none.

Gregarious, on lower portion of Carex stems, in marshes, willow swamps, etc. Ann Arbor. October-November. Common locally.

Differs from *M. candidus* Fr. in the sense of all authors, in that the pileus is not umbilicate nor hemispherical, in its naked, inserted base of the stem, and probably in the spores. Quelet (Jura et. Vosges) gives the spores of the same length for *M. candidus.* Cooke (Ill.) gives minute spores, and Patouillard (Tab. Analyt.) figures them fusiform for *M. candidus.* Hard's photograph (Mushrooms, Fig. 107, p. 142, 1908) can scarcely be considered as the *M. candidus* of Fries, whose plant is described as minute, but is apparently *M. magnisporus* Murr. Manifestly, *M. candidus* Fr. is not well understood.

The trama of the pileus is composed of compact long, thickish, hyaline hyphae, differentiated at the surface into globose, hyaline cells 6-7 micr. in diameter.

SUBGENUS MYCENA: Margin of pileus at first straight and appressed. Stem *horny,* tubular, sometimes stuffed, tough and dry. Pileus submembranaceus.

Section IV. Chordales. Stem radicating or attached by floccose-radiating hairs.

46. Marasmius cohoerens Fr.—Bres.

Epicrisis, 1836-38 (as Mycena).

Illustrations: Fries, Icones, Pl. 80, Fig. 1 (as *Mycena cohoerens*).
Ricken, Blätterpilze, Pl. 25, Fig. 4.
Atkinson, Mushrooms, Fig. 127, p. 133, 1900.
Hard, Mushrooms, Fig. 106, p. 141.

PILEUS 1-2.5 cm. broad, campanulate-expanded, obtuse, sometimes umbonate, even, or striatulate when moist, *soft-velvety*, vinaceus-cinnamon to chestnut color, fading to alutaceus, margin at length repand-wavy. FLESH thin, concolor. GILLS adnate, rounded behind or sinuate, seceding, moderately broad, ventricose, close to subdistant, pallid at first, soon colored, brown, brick red to reddish-brown from the dark-colored, spiculate cystidia, sometimes intervenose. STEM 5-15 cm. long, 4-6 mm. thick, elongated, subequal, *horny, tubular*, even, glabrous and shining, sometimes obscurely velvety from spicules, *bay-brown to chestnut*, pallid at dilated apex, base darker and densely floccose with interwoven hairs which join the stems and attach them to substratum. SPORES variable in size, 6-8.5x4-5 micr., oval-elliptical, smooth, white. CYSTIDIA numerous over entire surface of gills, *lanceolate-aciculate*. 65-95x8-10 micr., *reddish-brown*. ODOR "somewhat disagreeable." (Ricken.)

Caespitose and coherent, on the ground or much decayed wood, in frondose woods. Throughout the state. July-September. Not infrequent.

The rigid, horny, dark stems, joined at base by a mass of white mycelial threads, the numerous cystidia and the size, distinguish this well-marked plant. Sometimes they grow singly. *Collybia lachnophylla* Berk and *Collybia spinulifera* Pk. have been shown by Atkinson to be identical with it. It is often referred to as *Mycena cohoerens*. The surface of the pileus and of the stem are usually covered by dark spicules like those of the gills, and the color of any of these parts varies in proportion to their abundance. These spicules are microscopic in size.

47. Marasmius elongatipes Pk.

N. Y. State Mus. Rep. 26, 1874 (as *M. longipes* Pk.).

"PILEUS 8-12 mm. broad, convex, glabrous, finely striate on the margin, *tawny-red.* FLESH membranacous. GILLS adnate, close, white. STEM 5-12 cm. long, filiform, *tall, straight,* equal hollow, *pruinose-tomentose,* radicating, brown or fawn color, apex white." SPORES 7-8x3.5 micr. (Pennington.) Among fallen leaves in woods. Rare.

It has been suggested that this is identical with *M. chordalis* (Fr.) Bres. I will, therefore, append Bresadola's description of that species:

"Pileus 1-2.5 cm. broad, convex, soon umbilicate, then expanded, dry, *umber, then livid-whitish, marked with reddish spots,* pruinose under a lens, with an incurved, at first striate then sulcate margin. FLESH membranaceus. GILLS adnate to subdecurrent, distant, whitish, *at length straw yellow and reddish spotted.* STEM 7-10 (rarely 15) cm. long, 1-2 mm. thick, straight, stuffed by a pith, (then hollow), *date-brown,* apex whitish, densely gray pruinose, in wet weather the surface is shiny from yellowish watery drops. SPORES fusoid-ventricose, 8-10x6 micr., hyaline under microscope. CYSTIDIA fusoid. BASIDIA clavate, 40x4-6 micr. ODOR none."

It is evident that here are two forms of Marasmius, clearly distinguishable by the colors. Specimens have been sent from Europe, according to Pennington (information by letter) marked *M. chordalis,* which had the color of our *M. elongatipes.* It seems probable that there are two species in Europe which are confused under the one name. Bresadola's figure does not illustrate our plants and Peck's name should be retained. It was originally called *M. longipes,* a name which had been pre-empted.

48. Marasmius papillatus Pk.

N. Y. State Mus. Rep. 24, 1872.

PILEUS 5-15 mm. broad, convex-expanded, *markedly papillate,* striatulate on margin, *dingy whitish with pink tinge,* opaque, slightly subtomentose or glabrous. FLESH submembranaceus. GILLS broadest behind, decurrent by tooth, narrow in front, close to subdistant, whitish or tinged yellowish. STEM 2-5 cm. long, 1 mm. thick, equal, elastic, toughish, hollow, *pruinose,* pallid, tinged flesh color, slightly darker below, *distinctly rooting.* SPORES 10-11 x3-4 micr., subcylindrical, smooth, white. CYSTIDIA few, scattered, narrowly lanceolate, about 50x5-6 micr., acuminate.

Gregarious, on decayed, mossy logs in coniferous regions. Bay View, New Richmond. July-September. Infrequent.

Easily known by its habitat, the small rounded umbo on the cap and the incarnate tinge of cap and stem.

49. Marasmius siccus (Schw.) Fr.

Synop. Fung. Car., 1822 (as *Mycena siccus*).
N. Y. State Mus. Rep. 23, 1870 (as *M. campanulatus* Pk.).
N. Y. State Mus. Bull. 105, 1906.

Illustration: Hard, Mushrooms, Pl. 17, Fig. 110, p. 146, 1908.

PILEUS 1-2.5 cm. broad, or sometimes smaller, at first subconical, broadly campanulate, at length often depressed in center, dry, glabrous, *distantly radiately striate-sulcate to the disk,* ochraceus-reddish to bright rose-madder, darker on disk, in age sometimes ferruginous. FLESH membranaceus. GILLS free or slightly attached, *narrowed toward stem,* broad in front, *distant,* white or tinged by color of pileus, subvenose. STEM 4-8 cm. long, slender, horny, *glabrous and shining,* blackish-brown, often pallid to white at apex, tubular, attached to leaves, etc., by small mycelioid base. SPORES elongated oblong-lanceolate, narrowed to the pointed apiculus, variable in size, 13-18 (up to 24) x3-4.5 micr., smooth, white. ODOR mild.

Gregarious, on fallen leaves, twigs and debris in frondose woods. Throughout the State. July-September. Frequent.

One of our most beautiful species of Marasmius, due to its bright colors when in full luxuriance. The color varies considerably and in age is often rusty-reddish on the cap. The stem is paler at times when young. The spores are very variable, and either continue to mature, or in wet weather become elongated by the first stages of germination. Peck referred it to the species of Schweinitz, whose specimens of *M. siccus* are preserved in the herbarium of the Philadelphia Academy of Science. This species has been reported by De Seynes as occurring in the region of the Congo in Africa.

50. Marasmius felix Morg.

Jour. Mycol., Vol. 12, 1906.

PILEUS 3-8 mm. broad, convex-plane, dry, glabrous, striate-rugulose when dry, *rufescent.* FLESH membranaceus. GILLS adnate, not broad, *distant,* white, venose, sometimes forked. STEM 2-8 cm. long, filiform, brownish to blackish-brown, sometimes whitish at apex, minutely brown-pubescent or velvety, instititious, slightly brown-hairy at insertion, base attached to veins of fallen oak leaves. SPORES elliptical, 7-9x4-5 micr., smooth, white. In frondose woods. Ann Arbor.

Section V. Rotulae. Stem instititious, filiform, horny or rigid-setaceous. (Attached to leaves, twigs, etc.)

51. Marasmius rotula Fr.

Syst. Myc., 1821.

Illustrations: Cooke, Ill., Pl. 1129.
  Gillet, Champignons de France, No. 443.
  Berkeley, Outlines, Pl. 14, Fig. 7.
  Ricken, Blätterpilze, Pl. 25, Fig. 10.
  Hard, Mushrooms, Fig. 108, p. 143.
  Conn. State Geol. & Nat. Hist. Surv., Bull. 15, Pl. 5.

PILEUS 4-10 mm. broad (rarely broader), pliant, hemispherical-convex, subumbonate-*umbilicate, white* or whitish, umbilicus darker, *radiately plicate,* glabrous, margin crenate. FLESH membranaceus. GILLS *attached to a free collar behind,* distant, broad, whitish-pallid. Stem 2-5 cm. long, filiform, horny, tubular, black or brownish-black, whitish at apex, entirely naked, instititious. SPORES lanceolate-fusiform, 6-9x3-4 micr., smooth, white. ODOR none.

On fallen twigs, leaves and around base of living trunks, gregarious. Throughout the State. May-September. Very common.

Often in great abundance after rains in woods, around shade trees, thickets, etc., and is our commonest Marasmius. Its beautifully pleated white cap and black stem cause it to be a striking little plant when moist and fully expanded. Sometimes the plants arise in series along a prostrate black strand, and are then often sterile.

52. Marasmius graminum Libert.

Plant. Crypt., 1837.

Illustrations:· Cooke, Ill., Pl. 1129.
Berkeley, Outlines, Pl. 14, Fig. 8.
Gillet, Champignons de France, No. 443.
Ricken, Blätterpilze, Pl. 25, Fig. 9.
Patouillard, Tab. Analyt., No. 325.

"PILEUS *minute,* 2-4 mm. broad, nearly plane, umbonate, *pale rufous, sulcate,* the furrows paler, umbo brown. GILLS few, subventricose, cream-colored, intervenose, *attached to a free collar.* STEM 2-4 cm. long, capillary, shining-black, apex white, entirely naked." SPORES obovate, 5-6 micr. long (Sacc.) ; lanceolate, 12-15 x3-4 micr. (Ricken) (Schroeter) ; globose, 3-4 micr. diam. (Massee) (Cooke).

Gregarious, attached to grass-leaves. Southern Michigan.

The description is adapted from Berkeley. Ricken and Schroeter describe it somewhat differently: "PILEUS bright reddish-yellow or brownish-orange, depressed and darker in center. GILLS very distant, all the same length, white or whitish. STEM entirely brownish-black or whitish at apex, hair-like in form, tough and hard." (Otherwise as above, but with long spores.) The very different sizes reported for the spores, show it to be as yet an uncertainly understood species. I have no record of the spores.

53. Marasmius androsaceus Fr.

Syst. Myc., 1821.

Illustrations: Cooke, Ill., Pl. 1129.
Gillet, Champignons de France, No. 439.
Ricken, Blätterpilze, Pl. 25, Fig. 6.
Hard, Mushrooms, Fig. 103, p. 138, 1908.

PILEUS 6-12 mm. broad, at first subhemispherical, soon expanded and depressed-umbilicate, *reddish-brown or with purplish-tint,* sometimes whitish, distantly sulcate-striate or radiately wrinkled, glabrous. FLESH membranaceus. GILLS *adnate,* thickish, *distant,* moderately broad, sometimes forked, flesh-color or rufescent. STEM 3-6 cm. long, *capillary, tubular,* tough and hard, glabrous-shining, *black,* apex paler, equal or dilated at apex, instititious. SPORES lanceolate, 6-8x2.5-3 micr., smooth, white. ODOR *none*.

Gregarious, attached to fallen leaves, twigs, pine needles, etc. Houghton, New Richmond and probably throughout the state. July-September.

Not to be confused with *M. perforans* Fr. which has a similar appearance, but differs in possessing a strong, specific odor (not of garlic), and in its minutely-velvety stem covering.

54. Marasmius epiphyllus Fr.

Syst. Myc., 1821.

Illustrations: Cooke, Ill., Pl. 1137.
        Patouillard, Tab. Analyt., No. 219.

PILEUS 2-8 mm. broad, convex, at length flattened and depressed or subumbilicate, subpruinose or glabrous, *milk-white* rugulose. FLESH membranaceus. GILLS adnate, few, *very distant,* white. STEM 1-4 cm. long, filiform, equal, *reddish-brown,* paler or whitish at apex, *pruinose, pubescent* toward base, instititious, tough. SPORES narrowly fusiform-lanceolate, 9-12x3-4 micr., smooth, white. CYSTIDIA moderately abundant, on sides and edge of gills, 40-50x7-8 micr., subacuminate, narrowly lanceolate. BASIDIA 30x7 micr., 4-spored. ODOR none.

Gregarious, on fallen leaves of oak, etc., attached to midrib and veins. Ann Arbor. October.

Distinguished from the preceding by the pruinose stem. *M. instititious* Fr. is said to differ by the sulcate-plicate pileus and the thicker stem which tapers downward. The spore-sizes given by various authors clash here as in many other cases. Massee and Cooke give them as 3x2 micr.; Morgan (ex Saccardo) as 6-7x2. Our plants appear to be those of Ricken.

55. Marasmius capillaris Morg.

Ann. Soc. of Nat. Hist. Jour., Vol. 6, 1883.

PILEUS 2-6 mm. broad, convex, umbilicate, plicate-sulcate, alutaceus sometimes darker, *with white umbilicus,* glabrous. FLESH membranaceus. GILLS *adnate to a free collar,* moderately broad, white, distant. STEM 3-5 cm. long, capillary, equal, long, black, scarcely whitish at very apex, glabrous-shining, tubular, tough, instititious. SPORES oblong-lanceolate, 8-10x4-5 micr., smooth, white. ODOR none.

Gregarious on fallen leaves of oak, etc., twigs and sticks in woods. Ann Arbor. September.

Known by its long, filiform black stem and the white umbilicus which is in marked contrast to the color of the rest of pileus.

Heliomyces Lev.

(From the Greek, *helios,* the sun, and *myphes,* a fungus.)

Flesh tremelloid, subcoreaceous, reviving in moist weather. Pileus rugose, sulcate or reticulate-ridged. Stem central, confluent with the pileus, tough. No veil. Gills with acute edge.

Marasmius-like plants with a gelatinous trama, usually lignicolous. The species are few and have been poorly studied; probably most of them occur in the tropical regions. It is highly desirable to know the microscopic structure of the species so far referred here. *Pleurotus subpalmatus* is closely related to this genus, and should perhaps be included. Only two species are represented in my collections.

56. Heliomyces nigripes (Schw.) Morg.

Epicrisis, 1836-38.

Illustrations: Hard, Mushrooms, Fig. 115, p. 152, 1908.
Lloyd, Myc. Notes, No. 5, Fig. 19 and 20, p. 46.

PILEUS 1-2 cm. broad, very thin, *pure chalk-white,* convex then expanded, pruinose, rugulose-subsulcate; *trama* composed of *sub-gelatinous hyphae* much interwoven. GILLS adnate or adnato-decurrent, subdistant, unequal, intervenose, some forked, *white,* rufescent. STEM 2-4 cm. long, 1-2 mm. thick, enlarged and usually compressed above, tapering downward, *instititious,* cartilaginous-tough, *black,* white-pruinose at first, minutely tubular, black within. SPORES coarsely stellate, 3-5 rayed, hyaline, 8-9 micr. diam. CYS-TIDIA none.

On sticks, stems of Equisetum, fallen leaves, etc., in mixed woods. New Richmond. September.

In age the colors of the whole plant change to alutaceous. This species has usually been referred to Marasmius. It is an American plant and was placed in that genus by de Schweinitz. In his North

American Species of Marasmius (Jour. Mycol., Vol. 12, p. 98), Morgan included it under Heliomyces, where it probably belongs, although the gelatinous character of the trama is not very strongly developed. Its peculiar spores set it off from all others; Lloyd has given us a photograph showing their stellate character.

57. Heliomyces pruinosipes Pk. var.

N. Y. State Mus. Bull. 167, 1913.

PILEUS 1-2 cm. broad, *tremelloid,* convex then plane, minutely pubescent, hygrophanous, dark chestnut-brown, becoming paler, *surface marked by convolute, crowded, obtuse ridges,* not viscid. FLESH thick, becoming tough and slightly horny when dry, reddish-pallid. GILLS adnate running down the stem by short lines, medium broad, close, thin, pallid to dingy ochraceous, becoming brownish-yellow on drying, edge entire. STEM 3-4.5 cm. long, 3 mm. thick, equal, hollow, compressed, somewhat twisted and canaliculate on drying, fibrous, tough, *dark chestnut brown,* fading, clothed by a short tomentose pubescense. SPORES minute, oblong, 5x2.5 micr., smooth, white. TRAMA of cap of large, gelatinous, interwoven hyphae, which in cross-section have a very refractive center; that of gills of similar but more slender hyphae. ODOR and TASTE mild.

The specimen was sent by Mrs. Cahn, from Detroit, in July. The description applies only to our plant. It departs from the description of Peck in that the cap does not at first possess the bright orange-red colors and although our specimens were rather fresh such a loss of color by fading might be expected. A more important difference is the distinct cerebrose surface of the pileus in our plant, not mentioned at all by Peck; for the present it may be considered var. *cerebrosus,* until further data are at hand. It is evidently rare, but there is a curious coincidence in its discovery in the same year at three separate localities, viz., Vaughns and Ithaca, N. Y., and Detroit, Michigan.

LACTARIEÆ

Context of fruit-body fleshy, putrescent, *vesiculose;* stem confluent with pileus and gills, central; gills brittle, attached, acute on edge, mostly with cystidia in the hymenium; spores sphoeroid, rough, white, yellowish or ochraceous.

This subfamily is sharply set off from the others by the vesiculose trama of the fruit-body and the echinulate or otherwise roughened, globose spores. With the exception of the Cortinarii, no other groups develop such a variety of bright-colored pilei. Many of them possess a strong acrid taste, and nearly all of them have specially differentiated hyphae scattered through the trama, which in the Lactarii secrete a milky or colored juice. The hymenium is composed of cylindric-clavate basidia intermingled with cystidia; the latter often extend into or below the subhymenium, and in the young plant project above the basidia; later they are often even with the rest of the hymenium. In a few cases the cystidia are scanty or lacking. The subhymenium is differentiated to a greater or less extent in the different species, consisting of a tissue of small roundish cells between basidia and trama.

The group is apparently derived from Hygrophorus, probably by several paths. The gills have a somewhat waxy consistency in some species, reminding one of the gills of that genus. There are two well-marked genera:

Lactarius, exuding a milky juice when wounded.

Russula, without this juice.

Lactarius Fr.

(From the Latin, *lac,* milk.)

Veil none; the trama composed of *vesiculose* tissue, and *with a milky or colored juice* which exudes when plant is broken; gills rigid, fragile, acute on edge; stem central, confluent with the pileus; spores globose or subglobose, usually echinulate or verrucose, white or yellowish.

Fleshy and putrescent fungi, often of large size, mostly terrestrial, sometimes on much decayed wood. The genus is very distinct and

most closely related to Russula, from which it differs by the exudation of a milky or colored juice from the gills and elsewhere when
wounded. The abundance and size of many species which are *edible*
makes this an important genus economically; but a number of
species are believed to be *poisonous* and must be carefully distinguished.

The PILEUS may be white, yellow, orange, green, blue, reddish,
tan, gray, etc., often with the colors in variegated zones of related
hues. It is either dry or viscid, glabrous, velvety or tomentose, and
the margin which is at first involute is usually much more velvety
or tomentose than the center of the pileus; in some species, however,
the margin is naked. The GILLS are usually adnate at first or
acuminate on the stem, becoming spuriously decurrent in many
cases as the margin of the pileus is elevated at maturity or in age.
They are usually rigid-brittle, and exude the milky juice to best
advantage when quickly cut by a sharp-pointed instrument. They
are usually of unequal length and often forked, sometimes dichotomously as in *L. piperatus*. The color of the gills varies from
white to yellowish or grayish, and in many cases they become distinctly darker in age, a character on which the main division has
been based. In one group they become dusted by the spores and are
said to be pruinose in age. The STEM has a rigid cortex with a
spongy-stuffed interior, and becomes rather brittle. It is never
fibrous but may become hollow or cavernous with age. It is either
white or has the color of the pileus, but often diluted. Its rigid,
stiff-looking appearance, which is due to the vesiculose structure of
the flesh, gives both the species of this genus as well as those of
Russula a characteristic pose by which these two genera are soon
easily recognized. The TRAMA has a structure which, along with
that of the Russulas, is unique among the Agaricaceae. The hyphae
of the usual slender, filamentous type of other genera are rather
scanty, and interweave among clusters of thin-walled, parenchyma-
like, isodiametric cells, forming the so-called vesiculose tissue.
Mixed with the filamentous are the milk-bearing hyphae, called
"latex-tubes" or "lactiferes." These extend longtitudinally up
through the stem, spread out in the pileus and extend through the
gills. The "MILK," as it is called, is usually white as it comes from
a sudden wound, but in several species it is colored blue, orange or
red. After the white milk is exposed to the air for a few minutes, it
either remains unchanged or becomes yellow, lilac, pink, greenish
or grayish. In many species this change is only noticeable where
the milk touches the flesh, and the latter takes on the corresponding

color. In a few species the juice is watery or a diluted white; this was considered by Fries as a degenerate condition due to the habitat. During very dry weather or in old specimens the juice is dried up and does not respond to the wounding of the tissue. Some species of Mycena are also supplied with a colored juice, but these lack the vesiculose trama and are very slender-stemmed plants. The TASTE of the milk and flesh is often very acrid in fresh plants and continued sampling of many specimens the same day is apt to produce a sore tongue. It is, however, necessary to know whether a species is acrid or mild, hence cautious tasting of minute pieces of the gills is not objectionable and if kept in the mouth but a short time and not swallowed, no harm results. This character is of great importance in determining the species of this genus. Some species, usually called mild, have a woody or bitterish taste. The SPORES are globose to almost broadly e'liptical in some species. The epispore is decorated with minute spines, reticulations, etc. The color varies from white to yellowish, not nearly as variable as in the genus Russula. The size of the spore is not sufficiently different to be of much use in ordinary diagnosis of species. CYSTIDIA are abundant in many of the species, and are apparently of the same nature as in Russula.

Many species, especially those with a mild taste, are EDIBLE, and are much prized by mycophagists; such are *L. deliciosus, L. volemus, L. hygrophoroides, L. indigo,* etc. The very acrid species should be tried cautiously. Some are considered poisonous and have been so marked. The poison is, however, not of the same order as in the Amanitas, and there is a growing belief that if properly prepared most, if not all of them, may be eaten with impunity. *L. piperatus,* whose milk has a most excruciatingly biting effect on the tongue when taken from a fresh plant, is known to be perfectly safe after it is cooked. All serious accidents which have come to my notice in the state, have been traced with fair certainty to the Amanitas. Any mushroom, however, especially if fried, may cause illness to people with poor digestion in the same way as many other delicious articles of food.

The Lactarii are most abundant during July and August, with a similar seasonal range as the Russulas. They often occur in large numbers in the open woods of higher ground, although some species are mostly limited to swamps, bogs and low rich woods. I have seen hundreds of individuals of several species, including *L. vellereus,* in an area several rods in extent. Others like *L. indigo* are mostly few in a place and occur in widely separated localities.

The Friesian arrangement into two main groups is here retained. Other groupings which have been attempted, seem to me to have brought out no clearer relationships and tend only to complicate matters. The main divisions are here considered as subgenera. These have been subdivided into sections, depending on the character of the surface of the pileus, and on the taste. The key includes only the species so far identified from plants gathered within the state.

Key to the Species

(A)   Milk brightly colored from the first. [See also (AA) and (AAA)].
  (a)   Young gills and milk indigo-blue. 78. *L. indigo* Schw.
  (aa)   Not indigo-blue.
    (b)   Young gills and milk dark red. 76. *L. subpurpureus* Pk.
    (bb)   Young gills and milk orange. 77. *L. deliciosus* Fr.
(AA)   Milk at first white, changing color on exposure to the air, at least on the flesh.
  (a)   Milk becoming lilac or violet-lilac, at least on the bruised flesh.
    (b)   Pileus zonate, 8-12 cm. broad; stem spotted. 75. *L. maculatus* Pk.
    (bb)   Pileus azonate, 3-7 cm. broad; stem not spotted. 74. *L. uvidus* Fr.
  (aa)   Milk not changing to lilac.
    (b)   Milk becoming pinkish-red, at least on the bruised flesh.
      (c)   Pileus chocolate-brown to pale sooty-brown, usually rugose. 80. *L. lignyotus* Fr.
      (cc)   Pileus grayish-brown to isabelline, even. 79. *L. fulginosus* Fr.
    (bb)   Milk not changing to pinkish red.
      (c)   Milk becoming yellow, at least on the bruised flesh.
        (d)   Margin of pileus tomentose-hairy.
          (e)   Stem spotted; pileus straw-color to ochraceous. 60. *L. scrobiculatus* Fr.
          (ee)   Stem not spotted; pileus buff tinged with flesh color. 62. *L. cilicioides* Fr.
        (dd)   Margin of pileus glabrous or nearly so.
          (e)   Pileus azonate, dry or scarcely viscid, some shade of reddish-brown.
            (f)   Odor strong, disagreeable. 69. *L. theiogalus* Fr.
            (ff)   Not with marked odor.
              (g)   Pileus substriate on margin, fading to isabelline. 88. *L. isabellinus* Burl.
              (gg)   Pileus even on margin, color of *L. comphoratus*. 87. *L. colorascens* Pk.
          (ee)   Pileus zonate, at least toward margin.
            (f)   Pileus very viscid when moist, orange-yellow. 86. *L. croceus* Burl.
            (ff)   Pileus subviscid.
              (g)   Pileus distinctly spotted-zoned with dull-orange zones; milk very acrid. 68. *L. chrysorheus* Fr.
              (gg)   Pileus faintly zonate; milk tardily acrid or bitterish. 69. *L. theiogalus* Fr.
      (cc)   Milk not changing to yellow.
        (d)   Milk becoming greenish on the bruised flesh.
          (e)   Pileus dark live-green, rather rigid, zonate. 59. *L. atrovirides* Pk.
          (ee)   Pileus livid-smoky-gray, azonate. 73. *L. trivialis* var. *viridilactis.*
        (dd)   Milk not changing to green or brownish on flesh.
          (e)   Gills stained gray where bruised.

    (f)   Pileus olive-brown to umber, rigid, 6-12 cm. broad. **58.** *L. turpis* Fr.

    (ff) Pileus drab-colored to lilac-grayish, 3-6 cm. broad. **85.** *L. vietus* Fr.

  (ee) Milk changing to brown on the flesh. **94.** *L. luteolus* Pk.

(AAA) Milk white, unchanging.

 (a) Pileus viscid when moist.

  (b) Margin of pileus distinctly tomentose-hairy; pileus incarnate-tinged. **61.** *L. torminosus* Fr.

  (bb) Margin of pileus glabrous or nearly so.

    (c) Pileus distinctly zonate, more or less copper-orange color. **70.** *L. insulsus* Fr.

    (cc) Pileus not or obscurely zonate.

      (d) Pileus large, usually 8-15 cm. broad.

        (e) Pileus pale yellowish or subochraceous; gills broad. **71.** *L. affinis* Pk.

        (ee) Pileus white soon spotted-stained; gills becoming flesh-colored. **65.** *L. controversus* Fr.

        (eee) Pileus livid-smoky gray or tinged slightly with lilac-purplish. **73.** *L. trivialis* Fr.

      (dd) Pileus medium to small, less than 8 cm. broad.

        (e) Pileus drab or lilac-gray; gills pruinose. **85.** *L. vietus* Fr.

        (ee) Pileus some other color.

          (f) Pileus and stem cinereus, glabrous, small. **84.** *L. cinereus* Pk.

          (ff) Pileus reddish.

            (g) Pileus unbonate-papillate, reddish-fulvous, 1-2 cm. broad. **96.** *L. oculatus* (Pk.) Burl.

            (gg) Pileus umbilicate-depressed, reddish-brown, 5-7 cm. broad. **72.** *L. hysginus* Fr.

 (aa) Pileus not viscid.

  (b) Pileus minutely tomentose, scaly, pubescent or with velvety-bloom.

    (c) Taste mild, never acrid; pileus reddish-brown to pale tawny.

      (d) Gills close; pileus rugose-reticulate, velvety-pubescent. **92.** *L. corrugis* Pk.

      (dd) Gills distant; pileus even or slightly rugulose, almost glabrous. **93.** *L. hygrophoroides* B. & C.

    (cc) Taste acrid or slowly acrid, if mild then pileus not reddish-brown.

      (d) Odor aromatic, rather -strong.

        (e) Pileus ashy to smoky-brown. *L. glyciosmus* Fr.

        (ee) Pileus tawny to isabelline; in swamps and bogs. **81.** *L. helvus* Fr.

      (dd) Odor none.

        (e) Pileus white or whitish.

          (f) Pileus persistently velvety-tomentose on entire surface. **63.** *L. vellereus* Fr.

          (ff) Pileus glabrous on center, margin densely cottony-tomentose. **64.** *L. deceptivus* Fr.

        (ee) Pileus not white.

          (f) Pileus 1-3 cm. broad, gray; often on much decayed wood. **83.** *L. griseus* Pk.

          (ff) Pileus 2-7 cm. broad; flesh reddish or flesh-color where bruised.

            (g) Pileus chocolate-brown to pale sooty-brown, rugose on center. **80.** *L. lignyotus* Fr.

            (gg) Pileus grayish-brown to isabelline. **79.** *L. fuliginosus* Fr.

  (bb) Pileus glabrous.

    (c) Pileus etc. white; gills very crowded, dichotomously forked.

66. *L. piperatus* Fr.
(cc) Pileus not white.
  (d) Pileus some shade of gray or brown.
    (e) Gills becoming dingy greenish-brown where bruised.
      (f) Pileus 1-3 cm. broad, pale lilaceous-umber. 89. *L. parvus* Pk.
      (ff) Pileus 3-6 cm. broad, grayish-buff. 90. *L. varius* Pk.
    (ee) Gills not changing to greenish-brown when wounded; pileus zoned, gray to brownish-gray. 67. *L. pyrogalus* Fr.
  (dd) Pileus some shade of red or yellow.
    (e) Gills distant; pileus pale brownish-orange. 93. *L. hygrophoroides* B. & C.
    (ee) Gills close or subdistant.
      (f) Taste acrid.
        (g) Pileus bay-red to rufus. 82. *L. rufus* Fr.
        (gg) Pileus pale yellowish to subochraceus. 71. *L. affinis* Pk.
      (ff) Taste mild or nearly so.
        (g) Odor aromatic, sometimes faint.
          (h) Pileus even, brown-red; color persisting. 97. *L. camphoratus* Fr.
          (hh) Pileus rimulose, areolate, brown-red, fading. 98. *L. rimosellus* Pk.
        (gg) Odor none.
          (h) Pileus 5-12 cm. broad, brownish-orange to fulvous; stem solid. 91. *L. volemus* Fr.
          (hh) Pileus 2-5 cm. broad, brownish-red to isabelline; stem stuffed to hollow. 95. *L. subdulcis* Fr.

PIPERITES: Gills not becoming darker nor pruinose-sprinkled in age.

In this group the milk is either colored or white. In some species it changes on exposure to the air and stains the gills so that they assume a different color than at first; such species must not be referred to the second group, since there the gills assume a darker color without reference to the milk.

Section I. Pileus, especially on margin, shaggy, scabrous, tomentose or hairy-fringed; taste *acrid*.

58. Lactarius turpis Fr.

Epicrisis, 1836-38.

Illustrations: Fries, Sverig. Svamp., Pl. 60.
  Cooke, Ill., Pl. 987.
  Gillet, Champignons de France, No. 397.
  Ricken, Blätterpilze, Pl. 9, Fig. 4.

PILEUS 6-12 cm. broad, *rigid,* convex-umbilicate, then expanded and depressed, *olive-brown to umber,* darker on disk, azonate, somewhat roughish-floccose, *fibrils glutinous when moist,* at length sub-glabrous, margin at first involute with an olivaceus-yellow villosity. FLESH whitish, compact, thick. GILLS adnate, decurrent, narrow, close to crowded, dingy cream-colored, *stained gray or nearly black where bruised.* STEM 3-4 cm. long, 1.5-2.5 cm. thick, stout, short, firm, scarcely viscid, glabrous, concolor or paler than pileus, *often spotted with darker spots,* even, stuffed, sometimes hollow. SPORES "globose, echinulate, 6.5-8 micr." (Burl.) MILK white, unchanging, causing gray stains on gills, *acrid.* ODOR slight. *Edible.*

Gregarious or solitary. On the ground in the north, in mixed woods of hemlock, balsam, poplar, maple, etc. Presque Isle, Marquette. August-September. Rare or frequent locally.

It is very distinct from *L. atroviridis* in its colors and in the character of the surface of the pileus, etc. Dried specimens are grayish-black. *Lactarius sordidus* Pk. is without doubt the same. It is said to be eaten in Europe, although as Fries remarks, it has a loathsome appearance. It has somewhat the habit of *Paxillus involutus* and like the latter, prefers coniferous woods.

59. Lactarius atroviridis Pk.

N. Y. State Mus. Rep. 42, 1889.

Illustration: Hard, Mushrooms, Fig. 139, p. 175, 1908 (not typical).

PILEUS 6-15 cm. broad, *subrigid,* convex-expanded, soon depressed, *dry,* rough-scabrous to scabrous-hairy, often rugose, *dark olive-green,* becoming blackish-green, sometimes obscurely mottled-zonate toward margin, which is at first involute then spreading and thin. FLESH whitish, thick and compact on disk. GILLS adnate or subdecurrent, close, distinct, rather narrow, whitish at first, *stained with dark green where bruised* or in age, intervenose, few forked. STEM *short,* 2-5 cm. long, 1-2.5 cm. thick, stout, subrigid, equal, dry, glabrous, *dark greenish,* soon hollow or cavernous. SPORES "subglobose, echinulate, 7-8 micr., white." (Burl.) MILK white, unchanging, causing dark green stains on gills, *acrid.*

Gregarious. On the ground in frondose woods. Ann Arbor, Detroit. August. Infrequent.

Blackish when dried. A very curious and repellent mushroom, concerning whose edibility nothing is known. It is quite distinct and easily recognized by its blackish-green colors, rigid flesh and short stem. The pileus is relatively much broader than the stem and is often exceedingly rough-scabrous on the surface, especially in dry weather. It seems distributed over the northeastern portion of the United States, but is not often collected. The stem is often spotted with darker spots.

60. Lactarius scrobiculatus Fr. (Poisonous)

Syst. Myc., 1821.

Illustrations: Cooke, Ill., Pl. 971.
  Gillet, Champignons de France, No. 392.
  Patouillard, Tab. Analyt:, No. 409.
  Michael, Führer f. Pilzfreunde, Vol. II, No. 53.
  Hard, Mushrooms, Fig. 133, p. 169, 1908.
  Ricken, Blätterpilze, Pl. 9, Fig. 2.

PILEUS 7-17 cm. broad, convex-depressed, at length infundibuliform, varying azonate to markedly zonate, *viscid when moist,* often covered by a thin, hairy tomentum, *straw-yellow to dark ochraceus,* becoming subferruginous and areately cracked when dry, *margin* at first involute and *tomentose-hairy or densely fringed.* FLESH compact, firm, white, changing to yellowish from the milk. GILLS adnate, subdecurrent, narrow, crowded, sometimes forked or anastomosing on stem, whitish or yellowish, darker where wounded. STEM 3-6 cm. long, 2.5-3 mm. thick, *stout,* short, equal, stuffed then hollow, glabrous, concolor or paler than pileus, *with depressed, roundish spots of a brighter color.* SPORES subglobose-elliptical, "minutely echinulate, 6.5-7x8-10 micr., white." (Burl.) MILK white, *changing quickly to sulphur-yellow, acrid. Poisonous.*

Gregarious. On the ground in moist woods, or along mossy margins of swamps, mostly in coniferous regions. Bay View, Huron Mountains, New Richmond. July-August. Infrequent.

The well-marked depressed spots on the stem and the tomentose-hairy margin distinguish it. The margin finally becomes spreading or elevated and the tomentosity gradually disappears. The zones of the pileus may be very obscure or quite distinct; in one large specimen I counted seventeen zones. It is a magnificent mushroom when in full luxuriance, but is not often found.

61. Lactarius torminosus Fr. (POISONOUS)

Syst. Myc., 1821.

Illustrations: Fries, Sverig. Svamp., Pl. 28.
  Cooke, Ill., Pl. 972.
  Gillet, Champignons de France, No. 395.
  Michael, Führer f. Pilzfreunde, Vol. I, No. 38.
  Hard, Mushrooms, Fig. 127, p. 165, 1908.
  Atkinson, Mushrooms, Fig. 118, p. 119, 1900.
  Ricken, Blätterpilze, Pl. 9, Fig. 3.

PILEUS 4-10 cm. broad, convex, depressed to subinfundibuliform, viscid when young or moist, ochraceus-buff *tinged with rosy-flesh color,* spotted-zoned, sometimes paler and azonate, *margin* at first involute and *persistently tomentose-hairy or fringed,* disk glabrous. FLESH rather soft, thick, white or tinged incarnate. GILLS decurrent, narrow, thin, close, some forked at base, whitish to creamy, *at length incarnate or reddish-yellow.* STEM 3-6 cm. long, 1.5-2 cm. thick, short, equal or tapering downwards, glabrous or pruinose, even, stuffed then hollow, flesh-color, paler below, sometimes spotted. SPORES "elliptical, echinulate, 8-10x6-8 micr., white." (Burl.) MILK white, *unchanging, very acrid. Poisonous.*

Gregarious. On the ground in mixed forests of birch and hemlock, etc., and in frondose woods of oak, maple, elm, etc.

Throughout the state, from the southern limits to Isle Royale. July-September. Frequent.

Known by the tomentose-fringed margin of the pileus, the zones on the surface, the white, acrid milk which remains unchanged, and the pinkish-yellow or ochraceus color. It must be carefully distinguished from the edible species like *L. deliciosus.* It is usually much paler than the latter, but occasionally approaches it in its colors, and *L. deliciosus* has colored milk and the margin of pileus is naked. *L. torminosus* is poisonous, yet the Russian peasants are said to preserve it and eat it seasoned with oil and vinegar.

62. Lactarius cilicioides Fr. (POISONOUS)

Syst. Myc., 1821.

Illustration: Cooke, Ill., Pl. 973.

"PILEUS 4-10 cm. broad, broadly convex or nearly plane, umbilicate or centrally depressed, occasionally subinfundibuliform, *covered with long matted hairs or tomentum,* the center sometimes naked with age, *azonate,* viscid when moist, white, reddish, buff or dingy incarnate. FLESH soft. GILLS adnate or slightly decurrent, thin, rather narrow, close, some forked, white or tinged with yellow or incarnate. STEM 2-3 cm. long, 6-12 mm. thick, *short,* equal or tapering downward, pruinose, stuffed then hollow, *not spotted,* white or whitish. SPORES globose-elliptical, 6-8 micr., white. MILK white, sparse, slowly changing to pale yellow, *acrid.*

"In pine woods. September-October."

The description is adapted from Peck (N. Y. Mus. Rep. 38) who remarks that it is distinguished from all others by its conspicuously woolly pileus. The hairs or fibrils are long and intricately matted, and very viscid in wet weather. The milk is said to be very sparse, and in a white variety, sometimes wanting. I have not yet found it in the state, but as it is said to be *poisonous* like the preceding, to which it is closely related, it seemed desirable to include it. The white variety might be mistaken for a Russula.

63. Lactarius vellerius Fr. (SUSPECTED)

Syst. Myc., 1821.

Illustrations: Cooke, Ill., Pl. 980.
    Bresadola, Fungh. Mang. e. Vel., Pl. 67.
    Gillet, Champignons de France, No. 400.
    Ricken, Blätterpilze, Pl. 10, Fig. 2.
    Hussey, Illust. Brit. Myc. I, Pl. 63.
    White, Conn. Geol. Nat. Hist. Surv., Bull. 15, Pl. 13.

PILEUS 6-12 cm. broad, subrigid, convex-umbilicate, at length expanded and concave-depressed, *dry, white or whitish, entirely minutely tomentose,* velvety to the touch, margin at first involute then spreading or elevated. FLESH compact, thick white or *stained* from the milk. GILLS adnate-subdecurrent, *subdistant to distant,* moderately broad, somewhat forked, whitish to creamy-yellow becoming brownish-stained. STEM 1.5 cm. long, 1.5-3 cm. thick, equal or tapering downward, *short, stout, pruinose-pubescent,* white, rigid, solid. SPORES subglobose to broadly elliptical, *nearly smooth,* 7-9 micr., white. MILK white, unchanging or temporarily cream-colored, sometimes lacking, *acrid. Poisonous.*

Gregarious. On the ground in mixed and frondose woods, often very abundant.

Throughout the state from the southern limits to Lake Superior. July-September. Rather frequent locally.

This differs from *L. piperatus* in the velvety-tomentose pileus and rather distant gills. *L. deceptivus* has a thick, cottony tomentum on the involute margin, but is almost glabrous elsewhere. Sometimes the milk of *L. vellerius* seems to be lacking, when it might be mistaken for *Russula delica;* the latter, however, lacks the tomentosity of the pileus as a rule, and often has a greenish tinge on the apex of the stem and the edge of the gills. Its edibilty is questioned, but McIlvaine ate it for years. Others also consider it edible since it loses its acridity when cooked. Without doubt it can be eaten by some, but like *Lepiota morgani,* causes bad effects in others. The nature of its harmful principle should be investigated.

64. Lactarius deceptivus Pk. (EDIBLE)

N. Y. State Mus. Rep. 38, 1885.

Illustrations: Peck, N. Y. State Mus. Rep. 54, Pl. 70, Fig. 7-I, 1901.
    White, Conn. Geol. & Nat. Hist. Surv., Bull. 3, Pl. 8, op. p. 30.
    Hard, Mushrooms, Fig. 129, p. 167 (poor).

PILEUS 7-15 cm. broad, firm, convex-umbilicate, then expanded-depressed or subinfundibuliform, dry, glabrous or nearly so except the margin, *white or whitish,* often with dingy rusty stains, *margin* at first involute and *densely cottony-tomentose,* then spreading or elevated and fibrillose. FLESH compact, thick, white. GILLS adnate-subdecurrent, *rather broad,* subdistant, some forked, white or cream-yellow. STEM 3-7 cm. long, 1-4 cm. thick, stout, short, *solid,* equal or tapering downward, pruinose-pubescent, white. SPORES subglobose to broadly elliptical, 9-12 micr., echinulate, white. MILK white, unchanging, *acrid. Edible.*

Gregarious. On the ground, especially in coniferous woods, occasionally in frondose woods.

Isle Royale, Huron Mountains, Marquette, Houghton, Detroit; throughout the state. July-September. Sometimes very abundant in the north.

Easily confused with *L. vellerius,* from which it differs in the thick, cottony inrolled margin of the pileus and its glabrous surface elsewhere. It has also large spores as compared with *L. vellerius.* It has been eaten in quantity by Peck who pronounces it of fair quality, since the acrid taste disappears in cooking; with us it is far

more abundant in the Northern Peninsula, apparently prefering
the colder latitude or altitude. It is said to be most abundant in
the mountainous regions in the eastern United States.

65. Lactarius controversus Fr.

Syst. Myc., 1821.

Illustrations: Fries, Sverig. Svamp., Pl. 29.
  Bresadola, Fungh. mang. e. vel., Pl. 61.
  Gillet, Champignons de France, No. 381.
  Cooke, Ill., Pl. 1003 (extreme form).

PILEUS 8-20 cm. broad, firm, convex and broadly umbilicate or
depressed, at length infundibuliform, *viscid* when moist, appressed
subtomentose or flocculose, *white at first,* at length tinged incarnate
and *stained with brownish flesh colored spots, obscurely* zoned toward margin which is at first involute but soon spreading and elevated or reflexed. FLESH white or at length slightly incarnate.
GILLS attenuate behind, at length ascending-decurrent, abrupt,
narrow, crowded, whitish at first *then strongly incarnate* to pink-
incarnate, thin, rather easily separable from pileus. STEM 3-4 cm.
long, 1-3 cm. thick, *often eccentric,* equal or narrowed downward,
solid, firm or spongy, subflocculose, glabrescent, even, not spotted,
white within and without. SPORES subglobose, echinulate, 5-7
micr., white or slightly incarnate-tinged. MILK white, unchanging,
slowly acrid, often rather scanty.

Gregarious. On the ground in low, moist, frondose woods. Ann
Arbor, Jackson, Detroit, etc. August-September. Frequent in the
southeastern part of the state.

This interesting species I have seen frequently and it appeared
to be undescribed. A comparison of figures and descriptions has
convinced me that it is an American form of *L. controversus.* The
spots on the cap do not become so deeply colored as described for
the European plant, but otherwise there is very little discrepancy.
When young the plants are white and are easily mistaken for *L.
piperatus,* but soon the gills, etc., take on the characteristic flesh-
color. The color of the gills is often bright incarnate while that of
the cap, flesh and stem is slightly so only in age. The stem is sometimes somewhat proemorsely rooted. The European plant is said
to be edible. A form occurs which has a hollow stem but otherwise
not very distinct; this may be *L. pubescens* Fr. The latter is said
to be much smaller.

Section II. Pileus glabrous, *dry;* taste acrid.

66. Lactarius piperatus Fr. (EDIBLE)

Syst. Myc., 1821.

Illustrations: Fries, Sverig. Svamp., Pl. 27.
    Cooke, Ill., Pl. 979.
    Patouillard, Tab. Analyt., No. 119.
    Michael, Führer f. Pilzfreunde, Vol. I, No. 37.
    Ricken, Blätterpilze, Pl. 10, Fig. 3.
    Marshall, Mushroom Book, Pl. 36, p. 92, 1905.
    Atkinson, Mushrooms, Fig. 119, p. 120, 1900.
    Hard, Mushrooms, Fig. 128, p. 166, 1908.
    White, Conn. Geol. & Nat. Hist. Surv., Bull. 3, Pl. 9, op. p. 30.
    Plate IX of this Report.

PILEUS 4-12 cm. broad, firm, convex-umbilicate, then expanded-depressed, at length infundibuliform, *dry, glabrous,* azonate, *white,* even, *margin* at first involute and *naked,* at length spreading or elevated. FLESH white, compact, thick. GILLS attenuate-sub-decurrent, *narrow, very crowded,* dichotomously *forked,* white then cream-yellow. STEM 2-6 cm. long, 1-2 cm. thick, equal or tapering downward, dry, firm, *solid,* glabrous or pruinose, white. SPORES subglobose, nearly smooth, 6-7.5 micr., white. MILK white, unchanging, *very acrid,* copious. *Edible.*

Gregarious or scattered. On the ground in frondose woods of maple, oak, etc.

Throughout the Southern Peninsula, less frequent northward. July-September. Common.

This has the most intensely biting taste of all Lactarii. The acridity disappears in cooking and it can then be eaten with impunity. McIlvaine advises its use in gravy. This species is distinguished from its near relatives by its naked margin and very crowded and dichotomously forked gills which become dingy pale yellowish in age. The photograph of Marshall and the figure of Michael show extreme forms if they refer to this plant. *L. pergamenus* Fr. is said to differ in its longer and stuffed stem, and the pileus is thinner and wrinkled, and is not umbilicate at first; some consider it only a variety. A form occurred near Marquette with merely close gills, and in which the milk changed to pale sulphur-yellow; it had a pleasant odor and is var. *fragrans* Burl. (See Torr. Bot. Club Bull. 14, p. 20, 1908.)

67. Lactarius pyrogalus Fr. (POISONOUS)

Syst. Myc., 1821.

Illustrations: Gillet, Champignons de France, No. 390.
    Ricken, Blätterpilze, Pl. 11, Fig. 2.
    Patouillard, Tab. Analyt., No. 121.

PILEUS 4-6 cm. broad, convex then plane and depressed, *gray to livid-gray or brownish-gray,* darker in the center, *zoned* toward margin, moist in wet weather but *not viscid,* glabrous, margin at first involute then spreading. FLESH white, compact, thick. GILLS adnate-subdecurrent, *subdistant to distant,* firm, thin, moderately broad, *yellowish.* STEM 3-5 cm. long, 6-10 mm. thick, equal or tapering downwards, glabrous, becoming hollow, concolor or paler, white-mycelioid at base. SPORES subglobose, echinulate, 6-8 micr., pale ochraceous. CYSTIDIA abundant, subcylindrical, 67-70x9 micr. MILK white, *very acrid,* abundant, persisting as coagulated yellowish globules on the edge of the gills. *Poisonous.*
On the ground in woods. Bay View, Marquette, Ann Arbor. July-August. Infrequent.
Known by its distant gills which become yellowish, the subzonate gray pileus and the milk. The milk often remains as coagulated drops on the gills.

68. Lactarius chrysorheus Fr. (POISONOUS)

Epicrisis, 1836-38.

Illustrations: Cooke, Ill., Pl. 984.
    Gillet, Champignons de France, No. 379.
    Ricken, Blätterpilze, Pl. 13, Fig. 4.
    Atkinson, Mushrooms, Fig. 123, 1900.

PILEUS 4-10 cm. broad, convex and broadly umbilicate, then expanded-depressed to subinfundibuliform, *dry or subviscid,* glabrous, color variable, *whitish to yellowish tinged incarnate, zoned with dull orange or yellow,* sometimes almost fulvous, spotted, margin at first involute then pruinose-tomentose, then elevated. FLESH whitish then yellowish from the milk, medium thick. GILLS adnate-decurrent, *crowded,* less so in age, *narrow,* some forked at base, thin, white at first, soon dingy yellowish, stained darker in age. STEM 4-6 cm. long, 1-1.5 cm. thick, equal or subequal, pruinose, glabrescent, even, stuffed then hollow, white, changing to color of pileus with age, sometimes spotted. SPORES subglobose, echinulate, 7-8 micr., white. MILK white, *changing to sulphur-yellow,* copious, very acrid. *Poisonous.*

Subcaespitose or gregarious. On the ground in frondose woods. Ann Arbor, Detroit, Marquette, etc., throughout the state. August-September.

Closely related to *L. theiogalus.* The latter has a more truly viscid pileus which is usually not zoned, and an odor which is well-marked and disagreeable. *L. chrysorheus* is sometimes frequent locally but I have so far not happened upon it in many localities. It may be that it is quite strongly restricted to certain seasons. Fries, Ricken and other European authors describe the pileus as always dry but in the United States it is often subviscid in moist weather. The milk sometimes turns slowly and the taste is occasionally bitter-acrid.

69. Lactarius theiogalus Fr. (SUSPECTED)

Syst. Myc., 1821.

Illustrations: Gillet, Champignons de France, No. 396.
Ricken, Blätterpilze, Pl. 13, Fig. 5.
Burlingham, Torr. Bot. Club Mem. 14, Fig. 12, p. 70, 1908.

PILEUS 3-8 cm. broad, convex then expanded, *umbonate, obtuse or depressed,* dry or subviscid, even or wrinkled-uneven, glabrous, *incarnate-isabelline to pale tawny-reddish or fulvous,* obscurely zonate to azonate, margin at first involute soon spreading. FLESH medium thick, compact, white then yellowish from the milk. GILLS adnate-subdecurrent, close, rather narrow, some forked near base, pallid to yellowish-flesh color, reddish-brown where bruised or in age. STEM 3-7 cm. long, 6-12 mm. thick, subequal, firm, *undulate-uneven,* stuffed then hollow, glabrous, concolor or paler, substrigose at base. SPORES "subglobose to broadly elliptical, minutely echinulate, 8-9x6-7 micr., whitish." (Burl.) MILK white, *changing to sulphur-yellow,* tardily but very acrid. ODOR *strong,* pungent, disagreeable. *Suspected.*

Gregarious. On the ground in coniferous woods, sometimes in swampy places. Marquette, Huron Mountains, Houghton, Bay View, New Richmond. July-October. Frequent locally.

This species differs as a rule from the preceding by its umbonate or obtuse pileus, but this is not always reliable. It is necessary to

take into account the odor of the fresh plant, the undulate surface
of the stem and the color of the pileus. Usually it lacks the zones
which are marked in *L. chrysorheus,* but I have specimens from a
sphagnum swamp which show the zones quite well. Miss Burlingham states that it is more zonate in wet places. *L. brevis* Pk. and
L. brevipes Longyear, are considered by Miss Burlingham as
ecological forms of this species. Ricken refers this to the group
with pruinose gills; it is, however, too close to the preceding to be
placed so far away. Its taste is sometimes bitter at first.

Section III. Pileus glabrous, *viscid;* taste *acrid.*

70. **Lactarius insulsus** Fr. (SUSPECTED)

Syst. Myc., 1821.

Illustrations: Cooke, Ill., Pl. 975.
    Bresadola, Fungh. mang. e. vel., Pl. 62.
    Gillet, Champignons de France, No. 386.
    Hard, Mushrooms, Fig. 135, p. 171, 1908.
    Ibid, Fig. 132, p. 168 (as *L. regalis* Pk.).
    Plate X of this Report.

PILEUS 5-10 cm. broad, rigid, convex-umbilicate, then expanded-
depressed to infundibuliform, *coppery-orange,* with alternate *zones*
of deeper or lighter tones, sometimes paler throughout, *viscid,* glabrous, somewhat uneven, margin at first involute then elevated and
arched, naked. FLESH scarcely compact, thick, white. GILLS adnate then decurrent, thin, *narrow,* some forked at base, white then
pallid. STEM 2-5 cm. long, 8-15 mm. thick, equal or tapering downward, glabrous, stuffed then hollow, paler than pileus. SPORES
globose, strongly echinulate, 7-9.5 micr., pale yellowish. MILK
white, unchanging, *very acrid.*
    Gregarious to caespitose. On the ground in open frondose
woods. Ann Arbor. July-October. Frequent.
    This species does not yet seem to be clearly understood. Ricken
describes a plant which is scarcely zoned except on the margin and
which has very large spores—12-15x10-12 micr. The spore-measurements of Bresadola and Saccardo, on the other hand, agree with
ours. Peck's description (N. Y. State Mus. Rep. 38, p. 122) is that
of the paler form and has been copied by McIlvaine. Our plants are
mostly of the dark yellow to orange type as described by Miss Burlingham, but paler forms also occur. Specimens of the dark form

were sent to Peck who referred them to *L. regalis* Pk. and Dr. Fischer's photograph of it is so named in Hard's book. It is possible that some of our forms represent *L. zonarius* Fr. which is said to have a solid stem, pale orange to yellow-gilvus pileus with a thinner margin. According to Fries (Monographia) *L. insulsus* has the habit and size of *L. deliciosus,* differing in paler colors, acrid taste and white unchangeable milk. Cooke's figure represents our plants well except that they may become darker with age. *L. regalis* is referred by Peck to a variety of *L. resimus* Fr., and is said to be an almost entirely white plant with scarcely noticeable zones, not at all related to *L. insulsus;* its milk changes to sulphur-yellow. The gills of our form of *L. insulsus* sometimes become dingy yellowish in age or where bruised, but the milk is unchangeable. The plants referred to *L. insulsus* by McIlvaine were edible.

71. Lactarius affinis Pk.

N. Y. State Mus. Rep. 23, 1872.
Ibid, (as *L. platyphyllus* Pk.).

PILEUS 6-15 cm. broad, firm, convex-umbilicate then expanded-depressed, *pale yellowish to yellowish-incarnate* or ochraceous-yellow, *azonate, viscid,* glabrous, even, margin involute at first spreading and arched. FLESH white, moderately thick. GILLS adnate-subdecurrent, *broad* or moderately broad, close to subdistant, forked toward base, *creamy-yellowish.* STEM 5-10 cm. long, 1-2 cm. thick, equal, glabrous, stuffed *then hollow,* yellowish to whitish, often spotted. SPORES globose to broadly elliptical, 9-11 micr., echinulate, whitish. MILK white, unchanging, *acrid.*

Gregarious. On the ground in mixed or frondose woods. Marquette, Ishpeming, South Haven, New Richmond, Detroit. July-September. Rather rare.

Often a very large plant, whose pale yellow, zoneless cap and broad subdistant gills set it apart from others. The whole plant has a tendency to be unicolorous, sometimes dark, sometimes paler. Miss Burlingham states that the milk sometimes dries to a pale dull green shade on the gills. Whether it is edible is unknown.

72. Lactarius hysginus Fr.

Syst. Myc., 1821.

Illustrations: Fries, Icones, Pl. 169, Fig. 2.
  Cooke, Ill., Pl. 989.
  Ricken, Blätterpilze, Pl. 12, Fig. 4.

"PILEUS 5-7.5 cm. broad, rigid, convex, then plane, umbilicate or slightly depressed, even, *viscid,* obscurely zonate or azonate, *reddish-incarnate, tan-color or brownish-red,* becoming paler with age, the thin margin involute, GILLS adnate-subdecurrent, close, whitish, becoming yellowish or cream-colored. STEM 2-5 cm. long, 6-15 mm. thick, equal, glabrous, stuffed or hollow, colored like the pileus or a little paler, sometimes spotted. SPORES subglobose, whitish or yellowish, 9-10 micr. MILK white, acrid."

On the ground, mixed woods. Houghton. July.

This was found only in the locality mentioned. The description is that of Peck, with which the fresh plants agreed, except that the gills were almost subdistant. The pileus was obscurely zonate. It was found several times, always solitary.

73. Lactarius trivialis Fr. (SUSPECTED)

Syst. Myc., 1821.

Illustrations: Cooke, Ill., Pl. 976.
  Hard, Mushrooms, Fig. 134, p. 170, 1908.

PILEUS 5-15 cm. broad, convex, soon nearly plane and depressed, glabrous, *viscid, azonate,* color varable, *livid-gray to smoky-gray* or with a lilac-purplish tint, lead-colored or pinkish-brown, margin soon arched, at first pruinose, thin. FLESH thickish, rigid-fragile, pallid. GILLS adnate-subdecurrent, close, thin, moderately broad or rather narrow, some forked, cream-yellowish, *becoming dingy-greenish stained when bruised or in age.* STEM 4-12 cm. long, 1-2 cm. thick, equal, or irregularly undulate, glabrous, even, not spotted, stuffed then *hollow,* firm, concolor or paler than pileus, often pallid. SPORES elliptical, echinulate, 8-10 micr., *yellowish.* MILK white or creamy-white, unchangeable, *acrid. Suspected.*

Gregarious, subcaespitose or scattered. On the ground in frondose and coniferous woods.

Throughout the state, from the southern limits to Isle Royale. July-October. Common.

This is one of our commonest Lactarii during some seasons, usually among the first to appear, especially in the frondose regions. It is found in pine, hemlock, mixed, or oak and maple woods throughout the state. The northern form varies somewhat and needs further study; a variety also occurs in the north whose milk turns sordid green after exposure to the air, with broader and more distant gills and a spotted stem. This may be called var. *viridilactis* var. nov. Peck has described var. *maculatus* with zonate pileus and spotted stem, and var. *gracilis* which is quite a small and slender plant. The common form is a rather large plant; the pileus is sometimes up to 18 cm. broad with a dark livid or lurid, indescribable color, and white or creamy-yellowish, acrid milk. When old or faded the pileus becomes much paler and is often pale leather-colored or incarnate-tan. The flesh of the pileus though rigid is rather fragile and the stem is firm but soon hollow or cavernous.

74. Lactarius uvidus Fr. (Poisonous)

Syst. Myc., 1821.

Illustrations: Cooke, Ill., Pl. 991.
Gillet, Champignons de France, No. 399.
Ricken, Blätterpilze, Pl. 11, Fig. 4.
Patouillard, Tab. Analyt., No. 209.
Hard, Mushrooms, Fig. 144, p. 180, 1908.

PILEUS 3-7 cm. broad, convex then plane and depressed, rather firm, often subumbonate, *viscid,* obscurely or not at all zonate, sometimes spotted, *cinereus with lilac tinge or livid brownish--gray,* margin at first involute and subpruinose, thin and spreading. FLESH whitish, *becoming lilac or violet when cut,* usually rather soft when moist. GILLS adnate-subdecurrent, thin, close, rather narrow, white or yellowish, *quickly becoming violet or lilac when bruised.* STEM 4-7 cm. long, 6-12 mm. thick, subequal, glabrous, uneven-undulate, viscid, white or dingy yellowish, stuffed then hollow or cavernous. SPORES subglobose or broadly elliptical, 8-10 micr., echinulate, white. MILK white, *changing quickly when in contact with the flesh to lilac-violet,* bitterish-acrid.

Gregarious. On the ground in low, mossy places in swamps, thickets, etc. Bay View, Houghton, Marquette. August-September. Infrequent.

Known by the flesh changing to lilac or violet when cut or bruised. It is found in rather wet places, sometimes attached to moss and sphagnum and then the base of the stem is white-tomentose. It seems to be most frequent in the Northern Peninsula. Its edibility is uncertain; it is considered poisonous in Europe.

75. Lactarius maculatus Pk. (Suspected)

N. Y. State Mus. Rep. 41, 1888.

PILEUS 8-12.5 cm. broad, convex-umbilicate, then expanded-depressed to infundibuliform, grayish-buff to grayish-lilac, *distinctly zoned with concentric darker spots,* viscid when moist, glabrous, margin at first involute, naked, then spreading and substriate. FLESH grayish, *becoming lilac where bruised,* rather compact. GILLS adnate-subdecurrent, close, broadest in the middle, attenuate behind, whitish to cream-color, *lilac-vinaceous where wounded.* STEM 3-7 cm. long, 1.5-3 cm. thick, subequal, ventricose or tapering, hollow, sometimes compressed, *spotted-variegated,* concolor, glabrous. SPORES "subglobose, echinulate, 10-12.5 micr." (Peck.) MILK at first white to cream color, unchanged or becoming lilac on the flesh, *acrid.*

On sandy ground, oak and maple hillside along Lake Superior, Marquette. August. Rare.

This is closely related to *L. uvidus,* differing from it in its distinctly zonate pileus, larger size and spotted stem. The milk in our specimens remained unchanged. It is likely that the milk in both *L. uvidus* and *L. maculatus* sometimes turns lilac-vinaceous, that at other times it remains unchanged except to cause the broken flesh where it is touched by the milk to assume a lilac-vinaceous color.

Section IV. Pileus glabrous, viscid; taste *mild; milk bright-colored from the first.*

76. Lactarius subpurpureus Pk. (Edible)

N. Y. State Mus. Rep. 29, 1878.

Illustrations: Peck, Ibid, 54, Pl. 70, Fig. 1-6.
　　　　　　　Burlingham, Torr. Bot. Club Mem. 14, Fig. 8, p. 61, 1908.

PILEUS convex-umbilicate, then expanded-depressed to subinfundibuliform, *dark red,* pink-zoned, with a grayish lustre, spotted with emerald-green, subviscid when moist, glabrous, margin at first involute, pruinose, then spreading. FLESH whitish to pinkish, *becoming red when broken especially* next to the gills. GILLS adnate-subdecurrent, close to subdistant, broadest in middle, medium broad, *dark-red,* fading and *greenish with age.* STEM 3-7 cm. long, 6-15 mm. thick, equal or tapering upwards, glabrous, sometimes pruinose, stuffed then hollow, *dark red, spotted more deeply,* floccose-hairy at base. SPORES "broadly elliptical, echinulate, 8-10x7-8 micr., yellowish." (Burl.) MILK *dark red,* mild. *Edible.*

Gregarious. Low moist woods of hemlock or mixed with hemlock. Bay View, Huron Mountains. August-September. Infrequent.

Easily distinguished by its dark red milk which stains the flesh of the broken plant; later the stains assume a greenish hue. Dried specimens do not show this character well, since they become much paler.

77. Lactarius deliciosus Fr. (EDIBLE)

Syst. Myc., 1821.

Illustrations: Fries, Sverig. Svamp., Pl. 6.
    Gillet, Champignons de France, No. 382.
    Cooke, Ill., Pl. 982.
    Bresadola, Fungh. manger. e. vel., Pl. 64.
    Peck, N. Y. State Mus. Rep. 48, Pl. 29, 1896.
    Atkinson, Mushrooms, Pl. 35, Fig. 1, 1900.
    Gibson, Edible Toadstools, Pl. 18, p. 169, 1903.
    Michael, Führer f. Pilzfreunde, Vol. I, No. 37.
    Swanton, Fungi, Pl. 15, Fig. 6-7.
    Plate XI of this Report.

PILEUS 5-10 cm. broad, convex-umbilicate, then expanded-depressed to subinfundibuliform, viscid when moist, glabrous, *orange or grayish-orange,* fading to grayish in age, *zoned,* zones or spots brighter-colored, involute at first then arched-spreading. FLESH white soon stained orange when broken, then greenish, especially at junction of gills and pileus. GILLS adnate-decurrent, close, rather narrow, intervenose and more or less forked, *bright orange with yellowish sheen,* becoming greenish in age or where bruised. STEM 3-8 cm. long, 8-15 mm. thick, *equal,* even, stuffed then hollow, pruinose, glabrescent, *orange-yellow, orange-spotted or at length greenish-variegated.* SPORES subglobose, echinulate, 8-10x7-8 micr., yellowish. MILK *orange* or *saffron-yellow, mild.*

Gregarious-subcaespitose. On the ground in moist mossy woods in coniferous regions, under hemlock, balsam-fir, spruce, cedar, birch, etc. Isle Royale, Huron Mountains, Marquette, Munising, Houghton, Bay View. July-September. Frequent locally.

The most desirable perhaps of all the Lactarii for the table, but not very common in southern Michigan at least. Its orange milk and the beautiful zones of the cap have frequently attracted the artist, and it has often been illustrated. Its range with us seems to be mostly northward. This statement is based on seven years of collecting in southern Michigan, but does not exclude the possibility of the appearance of *L. deliciosus* when least expected and perhaps in quantity. Such sporadic fruiting is not infrequent in other mushrooms after they seem to be absent from a region. Peck says it occurs in all kinds of woods, but so far it has been found in quantity only in the northern part of the state. Michael says that because of its strong aromatic taste it is not so desirable as food when served alone but as an addition to other dishes it is excellent.

78. Lactarius indigo Schw. (EDIBLE)

Syn. Fung. Carol. Super., 1818.
(Fries, Epicrisis, 1838).

Illustrations: Atkinson, Mushrooms, Pl. 35, Fig. 3, 1900.
McIlvaine, Thousand Amer. Fungi, Pl. 41, Fig. 2.

PILEUS 5-12 cm. broad, convex-subumbilicate, then expanded-depressed to infundibuliform, *indigo-blue or paler,* fading when dry, with a silvery-gray lustre, *zonate,* glabrous. FLESH blue, greenish in age. GILLS adnate-decurrent, close, rather broad, *indigo-blue or paler,* at length pale greenish. STEM 2-5 cm. long, 1-2 cm. thick, equal or tapering downward, glabrous, even, stuffed then hollow, *indigo-blue,* often paler and *spotted.* SPORES "globose to broadly elliptical, echinulate, 7 micr., yellowish." MILK *dark blue, mild. Edible.*

Gregarious. On the ground in oak and maple woods, and sandy pine forests. Ann Arbor, Huron Mountains. Evidently throughout the state. August. Rather rare.

No one can mistake this mushroom as it has no double. It occurs sparingly, but is widely distributed. Schweinitz should be given full credit for naming this striking plant. It seems to be exclusively North American.

RUSSULARIA: Gills becoming darker in age, and then pruinose.

Section V. Pileus minutely scaly, tomentose, pruinose-velvety, dry; taste slowly or slightly acrid.

79. Lactarius fuliginosus Fr. (SUSPECTED)

Syst. Myc., 1821.

Illustrations: Cooke, Ill., Pl. 996.
    Gillet, Champignons de France, No. 384.
    Patouillard, Tab. Analyt., No. 322.
    Ricken, Blätterpilze, Pl. 12, Fig. 5.
    Atkinson, Mushrooms, Fig. 117, p. 119, 1900.

PILEUS 2-6 cm. broad, convex, soon expanded-plane or obtuse, sometimes depressed, *dry, even,* minutely velvety-tomentose or glabrous, *azonate,* isabelline or grayish-brown, *clouded with a smoky shade,* margin at length crenate-wavy. FLESH thin on margin, whitish, *becoming tinted with flesh-pink to salmon-color when broken.* GILLS adnate, at length subdecurrent, distinct, close to subdistant, moderately broad, *pruinose,* pallid then pale ochraceus, *becoming pinkish or salmon when bruised.* STEM 2-6 cm. long, *often short,* 3-10 mm. thick, subequal or tapering downwards, stuffed then hollow, minutely pruinose-velvety or glabrous, pallid-grayish-isabelline or smoky-clouded, pinkish-stained where bruised. SPORES globose, echinulate, 7-9 micr. with long sterigmata, *pale ochraceous-yellow.* MILK white at first, then *changing slowly to flesh-pink or salmon* where in contact with the flesh, *slowly acrid.*

Gregarious. On the ground in frondose woods of oak and maple. Ann Arbor. August. Infrequent.

In Europe it is said to occur also in pine woods. It is known by its smoky-clouded often "snuff-brown" pileus, and the tendency of the flesh to assume a flesh-pink or pale salmon color where bruised. Dry weather plants often respond slowly to bruising. The margin of the pileus in age is apt to be wavy or scalloped. *L. gerardii* Pk. is considered by Atkinson as probably a variety.

80. Lactarius lignyotus Fr. (POISONOUS)

Monographia, 1863.

Illustrations: Fries, Icones, Pl. 171, Fig. 1.
    Michael, Führer f. Pilzfreunde, Vol. II, No. 58.
    Atkinson, Mushrooms, Fig. 116, p. 117, 1900.
    Hard, Mushrooms, Pl. 21, Fig. 236, p. 172, 1908.
    Peck, N. Y. State Mus. Bull. 150, Pl. 123, 1911.

PILEUS 3-7 cm. broad, convex, soon almost plane, *umbonate,*
sometimes slightly depressed and then obsoletely umbonate, *dry,*
azonate, *pruinose-velvety,* even or *mostly uneven-rugulose* toward
the center, chocolate or seal-brown to sooty, margin wavy or sub-
plicate in age. FLESH white, *slowly pinkish or reddish where
wounded.* GILLS adnate-subdecurrent, close to subdistant, moderately broad, *at first pure white,* then ochraceus, reddish or pinkish
where bruised. STEM 4-8 cm. long, 4-12 mm. thick, equal or *abruptly plicate at apex,* pruinose-velvety, sometimes scarcely velvety,
sooty-brown, spongy-stuffed. SPORES globose, 8-9 micr., echinulate,
yellowish, sterigmata long. MILK white, changing slowly to red-
dish-pink where in contact with flesh, *mild* or subacrid. *Poisonous.*

Gregarious. On the ground in woods, especially in coniferous
regions. Marquette, Huron Mountains, Bay View, Ann Arbor.
July-September. Infrequent.

Differs from the preceding in the darker color, the rugose pileus
and longer and more velvety stem. Efforts which I made to differentiate the two by microscopical characters remained abortive.
Both possess slender, cylindrical, aculeate sterile cells on the edge
of the gills, about 4 micr. in diameter. The trama of the gills in
the specimens examined was more filamentous in *L. lignyotus* and
had a floccose structure of spherical cells in *L. fuliginosa.* The two
species, however, appear to run into each other at times.

81. Lactarius helvus Fr.

Syst. Myc., 1821.

Illustrations: Cooke, Ill., Pl. 994.
    Bresadola, Fung. Trid., Pl. 127 and 39.
    Ricken, Blätterpilze, Pl. 13, Fig. 2.

PILEUS 4-12 cm. broad, *fragile,* convex then plane and depressed with decurved margin, with or without an obscure umbo, azonate, *dry, floccose-scaly, tawny-isabelline,* fading, margin at first involute then spreading. FLESH somewhat watery. GILLS subdecurrent, thickish, close to subdistant, rather narrow, broadest behind, whitish then ochraceous tinged incarnate, pruinose. STEM 5-8 cm. long, (up to 15 cm. long on sphagnum), 5-15 mm. thick, subrigid-fragile, subequal, *pruinose-pubescent,* stuffed then cavernous, concolor, white-mycelioid at base. SPORES globose, 7-9 micr., echinulate. MILK *watery,* rarely white, sparse, mild or scarcely acrid. ODOR *fragrant,* like that of *L. camphoratus.*

Gregarious or scattered. On the ground or on moss in low swampy woods, or on sphagnum in peat-bogs, sometimes among moss along exposed borders of lakes, etc. Ann Arbor and elsewhere in the lake regions of the interior. July-Sept. Frequent locally.

This is for the most part included under var. *aquifluus* by Peck but the watery character of the milk is apparently merely a result of the moist habitat.

82. Lactarius rufus Fr. (POISONOUS)

Epicrisis, 1836-38.

Illustrations: Fries, Sverig. Svamp., Pl. 11.
Cooke, Ill., Pl. 985.
Gillet, Champignons de France, No. 391.
Ricken, Blätterpilze, Pl. 13, Fig. 3.
Michael, Führer f. Pilzfreunde, Vol. I, No. 36.
Swanton, Fungi, Pl. 7, Fig. 3-4.

PILEUS 4-10 cm. broad, convex then expanded-depressed to infundibuliform, *umbonate,* flocculose-silky, *glabrescent,* azonate, dry, *bay-red to rufous,* not fading, subshining, margin at first involute. FLESH rather thin, rather soft when moist. GILLS adnate-decurrent, close, at length pruinose, narrow, *ochraceous then rufous.* STEM 5-8 cm. long, (longer in moss), 6-12 mm. thick, equal, dry, glabrous, sometimes pruinose, stuffed then hollow, firm, *rufous or paler,* often strigose-hairy at base. SPORES sub-globose, 7-8 micr., slightly echinulate, white. MILK white, unchanging, *very acrid.* ODOR *none. Poisonous.*

On the ground in hemlock and pine woods. New Richmond. September. Infrequent or local.

Known by its red-brown color, umbonate pileus, very acrid taste and rather large size as compared with others of the same color. Peck has segregated a species on the lack of the umbo, the hollow stem and scanty milk; it is edible. This he named *L. boughtoni* Pk. (see N. Y. State Mus. Bull. 150, p. 32, and Pl. 6, Fig. 1-7). It seems to be an extreme form of *L. rufus* and may be referred to as var. *boughtoni* Pk. Longyear has reported *L. rufus* from a swamp near Lansing where it occurred in large numbers. I have seen it only in the Adirondack Mountains, New York.

83.   Lactarius griseus Pk.

N. Y. State Cab. Rep. 23, 1872.

Illustrations: Burlingham, Torr. Bot. Club, Mem. 14, Fig. 14, p. 18, 1908.
>   Hard, Mushrooms, Fig. 138, p. 174, 1908.

PILEUS 1-4 cm. broad, soon flaccid, convex then depressed to infundibuliform, *papillate, dry,* azonate, *minutely tomentose,* becoming floccose, *grayish* or brownish-gray, variegated smoky-gray, margin at first incurved. FLESH white, *thin.* GILLS adnate-decurrent, close to subdistant, pruinose, broader than the thickness of the pileus, white *then cream-colored to honey-yellow.* STEM 1-5 cm. long, 2-5 mm. thick, equal, dry, glabrous, stuffed then hollow, whitish to grayish. SPORES broadly elliptical to subglobose, 8-9x6-7 micr., echinulate, white. MILK white, unchanging, *slowly acrid.*

Gregarious or scattered. On the ground or on much decayed logs in woods of the coniferous regions of the state. Marquette, Houghton, Huron Mountains, Sault Ste. Marie, Bay View, New Richmond.

Distinguished by its small size, gray color and tomentose-flocculose cap. It differs from *L. cinereus* in its dry, non-glabrous pileus and in the gills becoming cream-yellow in color. It seems to be limited to regions with conifer trees, although it is also found in frondose woods of such regions.

Section VI.   Pileus glabrous, *viscid;* taste *acrid.*

84.   Lactarius cinereus Pk.

N. Y. State Mus. Rep. 24, 1872.

Illustrations: Burlingham, Torr. Bot. Club, Bull. 14, Fig. 11, p. 67, 1908.
>   Hard, Mushrooms, Fig. 137, p. 173, 1908.

PILEUS 1-5 cm. broad, lax, convex-umbilicate, soon expanded-depressed to subinfundibuliform, *viscid* when moist, azonate or sub-zonate, *glabrous,* even, *cinereous,* margin involute at first then spreading. Thin. FLESH white. GILLS adnate, close, narrow, *white,* not yellowish in age, often pruinose. STEM 2-6 cm. long, 6-12 mm. thick, subequal or tapering slightly upwards, stuffed-spongy then hollow, glabrous, *cinereus,* tomentose at base. SPORES sub-globose, echinulate, 6-7.5 micr., *white.* MILK white, unchanging, *acrid.*

Gregarious. On the ground in coniferous and mixed woods of the hemlock regions of the state. Isle Royale, Huron Mountains, Marquette, Houghton, New Richmond. July-September. Infrequent.

Miss Burlingham distinguishes a distinct species which is named *L. mucidus* Burl., which differs from *L. cinereus* in its putty-colored cap with sepia center, and in that the milk stains the flesh and gills blue-grayish-gray. It is said to occur under hemlock but according to this author the true *L. cinereus* is said to be restricted to beech woods. Our plants grew under hemlock, birch, maple and pine. I have no record concerning beech. It is probable that our plants are to be referred to *L. mucidus;* in that case I have no record of *L. cinereus* to which I have always referred these collections. My notes are not sufficient to settle the matter.

85. Lactarius vietus Fr.

Syst. Myc., 1821.

Illustrations: Fries, Icones, Pl. 170, Fig. 1.
Cooke, Ill., Pl. 1009.
Gillet, Champignons de France, No. 401.
Michael, Führer f. Pilzfreunde, Vol. III, No. 71.
Ricken, Blätterpilze, Pl. 14, Fig. 1.

PILEUS 3-6 cm. broad, convex then depressed or subinfundibuli-form, *viscid* when moist, *azonate,* minutely silky-tomentose when dry, *drab-colored or lilac-grayish,* margin involute at first then elevated and arched. FLESH whitish. GILLS adnate-decurrent, close, narrow, *pruinose,* cream color then drab or dingy yellowish, *stained grayish when bruised.* STEM 3-7 cm. long, 5-10 mm. thick, equal or tapering upwards, stuffed then hollow, glabrous or glaucous, rivu-lose-wrinkled, concolor, tinged drab within. SPORES, globose, echinulate, 6-8 micr., cream-buff in mass. MILK white, unchanged, *very slowly acrid.*

Gregarious on the ground, mixed hemlock, beech and maple woods. New Richmond. Infrequent.

Sometimes the whole plant including the gills is pinkish-buff or incarnate. The grayish hue is more marked in age. It is said to be under suspicion.

86. Lactarius croceus Burl.

Torr. Bot. Club, Mem. 14, 1908.

Illustration: Ibid, Fig. 3, p. 38.

PILEUS 5-10 cm. broad, broadly convex-umbilicate then depressed to infundibuliform, *viscid,* azonate or obscurely zonate, micaceous when dry, *orange to saffron-yellow,* glabrous, margin at first involute and pruinose-downy. FLESH rather thin, whitish, *staining yellow or ochraceous where cut.* GILLS adnate-decurrent, close to *subdistant,* moderately broad, rarely forked, pallid to pale yellow or incarnate-tinged, *changing to cadmium-yellow where bruised.* STEM 3-6 cm. long, 1-2 mm. thick, equal, stuffed then hollow, glabrous, pale orange-yellow, spotted. SPORES globose to broadly elliptical, echinulate, 6-8 micr., pale yellow. MILK white, scanty, slowly changing to yellow, acrid or bitter, often slowly acrid.

Gregarious or scattered. On the ground in woods of oak, maple, elm, etc. Detroit. August-September. Local.

This approaches *L. aurantiacus* Fr. if indeed it is not identical. That species is said to be poisonous. The milk, flesh and gills of the European species do not change color like ours. I have found it at different times, always in the same woods near Detroit. Miss Burlingham reports it from Vermont and North Carolina, and identified our specimens as the same.

Section VII. Pileus glabrous, *dry;* taste *acrid or bitter-astringent.*

87. Lactarius colorascens Pk.

N. Y. State Mus. Bull. 94, 1905.

PILEUS 2-6 cm. broad, nearly plane, then depressed, whitish at first, then *reddish-buff to brownish-red,* azonate, dry or subviscid, glabrous. FLESH thin. GILLS adnate, narrow, crowded to close, whitish *soon brownish-red.* STEM 3-6 cm. long, 5-10 mm. thick, glabrous, equal, stuffed, often compressed, even, whitish, *soon concolor.* SPORES "globose, echinulate, 8 micr." (Peck.) MILK white, *changing to sulphur-yellow,* bitter or slightly astringent.

On the Ground in mixed woods. Marquette, New Richmond. August-September. Rare or local.

It has the color of *L. camphoratus* when mature, but the milk turns decidedly sulphur-yellow.. Found so far only in coniferous regions.

88. Lactarius isabellinus Burl.

Torr. Bot. Club, Bull. 34, 1907.

Illustration: Ibid, Fig. 15, p. 103.

PILEUS 2-5 cm. broad, convex then expanded-depressed, sub-umbonate, azonate, *dry,* glabrous, wrinkled on disk, *red-fulvous* when moist, paler on margin, fading, margin at length short-striatulate. FLESH thin, white, *staining yellowish from the milk.* GILLS adnate-subdecurrent, thin, close, narrow, forking toward base, pale yellowish, *soon ochraceous-fulvous.* STEM 2-4 cm. long, 4-6 mm. thick, equal, stuffed then hollow, glabrous, *concolor,* white-tomentose at base. SPORES "slightly echinulate, white, 7-8.5x6-7.5 micr." (Burl.) MILK white or watery, at *length sulphur-yellow on flesh,* abundant, slowly *acrid or astringent.*

On the ground in mixed woods, in coniferous regions. Marquette. August. Rare or local.

Could easily be mistaken for a large form of *L. subdulcis,* but the striations of the pileus, the taste and the changing milk differentiate it. No specimens were retained. In age, the milk seems to be sparse and its change can not then be noticed.

89. Lactarius parvus Pk.

N. Y. State Mus. Rep. 29, 1878.

PILEUS 1-3 cm. broad, broadly convex then expanded, sub-depressed, obsoletely papillate, *dry,* azonate, glabrous, *pale lilaceus-umber,* fading, margin at first involute. FLESH thin. GILLS adnate-decurrent, close to crowded, narrow, few forked at base, dingy white or ochraceus-tinged, *becoming obscurely greenish then dingy-brown where bruised.* STEM 2-3 cm. long, 3-5 mm. thick, subequal, glabrous or pruinose above, stuffed then hollow and *often*

compressed, sometimes sulcate, tinged with same color as pileus.
SPORES subglobose, slightly echinulate, white, 6.5-8 micr. MILK
white, unchanging, sometimes slightly changed on flesh, *acrid.*
ODOR none.

Gregarious or scattered. On the ground or much decayed wood
in forests of hemlock and pine or in cedar swamps. New Richmond.
August-September. Frequent locally.

This is one of our smallest Lactarii. The umber color of cap and
stem, and the peculiar dingy-greenish tints assumed by the wounded
gills characterize it. It closely approaches *L. varius.*

90. Lactarius varius Pk.

N. Y. State Mus. Rep. 38.

PILEUS 3-6 cm. broad, convex then plane and depressed, *grayish-
buff or darker,* with tinge of lilac, *dry, micaceous-shining,* azonate
or slightly zonate on margin. Flesh thin, white. GILLS adnate-
subdecurrent, close, narrow, subventricose, whitish to cream-colored,
stained dingy greenish-brown where bruised. STEM 2-5 cm. long,
4-6 mm. thick, equal, glabrous, firm, *spongy-stuffed,* concolor or
paler. SPORES globose, white, 7-8 micr. MILK white, unchanging,
slowly acrid. ODOR none.

Gregarious. On the ground in mixed woods. Marquette. August.

This species is very close to the preceding. It is known by its
pale colors both when fresh and in herbarium specimens. It was
found only in the Northern Peninsula.

Section VIII. Pileus glabrous or pruinose velvety, *dry;* taste
mild.

91. Lactarius volemus Fr. (EDIBLE)

Syst. Myc., 1821.

Illustrations: Fries, Sverig. Svamp., Pl. 10.
      Cooke, Ill., Pl. 999.
      Gillet, Champignons de France, No. 402.
      Bresadola, Fungh. mang. e. vel., Pl. 66.
      Ricken, Blätterpilze, Pl. 14, Fig. 3.
      Patouillard, Tab. Analyt., No. 323.
      Peck, N. Y. State Mus. Rep. 48, Pl. 30.
      White, Conn. Geol. & Nat. Hist. Surv., Bull. 3, Pl. 10.

Michael, Führer f. Pilzfreunde, Vol. I, No. 35.
Hard, Mushrooms, Fig. 142, p. 179.
Plate XII of this Report.

PILEUS 5-12 cm. broad, firm, convex then expanded-depressed, plane or obtuse, *dry,* azonate, *glabrous,* even or becoming rimose-areolate or rivulose, *unicolorous, orange-fulvous or brownish orange* to tan-brown, often pale, margin at first involute then spreading. FLESH compact, rigid, whitish, sometimes brownish. GILLS adnate-decurrent, close, moderately broad, white or yellowish, darker with age or brownish where bruised, somewhat forked. STEM 3-10 cm. long, 1-2 cm. thick, subequal, glabrous or pruinose, *solid,* rarely cavernous, concolor or paler. SPORES globose, echinulate, 7-10 micr., white. MILK white, unchanging, *mild, abundant.* ODOR slight when fresh, strong on drying. *Edible.*

Gregarious or scattered. On the ground in frondose woods and open places, throughout the southern part of the state. July-September. Common.

Like *L. deliciosus,* this species is very delicious when properly prepared. It can be cut up and dipped in egg and bread crumbs and fried like oysters; it is also excellent when grated and then baked and served on toast. The milk is copious and white. It is not likely to be confused with others except *L. corrugis and L. hygrophoroides,* both of which are similarly colored, but as they are edible no harm results. It must not be confused, however, with *L. rufus* which is considered poisonous. I have been unable to find *L. volemus* in the coniferous regions of the northern and western parts of the state, although it probably occurs there.

92. Lactarius corrugis Pk. (EDIBLE)

N. Y. State Mus. Rep. 32, 1880.

Illustrations: Atkinson, Mushrooms, Fig. 115, p. 115, 1900.
Hard, Mushrooms, Fig. 141, p. 177, 1908.

PILEUS 6-12 cm. broad, firm, convex then depressed-expanded, dry, azonate, *minutely velvety* (spicules!), *corrugate or rugose-reticulate,* dark reddish-brown to rufous-tawny, sometimes paler, margin involute at first then spreading and arched. FLESH compact, white, thick. GILLS adnate-decurrent, close, somewhat narrow, sometimes forking, yellowish-cinnamon, *becoming fulvous-brown where bruised,* provided *with dark-colored spicules* which give them the brown color. STEM 6-7 cm. long, 1.5-2.5 cm. thick, *stout,* firm, solid, equal, dry, more or less tinged concolor and subvelvety. SPORES globose, echinulate, 9-12 micr., white. MILK white, unchanging, *mild,* copious. ODOR slight.

Gregarious or solitary. On the ground in frondose woods or open places. Detroit, Ann Arbor. August-September. Infrequent.

Closely related to the preceding, of which it might be considered a variety. The rugose or corrugated pileus and the abundance of brown spicules on the gills are the main distinguishing characters.

93.   Lactarius hygrophoroides B. & C.   (EDIBLE)

Ann. & Mag. Nat. Hist., Vol. III, 1859.

N. Y. State Cab. Rep. 23, 1872 (as *L. distans* Pk.).

Illustrations: Peck, N. Y. State Mus. Mem. 4, Pl. 53, Fig. 7-11, 1900.

PILEUS 3-8 cm. broad, rarely broader, firm, convex then expanded, umbilicate or subdepressed, glabrous or minutely velvety-pubescent, *dry,* sometimes rugose-wrinkled or rimose-areolate, *yellowish-tawny, fulvous or paler,* margin involute then spreading. FLESH somewhat brittle, whitish, thick. GILLS adnate-subdecurrent, *distant,* narrow, often intervenose, whitish to cream-yellowish. STEM 2-4 cm. long, *short,* 8-16 mm. thick, equal or tapering downward, *solid,* glabrous or pruinose, *concolor.* SPORES globose to broadly elliptical, 9-11 micr., minutely echinulate, white. MILK white, unchanging, *mild. Edible.*

Gregarious or scattered. On the ground in frondose woods or open places. Ann Arbor, Lansing, etc., throughout southern Michigan. July-August. Sometimes common.

This species has the color of *L. volemus* but has distant gills, a short stem and is usually smaller in size. It was described as *L. distans* by Peck and it is regrettable that this appropriate name could not be retained, as the distant gills are its most striking characteristic. However, specimens of Curtis' collections are still in existence and show the plant to have been described by Berkely, as *L. hygrophoroides.* It is equally as good to eat as *L. volemus.*

94. Lactarius luteolus Pk.

Torr. Bot. Club, Bull. 23, 1896.

Illustrations: N. Y. State Mus. Bull. 67, Pl. 83, Fig. 7-11, 1903.

PILEUS 3-7 cm. broad, firm, convex or nearly plane, sometimes umbilicately depressed and subpapillate, *minutely pruinose-velvety, dry,* azonate, more or less rugose, yellowish or dingy buff, margin involute at first. FLESH white, *becoming brown when bruised.* GILLS adnate-subdecurrent, close, narrow, whitish, *becoming brown when bruised.* STEM 2.5-5 cm. long, 3-10 mm. thick, subequal, dry, glabrous or pruinose, firm, spongy-stuffed, *whitish or buff.* SPORES globose, echinulate, 7-8 micr., white. MILK white or whitish, *changing to brown on the flesh,* copious, mild. ODOR mild or foetid.

On the ground in mixed woods. Marquette. August. Rare.

To this species evidently belongs *L. foetidus* Pk. (N. Y. State Mus. Bull. 54, p. 949, 1902), which is a form with a foetid odor.

Section IX. Pileus glabrous, dry or subviscid, taste *mild;* milk white, pale or watery.

95. Lactarius subdulcis Fr. (EDIBLE)

Syst. Myc., 1821.

Illustrations: Gillet, Champignons de France, No. 393.
    Cooke, Ill., Pl. 1002.
    Michael, Führer f. Pilzfreunde, Vol. II, No. 55.
    Murrill, Mycologia, Vol. 3, Pl. 49, Fig. 5.
    Hard, Mushrooms, Fig. 140, p. 176.

PILEUS 2-5 cm. broad, firm, convex then depressed or subinfundibuliform, often papillate, *azonate, dry,* glabrous, *brownish-red,* isabelline or reddish-fulvous, sometimes paler, *not fading,* even or subwrinkled. FLESH whitish or tinged fulvous. GILLS adnate-decurrent, close, *pruinose,* sometimes forked, rather narrow, whitish soon pallid yellowish-flesh color, often fulvous-stained. STEM 4-7 cm. long, 2-8 mm. thick, subequal, stuffed then hollow, glabrous or pubescent to tomentose toward base, even or wrinkled-lacunose, *concolor or* paler than pileus. SPORES globose, echinulate, 7-8 micr., white. MILK white or watery-white, unchanging, *mild* or slightly acrid or bitterish in the throat. *Edible.*

On the ground in low woods, fields, copses, swamps and wet places or in mixed or frondose woods. Throughout the state. June-October. Very common.

This species occurs in dry weather when hardly any other mushroom is to be found, and a swamp or bog must be very dry if it does not yield some. In wet weather it is to be found on high ground as well, either in the woods or the bare soil in fields or roadsides, sometimes even on decayed wood. It is very variable and several varieties have been named, e. g. (a) with cinnamon-red pileus; (b) with chestnut-red pileus and spongy stem, and (c) with varnished-shining bay-red cap and hollow stem. Ricken says the European form is best known by the red-strigose base of the stem and the tufted mode of growth. With us it is usually gregarious or scattered. It must not be confused in dry weather with *Clitocybe laccata* when the latter is moist and then similarly colored. That species differs in its distant gills and fading pileus, and never possesses milk.

96. Lactarius oculatus (Pk.) Burl. (Edible)

Torr. Bot. Club, Bull. 34, 1907.

Illustration: Peck, N. Y. State Mus. Bull. 67, Pl. 83, Fig. 20-24 (as *L. subdulcis* var. *oculatus* Pk.).

PILEUS 1-2 cm. broad, convex-expanded, *abruptly papillate-umbonate,* viscid when moist, glabrous, *fulvous,* fading to pinkish, umbo-darker and scarcely fading, margin at first involute then spreading. FLESH whitish, thin. GILLS subdecurrent, medium close, *broad,* pruinose, pallid then yellowish. STEM 2-4 cm. long, 2-5 mm. thick, equal, glabrous, stuffed, *concolor* or paler. SPORES globose to broadly elliptical, echinulate, 7-9.5 micr., white. MILK white, sparse, unchanging, *mild.*

On the ground in moist places in woods, or on moss. Ann Arbor. July-September. Infrequent.

Related to the preceding, but often with a distinct viscidity on the expallent pileus. Its definite and persistent papilla has been called the "eye spot" of the cap, since its darker color, especially after the rest of the pileus is faded, makes it appear prominent.

97. Lactarius camphoratus Fr. (EDIBLE)

Epicrisis, 1836-38.

Illustrations: Cooke, Ill., Pl. 1013.
Ricken, Blätterpilze, Pl. 14, Fig. 7.
Plate XIII of this Report.

PILEUS 1-4 cm. broad, firm, rigid-fragile, convex, often umbonate, at length depressed, *fulvous to dark brownish-red,* azonate, dry, glabrous, often wrinkled-uneven, *opaque,* margin arched-decurved. FLESH concolor or paler, rather thin. GILLS adnate-subdecurrent, close, rather narrow, pruinose, dull yellowish to reddish-brown. STEM 1-3 cm. long, 3-8 mm. thick, subequal, glabrous or pruinose, sometimes compressed-wrinkled, spongy-stuffed, *concolor.* SPORES globose, echinulate, 6-7.5 micr., white. MILK white, unchanging, either copious or in dry weather often watery white and scanty, *mild.* ODOR *aromatic, agreeable,* usually very distinct. *Edible.*

On the ground in wet places, swamps, very rotten wood in mixed or frondose woods. Throughout the state. July-August. Common.

Known by its peculiar rigid-fragile consistency, its aromatic odor and dark reddish-brown color. Distinguished from *L. rufus* which grows in similar situations, by its smaller size, odor and non-acrid taste; from *L. subdulcis* by darker color and odor. The odor is not of camphor as the name would indicate; it has been variously characterized as like that of dried melilot, slippery-elm bark, or chicory, or similar to that of *L. helvus.* Like *L. subdulcis,* it is often to be found when other mushrooms are absent.

98. Lactarius rimosellus Pk.

N. Y. State Mus. Bull. 105, 1906.

Illustration: Ibid, Pl. 95, Fig. 7-11.

"PILEUS 3-6.5 cm. broad, rather firm, convex umbonate, then depressed, *brownish terra-cotta,* fading somewhat, azonate, dry, glabrous, rugose from the center, *at length minutely rimose-areolate.* FLESH thin, isabelline then concolor. GILLS decurrent, close, medium broad, few forking, whitish then somewhat ochraceous. STEM 2-6 cm. long, 5-10 mm. thick, equal or tapering upwards, stuffed then hollow, pruinose above, *tomentose to strigose downwards,* concolor. SPORES broadly elliptical, echinulate, 7-8 micr., white. MILK *watery or watery-white,* unchanged, mild or slightly woody. ODOR faint, somewhat like that of *C. camphoratus."*

On the ground in open places or in wet places in woods. Ann Arbor. August. Rare.

Differs from *L. camphoratus* in that the pileus becomes rimose-areolate and fades somewhat in age, and in its more tomentose stem.

Russula Fr.

(From the Latin, *russula,* reddish.)

Veil none; the trama composed of *vesiculose* tissue, *without a milky juice;* gills rigid, fragile, acute on edge; stem central, confluent with the pileus; spores globose or subglobose, usually echinulate or verrucose, white cream-color, yellow or ochraceous.

Fleshy, putrescent, rigid-brittle mushrooms, mostly terrestrial, a few on much decayed wood, on sphagnum or on other mosses. A very distinct genus, most closely related to Lactarius, from which it differs by its lack of a milky juice. Hygrophorus differs in the thicker and more waxy nature of the gills although here there are evident certain signs of relationship with species of Russula. Almost all of the species are *edible* after careful cooking since even the peppery forms then lose their sharp taste; in any case the mild species are perfectly safe when fresh, young and clean.

The PILEUS may be red, purple, violet, bluish, yellow, green or white, except in the Compactae, a differentiated pellicle is present on the surface of the cap. This pellicle is often composed of more or less gelatinous hyphae and becomes viscid in wet weather, or it may remain dry and become pruinose or velvety. The pellicle is somewhat separable along the margin of the pileus and in many of the Fragiles can be peeled easily on the whole surface. The margin of the pileus is often striate at least in age. In the species with a thin cap, the lines of attachment of the gills to the cap show through as raised ridges which are often tuberculate because of the presence of the interspacial veins beneath and these striae may extend far toward the center of the pileus. In the species with firm and thick caps, the striations are not as marked or are obscurely developed on the margin only when the plant becomes old. Still, this character is so variable that it must be used with caution as a diagnostic character. The surface is usually glabrous or merely pruinose to velvety; the latter appearance is due to cystidia-like erect hyphae closely covering the pellicle. The GILLS of the different species are of all shades between shining white and egg-yellow, and this fact alone separates them from any one of the spore-color groups of the Agaricaceae. Some authors consider the forking of the gills as well as the veining in the interspaces of the gills important diagnostic characters. These two characters are intimately related and forking is for the most part merely a pronounced development of veining. In fact such a large number of species have been observed with veined interspaces and some forked gills that this character loses most of its value. In *R. variata* the forking is dichotomous or mostly so and reaches its highest development. The different lengths of the gills are, on the contrary, much more important characteristics. They may be alternately long and short as in the Compactae, or they may be all of one length with rarely any secondary or shorter gills. Intermediate cases occur in the Subrigidae, but even here the short gills are not numerous. Their shape and width are also of value, since the anterior and posterior ends have a characteristic width which accompanies other characters of the given subgenera. The STEM is usually white, sometimes red or slightly ochraceous, in some species changing to ashy, etc., with age. The reticulations on the surface are obscure and of no diagnostic value. It is usually spongy-stuffed within and may become cavernous in age or hollowed by grubs; in the Compactae, however, it is usually solid. The TRAMA is composed of large bladder-like cells arranged in groups and surrounded by strands of slender hyphae, as in Lactarius. Such a structure is said to be *vesiculose* and accounts for the more or less brittle consistency of the plants. Since the difference in this consistency is accompanied by other good characters, it is made the basis of a division of the genus into its subgenera. The TASTE as in the Lactarius, is sharply acrid in some species, slowly or slightly acrid in others, and entirely mild in a considerable number. This is an important character for the identification of the species and is fairly constant. It is necessary to have fresh plants to be sure in some cases that the acidity is present. Sometimes plants which are apparently mild will be found to have a slight acridity only when very young, or only in the gills and not elsewhere. The ODOR of some species, e. g., *R. foetans, R. foetantula, R. compacta,* etc., is quite characteristic and should never be unconsidered. One must not confuse this test by applying it to plants already in the first stages of decay. SPORE PRINTS are considered by most as the most essential means of settling the identity of closely related species. It has been claimed that the color is constant and with this claim I agree. It is also known that the spore prints fade or change after a time, and hence old herbarium spore-prints are not reliable unless accompanied by careful notes of the print when fresh.

The genus may be divided into four natural groups which are here considered as subgenera: Compactae, Rigidae, Subrigidae and Fragiles. Of these, the first and last correspond to the tribes of that name in Fries. (Hymen. Europ.) As shown in a former paper, (Kauffman, Mich. Acad. Sci., Rep. 11, p. 60, 1909), the forking of the gills and the striations on the pileus are not very reliable for the characterization of the main groups. It has seemed practicable to establish a new division, viz., the Subrigidae, to include forms with a pruinose or velvety dry pellicle and rather firm consistency, which are out of place elsewhere, and seem to be closely related. Some have divided the genus into two large groups on the basis of the mild and acrid taste (Massee, British Fungus Flora, Vol. III.). Others have used the spore-color (Schroeter, Pilze Schlesiens and Hennings, Engler. u. Prantl Pflanzenfamilien). Earle has raised the five "tribes" to generic rank (Bull. N. Y. Bot. Gard. 5, p. 373, 1909), and finally, Maire has proposed a division of the genus into eight sections based in part on microscopical characters (Soc. Myc. de. France, Bull. 26, p. 120, 1910). The last author appreciates that the groups of Fries are fairly natural and has kept the main features, while emphasizing the presence or absence of cystidia-like spicules on the surface of pileus and stem. These "cystidia" cause the velvety or pruinose character which I have used in the group Subrigidae. Further studies of all young buttons and their development will aid materially in a proper arrangement, especially with reference to the character of the margin of the very young pileus.

The claim of Maire (1. c.) that microchemical tests can be used to advantage, has been given a trial in ten of the following species. This work was done at my request by Dr. W. B. McDougall in our laboratory during the summer of 1912. The results are appended under the corresponding descriptions of the species studied.

The abbreviations of Maire are used as follows: G = Tincture of Guaiac. S V=Sulfovanilline. F S=Sulfoformalin. The last two are prepared as follows:

Sulfovanilline.

Distilled water	2.cc.
Sulfuric acid, pure	2.cc.
Vanilline (c. p.)	25 g.

Sulfoformalin.

Distilled water	25 drops
Sulfuric acid, pure	5.cc.
Formalin (4% sol.)	75 drops

The action of *guaiac* is to turn the flesh blue and should react in one or two minutes. Sometimes only certain parts of the plant react, e. g., in *R. subpunctata,* the gills are unaffected. The *sulfovanilline* turns the parts blue, sometimes at first pink, while the *sulfoformalin* intensifies the brownish color of the cystidia and the lactiferous hyphae in the gills. We did not test the "cystidia" of the surface of the pileus and stem, where the test was effectively used by Maire. In *R. virescens* and *R. crustosa* the last two chemicals had hardly any effect as compared with the quick reaction in other species. Our work has been merely preliminary and covered only a small number of species.

The key includes a few species not yet found in the state. Every season seems to differ in the particular species one finds and a number of forms still remain unidentified, but the following list comprises all the species frequent from year to year, at least in the southern part of the state.

The genus has been largely gone over and revised since the publication of the Monograph (Mich. Acad. Rep. 11, 1909), and several additional species have been included and others more fully described and discussed. The recent critical papers by Maire, Romell, Battaille, Ricken, and others in Europe, have thrown much needed light on a number of species.

Key to the Species

(A) Gills unequal, alternately long and short, flesh thick to the margin of the pileus, which is at first incurved and never has striations. (Compactae).
  (a) Flesh white, unchangeable.
    (b) Gills subdistant; plant entirely whitish; pileus 8-15 cm. 99. *R. delica* Fr.
    (bb) Gills close.
      (c) Pileus whitish then sooty-gray, 5-7 cm. broad. 102. *R. adusta* Fr.
      (cc) Pileus not becoming sooty in age.
        (d) Odor strong, alkaline; pileus large, 10-30 cm. broad, whitish then pale rusty-ochraceus. *R. magnifica.* Pk.
        (dd) Odor none; pileus 4-8 cm. broad, whitish. 99. *R. decila* var. *brevipes* Pk.
  (aa) Flesh changing to reddish or blackish in age or when bruised.
    (b) Flesh at length incarnate or rusty-reddish; odor disagreeable when drying. 104. *R. compacta* Frost.
    (bb) Flesh at length blackish.
      (c) Gills subdistant to distant; flesh at first reddish when bruised, then black. 100. *R. nigricans* Fr.

(cc)   Gills close or crowded.
  (d)   Gills etc. becoming reddish then black; gills crowded. 101.
    R. densifolia Secr.
  (dd) Gills etc. becoming bluish-black, not at first red; pileus dry.
    103. *R. sordida* Pk.
(AA) Gills mostly equal, sometimes with shorter ones scattered promiscuously.
  (a) Gills dichotomously forked throughout; pileus dull pink to pur-
    plish when young, later olivaceous, or greenish-umber. 116. *R.*
    variata Bann.
  (aa) Gills forked only at the base, or forking not extensive or lack-
    ing.
    (b) Spores white in mass.
      (*R. acruginea, R. foetentula, R. rosacea, R. mariae* and *R. ·sub-*
      punctata have creamy-white spores).
      (c) Pileus white.
        (d) Taste acrid. 133. *R. albidula* Pk.
        (dd) Taste mild.
          (e) Pileus viscid, sometimes tinged yellowish; remaining
            white when dried. 139. *R. albida* Pk.
          (ee) Pileus dry, sometimes tinged pink. 133. *R. albella* Pk.
      (cc) Pileus some shade of green or dingy greenish-white. [See
        also (ccc)].
        (d) Pileus with a continuous separable pellicle; taste mild.
          120. *R. aeruginea* Lindb.
        (dd) Pellicle adnate, becoming pulverulent or areolate-cracked;
          gills close.
          (e) Pileus dry, dark green when young, substriate on margin.
            105. *R. virescens* Fr.
          (ee) Pileus viscid, glabrous on disk, mouldy-white to pale
            greenish-white, striate on margin. 106. *R. crustosa* Pk.
      (ccc) Pileus some shade of red, pink, purple or bluish. [See
        also (cccc)].
        (d) Taste mild.
          (e) Gills floccose-crenulate on edge; pileus viscid, shining
            blood-red; stem tinged red. 141. *R. purpurina* Q. & S.
          (ee) Edge of gills not crenulate.
            (f) Pileus firm and hard, or compact; pellicle adnate or
              disappearing in places.
              (g) Pileus pruinose-velvety, dark red, or purple-red; stem
                rosy or dark red; gills at length dingy cream-color.
                119. *R. mariae* Pk.
              (gg) Pileus not markedly pruinose.
                (h) Pileus 5-10 cm. broad.
                  (i) Pileus pale bluish-purple, at length rosy to white
                    on disk, viscid, stem white. 117. *R. cyanoxantha*
                    Fr. var.
                  (ii) Pileus pale red, soon dry, unpolished; stem rosy-
                    tinged or white; taste rarely slightly acrid. 108.
                    R. lepida Fr.
              (hh) Pileus 3-6 cm. broad.
                (i) Pileus dull lilac-purplish. *R. lilacea* Quel.
                (ii) Pileus incarnate to pale livid pink. 114. *R.*
                  vesca Fr.
             (ff) Pileus rather thin, fragile or subfragile.
               (g) Pileus usually 2-4 cm. broad, clear pink; in oak woods.
                142. *R. uncialis* Pk.
              (gg) Pileus 4-6 cm. broad, dark violet-purple or purplish-
                red, silky-shining, in conifer woods. 143. *R. seri-*
                ceoniteus Kauff.
              (ggg) Pileus 6-12 cm. broad, bright rose-red with yellowish
                spots; stem white. 140. *R. subdepallens* Pk.
        (dd) Taste very acrid.

(e) Pileus 2-6 cm. broad.
  (f) Spore-mass pure white; stem white, fragile.
    (g) Pileus uniform rosy-red; gills close to subdistant. 131. *R. fragilis* Fr.
    (gg) Pileus rosy-red on margin, disk olivaceous or purplaces. 132. *R. fallax* Cke.
      plish and livid; gills subdistant; usually in mossy
  (ff) Spore-mass creamy white; stem white or rosy.
    (g) Pileus rigid, not striate, soon dry; cuticle adnate, unpolished, red. 115. *R. subpunctata* sp. nov.
    (gg) Pileus subfragile; pellicle separable and striate on margin, viscid, shining rosy-red. 134. *R. rosacea* Fr. *R. sanguinea* Fr.
 (ee) Pileus 5-10 cm. broad, rarely larger.
  (f) Rigid. Pileus dark red, not fading, cuticle adnate, even on margin. 118. *R. atropurpurea* Maire.
  (ff) Fragile; pileus rose-red to scarlet.
    (g) Taste tardily acrid. 130. *R. rugulosa* Pk.
    (gg) Taste quickly acrid.
      (h) On sphagnum; in troops. 129. *R. emetica* var. *gregaria*.
      (hh) On debris of very rotten wood and on the ground. 129. *R. emetica* Fr.
(cccc) Pileus some shade of brown, yellowish, etc.
 (d) Odor aromatic, becoming foetid; pileus very striate.
(c) Pileus 7-12 cm. broad, sordid yellowish-whitish. 111. *R. foetens* Fr.
(cc) Pileus 3-7 cm. broad, pale livid ochraceous; base of stem with rusty-red stains. 110. *R. foetentula* Pk.
 (dd) Odor not aromatic.
  (e) Pileus 6-12 cm. broad, straw-color to ochraceous-reddish, rigid, not striate. 107. *R. ochraleucoides* sp. nov.
  (ee) Pileus 3-6 cm. broad.
    (f) Taste acrid; pileus grayish-brown, substriate. 113. *R. sororia* Fr.
    (ff) Taste mild.
      (g) Pileus yellow or yellowish, at least when young, not ashy under the cuticle.
        (h) Pileus 5-8 cm. broad, scarcely striate in age, chrome yellow; stem yellow. *R. flavida* Frost.
        (hh) Pileus 3-5 cm. broad, very tuberculate-striate in age, at first sulphur-yellow then dingy yellowish-brown. 109. *R. Pulverulenta* Pk.
      (gg) Pileus pale yellowish-brown, ashy under the cuticle, strongly striate. 112. *R. pectinatoides* Pk.
(bb) Spores and gills some shade of ochraceous, yellowish or creamy-yellowish (spore-print necessary).
 (c) Stem whitish, changing to ochraceous-brown where bruised or handled; odor disagreeable in age; color of pileus purplish-red, olivaceous, yellowish, etc., very variable, colors mixed. 121. *R. xerampelina* Fr. 122. *R. squalida* Pk.
 (cc) Stem not with this peculiarity.
  (d) Pileus some shade of red.
    (e) Taste acrid; fragile.
      (f) Pileus reddish-buff to purplish; spores pale yellow; in swamps. 137. *R. palustris* Pk.
      (ff) Pileus rosy-red to scarlet.
        (g) Gills straw yellowish to pale ochraceous;' margin of pileus even, rather firm. 135. *R. veternosa* Fr.
        (gg) Gills deep ochraceous-yellow; margin of pileus striate, gills and pileus fragile. 136. *R. tenuiceps* Kauff.
    (ee) Taste mild.

   (f) Stem at length ashy or blackish where bruised.
    (g) Wound at first reddish then black; pileus dull red,
         variegated with yellow etc., firm. 126. *R. rubescens*
         Beards.
    (gg) Wound not at first reddish.
     (h) In coniferous regions; stem stout.
       (i) Pileus 5-12 cm. broad, orange-red. 123. *R. de-
            colorans* Fr.
       (ii) Pileus 5-10 cm. broad, crimson-red. 123. *R. de-
             colorans* var. *rubriceps* Kauff.
      (hh) In frondose regions; stem not very stout; pileus
            dark red to blackish on disk. 125. *R. obscura*
            Rom.
  (ff) Stem not becoming ashy.
    (g) Pileus 5-10 cm. broad or more.
     (h) Plants usually solitary or scattered.
       (i) Pileus firm, large, dingy or dull red to purplish,
            often faded; gills ochraceous from the first. 128.
            R. alutacea Fr.
       (ii) Pileus and stem very fragile; colors of pileus
             mixed varying pink, incarnate, yellowish; spores
             bright yellow. 145. *R. amygdaloides* sp. nov.
       (iii) Pileus firm, blood-red. 127. *R. borealis* Kauff.
      (hh) Closely gregarious, sometimes in troops; fragile.
       (i) Pileus dull and variable in color, not bright red;
            gills white at first, then creamy-yellowish to pale
            ochraceous. 144. *R. integra* Fr. and forms.
       (ii) Pileus dark violet-purple to dark red; rather firm;
             spores ochraceous-buff. *R. ochrophylla* Pk.
    (gg) Pileus 2-5 cm. broad or less.
     (h) Spores pale yellow or cream color.
       (i) Pileus umbonate, very fragile; on sphagnum. 148.
            R. sphagnophila Kauff.
       (ii) Pileus not umbonate; stem and gills translucent,
             honey-yellowish in age; fragile. 147. *R. puel-
             laris* Fr.
      (hh) Spores truly ochraceous in mass.
       (i) Stem rosy-dusted; pileus rose-red, fragile. 146.
            R. roseipes (Sec.) Bres.
       (ii) Stem white; pileus pinkish red, lilac etc., fading
             to yellowish. 149. *R. chamaeolentina* Fr. 150.
             R. abietina, etc.
(dd) Pileus some shade of yellow.
  (e) Flesh of stem cinereous when old.
    (f) Pileus orange-red, fading in age. 123. *R. decolorans*
         Fr.
    (ff) Pileus dull yellow (flavus), color not changing, scarcely
          viscid. 124. *R. flava* Rom.
  (ee) Flesh not becoming ashy.
    (f) Edge of gills vivid lemon-yellow. *R. aurata* Fr.
    (ff) Edge of gills concolor.
      (g) Taste mild; pileus 2-6 cm. broad, gills egg-yellow. 151.
           R. lutea Fr.
      (gg) Taste tardily acrid; pileus 5-10 cm. broad; gills pale
            yellow. 138. *R. aurantialutea* Kauff.

COMPACTAE Fr. Flesh thick, compact and firm. Pileus without a separable pellicle, its margin non-striate and at first involute.
With entire and short gills alternating regularly. Spores white in
mass.

This group is closely related to the Piperites division of the genus Lactarius. Some of the species, e. g. *R. delica,* are very similar to *L. vellerius, L. deceptivus,* etc., when the latter are dried out by the wind or dry weather and then lack the milky juice. The Compactae are a very natural group, easily distinguishable.

99. Russula delica Fr. (EDIBLE)

Epicrisis, 1836-38.

Illustrations: Cooke, Ill., Pl. 1068.
  Gillet, Champignons de France, No. 607.
  Bresadola, Fung. Trid., Vol. 2, Pl. 201.
  Ibid, Fung. mang. e. vel., Pl. 68.
  Ricken, Blätterpilze, Pl. 15, Fig. 1.
  Patouillard, Tab. Analyt., No. 514.
  Peck, N. Y. State Mus. Rep. 54, Pl. 71, Fig. 1-5 (as *R. brevipes* Pk.).
  Ibid, N. Y. State Mus. Rep. 43, Pl. 2, Fig. 5-8 (as *R. brevipes* Pk.).

PILEUS 8-15 cm. broad, firm, convex-umbilicate then depressed to infundibuliform, *dull white,* sometimes with rusty-brown stains, *unpolished,* glabrous, pubescent or obscurely tomentose, even, *dry,* margin at first involute not striate. FLESH compact, white or whitish, not changing where bruised. GILLS subdecurrent, narrowed behind, broader in the middle, *subdistant,* or distant, thickish, short and long alternating, few forked, *white or whitish,* edge often distinctly greenish. STEM 2-5 cm. long, 1.5-2 cm. thick, *short,* stout, *solid,* equal or subequal or tapering down, white becoming dingy, *not turning blackish* when bruised, glabrous or subtomentose above, often with a narrow pale-green zone at apex. SPORES globose, 9-10 (rarely 11 or 12) micr., tuberculate, white in mass. TASTE mild to tardily but weakly acrid. ODOR none.

Gregarious, in sandy soil. In maple, birch, oak and coniferous woods throughout the state; most abundant along the Great Lakes in conifer regions. July-October. Common locally.

Var. *brevipes* Pk. (=*R. brevipes* Pk., N. Y. State Mus. Rep. 43, 1890), has been found at New Richmond. The gills are crowded and the pileus is smaller, 4-6 cm. broad. It was found in hard clay soil, through which it pushed with difficulty. It is apparently an ecological variety conditioned by dry weather and hard soil. It is uncommon.

The typical *R. delica* is usually a large plant, simulating. *Lactarius vellerius* in size, color, etc. Fries in the Epicrisis says the cap is "shining." This error was omitted in his Monographia but copied again in Hymenenomycetes Europaei. The error has since been repeated by other authors, including Cooke on his plate in the Illustrations. The Michigan plants are exactly like those growing in Sweden, where in some of the specimens the edge of the gills and the apex of the stem were tinged green, as is the case in ours, especially in the plants of the northern part of the state. *R. lactea* Fr. is said to have very broad, distant, free gills and milk-white cap and stem. I have not seen any plants with the glaucous green gills of *R. chloroides* Bres.

100. Russula nigricans Fr. (EDIBLE)

Epicrisis, 1836-38.

Illustrations: Cooke, Ill., Pl. 1015.
Gillet, Champignons de France, No. 625.
Michael, Führer f. Pilzfreunde, Vol. III, No. 75.
Ricken, Blätterpilze, Pl. 15, Fig. 2.
Peck, N. Y. State Mus. Rep. 54, Pl. 71, Fig. 6-9.
Hard, Mushrooms, Fig. 146, p. 184, 1908.

PILEUS 7-15 cm. broad, subrigid, convex then depressed to subinfundibuliform, margin at first incurved then spreading and elevated, often irregularly wavy, at first whitish and clouded with umber, *soon smoky-umber,* subviscid at first, glabrous, even on margin. FLESH compact, white, *changing to reddish* where bruised, *then blackish.* GILLS narrowed or rounded behind, adnexed, *thick* and firm, *subdistant to distant,* sometimes intervenose, short and long alternating, white becoming grayish, reddish at first when bruised. STEM 2-6 cm. long, 1-3 cm. thick, *solid,* hard, stout, glabrous, even or lacunose-depressed in places, white at first, *at length smoky-umber,* reddish then blackish where bruised. SPORES subglobose, 8-10 micr., echinulate, whitish in mass. TASTE mild, sometimes tardily but slightly acrid. ODOR none.

Gregarious or solitary. On the ground in coniferous or frondose woods. Throughout the state, rarely in the southern part, more plentiful in the north. July-September.

This Russula usually persists in ordinary weather without decaying and is then frequently inhabited by another mushroom,

Nyctalis asterophora, as shown in the illustration. It is usually a rather large, firm plant, distinguished from the following by the subdistant, thick gills. The flesh of all parts when bruised turns first reddish then blackish, but the red stain may not appear in old plants; this is to be expected because of the drying up of the scanty juice which is supposed to cause this phenomenon where it is exposed to the air. Peck, McIlvaine and others have eaten it and consider it fairly good.

101. Russula densifolia Secr. (EDIBLE)

Mycographie I, 1833.

Illustrations: Cooke, Ill., Pl. 1017.
    Gillet, Champignons de France, No. 608.
    Patouillard, Tab. Analyt., No. 319.
    Hard, Mushrooms, Figs. 157 and 145, 1908.
    Kauffman, Mich. Acad. Sci. Rep. 11, Fig. 1, op. p. 90, 1909.

PILEUS 5-12 cm. broad, somewhat firm, convex then depressed to subinfundibuliform, margin at first incurved then elevated, dull whitish at first, *soon clouded with pale smoky-brown,* without a pellicle, usually *subviscid,* even, pruinose when dry. FLESH compact, thick, grayish-white, pale smoky in age, *changing to reddish* when bruised, *then blackish.* GILLS narrowly adnate to subdecurrent, *rather narrow,* thick, *crowded* then close, alternately long and short, few forked, subvenose, whitish soon dingy grayish, reddish when bruised then black. STEM 5-6 cm. long, 1.5-2.5 cm. thick, stout, equal or tapering downward, rigid, spongy-solid, whitish then cinereous, soon dark ashy within, *turning reddish then blackish where bruised,* obscurely wrinkled, glabrous or subpruinose. SPORES globose, coarsely reticulate, 7-9x6-8 micr., white in mass. STERILE CELLS on edge of gills, hyaline, slender, flexuous, acuminate, 60x3-4 micr., abundant. TASTE slowly acrid in fresh plant. ODOR none.

Gregarious, subcaespitose or solitary. On the ground in frondose woods among fallen leaves. Ann Arbor, Detroit, Palmyra. July-September. Usually rare, but abundant in August, 1912, in oak woods at Ann Arbor.

As pointed out by Peck, the American plant is slightly subviscid on the cap but this character is easily overlooked. The viscidity is slight, even after rains. It comes nearest to *R. adusta,* in size, natural coloring and gills, but differs in the change which the flesh undergoes when bruised. Authors consider *R. adusta* to have a mild taste and if this is true our plant differs also in this respect. The gills are usually markedly crowded and narrow, while those of *R. nigricans* are broad and subdistant. The latter is more common in coniferous regions, while *R. densifolia* has so far been found in Michigan only in frondose woods. Maire (Bull. Soc. Myc. France, 26, p. 87) states that *R. densifolia* lacks the hair-like sterile cells on the edge of the gills; that they are abundant in *R. nigricans* and less numerous in *R. adusta*. In our specimens of *R. densifolia* they were abundant, which would indicate that this is not a very constant character.

102. Russula adusta Fr.

Epicrisis, 1836-38.

Illustrations: Cooke, Ill., Pl. 1051.
    Michael, Führer f. Pilzfreunde, Vol. II, No. 64.
    Ricken, Blätterpilze, Pl. 15, Fig. 3.

"PILEUS 5-7 cm. broad, convex then depressed or subinfundibuliform, *white or whitish,* becoming brownish or sooty-gray, glabrous, dry, even. FLESH compact, white, *not changing when bruised.* GILLS adnate to subdecurrent, *thin, close,* short and long alternating, narrow, white becoming sordid. STEM 2-5 cm. long, about 1.5 cm. thick, *short, solid,* equal or subequal, glabrous, even, *white then sooty-gray.* SPORES subglobose, slightly echinulate, 6-9 micr., white in mass. Taste *mild. Odor* slight."

Gregarious or solitary. On the ground in mixed woods of northern Michigan. July-September. Infrequent.

The smaller size, unchanging flesh when bruised, and thin close gills characterize it. At first the whole plant is nearly white, but it gradually takes on a grayish or sooty cast. Michael, who gives an excellent figure, says it has a rather strong odor which is almost nauseating. This seems not to have been noticed by others. In Europe, also, it is said to be soon attacked by grubs especially in the stem; as the same insects do not always occur in this country, such facts are only of local interest. It usually hugs the ground closely.

103. Russula sordida Pk. (EDIBLE)

N. Y. State Mus. Rep. 26, 1874.

Illustrations: N. Y. State Mus. Bull. 105, Pl. 98, Fig. 1-3, 1905.
Plate XIV of this Report.

PILEUS 5-12 cm. broad, *dry,* convex-depressed, margin at first incurved, glabrous, even, *dingy white becoming smoky with age.* FLESH whitish, compact, *becoming blackish-brown or bluish-black* when bruised, *without first turning reddish.* GILLS adnate to sub-decurrent, rather narrow, *close,* long and short alternating, *white becoming blackish in age,* few forked. STEM 3-5 cm. long, 1-2 cm. thick, short, solid, rigid, equal, whitish becoming black when handled. SPORES globose, 7-8 micr., white in mass. TASTE mild or tardily and slightly acrid. ODOR none.

Gregarious or solitary. On the ground in the hemlock regions of the north, rarely in southern Michigan. July-August. Infrequent.

This differs from the European *R. albonigra* (Kromb.) in its dry pileus. A species has been named by Peck with viscid cap, viz., *R. subsordida;* this is probably identical with *R. albonigra.* Our plant has a dry pileus and differs from *R. nigricans* and *R. densifolia* in the lack of the change to red immediately after bruising. In specimens found near Ann Arbor the gills of the young plants were easily separable from the trama of the pileus; whether this is a constant character I cannot say. Peck found the same to be true in specimens of *R. densifolia.* The stems are said to be often infested with grubs.

104. Russula compacta Frost & Peck (EDIBLE)

N. Y. State Mus. Rep. 32, 1879.

Illustration: Peck, N. Y. State Mus. Bull. 116, Pl. 109, 1907.

PILEUS 5-10 cm. broad, firm, convex then depressed to subinfundibuliform, margin at first incurved, thin, then elevated, *dry, unpolished,* minutely tomentose in age, even, whitish when young, *at length sordid-pale-reddish or rusty-ochraceous* either wholly or in spots. FLESH thick, compact, rather brittle, white, *changing to reddish in age or when wounded.* GILLS narrowly adnate, close, rather *narrow,* alternately short and long, sometimes much forked toward base, sometimes few forked, white at first, then stained

sordid reddish or reddish-brown.   STEM 3-6 cm. long, 1.5-3 cm.
thick, *stout*, spongy-stuffed, *rather brittle*, equal or tapering down,
uneven, white at first becoming reddish or reddish-brown in age or
from handling.   SPORES subglobose, echinulate, with large oil-
globule, 8-10x7-8 micr., white in mass.   TASTE mild or slightly and
tardily acrid.   ODOR *becoming disagreeable* in age or on drying,
like that of *R. squalida* Pk.

Gregarious.   On the ground in beech and maple woods.   New
Richmond.   August-September.   Rare.

This is a very distinct species.   The whole plant becomes diffused
with the rusty-reddish color which is at first pale incarnate, but becomes more marked as the plant ages.   The stem has the consistency
of that of *Boletus castaneus* or *B. cyanescens* but the interior becomes cavernous less readily than in those plants.   The scanty juice
which causes the color change has the same relation to the flesh as
that which causes the reddish and then blackish color in *R. nigricans*.
The disagreeable odor of the drying plant is quite marked, and is
an aid to its identification.   It is probably quite rare; it was found
only a few times in New York by Peck but has been reported by
Van Hook from Indiana.   *R. incarnata* Morgan (Cinn. Soc. Nat.
Hist., 1883) is probably identical.   The edges of the gills are provided with microscopic, subcylindrical, sterile cells.   In age the plant
becomes quite fragile.   Peck's figure is not at all illustrative of the
colors.

RIGIDAE.   Flesh compact, rather thick.   Pileus rigid, provided
with an adnate cuticle which often cracks or disappears in parts of
the surface, especially on disk, mostly separable only at the margin.
Gills usually somewhat forked, and with shorter ones intermingled.

The subgenus differs from the Compactae in that the gills do not
alternate regularly as long and short and by the presence of an
adnate pellicle; it differs from the Subridgidae and Fragiles, by the
more rigid substance of the pileus, the adnate pellicle, the presence
of short gills and usually by the forking of some of the gills
especially at or near the stem.   Most of the species are mild or
very slightly acrid.

Section I.   Margin of pileus obtuse, cuticle soon dry, at length
pulverulent, granular or rimosely-cracked in places.   Gills broader
anteriorly.

105. Russula virescens Fr. (EDIBLE)

Epicrisis, 1836-38.

Illustrations: Cooke, Ill., Pl. 1039.
  Gillet, Champignons de France, No. 639.
  Bresadola, Fungh. mang. e. vel., Pl. 69.
  Michael, Führer f. Pilzfreunde, Vol. II, No. 62.
  Atkinson, Mushrooms, Pl. 36, Fig. 1, 1900.
  Marshall, Mushroom Book, Pl. 18, p. 69 (poor).
  Gibson, Edible Toadstools and Mushrooms, Pl. 11, p. 126, 1903.
  Peck, N. Y. State Mus. Rep. 48, Pl. 31, 1896.
  Hard, Mushrooms, Fig. 150, p. 189, 1908.
  McIlvaine, Amer. Fungi., Pl. 44, Fig. 6, p. 184, 1900.

PILEUS 5-12 cm. broad, at the very first globose, soon convex and expanded, often somewhat depressed on disk, firm, *dry,* as if velvety, the surface (especially the disk) broken into many floccose or pulverulent *areas or patches, green* or grayish green, the margin *not striate* or rarely so, cuticle scarcely distinguishable or separable. FLESH white. GILLS *white.* rather close, narrowed toward the stem, almost or entirely free, few shorter or forked. STEM 3-7 cm. long, 1-2 cm. thick, white, firm, equal or subequal, solid or spongy. SPORES white, subglobose, 6-8 micr. CYSTIDIA none. No differentiated subhymenium. TASTE *mild.* ODOR none.

Oak and maple or mixed woods, probably throughout the state. Occasional. July and August.

Under this name was included in this country, for a time, a more common form with viscid striate cap which has been segregated by Peck under the name of *R. crustosa.* The two seem to run into each other at times, but Peck distinguishes the pileus of *R. crustosa* "by its smooth, not warty center, its paler color and usually striate margin." The latter is also distinctly viscid when young but this depends considerably on the weather conditions. *R. virescens* might be confused with green specimens of *R. variata* whose surface is sometimes areolate, but the gills of *R. virescens* are not as pure white, are not decurrent nor much forked, and the taste is mild.

Microchemical tests: G. (Flesh and gills slowly bright blue.) F S. (No effect.) S V. (No effect.)

106. Russula crustosa Pk. (Edible)

N. Y. State Mus. Rep. 39, 1886.

Illustration: N. Y. State Mus. Bull. 67, Pl. 84, Fig. 1-7, 1903.

PILEUS 5-12 cm. broad, firm, convex then expanded and depressed in the center, surface cracked except on disk, the *areas crustlike,* sordid cream-color, dirty brownish or ochraceous, usually tinged with olive or green, *viscid* when young or moist, especially on the disk, *striate on margin* when mature. FLESH white. GILLS *dull white,* becoming somewhat dingy cream color in age, rather broad in front, narrowed toward the stem, adnexed or free, *thick, distinct,* not crowded, rather brittle, few forked, few short. STEM 3-6 cm. long, 1-2.5 cm. thick, short, stout, spongy-stuffed, subequal or ventricose, white. SPORES white, subglobose, 8-10 micr. CYSTIDIA rather numerous, extending clear through the subhymenium. *Subhymenium* sharply separated from gill-trama. TASTE *mild.* ODOR none.

Scattered or gregarious. Oak and maple woods in southern Michigan. July to September. Common.

This is near *R. virescens* and is apparently much more common. It seems to be still referred to *R. virescens* by some authors, although in that case the Friesian description will have to be modified to include it.

Michochemical tests: G. (Flesh and gills become deep blue.) S V. (Gills and flesh very slowly tinged blue.) F S. (Cystidia colored brown.)

107. Russula ochraleucoides sp. nov.

Illustration: Plate XV of this Report.

PILEUS 6-12 cm. broad, *large, rigid,* convex, soon expanded-plane, varying *straw-yellow to pale ochraceous,* usually dull ochre to reddish-ochre toward center, pellicle adnate, soon dry, and *pulverulent* or subrimose, *even* on the *obtuse* margin. FLESH *thick,* compact, white, unchanging or slightly sordid in age. GILLS adnexed or free, *rather narrow,* rounded and slightly broader in front, *white* or whitish, close to subdistant, shorter ones intermingled, often forked in posterior part, intervenose. STEM 4-6 cm. long, 1.5-2 cm. thick, short, *rigid,* equal or tapering slightly downward, *white,* glabrous or subpruinose, spongy-solid, even or obscurely wrinkled. SPORES globose, very minutely rough, 7-9 micr. (incl. apiculus), *white in mass*. CYSTIDIA very few. BASIDIA about 40x9 micr. TASTE tardily and slightly bitterish-acrid or disagreeably bitter. ODOR faintly aromatic or none.

Gregarious. On the ground in open oak-maple woods. Ann Arbor. August. Rare.

Related to *R. virescens* by its rigidity and the nature of the surface of the pileus. The surface is pulverulent, somewhat rimose in age, soft to the touch and under the microscope is seen to be composed of slender, hyaline, erect cystidia-like hairs. A subhymenium is lacking. It has a short, stout stem and relatively much broader cap. It differs from *R. ochraleuca* in size and in the thick flesh of the .cap, in that the flesh of the stem does not become ashy when bruised, as well as in the bitter taste and the unpolished pileus. *R. granulosa* Cke. is said to have a granular stem and pileus, and many cystidia in the hymenium according to Massee. It is far from belonging to the Fragiles where Fries placed *R. ochraleuca*. *R. granulata* Pk. is said to be tubercular-striate on the margin of the cap and is smaller. The gills are often abundantly forked toward the stem.

108. Russula lepida Fr. (non Bres.) (EDIBLE)

Epicrisis, 1836-38.

Illustrations : Fries, Sverig. Swamp., Pl. 59, form minor.
    Cooke, Ill., Pl. 1072.
    Gillet, Champignons de France, No. 620.
    Ricken, Blätterpilze, Pl. 16, Fig. 4.
    Hard, Mushrooms, Fig. 149, Pl. 188, 1908. (Doubtful.)
    Gibson, Edible Toadstools, etc., Pl. 12, p. 131, 1903. (Doubtful.)
    Atkinson, Mushrooms, Pl. 36, Fig. 3, p. 126, 1900. (Doubtful.)

PILEUS 4-10 cm. broad, *rigid,* convex, then expanded-depressed, cuticle adnate and disappearing on disk, *unpolished, soon dry,* rose-red to pale blood-red, *fading,* disk soon pallid or variegated with paler yellowish-reddish hues, sometimes rimulose-cracked or rugulose on disk, margin obtuse, not striate. FLESH compact, *white* or reddish under the cuticle, thick, abruptly thin on margin. GILLS narrowed behind and narrowly adnate or almost free, close, *rather narrow,* broader and rounded in front, *white then whitish* (albus), few shorter, occasionally forked. STEM 4-7 cm. long, 1-2 cm. thick, equal or slightly tapering downward, *white or tinged rosy-pink,* spongy-stuffed, rather rigid, obscurely wrinkled. SPORES subglobose, 9-10 x 7-8 (incl. apiculus), with oil-drop, rough or partly smooth, *almost pure white in mass.* ODOR none or very slightly disagreeable. TASTE *mild,* sometimes slightly bitterish-subacrid. CYSTIDIA moderately abundant, subcylindrical, 70-75x10-12 micr.

Gregarious or solitary. On the ground in frondose woods. Ann Arbor, Detroit. July-August. Rather rare.

This plant occurs rather rarely in southern Michigan. It differs from the description given by Bresadola (see translation Mich. Acad. Rep. 11, p. 68, 1909) in that the spore-mass is nearly white, not straw color, and the gills are only slightly thickish. I have found specimens only during a few seasons. Peck also reports it uncommon in New York. The margin of the pileus is sometimes slightly viscid and the cuticle slightly separable on the margin. It must not be confused with *R. mariae* whose cap and stem are less rigid and more deeply colored, and which has creamy-yellowish spores and larger cystidia. Our plant sometimes has an entirely rose-red cap, sometimes, especially when older, approaching the colors of *R. decolorans* but paler and duller, subpruinose when dry and variegated with pinkish, yellowish or pale-orange hues becoming white in spots. It is often rigid for a long time.

Section II. Margin of pileus acute or subacute, at first incurved; cuticle *viscid,* slightly separable only on margin, often disappearing on disk or in spots.

109. Russula pulverulenta Pk.

Torr. Bot. Club, Bull. 29, 1902.

Illustration: Plate XVI of this Report.

PILEUS 3-5 cm. broad, rather rigid at first, *then fragile,* rather thin, broadly convex at first, expanded and depressed to subumbilicate, at first even on the margin, at length *distinctly tuberculate-striate,* cuticle adnate, viscid, separable on margin, in very young stage sulphur-yellow, soon ochraleucous, finally *dingy yellowish brown,* surface *dotted* by small, numerous, *pale yellow, somewhat mealy or flocculent scales or granules,* margin at very first incurved-subinrolled. FLESH white, at first firm and tough, finally soft. GILLS narrowly adnate, close, rather narrow, broader toward front, *white,* unchanging, often bifurcate at stem, intervenose. STEM 3-5 cm. long, 1-1.5 cm. thick, subequal or irregularly enlarged, *rigid-fragile,* surface at the very first covered by a sulphur-yellow pulverulence, *at length dotted by sulphur-yellow granules, especially at base,* white beneath, spongy-stuffed, *becoming cavernous.* SPORES globose, echinulate, 6-8 micr. (incl. apiculus), *white in mass.* CYSTIDIA numerous, subhymenium scarcely differentiated. BASIDIA 45x9 micr., 4-spored. TASTE and ODOR slight or somewhat disagreeable.

Gregarious. On lawns, roadsides, or in frondose woods among grass, etc. July-September. Southern Michigan. Not infrequent during a few seasons.

This Russula is closely allied to the preceding section. Its development has been carefully studied. When the caps are 4 mm., or less broad the margin is definitely subinrolled. The texture of the trama is then very firm and tough and the entire surface of both cap and stem is covered, as seen under the microscope, by a differentiated thin layer composed of short, dense, erect yellow hairs or hyphae. These hyphae are continuous at first with the trama but become separated in masses as the pileus and stem enlarge, adhering at length to the surface of the mature pileus and stem as delicate, appressed, pulverulent-flocculose, sulphur-yellow granules. The hymenium contains very numerous cystidia with a dark-brown, granular content, which project into the subhymenium and often connect with similarly colored hyphae which intermingle with the gill-trama. (Lactiferes.) The young cystidia project above the basidia but later are even with them. These brownish cystidia give a brown-dotted appearance to the sides of the gills as seen under low power of the microscope.

Microchemical tests: G. (Flesh and gills become rapidly light blue, then dark blue.) S V. (Gills first turn reddish then slowly blue; flesh scarcely affected.) F S. (Cystidia colored brown.)

This species is easily confused in the old, discolored stage with *R. pectinatoides* and *R. foetentula,* since both have a livid yellowish-brown cap at times when mature, well marked tuberculate striations, and are about the same size. They lack, however, the peculiar yellow granules of *R. pulverulenta.* (For further remarks see Mich. Acad. Rep. 11, p. 77, 1909.)

110. Russula foetentula Pk.

N. Y. State Mus. Bull. 116, 1907.

PILEUS 3-7 cm. broad, soon fragile, at first subhemispherical then convex to plane and depressed, *viscid, livid-ochraceous, russet-tinged,* disk darker and innately granular, long tuberculate-striate. Margin at first incurved. FLESH thin, whitish. GILLS adnexed or nearly free, close, rather narrow, broader in front, thin, whitish, *often spotted or stained reddish.* STEM 2.5-5 cm. long, 6-12 mm. thick, subequal, somewhat firm, spongy-stuffed, soon cavernous, whitish or sordid-white, *stained at the very base by cinnabar-red stains.* SPORES 7-9 x 6-7 micr., echinulate, *creamy-white in mass.* CYSTIDIA moderately abundant. BASIDIA 40-45x9 micr., 4-spored; *subhymenium* scarcely differentiated. OROR none or somewhat like oil of bitter almonds, varying in intensity. TASTE very slightly acrid.

Scattered or gregarious. On the ground in frondose woods. Ann Arbor. Abundant in 1911.

This species has characters intermediate between *R. foetens* and *R. pectinatoides* and is most easily distinguished from both by the reddish stains at the base of the stem; this character was very constant in many individuals during a single season. The odor varies much in intensity and is often lacking. The pileus is sometimes tinged with reddish-yellow but most of our plants had a decided russet color at maturity. Micro-chemical tests as in *R. pulverulenta.*

111. Russula foetens Fr.

Syst. Myc., 1821.

Illustrations: Fries, Svamp. Sverig., Pl. 40.
      Cooke, Ill., Pl. 1046.
      Gillet, Champignons de France, No. 612.
      Michael, Führer f. Pilzfreunde, Vol. I, No. 45.
      Ricken, Blätterpilze, Pl. 19, Fig. 4.
      Hard, Mushrooms, Fig. 147, p. 185, 1908.
      Plate XVII of this Report.

PILEUS 7-12 cm. broad, fleshy, hard then fragile, *subglobose* then expanded and depressed, viscid when moist, thin margin at first incurved, *tuberculate-sulcate* when expanded, yellowish or dingy ochraceous, pellicle adnate. FLESH thin, rigid but fragile, dingy white. GILLS white, at *first exuding drops of water,* sordid when old or bruised, rather close, adnexed, few forked, interspaces venose, shorter ones present. STEM 4-6 cm. long, 1-2.5 cm. thick, whitish, short, stout, stuffed then cavernous. SPORES *white* in mass, sub-globose, 7.5-10 micr. CYSTIDIA numerous; subhymenium narrow, not sharply differentiated. TASTE *acrid.* ODOR *strongly amygdaline, becoming foetid.*

Gregarious. In mixed woods in the north; in oak, maple, etc., in southern Michigan. July, August and September.

The odor of the fresh young plant is like oil of bitter almonds or cherry bark; when old or decaying it becomes quite disagreeable. The margin of the young pileus is strongly incurved. Not edible.

Micro-chemical tests: G. (Flesh and gills quickly light blue, then dark blue.) S V. (Gills slowly deep blue.) F S. (Cystidia coloreu brown.)

112. Russula pectinatoides Pk.

N. Y. State Mus. Bull. 116, 1907.

Illustrations: Ibid, Pl. 105, Fig. 6-10.

PILEUS 3-7 cm. broad, rather firm, *becoming fragile, thin,* convex, then plano-depressed, viscid when moist, covered by a thin separable pellicle, radiately rugose-striate on the margin, often halfway to the center, or *strongly tubercular-striate,* dingy straw color, brown-ish, yellowish-brown or umber-brown. FLESH white, thin, becoming fragile, slightly *ashy under the cuticle,* not changing. GILLS whitish, close to subdistant, thin, distinct, equal, moderately broad, broadest in front, narrowed behind, often stained or broken halfway from stem, some forked at base. STEM 2-5 cm. long, .5 to 1 cm. thick, white or dingy, subequal, glabrous, spongy-stuffed *then hollow,* even. SPORES whitish or creamy-white in mass, subglobose, 6-8 micr. diam. TASTE mild or slightly and tardily acrid. ODOR *not noticeable.*

Gregarious. Grassy places, lawns, groves and woods. Through-out the state. July and August.

Cooke's illustrations of *R. pectinata* and *R. consobrina* var. *sororia* remind one very much of this plant. Peck points out that it differs from these by its mild taste, adnate gills and grayish color under the cuticle. It is also close to *R. foetentula,* which sometimes lacks the odor. *R. subfoetens* Smith as known to Romell, also reminded me of this species. The color of *R. pectinatoides,* the long striations and the medium size are the best recognition marks in the field. It differs, of course, from *R. foetens* by lack of a strong odor. Whether the margin is at first incurved is nowhere noted.

113. Russula sororia Fr.

Epicrisis, 1836-38 (as subspecies of *R. consobrina*).

Illustration: Cooke, Ill., Pl. 1057.

PILEUS 3-6 cm. broad, rather firm, convex then subexpanded, *viscid* when moist, margin substriate when mature, pellicle somewhat separable along margin, *gray,* olivaceous-brown or grayish-brown. FLESH white, unchanged. GILLS narrow, subdistant, distinct, white for a time, then discolored, adnate, shorter ones intermingled, rarely forked, interspaces venose. STEM 2.5-5 cm. long, 1-2 cm. thick, white, not becoming cinereous, short, spongy-stuffed. SPORES *white.* TASTE *acrid.* ODOR none.

Solitary. Woods in southern Michigan. August and September. Rare. This species used to be placed under *R. consobrina.*

114. Russula vesca Fr.-Bres.

Epicrisis, 1836-38.

Illustrations: Cooke, Ill., Pl. 1075.
Bresadola, Fungh. mang. e. vel., Pl. 72.
Ibid, Fung. Trid., Pl. 128 (as *R. lilacea* var. *carnicolor*).
Michael, Führer f. Pilzfreunde, Vol. I, No. 41 b.

PILEUS 3-6 cm. broad, fleshy, firm, convex then expanded and depressed in the center, *viscid, soon dry,* more or less rugulose or wrinkled, reddish, *pale livid-pink,* or sordid flesh-red, becoming paler, cuticle thin and disappearing, *not quite reaching the edge of the pileus* so that a narrow white exposed margin results, margin even and spreading. FLESH white. GILLS white, thin, at length *stained* lurid-brownish or rusty, close, moderately narrow, adnate, forked or anastomosing at base. STEM white, obscurely rivulose, *hard* and compact, subequal, solid, 3.5-4.5 cm. long, 1.5 cm. thick, often discolored by yellowish-rusty stains. SPORES *white in mass,* subglobose, minutely echinulate, 7-8 micr. TASTE *mild.* ODOR none. Rare.

Only a few doubtful collections have been made in southern

Michigan. The above description is taken from my notes of the Swedish plant as known to Romell, and agrees mostly with that of Bresadola. Most modern mycologists consider the Friesian "rugulose-reticulate" character of the stem as too uncertain to be practicable. The important characters are: the hard consistency, the wrinkled or veined rarely "cutefracta" surface of the cap, the cuticle not reaching to the margin of the cap, and the gills discolored in spots. The cuticle apparently ceases to grow so that the surface of the expanding pileus may become somewhat areolate cracked and the margin naked.

115. Russula subpunctata sp. nov.

PILEUS 2-5 cm. broad, *rigid,* convex then expanded-plane to depressed, cuticle adnate and scarcely separable on margin, subviscid, soon dry, *pale dull red to rosy-red,* often white-spotted where cuticle disappears, minutely rivulose or subgranular, margin even, acute. FLESH compact, firm, rather thick on disk, abruptly thin on margin. GILLS adnate to subdecurrent, thin, slightly attenuate at both ends, not broad, close to subdistant, whitish *then pale cream-colored,* few short or forked at base, pruinose, intervenose. STEM 2-4 cm. long, 4-10 mm. thick, subequal or tapering down, spongy-stuffed, *becoming cavernous,* white or rosy-tinged, unchanging, attached at times to roots and forming mycorhiza. SPORES subglobose, rough-reticulate, 9-11x7-9 micr. (incl. apiculus), *creamy-white in mass.* CYSTIDIA abundant, subcylindrical, rough, with dark brown granular content, 90-110x8-12 micr. BASIDIA about 65x9 micr. *Subhymenium* markedly differentiated. TASTE *quickly and very acrid.* ODOR none.

Gregarious. On the ground in frondose woods. Ann Arbor. July-August. Infrequent.

The appearance of this Russula is well shown in Patouillard's figure of *R. punctata* Gill. (Tab. Analyt., No. 621) with which it agrees except in its very acrid taste. The gills of our plants have only rarely a red edge. The spore print is cream-colored or almost light yellowish. Dr. McDougal found one group of specimens forming mycorhiza on roots of *Tilia americana.*

Micro-chemical tests: G. (Flesh slowly light blue; gills unaffected.) S. V. (Flesh and gills quickly deep blue.) F. S. (Cystidia colored brown.)

116. **Russula variata** Banning—Pk. (Edible)

N. Y. State Mus. Bull. 105, 1906.

Illustrations: Ibid, Pl. 101, Fig. 1-5.
    Hard, Mushrooms, Fig. 154, p. 194, 1908 (as *R. furcata*).

PILEUS 5-12 cm. broad, fleshy, firm, convex then depressed to subinfundibuliform, viscid, *not striate,* purplish or *deep rose pink when young,* later variegated with olive or dark umber or sometimes *greenish* with only a trace of *purple,* opaque and reticulate-wrinkled under lens, the thin pellicle slightly separable on the thin margin, with a subsilky or dull luster when dry. FLESH white, firm, cheesy, tinged grayish under pellicle. GILLS shining and *persistently white,* adnato-decurrent, thin, *rather crowded,* narrowed at both ends, not broad, *subdichotomously forked,* interspaces venose. STEM 4-7 cm. long, 1-3 cm. thick, white, firm, solid, equal or subequal, sometimes tapering downward, even. SPORES *white in mass,* subglobose, 7-10 micr. TASTE *mild to tardily acrid* or slightly astringent. CYSTIDIA very few and short. *Subhymenium* not clearly differentiated. ODOR none.

Gregarious. Under conifers at Marquette, in deciduous woods about Ann Arbor. July, August and September. Frequent.

Superficially nearest to the descriptions of *R. furcata* Fr. and *R. virescens* Fr. The former species is rare in Europe, and most authors have consigned it to oblivion or consider it a variety of *R. cyanoxantha.* The plants which used to be referred to *R. furcata* in this country, have found a more appropriate resting place in *R. variata.* The figures of *R. cutefracta* Cke. (Cooke, Ill., Pl. 1024 and 1040) show the color of the young and old plants much better than do Peck's figures, and if Cooke's species had pure white spores and white and dichotomously forked gills, they could be considered identical; however, these points are not clear. Peltereaux thinks *R. cutefracta* Cke. occurs in France and has ochraceous spores and that the cracked margin of the cap is a weather effect; this then could not be our species with white spores. When one finds single old plants with much green, it is quite difficult to distinguish them from *R. virescens;* they are to be separated by their dichotomously forked gills which are slightly decurrent and more persistently white, and by the slight acridity. The cuticle is sometimes cracked toward the margin as in *R. virescens,* but its margin is at first incurved while in *R. virescens* it is straight on the stem. Peck says it has a good flavor after cooking, which destroys the slight acrid taste.

Micro-chemical tests: G. (Flesh and gills quickly deep blue.) S V. (Gills slowly blue; flesh slightly blue-tinged.) F S. (No effect.)

117. Russula cyanoxantha Fr. var. (EDIBLE)

Monographia, 1865.

Illustrations: Michael, Blätterpilze, Vol. II, No. 59.
Gillet, Champignons de France, No. 605.
Cooke, Ill., Pl. 1076 and 1077. (Doubtful.)
Bresadola, Fungh. Mang. e. vel., Pl. 71. (Doubtful.)

PILEUS 5-10 cm. broad, *rigid,* convex then expanded and depressed in the center or subinfundibuliform, *dark bluish-purple or lilac* on margin, *disk dingy white tinged rose-pink,* cuticle thin and adnate, *viscid,* separable on margin, *even,* or substriate only near edge, surface somewhat wrinkled or streaked. FLESH white, compact, purplish or lilac under cuticle. GILLS *white,* a few forked toward base, few shorter, moderately broad, not very distant, narrowed behind, intervenose. STEM 6-9 cm. long, 1-2 cm. thick, *white,* subequal, spongy-stuffed, cortex hard, sometimes cavernous and compressed, glabrous, even or obscurely wrinkled. SPORES *white in mass.* TASTE *mild.* ODOR none.

Scattered or gregarious. Maple and birch, or mixed woods of northern Michigan, oak and maple woods of the southern part. July-August. Not infrequent.

The above description applies to a definite form which occurs in Michigan and is quite constant. It does not agree with the species understood by Romell, Maire and Pelteraux in Europe, whose typical plant has creamy-white gills and spores. Our species approaches *R. azurea* Bres. in color, but that plant is rather fragile and is related to the *R. emetica* group. Michael's figures show the colors of the cap when young and not yet decolorized on the disk. It is more frequent northward and may be distinct from the European plant.

118. **Russula atropurpurea** Maire (ex. Kromb. non Pk.)

Bull. Sco. Myc. de France, Vol. 26, p. 167, 1910.

Illustrations: Cooke, Ill., Pl. 1025 and 1087 (as *R. rubra*).

PILEUS 5-14 cm. broad, rigid, medium to large size, convex then plane, soon depressed, rather firm, viscid, pellicle adnate and scarcely separable on the margin only, scarlet to dark crimson when fresh and young, *becoming darker to purplish when mature or on drying, pruinose,* disk often darker, sometimes blackish-red to livid olivaceus-purple, sometimes yellow spotted, margin even or only slightly striatulate in age. FLESH dark red under the pellicle, white elsewhere, not changing to ashy. GILLS *white,* dingy in age, *rather narrow,* close behind, subdistant in front, adnexed, few short, interspaces venose. STEM 4.7 cm. long, 1-3 cm. thick, subequal, medium stout, white with a dull lustre, *pruinose,* even, spongy-stuffed, apex floccose-punctate. SPORES white in mass, oval, 8-10 micr. diam., strongly echinulate, nucleate, apiculus long and stout. TASTE *acrid.* ODOR none.

Gregarious or solitary. On the ground, on much decayed logs or debris, sometimes at base of white pine or beech trees, in pine-beech woods. New Richmond. Sept. Frequent locally.

Distinguished among the "ruber" group by the mode of coloi change while maturing, the white gills, spores and stem, and the acrid taste. In wet weather the cap is viscid, on drying its surface is distinctly pruinose. Except for the colors of the pileus it agrees with *R. ruber* Fr. in the sense of Peck. The stem is rarely inclined to ashy in age but not distinctly so. According to Maire's concep-tion the species is quite variable and includes plants whose stem readily turns ashy.

SUBRIGIDAE. Pileus subrigid, rather compact; cuticle soon dry, *pruinose or pruinose-velvety;* margin obtuse. Gills broader in front, equal. Spore-mass never pure white.

This group approaches the preceding by its rather compact and thick pileus, and the following by its equal gills. The pellicle is soon dry and pruinose or pruinose-velvety by which character the species are best recognized. Several aberrant species are, however, included, e. g., *R. xerampelina* with intermixed short gills and *R. mariae* with margin of pileus at first incurved.

119. Russula mariæ Pk. (EDIBLE)

N. Y. State Mus. Rep. 24, 1872.

Illustrations: N. Y. State Mus. Bull. 75, Fig. 1-8, 1904.
Plate XVIII of this Report.

PILEUS 3-9 cm. broad, firm, subhemispherical at first, then broadly convex to plane and depressed, *dry,* subviscid when wet, *pruinose-velvety,* dark crimson, *reddish-purple* or maroon-purple, *even,* substriate only when old, margin at first incurved. FLESH thick, thinner toward margin, compact, becoming softer, white, sometimes reddish under pellicle. GILLS narrowly adnate or almost subdecurrent, *rather narrow,* of nearly uniform width, *white then dingy cream-color,* close to subdistant, equal, bifurcate at base. STEM 3-9 cm. long, 8-15 mm. thick, subequal or tapering downward, firm then fragile, spongy-stuffed, *pruinose, rosy-red to dull purplish-red,* especially in the middle, rarely white except at ends, white within and unchanging. SPORES globose, tuberculate-crystallate, 7.8 micr., *creamy-whitish in mass,* scarcely yellowish-tinged. CYS-TIDIA rather abundant, lanceolate, 90-95x12 micr. BASIDIA 36-42 x9 micr. *Subhymenium* of small cells, not sharply limited. TASTE mild or rarely very slightly acrid. ODOR none.

Gregarious. On the ground in frondose woods. Southern Michigan. July-August. Infrequent.

I have examined the type specimens and submitted drawings, photographs and specimens to Peck. His plants average smaller and his figures and descriptions are deceptive as to size as compared with most of the specimens found in Michigan. With us *R. mariæ* is nearly always larger and has much of the appearance of Cooke's figure of *R. expallens* (Ill., Pl. 1029), but that species is said to have a very acrid taste. The pileus varies scarlet-red, reddish-purple, maroon or dark purple. The caps of the purple forms have the appearance of those of *R. queletii, R. purpurea* and *R. drimei* of Cooke's plates; but all of these have a very acrid taste. The red forms agree quite well with Gillet's and Michael's figures of *R. linnaei,* but Romell, Maire, Bresadola and others consider *R. linnaei* as a doubtful species. The stems of *R. mariæ* are nearly always somewhat colored. The pruinosity of the cap and stem is due to minute tufts of purplish or reddish hairs as seen under the microscope. The plant was named by Dr. Peck in honor of his wife Mary. The interpretation of this species in my previous paper (Mich. Acad. Rep. 11, p. 70, 1909) was an error.

120. **Russula aeruginea** Lindb. (non Fr.) (EDIBLE)

Svampbok, 1902.

Illustrations: Ibid, Fig. 52.
    Cooke, Ill., Pl. 1044 (as *R. heterophylla* Fr.). (Doubtful.)
    Michael, Führer f. Pilzfreunde, Vol. II (as *R. livida* Pers.).
    Ricken, Blätterpilze, Pl. 16, Fig. 2(as *R. graminicolor* Quel.).

PILEUS 5-8 cm. broad, *moderately firm,* then fragile, convex to
expanded, subdepressed, *dull greenish, dark green* to smoky-green,
paler on margin, pellicle adnate, subviscid when moist, soon dry with
a dull luster and *subpulverulent to pruinose-velvety,* slightly separable on margin, even or substriate in age. FLESH thick on disk,
thin on margin, white, sometimes cinereous to greenish under pellicle. GILLS narrowly adnate or almost free, close to subdistant,
rather narrow, slightly broader in front, entire or very few short
ones, distinct, white at first *then pale creamy-white,* becoming dingy
in age, bifurcate at base, intervenose. STEM 4-5 cm. long, 1 cm.
thick, subequal or tapering downward, glabrous, *white,* spongy-
stuffed, firm, even. SPORES subglobose, *creamy-white,* 6-9 micr.
TASTE *mild.* ODOR none.

Gregarious or solitary. On the ground in coniferous or mixed
woods of the Northern Peninsula. Marquette, Sault Ste. Marie.
July-September. Infrequent.

This species is considered identical with *R. graminicolor* Quel.
by the French mycologists. The "shining-white gills" (candidae)
of the Friesian description is probably an error. *R. heterophylla*
Fr. is now limited by most writers to a plant with pure white gills
and spores and is rare. *R. olivascens* Fr., reported (Mich. Acad. Sci.
Rep. 11, p. 76, 1909), has been omitted as it appears too close to this
species; the specimens referred to it had a more yellowish tint to
the spore-mass.

121. Russula xerampelina Fr. (SUSPECTED)

Epicrisis, 1836-38.

Illustrations: Cooke, Ill., 1041 (as *R. olivacea*).
    Gillet, Champignons de France, No. 628 (as *R. olivacea*).
    Ricken, Blätterpilze, Pl. 18, Fig. 4 (as *R. olivacea*).

PILEUS 5-10 cm. broad, *firm,* convex then plano-depressed, dry
or very slightly viscid in wet weather, pellicle hardly separable,

not striate on margin, surface glabrous or subpruinose, purplish-
red to purplish-olive, disk olivaceous, variegated. FLESH *compact,*
whitish then dingy. GILLS *creamy-white* to creamy-yellowish, then
sordid, rather close, adnexed, moderately broad throughout, thickish, often forked, shorter ones usually intermingled, interspaces
venose. STEM white or *rosy-tinged,* soon dingy olivaceous-yellowish where handled, 5-7 cm. long, 1.5-2.5 cm. thick, firm, subventricose or equal, spongy-stuffed, even or obscurely wrinkled, *changing*
where bruised *to dirty ochraceous-brown.* SPORES creamy-yellowish, globose, echinulate, 9-10 micr. TASTE *mild.* ODOR *disagreeable with age* or when drying.

Scattered. Hemlock and coniferous or mixed woods of the
Northern Peninsula. July and August.

This has usually been referred to *R. olivacea* Fr. in this country.
In Europe, *R. olivacea* is a very much debated species. Fries' description requires truly yellow gills (luteis), and with this character it has seldom been found. Romell has never seen such a plant
in Sweden and unites *R. olivacea* and *R. xerampelina* under the
name *R. graveolens.* The series of color forms included under the
last name is quite common about Stockholm, and as far as I could
see it is the same as our northern Michigan species. I assume, then,
that we can drop the name *R. olivacea* from our list of American
Russulas, in which case our olive form goes into the present species.
Our plant is near *R. squalida* Pk. as the latter is diagnosed in this
paper. It differs, however, from that species in the more firm consistency, in the stem being often reddish, and its habitat in coniferous regions. *R. squalida* is soft and flexible in age.

122. Russula squalida Pk. (Suspected)

N. Y. State Mus. Rep. 41, 1888 (as *R. atropurpurea* Pk.).
N. Y. State Mus. Bull. 116, 1907.

Illustration: Kauffman, Mich. Acad. Sci. Rep. 11, 1909.

PILEUS 7-11 cm. broad, convex then plano-depressed,
firm, soon subflaccid, margin *even when young,* becoming
slightly tubercular-striate in age, the pellicle continuous but
rather adnate, not easily separable, subviscid in wet weather,
soon dry and then *pruinose-velvety,* even, color varying from
reddish-purple to pallid and mixed with olivaceous, tan
or ochraceous, often shades of all these colors are seen in
one cap, opaque and dull, not shining. FLESH white, thick on

disk, rather thin elsewhere, grayish or grayish-purple under the *cuticle.* GILLS white when young, later *creamy-yellow to ochraceous,* subdistant, becoming fragile, moderately broad, broadest toward the front, more or less forked toward base, few shorter ones, interspaces venose. STEM *white, changing to ochraceous if bruised* when fresh and young, when older becoming dirty-brown or ochraceous-brown where handled, equal and subcylindrical, rather long, 5-9 cm. by 1.5 cm. thick; glabrous, spongy-stuffed, obscurely rivulose. SPORES ochraceous to buff, globose, 7.5-10 micr. TASTE *mild.* ODOR *unpleasant,* very characteristic when plants are old or drying.

Solitary or gregarious. Hemlock and maple woods in the north, oak and maple woods in southern Michigan. July, August and September.

This is our early, abundant Russula about Ann Arbor. It occurs in great quantities during July if the weather is favorable and only sparingly later. Once recognized by its odor and changeable flesh, its many color disguises are not as deceptive as they at first seem. The colors run into each other in a rather definite way, so that the general effect to the observer, after he has compared many individuals, is quite characteristic for the species. Hundreds of individuals were examined about Ann Arbor and all had white stems, never red. When old the effect of the whole plant is that of dinginess. Although the above description extends beyond the limits allowed by Peck's description, it is doubtless his species. Originally it included only the purple or dark red forms and was called *R. atropurpurea* Pk. but since this name was pre-empted, he changed it to *R. squalida.* It seems close to the preceding.

123.   Russula decolorans Fr.   (EDIBLE)

Syst. Myc., 1821.

Illustrations: Cooke, Ill., Pl. 1079.
　　　　　　　Ricken, Blätterpilze, Pl. 17, Fig. 5.

PILEUS 5-12 cm. broad, *often large,* firm, *globose at first* then convex and plano-depressed, *orange red,* usually ochre on disk and dark red on margin, pellicle separable, subviscid, margin even, slightly striate in age. FLESH white, *becoming cinereous* with age or where broken, becoming fragile. GILLS pale yellowish-ochraceous at maturity, white at first, thin, fragile, moderately broad, close, adnexed, forked at base, few short. STEM 5-12 cm. long,

1-2.5 cm. thick, *stout,* long, spongy or solid, wrinkled-rivulose, white, *the flesh becoming cinereous with age or where bruised.* SPORES subglobose, echinulate, pale ochraceous-yellow, 7-9 micr. TASTE *mild.* ODOR none.

Solitary or scattered. In coniferous or mixed woods of northern Michigan. July, August and September. Frequent.

The large size, globose young pileus, orange-red color and the changing flesh easily distinguish it. *R. depallens* Fr. in which the flesh turns ashy has not with certainty been found. It is said to have whitish gills, and the color of the pileus is dirty red to fawn. *R. decolorans* appears to prefer the regions of the pine and fir, both in this country and in Europe.

Var. *rubriceps* Kauff.

Mich. Acad. Sci. Rep. 13, p. 215, 1911.

The shape of the young and old pileus of this variety is well represented in Cooke's figure of *R. decolorans,* Plate 1079. The color of the pileus is, however, *ruber-red* (Sacc. colors) and persistent, changing only in age or on drying as a result of the cinerescent flesh. The pellicle is adnate, scarcely separable except on the margin, vanishing on the disk and sometimes ochraceus-spotted where the pellicle has disappeared. It is firm and the margin is not striate or very slightly so in age. These characters ally it to the Rigidae. It is slightly viscid. FLESH is firm, white, tinged ashy in age, *becoming dark cinereous on the stem where bruised.* The taste is *mild* and when fresh was taken for *R. lepida.* SPORES creamy-white in mass. It is smaller, at least in our specimens, than the type.

On the ground in beech and white pine woods. New Richmond, Allegan County. September. Apparently rare.

124. Russula flava Romell (EDIBLE)

Lönnegren's Nordisk Svampbok, 1895.

Illustration: Mich. Acad. Sci. Rep. 11, p. 55, Fig. 3.

PILEUS 5-8 cm. broad, *rather fragile,* convex, then plano-depressed, *even or slightly striate* in age, dry in dry weather, somewhat viscid when moist, pellicle separable, *dull yellow* (flavus, Sacc.), color hardly fading, but sometimes ashy, discolored in age. FLESH white *becoming cinereous* with age. GILLS white at first, becoming yellowish, broadest towards front, narrowly adnate, close, distinct, becoming slowly gray in age. STEM chalk-white at first, the flesh becoming ashy, equal or subequal, spongy-stuffed, obscurely reticulate-rivulose, rather fragile, 6-8 cm. long, 1-2 cm. thick. SPORES *yellowish,* globose, echinulate, 8-9 micr. TASTE *mild.* ODOR none.

Solitary or scattered. In coniferous or mixed woods of northern Michigan. July, August and September. Frequent.

This mild, dull or pale yellow, rather large Russula, with flesh, gills and stem becoming ashy when old, is quite easily recognized. This is *R. constans* Karst. which name was pre-empted. It differs from *R. ochraleuca* Fr. in the mild taste and unpolished pileus, etc. Its habit is very similar to that of *R. decolorans,* but it rarely reaches the same size and differs constantly by its yellow cap.

125. Russula obscura Romell (EDIBLE)

PILEUS 4-7 cm. broad, rather pliant; convex then plano-depressed, dull, *dark blood-red,* pileus sometimes blackish on disk, thin, the pellicle continuous and separable, hardly viscid when moist, *subpruinose* when dry, even or slightly striate in age. FLESH whitish, becoming ashy. GILLS white at first, then dingy straw-color, moderately broad, narrowly adnate, close, mostly forked at base, equal, interspaces sometimes venose. STEM white, *becoming ashy or blackish,* rarely tinged red, subequal, 4-6 cm. long, 10-15 mm. thick, spongy-stuffed, rigid, soon soft, obscurely wrinkled. SPORES *pale ochraceous in mass.* TASTE mild. ODOR none.

Gregarious or scattered, in low woods of southern Michigan. July and August.

It is found frequently around Stockholm. The examples pointed out by Romell did not seem to possess such a blackish stem as some of ours. This species does not remind me of *R. decolorans,* being a more slender and smaller plant. It might be confused with *R. nigrescentipes* Pk., but that species is said to have white spores. Romell (Hymen. Lapland, 1911) suggests that a better name for this plant is *Ř. vinosa* Lindb. since the latter name was used by Lindbladt in his Svampbok prior to the use of *R. obscura.*

126. Russula rubescens Beards. (EDIBLE)

Mycologia, Vol. 6, p. 91, 1914.

Illustrations: Beardslee, Mycologia, Vol. 6, Pl. 121, Fig. 1.
Plate XIX of this Report.

PILEUS 4-10 cm. broad, firm, becoming fragile, convex-plane, *dull-red, variegated* with yellowish, ochraceous or olivaceous-purplish hues, at first darker, *fading,* pellicle adnate, *dry,* scarcely separable and substriate on the margin, subglabrous, margin acute and at first straight. FLESH whitish, *staining slowly red then black where wounded,* becoming cinereous from age. GILLS narrowly adnate, broader in front, close to subdistant, medium broad, *equal,* rarely forked, white at first *then pale creamy-ochraceous,* intervenose. STEM 3-7 cm. long, 1-2.5 cm. thick, subequal or tapering down, spongy-stuffed, glabrous, even, white, becoming cinereous in age, *changing slowly* to red then blackish where bruised. SPORES globose, pale ochraceous, 7-10 micr. CYSTIDIA few and short, *subhymenium* not differentiated. TASTE *mild.* ODOR none.

Gregarious or scattered. On the ground in frondose woods. Ann Arbor. July-August. Infrequent.

Remarkable among the Subrigidae for the changes which the flesh assumes on bruising. It approaches *R. nigrescentipes* Pk., but that species is said to have a shining red cap and crowded white gills, and the stem turns blackish; no mention is made of any red stains preceding the black and since the change is slow it could scarcely be overlooked. Our species has appeared from season to season but never in abundance. It is a firm plant when fresh, becoming fragile only in age. It is apparently also related to *R. depallens* Fr. but Maire says "nobody knows this, even in Sweden." *R. obscura* Rom. has a velvety-pruinose pileus whose color is rather uniform, and whose flesh is of a different consistency.

Micro-chemical tests: G. (Gills and flesh turn blue.) S V. (Gills and flesh turn bluish very slowly.) F S. (Cystidia colored brown).

As this report was ready for the press there appeared in print the above name applied by Beardslee to a species from Asheville, N. C., which seems identical with ours.

127. Russula borealis Kauff. (EDIBLE)

Mich. Acad. Sci. Rep. 11, p. 69, 1909.

PILEUS 5-9 cm. broad, *firm and rather compact,* convex then
plano-depressed, outline broadly elliptical, often with a sinus on
one side, *blood-red,* disk darker or color uniform and not fading,
pellicle somewhat separable, hardly viscid, margin even or obscurely striate. FLESH white, red under the cuticle, not very
thick. GILLS *ochraceous,* subdistant or moderately close, *medium
broad,* broader in front, narrowly adnate, rather distinct, edge often
reddish anteriorly, equal, a few forked toward base, interspaces
venose. STEM white and *tinged red* in places, *firm,* spongy-stuffed,
thickened below, 5-7 cm. long, 1.5-2 cm. thick. SPORES deep
ochraceous-yellow in mass. TASTE *mild,* sometimes slightly and
tardily acrid. ODOR none.

Solitary. In mixed woods of hemlock, yellow birch and hard
maple, in the Northern Peninsula. Huron Mountains, Marquette
and Munising. August.

Russula alutacea is usually larger, stouter, the cap dull or sordid
red, and with broader gills. *Russula ochrophylla* occurs in oak
woods, has "buff spores, dusted" on yellow gills, and has violaceous-
purple or purple-red cap. Peck saw our plant but did not refer
it to either species. This species and *R. alutacea* show the futility
of using the striations on the margin of the cap as an important
character to distinguish the main groups. A true pellicle is present
in both and is often quite easily separated especially on the margin,
and this with the character of the gills connects them very closely
with the Fragiles. *R. linnaei,* which is not well known in Europe,
looks like it according to Cooke's figures, but is said to have white
gills and spores.

128. Russula alutacea Fr. (EDIBLE)

Syst. Myc., 1821.

Illustrations: Cooke, Ill., Pl. 1096 and 1097.
        Gillet, Champignons de France, No. 597.
        Berkley, Outlines, Pl. 13, Fig. 8 (reduced in size).
        Bresadola, Fungh. mange. e. vel., Pl. 76.
        Patouillard, Tab. Analyt., No. 513.
        Michael, Führer f. Pilzfreunde, Vol. II, No. 65 (as *Rus-
        sulina alutacea*).

Atkinson, Mushrooms, Pl. 36, Fig. 2, 1900 (much reduced in size).

Gibson, Edible Toadstools and Mushrooms, Pl. 12, Figs. 2, 4, 6, p. 131, 1903 (much reduced in size).

PILEUS 8-15 cm. broad, large, firm, convex then depressed, with dull colors, dark reddish-purple, sordid red, sometimes mixed with other shades, the reddish color predominating, *with somewhat separable pellicle,* glabrous, somewhat viscid in wet weather, soon dry, *pruinose and subgranulose,* margin even or somewhat short-striate in age. FLESH white, thick. GILLS *ochraceous from the beginning,* deeper ochraceous to tan-colored when mature, *rather broad,* thick, *subdistant,* broader in front, rounded adnexed, of *equal* length. STEM 7-10 cm. long, 3-4 cm. thick, very *firm, stout,* solid, *tinged red* or entirely white, subequal or ventricose, almost even. SPORES ochraceous-yellow to alutaceous, subglobose, 9-11 micr. TASTE *mild.* ODOR none or pleasant.

Usually solitary and rather late. Oak and maple woods of southern Michigan. Not very common. August and September.

As limited above, no bright or shining red forms are admitted from our territory. This species and *R. integra* have been the receptacle for a good many reddish species with ochraceous gills, and even experienced mycologists cannot agree on their identification. I have kept this name for a large, solitary, often late plant, with firm or hard consistency and dull, dark red and purplish cap, with truly ochraceous gills and spores. *R. integra* has cream-colored or at least paler spores and is more fragile and often grows in troops. The descriptions of this and R. *ochrophylla* run close together. Cooke's illustration of *R. alutacea* fits our plants well.

FRAGILES. Pileus thin, fragile, the viscid pellicle continuous and quite separable, margin connivent, not incurved when young, usually strongly striate. The gills are of equal length, broader anteriorly, narrowed behind.

Section I. Taste acrid. Spores white in mass.

129. Russula emetica Fr.

Syst. Myc., 1821.

Illustrations: Fries, Sverig. Svamp., Pl. 21.
    Cooke, Ill., Pl. 1030.
    Gillet, Champignons de France, No. 610.

Bresadola, Fungh. mang. e. vel., Pl. 68.
Marshall, Mushroom Book, Pl. 17, p. 68, 1905 (reduced).
Gibson, Edible Toadstools and Mushrooms, Pl. 13, p. 139,
    1903 (reduced).
Atkinson, Mushrooms, Pl. 36, Fig. 4, 1900 (reduced).
McIlvaine, American Fungi, Pl. 41, Fig. 2, 1900.

PILEUS 5-10 cm. broad, fleshy, soon *fragile,* convex to plano-depressed, *rosy to blood-red,* sometimes faded to white, pellicle
separable, *margin strongly tubercular-striate* or even sulcate, viscid
and shining. FLESH white, *red under the cuticle.* GILLS *pure
white,* subdistant or close, distinct, rather broad, equal, broadest
toward front, narrowly adnexed or free, interspaces venose. STEM
4-7 cm. long, 1-2 cm. thick, white or tinged red, subequal, spongy-
stuffed, even. SPORES *white in mass,* globose, echinulate, 7.5-10
micr. TASTE *very acrid.* ODOR none.

Scattered or gregarious. On the ground or on debris of very
rotten logs in woods. Throughout the state. July to October.
Common.

The mycelium has been found to be attached to oak tree roots
where it forms mycorrhiza. The very acrid taste gives it a bad
reputation and it is avoided by mushroom-eaters. Some think it
is harmless when thoroughly cooked. There are variations of habitat. It grows quite constantly on the crumbling remains of wood
or logs, where its white strings of mycelium are easily seen; here
the gills are close. One form has been found growing in troops;
such were found in a tamarack swamp in late October, growing on
thick beds of sphagnum. They had developed somewhat differently
in this habitat as was to be expected. The stems were white, long
and stout, narrower above and obsoletely wrinkled. The gills were
subdistant. The taste was sharp but not as excruciating as that of
the type. The disk of the pileus was glabrous and very viscid. It
was a beautiful plant, apparently appearing late; it might be referred to as var. *gregaria.*

130. Russula rugulosa Pk.

N. Y. State Mus. Rep. 54, 1901.

Illustration: Ibid, Pl. 72, Fig. 12-18.

PILEUS 5-10 cm. or more broad, thin, *fragile,* convex then plano-
depressed, *dark rose-red,* color sometimes thin, *surface* almost entirely *rugulose,* the rugae radiating somewhat, rather viscid, pellicle

separable, margin at length distinctly tubercular-striate. FLESH thin, white, red under the pellicle. GILLS shining white, rather close, narrowly adnate, not very broad, broadest in front, few forked, equal, interspaces venose. STEM white, subequal, unchanged, glabrous, spongy-stuffed, 6-7 cm. long, 1-2 cm. thick. SPORES *white in mass,* globose, echinulate, 8-9 micr. TASTE tardily but very acrid.

In troops. Hemlock and mixed woods on the ground. August and September. Northern Michigan.

Differs from *R. emetica* in that its acrid taste develops slowly, in the uneven and rather dull pileus and in the habit of appearing in troops on the ground. It was formerly referred to *R. emetica,* and is close to it.

131. Russula fragilis Fr.

Syst. Myc., 1821.

Illustrations: Cooke, Ill., Pl. 1091.
　　　　Gillet, Champignons de France, No. 614.
　　　　Patouillard, Tab. Analyt., No. 622.
　　　　Michael, Führer f. Pilzfreunde, No. 43 (var.).
　　　　Ricken, Blätterpilze, Pl. 19, Fig. 3.
　　　　Hard, Mushrooms, Fig. 172, p. 192, 1908.

PILEUS 2.5-5 cm. broad, *very thin* and fragile, convex then plano-depressed with a thin viscid pellicle, tubercular-striate on the thin margin, glabrous, rather uniform rosy or *pale red,* sometimes faded or bleached to white. FLESH *white under the pellicle,* thin. GILLS white, thin, close, crowded, adnexed, ventricose, moderately broad. STEM 2.3-5 cm. long, .5-1 cm. thick, white, spongy then hollow, equal, fragile. SPORES *white in mass,* subglobose, 8-9 micr. TASTE promptly and *very acrid.* ODOR none.

Scattered. On the ground in woods. Throughout the state. July-August. Infrequent.

This species, as limited here, is only distinguishable from *R. emetica* relatively; it is smaller, color paler, flesh thinner and more fragile and white under the cuticle. Maire says the taste is more quickly acrid on the tongue than *R. emetica,* but not as violent. It grows in somewhat dryer situations. Var. *nivea* is a white plant, otherwise the same. *R. fallax* Cke. used to be considered a variety of it.

132. Russula fallax Cke.

Illustration: Cooke, Ill., Pl. 1059.

PILEUS 3-7 cm. broad, *thin, fragile,* color incarnate or pale rose, the *disk* pale *olivaceous or livid,* sometimes darker or purplish, soon plane or slightly depressed on disk, quite viscid, margin striate and becoming elevated, surface faintly rugulose under lens. FLESH white. GILLS white, unchanged, subdistant, attached by a point, *narrow,* edge even. STEM 3-4 cm. long, 6-10 cm. thick, pure white, cylindrical or compressed, equal, spongy-stuffed, soon hollow, longitudinally-wrinkled under a lens. SPORES *white in mass,* subglobose, 7.5 micr. TASTE promptly and very acrid.

Solitary or gregarious. In sphagnum bogs, low mossy ground in woods, etc., often attached to sphagnum. Distributed throughout the state. Not rare. July, August and September.

This species differs in two important particulars from *R. fragilis.* The gills are subdistant and the pileus is livid or olivaceous in the center. It is very characteristic of the sphagnum flora of the state. It has often been referred to *R. fragilis* as a variety. The pileus is not as lilac as shown in Cooke's figure.

133. Russula albidula Pk.

Torr. Bot. Club, Bull. 25, 1898.

PILEUS 2.5-5 cm. broad, *white,* broadly convex, glabrous, the pellicle *viscid* and separable when fresh, the margin even. FLESH white, subfragile. GILLS white, rather crowded, adnexed, not broad, *of equal length,* some basifurcate, interspaces venose. STEM 2.5-4 cm. long, 8-12 mm. thick, white, equal, spongy-stuffed, even. SPORES white in mass, subglobose, 7-10 micr. TASTE acrid. ODOR none.

Solitary. In oak woods. Ann Arbor. July and August.

In dried specimens the pileus and gills are ochraceous to yellowish, and stem whitish. The taste and viscidity seem to be the only marked differences between this species and the other two white Russulas of Peck, *R. albida* and *R. albella.* All three are rather fragile, while *R. lactea* is a compact firm plant with thick, broad, distant gills. There is a white variety of *R. emetica* which is very acrid and fragile and whose striations on the margin of the cap are like those of that species.

Section II. Taste acrid. Spore-mass cream-color, yellowish, ochraceous to alutaceous.

134. Russula sanguinea Fr. (*R. rosacea* Fr.)

Epicrisis, 1836-38.

Illustrations: Cooke, Ill., Pl. 1020 (as *R. rosea*).
    Michael, Führer f. Pilzfreunde, Vol. II (as *R. rosacea*).

PILEUS 3-6 cm. broad, rather firm at firs*t, subfragile,* convex-plane or depressed, *rosy-red, viscid,* margin acute and thin, pellicle subadnate, easily separable on margin and tubercular-striate. FLESH rather thin, white, red under the pellicle. GILLS slightly adnate, close to subdistant, *equal,* not broad, *creamy-white.* STEM 4-6 cm. long, subequal or tapering down, often eccentric, *white or tinged rosy-red,* spongy-stuffed then cavernous, rather fragile, glabrous, even. SPORES *creamy-white in mass.* TASTE tardily but truly acrid.

Gregarious. On the ground among grass in frondose woods. Ann Arbor. September-October. Infrequent.

The plants referred here are *R. rosacea* in the sense of Romell, and *R. sanguinea* according to most of the modern French mycologists. They are distinguished by the cream color of the spores and gills. The gills are not decurrent as they are supposed to be in *R. rosacea,* but the stem is often eccentric as that species is described by Fries. Bresadola, Maire, etc., conceive *R. rosacea* Fr. as a plant with pure white gills and spores. Our plant agrees with a species, common around Stockholm, whose gills are usually creamy-white. It was placed by Fries among the rigid forms but is almost too fragile. It is not large and except for the color of the spores small forms might be mistaken for *R. fragilis.*

135. Russula veternosa Fr.

Epicrisis, 1836-38.

Illustrations: Bresadola, Fungh. mang. e. vel., Pl. 75.
    Cooke, Ill., Pl. 1033.

PILEUS 5-7.5 cm. broad, convex then expanded, with a somewhat separable pellicle, *indistinctly striate* on the margin, deep rose-red (like *R. emetica*), viscid when moist. FLESH white, red under the cuticle. GILLS white at first, *then straw-color or pale ochraceous,* narrow, adnate, close, broader in front, equal or few shorter, few forked, interspaces venose. STEM white, *never red,* equal or subequal, spongy-stuffed, somewhat slender, fragile, hollow, even, 1.5 cm. long, 1-1.5 cm. thick. SPORES pale *yellowish-ochraceous,* subglobose, echinulate, 8-9 micr. TASTE *very acrid.* ODOR none.

Scattered or gregarious. Oak and maple woods of southern Michigan. July and August.

This represents a group of red Russulas with acrid taste and gills varying pale ochraceous or somewhat yellowish in the different forms. I have limited the name to those with white stem and a rather firm and hardly striate pileus, although it may include several forms of which only the spore-color has so far been a distinguishable character. The separable, viscid, distinct pellicle and rather fragile stem, relates it to the Fragiles. From *R. tenuiceps* it is separated by the less deep ochraceous spores and gills, the firmer consistency of pileus and gills, and the uniform red color and even margin of the pileus.

136.   Russula tenuiceps Kauff.

Mich. Acad. Sci. Rep. 11, p. 81, 1909.

Illustration: Plate XX of this Report.

PILEUS 7-12 cm. broad, thin, fragile, convex to expanded, the somewhat viscid pellicle easily separable, margin at first connivent, *striate,* deep rosy-red or blood-red, sometimes white, spotted or tinged with orange blotches, sometimes uniform red, with or without minute rugae. FLESH white, red beneath the cuticle, *very fragile at maturity.* GILLS white, then yellow-ochraceous, *crowded,* narrow, *fragile,* narrowly adnate to free, few forked, interspaces venose, equal. STEM fragile, white or rosy-tinged, spongy-stuffed, subequal or ventricose, obscurely rivulose, white within and unchanged, 5-9 cm. long, 2-2.5 cm. thick. SPORES *yellow-ochraceous,* subglobose, 6-8 micr., echinulate. TASTE acrid, sometimes tardily but very acrid. ODOR not marked.

Gregarious. Mixed woods at Marquette; in oak and maple woods at Ann Arbor. July and August. Rather frequent.

As in *R. veternosa,* it is probable that several forms are represented here. The red Russulas are very troublesome, and we seem to have a considerable number of forms with acrid taste and yellowish to deep ochraceous gills, which cannot be easily kept separate. All efforts to refer them to old species like *R. sardonia, R. rugulosa,*

R. rosacea, etc., failed repeatedly; the fragile flesh and ochraceous, almost alutaceous gills are too distinctive. The maturing of the spores is sometimes slow and care must be taken to get a good spore print in these red species. All the collections which I have referred here showed red on some or all of the stems of each collection. Their edibility was not tested.

137. Russula palustris Pk.

N. Y. State Mus. Rep. 53, 1900.

PILEUS 4-7.5 cm. broad, *fragile,* subglobose or hemispheric, then convex or nearly plane, viscid, pellicle separable, obscurely tubercular-striate on margin, *reddish*-buff or purplish-red especially on disk, glabrous. FLESH white, thin, tinged with the color of the pileus under the pellicle. GILLS narrowed behind, broader in front, close to subdistant, entire, *whitish then yellowish,* intervenose. STEM 3-7 cm. long, 6-12 mm. thick, equal, glabrous, spongy-stuffed then hollow, fragile, white or tinged red. SPORES subglobose, *pale yellow in mass,* 7.5-10 micr. TASTE *tardily acrid.*
Gregarious or scattered. In low woods or swamps. Marquette, New Richmond, Ann Arbor. August-September. Infrequent.
The pileus is sometimes faintly glaucous.

138. Russula aurantialutea Kauff.

Mich. Acad. Sci. Rep. 11, p. 81, 1909.

PILEUS 5-10 cm. broad, *thin,* fragile, convex then plano-depressed, *yellow* (citron to luteus), *or with orange shades* intermingled, especially on the margin, slightly tubercular-striate, pellicle viscid, shining and somewhat separable for some distance. FLESH *white,* thin toward the margin, *unchanged with age.* GILLS *pale yellow,* close, or subdistant at the outer extremity, equal or a few shorter, narrowly adnate, seceding with age, broadest toward front, often forked at the base, rarely elsewhere, interspaces venose. STEM 4-8 cm. long, 1.5-2 cm. thick, white, flesh concolor and unchanged, subequal, glabrous, even, spongy-stuffed. SPORES *ochraceous-yellow,* subglobose, 8-9 micr. TASTE acrid in all its parts, often very acrid. ODOR not noticeable.
Solitary or scattered. On debris or forest mould in hemlock or mixed woods of northern Michigan, in deciduous woods in the southern part of the state. July, August and September. Earlier in southern Michigan. Infrequent.

R. ochraleuca Fr. differs in having white to pallid gills and spores, and a cinerescent stem; *R. granulosa* Cke. has white gills and spores and a granular cap and stem; *R. fellea* Fr. has ochraceous or straw-yellow flesh and the more firm pileus is either straw or gilvous color, and its gills exude watery drops; *R. claroflava* Grove has a cinerescent stem and its gills are white then lemon yellow with an ochre tinge; *R. ochracea* Fr. has a mild taste, and the flesh of the cap, gills and stem is ochraceous; *R. simillima* Pk. has white spores and a pale ochraceous pileus and stem; and *R. decolorans* Fr. has cinerescent flesh and is stouter. Our species could be made on ecological variety of almost any of the above species, depending on the guess of the author who so interpreted it.

Section III. Taste mild. Spore-mass white.

139. Russula albida Pk.

N. Y. State Mus. Bull. 2, 1887 (*R. albida*).
N. Y. State Mus. Rep. 50, 1897 (*R. albella*).

Illustration: N. Y. State Mus. Bull. 105, Pl. 96 (*R. albida*).

PILEUS 3-6 cm. broad, *thin, fragile,* broadly convex to plane, slightly depressed in the center, white or whitish, even or slightly striate on the margin, not shining. FLESH white, fragile. GILLS white or whitish, thin, moderately close, entire, equal, not broad, broadest in front, rarely forked at base, adnate or subdecurrent. STEM 2.5-6 cm. long, white, subequal, glabrous, spongy-stuffed or solid. SPORES about 8 micr. diam., *white.* TASTE mild or *slightly bitterish.*

Solitary. Hemlock or mixed woods in the Northern Peninsula. July and August.

Peck's description of both *R. albida* and *R. albella* differs in minor particulars from our plants. The pileus of *R. albida* has a viscid, separable pellicle, while that of *R. albella* is dry. *R. albida* is said to have a "slightly bitterish or unpleasant taste," while our plants were sometimes bitterish, sometimes tardily and slightly acrid. *R. albida* is described with a stuffed or hollow stem; in one of my collections the stem was solid, in another it was spongy-stuffed. It is worth noting whether the spore prints are pure white or with yellow tinge; some of Peck's specimens of *R. albida* had spores with a faint yellowish tinge. In my specimens the whole plant is ochraceous when dried; specimens seen at the N. Y. Botanical Gardens were white when dry. As these species occur so seldom and far apart, it is difficult to obtain exact data with regard to their characters. *R. anomala* Pk. and *R. albidula* differ in the acrid taste.

140. Russula subdepallens Pk. (EDIBLE)

Torr. Bot. Club Bull., Vol. 23, 1896.

PILEUS 5-14 cm. broad, *fragile,* convex then plane and depressed, margin elevated in age, *bright rosy-red,* shading into yellowish blotches as if the red color were put over the yellow, disk paler in old specimens, disk dark-red in very young plants, with a thin, separable, viscid pellicle, *tubercular-striate* on margin, obscurely wrinkled elsewhere. FLESH white, rosy under the cuticle, becoming slightly cinereous, *very fragile.* GILLS *white,* broad in front, narrowed behind, adnate, subdistant, few forked, interspaces venose. STEM white, spongy-stuffed, rather stout, 4-10 cm. long, 1-3 cm. thick, subequal. SPORES *white in mass,* globose, echinulate, 7.5-8 micr. TASTE mild. ODOR none.

Gregarious. In woods of maple, yellow birch and hemlock of northern Michigan. August.

Found in a number of places in considerable abundance. The fragile character, especially of the gills, is very marked and the mild taste, white gills and red cap help to distinguish it. The flesh does not turn so strongly ashy as in Peck's plants, and this character did not seem to be always noticeable. It is distinguished from *R. purpurina,* the brilliant-red Russula, by its gregarious habit, large size and less viscid cap; also the gills are not crenulate. Our specimens had the stature and appearance of *R. rugulosa* and *R. emetica* var. *gregaria.* Peck's plants were found in Pennsylvania by Dr. Herbst, and reported but once; the species is not included in Peck's New York monograph. Our plant has so far been limited to the north.

141. Russula purpurina Quel. & Schultz (EDIBLE)

Hedwigia, 1885.

Illustrations: McIlvaine, American Fungi, Pl. 45 [a, p.] 188, 1900.
    Plate XXI of this Report.

PILEUS 3-7 cm. broad, fragile, *viscid,* usually very viscid, subglobose then expanded and slightly depressed at the disk, *brilliant rosy-red* to blood-red or even darker, pellicle somewhat separable, margin thin but *not striate* except when fully expanded, surface when dry as if with a bloom. FLESH white, red under the cuticle, thin, fragile, unchangeable. GILLS *white,* later dingy-white or "yellowish," medium close to subdistant, adnexed, not broad, broadest in front, mostly equal, few or none forked, interspaces sometimes venose, *edge floccose-crenulate.* STEM rather long, 5-8 cm., 8-12 mm. thick, sprinkled rosy-pink, equal or subequal, spongy-stuffed, fragile but rather soft. SPORES *white in mass,* globose, 8-10 micr. TASTE mild. ODOR none.

Solitary or scattered. In mixed or maple-birch woods of the Northern Peninsula. Infrequent. August and September.

Distinguished by its brilliant red, viscid cap, small to medium size, mild taste and white crenulate gills and spores. Peck also notes the floccose-crenulate edge of the gills, which is due to cystidia. *R. uncialis, R. sericeonitens* and *R. subdepallens* are the only others of the Fragiles group with mild taste, red cap and white spores. From *R. unciales* it differs by the deep color, character of gills and habitat. *R. sericeonitens* is hardly viscid and becomes silky-shining; it has a different stature and color. Maire points out that *R. punctata* Gill. and *R. pseudointegra* A. & G. have gills with a floccose-crenulate edge.

142. Russula uncialis Pk. (EDIBLE)

N. Y. State Mus. Bull. 2, 1887.

Illustrations: Peck, N. Y. State Mus. Bull. 116, Pl. 107, 1907.

PILEUS 2-5 cm. *broad,* thin, rather fragile, convex then expanded-depressed, *pink or bright flesh-color, unicolorous,* the rather adnate pellicle slightly separable, slightly viscid when moist, pruinose and pulverulent when dry, margin not striate till old. FLESH white, pink under the pellicle, unchanged. GILLS pure *white,* hardly changed, *rather broad,* broadest in front, narrowed behind and adnate, subdistant or moderately close, distinct, entire on edge, few forked, interspaces venose. STEM white, rarely tinged pink, rather short, 1-3.5 cm. long, 4-10 mm. thick, spongy-stuffed, equal, glabrous. SPORES *white in mass,* subglobose, echinulate, 7-8 micr. TASTE mild. ODOR none.

Gregarious. In oak woods of southern Michigan. July and August. Quite common in places.

The persistently white gills and spores, the mild taste, uniform pink color and size, distinguishes this Russula. It is sometimes more than an inch in width.

143. Russula sericeo-nitens Kauff. (EDIBLE)

Mich. Acad. Sci. Rep. 11, p. 84, 1909.

PILEUS 4-6 cm. broad, very *regular,* rather thin, convex then plano-depressed, *dark violet-purple* or dark blood-red tinted purplish, disk sometimes livid-blackish, the *separable pellicle* slightly viscid when moist, not striate or substriate in age, surface with a silky sheen. FLESH white, thin on margin, unchanged, purplish under the pellicle. GILLS *white,* subdistant or medium close, becoming flaccid, moderately broad, broad in front, narrowed behind, dry, equal, few forked near base, interspaces venose. STEM white, equal or thickened at apex, spongy within, unchanged, glabrous, even or obscurely rivulose, 3-5.5 cm. long, 1 cm. thick. SPORES *white in mass,* globose, echinulate, 6-7.5 micr. TASTE *mild.* ODOR none.

Usually solitary. In mixed woods of hemlock, maple and yellow birch in northern Michigan. July and August. Not uncommon.

Its thin pileus is *flexible* at maturity. The *silky sheen* and regular pileus are quite characteristic. The cap has the color of Cooke's figures of *R. queletii* Fr., *R. drimeia* Cke. and *R. purpurea* Gill. These three, including *R. expallens* Gill., have been placed together by some modern authors as one species, characterized by "a pruinose, violaceous, decolorate stem, and very sharp taste." The taste is said to be so peppery that even when the color is washed out by rains they can be recognized by this character. All of the four are violet or reddish on the stem. Our specimens all had a white stem and an impeachable mild taste.

Section IV. Taste mild; spore-mass cream-white, yellowish or ochraceous.

144. Russula integra Fr. (EDIBLE)

Epicrisis, 1836-38.

Illustrations: Cooke, Ill., Pl. 1093 and 1094.

PILEUS 5-10 cm. broad, firm, *soon fragile,* discoid, convex or campanulate then plano-depressed covered with *a viscid separable pellicle,* thin on the margin, at length *coarsely tubercular-striate,* variable as to color in different plants, *colors dingy or sordid,* from buff through to reddish-brown and dark dull red, *fading.* FLESH white, not changing. GILLS *white at first,* then creamy-yellow to buff-ochraceous, not strongly ochre, *broad, distinct,* equal, nearly free. STEM white, unchanged, *never red,* soon quite fragile, conic or short-clavate at first, then subequal or ventricose, spongy-stuffed, even. SPORES *creamy-yellow to pale ochraceous.* TASTE mild. ODOR none.

Gregarious. In woods, probably throughout the state. Ann Arbor. July and August. Not common.

This species is a sort of clearing house for various colored Russulas with broad, pale ochraceous gills and mild taste, especially reddish forms. I have given Fries' description above, supplemented for the most part from notes of my own collections about Stockholm. Romell describes the cap as "brown, blackish-brown, reddish-brown, dark red, violaceous, yellow or greenish, either unicolorous or with whitish or yellowish spots." I saw only the dirty reddish-brown, dark dull red and sordid-buff forms at Stockholm. In favorable weather or situations they occur in troops and seem very common in Sweden. Peck says they are rare in New York state. The European mycologists do not agree among themselves as to this species, but there seems to be a fair unanimity that the "dusting" of the gills by the spores is too deceptive for practical use in identification. *R. integra* is to be separated from *R. alutacea* by its gills being white at first, by the white fragile stem, the paler spores and more striate pileus; under certain conditions these two species are hardly distinguishable.

The two plates of Cooke referred to, give the best idea of the species as here limited. The figures of this species with bright red caps, shown by various authors, illustrate segregated species for the most part. Maire (Soc. Myc. Bull. 26, 1910) has named one form, *R. romelii,* and considers another to be *R. melliolens* Quel. As Fries pointed out long ago, it is easy to separate new species from the mass of plants usually referred here, and the more exact method with the microscope will doubtless produce many more. I have found this species rarely but then in quantity, as they usually cover quite an area from the same mycelium.

145. Russula amygdaloides sp. nov. (Edible)

(See under *R. barlae* Quel., Mich. Acad. Sci. Rep. 13, p. 221, 1911.)

PILEUS 4-8 cm. broad, thin, medium size, ovate at first with straight margin, then convex-plane or depressed, very viscid, *fragile, pale rosy-flesh color tinged with yellow,* sometimes *peach color,* sometimes dull citron-yellow, varying in color from young to old, pellicle continuous and entirely separable, *margin becoming* strongly tuberculate-striate. FLESH thin, white, not changing color, soft. GILLS *bright ochraceous-yellow* (flavus, Sacc.), white at first, *rather narrow,* broadest in front, narrowed and adnexed behind, subdistant at maturity, dusted by the spores. STEM 4-8 cm. long, 1-2 cm. thick, *subequal to ventricose, soft* and *fragile,* loosely stuffed then cavernous (but not from grubs), white, rarely tinged with delicate pink, slightly wrinkled, subglabrous. SPORES subglobose, 7-9 micr., echinulate, nucleate, bright ochre-yellow in mass. TASTE mild. ODOR none. CYSTIDIA very few. *Subhymenium narrow,* sharply differentiated from gill-trama.

Solitary or scattered. In mixed woods of hemlock and beech, among beds of white pine needles at New Richmond; among grass, etc., in oak woods at Ann Arbor. July-October. Frequent.

This very fragile Russula is known from the other members of the "Fragiles" group by its medium size, bright yellow-ochraceous spores and gills, the hollow, often subventricose stem, the mild taste and the pinkish-yellow to peach-colored pileus. The stem is sometimes enlarged at the apex, sometimes at the base, always fragile. Very few of our Russulas have such bright-colored spores and gills. The color of the cap varies rather rarely to a deeper red on the one hand or to ochraceous-tan and straw-color on the other. The flesh does not change on bruising, and the odor is not noticeable even in age. It is very different from *R. integra* Fr. It approaches *R. nitida* and is no doubt the plant usually referred to that species in this country. It differs in the lack of the nauseous, disagreeable odor which is known to be constant in *R. nitida.* I formerly referred it to *R. barlae* Quel. which, however, is described as compact and firm. *R. aurata* Fr. has gills with a chrome-yellow edge.

Micro-chemical tests: G. (Flesh turns blue quickly; gills become greenish-blue.) S V. (Flesh and gills slowly pinkish then blue.) F S. (Cystidia colored brown.)

146. Russula roseipes Secr.—Bres. (EDIBLE)

Fung. Trid., Vol. I, 1881.

Illustration: Ibid, Pl. 40.

PILEUS 2.5-5 cm. broad, *thin, fragile,* convex then plano-depressed, with a viscid, separable pellicle, margin tubercular-striate when mature, soon dry, *rosy-red or flesh-red,* disk tending to ochre-yellowish. FLESH white, thin, unchanged. GILLS soon truly *ochraceous,* subdistant, mostly equal, broadest in front, ventricose, narrowly adnate or almost free, few forked, interspaces venose. STEM white and *rosy-sprinkled,* stuffed then cavernous, equal or tapering upward, even, 2.5-5 cm. long, 5-12 mm. thick. SPORES *ochraceous,* globose, echinulate, 8-10 micr. TASTE mild. ODOR none or pleasant.

Solitary or scattered. In mixed woods, but usually under conifers. Only found in the northern part of the state. July and August.

A middle-sized to small plant, fragile, and with a rosy mealiness on the stem. This last is quite characteristic of the species. It occurs under spruces and balsams in moist places. It is quite distinct from *R. puellaris* Fr. to which Fries, who had never seen Secretan's plant, referred it as a variety. *R. purpurina* also has a rosy-sprinkled stem, but is very viscid and more brilliant shining red on the cap. Peck (Rep. 51, p. 307) says the stem is not rosy-sprinkled in his plants, but that the color resides in the stem; he does not seem to have had the typical plant.

147. Russula puellaris Fr.

Monographia, 1863.

Illustrations: Cooke, Ill., Pl. 1065.
    Bresadola, Fung. Trid., Vol. I, Pl. 64.
    Ricken, Blätterpilze, Pl. 17, Fig. 2.

PILEUS 2-4 cm. broad, *very thin,* convex then plano-depressed, viscid, *tubercular-striate* on the margin, livid-purplish or livid-brownish, then sometimes yellowish. FLESH white at first, soon watery subtranslucent, fragile. GILLS pallid white to pale yellow, watery honey-colored in age, equal, thin, subventricose, narrowed behind and adnexed, interspaces venose. STEM whitish, then *watery honey-colored toward base,* spongy-stuffed, soon cavernous, soft and fragile, subequal or subclavate at base, 4-5 cm. long, 7-10 mm. thick. SPORES subglobose, echinulate, *pale yellow,* 6-8 micr. TASTE mild or slightly acrid. ODOR none.

Found in low, moist places in conifer or mixed woods of Europe. It has not yet been reported from Michigan with certainty. I have given Bresadola's description as that of a typical plant, which is verified by my notes of the Stockholm plants. I have not seen the typical Swedish plant in this country, and Peck's specimens were evidently not typical as he says no yellowish stains occur in the stem. The stem soon becomes soft and then develops this characteristic, translucent, light-yellowish color. Several varieties occur in Michigan differing mainly from the above description in the red caps and non-lutescent stems; these are referred here for the present.

148. Russula sphagnophila Kauff.

Mich. Acad. Sci. Rep. 11, p. 86, 1909.

PILEUS 2-4.5 cm. broad, *very fragile,* convex, *umbonate,* margin at length elevated and disk depressed and purplish-red or rosy-red, the space between the umbo and the margin pale olive-brown, covered by a viscous pellicle, glabrous, margin slightly striate. FLESH reddish under the cuticle and under the surface of the stem fragile. GILLS white then pale ochraceous, narrow, adnato-decurrent, rather close, narrowed toward both ends, few forked here and there. STEM *rosy-colored,* usually ventricose or irregularly swollen, spongy-stuffed *then cavernous,* very fragile, rivulose-uneven, 4-5 cm. long, 7-12 mm. thick. SPORES cream-color, globose, echinulate, 6-7 micr. TASTE *mild.*

Scattered. On sphagnum, in swamps. Cold Spring Harbor. August and September. Rare.

Whole plant very fragile, always with an umbo, subpellucid and rosy stem, and pale gills. The only other Russula with an umbo, known to me, is *R. caerulea* Pers. which differs in color and habitat. The red color rubs off on paper when moist. In some points it is near *R. roseipes,* in others it is nearest *R. puellaris,* and might perhaps be referred to the latter as a variety but without settling anything as to its origin.

149. Russula chamæleontina Fr. (EDIBLE)

Epicrisis, 1836-38.

Illustrations: Cooke, Ill., Pl. 1908.
　　　Gillet, Champignons de France, No. 600.
　　　Ricken, Blätterpilze, Pl. 18, Fig. 2.

PILEUS 2-5 cm. broad, *rather small,* fragile, thin, plano-depressed, with a viscid separable pellicle, margin even at first then striatulate, *color varying for different pilei,* mostly some shade of red, purple, etc.. fading to yellowish especially on disk. FLESH white, thin. GILLS thin, crowded or close, adnexed or almost free, equal, rather broad, sometimes almost narrow, few forked, interspaces venose, *ochraceous or ochraceous-yellow.* STEM 2-5 cm. long, 4-6 mm. thick, white, spongy-stuffed then hollow, *slender,* equal or subequal to subventricose, sometimes subclavate, even or obscurely rivulose. SPORES *ochraceous.* TASTE mild. ODOR none.

Scattered or gregarious. In coniferous or mixed woods. So far reported only from northern Michigan.

Like *R. integra* this has to be considered at present a composite species, from which several species have, from time to time, been segregated. According to von Post, a pupil of Fries, the master himself included many forms which do not fit into his own description; and Romell follows the Swedish tradition and refers to *R. chamaeleontina* all small forms with mild taste and ochraceous gills not otherwise accounted for. "No subacrid forms are included" writes Romell. Specimens with the caps a uniform red, rose colored, purplish, lilac, etc., and accompanied with a yellowish tint, are always included; sometimes also, whitish, faded forms must be placed here.

150. Russula abietina Pk.

N. Y. State Mus. Rep*.* 54, 1901.

Illustration: Ibid, Pl. 72, Fig. 1-11.

"PILEUS 1-2.5 cm. broad, thin, fragile, convex becoming plane or slightly depressed in the center, covered with a viscid, separable pellicle, tubercular-striate on the thin margin, *variable in color,* purplish, greenish-purple or olive-green with a brown or blackish center, or sometimes purplish with a greenish center. FLESH white. GILLS narrowed toward the stem, subdistant, equal, rounded behind and nearly free, ventricose, whitish becoming *pale yellow.* STEM 1-2.5 cm. long, equal or tapering upward, stuffed or hollow, white. SPORES bright yellowish-ochraceous, subglobose, 8-10 micr. TASTE mild."

Its place of growth is only *under balsm fir.* It has been reported from Michigan, but the description given is that of Peck. The important characters seem to be the bright yellow tinged spores. It is separable from *R. puellaris,* "by the viscid cap, the gills rather widely separated from each other and nearly free, the stem never yellowish nor becoming yellow where wounded, and the spores having an ochraceous hue."

151. Russula lutea Fr. (Edible)

Syst. Myc., 1821.

Illustrations: Cooke, Ill., Pl. 1082.
    Gillet, Champignons de France, No. 622.
    Patouillard, Tab. Analyt., No. 321.
    Bresadola, Fungh. mang. e. vel., Pl. 79.
    Michael, Führer f. Pilzfreunde, No. 61.
    Ricken, Blätterpilze, Pl. 18, Fig. 3.
    Plate XXII of this Report.

PILEUS 3-6 cm. broad; *small, thin,* convex then plano-depressed, pellicle easily separable, viscid, margin *even,* becoming slightly striate in age, unicolorus, bright *yellow* or pale golden yellow. FLESH white, very thin, fragile. GILLS at length *deep yellow-ochraceous, subdistant,* rather broad in front, narrowed behind and free, equal, interspaces often venose. STEM white, unchanged, subequal, stuffed then hollow, soft, fragile, even or obscurely wrinkled, glabrous, 3-5 cm. long, 4-8 mm. thick. SPORES globose, echinulate, yellow, 8-10 micr. in diam. TASTE *mild.* ODOR none.

Solitary, in coniferous and mixed woods of northern Michigan, in frondose woods in the south. July and August. Infrequent and few in number.

Our plant is the same as the one occurring about Stockholm. It agrees with the characters as given in Hymenomycetes Europaei, except that the gills are subdistant, not truly narrow but relatively broad in front. The Stockholm specimens had the thin margins of the pileus at length slightly striate, as is also the case with the Michigan plants. Peck says he has found it but once in New York. I have found it a number of times in Michigan. *R. vitellina* Fr. which is said to resemble this species, is not known to Romell for Sweden, and he refers all their forms to *R. lutea.* It may be that *R. lutea* and *R. vitellina* represent extremes of the species. Our plant described above and that about Stockholm do not agree with either of the descriptions, but is a compromise between the two. Our plants are not strongly striate nor have they any marked odor like *R. vitellina;* on the other hand they have broader and more distant gills than is warranted by the description of *R. lutea.* According to Fries, *R. lutea* is found in beech forests and *R. vitellina* in coniferous woods. *R. flaviceps* Pk. is said to be larger, with narrow and close, pale yellow gills.

HYGROPHOREAE

Fruit body soft, fleshy. Stem central, confluent with the pileus. Gills with a waxy consistency, more or less distant, thick, well-developed, with acute edge.

This subfamily is well defined and set off from the others. The characteristics are not easily described in words, but the habit of the plants and the nature of the gills are soon learned by field study. The gills, although acute on the edge, thicken toward the pileus, and are built up of a thick central layer (the trama), coated on both surfaces by a thick, waxy, hymenial layer of long basidia, which is more or less removable.

Our species are included under two genera:

Spores white. *Hygrophorus.*
Spores blackish. *Gomphidius.*

Gomphidius Fr.

(From the Greek, *gomphos*, a wooden bolt or peg, referring to the shape of the young plants.)

Black-spored to smoky-olive-spored; *gills of a waxy* or subgelatinous *consistency*, decurrent, subdistant to distant, forked, edge acute; stem central, confluent with the pileus; pileus fleshy, *viscid;* partial veil when present membranous glutinous; spores elongated-subfusiform; cystidia abundant.

Terrestrial and putrescent fungi, very infrequent in this region, sharply distinct by the nature of its gills and spores. The genus appears to have some relationship with Hygrophorus on the one hand and with Paxillus on the other. In Europe, *G. viscidus* Fr. and *G. glutinosis* Fr. are a prominent part of the mushroom flora, although with us these two species seem to be entirely lacking, and no species can be said to be frequent. Peck has described five species from the United States; four of these came from the eastern states and are smaller than the two common European species mentioned above. Nothing is known of the edibility of our species.

The genus is best recognized by the smoky, decurrent and usually distant gills, the viscid or glutinous cap, and the spotted stem. In the young stage a viscid veil connects the margin of the pileus with

the stem; as the plant matures the veil collapses on the stem and
in most cases causes the stem to appear viscid and at length spotted
or blotched by the drying remnants of this veil. In our species
this veil is scanty and it apparently disappears very early, and in
most cases cannot be definitely seen. Our species occur in swampy
ground or in tamarack bogs. Only three species have been found
in the state. *G. nigricans* Pk. reported in the 8th Rep. Mich. Acad.
Sci., is doubtful. *G. rhodoxanthus* (Schw.) is referred to Paxillus.

Key to the Species

(a)   Pileus 2-5 cm. broad, obtuse or depressed; stem dry, becoming red-
      dish-black spotted, yellow at base. 152. *G. maculatus* Fr.
(aa) Pileus 1-2.5 cm. broad, often umbonate; stem at first viscid from
      the veil, slender.
  (b)   Stem yellow downwards. 154. *G. flavipes* Pk.
  (bb) Stem brick color to wine-reddish; not yellow at base. 153. *G.
        vinicolor* Pk.

152. Gomphidius maculatus Fr.

Epicrisis, 1836-38.

Illustrations: Ricken, Blätterpilze, Pl. 3, Fig. 2.
    Plate XXIII of this Report.

PILEUS 2-5 cm. broad, convex, obtuse, soon plane or depressed,
with a viscid, separable pellicle, glabrous, *brownish-incarnate to
pale clay color,* rugulose, spotted and shining when dry. FLESH
thick, soft, white or faintly incarnate. GILLS decurrent, narrowed
behind, thickish, subdistant to distant, distinct, subgelatinous to
soft-waxy, *dichotomously forked,* at first whitish, then *pale
olivaceous-gray, finally smoky,* moderately broad. Stem 4-7 cm. long,
apex 5-12 mm. thick, tapering downward, solid, firm, even, whitish
above or with a tinge of incarnate, at first dotted with reddish
scurf, glabrescent, *becoming black-spotted* or blackish in age or
when handled, *base yellow.* VEIL *none* or very evanescent.
SPORES variable in size, cylindrical-subfusiform to elongated-
elliptical, 15-23x6-7.5 micr., smooth, pale smoky-brownish under the
microscope. CYSTIDIA abundant on sides and edge of gills,
cylindrical, obtuse, variable, 100-135x15-25 micr. TASTE mild.
ODOR none or slight.

Gregarious, subcaespitose or scattered, under tamarack trees
(Larix), in bogs, on moss or debris. Between Chelsea and'Jackson. October-November. Rare or local.

Apparently this species occurs only in restricted localities in the
bogs near inland lakes. This is the largest form so far found in

the state, although it varies in size and the smaller plants have less distant gills, smoother stems and smaller spores. Probably because of the advance of cooler weather the plants mature slowly and the spores have not attained their full size in the small plants. The yellow color is sometimes confined to the base, sometimes it extends halfway or more than halfway the length of the stem. The latter condition may turn out to represent *G. flavipes* Pk. The plants turn blackish when dried, but differ from *G. nigricans* Pk. in the absence of a partial veil. Ricken considers *G. gracilis* Berk. to be identical, which is very probable. *G. furcatus* Pk. differs chiefly, according to Peck's description, in the lack of the yellow color at the base of the stem; it is said to occur under tamaracks also.

153. Gomphidius vinicolor Pk. minor.

N. Y. State Mus. Rep. 51, 1898.

PILEUS 1-2 cm. broad, convex then plane, sometimes umbonate, glabrous, even, with a viscid or glutinous separable pellicle, wine-red to rufous-cinnamon, fuscous in the center, paler toward margin. FLESH thick, pale incarnate. GILLS decurrent, subtriangular, rather distant, distinct, *thickish,* broad in the middle, *not or rarely forked,* olive-brown to fuscous-brown, sprinkled by dark spores. STEM 3-4 cm. long, 2-4 mm. thick, *slender, equal,* even, solid, *viscid* from the evanescent veil, flexuous, brick-color to vinaceous, concolor within, *not yellow at base,* silky-fibrillose. SPORES elongated-oblong to subfusiform, 13-16x6-6.5 micr., smooth, smoky-brown. CYSTIDIA abundant, subcylindrical, obtuse, 120-135 x 16-18 micr. ODOR very slight but disagreeable.

Gregarious or solitary. On the ground in low, swampy woods in region of hemlock and pine. New Richmond. September. Rare.

This species is referred here as a minor form of *G. vinicolor* Pk. from whose description it differs in the smaller size and smaller spores. My experience with *G. maculatus* leads me to suspect that the spores of small plants do not mature readily, as is shown also by the less smoky gills. Peck gives the spores 17.5-20x6-7.5 micr. and the type plants were much larger. I have found our plant on several occasions and as it seems to be constant, it may be necessary to separate it. When dried, it becomes black. Some consider *G. vinicolor* Pk. identical with *G. gracilis* B. & Br.; the latter is described with the base of the stem yellow.

154.   Gomphidius flavipes Pk.

N. Y. State Mus. Rep. 54, 1901.

Illustration: Ibid, Pl. I, Fig. 1-4.

PILEUS 1-2.5 cm. broad, convex or plane and sometimes umbonate, viscid, *dingy pink or yellowish, tinged reddish,* minutely
tomentose on center, slightly fibrillose on the margin.   GILLS
decurrent, arcuate, subdistant to distant, *scarcely forked,* whitish
then pale smoky-brownish.   STEM 3-5 cm. long, 3-7 mm. thick,
equal or tapering down, solid, slightly fibrillose, whitish at apex,
elsewhere yellow within and without.   SPORES elongated-fusi-
form, 20-30x6-7.5 micr., smooth, smoky-brown to brownish black.
CYSTIDIA present.

Solitary or gregarious.   On the ground in mixed woods.   Harbor
Springs.   September.   Rare.

Only one collection has been made of what seems to be this plant.
The spores were clearly immature and had not yet attained the
size given by Peck.

Hygrophorus Fr.

(From the Greek *hugros,* moist; and *phero,* to bear.)

White-spored.   *Consistency of the gills waxy;* of pileus and stem
waxy-fleshy or fleshy.   Hymenophore *continuous with the trama of
pileus and stem.*   Stem central.   Gills variously attached, soft, not
membranous, edge acute.   Hymenium loosely adherent to the trama
of the gills.   Trama of gills various: parallel, divergent or interwoven.

Putrescent, soft, terrestrial mushrooms, growing in woods,
meadows, etc., and uniformly harmless.   They are medium or small
in size and often brightly colored.   The gills are usually distant or
subdistant, characters which ordinarily distinguish them from the
species of Clitocybe for which those with decurrent gills might be
mistaken.   The genus corresponds to Gomphidius and Paxillus of
the ochre-spored group, but is distinguished from them by the gills
not easily separating from the trama of the pileus.

The PILEUS varies from conical to convex at first, in most cases
becoming plane at maturity, with or without an umbo and sometimes umbilicate.   In a great many species the expanded pileus is
obversely subconical, pulling the gills into an ascending position,

so that they appear decurrent, even in those cases where they were merely adnate or adnexed at first. With age, the margin of the pileus becomes recurved or split. The surface is viscid or glutinous in many cases, others are hygrophanous, but those of one subgenus include some with a dry pileus; a small number have minute squamules over the surface or on the disk. A great variety of colors is present; white, yellow, orange, red, green, ashy, brown, etc. Some have a striate margin, and others are even and glabrous. The FLESH is usually soft, and somewhat waxy or watery, often permeated by differentiated lactiferous hyphae or crystals of oxalate of lime. The GILLS are peculiar in structure, and furnish the main characters by which we separate the genus. Their edges are acute, but they gradually thicken towards their attachment with the pileus, so as to be narrowly triangular in cross-section. The hymenial layer becomes soft when mature and rubs off from the trama proper of the gills, leaving the skeleton of trama behind. They are mostly *subdistant to distant* or very distant, and this character, along with the waxy consistency and their shape in section, constitutes a set of marks by which, after a little experience, one can tell the genus. As McIlvaine says, "There is an indescribable, watery, waxy, translucent appearance about the gills, which catches the eye of the expert, and is soon learned by the novice." Their attachment varies from adnexed to adnate and decurrent. They are usually white, but may be similar in color to that of the pileus. The interspaces are often veined in a marked fashion. The STEM is central and similar in texture to the pileus, often very fragile or watery. It is either solid or if it is stuffed becomes quickly hollow. It often splits longitudinally with considerable ease. In the subgenus Limacium, the plant when young is sometimes enveloped by a slimy universal veil which breaks up into glutinous patches, scales or flocci on the stem or pileus, or by a partial floccose veil which is connected to the margin of the pileus and to the stem; as the plant expands or dries this partial veil breaks up into a floccose annulus or more often in the form of scabrous or punctate flocci at the apex of the stem. The plants of the other two subgenera do not possess either of these veils, but those species which are viscid develop this character from the cuticle of the pileus or stem which is gelatinous and which dissolves into a slimy substance in moist weather, as in *H. psittacinus*. The SPORES may be subglobose, oval, oblong, cylindrical or elliptical. Fries (Hymen. Europ), speaks of them as "globose" only, and Patouillard says they are ovoid. DeSeynes (Ann. Sci. Nat. Ser. 5, 1 (1864) Tab. 13, Fig. 3,) figures the spores of *H*.

ceraceus as obovate with an obscure constriction in the middle, and says they vary characteristically in this genus to reniform, irregular, etc. I am quite certain that the spores are often quite irregular, angular, etc., when immature, but have a regular outline when mature, although they often tend to be slightly thicker at one end in a number of species. In most species they appear granular-punctate, and usually have a transparent spot on one side, as if perforated. Between most of our species there is not much difference in spore-size, but sufficient difference to be of diagnostic value. The spores are white in mass, and hyaline under the microscope. The BASIDIA are quite characteristic within the genus; they are long and slender, tapering to a narrow stalk. They are said to be often 2-spored. CYSTIDIA are not present in the subgenus Limacium, but occur in some of the species of the other subgenera. The ODOR is not marked in any of our species. Several European species are said to have a characteristic odor; for example: in *H. cossus* Fr. it is disagreeable, like that of a kind of moth; in *H. nitratus* Fr. it is strongly alkaline; in *H. agathosmus* Fr., like oil of bitter almonds. The TASTE is usually mild, and most of them are to be classed *among our best edible mushrooms.* The HABITAT varies. They grow on the ground, usually in moist or wet situations, in woods, copses, fields and pastures, although in our climate they develop mostly in shaded places. Some appear in early summer, and others are found only in late fall—some species never develop till after the frosts appear. *H. hypothejus* (Ricken, Blätterpilze) is said to occur only after the first frost. *H. speciosus* is found, often in good condition, as late as December first.

The genus is divided into three subgenera, fundamentally limited by the structure of the gill-trama:

I.   Limacium (Hygrophorus proper).

II. Camarophyllus.

III. Hygrocybe.

These three subgenera are raised by some authors to the rank of genera, and from a scientific standpoint should be so considered. But for practical purposes the old arrangement seems better.

The key includes all species which are likely to be found within the limits of the state.

Key to the Species

(A) Plant white, disk of pileus with yellowish or reddish tints in some
      specimens. [See also (AA), (AAA) and (AAAA)]
  (a) Pileus viscid or glutinous.
    (b) Pileus entirely white, changing only in age.
      (c) Stem glutinous or viscid.
        (d) Apex of stem with white dots or squamules. Gills adnate
              to decurrent.
          (e) Stem floccose-tomentose below the glutinous annulus, apex
                at length reddish-dotted. 156. *H. rubropunctus* Pk. (syn.
                H. glutinosus Pk.).
          (ee) Stem glabrous, not annulate.
            (f) Stem firmly stuffed to hollow; plant persistently white.
                  156. *H. eburneus* Fr.
            (ff) Stem solid, plant changing color on drying. 156. *H.
                  eburneus* var. *unicolor* Pk.
            (fff) Stems solid, caespitose. 156. *H. eburneus* var. *de-
                    cipiens* Pk.
        (dd) Apex of stem not scabrous-scaly-dotted.
          (e) Gills emarginate-adnexed; pileus at first conical. *H.
                purus* Pk.
      (cc) Stem dry.
        (d) Pileus large, 8-15 cm. broad, stout; autumnal. 165. *H.
              sordidus* Pk.
        (dd) Pileus small, scarcely viscid, subumbilicate, thin, tough-
              ish. 170. *H. niveus* Fr.
    (bb) Pileus not entirely white.
      (c) Apex of stem decorated with yellowish granules or yellow
            glandular dots.
        (d) Pileus whitish, covered by yellowish or brownish gluten.
              159. *H. paludosus Pk.*
        (dd) Pileus white, with numerous golden yellow granules on
              margin. 155. *H. chrysodon* Fr.
      (cc) Apex of stem white-scaly-dotted or slightly floccose.
        (d) Disk of pileus pinkish or pale reddish-brown. 157. *H.
              laurae* Morg.
        (dd) Disk of pileus yellowish or reddish-yellow. 158. *H.
              flavodiscus* Frost.
  (aa) Pileus and stem not viscid nor glutinous.
    (b) Plant stout. Pileus 3-7 cm. broad, dry, white. 169. *H. vir-
          gineus* Fr. (See also *H. pratensis* var. *pallidus*.)
    (bb) Plant slender; pileus 1-3 cm. broad, whitish. 171. *H. borealis*
          Pk.
(AA) Plant yellow, bright green, olivaceous, orange or shades of these
      colors.
  (a) Pileus glutinous or viscid when moist.
    (b) Pileus at first olivaceous or green.
      (c) Pileus 3-5 cm. broad, color at length orange-yellow to tawny;
            gills yellow. 161. *H. hypothejus* Fr.
      (cc) Pileus 4-8 cm. broad; gills white-incarnate. 163. *H.
            olivaceoalbus* Fr.
      (ccc) Pileus 1-2.5 cm. broad, parrot green at first; gills yellowish
              or greenish. 184. *H. psitticinus* Fr.
    (bb) Pileus orange-yellow, yellow, yellowish or tawny.
      (c) Becoming blackish in age or when bruised; pileus conical; gills
            free. 180. *H. conicus* Fr.
      (cc) Not becoming black when bruised.
        (d) Gills emarginate-adnexed; pileus 2-5 cm. broad, citron to
              golden-yellow. 178. *H. chlorophanus* Fr.
        (dd) Gills broadly adnate to decurrent.
          (e) Pileus 3-8 cm. broad, yellow in age; in tamarack swamps
                in late fall. 160. *H. speciosus* Pk.

    (ee) Pileus 1-3 cm. broad.
      (f) Tough; pileus tawny-yellowish, not fading in age. 182.
          H. lactus Fr.
      (ff) Fragile; pileus wax-yellow to yellow.
        (g) Gills truly decurrent; pileus and stem fading to whitish in age. 181. *H. nitidus* B. & C.
       (gg) Gills adnate-decurrent; pileus not fading. 172. *H. ceraceus* Fr.
  (aa) Pileus not viscid nor glutinous.
    (b) Golden-orange-yellow; fragile; pileus and stem markedly fading; gills adnexed, deep orange-yellow. 179. *H. marginatus* Pk.
    (bb) Pale yellow; pileus 6-12 mm. broad; stem darker. *H. parvulus* Pk.
(AAA) Plant vermillion, scarlet, pink, flesh-color, rufous or shades of these.
  (a) Pileus viscid or glutinous.
    (b) Stem stout; pileus rather large, compact, firm.
      (c) Gills not becoming reddish-spotted.
        (d) Pileus scarlet, crimson or orange; stem viscid, in tamarack swamps. 160. *H. speciosus* Pk.
       (dd) Pileus tinged flesh color; stem dry. 164. *H. pudorinus* Fr.
      (cc) Gills becoming reddish-spotted. 163. *H. Russula* (Fr.).
    (bb) Stem medium or slender; pileus fragile.
      (c) Pileus 1-2 cm., pinkish-flesh-color; stem slender and viscous. 183. *H. peckii* Atk.
      (cc) Pileus 3-7 cm., scarlet or vermillion; stem moist, not viscid.
        (d) Gills arcuate-adnate; base of stem yellow or orange. 176. *H. coccineus* Fr.
       (dd) Gills slightly adnexed; base of stem white; spores larger. 177. *H. puniceus* Fr.
  (aa) Pileus not viscid nor glutinous.
    (b) Pileus 1-3 cm. broad, subglabrous to minutely scaly, vermillion to reddish-yellow. 175. *H. miniatus* Fr. *H. cantherellus* Schw.
    (bb) Pileus 3-7 cm. broad, flesh-color to tawny-reddish, glabrous. 168. *H. pratensis* Fr.
    (bbb) Pileus 3-10 cm. broad, salmon-rufous to testaceus; hoary when young; gills decurrent. 167. *H. leporinus* Fr.
(AAAA) Plant neither white, yellow, orange nor bright red.
  (a) Pileus and stem glutinous or viscid. [See also (aa) and (aaa)]
    (b) Gills pure white; pileus grayish-brown, cinereous or fuliginous.
      (c) Stem hollow, fuliginous. 185. *H. unquinosus* Fr.
      (cc) Stem solid, white or whitish. *H. fuligineus* Frost.
    (bb) Gills not pure white, or at least changing in age, adnate-decurrent.
      (c) Pileus purplish-red, virgate with darker fibrils; stem and gills concolor. *H. capreolarius* Bres.
      (cc) Pileus some shade of brown. [See also (ccc)]
        (d) Stem hollow, slender; plant fragile; pileus olive-brown, 1-2 cm. broad. *H. davisii* Pk.
       (dd) Stem solid, plant firm, larger.
         (e) Growing in sphagnum swamps; pileus white, covered with yellowish-brown gluten. *H. paludosus* Pk.
        (ee) In grassy woods; pileus smoky-olive, 3-6 cm. broad; spores 12 x 8 micr. *H. limacinus* Fr.
    (ccc) Pileus dark brownish olivaceous. 162. *H. olivaceoalbus* Fr.
  (aa) Pileus with a gelatinous, subviscid pellicle; stem dry.
    (b) Pileus violaceous to smoky-lilac, hygrophanous, fading to grayish; stem stuffed to hollow. 174. *H. pallidus* Pk.
    (bb) Pileus livid-rufescens to brownish, hygrophanous; stem stuffed to hollow; gills decurrent. 173. *H. colemannianus* Blox.
    (bbb) Pileus grayish-brown or blackish-brown; stem solid.
      (c) Spores 6-8 micr. long. 166. *H. fusco-albus* var.
      (cc) Spores 10-12 micr. long. *H. morrisii* Pk.

(aaa) Pileus and stem not viscid nor glutinous (slightly viscid in
        H. amygdalinus).
 (b)   Odor markedly noticeable.
   (c) Stem solid; pileus grayish-brown; gills adnate decurrent; odor
         of almonds. *H. amygdalinus* Pk.
   (cc) Stem stuffed then hollow; pileus hygrophanous.
     (d) Gills decurrent; pileus sooty-brown (moist); spores sub-
           globose, 5-6 micr.; odor "peculiar." *H. peckianus* Howe.
     (dd) Gills sinuate-adnexed; pileus yellowish-brown (moist), odor
           offensive. *H. mephiticus* Pk.
 (bb) Odor not marked; stem solid.
   (c) Plant stout; pileus smoky or blackish, virgate with fibrils;
         spores 8-9x5 micr. *H. carpinus* Fr.
   (cc) Plant slender; pileus grayish-brown to blackish-brown, glab-
         rous; spores 10-12x6-7 micr. *H. nigridius* Pk.

(Peck in his monograph, N. Y. State Mus. Bull. 116, 1907, of New
York species mentions the following as very rare: *H. virgatulus* Pk.,
H. burnhami Pk., *H. metapodius* Fr., *H. basidiosus* Pk., *H. sub-
rufescens* Pk., *H. immutabilis* Pk., *H. laricinus* Pk., *H. luridus* B.
& C., *H. minutulus* Pk. Peck has described also *H. serotinus* Pk.,
H. ruber Pk., *H. albipes* Pk., from Massachusetts; *H. elegantulus*
Pk. from Maryland and *H. sphoerosporus* Pk. from Iowa.)

SUBGENUS LIMACIUM: Provided with a glutinous universal
veil or a floccose cortina· or both. *Trama of gills of divergent
hyphae.*

Section I. Universales

Provided with *both* a universal veil and a floccose cortina; the latter is connate to the inner surface of the former along the stem,
sometimes forming a slight annulus at the apex of the stem, or a
floccose-downy edge on the incurved margin of the pileus. Stem
viscid, subglabrous to floccose-fibrillose, *shining or glistening-spot-
ted when dry,* apex scabrous-dotted or subglabrous.

This section is intended to include only those with a universal
veil. It corresponds to the subgenus Myxacium of the genus Cortinarius. This veil surrounds the very young button as a thick
gelatinous layer, which becomes attenuated on the stem as this
elongates and dissolves into a hyaline, or, in some species, into a
somewhat colored gluten in wet weather. The apex of the stem
is glandular or scabrous-dotted in those species in which the margin
of the pileus is at first inrolled, but in those in which the margin of
the pileus is merely incurved and continuous with the cortina, the
apex of the stem is subglabrous and not floccose-dotted. *H. speciosus*
is an example of the latter group.

155. Hygrophorus chrysodon Fr. (EDIBLE)

Syst. Myc., 1821.

Illustrations: Atkinson, Mushrooms, Fig. 112, p. 110, 1900.
Cooke, Ill., Pl. 885.
Ricken, Blätterpilze, Pl. 6, Fig. 4.

"PILEUS 3-7 cm. broad, convex then expanded, viscid (moist), shining (dry), white, *concolorous except for the numerous golden granules on the margin,* or sometimes over entire surface, margin involute at first. FLESH white, rather thick. GILLS decurrent, distant, *white or yellow-powdered on the edge,* interspaces venose. STEM 4-7 cm. long, 6-10 mm. thick, soft, equal, stuffed, white, *apex decorated by yellowish granules,* sometimes in the form of an imperfect ring. SPORES oval-elliptical, smooth, 7-10x4-6 micr., white.

"Gregarious. In late summer or autumn. On the ground in open woods."

Not yet reported from Michigan.

156. Hygrophorus eburneus Fr. (EDIBLE)

Syst. Myc., 1821.

Illustrations: Atkinson, Mushrooms, Pl. 34, Fig. 113, p. 111, 1900.
Murrill, Mycologia, Vol. 6, Pl. 131.
Hard, Mushrooms, Fig. 164, p. 207, 1908.
Marshall, Mushroom Book, Pl. 30, p. 84, 1905.
Peck, N. Y. State Mus. Bull. 54, Pl. 77, Figs. 13-14, 1902. (As *H. laurae* var. *unicolor.*)
Peck, N. Y. State Mus. Bull. 94, Pl. 88, Figs. 8-11, 1905. (As *H. laurae* var. *decipiens.*)
Cooke, Ill., Pl. 886.
Ricken, Blätterpilze, Pl. 6, Fig. 5.

PILEUS 2-7 cm. broad, convex-expanded, *pure white* when fresh, glutinous, *shining,* even, glabrous, margin at first involute and floccose-pubescent. FLESH white, rather thick and firm. GILLS adnate to decurrent, subdistant, moderately broad behind, narrowed in front, subvenose, *white,* often dingy yellowish in age, trama of divergent hyphae. STEM 6-15 cm. long, 3-8 mm. thick, elongated, subequal, tapering or fusiform, often flexuous, glutinous, shining-spotted when dry, *persistently stuffed or becoming hollow,* glab-

rous, apex with white dots or squamules, not annulate, *white* often
becoming dingy in age. ODOR and TASTE mild. SPORES cylin-
drical-elliptic, smooth, 6-8x4-5.5 micr. BASIDIA slender, 4-spored,
40-42x7 micr.

Gregarious or subcaespitose in woods, thickets, etc., often among
grass. October-November. Frequent. Ann Arbor and probably
throughout the State.

Var. *unicolor* Pk. This is said to differ by its solid stem and
change of color on drying. It was referred by Peck to *H. laurae*
as a variety. If it is distinct at all it appears to be better to attach
it to *H. eburneus*. Gillet says the stem of *H. eburneus* is solid or hollow. There is so much variation in this respect in our plants—some
having a persistent pith and appearing solid, and others becoming
hollow—that it seems to me best to merge the variety in the species.
Berkeley notes that sometimes the English plants turn "fox-red in
parts" when they decay.

Var. *decipiens* Pk. is closely related to the preceding variety, but
is caespitose and the gills are said to remain white. It was also
attached to *H. laurae* by Peck.

All these have a uniform white color when young or fresh, and
are provided with a hyaline, glutinous, universal veil which makes
the cap and stem slippery and difficult to pull up or to handle.
The shining pileus when dry reminds one of *Tricholoma resplendens,*
but the pileus averages smaller than in that species, and the stem
is glutinous. *Hygrophorus rubropunctus* Pk. is also said to be a
white plant, but differs from the preceding by its stem being floccose-tomentose below the glutinous annulus, and studded at the
apex with drops of moisture which in drying form glandular red
dots; its stem is short but thick; and the spores measure 7.5-10x5-6
micr. It has not been detected by me in Michigan. These white
forms are all closely allied, and may be considered variations of
one species.

157. Hygrophorus laurae Morg. (EDIBLE)

Cincinnati Soc. Nat. Hist., Vol. 6, 1883.

Illustrations: Ibid, Pl. 9.
      Peck, N. Y. State Mus. Bull. 54, Pl. 77, 1902.
      Hard, Mushrooms, Fig. 170, p. 214, 1908.
      Murrill, Mycologia, Vol. 2, Pl. 27, Fig. 10.

PILEUS 3-10 cm. broad, convex-expanded or depressed on disk, umbonate, more or less irregular, pinkish-brown or reddish on disk, white on margin, glutinous when fresh, glabrous, even, margin at first involute. FLESH thickish, white. GILLS adnate to decurrent, subdistant, rather narrow, white or tinged with cream-flesh-color, trama of divergent hyphae. STEM 3-8 cm. long, 6-12 mm. thick, equal or tapering downward, *solid, glutinous,* white or yellowish-white, upper half often squamulose-scabrous, the apex dotted with scabrous points. SPORES elliptical, smooth, apiculate, 7-9x 4-5.5 micr., white in mass. BASIDIA slender, about 38x6 micr. ODOR and TASTE mild.

Gregarious or subcaespitose. On the ground in frondose woods, thickets, etc., among fallen leaves. Detroit, Ann Arbor, New Richmond. August-November. Frequent.

This species usually has a cap which is wider than the length of the stem, while *H. eburneus* usually has an elongated stem and narrow pileus. There is some discrepancy in the spore-measurements as given by Morgan and Peck. The latter author gives them as 6-7.5 micr. long. Such discrepancy usually points to different species studied by the different authors, but in the genus Hygrophorus, as in some other white-spored genera, the spores often mature slowly, and it is often not easy to distinguish mature from immature plants, so that the best of observers may disagree. *H. laurae* is said to stain one's fingers as if with sumach. (S. Davis, Rhodora, 13, p. 63, 1911.)

158. Hygrophorus flavodiscus Frost (EDIBLE)

N. Y. State Mus. Rep. 35, 1884.

Illustrations: Peck, N. Y. State Mus. Mem., Vol. 3, Pl. 50, Fig. 1-6.
Hard, Mushrooms, Fig. 167, p. 210, 1908.
Murrill, Mycologia, Vol. 4, Pl. 56, Fig. 11.

PILEUS 3-7 cm. broad, convex or nearly plane, *glutinous* when fresh, *pale yellow or reddish-yellow on disk,* white elsewhere, glabrous, even, margin at first involute. FLESH white. GILLS adnate to decurrent, subdistant, white sometimes with a slight flesh-colored tint, trama of divergent hyphae. STEM 3-7 cm. long, 6-12 mm. thick, nearly equal, *solid,* very glutinous, apex with white scabrous points, white or yellowish below. Spores elliptical, inequilateral, 6-7.5x4-5 micr., white.

Gregarious. On the ground in hemlock and beech woods. New Richmond. September.

This is close to the preceding, and may be a form of it peculiar to conifer woods. Peck thinks it belongs nearest to *H. fuligineus,* in whose company he has found it. According to this author, there are no scabrous points at the apex of the stem. In my specimens they were present, at least in the younger stages. The species was first published by Peck who obtained the name from Frost's manuscript description. The pileus has a thick fleshy disk, its margin is at first inrolled and is densely white-floccose on the side next the stem. The gills are sometimes intervenose; at first they are simply adnate, but on the expansion of the pileus become decurrent. This change from the young to the old gills has caused some discrepancies in the descriptions by different authors of this and the preceding species. The layer of glutinous tissue is very thick on the cap, thin on the stem.

159. Hygrophorus paludosus Pk.

Torr. Bot. Club Bull., Vol. 29, 1902.

"PILEUS 2-4 cm. broad, convex, obtuse, *whitish,* covered with a thick *yellowish or brownish gluten.* FLESH white. GILLS adnate or slightly decurrent, subdistant, whitish, *stained with greenish-yellow when old.* STEM 5-10 cm. long, 4-6 mm. thick, subequal, *long and slender,* flexuous, often curved at the base, *solid,* glutinous, white with yellow glandular dots at the top, streaked with brownish fibers or shreds of the dried gluten when dry. SPORES broadly elliptical, 8-10 x 5-7 micr., white. ODOR earthy. TASTE slightly *acrid."*

Growing among peat mosses. Greenville. September. Reported by Longyear.

The yellowish dots at the apex of the stem are said to become black on drying, and there are yellowish stains at the base of the stem. The plant seems rare, as it has not been reported since its discovery. It needs further study to show its relationship.

160. Hygrophorus speciosus Pk. (EDIBLE)

N. Y. State Mus. Rep. 29, 1878.

Illustrations: Peck, N. Y. State Mus. Mem. 4, Pl. 51, Fig. 21-28. 1900, and Rep. 29, Pl. 2, Fig. 1-5, 1878.
Hard, Mushrooms, Fig. 168, p. 211, 1908.
Fries, Icones, Pl. 166 (*Hygrophorus aureus* Fr.).

Bresadola, Fungi Trid., Vol. I, Pl. 9 (*Hygrophorus bresa-dolae* Quel.).

Plate XXIV of this Report.

PILEUS 2-8 cm. broad, oval, subconic or flattened convex when young, broadly convex and at length almost plane when mature, or varying subcampanulate and umbonate, umbo usually subobsolete, *glutinous* when fresh, *bright red or orange-vermillion* when young or in full vigor, becoming paler with age or after freezing, often subvirgate, even or slightly rugulose from the drying gluten, margin at first incurved then decurved or spreading. FLESH white or tinged orange under the separable pellicle, soft, rather thick. GILLS decurrent, *distant, moderately* broad in middle, acuminate at ends, arcuate, thick, intervenose, white or tinged yellowish, trama of divergent hyphae. STEM stout, 3-10 cm. long, 8-20 mm. thick, variable in length, equal or irregularly subcompressed, soft and spongy within, *not hollow,* straight or flexuous, *hyaline-white, floccose-fibrillose to the apical, obsolete annulus,* almost glabrous at times, variegated with glistening spots from the drying of the gluten, sometimes ochraceous-stained when old, apex subglabrous to silky, base usually deeply imbedded in substratum or subrooting. UNIVERSAL VEIL of hyaline gluten. SPORES 8-9.5 x 5-6 micr., broadly elliptical, smooth, white in mass. BASIDIA slender, 50-60 x 6-8 micr., 4-spored, sterigmata long and prominent. ODOR and TASTE mild.

In troops, etc., solitary or caespitose. In tamarack swamps. Ann Arbor. October-November. Frequent locally, appearing every fall in the same places.

This is the American form of *Hygrophorus aureus* of Europe. The illustrations of European authors as well as those of Peck, indicate a smaller average size and a pileus markedly umbonate. In our region as well as in the Adirondack Mountains I have seen such plants occur with the rest, but the majority are broadly convex with or without an obsolete umbo and as a rule are larger than the European form. Sometimes vestiges of a distinct floccose annulus occur, but more often this cannot be seen; on the other hand, the stem is usually covered by a white, floccose-fibrillose, appressed sheath which becomes dingy ochraceous or pale sordid reddish on drying, especially where gluten has dropped from the margin of the cap on the stem. Plants in the same patch vary greatly in the size of the pileus and the stem. The stem of the young plant is at first large and stout as compared with the flat or convex, narrow young pileus. The partial veil is floccose-fibrillose. The margin of the pileus is merely incurved at first, not inrolled as it is said to be in *H. glutinifer* Fr. The color of the pileus of the typical American plant is a brighter red than that in Europe. This, however, is not unusual, as the reverse is true in *Amanita muscaria*. The pileus usually becomes pallid yellowish after exposure to sun and wind, or after being frozen. In the Adirondack Mountains I collected a color variety growing with the species, which differed from it at every stage of its development by its cadmium-yellow pileus. *Hygrophorus coloratus* Pk. is said to differ from *H. speciosus* by having a stuffed or hollow stem and a partial, floccose, white veil. As the latter is sometimes noticeable in the Michigan plants, and because of the soft structure of the interior of the stem in our plants, I doubt whether *H. coloratus* is more than a variety of the species.

161. Hygrophorus hypothejus Fr. (EDIBLE)

Syst. Myc., 1821.

Illustrations: Cooke, Ill., Plate 891.
    Patouillard, Tab. Analyt., No. 510.
    Gillet, Champignons de France, No. 337.
    Ricken, Blätterpilze, Pl. 5, Fig. 5.

"PILEUS 3-5 cm. broad, convex-expanded, at length depressed in center, obtuse, glutinous, *olive-brown,* virgate with radial fibrils, even, *becoming pale, or citron-golden-yellow, tawny after the disappearance of the olive-brown superficial gluten.* FLESH pale yellowish with a yellow periphery, thin. GILLS decurrent, distant, *yellow* to orange-yellow, thickish. STEM 5-7 cm. long, 6-8 mm. thick, equal, stuffed to hollow, yellow to pale yellowish, glabrous, glutinous, *evanescently annulate from the partial floccose veil.* SPORES cylindrical-elliptical, smooth, 7-9 x 4-5 micr. ODOR and TASTE mild."

This species has not yet come to my notice within the State. It is said to be more common farther south, although its known northern limit should include Michigan. It is an inhabitant of pine woods, and Ricken says it never appears until after the first frost in the autumn, when it flourishes till the snow falls. Its yellow gills distinguish it from related species. Some consider *H. fuligineus* Frost identical.

162. Hygrophorus olivaceoalbus Fr.

Syst. Myc., 1821, and Fung. Trid., 1881.

Illustrations: Fung. Trid., Vol. I, Pl. 92.
Plate XXV of this Report.

PILEUS 4-8 cm. broad, at first acorn-shaped or rounded-campanulate, then convex to subexpanded, umbonate, umbo often obsolete, *covered by a thick gluten, dark, olive-gray,* stained ferruginous in age, at length somewhat wrinkled from the drying gluten, margin at first involute. FLESH white, thick, rather soft. GILLS adnate to decurrent, subdistant to close, moderately broad, distinct, white or slightly incarnate, trama of divergent hyphae. STEM rather stout, 4-7 cm. long, 8-15 mm. thick, equal or tapering downward, *peronate at first and floccose-scaly from the glutinous veil,* at length marked by rusty-fuscous, subannular, irregular stains, apex at first beaded with drops and densely white-scaly-dotted, solid, subrooting and curved at base. SPORES broadly elliptical, smooth or slightly rough-punctate, 9-12 x 6-7 micr. BASIDIA elongated, 50 x 8-9 micr. ODOR and TASTE mild.

Gregarious or subcaespitose. On the ground in woods of oak, maple, etc. Ann Arbor. October. Found but once.

This is a very marked species. The sheathed, floccose stem with its several rings of staining gluten separates it from nearby species. The base of the stem is usually deep in the ground. Bresadola's figures show a darker plant, while Gillet, Michael and Ricken figure a more slender plant. The colors of our plants approach more nearly those of the last three authors.

Section II. Partiales. Universal veil none. Partial veil or cortina floccose, adhering to the involute margin of the pileus. Stem *dry,* apex floccose-scabrous or subglabrous.

This section corresponds to the subgenus Phlegmacium of the genus Cortinarius. The stem is dry except when the gluten of the cap falls upon it. The viscidity of the pileus is due to a gelatinous layer on its surface which becomes glutinous in some species in wet weather.

CLASSIFICATION OF AGARICS185

163. Hygrophorus Russula Fr. (Edible)

Syst. Mycol., 1821 (as Tricholoma).

Illustrations: Hard, Mushrooms, Fig. 51, p. 71, 1908. (As
  Tricholoma Russula.)
  Michael, Führer f. Pilzfreunde, Vol. II. (as *Tricholoma Rus-
  sula.*)
  Ricken, Blätterpilze, Pl. 4, Fig. 1.
  Peck, N. Y. State Mus. Bull. 54, Pl. 77, Fig. 1-5, 1902. (As
  Tricholoma Russula.)
  Bresadola, Fungh. mang. e. vel., Pl. 22. (As *Tricholoma
  Russula.*)
  Plate XXVI of this Report.

PILEUS 5-12 cm. broad, firm, convex, at length plane or depressed with margin elevated-wavy, *viscid* when moist, *pale pink to
rosy-red,* somewhat variegated, disk somewhat scaly-dotted, margin
at first involute and floccose-pruinose. FLESH compact, thick,
white or at length reddish-tinged. GILLS rounded behind, at
length spuriously decurrent, narrow, acuminate at ends, thickish,
white at first then reddish-spotted, *trama of divergent hyphae.*
STEM stout, usually short, 3-7 cm. long, 15-25 mm. thick, firm, solid,
dry, equal or subventricose, apex white-flocculose, *white, becoming
reddish in age.* SPORES narrowly elliptical, apiculate, smooth,
white in mass. BASIDIA slender, elongated, 45 x 5-6 micr. ODOR
and TASTE mild.

Solitary or caespitose in troops. On the ground, among leaves,
in frondose woods of oak, maple, etc. Ann Arbor, Detroit,
Marquette, New Richmond and throughout the State. September-
November. Common.

This Hygrophorus has usually been placed with the Tricholomas
with which it has some affinity; but the character of the gills,
which are somewhat waxy and whose trama is composed of divergent hyphae, the attenuated lower part of the basidia and its general characters ally it much better to Hygrophorus where Quelet
and Ricken also place it. The involute, slightly floccose margin of
the pileus is similar to that of *H. pudorinus.* It often occurs in
troops in late autumn, when it is covered by leaves which it pushes
up so as to form humps which betray its presence. It is among
the very best of edible mushrooms, especially after cold weather
sets in, at which time it is free from grubs. The bright color is
similar to that of some Russulas, hence the specific name. *Tricho-*

loma rubicunda Pk. is doubtless *H. Russula* in spite of the argument
for its autonomy by E. M. Williams in the Plant World, Vol. 4, p.
9, 1901. *H. erubescens* Fr. is similarly colored, but consistently of
a different habit, long stemmed and narrow-capped. The latter
species as I saw it in Sweden, seems to me to be quite distinct.

164. Hygrophorus pudorinus Fr. (Edible)

Syst. Myc., 1821.

Illustrations: Cooke, Ill., Plate 911.
        Gillet, Champignons de France, No. 347.
        Peck, N. Y. State Mus. Bull. 67, Pl. 83, 1903.
        Ricken, Blätterpilze, Pl. 4, Fig. 3, 1910.

PILEUS 2-10 cm. broad, firm, convex-campanulate, subexpanded,
obtuse, *viscid* when moist, *pale tan color, pinkish-buff or tinged incarnate,* glabrous, even, margin at first involute and minutely
downy. FLESH compact, thick, white or tinged flesh-color. GILLS
acuminate-subdecurrent, subdistant, thickish, narrow; sometimes
forked, interspaces venose, *usually connected at the stem by a narrow border,* trama of divergent hyphae. STEM 3-8 cm. long, 5-20
mm. thick, *stout,* compact, solid, *dry,* equal or tapering downward,
white, buff or incarnate-tinged, *floccose-scabrous at apex,* floccose-
fibrillose or glabrescent downwards. SPORES cylindric-elliptical,
smooth, 6-9 x 3.5-5 micr. BASIDIA slender, 45-50 x 6-7 micr., 4-
spored. ODOR and TASTE mild. *Edible.*

Gregarious to caespitose. On the ground, often among grass,
in hemlock or frondose woods or thickets. Ann Arbor, Detroit,
New Richmond. September-November. Frequent.

This is a variable species with us as regards size and coloration.
Late in the season a small form appears (form *minor*) which has
always a white stem, and forms considerable patches in oak woods.
It is possible that this form is *H. arbustivus* Fr. In the typical
and luxuriant specimens of *H. pudorinus* the stem is tinged flesh-
color to pale isabelline. Occasional specimens are larger than the
sizes given above, which are made to include form *minor*. All of
these are delicious food.

165. Hygrophorus sordidus Pk. (EDIBLE)

Torrey Bot. Club, Bull. 25, 1898.

Illustrations: Hard, Mushrooms, Fig. 176, p. 220, 1908.
Plate XXVII of this Report.

PILEUS *large,* 8-16 cm. broad, convex-expanded to plane, firm, *viscid* when moist, pure white, rarely tinged yellowish-buff, glabrous, even, margin at first incurved and slightly floccose. FLESH compact or somewhat soft, white, *thick.* GILLS adnate to decurrent, subdistant, rather broad in middle, attenuate at both ends, *white,* slightly yellowish in age, waxy, interspaces sometimes veined, trama of divergent hyphae. STEM *stout,* 6-10 cm. long, 15-30 mm. thick, *short,* solid, *dry,* equal or attenuated downwards, white, glabrous or obscurely floccose-mealy at apex, even. SPORES elliptical, smooth, 6-8 x 4-5 micr. ODOR and TASTE mild.

Gregarious. On the ground among leaves in frondose woods of maple, oak, etc. September-November. Ann Arbor, New Richmond. Frequent locally.

This is the largest and finest of the genus. Small individuals may be confused with *Tricholoma resplendens,* but due regard to broader pileus, shorter stem and the waxy gills which are decurrent in expanded plants, will distinguish it at once. Microscopically the divergent hyphae of the gills, as well as the basidia, are a certain distinction. It has been met with for a series of years, every autumn, and is consistently a large white plant, so that it can hardly be referred to *H. pudorinus.* When young, a floccose cortina is present. The universal veil is entirely lacking. It is edible, and vies with any mushroom in its abundant flesh and pleasant flavor. The pileus is sometimes quite obscured by adhering leaves or dirt.

166. Hygrophorus fusco-albus Fr. var. occindentalis var. nov.

Epicrisis, 1836-38.

Illustrations: Cooke, Ill., Plate 899.
Plate XXVIII of this Report.

PILEUS 2-5 cm. broad, convex-expanded, at length plane or depressed, *viscid* when moist, *livid grayish-brown to brownish-ashy,* sometimes blackish on disk, glabrous, even, becoming fragile, margin at first involute and floccose-downy. FLESH white, *rather thin,* rather soft. GILLS adnate to decurrent, subdistant to close, *rather narrow,* creamy-white, interspaces venose, *trama of divergent hyphae.* STEM slender, rarely stout, 3-7 cm. long, 4-6 mm. thick (rarely 10-12 mm.), equal or tapering downward, *dry,* solid, straight, or curved at base, sometimes flexuous, rather fragile, apex floccose-scabrous, *floccose-pruinose elsewhere,* glabrescent, *white or pallid.* SPORES elliptical, smooth, 6-8 x 3.5-4.5 micr., white. BASIDIA slender, 36-38 x 6-7 micr., 4-spored. ODOR and TASTE mild.

Gregarious or subcaespitose. On the ground in oak woods. Ann Arbor, Detroit. October. Infrequent.

This plant has been found in several places in successive years. It is well-marked, but differs in some respects from the published descriptions and figures of *H. fusco-albus.* It appears that there is no unanimity among European mycologists as to this species. It was first figured by Lasch. Ricken figures it as a stout plant with a viscid stem and says the stem is glutinous-peronate. This departs widely from the description of Fries, Gillet, Massee and others. Cooke's figure more nearly depicts our plant. Fries says the gills are broad, but in our specimens they were always rather narrow. Peck (N. Y. State Mus. Bull. 116) has included it under *H. fusco-albus,* in the sense of Fries, in his monograph. The spores of our plant are slightly smaller than given by Peck, and much smaller than those given by Cooke and Massee. In view of these discrepancies and differences, it has seemed best to bestow on our plant at least a varietal position. It seems to come halfway between *H. fusco-albus* and *H. livido-albus.* The partial floccose veil disappears early except on the involute edge of the pileus. The stem is delicately floccose and entirely dry when fresh or young.

167. Hygrophoius leporinus Fr.

Epicrisis, 1836-38.

Illustration: Cooke, Ill., Pl. 930.

PILEUS 3-10 cm. broad, at first oval-campanulate, at length expanded-plane, obtuse, often gibbous or irregular, opaque, *rufous-testaceous* to fulvous-rufescent, *variegated with a white, hoary, silkiness when young,* especially on margin, provided with a subviscid, separable, thin pellicle, becoming subfibrillose or subvirgate. FLESH thick, compact on disk, abruptly thin on margin, firm, pallid, tinged rufescent to rufous-fulvous. GILLS arcuate-*decurrent, rigid, thick, subdistant,* distinct, attenuate at both ends, *ferrugi-*

nous-fulvous to gilvous, pruinose, trama divergent. STEM 3-8 cm. broad, subequal or tapering downward, *attenuated at base,* often curved, rigid, 8-16 mm. thick above, at first with an appressed, glaucous silkiness, glabrescent, innately fibrous and shining, *solid, rufescent* within and without. SPORES narrowly elliptic-lanceolate to ovate, smooth, 7-9 x 4 micr., white. BASIDIA very slender, about 60 x 4 micr. ODOR none. TASTE mild.

Scattered or gregarious. On the ground among fallen leaves in frondose woods. October. Ann Arbor. Rare.

I have referred this large, well-marked plant to the above species on the strength of Cooke's figure, but with some hesitancy. It agrees well with that illustration. *H. leporinus* is usually placed under the subgenus Camarophyllus, but the divergent gill-trama of our plant indicates plainly its position in my grouping. The spore-measurements do not agree with those given by others. Massee says they are subglobose, 5-6 micr.; Ricken describes them as cylindric-elliptical, like ours, but smaller, 5-6 x 4 micr., which approximates somewhat closely. Berkeley says spores of *H. leporinus* are umber-colored; this is manifestly an error. The rather rigid habit and color suggest a large and deeply colored *Clitocybe laccata,* but otherwise they have nothing in common. The whole plant is more or less salmon-rufescent in color. The trama of the gills is composed of slender, diverging, compact hyphae, 5-7 micr. in diameter. The trama of the pileus is also pseudo-prosenchymatous, i. e., of narrow, compact hyphae. The species is variable in size and stout even when young. It is not found till late fall. It may turn out to be distinct.

SUBGENUS CAMAROPHYLLUS. Veil none. *Trama of gills of interwoven hyphae.* Pileus and stem usually dry. Stem glabrous or fibrillose, not scabrous-punctate at the apex.

Although this subgenus was separated by Fries from the subgenus Hygrocybe on account of its "firm, non-viscid" pileus, he nevertheless, placed under it a number of thin, viscid species like *H. fornicatus, H. niveus,* etc. In view of the fact that such typical species of this group as *H. pratensis* and· *H. virgineus* have a gill-trama of interwoven hyphae, and typical species of the subgenus Hygrocybe have a gill-trama of parallel hyphae, it seems that we have here a fundamental and natural separation of the two groups, as was insisted on by Fayod (Ann. d. Sci. Nat., 7 Ser., Vol. 9, p. 305). Thus, despite the statement of Peck and Earle, the dry character of the pileus cannot be retained to characterize this subgenus.

168. Hygrophorus pratensis Fr. (EDIBLE)

Syst. Myc., 1821.

Illustrations: Cooke, Ill., Pl. 917 and 932.
Ricken, Blätterpilze, Pl. 7, Fig. 2.
Gillet, Champignons de France, No. 345.
Swanton, Fungi, Pl. 9, Fig. 11-12, 1909.
Murrill, Mycologia, Vol. 2, Pl. 27, Fig. 1.
Peck, N. Y. State Mus. Rep. 48, Bot. ed., Pl. 28, Fig. 11-17, 1896.

PILEUS 2-7 cm. broad, disk compact, convex, subexpanded, often turbinate, obtuse or umbonate, glabrous, even, *reddish-fulvous or pale tawny,* moist when fresh, not viscid, margin thin. FLESH white or tinged like pileus. GILLS decurrent, distant, *thick,* whitish, yellowish or tinged like pileus, *intervenose,* very broad in the middle, trama of interwoven hyphae. STEM short, 4-7 cm. long, 7-12 mm. thick, equal or narrowed downwards, *glabrous,* even, persistently stuffed, white or tinged like the pileus. SPORES 6-8 x 4-5.5 micr., broadly elliptical or elliptic-ovate, smooth, white. BASIDIA slender, 40-42 x 5-6 micr. ODOR and TASTE mild.

Solitary, gregarious or caespitose. On the ground, woods, thickets, grassy places, etc. Marquette, Houghton, Bay View, New Richmond, Ann Arbor, etc. Most common apparently in the northern part of the State; mostly in frondose woods. July-October. Frequent.

Var. *pallidus.* Plant whitish (Detroit).

Var. *cinereus.* Plant cinereous or stem whitish. Otherwise like the typical form.

The dry surface of the pileus often becomes rimulose in expanded plants from the cracking of the cuticle. Such a condition is shown in Hard's Fig. 163, Plate 24, op. page 204; in other respects that illustration does not show the characteristic top-shaped pileus of the plant, nor the short stubby stem. It is distinguishable by its glabrous cap and stem, its top-shaped pileus and the compact flesh of the center of the cap. It grows more often in exposed, grassy places than our other Hygrophori.

169. Hygrophorus virgineus Fr. var. (EDIBLE)

Syst. Myc., 1821.

Illustrations: Hard, Mushrooms, Fig. 175, p. 219, 1908.
   Peck, N. Y. State Mus. Mem. 4, Pl. 52, Fig. 8-12, 1900.
   McIlvaine, American Mushrooms, Pl. 37, Fig 6, p. 146, 1900.
   Cooke, Ill., Pl. 892.
   Gillet, Champignons de France, No. 351.

PILEUS 2-5 cm. broad, convex, *often plane to depressed,.dry,* obscurely pruinose, even *white,* margin thin. FLESH thick in center of cap, white. GILLS decurrent, close to subdistant, thickish, white or at length tinged cream-flesh color, scarcely ever forked or veined, trama of interwoven hyphae. STEM short, 2-4 cm. long, 6-10 mm. thick, equal or tapering either way, solid, *white* within and without, *glabrous,* even. SPORES narrowly ovate or elliptic-ovate, smooth, 6-8 x 3.5-4 micr. ODOR and TASTE mild.

Solitary or gregarious. On sandy ground, in mixed, open woods of pine, beech and maple. New Richmond, Detroit. September-October. Found infrequently.

This species, it is said, is to be looked for among grass in meadows, etc., but the writer has not found it in such localities. The description applies to the American form, which is usually smaller, its cap is rarely distinguished by rimose cracks, and the spores are smaller than given for the European plant. The recorded European spore-measurements vary from 8-10 x 5 to 10-12 x 6-7 micr. Our plant is probably a distinct variety if not a species. It has also closer gills than the type. It is hard to distinguish from the pallid variety of *H. pratensis* except for its narrower spores, and less umbonate or turbinate pileus, which is commonly pure white.

170. Hygrophorus niveus Fr. (EDIBLE)

Epicrisis, 1836-38.

Illustrations: Michael, Führer f. Pilzfreunde, Ill. No. 89.
   Ricken, Blätterpilze, Pl. 7, Fig. 3.
   Cooke, Ill., Pl. 900.

PILEUS 1-3 cm. broad, convex or campanulate at first, then plane, *umbilicate, hygrophanous-white,* glabrous, slightly viscid, *striatulate when moist.* FLESH *thin,* white. GILLS decurrent, distant, narrow, white, thin, subvenose, trama of interwoven hyphae. STEM 2-8 cm. long, 2-5 mm. thick, stuffed then usually hollow, equal or tapering downward, *white,* glabrous. SPORES broadly elliptical, smooth, 7-8 x 5-6 micr. CYSTIDIA none. BASIDIA 40-45 x 5-6 micr., slender. ODOR none.

Gregarious. On moist ground in low woods or on mosses in swamps. Ann Arbor, New Richmond, Marquette. Throughout the State. August-September. Infrequent.

Most of our collections were composed of small plants, with slender stems often only 2 mm. thick. The pileus varies from truly convex to campanulate in the same patch. In some localities the pileus was tinged a slight cream-color, but otherwise the plant was the same. The umbilicus is sometimes obsolete. The pileus has a thin subviscid pellicle. This species, with us, differs from *H. borealis* in its more slender habit and its pileus, which is very thin and umbilicate on the disk. It is rather tough, and when moist the pileus is slightly viscid.

171. Hygrophorus borealis Pk. (EDIBLE)

N. Y. State Mus. Rep. 26, 1874.

PILEUS 1-3.5 cm. broad, convex then subexpanded, obtuse, *moist,* glabrous, *even,* white. FLESH thickish on disk, thin elsewhere, concolor. GILLS decurrent, arcuate, distant, intervenose, white. STEM slender, 2-5 cm. long, 2-5 mm. thick, firm, equal or tapering downward, straight or flexuous, stuffed, white, glabrous. SPORES 7-9 x 5-6 micr., broadly elliptical. ODOR none. TASTE mild.

Gregarious or subcaespitose. On moist ground in swamps or woods of birch, maple, hemlock, etc. Marquette, New Richmond, Ann Arbor. August-October. Infrequently found, but probably common in our northern woods.

This is a slightly larger and firmer species than the preceding. Its pileus is rarely striate and is not viscid. It is, however, closely related to *H. niveus.* No data are at hand to determine what may be the structure of the gill-trama.

Var. *subborealis,* var. nov. A plant has been found which simulates *H. borealis,* whose spores are markedly larger. If these prove to be constant, it deserves to be considered a separate species. The full description follows:

PILEUS 1-3 cm. broad, convex, broadly umbonate, obtuse or sometimes depressed-umbilicate, *thick on disk,* firm, watery white, *sub-hygrophanous,* not shining, *glabrous,* even, the thin margin at first slightly incurved, at length spreading. FLESH white. GILLS decurrent, distant, *veined,* forked, concolor, trama of interwoven hyphae. STEM 3-4 cm. long, 4-7 mm. thick, tapering downward, dull white, stuffed then hollow, glabrous or innately silky-fibrillose. SPORES *cylindric-elliptical,* smooth, 10-12 (rarely 13) x 4-5.5 micr. BASIDIA slender, 45-50 x 6-7 micr., with sterigmata about 6 micr. long. ODOR none. TASTE mild.

Ann Arbor, New Richmond. August-October.

172. Hygrophorus ceraceus Fr. (EDIBLE)

Syst. Myc., 1821.

Illustrations: Michael, Führer f. Pilzfreunde I, No. 33.
Hard, Mushrooms, Fig. 174, p. 218.
Cooke, Ill., Pl. 904 (B).
Murrill, Mycologia, Vol. 2, Pl. 27, Fig. 2.

PILEUS 1-4 cm. broad, convex-capmanulate, obtuse, soft and *fragile, viscous,* pale ceraceus to lemon-yellow, sometimes tinged orange, *not pallescent,* pellucid-striate, glabrous. FLESH concolor, fragile. GILLS broadly adnate to subdecurrent, broad behind to subtriangular, thickish, subdistant, pale yellowish or whitish, trama of interwoven hyphae. STEM 2-5 cm. long, 2-4 mm. thick, equal, terete or compressed, *hollow,* glabrous, slightly viscid, soon dry, shining-undulate, waxy-yellow, sometimes tinged orange. SPORES 6-8 x 4 micr., short-elliptic, smooth. CYSTIDIA none.

Gregarious. On moist ground, in woods of the northern and western part of the State. July-September. Frequent.

This little species is usually placed under the subgenus Hygrocybe, but the interwoven hyphae of the gills bar it. It is distinguished from *H. nitidus,* a very similar species, by the color of the cap not fading as in that species; and from *H. chlorophanus* by the broadly adnate or subdecurrent gills. It seems to prefer the region of conifer woods, although it is not necessarily found only among conifers.

173. Hygrophorus colemannianus Blox.

Outlines of British Fungology, Berkeley, 1860.

Illustrations: Cooke, Ill., Pl. 903.
Bresadola, Fung. Trid., Vol. 2, Pl. 125.
Ricken, Blätterpilze, Pl. 7, Fig. 5.
Plate XXIX of this Report.

PILEUS 1.5-4 cm. broad, convex with obtuse umbo, *finally turbinate* and plane to depressed, *hygrophanous,* with a thin, separable, subviscid pellicle, even or at length pellucid-striate, glabrous, livid rufescent then *brownish-flesh color,* margin soon spreading. FLESH thin except disk, rather fragile, concolor. GILLS *decurrent* from the first, distant, not broad, acuminate at ends, very veiny, whitish, tinged grayish-brown, *trama of interwoven hyphae.* STEM 3-6 cm. long, 3-6 mm. thick, *equal or subequal,* elastic, innately fibrillose-striatulate, apex naked, stuffed or at length hollow, *whitish.* SPORES broadly elliptical, smooth, 6-9 x 5-6 micr., white. BASIDIA slender, 40 x 6 micr., 4-spored. CYSTIDIA none. ODOR none. TASTE mild.

Gregarious or solitary. On the ground in mossy or grassy moist places, in low woods or edge of swamps. Ann Arbor, New Richmond. Infrequent.

Bresadola gives a good figure, though our plants average smaller than his. It has the shape of *H. pratensis* but is hygrophanous and thinner, and must not be confused with the gray variety of that species. It prefers springy or moist places. The entire lack of odor separates it from *H. foetens* Phil. and *H. peckianus* Howe.

174. Hygrophorus pallidus Pk.

Torrey Bot. Club, Bull. 29, p. 69, 1902.

Illustration: Plate XXIX of this Report.

PILEUS 2-6 cm. broad, convex-campanulate, then expanded-plane to subdepressed, subturbinate, *hygrophanous,* glabrous, *smoky-violaceous or smoky-lilac when fresh and moist,* fading to pale gray, *with a thin gelatinous pellicle,* subviscid when moist, soon dry and shining, even. FLESH white, rather thin. GILLS arcuate-adnate to decurrent, *distant,* not broad, intervenose, *colored like the pileus when moist,* at length whitish or grayish-white, trama of interwoven hyphae. STEM 3-6 cm. long, 2-8 mm. thick, slender or stout, equal or narrowed downwards, slightly fibrillose or glabrous, *apex naked,* at first *stuffed by a large soft pith which disappears,* at length hollow and easily splitting, white or pale silvery-gray. SPORES ovate-subglobose, smooth, 5-6.5 x 4-5 micr. BASIDIA short, 30 x 6-7 micr. ODOR none. TASTE mild.

Gregarious or solitary. On moist ground in low woods or swamps. Ann Arbor, Marquette, Negaunee, New Richmond. Rather rare.

A beautiful Hygrophorus when fresh and moist, but very variable in the degree of color and viscidity. The deep color and the viscidity of the pileus disappear quickly on exposure to the wind, causing it to appear like quite a different plant. The gelatinous cuticle can, however, be demonstrated in all conditions by means of the microscope. Examples of our specimens were seen by Simon Davis, who collected the type specimens which were named by Peck. *Hygrophorus subviolaceous* Pk. is very close to it, according to the description, differing only in its solid stem; Peck has, however, referred it to the subgenus Limacium. I suspect that *H. caerulescens* B. & C. is the same plant.

SUBGENUS HYGROCYBE. Veil none. *Trama of gills of parallel hyphae.* Entire fungus thin, watery succulent, fragile. Pileus viscid when moist, shining when dry, rarely floccose-scaly. Stem *hollow,* not scabrous-punctate at apex.

Most specimens of this subgenus are brightly colored, are soft, and grow in moist or wet places. As no data are at hand concerning the gill-trama of several species, these have been included temporarily under the subgenus Hygrocybe.

175. Hygrophorus miniatus Fr. (EDIBLE)

Syst. Myc., 1821.

Illustrations: Hard, Mushrooms, Fig. 171, p. 215.
  Marshall, Mushroom Book, Pl. X, p. 60, 1903.
  Peck, N. Y. State Mus. Rep. 48, Pl. 28, Fig. 1-10, 1894.
  White, Conn. State Nat. Hist. Surv., Bull. 15, Pl. 18, 1910.
  Cooke, Ill., Pl. 921 (A).
  Ricken, Blätterpilze, Pl. 8, Fig. 9.

PILEUS 1-3 cm. broad, convex-subexpanded, at length *umbilicate,* never viscid, vermillion, reddish-yellow or yellow, fading, *minutely tomentose, at length minutely scaly, sometimes glabrous,* even, fragile. FLESH thin, yellowish to pale. GILLS adnate to subdecurrent, subdistant, orange-red or yellow, at length paler, thickish, trama of parallel hyphae. STEM 2-7 cm. long, 3-5 mm. thick, equal, almost cylindrical, orange-red or yellow, stuffed, at last hollow, *dry,* glabrous. SPORES *variable,* broadly elliptical, 7-9.5 x 5-6 micr. ODOR and TASTE mild.

Var. *Cantheréllus* Schw. (*Hygrophorus Cantherellus* Schw.) Stem longer and more slender, pileus narrower, gills a little more decurrent, spores the same.

Illustrations of the variety:
    Hard, Mushrooms, Fig. 165, p. 208, 1908.
    Murrill, Mycologia, Vol. 2, Pl. 27, Fig. 9.
    Marshall, Mushroom Book, Pl. X. p. 60, 1903.
    Peck, N. Y. State Mus. Rep. 54, Pl. 76, Fig. 8-20, 1901.

The var. *Cantherellus* is much more common with us than the
type, but it intergrades so much that it is often difficult to decide
on the identity. The characters usually given for its separation,
viz., the decurrent gills, minutely scaly pileus and slender stem, do
not always hold good, so that it can hardly be an autonomous species.
Numerous collections show all possible combinations, although the
commonest type in Michigan is the plant with narrow pileus and a
stem 2-3 mm. thick and 5-7 cm. long. A number of *color forms* of
both have been named as varieties: (a) with red or orange cap
and yellow stem; (b) with yellow pileus and red stem; (c) with
both stem and pileus pale yellow. Var. *sphagnophilus* Pk. is more
marked, grows in sphagnum bogs, is very fragile and the white
base of the stem is imbedded and attached to the moss. The spores
of the whole series are rather variable, even in the same collection,
but fall within the limits given above. Massee and Cooke give the
spore lengths a little large for our plants. The color varies greatly
and fades in age.

Gregarious or subcaespitose. On the ground in moist conifer or
frondose woods or on mosses. Throughout the State. June-October. Quite common.

176. Hygrophorus coccineus Fr. (EDIBLE)

Syst. Myc., 1821.

Illustrations: Swanton, Fungi, Pl. 9, Fig. 4-6.
    Cooke, Ill., Pl. 920.
    Murrill, Mycologia, Vol. 2, Pl. 27, Fig. 7.
    Plate XXX of this Report.

PILEUS 2-7 cm. broad, *campanulate* or sometimes convex,
scarcely expanded, obtuse, subviscid, *cherry red or blood-red, fading,* glabrous, even. FLESH thin, *fragile, concolor.* GILLS
arcuate-adnate, somtimes with decurrent tooth, *subdistant* to *distant,* orange-red to yellow, at length glaucous, thickish, intervenose,
trama of parallel hyphae. STEM 4-7 cm. long, 3-9 mm. thick, varying much in thickness, subequal or tapering downward, often *com-*

pressed and furrowed, hollow, blood or cherry-red, *orange or yellow at base,* often undulate-uneven, *naked.* SPORES *broadly elliptical,* 7-9 x 5-6 micr. BASIDIA 40-50 x 6-7 micr. ODOR and TASTE none.

Gregarious. On the ground, in low meadows or moist woods, thickets, clearings, etc., of conifer or hardwood regions. Marquette, Houghton, Detroit. Throughout the State. July-October. Infrequent; more frequent in the northern part of the State.

Among the largest of the bright-colored species of this group, approaching *H. puniceus* in size in spite of the notes of some authors that it is smaller. It is variable in size, has a firm appearance, but is rather brittle. This is one of our most beautiful mushrooms when well developed. It is easily confused with *H. puniceus,* from which it is to be separated by its *spores,* the yellow base of the stem, the more distinctly adnate gills and the entirely glabrous stem. European authors disagree as to the spore sizes of *H. coccineus* and *H. puniceus,* but two species which agree in the other characters with the published descriptions and figures, and the spores of which are consistently of the two types given under these two species, are found in Michigan. They vary somewhat in size in each case, but the narrower and longer spore of *H. puniceus* is well-marked.

177. Hygrophorus puniceus Fr. (EDIBLE)

Syst. Myc., 1821.

Illustrations: Peck, N. Y. State Mus. Mem. 4, Pl. 52, Fig. 1-5, 1900.
　　　　Michael, Führer f. Pilzfreunde, Vol. I, No. 34.
　　　　Cooke, Ill., Pl. 922.
　　　　Murrill, Mycologia, Vol. 2, Pl. 27, Fig. 5.
　　　　Ricken, Blätterpilze, Pl. 8, Fig. 2.

PILEUS 3-7 cm. broad, campanulate, obtuse, *expanded at length and then wavy or lobed,* bright red or scarlet, *viscid,* fading, glabrous. FLESH fragile, white, yellow under the thin separable pellicle. GILLS *narrowly adnexed,* thick, distant, yellow to scarlet, intervenose, trama of parallel hyphae. STEM 5-8 cm. long, 5-12 mm. thick, ventricose, unequal or tapering, hollow, yellow, or scarlet and yellow, *white at the base,* dry, *fibrillose-striate.* SPORES cylindrical-elliptical, smooth, 9-12 x 4-5 micr. BASIDIA 40-42 x 5-6 micr. ODOR none, TASTE mild.

Gregarious or solitary.   On the ground, in moist places, bare ground, woods, thickets, etc.   August-October.   Ann Arbor, Detroit. Infrequent.

This species is similar to the preceding in general appearance.   It is separable from it by its large spores, the slightly adnexed gills and the white base of the stem; it has also a more viscid cap and a somewhat fibrillose stem.   It also differs from *H. chlorapanous* in its red colors and dry stem.

Var. *flavéscens* Kauff.   (8th Rep. Mich. Acad. of Sci., 1906.)

PILEUS smaller, 2-6 cm. broad, "luteus" yellow, varying to orange tints in places, then citron yellow, fragile, convex-campanulate, expanded, glabrous, even, viscid, sometimes wavy.   GILLS adnexed, rather broad, close to sub-distant, *pale yellow or white,* subveiny.   STEM 4-7 cm. long, 3-6 mm. thick, hollow, compressed, sulphur or citron-yellow, *base white,* moist, *pellucid-shining, glabrous,* sometimes pellucid-striate.   SPORES *smaller,* 6-7.5 x 4-5, elliptical.

Gregarious, in wet places, moss, etc., in cedar swamps or low woods, in northern Michigan.   Rather frequent.

The viscidity of the pileus is not very marked.   It has much the habit and coloring of *H. chlorophanous,* but the stem is never viscid and varies in color to a distinct citron-yellow with white base, and is usually compressed.   It is a distinct species as shown by its spores.

178.   Hygrophorus chlorophanus Fr.   (EDIBLE)

Syst. Myc., 1821.

Illustrations: Gillet, Champignons de France, No. 329.
  Fries, Icones, Pl. 167, Fig. 4.
  Cooke, Ill., Pl. 909.
  Peck, N. Y. State Mus. Mem. 4, Pl. 51, Fig. 13-20, 1900.
  Murrill, Mycologia, Vol. 2, Pl. 27, Fig. 3.

PILEUS 2-5 cm. broad, convex or campanulate, then nearly plane, obtuse, *viscid,* citron, sulphur or golden yellow, glabrous, sometimes pellucid-striate on margin.   FLESH *fragile,* not becoming black when bruised.   GILLS *adnexed, ventricose, becoming emarginate, thin,* subdistant, rather broad, pale citron-yellow, trama of parallel hyphae.   STEM 3-7 cm. long, 4-8 mm. or less in thickness, *equal* or nearly so, sulphur or pale citron-yellow, *unicolorous,* hollow, rarely compressed, *viscid,* glabrous, even. SPORES narrowly elliptical, 6-8 x 4-5 micr., smooth.

Gregarious. Low, moist places in woods. Throughout the state. June-September. Common.

Known by its unicolorous viscid stem, and the adnexed, rather broad gills. The stem often dries quickly when exposed to the wind. Var. *flavescens* of the preceding species is almost as closely allied to this species, but its stem is fundamentally distinct.

179. Hygrophorus marginatus Pk. (SUSPECTED)

N. Y. State Mus. Rep. 28, 1876.

Illustrations: Hard, Mushrooms, Fig. 173, p. 217, 1908.
Plate XXXI of this Report.

PILEUS 1-4 cm. broad, *fragile,* irregularly convex or campanulate, gibbous at times, at length plane, obtuse or broadly umbonate, *hygrophanous,* glabrous, varying *golden yellow to orange or variegated with olivaceous (moist), fading* and pale yellowish (dry), striatulate or rimose on margin. FLESH thin, fragile, concolor. GILLS arcuate adnate, becoming emarginate, subdistant, ventricose, rather broad, deep yellow or orange, *color persisting,* intervenose. STEM 2-5 cm. long, 3-8 mm. thick, fragile, hollow, *dry,* often flexuous or irregularly compressed, glabrous, yellow or tinged orange, *fading* to straw-color. SPORES broadly elliptical, smooth, 7-8 x 4-5 micr. (rarely longer). ODOR and TASTE not marked.

Gregarious or subcaespitose. On the ground in low, moist places in swamps of conifers or in frondose woods. Ann Arbor, Sault Ste. Marie, Marquette, Houghton, Huron Mountains. July-August. Infrequent.

The striking characteristic of this species is the orange-yellow gills which retain their color even after drying, while the pileus and stem fade considerably; this is shown well in Hard's figure. The edge of the gills is sometimes more deeply colored. The whole plant is very fragile, and it is difficult to get good herbarium specimens. The plants found in the Northern Peninsula were mostly variegated with olive, while those in the frondose woods of the south lacked this character, which, however, soon disappears as the pileus fades. None of my specimens were viscid. It is a well-marked species. The stems are sometimes more elongated.

180. Hygrophorus conicus Fr. (SUSPECTED)

Syst. Myc., 1821.

Illustrations: Hard, Mushrooms, Fig. 166, p. 209, 1908.
   White, Conn. State Nat. Hist. Surv., Bull. 3, Pl. 13, p. 34,
      1905.
   Michael, Führer f. Pilzfreunde, Vol. II, No. 48.
   Ricken, Blätterpilze, Pl. 8, Fig. 4.
   Cooke, Ill., Pl. 908.
   Murrill, Mycologia, Vol. 2, Pl. 27, Fig. 8.
   Gillet, Champignons de France, No. 332.

PILEUS 1-3 cm. broad and high, *conical*, unexpanded, subacute
at apex, often splitting-expanded, or lobed on margin, viscid when
moist, shining when dry, glabrous, yellow, orange or orange-red,
subvirgate, *often stained black in age*. FLESH concolor, very thin,
becoming black when bruised or old. GILLS almost *free*, ventricose, broad, almost triangular at times, thick, rather close to subdistant, pallid to sulphur-yellow, when old black stained, trama of
parallel hyphae. STEM 3-9 cm. long, 2-6 mm. thick, subcylindrical,
soft, *dry, fibrillose-striate,* usually *twisted,* hollow, citron to golden
yellow, *becoming black stained with age,* splitting longitudinally.
SPORES broadly elliptical, 8-10 x 5-6.5 micr., smooth. CYSTIDIA
none. BASIDIA 35-38 x 8 micr., slender.

Gregarious or solitary. In low, moist, conifer or frondose woods,
grassy places, etc. Throughout the State. May to October.
(Earliest record May 8; latest October 15.) Very common.

Easily recognized by its conical pileus and the blackening flesh.
The whole plant usually turns black in drying. It is not unusual
to find olive tints in the pileus, and the shades of yellow or orange
to red vary much as the plant matures or ages. After having become rain-soaked, the whole plant is sometimes black.

181. Hygrophorus nitidus B. & C. (NON. FR.)

Centuries of N. Amer. Fungi (Exsicatti), see also Peck, N. Y.
   State Mus. Rep. 23, 1870.

Illustrations: Peck, N. Y. State Mus. Bull. 94, Pl. 88, Fig. 1-7,
      1905.
   Murrill, Mycologia, Vol. 2, Pl. 27, Fig. 6.

PILEUS 1-2.5 cm. broad, fragile, convex, *umbilicate,* viscid when moist, *wax-yellow to lemon-yellow, whitish when dry, pellucid-*striatulate and shining when moist, glabrous. GILLS arcuate, decurrent, distant, pale yellow, intervenose. STEM 3-7 cm. long, 2-4 mm. thick, *slender,* fragile, hollow, equal or narrowed downwards, sometimes flexuous, *viscid* at first, wax-yellow, at length whitish. SPORES elliptical, 6-7 x 3-4 micr. ODOR and TASTE not marked.

Gregarious or subcaespitose. On the ground in swamps or low woods in the conifer regions of the State. Marquette, Houghton, Huron Mountains, New Richmond. July to September. Frequent locally.

A slender Hygrophorus whose cap and often also the stem, fade considerably on drying. This characteristic distinguishes it from *H. ceraceus.* It has hitherto been found only in mixed woods of hemlock, birch and maple or of maple and oak in the northern and western parts of the state. The gills are usually quite decurrent, narrowed to a point on the stem, and their persistent color contrasts markedly with that of the stem and pileus as the plant dries. There is no universal viscous veil as in the plant of the same name described by Fries. The latter plant is now called *H. friesii* Sacc.

182. Hygrophorus laetus Fr. (EDIBLE)

Syst. Myc., 1821.

Illustrations: Ricken, Blätterpilze, Pl. 8, Fig. 8.
     Fries, Icones, Pl. 167, Fig. 2.
     Cooke, Ill., Pl. 938.
     Gillet, Champignons de France, No. 338.

"PILEUS 1.5-3 cm. broad, convex-plane, *subobtuse,* viscid when moist, shining, *tawny, not fading,* pellucid-striate. FLESH concolor or paler, *tough,* thin. GILLS subdecurrent, broadly adnate, subtriangular, distant, thin, yellow, greenish-yellow, grayish-yellow or at length pale orange. STEM slender, 3-5 cm. long, 3-6 mm. thick, *tough,* glabrous, *very viscid,* equal, *tawny,* undulate-uneven. SPORES elliptical, 6-7 x 4 micr. BASIDIA 30 x 5-6 micr. ODOR and TASTE not marked."

Gregarious. In meadows, pastures, cedar swamps, etc. Lewiston, Houghton. July-August. I have given Ricken's description. Doubtless it is often confused with *H. peckii.* The dry state of the latter seems to imitate it, and differs only in its fragility, the subumbilicate pileus, and gills which are at first whitish.

183.   Hygrophorus peckii Atk.

Jour. of Mycol., Vol. 8, 1902.

PILEUS 1-2 cm. broad, fragile, convex-plane, *broadly umbilicate* or depressed, glutinous when moist, color varying pale yellowish-flesh color, *pinkish or vinaceous-buff*, rarely tinged greenish, glabrous, pellucid-striatulate when moist, fading somewhat on drying. GILLS arcuate-decurrent, distant, rather broad, whitish to pale flesh color, trama of parallel hyphae. STEM 3-8 cm. long, 2-4 mm. thick, slender, equal, *very viscid*, shining, concolor, rarely greenish at apex, hollow, terete, even. SPORES broadly elliptical, 6-8 x 5 micr. ODOR present or absent; taste mild.

Gregarious or solitary. On the ground, moss, etc., of low, wet woods or swamps of cedar and balsam in northern Michigan, maple and oak woods of the southern part of the State. Isle Royale, Marquette, New Richmond, Ann Arbor, etc. July-August, rarely September. Frequent.

This is much more common apparently than *H. laetus,* and may represent an American variety of that species. It differs from *H. psitticinus* by the form of the pileus; in that species it is obtuse or umbonate, and the green color persists longer and is practically always present in the young plant, while in *H. peckii* the green tinge is rare. Both these species are very slippery on the stem and cap when fresh or young.

184.   Hygrophorus psitticinus Fr.

Syst. Myc., 1821.

Illustrations: Ricken, Blätterpilze, Pl. 8, Fig. 6.
   Michael, Führer f. Pilzfreunde, No. 65.
   Swanton, Fungi, Pl. 9, Fig. 7-8, 1909.
   Cooke, Ill., Pl. 910.
   Gillet, Champignons de France, No. 346.
   Murrill, Mycologia, Vol. 2, Pl. 27, Fig. 4.

PILEUS 1-3 cm. broad, *campanulate,* then convex-expanded or plane, *umbonate or obtuse,* glutinous and slippery, *at first parrot-green,* at length varying livid-reddish, pinkish-flesh color or dingy citron-yellowish, pellucid-striate. FLESH thin, subconcolor. GILLS adnate, ventricose, thick, subdistant, greenish or incarnate-reddish to yellowish, intervenose, trama of parallel hyphae. STEM

4-7 cm. long, 2-5 mm. thick, equal, *toughish,* even, *very viscid* when fresh, glabrous, undulate-uneven, subpellucid, *green above,* usually tinged reddish-orange, flesh-colored or yellowish elsewhere, hollow. SPORES short elliptical, smooth 6-7.5 x 4-5 micr. BASIDIA slender, 36-40 x 5-6 micr.

Gregarious or subcaespitose. On the ground in low, mossy woods or swamps, or in grassy places. Marquette, Houghton, New Richmond, Detroit, Ann Arbor. Throughout the State. July-October. Rather frequent.

This striking species is one of the few bright green mushrooms. As in the case of *Stropharia aeruginosa* and *Pholiota aeruginosa,* it is always a delight to come across this beautiful little plant. The green color soon fades out when exposed to the wind and light, whereas those individuals which are protected by leaves, etc., retain this color for some time. There is no cortina in the young stage, and the gluten is derived from the cuticle of the pileus and stem; otherwise, except for the structure of the gill-trama, it might be confused with the subgenus Limacium. Its colors are sufficiently characteristic in the early stage to prevent anyone from confusing it with other Hygrophori.

185. Hygrophorus unquinosus Fr.

Syst. Myc., 1821.

Illustrations: Cooke, Ill., Pl. 924.
Gillet, Champignons de France, No. 350.

PILEUS 2-5 cm. broad, fragile, hemispherical-campanulate, then subexpanded, obtuse, *gray or smoky brown, glabrous,* pellucid striate, *very viscid,* radiate-wrinkled in age. FLESH pallid, thin, very fragile. GILLS broadly adnate, subventricose, *pure white,* thickish, subdistant. STEM 3-8 cm. long, 3-8 mm. thick, subequal or variously thickened, hollow, compressed, *viscid-slippery,* glabrous, *lead-gray.* SPORES elliptical, 7-8 x 4-5 micr. BASIDIA 30-35 x 5-6 micr. Trama of gills parallel. ODOR none when young. TASTE mild.

Gregarious or subcaespitose. On the ground or moss of low woods or swamps. Detroit, Marquette, Houghton. July-September. Rather rare.

This species must not be confused with *H. fuligineus* which belongs to the subgenus Limacium, and has a solid stem and a veil.

AGARICEÆ

Context of fruit-body fleshy, putrescent, that of pileus sometimes membranous, of stem sometimes cartilaginous or horny; neither leathery, nor vesiculose. Stem central, eccentric, lateral or lacking. Gills well-developed, acute on edge. Spores with a hyaline or colored epispore; their deposit in mass on white paper yields a series of "prints" of various shades of white, pink, ochraceous, brown, purple or black. This series is arbitrarily divided into five artificial groups as follows:

(a) Black-spored. (*Melanosporae*) : Spore-print black.
(b) Purple-brown-spored. (*Amaurosporae*) : Spore-print dark purple or purple-brown.
(c) Rusty-spored or ochre-spored. *(Ochrosporae):* Spore-print rusty-yellow, rusty-brown, ochraceous or cinnamon-brown.
(d) Pink-spored. *(Rhodosporae):* Spore-print flesh-colored, rosy or pale pink.
(e) White-spored. *(Leucosporae):* Spore-print white.

The spore-print is in many cases indispensable in determining the proper group to which the mushroom belongs. It is obtained easily by cutting off the stem just below the gills and laying the cap, with gills down, on a piece of white paper and covering it over night with a dish to prevent premature drying. Mushrooms which have been kept on ice do not seem to deposit spores thereafter, nevertheless it is well to avoid too warm a place, else the specimen may putrefy. The color of the spores may often be detected at the time of collecting by the deposit already made on the ground beneath it or on other mushrooms when growing in a cluster. In mature specimens the gills usually become colored by the color of the spores, but when young the gills are generally white; in some species, however, the gills are themselves colored, e. g., *Clitocybe illudens* and *Mycena leijana.* After some experience, it is usually possible to determine the group to which a species belongs by means of the microscope. The delicate tint of the color for each group is then discernible in the episphere of each mature spore. This method is especially useful in cases where it is a question of the presence of the purple tint of the purple-brown-spored plants; the spore-mass or gills often appear entirely dark brown to the naked eye in species whose separate spores have a purple tint under the microscope.

MELANOSPORAE

Coprinus Pers.

(PROF. L. H. PENNINGTON)

(From the Greek, *kopros,* dung.)

Spores dark brown or black; gills free or slightly attached, *at first closely in contact laterally,* separated in many cases by projecting cystidia, soon deliquescing, or drying quickly to a black line upon the lower side of pileus. Many small species develop at night and almost entirely disappear by morning. The flesh of the pileus is thin, in the smaller species often membranaceous or apparently lacking entirely. A universal veil is present in a majority of the species. The stem is fleshy to fibrous. Most of the species grow upon dung or richly manured ground, several upon wood or vegetable debris, and a few upon lawns, sand, or even upon walls in cellars.

The spores of the dung inhabiting species usually germinate readily to produce a fine white or colorless mycelium upon which sporophores will often appear within 7-10 days after the spores are sown. *C. radiatus,* various forms of *C. ephemerus, C. patouillardi, C. semilanatus, C. narcoticus* and several similar kinds are readily grown in pure cultures in the laboratory. *C. sclerotigenous* grows from rather small black sclerotia in dung or in a mixture of soil and dung. Some of the wood inhabiting species, *C. laniger* and *C. radians* are often found growing from dense masses of fine yellow mycelial threads, called *ozonium.* Others, e. g. *C. quadrifidus,* grow from tough coarse black fibres, termed *rhizomorphs.* The pileus is scaly from the breaking up of the cuticle into rather large squamose scales in the Comati; into fine innate fibrils in the Atramentarii; smooth but covered at first with floccose, mealy or granular scales, which wholly or partly disappear in the Picacei and Tomentosi; or pruinose with minute hairs in forms of *C. ephemerus* and *C. radiatus.* The stem is stuffed or hollow, fleshy or fleshy-fibrous, often very fragile. It differs in texture from the trama of the pileus and usually separates easily from it. The gills are white at first. In some species they become purplish then black, in others they become brown or smoky, then black. They are free or slightly attached, or adnate in a few species.

The universal veil is usually seen as scales, fibrils or granules at the base of the stem or upon the pileus. In a few instances it forms a movable ring upon the stem in *C. comatus, C. bulbilosus* and frequently in *C. sterquilinus;* in the last named species the veil may form a distinct volva at the base of the stem. The taste is mild and the odor is usually pleasant. A few species, as *C. quadrifidus* and *C. narcoticus,* have a strong disagreeable odor. None of the species of Coprinus are considered poisonous and many are highly esteemed by the mycophagist.

The spores are very dark brown or sooty black in mass. By transmitted light they vary from light brown to very dark brown or smoky black. There is a wide variation in the size and shape of the spores. Some species may be identified by the spores alone as *C. insignis, C. boudieri* and some forms of *C. ephemerus,* etc.

The genus can be divided into two fairly distinct groups (see Massee, Ann. Bot., Vol. 10, p. 123, 1896) according to the size of the plant and the thickness of flesh or cuticle covering the gills; these groups can be further subdivided into sections as follows:

A. Pelliculosi:
    I. Comati
    II. Atramentarii
    III. Picacei
    IV. Tomentosi
    V. Micacei
    VI. Glabrati (No species reported)
B. Veliformes:
    VII. Cyclodei
    VIII. Lanulati
    IX. Furfurelli
    X. Hemerobii

Key to the Species

(A) Plants large, usually over 3 cm. broad; pileus fleshy or sub-fleshy.
  (a) Pileus with cuticle torn into distinct scales or almost smooth.
    (b) Cuticle torn into distinct scales; ring or volva present.
      (c) Spores over 20 micr. long; volva usually evident. 188. *C. sterquilinus* Fr.
      (cc) Spores less than 20 micr. long; movable ring usually present upon stem.
        (d) Pileus cylindrical; spores 15-17 micr. long. 186. *C. comatus* Fr.
        (dd) Pileus ovate; spores less than 15 micr. long. 187. *C. ovatus* Fr.
    (bb) Pileus smooth or with innate fibrils.
      (c) Spores smooth, plants usually densely caespitose. 189. *C. atramentarius* Fr.
      (cc) Spores distinctly warted. 190. *C. insignis* Pk.
  (aa) Cuticle not torn into scales; veil breaking up into superficial patches, scales, or granules.

(b) Veil felt-like, breaking up into areolate patches.
 (c) Rhizomorph or ozonium not evident; plants densely caespitose.
  192. *C. ebulbosus* Pk.
 (cc) Rhizomorph or ozonium present.
  (d) Plants growing from rhizomorph; 5-8 cm. broad. 191. *C.*
   quadrifidus Pk.
  (dd) Plants growing from fine yellow ozonium; 1-3 cm. broad.
   193. *C. laniger* Pk.
(bb) Veil not as above.
 (c) Veil of fibrillose scales or a dense coat of white mealy vesicles.
  (d) Spores less than 10 micr. long.
   (e) Gills broad; growing upon sand. 199. *C. arenatus* Pk.
   (ee) Gills narrow.
    (f) Disk livid; upon rotten wood in forest. 197. *C. lago-*
     pides Karst.
    (ff) Disk buff; upon cellar walls. 198. *C. jonesii* Pk.
  (dd) Spores more than 10 micr. long.
   (e) Gills attached.
    (f) Disk obtuse; reddish or reddish brown. 202. *C. domes-*
     ticus Fr.
    (ff) Disk narrow, not colored; veil often composed of mealy
     vesicles. 200. *C. niveus* Fr.
   (ee) Gills free.
    (f) Pileus at first cylindrical. 196. *C. tomentosus* Fr.
    (ff) Pileus not cylindrical.
     (g) Veil more or less mealy; plants small, not in troops.
      (h) Spores 11-13 micr. long. 201. *C. semilanatus* Pk.
      (hh) Spores 15-17 micr. long. 200. *C. niveus* Fr.
     (gg) Veil never mealy; plants large; in troops upon dung
      heaps.
      (h) Stem not rooting. 194. *C. fimetarius* Fr.
      (hh) Stem rooting. 195. *C. fimetarius* var. *macrorhizus*
       Fr.
 (cc) Veil of small granules or micaceus particles.
  (d) Spores less than 10 micr. long.
   (e) Plants not growing from ozonium; densely caespitose.
    203. *C. micaceus* Fr.
   (ee) Plants from ozonium or at least with radiating mycelium
    at base of stem, single or caespitose. 204. *C. radians* Fr.
  (dd) Spores 10-12 micr. long. 209. *C. micaceus* var. *conicus* Pk.
(AA) Pileus thin, plicate; if subfleshy then less than 3 cm. broad when
 expanded.
 (a) Veil present as superficial scales or granules.
  (b) Ring present upon the stem. 205. *C. bulbilosus* Pat.
  (bb) Ring absent.
   (c) Pileus covered with a dense white floccose or mealy coat.
    (d) Spores 12 micr. or more long.
     (e) Spores 12-13 micr. long. 201. *C. semilanatus* Pk.
     (ee) Spores 15-16 micr. long. 200. *C. niveus* Fr.
    (dd) Spores less than 12 micr. long.
     (e) Plants growing from black sclerotia in dung. 207. *C.*
      sclerotigenous E. & E.
     (ee) Not growing from sclerotia.
      (f) Plants growing upon plant stems. 209. *C. brassicae* Pk.
      (ff) Plants growing upon dung or soil.
       (g) Odor strong; spores 10-11 micr. long. 208. *C. nar-*
        coticus Fr.
       (gg) Little or no odor; spores 6-8 micr. long. 206. *C.*
        stercorarius.
   (cc) Pileus with a few micaceus particles or granules.
    (d) Spores ovate triangular or pentagonal, compressed. 210.
     C. patouillardi Quel.
    (dd) Spores elliptical. 211. *C. radiatus* Fr.

(aa) No véil present.
  (b) Spores angular.
    (c) Spores key-stone shaped; plants growing upon ground in
       woods. 214. *C. boudieri* Quel.
    (cc) Spores not key-stone shaped; plants upon dung. 213. *C.*
       ephemerus Fr. form.
  (bb) Spores not angular.
    (c) Plants growing upon dung or recently manured ground. 213.
       C. ephemerus Fr.
    (cc) Not growing upon dung.
      (d) Growing among grass; spores broadly ovate, compressed.
        215. *C. plicatilis* Fr.
      (dd) Growing in woods; spores gibbous-ovate. 213. *C. silva-*
        ticus Pk.

PELLICULOSI. Pileus covered with a distinct fleshy or membranous cuticle, not splitting along the lines of the gills but becoming lacerate and revolute. Plants usually large.

Section I. *Comati.* Ring formed from the free margin of the volva; cuticle torn into scales.

186. Coprinus comatus Fr. (EDIBLE)

(The Shaggy Mane)

Fries, Epicr., p. 242.

Illustrations: Cooke, Ill., Pl. 658.
    Murrill, Mycologia, Vol. 1, Pl. 3, Fig. 3.
    Atkinson, Mushrooms, Fig. 31-38.
    Hard, Mushrooms, Figs. 269, 270.
    Gillet, Champignons de France, No. 174.
    Patouillard, Tab. Analyt., No. 448.

PILEUS 7-10 cm. high, cylindrical, then more or less expanded, at first even, the cuticle becoming torn into broad adpressed scales, pale ochraceous, becoming darker in age, interstices whitish. GILLS up to 12 mm. broad, almost free, white, crowded, then pinkish, at length black. STEM 10-15 cm. long, 12-17 mm. thick, subequal, slightly attenuated upwards, white, even, hollow, more or less bulbous, bulb solid, ring movable. SPORES almost black, elliptical, 13-18 x 7-8 micr.

Gregarious. In lawns and fields, very common in autumn, occasional in spring.

The Shaggy Mane is probably more generally used for food than any other Coprinus. By many people, however, it is not considered equal in quality to *Coprinus micaceus*.

187. Coprinus ovatus Fr. (EDIBLE)

Fries, Epicr., p. 242.

Illustrations: Schaeffer, Icon., Tab. 7.
    Cooke, Ill., Pl. 659.

PILEUS about 5 cm. across when expanded, at first ovate and covered with an even pale ochraceous cuticle, which becomes broken into large concentric scales, the apical portion remaining intact like a cap, margin striate. FLESH, thin, white. GILLS about 4 mm. broad, free, distant from the stem, whitish then black. STEM 6-10 cm. long, 10 mm. thick, attenuated upwards, flocculose or fibrillose, white, hollow, the lower portion bulbous, solid, rooting, ring evanescent. SPORES smoky black, 11-12 x 7-8 micr.

This plant, which is often considered as a smaller form of *Coprinus comatus* Fr., was found but once growing upon a lawn at Palmyra, Mich. It differs from *Coprinus comatus* Fr. in that it has a smaller ovate pileus and smaller spores. In the specimens found the pileus was about 3 cm. high and the spores 11-13 x 7 mm. But for its much smaller spores the plant might easily be taken for a form of *Coprinus sterquilinus* growing in soil. In shape and color the spores of *Coprinus comatus, C. ovatus* and *C. sterquilinus* are very similar. In size, however, there is much variation, the measurements running from 11 microns in *C. ovatus* to 26 microns in *C. sterquilinus.*

188. Coprinus sterquilinus Fr. (EDIBLE)

Fries, Epicr., p. 242.

Illustrations: Patouillard, Tab. Analyt., No. 437.
    Gillet, Champignons de France, Pl. 130 (as *C. oblectus* Fr.).
    Cooke, Ill., Pl. 660.
    Murrill, Mycologia, Vol. 3, Pl. 49, Fig. 3.
    Plate XXXII of this Report.

PILEUS 5-6 cm. broad when expanded, at first short cylindrical, conical then expanded, white tinged with brown or fuscous at disk, cuticle at first villous or silky, later torn into squarrose scales especially at disk. FLESH thin, white, sulcate half way to disk. GILLS free, white then purplish, soon becoming black. STEM 10-15 cm. high, slightly attenuated upward, subfibrillose, white slowly becoming discolored when bruised, often entirely black with spores, hollow, base solid, thickened, peronate, the sheath or volva with a free margin. SPORES 18-25 micr., smoky black.

In old manure, straw, or in manured ground. June.

This plant has been reported as *Coprinus stenocoleus* Lindb. It is also *Coprinus macrosporus* Pk. When growing in manured ground, the volva is not as evident as when the plant grows in old manure or straw. From plates and descriptions it appears that this plant has also been called *Coprinus oblectus* Fr. In the herbarium of the New York Botanical Garden a specimen from Kew labeled *Coprinus oblectus* Fr. is very plainly *Coprinus sterquilinus* Fr. Moreover in a collection of many individuals, specimens may be picked out which fit the description of *C. sterquilinus, C. stenocoleus, C. oblectus* and *C. macrosporus* respectively. It is very probable that these names are all synonyms.

The plants are frequently found in June upon old manure which has been lying out in the open over winter or in heavily manured ground. The young unexpanded plants resemble rather small short specimens of *C. comatus* Fr. Undoubtedly *C. sterquilinus* Fr. is frequently taken for *C. comatus* or *C. ovatus*. In fact the writer has had typical specimens of *C. sterquilinus* pointed out to him by a mushroom collector as "the shaggy mane mushroom, very good to eat."

The gills sometimes remain perfectly white for several hours and then change rapidly through a purplish color to a smoky black. The flesh is thin and, as the pileus expands, it often becomes revolute and in bright sunshine it dries in this condition. Sometimes the stem becomes dark when bruised or when dried. Usually, however, it remains white unless it becomes covered with spores.

This mushroom is edible and has a more pronounced "mushroom" flavor than the ordinary Coprinus. McIlvaine says, *"Coprinus macrosporus* is an excellent species, higher in flavor than any other Coprinus."

Section II.   Atramentarii.   Ring imperfect, not volvate, squamules of pileus minute, innate.

189.   Coprinus atramentarius Fr.   (EDIBLE)

Fries, Epicr., p. 243.

Illustrations: Cooke, Ill., Pl. 622.-
    Gillet, Champignons de France, No. 172.
    Atkinson, Mushrooms, Fig. 39-42.
    Hard, Mushrooms, Fig. 271-272.
    Murrill, Mycolgia, Vol. 1, Pl. 3, Fig. 4.

PILEUS 5-8 cm. broad when expanded, ovate then expanded, firm, often lobed and plicate, grayish, silky fibrous, or minutely mealy, apex brownish, often minutely squamulose.   FLESH thin. GILLS crowded, broad, ventricose, free, white then black, often with a purplish tinge.   STEM 10-15 cm. high by 1-2 cm.. thick, white, silky shining, hollow, ring basal, very evanescent.   SPORES 11-12 x 5.5-6 micr.   CYSTIDIA numerous, large, subcylindrical.

Common, gregarious or densely caespitose, about stumps or on rich soil, but not upon dung.

Both the smooth and the scaly, or squamulose, forms are found. These characters often seem to depend upon weather conditions, the smooth form being found under moist atmospheric conditions and the scaly form under dry atmospheric conditions.

Its close broad gills make it very thick and meaty in the unexpanded condition.   For this reason some people consider this species the most desirable Coprinus for the table.

190.   Coprinus insignis Pk.

Peck, N. Y. State Mus. Rep. 26, p. 60, 1874.

Illustration: Plate XXXIII of this Report.

PILEUS 5-7.5 cm. broad, ovate then campanulate, thin, sulcate-striate to the disk, grayish brown, glabrous or with a few innate fibrils, disk sometimes cracking into small areas or scales.   GILLS free, ascending, crowded.   STEM 10-14 cm. high, 10 mm. thick, hollow, slightly fibrillose, striate, white.   SPORES 10 x 7 micr., rough.

About trees in woods.

This plant was found but twice in low woods at Ann Arbor.   It resembles *C. atramentarius* in some respects but differs very decidedly in the distinctly warted spores.

Section III. Picacei. Universal veil flocculose, at first continuous, then torn into superficial areolate patches by the expansion
of the pileus.

191. Coprinus quadrifidus Pk.

N. Y. State Mus. Rep. 50, p. 106, 1897.

Illustration: Plate XXXIV of this Report.

PILEUS 5-8 cm. broad, oval then campanulate, finally more or
less expanded, thin, margin becoming revolute; covered at first with
a floccose-tomentose veil, which soon breaks into evanescent flakes
or scales and reveals the finely striate surface of the pileus; whitish, becoming gray or grayish brown with age; margin often wavy
or irregular. GILLS broad, thin, crowded, free, at first whitish,
then dark purplish brown, finally black. STEM 7-10 cm. long by
6-8 mm. thick, equal or slightly tapering upward, hollow, white,
floccose-squamose, sometimes with an evanescent ring at the base.
SPORES 7.5-10 x 4-5 micr.

Gregarious or caespitose upon or near decaying stumps or logs,
growing from an abundant rhizomorph. Ann Arbor, Bay View.

Although nothing is said in the original description about the
rhizomorph, some few strands may be seen at the base of the stem
in some of the type specimens. The writer has found this plant
growing in New York from richly developed rhizomorph upon the
roots and trunk of dead basswood.

192. Coprinus ebulbosus Pk.

Bull. Torr. Bot. Cl. 22, 1895.

Illustrations: Hard, Mushrooms, Fig. 274.
Plates XXXV and XXXVI of this Report.

PILEUS 5-7 cm. broad, thin, campanulate, somewhat striate,
grayish brown, margin at length revolute, lacerated, cuticle breaking into broad superficial persistent whitish scales. GILLS narrow, thin, crowded, free, slate-colored becoming black. STIPE 7-15
cm. long, 10-15 mm. thick, equal, hollow, white. SPORES 7.5-10 x
5 micr., elliptical.

Caespitose near or upon decaying trees or stumps.

193. Coprinus laniger Pk.

Bull. Torr. Bot. Cl. 22, 491, 1895.

Illustration: Plate XXXVII of this Report.

PILEUS 12-25 mm. broad, thin, conical or campanulate, pallid, tawny or grayish-ochraceous, sulcate-striate, covered with tawny, tomentose or floccose scales, which wholly or partly disappear. GILLS crowded, whitish, then brownish black. STEM 2.5 cm. long, 2-4 mm. thick, slightly thickened at base, hollow, white, pruinose. SPORES 7-10 x 4 micr., oblong-elliptical.

Caespitose or gregarious upon or near decaying wood. Unfortunately the type specimens of this species have been lost. The plants referred to this species are found growing from a more or less profusely developed yellow ozonium upon various kinds of decaying wood.

The three species *C. laniger, C. ebulbosus* and *C. quadrifidus,* seem to be distinct forms in a perplexing group of brown-spored wood-inhabiting Coprini, which are as yet very imperfectly known. *C. laniger* is smaller than either of the others and we have always found it associated with the fine strands of yellow ozonium. It resembles *C. radians,* but it has a thicker veil, which breaks into evident patches instead of minute particles as in *C. radians.*

C. quadrifidus and *C. ebulbosus* are not readily distinguished and may both prove to be the species which have been known as *C. flocculosus* (DC) Fr. or *C. (Agaricus) domesticus* Bolt.

Section IV. Tomentosi. Universal veil a loose villose web which becomes torn into distinct floccose scales.

194. Coprinus fimetarius Fr.

Fries, Epicr., p. 245.

Illustration: Plate XXXVIII of this Report.

PILEUS 2.5-5 cm. across, clavate then conico-expanded, soon split and revolute, grayish, apex tinged with brown, at first covered with white floccose scales, then naked, rimose-sulcate; disk even, flesh thin. GILLS free, lanceolate, becoming linear and wavy, very early becoming black with spores and rapidly deliquescing. STEM 12-15 cm. long, 4-6 mm. thick, hollow, thickened at the solid base, white, squamulose. SPORES 12-14 x 7-8 micr. CYSTIDIA large and numerous.

Solitary or in troops. Common upon dung heaps. The clavate caps already dark with spores may be found emerging late in the afternoon or in the evening. In the morning there will be little remaining except a small mass of inky fluid at the apices of the stems.

195. Coprinus fimetarius var. macrorhiza Fr.

Fries, Hym. Eur., p. 324.

Illustrations: Cooke, Ill., Pl. 670.
Massee, Ann. Bot., Vol. 10, Pl. X, Fig. 1.
Hard, Mushrooms, Fig. 275.
Gillet, Champignons de France, No. 178.

PILEUS at first with feathery squamules which become more or less squarrose, especially at the disk where they often form a crown. STEM short, villous, often sub-bulbous and with a more or less elongated base.

The type and this variety are very common, the latter being rather more frequently found than the former. In moist weather they may be found in almost any dung heap, a fresh troop appearing each evening and disappearing early the following day. There seems to be considerable variation in size, length of root and character of scales. In the typical form the root is usually reduced to a rather indefinite mass of hyphae, while the scales are more or less squarrose over the entire surface. In the variety the veil is more silky and closely appressed to the pileus, later becoming squarrose at the disk forming a crown of scales.

196. Coprinus tomentosus Fr.

Fries, Epicr., p. 246.

Illustration: Bulliard, t. 138.

PILEUS 2.5-4 cm. long, sub-membranaceous, cylindrical, narrowly conical, then expanding and splitting, striate, floccose-tomentose, pale gray, the floccose veil becoming torn into more or less persistent flakes or patches upon the expanded pileus. GILLS free, narrow. STEM 5-7 cm. long, 4-5 mm. thick, equal or slightly enlarged below, hollow, velvety, white or grayish. SPORES 12-13 x 7-8 micr., elliptical.

Solitary or gregarious upon dung or various kinds of debris. This is one of the earliest species of Coprinus to appear in the spring. The long cylindrical or narrowly conical pileus distinguishes this plant from the various forms of *C. fimetarius,* which usually appear a little later in the season.

This may be the *C. lagopus* of various authors.

197. Coprinus lagopides Karst.

Karsten, Hatts., 1, 535.

Illustrations: Massee, Ann. Bot., Vol. 10, Pl. 10, Figs. 20-22.

PILEUS 4-7 cm. broad, very thin, companulate, sulcate, grayish, disk livid, ornamented with free white scales joined by hairs. GILLS subcrowded, narrow, remote, black. STEM up to 17 cm. high, white, floccose, hollow, equal. SPORES 6-8 x 5-6 micr., apiculate. Upon very rotten wood in forest.

Found once at Bay View. We have found this plant in New York also.

198. Coprinus jonesii Pk.

Peck, Bull. Torr. Bot. Club 22, p. 206, 1895.

PILEUS 2.5-5 cm. broad, at first blunt, or truncate, becoming campanulate or broadly convex, submembranaceous, grayish, buff at apex, covered at first with white or tawny-cinereous floccose scales which wholly or partly disappear with age, striate, margin revolute and splitting. GILLS crowded, linear, free, whitish, becoming black. STEM 5-9 cm. long, 4-7 mm. thick, equal or slightly tapering upward, minutely floccose, hollow, white. SPORES 7.5-8.5 x 6 micr., broadly elliptical.

Fragile, sometimes caespitose. Found upon the wall in a cellar at Ann Arbor. Peck says "This species is closely related to *C. fimetarius* of which it might easily be considered a variety, but it is easily distinguished by the truncate apex of the young pileus, the differently colored pileus and smaller spores." It grew on what appeared like uncracked hard and dry plaster of the wall.

199. Coprinus arenatus Pk.

Peck, N. Y. State Mus. Rep. 46, p. 107, 1892.

PILEUS 2.5-5 cm. broad, thin, at first broadly ovate or sub-hemispherical, soon convex or campanulate, adorned with small white tomentose scales, striate on the margin, whitish or grayish-white, becoming grayish-brown with age, reddish brown in dried plant. GILLS crowded, broad, free, grayish-white, soon purplish-brown, finally black, furnished with numerous cystidia. STEM 2.5-5 cm. long, 2-4 mm. thick, equal, glabrous, hollow, white. SPORES 7.5-9 x 6-7.5 micr., broadly ovate or subglobose, purplish brown by transmitted light.

Solitary or gregarious in sandy soil, Ann Arbor. The mycelium binds the sand together in balls at the base of the stem.

200. Coprinus niveus Fr.

Fries, Epicr., p. 246.

Illustration: Cooke, Ill., Pl. 673 B.

PILEUS 1.5-2.5 cm. across, elliptical then campanulate and expanded, submembranaceous, almost persistently covered with snow-white floccose down. GILLS slightly attached, narrow, becoming blackish. STEM 4-8 cm. high, subequal or slightly attenuated upwards, villose, white, hollow. SPORES 16 x 11-13 micr.

This plant is frequently found upon dung heaps, street sweepings or in recently manured ground. Upon the pileus the veil is of a mealy nature but the tomentose character shows at the margin of the pileus and upon the stem. The spores are somewhat flattened, measuring 15-17 x 11 to 13 x 8-10 micr.

The plant referred to this species is *C. stercorarius* (Bull.) Fr. and has been distributed under that name in Sydow Mycotheca Marihoa, No. 2101.

201. Coprinus semilanatus Pk.

N. Y. State Mus. Rep. 24, p. 71, 1872.

Illustrations: N. Y. State Museum Report 24, Pl. 4, Fig. 15-18.

PILEUS 2-2.5 cm. broad, convex then expanded and revolute, sometimes split, submembranaceous, finely and obscurely rimose-

striate, farinaceo-atomaceous, white, then pale grayish-brown.
GILLS narrow, close, free. STEM 10-15 cm. high, slightly tapering
upward, fragile, hollow, white, the lower half clothed with loose
cottony flocci which rub off easily, upper half smooth or slightly
farinaceous. SPORES 12.5 micr., broadly elliptical. Rich ground
and dung.

This plant is frequently found on cow dung in woods and shaded
pastures. It resembles *C. niveus* Fr. but differs from it in its
smaller size, free gills and constantly smaller spores. The spores
in both species are broadly elliptical and somewhat flattened.
This fungus grows readily from spores in laboratory cultures.

202.   Coprinus domesticus Fr.

Fries, Epicr., p. 251.

Illustrations: Cooke, Ill., Pl. 684.
        Gillet, Champignons de France, No. 176.
        Plate XXXVIII of this Report.

PILEUS, 3-5 cm. across, thin, ovate, then campanulate, obtuse,
furfuraceous, squamulose, pale grayish-white, disk brown or reddish brown, undulate, sulcate, splitting. GILLS adnexed, crowded,
narrow at first, reddish white then blackish brown. STEM 5-7 cm.
long, 4-6 mm. thick, slightly attenuated upwards, subsilky, white,
hollow. SPORES 14-16 x 7-8 micr.

Usually caespitose, on various kinds of vegetable debris, sometimes in gardens where rubbish has been plowed under.

Section V. Micacei. Pileus at first covered with more or less
micaceous squamules or granules, which soon wholly or partly disappear.

203.   Coprinus micaceus Fr.   (EDIBLE)

Fries, Epicr., p. 247.

Illustrations: Cooke, Ill., Pl. 673.
        Atkinson, Mushrooms, p. 44, Figs. 43, 44.
        Murrill, Mycologia, Vol. 1, Pl. 3, Fig. 5.
        Hard, Mushrooms, Fig. 273.
        Plates XXXIX and XL of this Report.

PILEUS 4-6 cm. across, submembranaceous, elliptical then campanulate, coarsely striate, disk even, margin usually more or less repand, ochraceous-tan, disk darker, when young densely covered with minute glistening particles which usually soon disappear. GILLS sub-crowded, lanceolate, adnexed, whitish, then brown, finally nearly black. STEM 5-7 cm. long, 4-6 mm. thick, equal, even, hollow, silky white. SPORES 7-8 x 4-5 micr., dark brown in mass.

Very common, generally densely caespitose about stumps or trees, or growing from decaying wood buried in the earth. Under favorable conditions this Coprinus may be found from early spring until late autumn. It often appears at intervals of one to two weeks in the same place for a considerable length of time and it may be found year after year in the same place. It has a good flavor and is considered by many the best Coprinus for the table.

C. micaceus var. *conicus* Pk. (Not published.)

This variety differs from the type in having a distinctly conical pileus, darker colored, larger spores, 10-12 micr. long. It was found once at Palmyra, Michigan.

204. Coprinus radians (Desm) Fr.

Fries, Epicr., p. 248.

Illustrations: Cooke, Ill., Pl. 676 a.
  Lloyd, Mycological Notes, Vol. 1, p. 146, Fig. 69.
  Massee, Ann. Bot., Vol. 10, Pl. X, Figs. 6-8.

PILEUS 2-5 cm. across, ovate, conical or campanulate, yellowish-fulvous, soon becoming paler especially at the margin; striate to disk, covered with small brown granules which are more numerous at the disk. GILLS rather narrow, attached, pale then brownish black. STEM 3-6 cm. long, 2-3 mm. thick, equal or slightly swollen at base, hollow, white, smooth or minutely mealy at first, more or less evident yellow or white strands of mycelium radiating from the base. SPORES 7 x 4 micr., elliptical, brownish black.

Rather common, single or sub-caespitose, upon wood, rubbish, etc., or even in humus, sometimes growing from dense masses of yellow ozonium.

This is the plant illustrated by Lloyd and determined by Patouillard as *C. radians* (Desm.) Fr. It is also *C. pulchrifolius* Pk. It is possible also that it may be *C. granulosus* Clements. *C. radians* as figured by Cooke and Massee always has yellowish brown mycelium radiating from the base of the stem. Saccardo, Syll., Vol. 5, p. 1092, says that in Italy this plant grows upon *Ozonium stuposum* Fr. The writer has sometimes found our plant growing from masses of yellow ozonium, upon decaying maple, black locust and black ash logs. It appeared once in our laboratory cultures upon mycelium which was white at first then gradually became yellowish brown. This is not the only Coprinus, however, which grows from a yellow ozonium. *C. radians* resembles *C. laniger* from which it may be separated by the much smaller scales upon the pileus.

VELIFORMES. Pileus very thin, plicate-sulcate, splitting along the lines of the gills. Plants usually small.

Section VII. Cyclodei. Stem with a movable ring. Plants small.

205. Coprinus bulbilosus Pat.

Patouillard, Tab. Anal. Fung., 60.

Illustrations: Ibid, Fig. 658.
Plate XL of this Report.

PILEUS 8-10 mm. across, convex, margin striate, at first incurved then expanding, gray, disk tinged yellow, covered with white meal. GILLS narrow, gray. STEM 2-3 cm. long, slender, white, base bulbous, ring loose, at some distance from base, white. SPORES 8-9 x 7-8 x 4 micr., compressed, oval to subglobose.

On horse dung. Readily grown in cultures from spores. Saccardo, Sylloge, says "spores angular." In our specimens the spores are slightly angular as seen in one plane.

Section VIII. Lanulati. Pileus covered with a downy or cottony layer which often has the appearance of a dense coat of soft mealy vesicles.

206. Coprinus stercorarius Fr.

Fries, Epicr., p. 251.

Illustration: Cooke, Ill., Pl. 685 A.

PILEUS 1-25 cm. high, ovate then companulate, sometimes expanded and rolling up at the margin, very thin, margin striate, densely covered with a white glistening meal. GILLS adnexed,

2-3 mm. broad, sub-ventricose. STEM 7-12 cm. long, at first ovately bulbous then elongated and equally attenuated upwards from the base, hollow, white, at first mealy. SPORES black, 6-8 x 3-4.5 micr.

The specimens referred to this species are smaller than the dimensions given in the description. Otherwise they agree with the description in the sense of Saccardo. Massee, British Fungus Flora, Vol. 1, p. 326, gives the spore measurements as 14-15 x 8-9.

Found but once upon cow dung in woods near Ann Arbor.

207. Coprinus sclerotigenus E. & E.

Ellis & Everhart, Microscope, 1890.

Illustrations: Microscope, 1890, Fig.
      Massee, Ann. Bot., Vol. 10, Pl. XI, Figs. 26-28.
      Plate XLI of this Report.

PILEUS .5-1.2 cm. high and broad, ovoid or ovoid-oblong, then campanulate (at first covered with a white mealy veil which later becomes dark and sometimes almost entirely disappears). STEM 2.5-10 cm. high, slender, subequal, usually straight above and more or less flexuous below where it is downy. GILLS adnexed. SPORES obliquely elliptical, 8-10 x 5-6 micr.

Springing from an irregularly subglobose, rugulose, sclerotium which is black outside, white inside. On sheep's dung.

Although nothing is said in the original description about a veil, the type specimens at the New York Botanical Garden still show some of the mealy white covering of the pileus. This plant was first found at Ann Arbor and later in other localities. It was always found growing from sclerotia in dung which had apparently been upon the ground for some time, often over winter. These sclerotia were repeatedly grown from spores in the laboratory and, after a certain amount of drying out, sporophores grew from the sclerotia. By alternately moistening and drying the sclerotia several crops of sporohores were produced. This plant may be identical with *C. tuberosus* Quel.

208. Coprinus narcoticus Fr.

Fries, Epicr., p. 250.

Illustrations: Cooke, Ill., Pl. 680 b.
Plate XLI of this Report.

PILEUS 1-2 cm. across, *foetid*, very thin, cylindric-clavate then expanded, at length revolute, covered at first with recurved, white floccose scales, then naked, grayish white, hyaline, striate. GILLS free but nearly reaching the stem, white then black. STEM 3-5 cm. long, 2 mm. thick, fragile, at first covered with white down, then almost glabrous, hollow. SPORES 11 x 5-6 micr., elliptical.

On dung, caespitose. ODOR strong and disagreeable. Not common.

209. Coprinus brassicæ Pk.

Peck, N. Y. State Museum Rep. 43, 1878.

Illustrations: Peck, N. Y. State Mus. Rep. 43, Pl. 2, Fig. 9-14.
Murrill, Mycologia, Vol. 4, Pl. 56, Fig. 4.

PILEUS 8-10 mm. broad, at first ovate or conical, then broadly convex, squamulose, finely striate to the disk, white becoming grayish-brown, membranaceous, margin generally splitting and becoming recurved. GILLS narrow, crowded, reaching the stipe, brown with a ferruginous tint. STEM 16-20 mm. long, slender, glabrous, hollow, slightly thickened at the base, white. SPORES 7.5 x 5 micr., elliptical, brown. On decaying stems of cabbage and other vegetable debris.

Occasional upon vegetable debris of various kinds. Palmyra, Ann Arbor. We have found this fungus upon corn stalks, weed stalks and dead grass.

It seems very probable that this is the plant figured and described as *C. tigrinellus*, Boudier, Table 139, and *C. friesii* Quel. (Patouillard, Pl. 446.)

Section IX. Furfurelli. Pileus with micaceous particles or mealy granules.

210. Coprinus patouillardi Quel.

Quelet, Assoc. Fr., 1884, p. 4.

Illustration: Plate XLII of this Report.

PILEUS 1-3 cm. broad, ovate, oblong, then conico-campanulate and finally revolute, at first finely striate then deeply plicate, very thin, white or ashy with pulverulent particles, yellowish to brown at the center. GILLS narrow, free but close to stem, white then smoky brown. STEM 2.5-5 cm. long, 1-2 mm. thick, fragile, smooth or slightly tomentose or pulverulent at base, white. SPORES 8-7 x 4.5 micr., ovate-triangular to pentagonal.

Common on dung, usually appearing with *C. radiatus* or a little later. There seems to be considerable variation in this plant both in regard to size and color. In young stages, especially in dry weather, the pileus is densely covered with dead white to gray particles, which gradually become brown as the pileus develops. The shape of the spore is characteristic and the variation in size less than in many other Coprini. In young stages it is readily distinguished from *C. radiatus* by its longer, more cylindrical shape and by its thicker white veil.

211. Coprinus radiatus Fr.

Fries, Epicr., p. 251.

Illustration: Cooke, Ill., Pl. 682 a.

PILEUS 2-15 mm. wide, at first ovate or short cylindrical, then campanulate, finally nearly or quite plane and slightly depressed at the center, very thin, deeply plicate; pileus with a few brown granular flecks or scales, slightly pruinose with a few gland-tipped hairs, pale brown or yellowish brown, darker at disk, becoming gray. GILLS narrow, distant, free. STEM 2-6 cm. high, 1.5 mm. thick, slender, fragile, hollow, white, becoming darker with age, slightly pruinose with glandular hairs. SPORES 10-13 x 8-10 micr., regularly elliptical, very dark.

Very common upon dung. This is probably our most common dung-inhabiting Coprinus. It may be found at almost any time during the summer season upon dung in pastures. If fresh horse dung be placed in a damp chamber, troops of this fungus will appear within 10-14 days. Larger specimens appear at first; successive plants appear smaller and smaller until they are often only one or two millimeters in diameter and one or two centimeters high. Just as there is much variation in the size of the fungus there is wide variation in the size of the spores. Occasionally the specimens are found with small spores 7-10 x 5-8 micr., as given by Saccardo (Sylloge, Vol. 5, p. 1101). Usually, however, they average as large as given in our description. Specimens of this plant have been distributed in exsiccati under the name of *C. ephemerus* and *C. plicatilis*. The plant figured by Buller as *C. plicatiloides* (Researches in Fungi) is evidently *C. radiatus*.

Section X. Hemerobii. Pileus always glabrous or slightly pruinose with minute hairs. No universal veil. A few scurfy particles may be found by the breaking of the cuticle or trama when the pileus becomes plicate.

212. Coprinus ephemerus Fr.

Fries, Epicr., p. 252.

Illustrations: Cooke, Ill., Pl. 685 f.
    Plates XLII and XLIII of this Report.

PILEUS 1-2 cm. across, ovate, then campanulate, finally expanded, often splitting and revolute, margin sometimes uneven, striate, plicate when expanded, very thin, disk even or slightly elevated. Yellowish brown to reddish bay at the disk, at first slightly pruinose with minute hairs. GILLS linear, slightly adnexed or barely reaching the stem, usually white at margin. STEM 3-6 cm. high, 1-2 mm. thick, equal or slightly tapering upward, hollow, white. SPORES 15-17 x 7-8 micr., black in mass.

Common upon dung or freshly manured ground.

In an examination of different exsiccati, we have found abundant evidence of the truth of Saccardo's statement that many different species have been confused under the name of *C. ephemerus*.

We have found well-marked specimens of *C. radiatus*, *C. plicatilis*, and *C. spraguei* all under the name of *C. ephemerus*. Even as we have limited this species, there are many distinct forms which may be readily distinguished. We have grown several of these varieties from spores and have found them to be constant and, even in young stages, the differences are often apparent to the naked eye. One common form has shorter spores (11-13 micr.), which are distinctly angular when viewed in one plane. The deep bay disk and peculiar pruinose character of the plants make it possible to identify this form almost as soon as the buttons appear, see plates XLII, XLIII. A less common form resembles in the young stages very small specimens of *C. micaceus*. The spores are elliptical, 11-13 micr. long. We have grown another larger and lighter colored form with two-spored basidia.

213. Coprinus silvaticus Pk.

Peck, N. Y. State Mus. Rep. 24, p. 71, 1872.

Illustrations: Ibid, Pl. 4, Fig. 10-14.

PILEUS 12-30 mm. broad, convex, membranaceous, plicate-striate on margin, dark brown, disk very thin, fleshy. GILLS sub-distant, narrow, adnexed, brownish then black. STEM 5 cm. high, 1 mm. thick, slender, fragile, smooth, hollow, white. SPORES 12.5 micr. long, gibbous-ovate. On ground in woods.

This plant was found once at Ann Arbor and once at Bay View. The gibbous spores are very characteristic.

214. Coprinus boudieri Quel.

Quelet, Bull. Soc. Bot. Fr., 1877.
Peck, N. Y. State Mus. Rep. 26, p. 60, as *C. angulatus*.

Illustrations: Ibid, Tab. 5, Fig. 4.
Lloyd, Mycological Notes, Vol. I, Figs. 21-22, p. 47. (As *C. angulatus.*)

PILEUS 1-2.5 cm. broad, membranaceous, hemispherical, or convex, plicate-sulcate, reddish brown, smooth or minutely pruinose, disk smooth. GILLS subdistant, reaching the stem, whitish then black, the margins often remaining white. STEM 2.5-5 cm. long, 1-1.5 mm. thick, equal, smooth or sub-pruinose, white. SPORES 7-12 x 6-10 micr., compressed, *angular, key-stone shaped.*

Upon soil in woods. Rare.

The peculiar angular sub-ovate or key-stone shaped spores are very characteristic of this plant.

215. Coprinus plicatilis Fr.

Fries, Epicr., p. 252.

Illustrations: Cooke, Ill., Pl. 686 a.
    Massee, Ann. Bot., Vol. 10, Pl. XI, Figs. 23-25, 1896.
    Gillet, Champignons de France, No. 185.

PILEUS 1-2.5 cm. across, ovate-cylindrical, then campanulate, membranaceous, sulcate to disk, brown, then grayish; disk remaining darker, rather broad, becoming depressed. GILLS distant, narrow, *attached to a collar at some distance from the stem.* STEM 5-7 cm. long, 2 mm. thick, equal, white, smooth, hollow. SPORES 10-12 x 7.5 to 8.5 x 5-6 micr., compressed, broadly ovate.

Rather common among grass at roadsides, etc.

As in the case of *C. ephemerus* there has been considerable confusion of species under the name of *C. plicatilis.* We do not, however, find as much variation in this plant as in *C. ephemerus.*

Psathyrella Fr.

(From the Greek, diminutive of *Psathyra.*)

Black-spored. Gills at length uniformly dark-colored, *not deliquescing,* nor variegate-dotted. Pileus membranous, *striate or sulcate,* margin at first straight, not exceeding the gills. Stem slender, confluent. Veil inconspicuous.

Small, thin-capped mushrooms, growing on debris in woods, on the ground in low grassy places, in gardens, etc. With the exception of *P. disseminata,* the species are not well known. Peck has named twelve species found in the United States and a number of Friesian species are known to occur. The plants often have the appearance of the small, evanescent species of Coprinus, but the gills do not deliquesce. They differ from Panoeolus in the striate pileus, the non-variegated gills and the margin of pileus not exceeding the gills. I have definitely studied only two species.

216. Psathyrella disseminata Fr. (EDIBLE)

Syst. Myc., 1821.

Illustrations: Cooke, Ill., Pl. 657.
Gillet, Champignons de France, No. 586.
Patouillard, Tab. Analyt., No. 351.
Atkinson, Mushrooms, Fig. 49, p. 48, 1900.
Ricken, Blätterpilze, Pl. 23, Fig. 4.
Hard, Mushrooms, Fig. 280, p. 347, 1908.

PILEUS 5-10 mm. broad, oval then campanulate, at first white, then gray or grayish-brown, *prominently sulcate-plicate* to the small buff umbo, at first covered by microscopic, erect, one-celled hairs, scurfy, glabrescent. FLESH membranous, very thin. GILLS adnate, ascending, rather broad, ventricose, sub-distant, at first white, then ashy and finally uniformly black. STEM slender, 2-3 cm. long, .5 to 1 mm. thick, hollow, *white,* at first minutely hairy with spreading hairs, glabrescent. SPORES 7-10 x 4-5 micr., elongate-elliptical, smooth, purple-black under microscope. BASIDIA subcylindrical, 20-27 x 6-7 micr., 4-spored, interspersed with abundant sterile, inflated cells. CYSTIDIA none. ODOR none. TASTE mild.

On debris and on the ground in woods in extensive gregarious and caespitose clusters of numerous individuals.

Throughout the State. May-October. Common.

This species is well named; the thousands of plants which often cover the ground and debris around stumps are an attractive sight when fresh. It sometimes appears in greenhouses according to Atkinson. The microscopic structure of the hymenium is similar to that of the Coprini, and some authors (vide Ricken) refer it to that genus.

217. Psathyrella crenata (Lasch.) Fr.

Hymen. Europ., 1874.

Illustration: Cooke, Ill., Pl. 847.

"PILEUS 2-3.5 cm. broad, hemispherical, hygrophanous, rufescent or ochraceous, then pallid, atomate, *sulcate-plicate,* margin at length *crenate.* FLESH membranous. GILLS adnate, subventricose, yellowish-fuscous than black. STEM 6-7 cm. long, 1-2 mm. thick, slender, glabrous, whitish, striate and mealy at apex."

The description is adopted from Fries. Our plants had a more convex pileus, at first dark gray then rufescent or ochraceous; the gills were rather narrow, sub-distant, edge white-fimbriate; stem fragile, stuffed-hollow; the spores elliptic-oblong, 10-12.5 x 6-7 micr., smooth, purplish-black under microscope. CYSTIDIA few or none. The crenate folds of the margin of the cap included two to three striae. It agrees well with Cooke's figure.

Panœolus Fr.

(From the Greek, *panaiolus,* meaning all-variegated.)

Black-spored. Gills grayish-black, dotted by the spores, ascending, more or less attached but seceding. Stem central, polished, subrigid. Pileus *not striate,* rather firm but not very fleshy. Veil woven-submembranous or subsilky.

Dung-inhabiting, slender-stemmed, slightly persistent but putrescent mushrooms, whose otherwise glabrous pileus is either appendiculate or slightly white-silky on the margin by the collapsing of the more or less evanescent veil. Often ring-marked on the stem by the spores falling on the remnants of the veil. It is a rather small genus, and the rarer species are not well known. Peck has described five species, of which *P. epimyces* is to be looked for under Stropharia. The spores are opaque, black, smooth and usually lemon-shaped or elliptical; they remain aggregated in tiny clusters on the gills as these mature and so produce the dotted-variegated appearance of the gills. Later the gills become entirely gray-black to black.

218. Panœolus solidipes Pk. (EDIBLE)

N. Y. State Mus. Rep. 23, 1872.

Illustrations: Ibid, Pl. 4, Fig. 1-5.
> Hard, Mushrooms, Pl. 41, Fig. 278, p. 343.
> White, Conn. State Geol. & Nat. Hist. Surv. Bull., No. 3, Pl. 27, p. 53.
> Plate XLIV of this Report.

PILEUS 4-10 cm. broad, *large,* firm, at first hemispherical then broadly convex, obtuse, moist, glabrous, *white* when fresh, even, *at length rimose-scaly and yellowish,* especially on disk. FLESH rather thick, white, watery near the gills. GILLS ascending, narrowly adnate, *broad, ventricose,* close, white at first, then ashy to black, variegated by the spores, edge white-flocculose. STEM long and rather stout, 8-20 cm. long, 5-15 mm. thick, equal, firm, *solid,* fibrous, glabrous, *white* within and without, *apex striate* and beaded with drops, straight or curved at base, sometimes twisted. SPORES broadly elliptical, abruptly narrowed at base, smooth, 15-18 x 9-11 micr., black. STERILE CELLS on edge of gills, broadly lanceolate, 30-35 micr. long, subobtuse. BASIDIA short-clavate, about 33 x 14 micr., 4-spored. ODOR and TASTE slight. *Edible.*

Gregarious or subcaespitose. On manure piles rich in straw, on dung and on richly manured lawns. Ann Arbor. May-July. Spasmodic.

This is our largest Panœolus and an excellent species for the table. It is probably to be found throughout the southern part of the State; it has only appeared during a few seasons but then in abundance. The large size, white color when fresh, the solid stem and the marked striations on the upper portion of the stem are its distinguishing characters. The striations sometimes extend the whole length of the stem. Its flavor when cooked is quite agreeable. It is often a noble plant and our illustration does not do it justice.

219. Panœolus retirugis Fr. (SUSPECTED)

Epicrisis, 1838.

Illustrations: Gillet, Champignons de France, No. 509.
Murrill, Mycologia, Vol. 3, Pl. 40, Fig. 7.
Atkinson, Mushrooms, Pl. 11, Fig. 45, p. 45, 1900.
Hard, Mushrooms, Pl. 40, Fig. 276, p. 340, 1908.
Reddick, Ind. Geol. & Nat. Hist. Resour. Rep. 32, Fig. 9, p. 1231, 1907.

PILEUS 1-3 cm. broad, rather firm, at first elliptic-oval, then campanulate-hemispherical, obtuse, glabrous, *dark smoky when young and wet,* becoming paler, or in dry weather grayish, pale clay color or creamy-white, *shining-micaceous when dry,* surface usually *reticulate-veined on disk,* sometimes even, margin connected with *stem in young stage by a floccose-submembranous, ring-like veil,* veil soon broken and margin markedly *appendiculate* in expanded pileus. FLESH rather thin, equal. GILLS adnate-seceding, *broad,* ventricose, close, white then variegate-spotted by the black spores, edge white-flocculose. STEM 5-16 cm. long, 2-6 mm. thick, equal, cylindrical, sometimes flexuous, whitish, *rufescent* or tinged purplish within and without, darker below, hollow, *often covered with frost-like bloom,* sometimes minutely rimulose, bulbillate. SPORES broadly oval-elliptical, ventricose, 15-18 x 9-11 micr., smooth, black. *Sterile cells* on edge of gills, narrow, subcapitate.

Gregarious or scattered on dung-hills, manured lawns, fields, road-sides, etc., in woods or in the open. Throughout the State. May-October. Very common.

The most widely distributed of our species. In favorable weather it occurs abundantly where stock is pastured. In dry weather it is smaller and paler. In the woods or in drizzly weather the stems are large and the colors are very different. Some disagreement exists as to the size of the spores, which are variable in dimension but rather constant in shape. Ricken describes and figures a form which is scarcely our plant, and Cooke's figure is not convincing. It is not poisonous but is rather unattractive and usually avoided when collecting for the table. The older name is *P. carbonarius.* It is possible that this runs into *P. campanulatus* Fr. and is often confused with it.

220. Panœolus campanulatus Fr. (Suspected)

Epicrisis, 1836-38.

Illustration: Ricken, Blätterpilze, Pl. 69, Fig. 8.

"PILEUS 2-4 cm. broad, brownish-gray or yellowish-gray, *persistently conic-campanulate,* never expanded, *glabrous,* often somewhat silky-shining, *neither hygrophanous nor viscid,* margin somewhat appendiculate by the rather persistent veil. FLESH thin, concolor. GILLS adnate, ventricose-ascending, broad, close, variegated gray to black by the spores, edge white-flocculose. STEM 7-10 cm. long, 1-2 mm. thick, *straight,* rigid-fragile, equal, *reddish-brown,* pulverulent-pruinose, apex striate, black-dotted and beaded with drops in wet weather. SPORES lemon-shaped, 15-18 x 10-13 micr., smooth, opaque, black."

The description is adopted from Ricken. According to Godfrin (Bull. Soc. Myc. de France, 19, p. 45) this species differs from *P. retirugis* in the structure of the cuticle. In the latter species the surface cells of the pileus are four or five layers thick, gradually passing into the longer, tramal cells below; while in *P. campanu-*

latus there are only one or two rows of abruptly differentiated cells with large, clavate, erect cystidia-like cells intermingled. The species has not been uniformly conceived by different authors and needs further comparison. It is said to be very common in Europe and is widely reported in this country. The majority of authors give the same spore-size as Ricken.

221. Panœolus papillionaceus Fr. (Suspected)

Epicrisis, 1836-38.

Illustration: Ricken, Blätterpilze, Pl. 69, Fig. 3.

"PILEUS 2-4 cm. broad, subhemispherical, *at length* expanded, never viscid nor hygrophanous, *at length rimose-scaly or areolate, pallid or sordid-whitish* to smoky-gray or brownish-pallid, margin with evanescent, pallid veil. FLESH slightly thick, white. GILLS broadly adnate, often very broad, ventricose, close, variegated gray-blackish from the spores, at length black. STEM 6-8 cm. long, 2-5 mm. thick, cartilaginous-toughish, rigid, hollow, somewhat attenuated, *whitish*, with brownish base, apex striate and white-pruinose. SPORES lemon-shaped, 15-18 x 9-11 micr., smooth, black."

The description is adopted from Ricken. The spores are somewhat more narrow according to most authors. This species seems to be infrequent with us. Small forms occur which may be referred here, in which the pileus is less than a centimeter broad and the spores are smaller. The species is not too well known. Its main character seems to be the whitish stem but no doubt the forms with such a stem need segregation as shown by some of my collections.

222. Panœolus sp.

PILEUS 1-2.5 cm. broad, campanulate, obtuse, not expanded, 1-1.5 cm. high, hygrophanous, bibulous, *smoky gray when moist,* livid-buff when dry, glabrous, dull and subpruinose, at length coarsely crenate-wavy when dry; veil absent or fugacious. FLESH thickish, rather firm, concolor (moist), then pallid. GILLS rounded behind, adnate-seceding, not broadly attached, ventricose, crowded, gray then variegated black, edge white-flocculose. STEM 5-7 cm. long, slender, 1-2 mm. thick, equal, rigid-fragile, flexuous or straight, hollow, *livid smoky-gray,* concolor within, *pruinose,* glabrescent, base white-mycelioid. SPORES elliptical, ventricose, 9-10

x 6 micr., smooth, obtusely pointed, black. *Sterile cells* on edge of
gills, linear, subcapitate, 30-40 x 4-5 micr. ODOR none.

Gregarious. On horse dung and soil, in woods pastured by horses.
Ann Arbor. October.

This is close to *P. sphinctrinus* Fr. in most of its characters, but
differs in its much smaller spores and in the lack of a persistent,
appendiculate veil. The surface portion of the pileus has the same
structure that is given by Godfrin (l. c.) for *P. sphinctrinus.*

AMAUROSPORAE

Psalliota Fr.

(From the Greek, *Psallion,* a ring or collar.)

Purple-brown-spored. Stem *fleshy,* separable from the pileus,
provided with a persistent or evanescent *annulus.* Gills *free,* usually
pink or pinkish in the young stage.

Fleshy, mostly compact and large mushrooms, growing on the
ground in woods among fallen leaves, etc., or on lawns, pastures,
open ground or cultivated fields. They correspond to Lepiota of
the white-spored group. They are all *edible,* the larger ones being
among the best known and most widely used of edible mushrooms.
Several species have been cultivated a long time and are of considerable commercial importance, especially in Europe. (See remarks under *P. campestris.*)

The PILEUS is glabrous, fibrillose or fibrillose-scaly, either white
or whitish or dark colored by the color of the fibrils on its surface;
these fibrils compose a thin layer on the very young cap, and as the
cap expands are broken up, except at the slow-growing center, into
fibrillose scales. The young cap of these species is therefore much
more uniformly colored than later in the expanded stage. The surface of the whitish species is often stained somewhat with yellowish
of rufescent hues when bruised or in age. The *size* varies; most species may become quite large, *P. subrufescens* reaching a size of 20
cm. across the cap; a few are quite small. The surface is dry, or it
may be slightly viscid as in *P. cretacella.* The GILLS are free, as
in Lepiota. When the button is quite small it is white, but in some
species, e. g. *P. campestris,* becomes pink quickly. This character
has been used to separate the species, but is a difficult point for beginners to determine. As the spores begin to take on color, the pur-

plish-brown hues appear and when old, most gills appear blackish-brown because of the dense layer of spores. The STEM is either almost undifferentiated within and is then solid, or has a distinct pith which soon disappears and leaves it hollow, often in the form of a narrow tubule. It is fleshy and when fresh has no cartilaginous cortex; it is, however, of different texture from that of the pileus and easily separates from it.

The VEIL is single or double. When double the substance of the under layer is similar to that of the pileus and the base of the stem and is probably a part of a universal cuticle. Sometimes it is very voluminous and forms a large pendulous annulus, as in *P. placomyces* and *P. subrufescens*. Usually it is quite thick and persistent. The lower layer breaks off soonest, ceases expansion and cracks into radial patches which remain on the under side of the annulus; sometimes, as in *P. abruptibulba*, it is very evanescent.

The genus may be divided into two sections based on the structure of the veil. The Friesian grouping is entirely artificial, and the difference in the color of the young gills, used by some as a basis for grouping, seems too variable a criterion for the purpose.

Key to the Species

(A) Plants large; pileus normally much more than 4 cm. broad. (See
   P campestris.)
  (a) Growing in forests, thickets, groves, etc.
    (b) Pileus white, not fibrillose-scaly, usually glabrous.
      (c) Pileus turning yellowish on disk when rubbed; stem with small, abrupt bulb. 226. *P. abruptibulba* Pk.
      (cc) Pileus firm, chalky-white, not stained yellow; without abrupt bulb. 223. *P. cretacella* Atk.
    (bb) Pileus with fibrils or fibrillose scales on the surface.
      (c) Flesh turning pink to blood-red where broken; fibrils brownish-gray. 231. *P. haemorrhodaria* Fr.
      (cc) Flesh not or scarcely changing color.
        (d) Annulus single, not covered on under side with floccose patches; fibrils brown. 230. *P. silvatica* Fr.
        (dd) Annulus double, as shown by the patches on under surface.
          (e) Disk of pileus blackish, fibrils brown; odor not marked. 227. *P. placomyces* Pk.
          (ee) Disk reddish-brown, fibrils tawny; odor of almonds; large. 228. *P. subrufescens* Pk.
  (aa) Growing in fields, open places, cultivated grounds or lawns, not scaly.
    (b) Annulus as a broad band with spreading edges; gills very narrow as compared to the thick flesh; in cities. 224. *P. rodmani* Pk.
    (bb) Annulus different.
      (c) Pileus large, surface stained yellowish on disk when bruised; annulus double. 225. *P. arvensis* Fr.
      (cc) Pileus medium, surface unchanged; annulus lacerated, simple; gills bright pink. 229. *P. campestris* Fr.

(AA)   Pileus 1-5 cm. broad.
  (a)   Flesh of stem soon blood-red; in hot-houses.   235.   *P. echinata* **Fr.**
  (aa)   Flesh whitish, not turning red.
    (b)   Fibrils of pileus grayish-brown or brown; gills at first **gray.**
       232.   *P. micromegetha* Pk.
    (bb)   Not markedly fibrillose.
      (c)   Pileus creamy-white, with yellowish stains. 233. *P. comtula* **Fr.**
      (cc)   Pileus with pinkish to reddish-brown hues, slightly fibrillose.
        234.   *P. diminutiva* Pk.

Section I.   Bivelares.   Annulus double, with thick flocculose patches on under side.

223.   Psalliota cretacella Atk.   (EDIBLE)

Jour. of Mycology, Vol. 8, 1902.

PILEUS 4-7 cm. broad, convex to expanded, thin, *glabrous,* white, sometimes inclined to be slightly viscid in wet weather, even. FLESH white, sometimes with a tinge of pink.   GILLS free, crowded, narrow, 3-4 mm. broad, narrowed behind, white at first, *then slowly pink, later dark grayish-brown,* not becoming blackish. STEM 5-8 cm. long, 6-10 mm. thick, tapering from the enlarged base, white, glabrous above the annulus, chalky-white below and covered with minute, white, powdery scales often arranged in irregular concentric rings below, solid, but center less dense.   AN-NULUS *double,* persistent, white, smooth above, the lower surface with very fine floccose scales similar to those on the stem from which the annulus was separated.   SPORES 4-5 x 3 micr.   ODOR and TASTE of almonds as in *P. arvensis.*

Gregarious or subcaespitose.   On the leaf-mold, debris, etc., in coniferous regions.   Marquette, Bay View.   August-September.   In-frequent.

The description is adapted from that of Atkinson.   *P. cretacella* is closely related to *P. cretaceus* Fr. which differs, according to Fries' description, in the hollow stem, the blackish-fuscous gills when mature and in that the pileus becomes at length scaly.   Our plants have a glabrous chalky-white pileus and solid stem.   Ricken gives spores of *P. cretaceus* as 8-9 x 5-6 micr.

224. Psalliota rodmani Pk. (EDIBLE)

N. Y. State Mus. Rep. 36, 1884.

Illustrations: Peck, N. Y. Mus. Rep. 48, Pl. 9, Fig. 1-6, 1896.
Marshall, The Mushroom Book, Pl. 25, op. p. 76, 1905.
Atkinson, Mushrooms, Fig. 17, p. 19, 1900.
Hard, Mushrooms, Fig. 250, p. 309, 1908.
Plate XLV of this Report.

PILEUS 4-10 cm. broad, (more often medium size), at first de-pressed-hemispherical to broadly convex, at length subexpanded to plane, firm, dry, *glabrous,* subsilky, *white* or whitish, cream color to subochraceous in age, the margin at first incurved and surpassing the gills. FLESH *thick,* compact, white, not changed by bruising. GILLS free but nearly or quite reaching the stem, abruptly rounded behind, *narrow, width about one-third the thickness of pileus,* crowd-ed, at first dull pink, then purplish-brown, finally blackish-brown, edge entire. STEM *short,* 2-5 cm. long, 1-2.5 cm. thick, *stout, equal, solid,* glabrous below, apex slightly scurfy, white within and with-out, *provided at the middle or below with a band-like, double,* white ANNULUS, with somewhat spreading edges, sometimes narrow and merely grooved, or somewhat lacerated. SPORES minute, 5-6.5 x 4-4.5 micr., broadly elliptical or broadly oval, smooth, purplish-brown, blackish-brown in mass. BASIDIA 30-36 x 8 micr., 4-spored. ODOR and TASTE agreeable.

Solitary on the ground especially along city pavements, or caespitose on lawns or grassy places. Throughout the State. Ann Arbor, Detroit, Holland, Houghton, etc. May-October. Not infre-quent.

A well-marked species, whose margined, band-like annulus, nar-row gills, solid stem and squatty habit characterize it sufficiently. The young gills are white for a much longer time than in *P. campestris.* The pileus may become yellowish-tinged but the flesh is not changed by bruising except that it becomes slightly rufescent in the stem. Peck says the annulus is rather thick at times; in our specimens it was thin and almost membranous. Sometimes it occurs on lawns in dense, caespitose clusters of 50 to 100 individuals; such a growth was observed in Ann Arbor by myself, and the same condition has been reported to me by Dr. L. L. Hubbard at Houghton. It apparently prefers city conditions, as it is almost exclusively found there. It is edible and much prized by those acquainted with it.

225. Psalliota arvensis Fr. (EDIBLE)

Epicrisis, 1836.

Illustrations: Fries, Sverig. ätl. o gift. Swamp, Pl. 4.
    Cooke, Ill., Pl. 523.
    Gillet, Champignons de France, No. 571 (as Pratella).
    Berkeley, Outlines, Pl. 10, Fig. 4.
    Michael, Führer f. Pilzfreunde, Vol. I, No. 61.
    Ricken, Blätterpilze, Pl. 62, Fig. 2.
    Hard, Mushrooms, Pl. 34 and Fig. 252, p. 312.
    Swanton, Fungi, etc., Pl. 38, Fig. 13, op. p. 114.
    Peck, N. Y. State Mus. Rep. 48, Pl. 8,
    Plate XLVI of this Report.

PILEUS 5-20 cm. broad, *large,* subhemispherical at first, then
convex-expanded, disk plane, firm, even, *glabrous,* almost shining, or with appressed, small, fibrillose scales, dry, *white or tinged
yellowish-ochraceous on disk, especially when rubbed,* sometimes
rimose-areolate.   FLESH *thick, white,* at length yellowish-tinged.
GILLS free, crowded, rather broad, *at first whitish then slowly
grayish-pink, finally blackish-brown,* edge entire.   STEM 5-20 cm.
long, 10-30 mm. thick, *stout,* white, *yellowish-stained where bruised,*
silky-shining above the annulus, stuffed by a loose pith, *then hollow,*
equal-cylindrical above the abrupt, small and short bulb, *glabrous;*
ANNULUS thick, rather large, *double,* the lower layer radially
cracked into rather large ochraceous-tinged patches.   SPORES 6-7
x 4-4.5 micr., elliptical, smooth, purplish-brown, blackish-brown in
mass.   ODOR *of anise or of benzaldehyde.*

On the ground, cultivated fields, pastures, on grassy mounds in
woods, in the north on lawns; scattered-gregarious or solitary.
Throughout the State, more frequent in the Northern Peninsula.
July-October. Infrequent in the south part of State.

The "field mushroom" or "ploughed land mushroom" is not limited to cultivated fields.   It was found in several cities along Lake
Superior on lawns.   It is much prized by the inhabitants for the
table.   It is larger than *P. campestris,* and can be distinguished by
the tendency of the center of the cap and base of stem to turn yellowish-ochraceous when rubbed or bruised.   The gills, although pink for
a brief time at one stage, are white much longer than in the other
species.   Also there is often a slight but distinct odor of oil of bitter
almonds when the flesh is crushed.   It is curious to note the various
spore-measurements given by authors.   Ours agree practically with

the size given by Bresadola, Ricken and Massee. On the other hand, Karsten, W. Smith, Schroeter, Saccardo and Peck give them 9 (or 11) x 6 micr. and as one suspects from other remarks about the plant, some other species is probably at times mistaken for it. Ricken, whose figure is numbered, through an error, for that of *P. cretaceus,* emphasizes the point that in his plants the flesh of the stem becomes blackish in age. This has not been observed in our region and the dried specimens do not show it. Its edibility is not to be questioned.

226. Psalliota abruptibulba Pk. (EDIBLE)

N. Y. State Mus. Bull. 94, 1905 (as Agaricus).
N. Y. State Mus. Mem. 4, 1900 (as *Agaricus abruptus*).

Illustrations: Ibid, Pl. 59, Fig. 8-14, 1900.
Hard, Mushrooms, Fig. 254, p. 313, 1908.
Atkinson, Mushrooms, Fig. 19-20, 1900 (as *P. silvicola*).
Marshall, Mushrooms, Pl. 26, op. p. 77, 1905.
Plate XLVII of this Report.

PILEUS 7-15 cm. broad, convex then *expanded-plane,* brittle, dry, glabrous or covered with white, appressed silky fibrils, sometimes obscurely appressed-scaly, *white or creamy-white,* often with dingy yellowish stains on disk, silky-shining. FLESH moderately thick, *turning yellowish when bruised,* especially under the cuticle. GILLS free, *remote,* crowded, *narrow, soon pink,* then dark brown, edge entire. STEM 8-15 cm. long, 8-15 mm. thick, cylindrical or tapering upward from a small, *subabrupt bulb,* relatively slender at times, creamy-white, yellowish when bruised, stuffed then hollow, subglabrous. ANNULUS broad, *double,* smooth above, cracking below into thick, sometimes evanescent, yellowish patches. SPORES 5-6 x 3-4 micr., elliptical, smooth, purple-brown. ODOR and TASTE agreeable.

Scattered or subcaespitose on the ground among fallen leaves in frondose or mixed woods. Throughout the State. July-October. Fairly common.

The species is known by its habitat in woods, its flat cap at maturity which is shining-whitish, the rather slender, abruptly-bulbous stem and the tendency for the flesh of the cap and stem to become yellowish where bruised. It differs from *P. arvensis* in its very different stature; from *P. placomyces* in the absence of any brownish or rufous fibrils on the cap, and from *P. sylvaticus* Fr. by its bulbous stem. Peck first referred it to *P. arvensis* as a variety, later he called it *Agaricus abruptus;* but as this name was pre-empted it was changed to *abruptibulba.* Sometimes the veil appears to be single, but this is merely accidental. McIlvaine says "it has a strong, spicy, mushroom odor and taste and makes a highly flavored dish. It is delicious with meats; the very best mushroom for catsup." Since it occurs in the woods, it must be carefully distinguished from the deadly, white Amanitas.

227. Psalliota placomyces Pk. (Edible)

N. Y. State Mus. Rep. 29, 1878.

Illustrations: N. Y. State Mus. Rep. 48, Pl. 9, Fig. 7-12.
    Atkinson, Mushrooms, Fig. 21-23, pp. 23-24, 1900.
    Hard, Mushrooms, Fig. 255, 257, pp. 314-316, 1908.
    Clements, Minn. Mushrooms, Fig. 42, p. 74, 1910.

PILEUS 5-12 cm. broad, at first broadly ovate, convex-expanded, finally *quite plane,* sometimes subumbonate, not striate, *squamu-lose,* whitish, except where *dotted with the brown scales which are more dense toward the center,* forming a blackish-brown disk, in age the surface may be entirely brown. FLESH white or tinged yellowish under cuticle, *rather thin* except disk. GILLS free, crowded, thin, white at first, *soon pink* then blackish-brown, edge entire. STEM rather long, 7-12 cm. long, tapering upward or *clavate-bulbous,* 4-8 mm. thick, stuffed then hollow, whitish, the bulb sometimes yellowish-stained, glabrous. ANNULUS large, *superior, double,* the under layer cracking radially and leaving patches, finally darkened by the spores. SPORES 5-6 x 3.5-4 micr. (rarely few longer), elliptical-oval, nucleate, smooth, purplish-brown, blackish-brown in mass. ODOR not marked.

Solitary or scattered, sometimes a few caespitose, on the ground in frondose, hemlock or mixed woods, rarely on lawns. Ann Arbor, Lansing, New Richmond, probably throughout the State. July-September. Infrequent, during some seasons rare.

A beautiful plant when one comes across it at its best, with its artistically decorated cap and symmetrical stature. It differs clearly from all others. It is edible although the flesh is thinner than in the preceding species. It is known by the minute brown scales on the flattened cap, the clavate-bulbous stem and the large, flabby annulus. During some seasons, it seems to be absent even under favorable weather conditions.

228. Psalliota subrufescens Pk. (EDIBLE)

N. Y. State Mus. Rep. 46, 1893.

Illustrations: N. Y. State Mus. Rep. 48, Pl. 7, 1896.
Plates XLVIII, XLIX, L, of this Report.

PILEUS 8-18 cm. broad, *large*, at first hemispherical then convex, *finally plane*, becoming wavy and split on the margin, *silky-fibrillose at first*, the fibrillose surface soon breaking up to form *very numerous, appressed, pale tawny fibrillose scales*, disk reddish-brown and not scaly, sometimes rimose, not striate. FLESH white, unchangeable, *rather thin*, soft, fragile at maturity. GILLS free, not very remote, *narrow, crowded*, at first white, then pinkish, finally blackish-brown, edge at first minutely white-fimbriate. STEM 7-15 cm. long, *tapering upward*, 1-1.5 cm. thick at apex, twice as thick below, white and almost glabrous above the annulus, floccose-fibrillose to subscaly toward base, *stuffed by soft white pith then hollow*, the bulb varying clavate to more or less abrupt. ANNULUS very voluminous, reflexed, *double*, rather distant from the apex of the stem, smooth and white above, with soft, floccose, pale tawny scales below, becoming dark from spores. SPORES 6-7.5 x 4-5 micr., elliptical, smooth, dark purple brown, blackish-brown in mass. STERILE CELLS on edge of gills numerous, subcylindrical, very narrow, hyaline. ODOR when crushed, strong of almonds. TASTE of green nuts.

Caespitose, on masses of decaying fallen leaves in frondose woods and in richly manured hot-house beds. (It is also cultivated for the market.)

Ann Arbor, Detroit. August-October. Rather rare.

Our largest Psalliota, probably at times surpassing the size given above. The original description was made by Peck from old material, and later (48th Rep.) he points out that the cap is coated with fibrils which at length give it the scaly character. Peck's description of this species is, therefore, misleading, and probably his specimens did not show the full development of the scales shown in our photographs. Some of our specimens were sent to Dr. Peck who pronounced them *P. subrufescens* Pk. None of our other Psalliotas could be easily confused with *P. subrufescens* when it appears in the woods. Of the European species, *P. augusta* Fr. and *P. perrara* Bres. approach it in size. These are at once distinct, according to Ricken's descriptions, by their paler caps and larger spores. The spores of *P. augusta* are 12-14 x 6-7 micr., per Ricken; of *P. perrara,* 8-10 x 5 micr., per Bresadola. *P. silvatica* Fr. differs in the smaller size, the simple annulus and differently colored pileus. *P. subrufescens* sometimes appears in hot-house beds and has been reduced to cultivation, where its characters seem to be somewhat changed, so that Peck has made a lengthy comparison between it and *P. campestris,* to which the wild form has no close resemblance.

Section II. Univelares. Annulus simple, not with thick floccose-patches on under side.

229. Psalliota campestris Fr. (EDIBLE)

Syst. Myc., 1821.

Illustrations: (Selected, very numerous.)
>   Fries, Sverig. ätl. o. gift. Swamp., Pl. 5.
>   Cooke, Ill., Pl. 526.
>   Gillet, Champignons de France, No. 573 (As Pratella).
>   Michael, Führer f. Pilzfreunde, Vol. I, No. 60.
>   Bresadola, I. Fung. mang. e. velenos, Pl. 53.
>   Marshall, The Mushroom Book, Pl. 23, op. 74 and Pl. 24, op. 75, 1905.
>   Gibson, Our Edible Toadstools and Mushrooms, Pl. 5, p. 83 and Pl. 6, p. 89.
>   Murrill, Mycologia, Vol. I, Pl. 3, Fig. 1.
>   Hard, Mushrooms, Fig. 248 and 249, p. 307, 1908.
>   Atkinson, Mushrooms, Figs. 1-8, pp. 2-8, 1900.
>   Atkinson, Bot. Gaz., Vol. 43, p. 264 et. al., Pl. 7, 8, 9, 10, 11 and 12 (showing all stages of development).

PILEUS 4-7 cm. broad (occasionally larger, especially when cultivated), at first flattened hemispherical then convex-expanded or nearly plane, firm, even, *glabrous* or at length minutely floccose-silky or delicately fibrillose-scaly, dry, *white* (scaly forms are brownish, etc.), the margin extending beyond gills, edge often fringed when fresh by the tearing of the partial veil.   FLESH thick, white, not changing when bruised. GILLS free but not remote, rounded behind, ventricose, not broad, close, almost from the very *first delicate pink, then deep flesh color,* finally purplish-brown *to blackish,* edge even. STEM 5-7 cm. long, thick, usually *subequal or tapering downward,* rarely subbulbous, solid-stuffed,

usually rather short and firm, *white* or whitish, glabrous. AN-
NULUS above and near the middle, edge lacerate, often evanescent
in age, derived from the thin, simple, white, partial veil. SPORES
elliptical, 7-9 x 4.5-5.5 micr., purple-brown, *blackish-brown in mass,*
smooth. ODOR and TASTE agreeable.

On the ground in lawns, gardens, golf-links, roadsides, especially
in sheep-pastures, sometimes in cultivated fields.

Throughout the State. Less frequent in spring, usually in July-
October. Uncommon except locally during some seasons, rare at
other times.

This is the well-known "pink-gilled" or "edible" mushroom, by
many people in this country considered in addition to the "sponge
mushroom," *Morchella esculenta,* as the only mushroom safe to eat;
all others are dubbed "toadstools." Some persons, however, know
and eat a larger number of kinds; again, all others are "toadstools"
to them. The word toadstool, therefore, means nothing definite; it
only expresses the ignorance of people concerning those fungi of
which they are afraid. The two words refer to the same group of
plants and can be used interchangeably.

In the young or "button" stage the gills are soon tinged pink,
and as it is possible to mistake the button of the deadly, white
Amanita verna for it at this stage, every button should be broken
open while collecting. By the time the veil breaks the pink color
of the gills is quite marked. All who use this mushroom, should
read carefully the remarks under Amanita.

This mushroom has been eaten from time immemorial, and its
artificial cultivation carried on extensively for centuries. In and
around large cities, large establishments exist to raise it for the
market, selling it for 75c to 90c a pound in this country. "The an-
nual product of the Chicago mushroom beds is said to be from
sixty to seventy-five tons." (Nat. Hist. Surv. of Chicago Acad.
Sci. Bull. VII, part 1, p. 90.) Special underground mushroom
houses, caves, abandoned mines, cellars, etc., have been adopted for
the cultivation of this mushroom. Duggar states that in 1901 the
total product of the mushroom industry in the environs of Paris,
France, was 5,000 tons or 10,000,000 pounds. This shows the
extent to which Europeans eat mushrooms as compared with
our American consumption. About the same ratio exists in the
use of the many different edible wild species. In this country we
have hardly begun to realize the immense amount of palatable food
that goes to waste in our fields and woods.

Numerous varieties of *P. campestris* have been described. With us the white variety is the common form, although an occasional patch of the variety with brownish and more fibrillose caps may be found. The caps are apparently not as large as in more moist climates, although occasionally one finds large plants in cultivated fields. Var. *villaticus* Fr. has been raised to specific rank by Bresadola; the pileus of this species is large and scaly and the stem is scaly and coated or subvolvate by the inferior veil. I have not seen it. No discussion is given here of the cultivated varieties. Those interested in their cultivation should read Duggar's "The Principles of Mushroom Growing, etc." Bull. No. 85, Bureau of Plant Ind., U. S. Dept. Agr., or the chapter in Atkinson's Mushrooms, last edition.

230. Psalliota silvatica Fr. (Edible)

Epicrisis, 1836.

Illustrations: Bresadola, Fung. Trid., Vol. I, Pl. 90.
    Cooke, Ill., Pl. 530 (=*P. perrara* per Bres.)
    Michael, Führer f. Pilzfreunde, Vol. II, No. 68.

"PILEUS 8-11 cm. broad, campanulate then expanded, *at first cinereous* then yellowish-whitish with a rufous-fuscous center, *covered by brown scales.* FLESH rather thick except margin. GILLS free, remote, crowded, white at first, then rosy-flesh color, *at length reddish-cinnamon.* STEM 6-9 cm. long, 1-1.5 cm. thick, *hollow,* whitish, glabrous, or. subfibrillose, equal or with a bulbous base, bulb sometimes marginate, white within when broken, yellowish at apex, slightly rose-red on sides. ANNULUS *simple,* ample, distant, superior, white, substriate, flocculose. SPORES 6-7 x 3.5-4 micr., elliptical, incarnate-fulvous. BASIDIA clavate, 25 x 6-7 micr. ODOR and TASTE agreeable."

Reported by Longyear. In woods.

The description is adopted from Bresadola. The descriptions in our mushroom books are scarcely satisfactory. The figures of Cooke and Gillet are said to depart from the characteristics of the plant. It seems to be rare, and I have never collected it. The gray color of the young plant and the truly brown color of the scales, the hollow stem and spores ought to make it recognizable. Ricken emphasizes the change of gills and flesh to blood-red when bruised and considers *P. haemorrhoidaria* as an autumnal form. This complicates matters, especially in the absence of specimens of our own.

231   Psalliota hæmorrhodaria Fr.   (EDIBLE)

Hymen. Europ., 1885.

Illustrations: Cooke, Ill., Pl. 531.
Gillet, Champignons de France, No. 577 (as Pratella).
N. Y. State Mus. Rep. 54, Pl. 75, 1901.

PILEUS 5-10 cm. broad, at first subglobose to subovate then campanulate-expanded, nearly plane, covered by rather dense, fibrillose, brownish-gray, appressed scales, sometimes glabrous toward margin and paler, margin subpersistently incurved. FLESH white, *turning pink to blood-red when broken,* thick on disk, thin on margin. GILLS free, moderately broad, crowded, white at first, then rosy-flesh-color, finally dark brown. STEM 5-10 cm. long, 8-15 mm. thick, subequal, rarely bulbous, *stuffed then hollow,* floccose-fibrillose, glabrescent, white or pallid, darker in age. ANNULUS large, pendulous, persistent, superior, simple, white, at length colored by spores. SPORES 6-7 x 4 micr., elliptical, purplish-brown, smooth. STERILE CELLS on edge of gills, clavate, enlarged-rounded above. ODOR and TASTE agreeable.

Caespitose or scattered, on the ground or about the base of trees in low places in mixed woods, usually near birch and maple trees. Marquette, New Richmond. August-October.   Infrequent in the coniferous regions of the State.

Easily known by the change of the flesh to red, which color fresh plants immediately show when broken.   This character is said to be found also in the seashore mushroom, *P. halophila* Pk. which has a solid stem and has not been found inland.   Peck says its flavor when cooked is similar to *P. campestris,* and gives to the milk in which it is stewed a brownish color.   Ricken considers it a mere form of *P. silvatica,* but describes the latter differently from most authors.   It is certainly distinct.

232.   Psalliota micromegetha Pk.   (EDIBLE)

N. Y. State Mus. Rep. 54, 1901.   (As *Agaricus pusillus*).

Illustration: N. Y. State Mus. Bull. 116, Pl. 107, Fig. 1-6, 1907.

"PILEUS 2-7 cm. broad, fragile, convex becoming plane, some-times subdepressed in center, dry, *silky-fibrillose or fibrillose-scaly, grayish-brown or brown in center,* often with yellowish or ferruginous stains. FLESH white or whitish, *not changing color where wounded.* GILLS free, close, *grayish at first,* soon pinkish, finally brown. STEM 2-5 cm. long, 6-10 mm. thick, equal or slightly tapering upward, sometimes bulbous, stuffed or hollow, slightly fibrillose, white. ANNULUS *slight,* often evanescent. SPORES broadly elliptic or subglobose, 5 x 4 micr. Edible."

Solitary or caespitose, on grassy ground, in sandy or clay soil. September-November. Detroit.

The description is adapted from the revised one in N. Y. State Bull. 116, p. 44, 1907. The original description was made largely from smaller plants sent to Peck from Detroit by Dr. R. H. Stevens, and named *Agaricus pusillus;* later the name was changed to that given above, meaning small to large in size. I have not seen it.

233. Psalliota comtula Fr. (EDIBLE)

Epicrisis, 1836.

Illustrations: Fries, Icones, Pl. 130.
      Cooke, Ill., Pl. 533.
      Ricken, Blätterpilze, Pl. 62, Fig. 1 (as *P. rusiophylla*).
      Atkinson, Mushrooms, Fig. 24, p. 25, 1900.

PILEUS 2-4.5 cm. broad, convex-subexpanded, subumbonate or umbo obsolete, silky, creamy-white to grayish-white, *tinged with yellowish hues on disk,* sometimes rufous-tinged. FLESH whitish, becoming ochraceous under cuticle, thickish on disk. GILLS free, broader in front, narrowed behind, up to 5-6 mm. broad, dingy incarnate, at length smoky-umber. STEM 3-5 cm. long, 2.5-5 mm. thick, subequal, hollow, innately silky, pallid or slightly yellowish-stained. ANNULUS *median,* membranaceous, thin, whitish, often *subevanescent.* SPORES 5-6 x 3-3.5 micr., elliptical, smooth, dark purple-brown. BASIDIA 20 x 6 micr. STERILE CELLS on edge of gills inflated-clavate. ODOR not marked.

On the ground among fallen leaves in pine and beech woods. New Richmond. September. Infrequent.

The description shows a slight variation from that of other authors. Atkinson gives the spore measurements 3-4 x 2-3 micr. Ricken considers Fries' plant as identical with *P. rusiophylla* Lasch, and also gives small spores and basidia. Except for the pale color of the cap, our plants could be referred to Ricken's *P. sagata* Fr. The species needs further study.

234. Psalliota diminutiva Pk. (Edible)

N. Y. State Mus. Rep. 26, 1874.

Illustrations: N. Y. State Mus. Rep. 54, Pl. 74, Fig. 1-8, 1901.
Plate L of this report.

PILEUS 2-5 cm. broad, fragile, *convex then plane,* sometimes subdepressed, silky-fibrillose, the *fibrils forming delicate, pinkish-drab to reddish-brown scales toward center and on disk,* paler and denuded on margin, white or tinged gray under fibrils, not striate. FLESH thin, whitish. GILLS free, not remote, thin, close, moderately broad, ventricose, *edge entire.* STEM 3-5 cm. long (rarely longer), 2-5 mm. thick, equal or tapering upwards, stuffed by delicate white pith then hollow, glabrous, innately silky, even, whitish, sometimes subbulbous at base. ANNULUS delicate, thin, rather persistent, narrow, whitish. STERILE CELLS on edge none. BASIDIA 27 x 5-6 micr., 4-spored. ODOR and TASTE none.

Solitary or gregarious on mossy ground, or among leaf-mould in low moist frondose or mixed woods. Throughout the State. August-September (rarely in spring). Frequent.

This dainty little Psalliota is known by its delicate pinkish or reddish fibrils on the cap, the entire gills and persistent annulus. It is not supposed to possess, like the preceding, the yellowish stains on cap and base of stem, but specimens are found which have this character which do not seem to belong elsewhere. As they are rather scattered in occurrence no sufficient study has been made of these forms. It may be that several little species run into each other. Peck says they are very palatable when fried in butter, but their small size does not attract the collector who is looking for a meal.

235. Psalliota echinata Fr.

Syst. Myc., 1821.

Illustrations: Patouillard, Tab. Analyt., No. 155 (as Pholiota).
Cooke, Ill., Pl. 395 (as Inocybe).
Ricken, Blätterpilze, Pl. 31, Fig. 6 (as Inocybe).
Montagne, in Ann. Sci. Nat. 1836, Pl. 10, Fig. 3 (as *Agaricus oxyosmus*).

PILEUS 1-3 cm. broad, obtusely campanulate then expanded, margin at first incurved and somewhat appendiculate, then recurved, densely covered with smoky-brown, minute-floccose, wart-like or *pointed scales,* not striate, sometimes rimose in age. FLESH whitish at first, *then reddish,* thin. GILLS free, thin, narrow, crowded, bright pink to old rose-color, *finally dark purplish-red.* STEM 2-3 cm. long, 1-3 mm. thick, equal, stuffed with loose white fibrils then tubular, *elsewhere soon blood-red within,* surface floccosely-pulverulent with a smoky bloom below the annulus, often mycelioid-swollen at base. VEIL floccose-submembranaceus, easily lacerated, concolor, forming an imperfect ANNULUS. Spores minute, elliptical, 4-5 x 2-2.5 micr., smooth, *with a tinge of purple-brown* under microscope, many immature and hyaline, *cinnabar-purple brown in mass.* CYSTIDIA none. *Trama* of gills composed of large cells, about 20 micr. in diameter. ODOR and TASTE slight, not of cucumber, even after crushing.

Subcaespitose or gregarious, in a green-house of the Michigan Agricultural College, East Lansing. September. Rare.

As shown by the references, this plant has been placed in three different genera. It is therefore difficult of identification, the more so because of its rarity. It seems that the spores mature slowly, or perhaps in some regions or under hot-house conditions do not take on a purplish tinge. Under the microscope some of the spores of our specimens showed the usual delicate tint in the exospore which is characteristic of many of this group. Fries (in Hymen. Europ.) says he never saw them rosy. Patouillard says they are hyaline under the microscope but that on a white background they appear tawny ("fauve"). Ricken applies the word "erdfarbig." All the illustrations picture our plant well, which, to quote Berkeley, "is a most curious species." In Europe it occurs in hot-houses almost exclusively.

Stropharia Fr.

(From the Greek, *strophos,* a sword-belt, referring to the annulus.)

Purple-brown-spored. Stem fleshy, *confluent with the pileus;* annulus membranous or fibrillose-floccose. Gills *attached.* SPORES purple-brown or violet. Pileus usually *viscid.*

Putrescent, terrestrial or coprinophilous, of medium size, in fields, barnyards, dung hills or forest. They correspond to Armillaria of the white-spored, and Pholiota of the ochre-brown-spored groups in the adnate gills and annulate stem; differing from Hypholoma in that the veil collapses on the stem to form an annulus, instead of remaining as a fringe on the margin of the pileus.

It would be preferable, in my judgment, to limit the genus to those species with a viscid pellicle; but with the data at hand it seems best to defer this arrangement. Ricken divides the genus by the size of the spores, but this method neglects other more important morphological characters. On the other hand, some species could be better located in the genus Hypholoma as is done by Ricken for *S. caput-medusae* Fr., *S. scobinaceum* Fr. and *S. battarae* Fr. There are then two sections: Viscipelles and Spintrigeri.

Key to the Species

(a)   Pileus with bluish-green or olive shades, viscid.
  (b)   Stem 4-7 mm. thick, greenish-blue; pileus thick, green; on debris in woods. 236. *S. aeruginosa* Fr.
  (bb)   Stem 1.5-2 mm. thick, long and slender; pileus thin, olvaceous-gray; on dung and mud. (See 268. *Psilocybe uda* Fr.)
(aa)   Pileus without green or olive.
  (b)   Stem ventricose-radicating; pileus umber to tawny-alutaceus, viscid. 237. *S. ventricosa* Mass.
  (bb)   Stem not radicating.
    (c)   Parasitic on Coprinus, whitish. 244. *S. epimyces* (Pk.) Atk.
    (cc)   Not parasitic; pileus viscid or subviscid.
      (d)   Growing on dung.
        (e)   Pileus citron-yellow, 2-5 cm. broad; common.
          (f)   Pileus persistently hemispherical. 242. *S. semiglobata* Fr.
          (ff)   Pileus convex-subexpanded. 241. *S. stercoraria* Fr.
        (ee)   Pileus ochraceous-brown, 1-2.5 cm. broad, conic-campanulate. 243. *S. umbonatescens* Pk.
      (dd)   Not on dung.
        (e)   Pileus 5-10 cm. broad, cinnamon-drab, viscid, stem squarrose-scaly. 238. *S. depilata* Fr.
        (e)   Pileus 1-4 cm. broad.
          (f)   Gills strongly violet-purplish; pileus ochraceous-pallid. 240. *S. coronilla* Bres.
          (f)   Gills strongly gray-tinged; pileus white to buff. 239. *S. albonitens* Fr.

Section I. Viscipelles. Pileus provided with a distinct gelatinous pellicle, hence viscid; glabrous or scaly.

**Growing on the ground or on debris.*

236.   Stropharia aeruginosa Fr. (SUSPECTED)

Syst. Myc., 1821.

Illustrations: Cooke, Ill., Pl. 551.
    Gillet, Champignons de France, No. 650.
    Ricken, Blätterpilze, Pl. 63, Fig. 4.·
    Pattouillard, Tab. Analyt., No. 231.
    Swanton, Fungi, Pl. 38, Fig. 7-9.
    Harper, Wis. Acad. Sci. Trans., Vol. 17, pt. II, Pl. 64, 1913.

PILEUS 2-5 cm. broad (often rather small in our climate). Campanulate-convex, at length plane, subumbonate, *covered with verdigris-green, thick gluten,* hence viscid, sometimes dotted with scattered, white scales, especially on margin, at length fading to yellowish, pellicle separable. FLESH pallid, or tinged blue, rather soft, thickish. GILLS broadly adnate, sometimes emarginate-sinuate, rather broad, close, whitish at first, soon drab-gray or reddish-gray, finally purplish-chocolate-brown, *edge white and minutely flocculose.* STEM 5-7 cm. long, 4-7 mm. thick, equal, hollow, soft, *greenish-blue, viscid,* at first scaly or fibrillose below the annulus. ANNULUS distant˙from apex, narrow, submembranous, here and there floccose, subevanescent. SPORES pale, smooth, 7-8 x 4-5 micr., oval-elliptical. STERILE CELLS on edge of gills, clavate, lanceolate.

On debris in hemlock woods, and occasionally in frondose woods. Houghton, New Richmond, Detroit. August-October. Infrequent.

Although this is a brightly colored and striking plant, we have come across it infrequently, but in Europe it is said to be very common in forest, field and garden. The gills sometimes run down the apex of the stem in lines. The annulus is sometimes lacking. Our plants are well shown by the figures of European authors, and seem to agree perfectly. It is said to be *poisonous.* It is probably more common northward.

237. Stropharia ventricosa Massee

British Fungus Flora, Vol. I, p. 400, 1892.

Illustration: Cooke, Ill., Pl. 1188 (as *S. merdaria* var. *major*).

PILEUS 3-5 cm. broad, parabolic then convex-expanded, margin for long time decurved, *very viscid,* somewhat uneven when young, glabrescent and shining *pale umber at first, then tawny-alutaceus.* FLESH white, thick on disk, abruptly thin on margin. GILLS adnate, at length decurrent by tooth, close, *rather narrow,* pallid at first, then mouse-gray with purplish tinge, finally purplish-brown. STEM 8-12 cm. or more long, *ventricose-radicating,* up to 15 mm. thick at broadest part, thinner above, rooting-attenuate at base, sometimes subequal, white at first, becoming dingy yellowish, dry, *covered up to the annulus by squarrose scales,* markedly striate above, stuffed, whitish within. ANNULUS persistent, white, large, striate above. SPORES 9-12 x 5-6 micr., elliptical, smooth, with a purple tinge under the microscope, brown in mass. CYSTIDIA oval or short ventricose, obtuse at apex, about 45 x 24 micr., hyaline.

Caespitose on very decayed debris about stumps and roots in forest of hemlock, maple, etc. Bay View. September. Rare.

This has very much the stature of Cooke's figure of *Pholiota radicosa* (Ill., Pl. 361) and grows in similar places, but the pileus of our plants has a glabrous, viscid pellicle, and the spores are purple-tinged. The odor was not noted. The root-like prolongation pushes deep down into the debris and the mycelium was attached to dead roots. This agrees so well with Massee's description that I have ventured to refer it thither, in spite of its larger size and more scaly stem.

238. Stropharia depilata Fr.

Hymen. Europ., 1874.

Illustrations: Harper, Trans. Wis. Acad. Sci., Vol. 16, Pl. 62 and 63, 1913.

PILEUS 4-12 cm. broad, firm, convex to plane or broadly umbonate, obtuse, glabrous, *viscid*, light cinnamon-drab (Ridg.) when young and *with a smoky tinge*, at length dark olive-buff or pinkish-buff (Ridg.), even on the decurved margin which is sometimes appendiculate when young. FLESH whitish, thick except the thin margin. GILLS adnate, often subdecurrent and running down the stem in lines, close to crowded, broad, pallid at first, *soon pale purple-drab* (Ridg.) or *ashy*, at length purplish-black. STEM 6-12 cm. long, 8-15 mm. thick, subequal or subventricose, stuffed, whitish within and without, becoming yellowish-tinged, *clothed below annulus by subsquarrose, lacerate, fibrillose or floccose whitish or creamy-yellow scales*, apex glabrescent, often deeply immersed at base. ANNULUS distant, membranous, persistent, at first white, firm and erect, then deflected and clove-brown (Ridg.). SPORES elliptical, smooth, 9-12 x 5-6.5 micr., dark-gray with tint of purple under microscope. CYSTIDIA none. Edge of gills with sterile cells. ODOR none. TASTE tardily disagreeable.

Solitary or subgregarious, rarely subcaespitose; among debris or about logs and stumps in mixed woods of balsam, spruce, birch, etc. Northern Michigan. Frequent locally. September-October.

The large size, scaly stem and slate-gray gills are the striking characteristics of this species. Harper reports it from Neebish Island. It is also an inhabitant of the Adirondack Mountains, where I have collected it. It seems to fruit preferably in the autumn and in dry weather.

239. Stropharia albonitens Fr. (SUSPECTED)

Monographia, 1863.

Illustrations: Fries, Icones, Pl. 130, Fig. 2.
Ricken, Blätterpilze, Pl. 63, Fig. 3.

PILEUS 1-3 cm. broad, *campanulate,* then plane-subumbonate, with a *viscid* pellicle, *white to buff,* sometimes yellowish-tinged on disk, becoming gray on margin, shining when dry, glabrous, even. FLESH white, moist, thin. GILLS adnate becoming emarginate, *subdistant,* rather broad, ventricose, *gray to purplish-gray* then darker, edge minutely white-fimbriate. STEM elongated, 3-7 cm. long, 2-3 mm. thick, equal, stuffed with a white pith then hollow, whitish, *tinged yellow in age,* yellowish within, dry, pruinose or flocculose. ANNULUS superior, white, evanescent, soon colored by spores. SPORES 7-9 x 4-5 micr., elliptical, smooth, purple-brown in mass. CYSTIDIA. ODOR none.

On the ground in open, grassy woods. Ann Arbor. October.

Known by the gray color of the gills and the yellowish tinge to the stem in age.

240. Stropharia coronilla Bres. (SUSPECTED)

Fung. Trid., Vol. I, 1881 (Fr., Syst. Myc., 1821).

Illustrations: Ricken, Blätterpilze, Pl. 63, Fig. 5.
Patouillard, Tab. Analyt., No. 232.
Cooke, Ill., Pl. 535.

PILEUS 2-4 cm. broad, convex-expanded, subviscid, even, *ochraceous-whitish,* glabrous, subpruinose when dry. FLESH white, rather thick. GILLS adnate, rounded behind or sinuate, ventricose, close, moderately broad, *fuscous-violaceous then purple-blackish,* edge white-fimbriate. STEM 3-4 cm. long, 3-5 mm. thick, equal or slightly tapering upward, stuffed then hollow, dry, white, minutely flocculose above the annulus, fibrillose below then shining. AN-NULUS thickish-membranous, *persistent,* distant from apex, *striate above.* SPORES 8-9.5 x 4-5 micr., elliptic-ovate, violet-purple under microscope, smooth. CYSTIDIA short, broadly clavate, rounded but apiculate above. ODOR slight, unpleasant. On the ground in woods of white pine and beech. New Richmond. September. Infrequent.

This differs from *S. albonitens* in the strong violet color of gills and spores. The cap is more ochraceous and more convex. The gills are more crowded. This seems to be closely related to *S. melasperma* Fr., and the cystidia figured for that species by Patouillard (Tab. Analyt., No. 555) are characteristic of our specimens. *S. bilamellata* Pk. is a much larger plant, with larger spores, and the thick annulus has radiating gill-like ridges on its upper surface. (See Peck, Pl. 112, Fig. 5-10, N. Y. State Mus. Bull. 122, 1908 and Harper, Wis. Acad. Sci. Trans., Vol. 17, Pt. II, Pl. 65.)

**Growing on dung.

241. Stropharia stercoraria Fr. (EDIBLE)

Syst. Myc., 1821.

Illustrations: Cooke, Ill., Pl. 538.
        Harper, Trans. Wis. Acad. Sci., Vol. 17, Pt. II, Pl. 67.

PILEUS 2-6 cm. broad, convex-hemispherical, *then broadly convex or subexpanded,* viscid from the separable, gelatinous pellicle, glabrous, even, *citron-yellow,* buff or whitish when dry, often stained by the spores. FLESH white or tinged yellow, thin on margin, soft. GILLS adnate at length subdecurrent, *very broad,* close, umber-fuscous to purplish-olivaceous or blackish, *edge white flocculose.* STEM 6-18 cm. long, 2-6 mm. thick, *elongated-cylindrical,* stuffed by white pith then hollow, base thicker, yellowish-white, covered up to the evanescent, narrow *annulus* by the floccose-scaly thin remains of a membranaceus veil. SPORES large, elongated-elliptical, 15-21 x 8-12 micr., variable in size, smooth, violet-purple under microscope, blackish-purple in mass. "CYSTIDIA *on the sides* and edge of the gills, lanceolate, 50-70 x 12-18 micr." (Ricken.) TASTE of pellicle slightly bitter.

On dung hills, manure piles or similar places; gregarious.

Throughout the State. May-October. Common, apparently more common than the next, at least in southern Michigan.

So close in appearance to *S. semiglobata* that they are difficult of easy separation. *S. stercoraria* is apparently almost limited to dung or manure, while the other has a wider range. It differs microscopically according to Ricken, by the presence of cystidia which occur also on the sides of the gills and which are absent in *S. semiglobata* except on the edge. The pileus of the latter is more persistently hemispherical. *A sterile form* has been observed, in every particular like the above, except that the gills remained pale yellow or straw-color; spores were lacking at full expansion of the pileus and the hymenium was composed of large, inflated, sterile cells in place of the basidia.

242. Stropharia semiglobata Fr.   (Edible)

Syst. Myc., 1821.

Illustrations: Cooke, Ill., Pl. 539.
> Gillet, Champignons de France, No. 651.
> Patouillard, Tab. Analyt., No. 234.
> Ricken, Blätterpilze, Pl. 63, Fig. 2.
> Atkinson, Mushrooms, Fig. 30, p. 31, 1900.
> Hard, Mushrooms, Fig. 260, p. 320, 1908.
> Murrill, Mycologia, Vol. 4, Pl. 56, Fig. 3.

PILEUS 1-4 cm. broad, *persistently hemispherical,* very viscid from the pellicle, glabrous and naked, even, citron-yellow, shining when dry, faded in age, stained purplish-black by spores. FLESH thick on disk, thin on margin, pallid, soft. GILLS broadly adnate, *very broad,* close to subdistant, olive-gray to purplish-brown, clouded blackish, edge minutely white floccose. STEM 5-12 cm. long, 2-5 mm. thick, subequal or cylindrical, straight, *hollow,* rigid, often viscid when young or fresh, covered below up to the narrow annulus by the thin, membranous, flocculose veil. SPORES elliptical, 15-18 x 9-10 micr., smooth, violet-purple under the microscope, brownish-purple in mass. CYSTIDIA *only on edge of gills,* short-filamentous, 30-45 x 3-4 micr. (Ricken.)

On dung hills and grassy places in the open. Probably throughout the State. May-October. Frequent.

See notes on the preceding.

243.   Stropharia umbonatescens Pk.   (Suspected)

N. Y. State Mus. Rep. 30, 1878.

Illustrations: Harper, Wis. Acad. Sci. Trans., Vol. 7, Pt. II, Pl. 65, B.
> Plate LI of this Report.

PILEUS 1-2.5 cm. broad, *conico-campanulate,* at length more or less mammilately umbonate, with a viscid pellicle, pale ochraceous-brownish or grayish on margin, *umbo bright ochraceous brown to reddish-brown,* even or obscurely substriate, shining, glabrous. FLESH thin, pallid. GILLS adnate to adnate-decurrent, *broad to subtriangular,* close, at first whitish then gray, finally purplish-brown to blackish. STEM 5-10 cm. long, slender, equal, stuffed then hollow, toughish, *pallid, tinged ochraceous,* covered at first by thin, obscure, scaly remnants of the veil up to the fugacious AN-NULUS. SPORES 17-19 x 10 micr., elliptical, smooth, purple-brown under microscope, dark purplish in mass. ODOR *often strong of radish or foetid.*

Gregarious on dung hills or about manure heaps. September-October. Ann Arbor. Not infrequent.

Much more slender and with a thinner, smaller cap than the two preceding; also, the cap is very different in shape. Its rather foetid odor and large spores distinguish it from others. It is close to *S. paradoxa* P. Henn. in the shape of pileus and size of spores.

Section II. Spintrigeri. Pileus without a distinct pellicle, usually innately fibrillose, not viscid.

244. Stropharia epimyces (Pk.) Atk.

Plant World, Vol. X, Figs. 21-24, p. 121, 1907.
N. Y. State Mus. Rep. 35, 1884 (as *Panaeolus epimyces* Pk.).
Jour. Mycol., Vol. 8, 1902 (as *Stropharia coprinophila* Atk.).

Illustrations: Atkinson, Plant World.
    Hard,. Mushrooms, Fig. 227, p. 341, 1908 (as Panoeolus).
    Miss Sherman, Jour. Mycol., Vol. II, Pl. 80, opp. p. 169, 1905
        (as Panoeolus).

PILEUS 2-6 cm. broad, rarely larger, at first globose-oval, then convex-expanded, sometimes margin is elevated in age, silky-fibril-lose, *white* then dingy, even, margin at times appendiculate. FLESH thick except the thin margin, white. GILLS narrowly adnate, rather narrow, broader in front, close, thin, grayish at first then blackish-brown, *edge white-fimbriate.* STEM 2-7 cm. long, 5-15 mm. thick, fleshy, equal or tapering upward, solid-stuffed then hollow, soft, flocculose-mealy, striate, *white-annulate near the base* from the white floccose-veil, often abruptly obconic at base where it is in-serted in the depression (often volva-like) of the host mushroom. SPORES oval-elliptical, 7-8.5 x 3.5-5 micr., smooth, *dark purple-*

brown under microscope, almost black in mass.   CYSTIDIA on sides and edge of gills, clavate or subventricose on a slender stalk, obtuse at apex, 40-60 x 10-14 micr., abundant on edge.   BASIDIA 25-35 x 7-9 micr., 4-spored.   ODOR and TASTE mild.

Parasitic, from one to seven on the host; on *Coprinus atramentarius* and *Coprinus comatus.*

Ann Arbor, Detroit, Port Huron.   September-November.   Infrequent.

This curious Agaric, like *Nyctalis asterophora* and the European *Volvaria loveiana,* seems to have no other home than on the foundation furnished by some species of another Agaric.   Rumors have come to me that it occurs also on *C. micaceous,* but no specimens have been seen.   It is distributed over northeastern North America, having been seen in the states of New York, Michigan, Wisconsin, Minnesota and by Dr. Pennington in Canada as far west as Winnipeg.   It is a good Stropharia, although at first referred by Peck to Panoeolus with a suggestion that it might be put under Hypholoma. As Atkinson has shown (Plant World), the nature of the veil and annulus and the purple tinge to the spores are Stropharia characters.   The host mushrooms are deformed and may not develop sufficiently to be recognized.   Excellent specimens were received from Mr. A. W. Goodwin of Port Huron.   Harper has pointed out (Mycologia, Vol. 5, p. 167) that the figures of an European species, *Pilosace algeriensis* Fr., by Lanzi (Fung. Mang., Pl. 67, Fig. 3) may represent our plant.   An examination of these figures has convinced me that there is a probability that they illustrate our species.   It remains very doubtful, however, whether Lanzi's plant when fresh had free gills.   In any case, our plant is not a Pilosace, although collectors may disagree as to whether it is a Stropharia or a Hypholoma.

Hypholoma Fr.

(From the Greek, *hypha,* a web, and *loma,* a fringe; referring to the fringe left by veil on margin of pileus.)

Purple-brown-spored. Stem fleshy, confluent with the pileus; gills *adnate-seceding.* Veil *breaking away from the stem, leaving shreds or a silky border on the margin of the pileus,* flocculose-fibrillose. Margin of pileus at first incurved.

Putrescent fungi, growing on decaying wood or on the ground, often very caespitose around stumps or decayed roots of trees.   The genus corresponds to Tricholoma of the white-spored group, in the lack of a true annulus and by the attached gills. Many of the Hypholomas are, however, much thinner and more fragile than the Tricholomas. It differs from Stropharia and Psalliota in that the veil which is cortinate remains as a fringe on the margin of the pileus instead of forming an annulus on the stem. It is more difficult to separate the thin-capped species from Psilocybe. The latter differs in some cases only in a relative sense. The cortina-like veil in Psilocybe is only very slightly developed and leaves no shreds on the margin of the pileus or on the surface as in the hygrophanous species of Hypholoma. An account of the development of *H. sub-lateritium* by Miss Allen (Ann. Myc., Vol. 4, p. 387, 1906) shows that the young button is surrounded by a universal veil. This is probably also true of the hygrophanous species where this outer veil often leaves flocculent particles on the surface of the young cap.

The genus is divided into two sections whose species are notably different in their general appearance and the texture of the flesh. In the first section the PILEUS is thick, compact and firm; in the second, it is rather thin, somewhat fragile and soft. The former have usually brighter colors, while the latter are brownish, gray or white. The GILLS vary much in color during the course of their development. This character is often used to separate the species, but is less reliable for the purpose than in the genus Cortinarius. The STEM is fleshy, and in the fragile forms it is soon hollow. The SPORES are elliptical except in *H. populina* Britz. var., where they are variously shaped. In *H. velutinum* and *H. rugocephalum* they are more or less tuberculate. Many species have CYSTIDIA on the sides of the gills, or sac-shaped sterile cells on the edge. The large fleshy ones are *edible,* although at times they develop a disagreeable bitter taste. This is thought by some to be due to the passage of the larvae of insects through the flesh; needless to say, such bitter plants should not be eaten. Of the thin ones, *H. incertum* and allied forms are much sought after.

Key to the Species

(A) Pileus firm, compact, not hygrophanous, dull reddish or yellow; caespitose.
  (a) Pileus dark brick-red, especially on disk.
    (b) Gills at first whitish. 245. *H. sublateritium* Fr.
    (bb) Gills at first yellow. 245. *H. sublateritium* var. *perplexum* Pk.
  (aa) Pileus yellow or yellowish; no red.
    (b) Gills at first sulphur-yellow, soon green. *H. fasciculare* Fr.
    (bb) Gills at first pallid, never with green shades.
      (c) Gills gray or smoky gray. *H. capnoides.* Fr.

   (cc) Gills purple-gray, at length coffee-brown; stem long-radicating.
     H. epixanthium Fr.
(AA) Pileus rather fragile, sometimes hygrophanous, rarely red or
   yellow.
  (a) Pileus viscid, small, bay-brown. 246. *H. peckianum* sp. nov.
  (aa) Pileus not or slightly viscid.
   (b) Stem with a wine-colored juice when broken. 250. *H. vinosum*
     sp. nov.
   (bb) Stem not with a colored juice.
    (c) Pileus with innate hairy or fibrillose scales.
     (d) Pileus 1-3 cm. broad, with umber-brown hairy scales; spores
      irregular; gregarious-scattered. 249. *H. populinum* Britz.
      var.
     (dd) Pileus 3-10 cm. broad; caespitose.
      (e) Pileus whitish, dotted with brownish scales. 247.
       H. lachrymabundum (Fr.) Quel.
      (ee) Pileus tawny to yellowish; gills often beaded on edge.
       248. *H. velutinum* (Fr.) Quel.
    (cc) Pileus soon glabrous and naked.
     (d) Pileus 6-10 cm. broad, rugose, subviscid. 251. *H. rugoceph-*
      alum Atk.
     (dd) Pileus not over 6 cm. broad, hygrophanous.
      (e) Growing on lawns, fields or other grassy places, rarely in
       woods; densely gregarious-subcaespitose. 252. *H. incer-*
       tum Pk.
      (ee) In woods, swamps, thickets, etc.
       (f) Caespitose around stumps, etc.
        (g) Pileus when moist watery dark brown; gills at first
         grayish-brown; spores minute. 255 and 256.
         H. hydrophilum Fr.
        (gg) Pileus when moist honey-brown; gills at first per-
         sistently whitish. 253. *H. appendiculatum* Fr.
       (ff) Gregarious-scattered, singly; gills narrow.
        (g) Pileus 4-7 cm. broad, umber-brown when moist; gills
         very narrow. 254. *H. coronatum* Fr.
        (gg) Pileus 1-3 cm. broad, pale watery brown when moist;
         very fragile. 257. *H. saccharinophilum* Pk.
        (ggg) Pileus 3-6 cm. broad; pale honey brown when moist;
         stem 5-10 cm. long. 252. *H. incertum* var.
         sylvestris.

Section I. Fascicularia. Pileus fleshy, naked and glabrous,
margin at first silky, brightly colored, not hygrophanous.

     *Large, caespitose: pileus not viscid.

    245. Hypholoma sublateritium Fr. (Edible)

Epicrisis, 1836-38.

Illustrations: Cooke, Ill., Pl. 577.
   Gillet, Champignons de France, No. 357.
   Atkinson, Mushrooms, Fig. 25, opp. p. 26, 1900.
   Marshall, The Mushroom Book, Pl. 29, opp. p. 81, 1905.

Reddick, Ann. Rep. Geol. & Nat. Res. Ind. 32, p. 1231, Fig. 11, 1908.

Murrill, Mycologia, Vol. 1, (as *H. perplexum*).

Plate LI of this Report.

PILEUS 3-8 cm. broad, *firm,* convex-expanded, obtuse, *dark brick-red,* darker on disk, paler on margin, even, glabrous, naked except the decurved margin, which is white-silky from the veil. FLESH thick, *compact,* whitish, in age slightly yellowish. GILLS adnate, crowded, narrow, *at first whitish, then grayish to sooty-olive,* finally dark purplish-brown, edge minutely white-crenulate. STEM 8-12 cm. long, rather stout, 5-12 mm. thick, equal or attenuated downward, stuffed, whitish above, *ferruginous below,* floccose-fibrillose, glabrescent, ascending or curved from the crowded insertions. SPORES 6-7 x 3-4 micr., oblong-elliptical, smooth, purple-brown, blackish purple in mass. BASIDIA about 24 x 5 micr., 4-spored. CYSTIDIA few or scattered, obclavate with apiculate apex, 36 x 12 micr.; *sterile cells* on edge, shorter, inflated. ODOR none. TASTE mild or bitterish.

Very caespitose, forming large clusters in autumn, growing from the base of trees or stumps or on buried roots, etc.

August-November. Throughout the State. Very common.

Var. *perplexum* Pk. has the *gills yellow at first,* finally dark purple-brown, intermediate stage with olive tints. The STEM becomes hollow. The PILEUS has more yellow on the margin. SPORES etc. the same as in *H. sublateritium.*

This species is widely distributed and common in autumn. It is easily recognized by its dark brick-red cap, by the compact, thick flesh and caespitose habit. It is quite variable, and Peck seems to have based his species *H. perplexum* (N. Y. State Cab. Rep. 23, 1872) on such a variation. The conditions of weather, the nature of the wood and other factors no doubt produce some of these forms. An effort has been made by Peck, followed by McIlvaine (see the latter, p. 355, 1900) to provide a key for the separation of these two and of related European species. In the southern part of the state I have examined many clusters for the purpose of verifying this key but found that the mild or bitter taste, the stuffed or hollow stem, and the various shades of color which the gills possess during the process of maturing, were so variable and unreliable that no distinct species could be separated by them. I have not met the other European species: *H. capnoides, H. epixanthium* and *H. fasiculare,* which lack the *red* color of the pileus of our plants, and all of which are described with caps colored some shade of yellow.

Our plant is *edible,* and is eaten by many with safety and relish. In Europe, the same species is said to be poisonous, and is so marked by Ricken in the latest, extensive work of that country.

**Pileus viscid.

246. Hypholoma peckianum sp. nov.

PILEUS 1-2 cm. broad, convex, obtuse, subexpanded, *viscid,* glabrous, *bay-brown,* blackish on disk, paler on margin, even, margin bordered by white, silky fibrils from the veil. FLESH whitish, moderately thin, thicker on disk. GILLS adnate, rounded behind, 2-3 mm. broad, abruptly narrower in front, close, *at first flesh-colored* then dark purplish-brown, edge *white-fimbriate.* STEM 3-4 cm. long, 2-2.5 mm. thick, equal, white-floccose above, innately fibrillose elsewhere, *pallid to brownish,* brown within except the white pith, at length hollow, flexuous. SPORES 10-12 x 5-6 micr., ventricose-elliptical, pointed at ends, smooth, tinged purple under the microscope, purplish-brown in mass. CYSTIDIA none. STERILE CELLS on edge of gills, *clustered,* linear-cylindrical, obtuse, about 20 x 4 micr. BASIDIA subcylindrical, 30 x 6 micr., 4-spored. ODOR and TASTE none.

Scattered on debris of leaves and decayed wood in woods of hemlock, beech, maple, etc. New Richmond. September. Rare.

The viscid, dark-colored cap, the flesh-colored young gills and the small size, distinguish the species. The cortina is white and distinctly fibrillose.

Section II. Limbata. Pileus somewhat fleshy or thin, at first innately fibrillose or dotted with superficial floccose scales on the surface or margin.

This group approaches the genus Psilocybe, but the veil is always recognizable under favorable weather-conditions by the series of floccose remnants which border the margin of the fresh pileus; in wind and rain these rapidly disappear. In most of the species the remnants of the veil are scattered over the surface of the very young pileus as superficial flocculent particles or minute scales; these usually disappear early. In other species the veil remains hanging to the margin of the pileus in an appendiculate manner.

Pileus innately hairy, fibrillose-scaly or velvety.

247. Hypholoma lachrymabundum (Fr.) Quel. (EDIBLE)

Syst. Myc., 1821 (Pro parte) ; Jura et. Vosges, 1872.
(See Maire, Soc. Myc. de France, Bull. 27, p. 441, 1911).

Illustrations: Fries, Icones, Pl. 134, Fig. 1.
 Cooke, Ill., Pl. 543 (as *H. storea* var. *caespitosa*).
 Quelet, Bull. Soc. Bot. France, Vol. 23, Pl. 2, Fig 5 (as *Stropharia cotonea*).
 Plate LII of this Report.

PILEUS 4-10 cm. broad, convex then campanulate, obtuse or discoid, *ground-color whitish to buff,* then pale brownish-ochraceous, moist, covered except on disk by *scattered, rather large appressed brownish hairy scales,* paler on margin, not striate, margin at first incurved and appendiculate from the thickish, floccose-white veil, sometimes rugulose on disk. FLESH thick, thin on margin, firm, white. GILLS adnate-seceding, narrow, crowded, at first whitish, at length purplish-brown, edge white-flocculose, sometimes distilling bead-like drops. STEM 6-12 cm. long, 5-10 mm. thick, equal, hollow, striate above, fibrillose or subscaly below, glabrescent, *whitish* then sordid, base sometimes stained yellowish when bruised, white-mycelioid at base. SPORES 6-7.5 x 3-4 micr., elliptical, slightly curved, smooth, dark brownish-purple under microscope. CYSTIDIA on sides and edge of gills short, rather abundant, 30-40 x 12-15 micr., ventricose.

Densely caespitose at or about the base of trees, in beech, maple and birch woods of conifer regions. Bay View, Houghton. August-September. Rather rare.

This differs from *H. velutina* (which is the *H. lachrymabundum* of most books) in the whitish color, paler gills at first, the small spores and different cystidia. According to Maire (l. c.) the two species were originally combined by Fries, and later segregated by Quelet. It has been described under various names and much confusion has resulted. The unravelling of the tangle is due to Prof. Maire, with the result that the species ordinarily called *H. lachrymabundum* in this country is really *H. velutina*. *H. aggregatum* Pk. is in my opinion only a smaller form of the same plant. The gills of this species are rarely found "weeping," although in *H. velutina* they are usually "beaded with drops."

248. Hypholoma velutinum (Fr.) Quel. (EDIBLE)

Syst. Myc., 1821; Jura et. Vosges, 1872.
(See Maire, Soc. Myc. de France, Bull. 27, p. 144, 1911).

Illustrations: Cooke, Ill., Pl. 563.
     Gillet, Champignons de France, No. 358.
     Gillet, Champignons de France, No. 356 (as *H. lachrymabun-
     dum*).
     Patouillard, Tab. Analyt., No. 117 (as *H. lachrymabundum*).
     Berkeley, Outlines, Pl. 11, Fig. 2.
     Atkinson, Mushrooms, Fig. 28, p. 29, 1900 (as *H. lachryma-
     bundum*).
     Hard, Mushrooms, Figs. 263-264, pp. 325-326, 1908 (as *H.
     lachrymabundum*).
     Plate LIII of this Report.

PILEUS 3-10 cm. broad, convex then broadly campanulate, sometimes obtusely umbonate, finally plane, at first covered by a hairy
tomentum, *then appressed fibrillose-scaly,* not striate, *tawny to yellowish,* darker to umber on center, sometimes radially rugulose,
margin at first appendiculate from the veil, at length split. FLESH
thick on disk, soft, watery-brown to sordid yellowish. GILLS adnate-seceding, broad behind but sinuate, narrowed toward front,
crowded, not reaching margin of pileus, *at first pale yellowish then
umber* and dotted by spore masses, edge white-flocculose, *beaded
with drops.* STEM 2-8 cm. long, variable in length, 4-10 mm. thick,
equal, soon hollow, fibrillose to floccose-scaly and tawny up to the
obsolete annulus, whitish above; *veil* soft-fibrillose, soon breaking,
dingy, white, remnants clinging to the margin of the pileus.
SPORES oval to broadly elliptical, 9-12 x 7 micr., *tuberculate,* dark
purplish-umber under microscope. CYSTIDIA few or scattered on
sides of gills, cylindrical, in groups of several, about 60 x 9-10 micr.,
abundant on edge, cylindrical-subcapitate, 45-55 x 6-7 micr. ODOR
and TASTE earthy.

Caespitose, scattered or solitary on alluvial soil or swampy
grounds in woods. Throughout the State. July-October. Frequent.

This is the *H. lachrymabundum* Fr. of most authors. See notes
on the preceding. It is distinguished by its tawny or darker color,
very characteristic, tuberculate spores and cylindrical cystidia.
The gills usually distil drops from their edge in moist weather.
These drops are often dark colored from the spores, hence Fries

remarks that the edge is "nigro-punctate." Peck (N. Y. State Mus. Bull. 150, p. 81, 1911) has given (under *H. lachrymabundum*) spore measurements which are misleading; and the rest of the description applies to extreme forms.

249. Hypholoma populinum Britz. var.

Bot. Centralbl., Vol. 77, p. 402, 1899.

PILEUS 1-2.5 cm. broad, convex to subcampanulate, obtuse, at length expanded, innately pilose-scaly, not striate, hygrophanous, *grayish-buff, scales umber-brown to purplish-brown,* fading to pale grayish-white, margin appendiculate at first from the veil. FLESH concolor, rather thin. GILLS adnate-seceding, rounded behind, moderately broad, close, thin, at first whitish, soon drab, then dark purplish-brown, edge white-fimbriate. STEM 2-4 cm. long, 1.5-2 mm. thick, equal, *white, dotted with fuscous, fibrillose scales,* stuffed then hollow, shining when dry, base submycelioid. VEIL membranaceus, white, soon disappearing. SPORES *variously shaped,* subtriangular, inequilateral-elliptical, subangular, etc., sometimes curved, 6-7.5 x 4.5 micr., dark purple-brown. CYSTIDIA clavate to obclavate, or subventricose, stalked, not abundant, 50-40 x 15-18 micr. ODOR none.

On very rotten wood, scattered; in frondose low woods or swamps. Ann Arbor, May-June and September. Infrequent.

Characterized by the peculiarly shaped spores, which are often the shape of corn-kernels, or are elliptical, curved or very irregular. Britzelmayr's species is much larger, the cap measuring 7 cm. across; his spores also are a little larger. It is probably a distinct species.

250. Hypholoma vinosum sp. nov.

PILEUS 5-20 mm. broad, fragile, convex, then companulate, sub-umbonate, *pulverulent-floccose,* velvety in appearance, *umber-color-ed,* obscurely tinged with purple, darker in center, dry, even, obscurely rugulose, margin appendiculate at first by pale fragments of the veil. FLESH thin, dingy-white, fragile. GILLS adnate, seceding, crowded, rounded behind, ventricose and rather broad, *bright vinaceous-umber* (Sacc.) finally dark umber, edge entire. STEM 2-4 cm. long, 1-2 mm. thick, equal, except enlarged base, straight, slender, hollow, *vinaceous-umber, color persisting,* pulverulent like pileus, *with a slight purplish juice when broken* in the fresh condition. SPORES minute, 5-6 x 2.5-3 micr., oblong, smooth, obtuse at ends, purplish-black in mass, pale under microscope. CYSTIDIA none.

On very decayed wood, or logs in mixed woods of hemlock and beech, etc. Bay View, New Richmond. August-September. Infrequent.

This striking little Hypholoma is known by its tinge of dark wine-color mixed with umber, the purplish watery juice of the stem and the minute spores.   The trama of the gills and pileus is composed of large, inflated cells, 75-90 x 20 micr., and the surface layer of the pileus of globose cells, several rows thick, up to 30 micr. diameter, tinged smoky vinaceous. When fresh and young it is provided with a thin, evanescent veil, which sometimes forms a slight ring on the stem, and which soon disappears. It has no relationships to such plants as *Lepiota haematosperma* (Fr.) Bres. and *Armillaria haematites* Berk. & Br. which are much stouter plants, have whitish or red-tinged spores, and well developed annulus. It approaches more closely *Psalliota echinata* Fr., but the gills are not free, and the trama is composed of larger cells. The pileus never has pointed scales, and is differently colored.   The base of the stem is slightly bulbous.

**Pileus glabrous, rugose, not hygrophanous.*

251. Hypholoma rugocephalum Atk. (PROBABLY EDIBLE)

Mushrooms, 1900.

Illustration: Ibid, Pl. 8, Fig. 29, opp. p. 30.

PILEUS 6-10 cm. broad, convex-expanded to plane, the margin at length elevated, broadly umbonate, *strongly radiately rugulose,* moist or subviscid, glabrous, watery brown to tawny, then alutaceus-tan. FLESH thick on disk, thin on margin, tinged yellowish. GILLS adnate, seceding, rounded behind or sinuate, moderately close, rather broad, 5-7 mm., *black-sprinkled,* edge white-fimbriate. STEM 8-12 cm. long, 6-10 mm. thick, equal, subbulbous, even, glabrous, hollow, concolor below, paler above, subannulate by obscure threads of the veil, marked by the blackish stain from the spores. SPORES 9-11 x 6-8 micr., ventricose-elliptical, abruptly pointed at both ends, *minutely tuberculate,* inequilateral, dark purple brown, black in mass. CYSTIDIA on sides of gills cylindrical, enlarged at apex, clustered, hyaline; on edge narrowly flask-shaped. •ODOR and TASTE mild.

On the ground, subcaespitose or gregarious, in low or swampy frondose woods. Ann Arbor, South Haven, New Richmond. July-September. Not infrequent.

This species approaches *H. velutinum* in the character of the spore-surface and habit, the cap lacks the fibrillose covering of that species. The shape of the spores is distinctive.

*** *Pileus hygrophanous, at the first dotted with superficial flocculent particles or scales, glabrescent.*

252. Hypholoma incertum Pk. (Edible)

N. Y. State Mus. Rep. 29, 1878.

Illustrations: N. Y. State Mus. Bull. 25, Pl. 58, Fig. 13-20, 1899.
N. Y. State Mus. Mem. 4, Pl. 60, Fig. 1-9, 1900.
Marshall, The Mushroom Book, Pl. 28, opp. p. 80, 1905.
Atkinson, Mushrooms, Pl. 7, Fig. 26 and 27, p. 27, 1900.
Hard, Mushrooms, Pl. 37, Fig. 262, p. 324, 1908.
Murrill, Mycologia, Vol. 4, Pl. 56, Fig. 1 (as *H. appendiculatum*).
Plate LIV of this Report.

PILEUS 3-7 cm. broad, *fragile,* at first oval, obtuse, then broadly campanulate to expanded, at length split radially, hygrophanous, *pale honey-yellowish,* then buff to white as moisture disappears, white-flocculent or at length glabrous, even or slightly wrinkled when dry, the margin at first hung with loose shreds of the veil, *in age often violaceous, lilac towards margin.* FLESH thin, white. GILLS adnate-seceding, narrow, almost linear, thin, close, *at first white,* then pale dingy lilac or rosy-brown, finally purplish or darker, edge minutely white-fimbriate. STEM 3-8 cm. long, 3-6 mm. thick, rather slender, equal, hollow, subrigid, easily splitting lengthwise, even, *white,* innately silky, flocculose or mealy above. SPORES 7-8 x 4 micr., elliptic-oblong, obtuse, smooth, purple brown in mass. CYSTIDIA none on sides of gills. STERILE CELLS sac-shaped, i. e. inflated above, obtuse, 30-40 x 12-15 micr. BASIDIA 32 x 9 micr., short-clavate. ODOR and TASTE agreeable.

Densely gregarious or subcaespitose, sometimes scattered, among grass on lawns, roadsides, fields or rarely in woods among sticks and debris, nearly always around old stumps or buried remains of stumps, roots or decayed wood; sometimes in greenhouses.

Throughout the State. May to September. (Earliest record May 30.) Very common during rainy seasons in early summer.

This is probably the American form of *H. candolleanum* Fr. The single phrase, "gills at first violaceous," in Fries' description deterred Peck from referring it there. Ricken says "gills at first white, then sordid-rosy or violaceous"; this gives the gill-colors of the European plant without a doubt, and this condition is not much different from that in our plants. As in *H. sublateritium*, the gill-color varies somewhat with the conditions surrounding the development of the plant. Because of the abundance of individuals usually found in a patch, its well-known edibility makes it a plant much sought after. Although the caps are thin, the meat is crisp and of delicate flavor and it often grows at our very doors in the grass over some old hidden remains of a stump. This is also presumably the *H. appendiculatum* of many American authors.

A *variety* occurs in the woods, which only differs in that the plants are mostly *solitary* and long-stemmed, scattered here and there among decayed sticks or leaves; its spores are perhaps slightly longer and slightly variable in shape, but otherwise it is very similar. It may be called var. *sylvestris*.

Illustrations of *H. candolleanum* Fr.
> Cooke, Ill., Pl. 546.
> Gillet, Champignons de France, No. 352 (as *H. appendiculatum*).
> Ricken, Blätterpilze, Pl. 64, Fig. 4.
> Patouillard, Tab. Analyt., No. 350.

253. Hypholoma appendiculatum Fr. (EDIBLE)

Epicrisis, 1836-38.

Illustrations: Ricken, Blätterpilze, Pl. 64, Fig. 5.
> Patouillard, Tab. Analyt., No. 349 (faded condition).

"PILEUS 2-4 cm. broad, campanulate-hemispherical, hygrophanous, *dark-honey-brown* (moist) isabelline to ochraceous (dry), with a dull luster, *naked, but at first floccose or fibrillose on the surface or appendiculate from the white veil*, slightly wrinkled and almost atomate when dry. FLESH thin, pallid. GILLS broadly adnate, ascending, crowded, 6-7 mm. *broad*, almost equal in width, *at first and a long time whitish, then grayish-purplish*, at length purple-brown. STEM 5-10 cm. long, 3-6 mm. thick, fragile, narrowed upwards, often elongated, mostly curved worm-like, undulate, *white,* silky-shining above, apex mealy and striate, rarely with loose shreds forming a temporary ring. VEIL white, floccose-membranous, at first uniting the margin of the pileus with the stem, *very soon disappearing.* SPORES almost cylindrical-elliptical, 9-11 x 4-5 micr., smooth, red-brown under microscope. CYSTIDIA almost lanceolate, on sides and edge of gills, 40-45 x 10-13 micr."

"*Caespitose,* in beech woods on leaves and about stumps."

The description is adapted from Ricken's Blätterpilze. This species has been much discussed, and is reported in most American books. The pileus is brown when moist according to most European authors and occurs in the forests where it forms caespitose tufts. I have not been able to distinguish it in the southern part of the state, but have given a description from the most recent work on European Agarics, for the sake of comparison.

254. Hypholoma coronatum Fr.

Hymen. Europ., 1881.

Illustration: Fries, Icones, Pl. 134, Fig. 3.

PILEUS 4-7 cm. broad, *fragile,* at first oval, then convex-campanulate, hygrophanous, obtuse or subumbonate, *umber-brown on disk,* gradually paler toward margin, *whitish-tan or pale alutaceous when dry,* disk often retaining an umber shade and *at length blackish stained in spots,* at first dotted with white, flocculent, superficial scales, *soon denuded,* even or obscurely wrinkled on margin, margin hung by remains of veil in a dentiform manner. FLESH thin, *concolor.* GILLS narrowly adnate, seceding, *very narrow,* crowded, at first dingy-white, soon pale lilaceous-brown, *then umber-colored,* edge minutely white-fimbriate. STEM 5-7 cm. long, rather slender, 3-4 mm. thick, *tapering upward* or subequal, hollow, slightly toughish, *white,* dingy in age, often innately flocculose-scaly then glabrescent and *shining,* even, sometimes subcompressed. SPORES elliptical, 6-7 x 4 micr., smooth, purplish-brown. CYSTIDIA none. STERILE CELLS on edge of gills, broadly cylindrical, obtuse, abruptly short-stipitate, 36 x 10 micr. ODOR and TASTE pleasant.

Gregarious or scattered, attached to leaf-mould, fallen leaves and very rotten wood. Ann Arbor. July-August. Rare.

This differs from the solitary form of *H. incertum,* which also occurs in woods, by the umber color of the entire very young pileus

which has evanescent white-floccose scales sprinkled over it, and
in the less roseate hue of the gills in the intermediate stage. It
has the size and shape of *H. incertum.* The margin of cap does not
become violaceous-tinged in age. Fries says "caespitose" in habit,
and to that extent our plant is a variety.

255. Hypholma hydrophilum Fr. (sense of Ricken) (SUSPECTED)

Epicrisis, 1836-38. (Hymen. Europ. as Bolbitius.)

Illustration: Ricken, Blätterpilze, Pl. 64, Fig. 6.

PILEUS 2-6 cm. broad, fragile, campanulate-convex, then expanded, watery *cinnamon-brown to chestnut-brown when moist,*
hygrophanous, ochraceous-buff when dry, even or pellucid-substriate
on margin, often wavy, *margined with a delicate, superficial, white,
silky border* which represents the remains of the veil. FLESH thin,
concolor. GILLS adnate-seceding, thin, ventricose, not broad,
crowded, *at first grayish-brown, then purplish-umber or dark brown,*
edge minutely white-fimbriate when young. STEM 4-6 cm. long,
3-6 mm. thick, equal, hollow, splitting, elastic, *glabrous* except the
pruinose apex, *shining-white,* undulate, base mycelioid. SPORES
5-6 x 2.5-3 micr., *minute,* smooth, pale purplish-brown under microscope. CYSTIDIA few or none. STERILE CELLS on edge of
gills inflated-saccate, short, 30-8 micr. ODOR and TASTE none.

Caespitose in extensive clusters on or near stumps and decayed
wood, or at base of living trees. Ann Arbor, New Richmond, (probably throughout the State).

September-November. Not infrequent.

Fries says it distills drops of moisture along the edge of the
gills, but this is rare in our climate, although it does occur. It is
a very fragile plant, with a white stem and a watery-brown cap
which fades quickly in the wind as the moisture escapes. Its
minute spores distinguish it, although European authors are not
agreed on the spore size. Ricken and Massee give them as above.
Saccardo seems to be in error, or there may be two closely allied
plants as with us. We have another species, which is almost like
it.

256. Hypholoma hydrophilum Fr. (sense of Saccardo)

This differs from the preceding as follows: PILEUS at first
sprinkled over its surface with white, floccose particles or minute

scales, even on margin when moist. STEM fibrillose-flocculose, glabrescent. SPORES 7-8 x 4-5 micr., slightly unequally elliptical. CYSTIDIA on sides of gills scattered to somewhat numerous, ventricose-sublanceolate but obtuse, about 50 micr. long. STERILE CELLS pyriform-inflated, numerous on edge of gills.

In large or small tufts about logs, stumps, etc., in swampy woods. June-July. Ann Arbor, Detroit, Bay View. Not infrequent.

This may be *Psilocybe polycephala* (Paul.) (see N. Y. State Mus. Bull. 157, p. 98, Pl. 127, Fig. 1-9, 1912), which it approaches very closely. It is not *Psilocybe spadicea* and does not appear to be closely related to it. It is close to *H. hydrophilum* with which it agrees except in the points mentioned. Cooke's figure (Ill., Pl. 1157) which is doubtfully referred to *H. instratum* Britz. is perhaps the same; at least it is not Britzelmayr's plant which has rounded-triangular spores.

257. Hypholoma saccharinophilum Pk.

N. Y. State Mus. Rep. 25, 1873.

PILEUS 1-3 cm. broad, *fragile*, obtuse, ovate at first, then campanulate to plane, pale watery-brown and *even* when moist, pallid-ochraceous when dry, hygrophanous, *in age assuming a livid-gray or watery-soaked appearance when remoistened,* at first sprinkled with white flecks or flocculent scales, glabrescent and subatomate. FLESH soft, thin. GILLS adnate-seceding, narrow, sublinear or subventricose, close, white at first, slowly becoming pinkish to fuscous-purplish, edge white-fimbriate. STEM 3-7 cm. thick, *fragile,* subequal, undulate, white, silky-fibrillose, pruinose-floccose at apex, hollow, even, subbulbillate at base with radiating mycelium. VEIL delicate, flocculose-fibrillose, white, evanescent. SPORES 6-7 x 3-4.5 micr., elliptical-oblong, smooth, obtuse, purplish-brown in mass, pale under microscope. CYSTIDIA none on sides of gills. STERILE CELLS on edge, large, undulate-cylindrical, abundant, broadly obtuse, 40-50 x 9-11 micr.

Gregarious or scattered, attached to sticks, humus, decaying leaves and wood in low swampy woods of maple, elm, poplar, etc. Ann Arbor. July-August. Frequent.

Although this species was rejected by Peck in his monograph of the New York species (Bull. 150, 1911) it is revived here to supply a name for our species. The cap is characterized by its non-striate margin, and by its peculiar change in color when mature and when it again becomes moist. On drying the cap finally becomes grayish-white; mature specimens during wet weather assume a livid-gray appearance, which is also the case when kept moist in a box after collecting. It is a rather small, unimportant plant of swamps where it is sometimes plentiful.

Psathyra Fr.

(From the Greek, *psathyros,* friable.)

Purple-brown-spored. Stem *with a cartilaginous cortex,* rigid-fragile, slender and hollow. Gills adnate or adnexed. *Margin of pileus at first straight.* Veil either none or universal, in the latter case leaving delicate flecks or fibrils over the surface of the young pileus and stem. *Pileus hygrophanous.*

Putrescent, terrestrial or on decayed wood. The genus corresponds to Mycena of the white-spored group in that the stem is somewhat cartilaginous and the margin of the pileus is at first straight and appressed to the stem; the pileus. is therefore likely to be persistently campanulate as in Mycena. See Plate LVI. The species are slender, fragile and hygrophanous. It is somewhat difficult to tell some of the species from Psilocybe except in the presence of very young stages showing the straight margin of the cap.

The genus naturally falls into two sections, the first composed of species without cortina or universal veil; the second, where the young plants are surrounded by a delicate, usually white, fibrillose or flocculose universal veil. The veil breaks up early and leaves thin superficial flecks or scales on cap and stem, or sometimes merely white fibrils, which are unrecognizable in age or after rains. The species occur rather infrequently, but quite a number have been found in the state. Of these only a part are here presented, as it has been impossible to identify the others with any certainty. Their edibility has not been reported.

Key to the Species

(A) Pileus at first with fibrillose flecks or hairs.
  (a) Densely caespitose; pileus even, slightly pelliculose; stem short. 262. *P. microsperma* Pk.
  (aa) Gregarious; pileus and stem superficially white-hairy at first. 261. *P. semivestita* Berk.
(AA) Pileus glabrous; stem polished.
  (a) Caespitose on or near wood; pileus striatulate when moist; stem long. 259. *P. umbonata* Pk.

(aa) Not densely caespitose; solitary or gregarious.
  (b) Spores 7-9 micr. long; pileus umber. 259. *P. obtusata* Fr.
  (bb) Spores 10-12 micr. long; pileus rufous-brown. 260. *P. per-simplex* Britz.

Section I. Conopilae. (Incl. of Obtusatae Fr.) Surface of pileus glabrous; stem polished and shining.

258. Psathyra umbonata Pk.

N. Y. State Mus. Rep. 50, 1897.

Illustrations: Plates LV, LVI of this Report.

PILEUS 2-5 cm. broad at maturity, 2-3 cm. high, subcylindrical at the very first, then conico-campanulate, at length strongly and obtusely umbonate, hygrophanous, *dark bay-brown to purplish-brown and striatulate* (moist), grayish-white, even and atomate (dry), sometimes faintly rugulose when dry. FLESH thin, concolor. GILLS ascending, *adnate-seceding,* rather broad, 3-4 mm., narrowed in front, close, becoming dark purplish-brown, finally almost black, edge white-fimbriate. STEM 5-10 cm. long, 2-3 mm. thick, slender, flexuous, rigid-fragile, *equal,* hollow, sometimes twisted, *shining-white* becoming pallid. SPORES 13-15.5 x 7-8 micr., elliptical, obtuse, smooth, dark purplish under the microscope, black in mass. CYSTIDIA none on sides of gills; sterile cells on edge, cystidia-like, ventricose, apex obtuse. BASIDIA 4-spored, narrowly stalked, inflated above.

Caespitose or gregarious-subcaespitose, on decayed wood, usually stumps and logs. June-September. Ann Arbor, New Richmond. Not infrequent.

Forming large clusters of many individuals, often at the end of old moist logs. Its long slender stems and cone-shaped caps distinguish it at once from Hypholoma clusters. Sometimes only a few individuals occur in one place. It has the stature and general appearance of *P. conopilea* Fr., as shown in the published figures, but differs in the truly adnate gills and the striate margin of the moist cap. Peck compares it with *P. corrugis* Fr. (B) Another species sometimes occurs, which differs from the preceding mainly in the size of its spores: 15-18 x 7-8 micr. This differs from *P. elata* Mass., in the margin being long-striate. The size, shape and colors are the same as in *P. umbonata.* Because of its almost black spores it might be mistaken for *Psathyrella subatrata,* but that species does not grow on wood.

259. Psathyra obtusata Fr.

Syst. Myc., 1821.

PILEUS 1-3 cm. broad, campanulate-convex, *obtuse,* hygrophanous, *umber* and faintly or not at all striate *when moist,* pale
ochraceous to buff and atomate when dry, glabrous; veil none.
FLESH thin. GILLS ascending, adnate, *rather broad,* close to subdistant, umber when mature, edge white-fimbriate. Stem 5-8 cm.
long, 1-3 mm. thick, equal, glabrous, hollow, white then pallid, rigid-
fragile, flexuous, curved at base. SPORES elliptical, 7-9 x 4-4.5
micr., smooth, dark purplish-brown.

Solitary or subcaespitose, on very rotten wood. September.
New Richmond, Bay View. Infrequent.

Distinguished from the preceding by the obtusely convex pileus,
more scattered habit and shorter stems. Form *minor:* This varies
smaller, with a pileus .5-1 cm. broad and rather slender stem. The
spores, etc., are the same. Cook's figure (Ill., Pl. 593) does not
represent our plants.

260. Psathyra persimplex Britz.

Bot. Centralbl., Vol. 77, p. 436, 1899.

PILEUS 1-2.5 cm. broad, campanulate at first then campanulate-
convex, obtuse, *margin soon spreading,* hygrophanous, rufous-brown
to fuscous brown and striatulate when moist, whitish-buff to pale
ochraceous when dry, atomate, *glabrous.* Veil none. FLESH very
thin. GILLS ascending-adnate, rather broad, ventricose, close to
subdistant, whitish then gray to grayish-umber, edge white-fimbriate.
STEM 4-10 cm. long, *slender,* 1-2 mm. thick, equal, *whitish or pallid,*
somewhat fragile, stuffed by white pith then hollow, glabrous, shining, flexuous, pruinate at apex, rooting at base and attached to
wood by hairs. SPORES elliptical, 10-12 x 5-6.5 micr., obtuse,
smooth, dark purple-brown under the microscope. CYSTIDIA
scattered or few on sides of gills, up to 70 x 15 micr., sometimes
bifurcate at apex, ventricose-lanceolate; smaller on edge, 30-45 x
6-12 micr., obtuse. BASIDIA 30 x 10-12 micr., 4-spored. ODOR
none.

Gregarious on sticks and decayed wood in hemlock woods. New
Richmond. September. Rare.

This seems to be a segregate from *P. obtusata,* from which it differs in the size of its spores and the characteristic spreading of the margin of the pileus.

Section II. Fibrillosae. Stem and pileus when young flocculose or fibrillose from the universal veil.

261. Psathyra semivestita Berk. and Br.

Ann. Nat. Hist., p. 920, 1836.

Illustrations: Cooke, Ill., Pl. 578.
Ricken, Die Blätterpilze, Pl. 67, Fig. 4.

PILEUS 1-2 cm. broad, ovate-campanulate, subobtuse, hygrophanous, rufous-umber and pellucid-short-striate when moist, pale isabelline when dry, *surface sprinkled when young by superficial, white fibrillose flecks.* FLESH very thin, soon ochraceous-tinged. GILLS broadly adnate, *narrowed in front,* sometimes almost subtriangular, close, dark smoky-fuscous, edge at times white-fimbriate. STEM 4-6 cm. long, 1.5-2 mm. thick, *equal,* hollow, even, rigid-fragile, pale fuscous, pallescent, *closely sprinkled over with white, fibrillose flecks.* SPORES elliptical, 9-12 x 5-6 micr., variable in size, smooth, dark purple-brown. CYSTIDIA few on sides of gills, numerous on edge, ventricose-sublanceolate, obtuse, 50-60 x 12-15 micr. BASIDIA short and stout, 24 x 9-10 micr. ODOR none.

Gregarious, on horse-dung. New Richmond. September.

Known by the rufous tinge to the color of the pileus and the white fibrils which at the very first cover the cap and stem. *P. vestita* Pk. *is very similar,* if not the same, but the spore-sizes are given somewhat smaller; see description in N. Y. State Mus. Bull. 105, p. 28.

262. Psathyra microsperma Pk.

Torr. Bot. Club, Bull. 26, 1899.

PILEUS 1-2.5 cm. broad, at first ovate or subhemispherical, then convex-campanulate, often irregular, obtuse, *even,* hygrophanous, *slightly pelliculose,* pale watery-brown (moist) cinereous-buff (dry), at first with scattered flocculose white scales, *glabrescent,* margin at first straight. FLESH thin, concolor. GILLS adnate-seceding, close, *not broad,* subventricose, narrowed toward front, at first whitish then grayish-brown tinged purplish, edge white-fimbriate.

STEM 2-4 cm. long, 2-3 mm. thick, equal, rigid-fragile, hollow, *pure white,* apex subpruinose, subfibrillose, *at first covered by minute, white fibrils from the universal veil.* SPORES elliptical, 6-8 x 4-4.5 micr., smooth, purplish-brown.

Very caespitose, on grass or about stumps in or near woods. **Ann Arbor.** October. Rare.

This species was described by Peck from material sent from Ohio; he does not report it from New York State. The pileus is provided with a slight pellicle which is scarcely gelatinous. The stem separates rather easily from the pileus when the gills have receded from it. Our specimens grew out of the turf with no sign of nearby wood. They were sent to Peck who identified them as his species. It is easily mistaken for a Psilocybe, but the margin of the young cap is straight at first.

Psilocybe Fr.

(From the Greek, *psilos,* naked, and *kybe,* head, referring to the lack of veil-remnants on the pileus.)

Purple-brown-spored. Stem with a *cartilaginous cortex,* rigid-fragile or toughish. Gills adnexed to adnate-subdecurrent. *Veil scarcely noticeable or entirely lacking,* neither forming an annulus nor appendiculate on the margin of the pileus. *Margin of pileus at first incurved.*

Putrescent, terrestrial, on very decayed wood or around stumps, buried roots, sticks, etc. The genus corresponds to Collybia of the white-spored group in that the stem has a cartilaginous cortex and the margin of the pileus is at first incurved. The species are usually rather thin and fragile and not large. They are distinguished from the Hypholomas by the scanty or absent veil; those species which possess a veil often show no signs of it in windy or dry weather.

The PILEUS is convex or campanulate and expands in many cases until quite plane. The color is usually dull, even in those with reddish, yellow or olive hues. It is usually glabrous; a few species, however, like *P. canofacious,* have a somewhat fibrillose surface. The GILLS are broadly adnate and mostly slightly decurrent or triangular in the first section; in the other sections they are rounded behind or adnexed-emarginate. In age they are often sprinkled in a variegated manner by the spores. The STEM is neither stout nor truly fleshy. It is often white when young, but varies to brownish, reddish or grayish.

The genus is divided here into three sections, separated fundamentally by the broad, subdecurrent gills of the first group, the pellicle of the pileus in the second group, and the hygrophanous flesh of the plants in the third group. Few species have any record for or against their edibility; *P. foenisecii*, however, is known to be edible.

Key to the Species

(A) Pileus hygrophanous.
    (a) Spores in mass brick-reddish. 277. *P. conissans* Pk.
    (aa) Spores not red in mass.
        (b) Large; pileus 5-12 cm. broad, brown when moist. 270. *P. larga* sp. nov.
        (bb) Smaller; pileus 4 cm. or less in width.
            (c) Spores large, 13-18 micr. long; common on lawns and grassy places. 276. *P. foenisecii* Fr.
            (cc) Spores less than 13 micr. long.
                (d) Pileus subviscid and rufous-brown when moist; gills very broadly adnate.
                    (e) Growing on dung or pastured fields. 264. *P. subviscida* Pk.
                    (ee) Growing on the ground in woods. 265. *P. atrorufa* Fr.
                (dd) Pileus not subviscid; gills not subdecurrent.
                    (e) Stem pale fuscous, 10-15 cm. long; on sphagnum. 267. *P. atrobrunnea* Fr.
                    (ee) Stem white, shorter.
                        (f) Spores small, 6-7 micr. long.
                            (g) Pileus 1-4 cm. broad, livid-brown when moist and striate. 271. *P. cernua* Fr.
                            (gg) Pileus less than 1 cm. broad, dull-brownish when moist, spotted. 275. *P. submaculata* Atk.
                    (ff) Spores 8-10 micr. long or longer, pileus dark-brown when moist.
                            (g) Stem falsely bulbous from adhering sand, often subcaespitose and clavate. 273. *P. arenulina* Pk; *P. ammophila* Mont.
                            (gg) Stem not markedly enlarged by adhering sand, equal.
                                (h) Gills narrow; spores 10-12 x 6 micr.; stem slender, 1-2 mm. thick. 272. *P. murcida* Fr.
                                (hh) Gills medium broad; spores 7-9 x 4-5 micr.; stem 3-4 mm. thick, shorter. 274. *P. agrariella* Atk.
(AA) Pileus not hygrophanous.
    (a) Pileus with white fibrils or hairy scales on the surface; umber-colored. 268. *P. canofaciens* Cke.
    (aa) Pileus glabrous except margin, viscid or subviscid.
        (b) Stem long, 7-10 cm., pileus grayish-olive; on sphagnum or dung. 268. *P. uda* Fr.
        (bb) Stem shorter; pileus without olive tints.
            (c) On dung; pileus livid-brownish-yellow; gills broadly adnate; spores very large. 263. *P. merdaria* Fr.
            (cc) On the ground in woods; pileus tawny-fulvous; gills emarginate-adnate. 219. *P. ericaea* Fr.

Section I. Deconicae. Gills broad and broadly adnate, sometimes decurrent by a tooth; margin of pileus at first with a flocculose or fibrillose, delicate and very evanescent veil.

This section approaches Stropharia; it was raised to generic rank by W. G. Smith under the name Deconica. The veil, although usually very evanescent, may at times leave a slight annular mark on the stem so as to simulate Stropharia, and hence the species must be carefully compared with species of that genus.

263. Psilocybe merdaria Fr.

Syst. Myc., 1821 (as Stropharia in Hym. Europ.).

Illustrations: Fries, Icones, Pl. 130, Fig. 3 (as Stropharia).
    Cooke, Ill., Pl. 537 (?) (as Stropharia).
    Gillet, Champignons de France, No. 649 (as Stropharia).
    Ricken, Blätterpilze, Pl. 66, Fig. 1.

PILEUS 1-3 cm. broad, campanulate-hemispherical, finally plane, *livid-brownish to livid-yellow,* obtusely subumbonate, slightly darker on umbo, glabrous, *even, subviscid,* at first with slight flecks on the margin. FLESH pallid, thin. GILLS broadly adnate to triangular-subdecurrent, *broad, subdistant, yellowish at first,* then powdered by purple-brown spores, at length dark brown. STEM 2-4 cm. long, 1-3 mm. thick, equal, even or slightly ridged at apex by decurrent gills, delicately flocculose-fibrillose, glabrescent, *pale yellowish,* stuffed then hollow, often with slight annular remnants or fibrils. SPORES *large,* 14-17 x 7-8 micr., elliptical, smooth, purplish-brown under the microscope. CYSTIDIA none. ODOR mild.

On horse dung along with *Stropharia stercoraria.* Ann Arbor. May-June. Infrequent.

Not to be confused with *Naucoria semiorbicularis, N. pediades* and *N. platysperma,* the spores of which are smaller and lack the purple tinge. It is said to differ from *P. coprinophila* by the grayish young gills of the latter. I have followed Karsten and Britzelmayr (quoted by Sacc.) in referring this plant with large spores under *P. merdaria.* Other authors differ widely and it is clear that several species are either confused or that the plant needs segregation. Cooke, in the Illustrations, gives the size 8 x 5 micr.; W. G. Smith, 9 x 6 micr.; Ricken, 12-13 x 7-9 micr. Ricken says "the purplish color of the spores disappears in dried specimens," hence the study of exsicatti is of little value.

264. Psilocybe subviscida Pk.

·N. Y. State Mus. Rep. 41, 1888 (as Deconica).

PILEUS 5-15 mm. broad, fragile, ovate-campanulate then subexpanded and obtusely umbonate, hygrophanous, at first viscid and *chestnut-brown or rufous-brown and striatulate when moist,* very soon buff with or without an ochraceous umbo when dry, glabrous, *subviscid.* FLESH thin. GILLS broadly adnate, subtriangular, thickish, *subdistant, broad,* at first whitish, then umber. STEM 2-4 cm. long, 1-2 mm. thick, slender, equal or tapering downwards, pallid to fuscescent, varying to chestnut brown within and without, *at first covered with delicate white fibrils.* SPORES oval or ovate, 6-7 x 4-5 micr., smooth, pale brown tinged with wine-color under microscope. VEIL slight, fugacious.

In pastured fields among grass, on dung, and on moss in woods. April-June. Ann Arbor. Infrequent.

This approaches *P. physaloides* Fr. (sense of Ricken) in color, but the gills are not crowded and the spores are smaller. It also differs from *P. bullacea* Fr. in the subdistant gills. The latter species is doubtless native here, but the discrepancies in the descriptions by the different authors make it difficult to place. Saccardo following Fries, says cap of *P. bullacea* is fulvous-bay-color when moist, and gives the spores 6-10 x 4-7 micr.; Ricken describes the cap as chocolate-brown when moist, with spores like our *P. subviscida.* Which of these, if any, is *P. bullacea* is therefore hard to tell; nevertheless it is desirable to follow the description of Fries. The chestnut or rufous-brown color, and the visicidity quickly disappear and the pileus is then tan-colored and even.

265. Psilocybe atrorufa Fr.

Syst. Myc., 1821.

Illustration: Cooke, Ill., Pl. 571.

PILEUS 5-12 mm. broad, convex-hemispherical, obtuse, hygrophanous, *umber-brown then rufous-brown and striatulate when moist,* glabrous and pale alutaceus when dry, *not viscid,* margin faintly veiled. FLESH thin, concolor, broadly adnate or subdecurrent, subtriangular, close, at length umber-colored. STEM 3-4 cm. long, 1-2 mm. thick, slender, hollow, equal or tapering downward, obscurely flocculose-fibrillose, glabrescent, *rufous-bay color through-*

out. SPORES 5-8 x 4-5.5 micr., oval, somewhat pointed at ends, smooth, reddish-brown under microscope. CYSTIDIA none. STERILE CELLS on edge of gills, slender, lanceolate-subulate, 30-34 x 5 micr.

Gregarious, on the ground in woods. Ann Arbor, Bay View. (Probably throughout the State). June-July.

Differing from the preceding in the non-viscid pileus and closer gills. Here again two very different spore-sizes have been given, and although Cooke's figure is somewhat illustrative of our plant, his spores are too large, 10-12 x 6 micr.

Section II. Tenaces. Pileus with a pellicle, moist or subviscid when young; veil slight, cortinate. *Toughish and somewhat brightly colored.*

266. Psilocybe canofaciens Cke.

Grevillea, Vol. 14, p. 1, 1885.

Illustration: Cooke, Ill., Pl. 621.

PILEUS 1-3 cm. broad, campanulate-convex, then expanded, obtuse or subumbonate, even, *umber-brown, covered at first by delicate,* white, scattered fibrils, at length somewhat appressed fibrillose-scaly and fibrils concolor. FLESH thickish on disk, concolor. GILLS adnate, rather broad, *ventricose,* subdistant, *dark umber.* STEM 5-7 cm. long, 2-4 mm. thick, equal or slightly tapering, stuffed then hollow, *dark umber-color,* darker at base, covered with long fibrils which become matted, toughish. SPORES elliptical-oblong, slightly curved in one plane, *very variable in size,* 10-15 micr. long (rarely much longer), 4-5 micr. thick, purple-brown under microscope, umber in mass.

On the ground in woods. Negaunee. August. Rare.

Sent to me by Miss Rose M. Taylor. It is a very characteristic plant, with its dark colors, the fibrillose-hairy covering on the cap and stem and the variable spore-size. This plant is a striking commentary on the value of spore-characters in identification. Massee (British Fungus Flora) states that the spores vary very much in size in the English specimens, and in Michigan this peculiarity is also found.

267. Psilocybe atrobrunnea Fr.

Epicrisis, 1836-38.

Illustration: Plate LVI of this Report.

PILEUS 1-4 cm. broad, *campanulate-convex,* obtusely umbonate, hygrophanous, *umber when moist,* fading to dingy ochraceous, even, glabrous. FLESH thin, concolor. GILLS adnate but rounded behind, not uncinate, *seceding,* rather broad, *subdistant,* brownish-gray, then smoky-fuscous, edge whitish. STEM 5-15 cm. long, *elongated,* 1.5-4 mm. thick, slender, flexuous, equal or subattenuate at base, even, *pale fuscous, covered with white silky fibrils,* stuffed, concolor within, cartilaginous, toughish. SPORES elliptical, 10-12 x 5-6 micr., smooth, dark purplish-brown. ODOR and TASTE slight, somewhat farinaceous.

In tamarack bogs, among sphagnum. September-November. Ann Arbor. Local.

Known by its sphagnum habitat, dark color when moist and its long stems. The superficial white fibrils on the stem seem to indicate a veil.

268. Psilocybe uda (Fr.) Battaille

Syst. Myc., 1821, Bull. de la. Soc..Myc. de France, Vol. 27, p. 374, 1911.

PILEUS 1-2 cm. broad, *campanulate,* mammilate, with a viscid pellicle, *striatulate and grayish-olive with rufous-brown umbo* when moist, shining, fading to creamy white with pale-yellow umbo, glabrous. FLESH thin. GILLS adnate or slightly subdecurrent, very broad, close to subdistant, *gray* then violaceous-blackish, edge white-flocculose. STEM 7-10 cm. long, *slender,* 1.5-2 mm. thick, slightly thicker toward base, equal elsewhere, pallid-whitish, rigid, glabrous, even, hollow, sometimes *annulate* by the delicate, superior, fibrillose remains of the veil. SPORES elliptical, 17-20 x 9-10 micr., smooth, *bright violet-purple under the microscope,* purplish-blackish in mass. STERILE CELLS on edge of gills, narrow, linear. ODOR *none.*

On horse-dung, in low woods. New Richmond. September.

This species is slender-stemmed like *Stropharia umbonatescens,* and its spores are about the same size. It differs from *S. umbonatescens* in the olive-colored, striate pileus, and lack of odor.

This is referred to by Fries as var. *elongata* (Hymen. Europ.). The varietal name is used by Ricken for a plant which he calls *Hypholoma elongatum,* which has much smaller spores, while he claims that *P. uda* has no trace of a veil, but has the large spores. Battaille (l. c.) describes our plant well and emphasizes the deep violet color of the spores, which is quite marked in the Michigan specimens, as well as the slight evanescent annulus. The only discrepancy is that the habitat of *P. uda* is on dung instead of sphagnum and while this is important it is deemed best to refer it for the present to the above species. It is a better Stropharia.

269. Psilocybe ericæa Fr.

Syst. Myc., 1821.

Illustrations: Fries, Icones, Pl. 136, Fig. 1.
        Cooke, Ill., Pl. 568.

PILEUS 2-3 cm. broad, convex then subexpanded, obtuse or um-bonate, *even, subviscid,* with a gelatinous separable pellicle, *tawny-fulvous,* glabrous, at first with a whitish, fibrillose cortina on edge. FLESH firm, thickish, rather compact, pallid. GILLS adnate, be-coming emarginate, *broad,* close or almost crowded, whitish at first, then fulvous-brown and sprinkled with blackish spots, edge minutely white-fimbriate. STEM 5-8 cm. long, 3-4 mm. thick, equal, flexuous, *stuffed with a rather persistent pith,* glabrous, apex pruinose, pallid then fuscescent, curved at base and attached to fallen leaves, etc. SPORES oval-elliptical, inequilateral, 9-11 x 5-5.5 micr., pale pur-plish under the microscope, dark in mass.   CYSTIDIA none. STERILE CELLS on edge of gills, subcylindrical, elongate-narrow, 3-4 micr. diam. ODOR and TASTE mild.

On the ground in mixed woods. New Richmond. September.

Agrees well in size,. shape and color with the figures of Fries. Authors give conflicting spore-sizes and it seems impossible to be certain of the plant on this point.

Section III. Rigidae. Cortinate veil none or slight (except in *P. larga*), pileus *hygrophanous,* rigid-fragile when dry, scarcely or not at all pelliculose.

This section has the appearance of the second section of the Hy-pholomas except in the absence of or reduced development of the veil; the first species represents a connecting link between them.

270. Psilocybe larga sp. nov.

Illustration: Plate LVII of this Report.

PILEUS *large,* 4-14 cm. broad, oval-campanulate at first, at length expanded-plane and radially cracked or split on the margin, *fragile, hygrophanous, bay-brown* to ochraceous-brown and even *when moist, whitish-tan* and radiately rugulose *when dry, at first dotted with scattered, small, snow-white, floccose, superficial scales,* quickly denuded, often only with white-silky margin. FLESH rather thin, white when dry, scissile, homogeneous, with large cells. Gills adnate, rounded behind, *rather broad,* close to subdistant, white at first, then pale fuscous, *finally umber,* edge minutely white-fimbriate. STEM *stout,* 5-10 cm. long, 5-15 mm. thick, equal or tapering upward, soon *hollow,* terete or compressed, rather firm, *usually striate to sulcate,* furfuraceous but glabrescent, then shining, *white,* cortex subcartilaginous. SPORES elliptical, 8-9.5 x 4-5 micr., smooth, obtuse, *purple-brown under microscope,* umber in mass. CYSTIDIA abundant on sides and edge of gills, 70-80 x 12-15 micr., subventricose to subcylindrical, narrow-stalked, obtusely rounded above. BASIDIA 4-spored. ODOR and TASTE none.

Gregarious or caespitose around old stumps, buried roots, etc., in grassy clearings or woods. Ann Arbor. May-September. (More frequent in spring.) Not infrequent in elm swamps or clearings.

A large and striking species, related to *P. spadicea* and *Hypholoma sarcocephalum.* From the former it differs markedly in the presence of a veil, the adnate gills and the striate stem; from the latter, in its strongly marked hygrophanous character, and lack of any pellicle. Ricken suggests that these two species are identical. I suspect that all three are variations of the same plant, but at present this cannot be established. Our plant is often found without a sign of the floccose remnants of the veil, especially after a rain or in windy weather. Under favorable weather conditions, however, the developing plant shows the veil well. *Psilocybe spadicea* seems to be differently understood by authors. According to Quelet, Ricken and others it is a large plant, like *P. larga.* If this is true, Cooke's figures are very misleading, and as the English authors have followed his idea, it is not surprising to have it reported by Peck and others for this country in a way to suggest *Hypholoma hydrophilum,* which is a much smaller and more densely caespitose plant. I have not seen *P. spadicea* Fr. in the sense of Ricken and Quelet.

271. Psilocybe cernua Fr.

Syst. Myc., 1821.

Illustrations: Cooke, Ill., Pl. 574.
  Plate LVIII of this Report.

PILEUS 1-4 cm. broad, convex-campanulate, hygrophanous, *livid
watery-brown when moist and then striate,* whitish when dry, often
areolate cracked and rugulose in age, *veil entirely lacking.* FLESH
rather thin, whitish when dry. GILLS adnate-seceding, moderately broad, rounded behind, close, at first whitish, finally purplish-
umber, edge minutely white-flocculose. STEM 2-5 cm. long, 2-4 mm.
thick, equal or tapering below, delicately stuffed then tubular, *white,
rigid-cartilaginous* when dry, subfibrillose, apex pruinose, flexuous
or variously curved. SPORES oblong-elliptical, 6-7 x 3-4 micr.,
smooth, purple-brown under microscope. CYSTIDIA none.
STERILE CELLS on edge of gills, short, subsaccate, 25 x 7 micr.
ODOR and TASTE none.

Caespitose or subcaespitose-gregarious, at the base of trees.

Ann Arbor, New Richmond. September-October. Infrequent.

The pileus is rather firm when dry, not splitting easily on the
margin on drying. This species agrees well with the descriptions
and Cooke's illustration.

272. Psilocybe murcida Fr.

Syst. Myc., 1821.

PILEUS 2-4 cm. broad, obtuse, *fragile,* campanulate-convex,
then expanded, hygrophanous, *dark bay-brown and striatulate on
margin when moist,* fulvous-alutaceous or rufous-tinged when dry,
then subrugulose and atomate, glabrous. FLESH thin, subrigid
and fragile. GILLS adnate, almost close, *narrow,* attenuate in
front, subventricose, becoming fuscous-purplish, edge white-flocculose. STEM 6-8 cm. long, 1.5-2.5 mm. thick, *slender, fragile, white
at first,* then pallid, slightly fibrillose, glabrescent, stuffed with a
white pith then hollow, undulate. VEIL none. SPORES elliptical-
oblong, 10-12x6 micr., obtuse, smooth, purple-brown under microscope, purplish-black in mass. CYSTIDIA scattered, on sides and
edge of gills, ventricose-elongated, narrow above, 50-60 x 9 micr.
ODOR and TASTE none.

Solitary and scattered. On low, wet ground in low woods. Ann

Arbor, New Richmond. May, June and September. Not infrequent in wet weather.

Agrees well with the Friesian description. The gills are perhaps not truly subdistant but rather close. The color of the cap changes from umber to rufous then pale tan. The slender, white, equal stem is a marked character. When moist, the cap is somewhat shining, with a gelatinous appearance, but there is no pellicle and the trama is homogeneous.

273. Psilocybe arenulina Pk.

N. Y. State Mus. Rep. 30, 1878.

PILEUS 1-3 cm. broad, convex then plane, glabrous, hygropha-nous, *dark brown and coarsely striate on margin when moist,* dingy white when dry, margin at first incurved and fibrillose-flocculose. FLESH thin, concolor. GILLS adnate, close, not broad, ventricose, becoming brownish then purple-brown and dotted by spore-masses. STEM 3-5 cm. long, 1.5-2 mm. thick, tapering upward, hollow, *whit-ish,* the lower half covered with adhering sand and sometimes cla-vate. SPORES 10-11 x 5 micr., elliptical, smooth, purple-brown under the microscope. CYSTIDIA none.

Gregarious or subcaespitose, on sandy soil. Port Huron, New Richmond. September-October.

This seems to be close to *P. ammophila* Mont. (see illustration in Hard's Mushrooms, Fig. 268, p. 330, 1908). The spores of that species appear to be too large, and the habit is different. At least our plants were not like those figured by Hard.

274. Psilocybe agrariella Atk.

Ann. Myc., Vol. VII, p. 374, 1909.

PILEUS 1-3.5 cm. broad, campanulate-convex, obtuse, then ex-panded, *fragile,* hygrophanous, *obscurely rivulose or striatulate and umber-brownish to pale rufous when moist,* glabrous, pallid ochraceous or whitish when dry, margin at first incurved and deli-cately white-silky from the evanescent veil. FLESH thin, nearly homogeneous, of floccose cells, concolor. GILLS adnate, seceding, moderately broad, ventricose, *close,* at length purplish umber, edge white-fimbriate. STEM 4-6 cm. long, 3-4 mm. thick, equal, *fragile, white,* even, apex pruinose, glabrous, stuffed soon hollow, base white-mycelioid. SPORES elliptical, 7-9 x 4-5 micr., inequilateral, smooth, dark purple-brown under the microscope, blackish-purple in mass. CYSTIDIA scattered on sides of gills, more numerous on edge, 45-55 x 10-15 micr., ventricose-lanceolate, apex obtuse. ODOR and TASTE mild.

Gregarious or scattered, on the ground or leaf mould, in wet places of low frondose woods. Ann Arbor, New Richmond. May, June and September. Infrequent.

The color is somewhat variable in different localities but the other characters are the same. It differs from *P. cernua* in the presence of a very slight veil when young. The pileus is slightly rigid but fragile; its surface has a slight gelatinous feel when wet, but there is no distinct pellicle, merely a somewhat differentiated upper layer of more turgid cells.

A closely related species occurs in low wet ground in woods, which differs from this mainly in possessing a thin subgelatinous pellicle of horizontal narrow hyphae, with narrower gills and pellucid-white stem. The color of cap and stem and the microscopic characters are otherwise the same. Perhaps it is a variety of *P. ericaea* Fr., but the pileus is distinctly hygrophanous.

275. Psilocybe submaculata Atk.

Ann. Myc., Vol. VII, p. 375, 1909.

"PILEUS 4-10 mm. broad, convex, glabrous, hygrophanous, *dull brownish,* then dull white with dark watery and yellowish spots, margin at first incurved. FLESH with a surface layer of sub-pyriform to subglobose angular cells, inner portion floccose and grading into the surface cells. GILLS adnate, emarginate, *rather crowded,* brownish with a purple tinge, edge whitish. STEM 2-3 cm. long, 2-3 mm. thick, fistulose, even, somewhat flexuous, *white and shining,* apex white-mealy, base with white mycelium. SPORES suboblong, subelliptical, slightly inequilateral, 6-7 x 3-4 micr., purple-brown under the microscope. BASIDIA 4-spored. CYSTIDIA few on sides of gills, very numerous on edge, ventricose, apex crystalline. On very rotten wood."

The description is adapted from that of Atkinson, who reported specimens from Michigan. I have not studied it.

276. Psilocybe foenisecii Fr. (Edible)

Syst. Myc., 1821.

Illustrations: Cooke, Ill., Pl. 590.
   Gillet, Champignons de France, No. 592.
   Ricken, Die Blätterpilze, Pl. 66, Fig. 8.
   Swanton, Fungi, Pl. 9, Fig. 1.
   Murrill, Mycologia, Vol. 3, Pl. 40, Fig. 5.
   Hard, Mushrooms, Fig. 267, p. 329, 1908.
   Plate LIV of this Report.

PILEUS 1-2.5 cm. broad, rarely broader, campanulate-convex or subhemispherical, obtuse, seldom plane, hygrophanous, *dark grayish-brown to smoky-fuscous and even when moist,* sometimes rufescent, subzonate on drying, drab-tan-color to buff when dry, glabrous, veil entirely lacking. FLESH thin, dingy-pallid. GILLS adnate, almost subdistant, *broad,* ventricose, sometimes sinuate-emarginate, purplish-fuscous or fuscous-brown, *variegated,* edge white-fimbriate. STEM *slender,* 4-8 cm. long, 1.5-2 mm. thick, equal, rigid-elastic, fragile, hollow, even, glabrous, pruinose at apex, pallid to subrufescent, not rooting. SPORES *variable in size,* 13-18 x 8-10 micr., broadly elliptical, or in another plane broader at one end, *slightly tuberculate,* apiculate, purplish-brown under the microscope. CYSTIDIA none. STERILE CELLS on edge, narrow, 30-36 x 3-5 micr. ODOR and TASTE none.

Gregarious or scattered, among grass on lawns, roadsides, grassy places in woods, meadows and pastures. Throughout the State. May-June (less often, July-September). Very common.

The "haymarker's Psilocybe" is to be looked for during the warm spring months on our lawns everywhere. Its colors are dull and quite variable, but because of its abundance it can soon be recognized under its many guises. A zonate effect is often seen on the pileus as the moisture dries out. It is edible. The spore-sizes are given incorrectly by several authors, but this is not surprising because of their great variability, even in the same plant. The rough character of the surface of the spore distinguishes it from the others.

277. Psilocybe conissans Pk.

N. Y. State Mus. Rep. 41, 1888 (as Clitopilus).

PILEUS 2.5-5 cm. broad, broadly convex becoming plane, hygro-phanous, *watery-brown to pale chestnut when moist,* pale alutaceous to buff when dry, striatulate then subrugulose, glabrous or sub-pruinose, veil lacking. FLESH thin, whitish. GILLS adnexed, rounded behind, thin, close, brownish *then dusted by the reddish-cinnamon or vinaceous-red spores.* STEM 2.5-5 cm. long, 2-4 mm. thick, *equal,* rather slender, rigid-fragile, hollow, *white,* curved or flexuous, glabrous, pruinose at apex. SPORES elliptical or almost oblong, 7-9 x 4-5 micr. (rarely longer), smooth, hyaline but with reddish tinge under the microscope, brick-red in mass.

Caespitose around base of stumps in hemlock-maple woods. Marquette and Houghton. August-September. Rather rare.

A peculiar plant, whose spores might well lead one to look for it under the pink-spored group but whose general appearance is that of a Psilocybe. Under the microscope the spores are almost hyaline-white but the exospore is slightly tinged with reddish; when dusted on the cap and stem, as is often the case, they have a brick-red to vinaceous color. Peck originally referred it to Clitopilus, but in the N. Y. State Bull. 122, he changed it to Psilocybe.

OCHRASPORAE

Paxillus Fr.

(From the Latin *Paxillus,* a small stake.)

Ochre-spored. Stem confluent with the pileus, fleshy, tending to be eccentric or lacking. Gills mostly decurrent, forked behind and *anastomosing on the stem, easily separable from the trama of the pileus.*

Fleshy, putrescent, distinct fungi, growing on the ground, forest debris or decayed wood. When present the stems are stout and usually slightly eccentric, sometimes central; in two species the pileus is sessile and lateral, and the stem is lacking. The genus Paxillus is here limited to include only the plants placed by Fries under the tribe Tapinia. The white-spored species have been re-ferred to Clitocybe under the section Paxilloideae. *P. lepista* Fr., which is said to have reddish spores is not known to me. Ricken has placed some of the species of Clitopilus with reddish spores next to *Paxillus lepista,* an arrangement which hardly solves the problem.   Several species of Clitocybe and Tricholoma with a tint of reddish in the spore-print and with gills separable from the pileus are equally close to *P. lepista* as it is described, and an arrangement of these species under a single genus is desirable: such are *Tricholoma panoeolum* var. *caespitosum* and *Tricholoma nudum.* Karsten, Earle and others have raised the tribe Tapinia to the rank of a genus and include under it the species described below.   No uniformity of agreement has so far resulted and I prefer to retain the name Paxillus in this report because of its established use for our plants and therefore its practical convenience.

Key to the Species

(a) Stem present; pileus medium large.
  (b) Stem covered by blackish-brown, dense, tomentose hairs.   280.
      P. atrotomentosus Fr.
  (bb) Stem not tomentose-hairy.
    (c) Gills golden-yellow; pileus reddish-yellow-brown.   278.   *P. rhodoxanthus* Schw.
    (cc) Gills dingy olivaceous-yellowish, becoming brown when bruised. 279. *P. involutus* Fr.
(aa) Stem lacking; pileus lateral.
  (b) Gills orange-yellow, corrugate. 281. *P. corrugatus* Atk.
  (bb) Gills pale yellowish or yellowish tan; sinuous-crisped. 282. *P. panuoides* Fr.

278.   Paxillus rhodoxanthus Schw.

Synopsis Fung., 1822.

Illustrations: Cooke, Ill., Pl. 834 (as *P. paradoxus*).
    Bresadola, Fung. Trid., Pl. 207 (as *Phylloporus rhodoxanthus*).
    Fries, Icones, Pl. 115, Fig. 2 (*as Flammula tammii*).
    Gillet, Champignons de France, No. 136 (as *Clitocybe pelletieri*).
    Patouillard, Tab. Analyt., No. 354 (as *Paxillus tammii*).
    Ricken, Blätterpilze, Pl. 28, Fig. 1.
    Atkinson, Mushrooms, Pl. 47, Fig. 156, 1900.
    Hard, Mushrooms, Fig. 234, p. 289, 1908.

PILEUS 4-9 cm. broad, firm, convex, then expanded, depressed or obtuse, somewhat turbinate, color varying *reddish-yellow-brown to chestnut brown,* sometimes pale cinnamon-brown, minutely tomentose, glabrescent, dry, often rimosely cracked.   FLESH thick at disk, pallid tinged yellowish. GILLS long, decurrent, arcuate, thickish, rather broad toward stem, close to subdistant, *golden-yellow to chrome-yellow*, sometimes forked, *very intervenose*, sometimes reticulate-porose toward stem. STEM 4-8 cm. long, 5-10 mm. thick, equal or ventricose, solid, pale, reddish-yellow, yellow at base, punctate with small, reddish-brown scales or dots. SPORES elongated-oblong, almost fusiform, 9-12 x 3-4.5 micr., yellowish in mass. CYSTIDIA numerous on edge and sides of gills, clavate-lanceolate, 60-70 x 9-15 micr., filled with yellowish content. ODOR and TASTE mild.

Gregarious or scattered. On the ground or among mosses in frondose or conifer woods. Ann Arbor, Bay View. July-August. Infrequent.

This species appears to represent a link between the Boletaceae and the Agaricaceae. The top of the pileus may easily be mistaken for *Boletus subtomentosus* and in its extreme variation the gills anastomose to such an extent as to almost appear porose near the stem. The plant has been placed in Gomphidius, Flammula, and Clitocybe, while Bresadola erected the genus Phylloporus for it, where it might well be left. The plant was first described by Rev. David de Schweinitz from specimens gathered in North Carolina. It occurs also in Europe where it has had a variety of names.

279. Paxillus involutus Fr. (EDIBLE)

Syst. Myc., 1821.

Illustrations: Cooke, Ill., Pl. 875.
> Gillet, Champignons de France, No. 514.
> Berkeley, Outlines, Pl. 12, Fig. 5.
> Michael, Führer, f. Pilzfreunde, Vol. I, No. 30.
> Ricken, Blätterpilze, Pl. 28, Fig. 2.
> Swanton, Fungi, Pl. 40, Fig. 7-8.
> Atkinson, Mushrooms, Fig. 155, p. 166, 1900.
> Hard, Mushrooms, Fig. 232, p. 287, 1908.
> Peck, N. Y. State Mus. Rep. 48, Pl. 28, Fig. 18-23.

PILEUS 4-9 cm. broad, convex then expanded-depressed, firm, pliant in age, *ochraceous-rusty-brown, reddish-brown or olive-brown*, somewhat cottony-tomentose, margin *at first involute* then spreading and furrowed or ridged, sometimes subviscid, shining in spots when dry. FLESH thick, yellowish-pallid, becoming brownish when bruised. GILLS decurrent, arcuate, crowded, rather broad, *anastomosing, or reticulated-porose on the stem,* olivaceous-yellow *becoming brown when bruised.* STEM 4-6 cm. long, 1-2.5 cm. thick, solid, glabrous, even, central or eccentric, somewhat enlarged at base, dingy yellowish-brown or concolor. SPORES broadly elliptical, pallid, rusty-ochraceous, 7-9 x 5 micr., smooth. CYSTIDIA moderately abundant or scattered, lanceolate, 50-70 x 10-12 micr. ODOR and TASTE mild. *Edible.*

Solitary or scattered. On the ground or among forest debris, sometimes at the sides of logs or base of stumps, etc. More common in the coniferous regions of the State, rather infrequent elsewhere. Isle Royale, Houghton, Marquette, Bay View, New Richmond, Detroit, Ann Arbor, etc. July-October. Common in the north.

The dingy and dull colors are somewhat variable in various stages of development. It is not usually an attractive plant because of the hues assumed by the flesh, etc., in age. I have but seldom found it in the southern part of the State or where conifers are absent.

280. Paxillus atrotomentosus Fr. (EDIBLE)

Syst. Myc., 1821.

Illustrations: Cooke, Ill., Pl. 876.
>Gillet, Champignons de France, No. 512.
>Michael, Führer f. Pilzfreunde, Vol. I, No. 29.
>Ricken, Blätterpilze, Pl. 28, Fig. 4.
>Atkinson, Mushrooms, Fig. 157, p. 169, 1900.
>Hard, Mushrooms, Fig. 233, p. 288, 1908.

PILEUS 5-12 cm. broad, firm, tough, convex then plane or depressed, dry, more or less pruinose-tomentose, at length naked, *rusty-brown to blackish-brown,* even, margin at first involute, persistently incurved. FLESH thick, compact to spongy, white. GILLS adnate-decurrent, separable from the pileus, close, rather narrow, *forked behind* and often anastomosing, sometimes porose on stem. STEM 3-12 cm. long, 1-3 cm. thick, *often eccentric, stout,* solid, tough, straight or curved, arising from a rooting base, *covered by a blackish-brown velvety tomentum.* SPORES oval, smooth, 5-6 x 3-4 micr., yellowish in mass. CYSTIDIA none. ODOR and TASTE slight. *Edible.*

Solitary or caespitose. On decaying logs, stumps, etc., or base of trees, in coniferous woods. Huron Mountains, Bay View, Saginaw, New Richmond. July-September. Infrequent.

Very distinct by the blackish hairs which clothe the stem. It is apparently limited to wood or debris from coniferous sources. Occasional specimens attain quite a large size and often occur singly at the base of pine trees. The cap is sometimes nearly lateral especially when growing in tufts.

281. Paxillus corrugatus Atk.

Mushrooms, p. 170, 1900.

Illustration: Ibid, Pl. 48, Fig. 158.

PILEUS 2-5 cm. broad, *lateral, shelving,* narrowed down in an irregular wedge-form to the sessile base, convex then expanded, *maize-yellow to canary-yellow,* with a reddish-brown tinge near the base, glabrous or slightly tomentose, margin at first involute. FLESH pale yellow, spongy. GILLS 2-3 mm. broad, not crowded, regularly dichotomously forked, thin, *very wavy and crenulate,* sides corrugated, *orange-yellow,* easily separating from pileus. STEM lacking. SPORES minute, broadly-elliptical to oval, 3 x 1.5-2 micr., faintly yellow, olive-yellow on white paper. ODOR characteristic, disagreeable.

On hemlock stumps or wood. Houghton, Marquette. August-September. Infrequent or rare.

Known best by the deep orange-yellow color of the corrugated gills and the lack of a stem.

282. Paxillus panuoides Fr.

Syst. Myc., 1821.

Illustrations: Cooke, Ill., Pl. 878.
    Berkeley, Outlines, Pl. 12, Fig. 6.
    Michael, Führer f. Pilzfreunde, Vol. III, No. 50.
    Ricken, Blätterpilze, Pl. 28, Fig. 3.

PILEUS 3-12 cm. broad, *sessile,* or laterally extended to a stem-like base, *petaloid* or *conchate,* dull yellow to olivaceous-yellow, tinged with brown, downy at first, glabrescent, margin thin, acute, wavy or crisped. FLESH white, soft, not very thick. GILLS radiating from the base, forked, anastomosing, *often crisped,* close, pale yellow. STEM lacking. SPORES elliptical, smooth, 4-6 x 3-4, pale yellow in mass. CYSTIDIA none. ODOR and TASTE mild.

Gregarious or subimbricate. On decaying logs, etc., in coniferous woods.

Houghton, Munising, Bay View. July-August. Infrequent.

Paler and with less corrugated gills than the preceding. It is said to be very variable in form and habit. In Europe it occurs in dark places, in cellars, mines, etc., attached to the timbers. It appears to be much less common in this country.

Pholiota Fr.

(From the Greek *Pholis,* a scale.)

Ochre-brown or rusty spored. Stem continuous with the pileus, provided with a *membranous annulus,* which is formed from a partial veil; no volva, hence no universal veil; gills *adnate becoming emarginate* or decurrent by a tooth, sometimes adnexed.

Putrescent, terrestrial or lignicolous mushrooms, of great variability of types. They correspond to Armillaria of the white-spored group, and Stropharia of the purple-brown-spored group. The nearest genera are Flammula and Cortinarius whose veils differ, when present, in being cortinate. The large, wood-inhabiting species are often densely caespitose. None are known to be poisonous, and many are excellent when cooked.

The PILEUS varies according to the section to which it belongs. In one section it is often very scaly, in the others it is usually glabrous. It may be dry or hygrophanous. The color is usually whitish or dull yellowish in the first section. Those growing on wood are often very attractive, with bright yellow colors, in *P. aeruginosa* tinged with dark green, and in others a watery-brown. The GILLS are attached to the stem, adnate, adnexed, or decurrent by a tooth; in all these cases, the gills may secede from the stem during the expansion of the pileus, and they nearly always become emarginate or sinuate at maturity. This separates them from the genus Flammula whose gills never become sinuate. The color changes from the young condition to maturity and it is necessary in many cases to know the color of the young gills to identify the species; this is usually white or yellow, but at length changes to the color of the spores, which are either ochraceous, fuscous or ferruginous. The STEM is fleshy or fibrous, solid or stuffed, and provided with a membranous *annulus* which is either persistent or may break up into easily removed shreds, so that it may appear to be lacking in rainy weather. The SPORES are elliptical or oval, non-angular except obscurely so in a few species, e. g. *P. acericola, P. howeana* and *P. aegerita;* in *P. aggericola* they are often somewhat pear-shaped. The color when caught on white paper varies considerably, and has been used to subdivide the sections. CYSTIDIA are present only in two sections, as far as is known, viz. in the Humigeni and Hygrophani. This fact may serve as a basis for raising these sections to generic rank, as has been done by Earle and others.

The genus Pholiota furnishes some excellent species for the table. *P. praecox* and its near relatives are among the early edible mushrooms, and as they occur on lawns and grassy places are within easy reach. A number of the large, caespitose forms, like *P. squarrosa, P. squarrosoides* and *P. adiposa* are among those eaten, and in Europe *P. mutabilis* is highly prized as an ingredient of soups, and is often artificially cultivated on the wood on which it is found. On the other hand, wood-inhabiting Pholiotas as well as others, are apt to have a strong odor or taste, derived from the wood, and this does not always disappear on cooking. As far as known, no virulent poisons are present in any of this genus.

The genus is rather large, but many species are found rather infrequently. The following key includes most of the species reported for the north-eastern United States, and no doubt some which are not yet described will be discovered from time to time. Fries divided the genus into three sections; to these I will add the subdivision Hygrophani, as they seem to stand out sufficiently clear from the rest of the species. The four sections follow:

    I. Humigeni
   II. Truncigeni
  III. Hygrophani
  IV. Muscigeni

Key to the Species

(A) Pileus viscid when moist. [See also (AA) and (AAA).]
  (a) Pileus scaly; often very caespitose; on wood, sometimes on debris.
    (b) Pileus bright yellow.
      (c) Gills broad, adnate then emarginate, at first yellow; pileus very viscid, ochre-yellow.
     (cc) Gills narrow. 297. *P. adiposa* Fr.
      (d) Gills yellow at first; pileus sulphur-yellow, covered with tawny or reddish-brown scales; stem peronate. 299. *P. lucifera* (Lasch.) Bres.
     (dd) Gills whitish at first; pileus lemon-yellow. *P. limonella* Pk.
   (bb) Pileus not at all or tinged slightly with yellow.

  (c) Pileus tinged red, pink or purplish; subcaespitose; gills white or yellow-tinged at first. *P. ornella* Pk.

  (cc) Pileus not with red or pink.

    (d) Very caespitose; pileus and stem with dense, erect or recurved tawny scales on buff ground-color. 290. *P. squarrosoides* Pk.

    (dd) Solitary or very few in one tuft.

      (e) Edge of gills beaded with white drops; pileus yellowish-fulvous, spotted with removable scales. 291. *P. albocrenulata* Pk.

      (ee) Edge of gills not beaded; pileus yellowish-white or sometimes darker; stem bulbous-radicate. 289. *P. destruens* (Lasch.) Bres. (syn. *P. comosa* Fr.), (syn. *P. heteroclita* Fr.)

(aa) Pileus glabrous.

  (b) Spores large and variable, 10-15 micr. long, pileus dark brown or blackish brown; on the ground in woods. 288. *P. aggericola* Pk.

  (bb) Spores 9 micr. or less in length.

    (c) On decaying logs, etc.; pileus hygrophanous, rufous-cinnamon (moist). 304. *P. discolor* Pk.

    (cc) On lawns, grassy places, etc.; pileus whitish-buff or white, thick. 283. *P. praecox* Fr.

(AA) Pileus hygrophanous, not viscid.

  (a) Growing on moss or sphagnum; pileus small; stem slender to filiform; annulus membranous.

  (b) Pileus umbonate; stem solid; annulus slight. *P. minima* Pk.

  (bb) Pileus not umbonate; stem hollow; annulus persistent, entire. 308. *P. mycenoides* Fr.

  (aa) On decaying logs, stumps, chips, saw dust, etc., sometimes on debris in woods, or on the ground.

  (b) Gills at first yellowish or ochraceous.

    (c) Large; pileus 5-10 cm. broad, cinnamon (moist); annulus fugacious; flesh yellowish. *P. cerasina* Pk.

    (cc) Much smaller; annulus persistent.

      (d) Gills broadly adnate, subtriangular; appearance of *P. marginata*, subcaespitose. 305. *P. unicolor* Fr.

      (dd) Gills adnexed, relatively broad; solitary; pileus small, rugose. 307. *P. rugosa* Pk.

  (bb) Gills never with yellowish tints.

    (c) Very caespitose; pileus yellow-cinnamon to pale cinnamon; stem squarrose-scaly, below the blackish-brown annulus. *P. mutabilis* Fr.

    (cc) Gregarious; stem not scaly.

      (d) Annulus fugaceous, small, scarcely membranous; gills narrow; pileus watery-cinnamon. 306. *P. marginata* Fr.

      (dd) Annulus ample, membranous.

        (e) Pileus densely floccose-dotted, rufous-cinnamon to brick-red; very fragile. 303. *P. confragosa* Fr.

        (ee) Pileus glabrous, rugose-wrinkled, ochraceous-cinnamon then paler. 302. *P. acericola* Pk.

(AAA) Pileus neither viscid nor hygrophanous.

  (a) Pileus scaly; on wood, logs, trunks, etc.

  (b) Gills yellow, at length ferruginous.

    (c) Pileus silky, floccose-squamulose on disk, buff-yellow; taste bitter; annulus fugacious. *P. lutea* Pk.

    (cc) Pileus entirely squamulose.

      (d) Scales sulphur-yellow, superficial, pilose; stem squarrose-scaly, hollow. 298. *P. flammans* Fr.

      (dd) Scales innate, i. e., by the breaking up of the cuticle.

        (e) Gills narrow, adnato-decurrent; pileus golden-yellow to tawny; annulus ample, near apex of ventricose stem.

       296. *P. spectabilis* Fr.
  (ee) Gills broad.
    (f) Pileus and stem variegated yellow and green, or with greenish scales; on exposed, hard wood. 301. *P. aeruginosa* Pr.
    (ff) Pileus without green shades.
      (g) Stem hollow at length; pileus covered with ferruginous, pointed, fasciculate scales. 295. *P. muricata* Fr.
      (gg) Stem solid; pileus pale red or yellowish; gills subdistant. 300. *P. luteofolia* Pk.
  (bb) Gills not yellow at first, (becoming yellowish in *P. curvipes*).
    (c) Very caespitose; pileus and stem squarrose-scaly; gills pallid-olivaceous at first, narrow. *P. squarrosa* Fr.
    (cc) Solitary or subcaespitose.
      (d) Stem bulbous, subradicate, solid; gills rounded-adnexed or adnate. (Dry condition.) 289. *P. destruens* Fr.
      (dd) Stem equal, stuffed then hollow.
        (e) Pileus small, 2-3 cm. broad.
          (f) Pileus covered with superficial, erect, small spine-like scales, tawny-brown. 294. *P. erinaceella* Pk.
          (ff) Pileus with innate, flocculose minute scales. 293. *P. curvipes* Fr.
        (ee) Rather large, 6-12 cm. covered with appressed, tawny fibrillose scales; gills, narrow; annulus ample. 292. *P. fulvosquamosa* Pk.
(aa) Pileus not scaly; growing on the ground.
  (b) In moist, rich woods.
    (c) Moderately large.
      (d) Large; pileus covered with white flocci, lacunose-wrinkled; annulus large, persistent and movable. 284. *Pholiota caperata* Fr.
      (dd) Pileus glabrous; disk ochre-yellowish.
        (e) Gills adnexed or nearly free; stem solid; annulus thick. 285. *P. johnsoniana* Pk.
        (ee) Gills adnate, decurrent by a tooth; stem hollow; annulus ample; caespitose. 286. *P. aegerita* Fr.
    (cc) Small; pileus ochraceous; spores 7-8 x 3-4; annulus membranous, distant; gills yellowish. *P. togularis* Fr.
  (bb) On lawns, grassy places, etc., medium size.
    (c) Stem solid, hard. Pileus tan-color but variable; in cultivated fields and gardens. 284. *P. dura* Bolt.
    (cc) Stem stuffed then hollow; pileus varying white, whitish tinged with tan or yellowish.
      (d) Open places, in fields, thickets, etc. Spores 9-10.5 x 5-5.5, obscurely 5-angled. 287. *P. howeana* Pk.
      (dd) Annulus membranous, fragile, subfugacious, brown in mass. *P. duroides* Pk.
      (ddd) Annulus membranous, fragile, subfugacious.
        (e) On lawns, etc., in the spring; spores 8-10 x 5-6 micr., pileus whitish. 284. *P. praecox* Fr.
        (ee) Later in the season; spores 11-12.5 x 7-7.5 micr., similar to the preceding. 284. *P. vermiflua* Pk.

CLASSIFICATION OF AGARICS 293

Section I. Humigeni. Terrestrial, rarely caespitose, not hygrophanous, not attached to mosses, cystidia present or absent.

283. Pholiota præcox Fr. (EDIBLE)

Syst. Myc., 1821. (As *Psalliota praecox.*)

Illustrations: Atkinson, Mushrooms, Plate 42, p. 150, 1900.
Murrill, Mycologia, Vol. 3, Pl. 49, Fig. 1.
Harper, Wis. Acad. Sci. Trans., Vol. 17, Pl. 27 and 28, 1913.
Hard, Mushrooms, Fig. 209, p. 258, 1908.
Marshall, Mushroom Book, Pl. 30, p. 84.
Ricken, Blätterpilze, Pl. 55, Fig. 4.
Patouillard, Tab. Analyt., No. 112.
Peck, N. Y. State Mus. Mem. 4, Plate 57.
Plate LIX of this Report.

PILEUS 2-6 cm. broad, convex or nearly plane, *soft,* glabrous, or
nearly so, even, *moist,* in wet weather often slightly viscid to the
touch, *whitish* or *more or less tinged* with yellowish or leather-color
when old, margin at first incurved. FLESH white, medium thick.
GILLS adnate seceding or becoming emarginate, somewhat
rounded behind, close, of medium width, *at first whitish,*
then tinged gray, finally brownish or rusty brown, edge crenulate.
STEM 3-8 cm. long, 3-5 mm. thick, rather slender, equal or subequal,
usually straight, glabrous, apex pruinose, almost solid or *stuffed by*
a fibrous white pith, even or striate at apex, whitish. VEIL whitish,
thin and frail, *breaking variously,* sometimes forming a thin, fragile
ANNULUS, sometimes adhering in shreds to the margin of pileus.
Annulus apical, fugacious. SPORES elliptical, 9-13 x 6-7 micr.,
smooth, rusty-brown in mass. CYSTIDIA scattered, swollen-ventri-
cose with short, broad apex, 35-45 micr. long, 12-15 micr. thick.
ODOR farinose. TASTE mild.

Solitary or gregarious, rarely subcaespitose. On lawns, pastures,
roadsides, etc., sometimes in woods. Throughout the State. Common in May and early June, after heavy rains.

One of our early edible mushrooms; easy to get, as it grows at
our very doors. It has several near relatives and varies somewhat
when growing in the woods. Peck has called the wood form var.
sylvestris; the cap is darker, brownish to rusty-brown. Another
form, because of its small size (pileus 2-3 cm.) and appendiculate
margin of the pileus, was called var. *minor* by Fries.

The normal form varies also; in wet weather the pileus is sub-viscid, while ordinarily it is dry. The gills of different specimens are attached differently to the stem, adnexed, adnate or even slightly decurrent at times; on expansion of pileus, however, they become sinuate or emarginate; their edge is whitish-crenulate because of the cystidia. Sometimes the base of stem is attached to white strands which enter the turf. The stem is almost homogeneous at first. *P. vermiflua* Pk. is closely related to it. (See illustration: N. Y. State Mus. Bull. 75, Plate 73, 1904.) Authors differ somewhat as to the spore measurements, and may have confused other species with *P. praecox, P. dura* Fr. (see illustration: Hard, Mushrooms, Fig. 210, p. 259) has not been detected in Michigan but doubtless grows here. Its solid stem, tan to brownish pileus, which usually cracks on the surface into areas, and its preference for soil which has been cultivated, distinguish it. Ricken gives the spore-size of *P. dura* as 11-13 x 7-8 micr. *P. temnophylla* Pk. is separated by Peck, on account of its dingy-yellow or ochraceous cap and *very broad gills*. One specimen, which may be this species, was collected in hemlock and spruce woods, Sault Ste. Marie; the very broad gills were obliquely truncate at the inner extremity, but the spores were somewhat smaller than given by Peck. Otherwise it resembles *P. praecox*. Not infrequently specimens of *P. praecox* having the characters of the type rather than those of var. *sylvestris* are found in low, moist woods.

284. Pholiota caperata Fr.

Syst. Myc., 1821.

Illustrations: Cooke, Ill., Pl. 348.
    Ricken, Blätterpilze, Pl. 55, Fig. 2.
    Michael, Führer f. Pilzfreunde, Vol. I, No. 49 (as *Rozites caperata*).
    Gillet, Champignons de France, No. 520.
    Hard, Mushrooms, Pl. 31, Fig. 212.
    Harper, Trans. Wis. Acad. Sci. Arts & Let., Vol. XVII, Pt. 1, Pl. 24.

PILEUS 5-10 cm. broad, oval at first, campanulate-expanded, obtuse, markedly wrinkled or furrowed, dry, *at first with a super-ficial hoariness or floccosity*, straw-color to alutaceous, at length glabrous. FLESH white, thick on disk. GILLS adnate, then emarginate, medium close, whitish then *dingy* pale ferruginous, edge uneven or crisped. STEM *stout,* 7-12 cm. long, 10-20 mm. thick, subcylindrical, firm, solid, glabrous, dingy white, furnished *near the middle with a reflexed, persistant, whitish, membranous annulus.* SPORES 12-14 x 7-9 micr., inequilateral, elliptical, tuber-culate, yellowish. ODOR and taste mild.

Gregarious or scattered. On the ground in woods, especially of conifers. Ann Arbor, Bay View, Marquette, etc. August-September. Frequent locally.

This species has been separated from the Pholiotas by Karsten who invented the genus Rozites for it. It is quite distinct from the other species by its peculiar covering when young. Its stout stem, distinct annulus, large size and terrestrial habit make it easily recognizable.

285. Pholiota johnsoniana (Pk.) Atk. (EDIBLE)

N. Y. State Cab. Rep. 23, 1872 (as *Psalliota johnsoniana*).
N. Y. State Mus. Rep. 41, 1888 (as *Stropharia johnsoniana*).

Illustration: Atkinson, Mushrooms, Plate 44, p. 145, 1900.

PILEUS 4-10 cm. broad, convex then plane and subturbinate, *glabrous, ochre-yellowish,* often shading to whitish on margin which is *thin* and sometimes finely striate. FLESH *quite thick on disk,* white, soft. GILLS *adnexed or almost free,* rounded behind, thin, crowded, rather narrow, grayish-white at first, then rusty-brown, at length ascending toward front. STEM 5-10 cm. long (or more), 6-10 mm. thick, equal or slightly thickened at base, *solid,* glabrous, innately fibrillose, rarely floccose-torn, whitish. SPORES elliptical-oval, 5-6 x 3-4 micr., smooth, brown with a slight rusty tinge. CYSTIDIA none, but scattered over the hymenium are *clusters of stellate crystals.* ANNULUS *thick,* swollen, with obtuse edge.

(Dried: Pileus yellowish-alutaceous; gills fuscous-umber; stem buff).

Gregarious. On leaf-mould in rich woods; also said to occur in pastures. Ann Arbor. September. Rare.

As Atkinson points out, the plant is quite readily distinguished by its subturbinate (i. e. top-shaped) pileus and the thick annulus. Variations occur with erect tawny squammules on the center of the pileus, or with its surface innately floccose or fibrillose. The base of the stem is sometimes connected with the soil by white strands of mycelium. A constant peculiarity of the plant seems to be the clusters of stellate crystals which are scattered among the basidia as seen under the microscope.

286. Pholiota aegerita Fr.

Epicrisis, 1836-38.

Illustrations: Gillet, Champignons de France, No. 524.
Cooke, Ill., Plates 453, 365.

PILEUS 4-7 cm. broad, convex then plane, margin at length elevated, fragile, moist, glabrous, disk subrugulose, *ochraceous-yellow to fulvous,* paler on margin, edge even and thin. FLESH not thick, white. GILLS *adnate,* decurrent by a tooth, rather close, broad, whitish at first, then grayish fuscous, finally umber. STEM 8-12 cm. long, 4-8 mm. thick, slender, equal or slightly thicker at base, fibrillose-striate, floccose at base, *stuffed then hollow,* whitish. ANNULUS whitish, membranous, rather thin, sometimes disappearing. SPORES *obscurely* 5-angled, i. e. truncate at one end, subacute at the other, 9-11 x 5-6 micr., fuscous umber. CYSTIDIA scattered, ventricose, obtuse at apex, about 65-70 micr. long.

(Dried: Pileus fulvous-tan; gills fuscous-umber; stem dingy buff).

Caespitose. Among debris in low grounds, poplar, willow, etc., edge of hemlock woods. Houghton. July. Rare.

The figures and description given by Gillet fit our plant well. The spores agree with the size given by Ricken and Bresadola. The caespitose habit, uneven pileus and slender, hollow stem characterize it. It doubtless varies more as to form than my specimens indicate, and Cooke has given very aberrant examples in the figures cited. The peculiar outline of the spores is shown also in *P. acericola* and *P. howeana.* The flesh is very moist, almost hygrophanous, but in other respects differs from the section of hygrophanous species. It approaches *P. acericola,* which has slightly smaller spores and a large, persistent, curtain-like annulus, and is solitary or gregarious. Fries says the annulus is tumid, in which respect our specimens differ. Harper figures a plant under this name, which reminds one of a discolored form of *P. aeruginosa* Pk. Ricken says it has a strong, rather pleasant odor.

287. Pholiota howeana Pk.

N. Y. State Mus. Rep. 26, 1874.

PILEUS 1.5-5 cm. broad, convex expanded, fragile, subumbonate, dry, glabrous, even, pale ochraceous, unicolor or center darker. FLESH white. GILLS adnate, with a tooth, *narrow,* close, subventricose, white at first then rusty-brown, edge entire and concolor. STEM 3-7 cm. long, 1.5-4 mm. thick, *slender, equal,* rather rigid, corticate, glabrous, even, stuffed with white pith, whitish to pale ochraceous. ANNULUS apical, thin, membranous, and easily rubbed off. SPORES *obsurcly* 5-angled or sub-regular, truncate at one end, pointed at the other, 9-10.5 x 5-5.5 micr., fuscous-brown. CYSTIDIA none or very few. ODOR and TASTE mild.

(Dried: Pileus and stem pale-tan, gills rusty-brown.)

Gregarious. In grassy fields. Ann Arbor. June. Infrequent.

Our collections average smaller than Peck's description.   The slight angularity of the spores is obscure but easily made out. In shape it looks like a small *P. praecox* but the colors differ and the stem has a different texture.   The pileus is sometimes slightly pitted-lacunose on the margin. In size and appearance it resembles *Naucoria semiorbicularis,* but with an annulus; it also approaches Peck's *P. temnophylla;* but that species has very broad gills and the spores are larger.

288. Pholiota aggericola Pk.

N. Y. State Mus. Rep. 24, 1872.
N. Y. State Mus. Rep. 30, 1878 (as *Pholiota indecens* Pk.).
N. Y. State Mus. Bull. 28, 1899 (as *Pholiota aggerata* Pk.).

Illustrations: Marshall, Mushroom Book, p. 73.
(Compare Cooke's Ill., Plate 358 of *P. erebia.*)
Harper, Wis. Acad. Sci. Trans., Vol 17, Pl. 30 (as *P. erebia* Fr.).

PILEUS 1.5-4 cm. broad, convex then plane and at length with recurved margin, *viscid,* dark fuscous-umber, fading to cinnamon, glabrous, *even, rivulose* or *rugose,* margin obscurely striatulate. GILLS *adnate or arcuate subdecurrent,* close to subdistant, rather broad behind and subtruncate, pallid at first, then grayish, finally rusty-brown. STEM 3-6 cm. long, 4-7 mm. thick, equal or subequal, *fibrillose-striate,* stuffed then hollow, dark fuscous-umber below, pale at apex. ANNULUS membranous, thin, *fragile,* veil fuscous and striate above, pale below; veil sometimes adhering to margin of pileus. SPORES variable in size and shape, *long elliptical,* to *subpyriform,* 12-15 x 5-7 micr., sometimes dominantly 12 micr., sometimes 15, smooth, on slender sterigmata. BASIDIA *bispored.* CYSTIDIA nine-pin shaped, or lanceolate, 40-50 micr. long, scattered, fragile, shorter on edge of gills.

Gregarious. In hemlock mixed woods in paths or among debris, usually in moist ground. Bay View, Houghton, Marquette, New Richmond. July-October. Rather frequent locally.

This species has a confused history. It was given several names by Peck. Under *P. indecens* Peck gives spore-measurements 12-15 micr. long, but in his monograph of the New York State Pholiotas, they are said to be 10-12.5 micr. long. This discrepancy is due to spore variations in different individuals as I have assured myself. Often many spores of a specimen are less than 12 micr., but the majority of collections show a dominance of spores 15 micr. long. Often they vary much in the same specimen. This plant prefers low, moist hemlock woods although it is found elsewhere. Its viscid character disappears in dry weather, and the pileus in luxuriant plants is often very rugose; this is var. *retirugis* Pk. The European species, *P. erebia,* as figured by Cooke and Patouillard remind one very much of our plant. But the pileus of that species is described as hygrophanous although Fries says it is also subviscid. The cystidia are also figured differently by Patouillard, yet I should not be surprised if our plant were to turn out to be identical with *P. erebia* Fr. Some specimens have a distinct fuscous-purplish tinge to the gills, and the spores under the microscope suggest a Stropharia rather than a Pholiota; but this character also seems variable, even where spores and cystidia are the same.

Section II. Truncigeni. Lignatile, caespitose or solitary. Pileus scaly, not hygrophanous. Gills changing color. Cystidia lacking.

*Gills at first white or whitish.

289. Pholiota destruens (Fr.) Bres.

Fungi Tridentini, I, 1881.
Hymen. Europ., 1874. (As *Pholiota destruens* Fr., *Pholiota comosa* F*ʳ.*, and *Pholiota heteroclita* Fr.).

Illustrations: Bresadola, Fung. Trid., I, Plate 84.
Cooke, Ill., Pl. 600 (as *Pholiota comosa*).
Cooke, Ill., Plate 366 (as *Pholiota heteroclita*).
Gillet, Champignons de France, No. 522.
Gillet, Champignons de France, No. 521 (as *Pholiota comosa*).
Hard, Mushrooms, Fig. 214, p. 264, 1908 (as *Pholiota heteroclita*).
Harper, Wis. Acad. Sci. Trans., Vol. 17, Pl. 45 (as *P. comosa*).
Harper, ibid, Pl. 46 and 47 (as *P. heteroclita*).
Chicago Nat. Hist. Surv., Bull. VII, Plate 9, 1909 (as *Pholiota comosa*).
Plate LX of this Report.

"PILEUS 6-15 cm. broad, fleshy, convex then expanded, sometimes gibbous or broadly unbonate, *subviscid,* yellowish-white, disk fulvous, *elegantly covered with white, wooly, seceding scales,* margin at first involute and fibrillose. GILLS crowded, rounded-adnexed behind or adnate, decurrent by a line, *whitish at first* then cinnamon-umber. STEM 5-17 cm. long, 2-3 cm. thick, solid, attenuated at apex, bulbous-radicate at base, white-squamose, glabrescent in age, concolor. FLESH white, fulvous-cinnamon at base of stem. SPORES elliptical, or obovate, 8-10 x 4-6 micr., yellow under microscope. BASIDIA clavate, 20-25 x 6 micr. ODOR strong, somewhat nauseous. TASTE rather agreeable."

Solitary or subcaespitose. On trunks of poplar, birch and willow. Autumn. Detroit, Frankfort. Infrequent.

The description is that of Bresadola, who has shown the identity of the three species given by Fries (see above). It was collected by Dr. Fischer near Detroit and one of his photographs was published by Hard as *P. heteroclita*. It seems to be rare in the state. Harper recently reported it from Frankfort.

290. Pholiota squarrosoides Pk. (EDIBLE)

N. Y. State Mus. Rep. 31, 1879.

Illustrations: Peck, N. Y. State Mus. Rep. 54, Plate 73.
Hard, Mushrooms, Plate 21, p. 42, 1908.
Harper, Wis. Acad. Sci. Trans., Vol. 17, Pl. 36 and 37.
Conn. State Geol. & Nat. Hist. Surv. Bull. 3, Plate 21.

PILEUS 3-10 cm. broad, *firm,* subglobose when young, then convex, *viscid when moist, adorned with terete, erect, pointed, tawny scales,* more dense on disk, on a whitish ground-color. FLESH white, thick. GILLS rather narrow, adnate or arcuate subdecurrent, often becoming sinuate in age, close or crowded, whitish becoming brownish-ferruginous. STEM 5-10 cm. long, 5-10 mm. thick, equal, firm, *stuffed, rough* with numerous, thick, floccose, tawny scales, which terminate above in a lacerated, floccose ANNULUS, glabrous and white above the annulus. SPORES oblong, short-elliptical to ovoid, 5-5.5 x 2.5-3.5 micr., smooth, rusty-brown. CYSTIDIA scattered, about 30 micr. long, obtuse at apex.

(Dried: Ochraceous, with tawny scales.)

Very caespitose, up to 50 in a cluster. On trunks of living maple, birch and beech, also on dead wood: logs, stumps, etc., of deciduous trees. Northern Peninsula, frequent; not found elsewhere. August-September. Edible.

The "sharp scale" Pholiota is closely related to the European *P. squarrrosa.* It is said (N. Y. State Mus. Rep. 54, p. 183) to differ in the viscid pileus, emarginate gills and smaller spores. The gills, however, are not constant, and frequently I have seen our plant with arcuate-decurrent gills, without a sign of emargination. In 1908 in company of C. G. Lloyd, I came across a tuft of a Pholiota in the grounds of Upsala University, Sweden, which had all the macroscopic characters of our plant; it was slightly viscid (moist), and the colors were the same as in the specimens collected in northern Michigan. Unfortunately, I was unable to get the spore-measurements. Fries iñ Epicrisis, p. 166, says the color of *P. squarrosa* is croceo-ferruginous, and it is thus figured by Michael, Vol. II, No. 76, and Cooke, Ill., Plate 367. On the other hand, Patouillard in Tab. Analyt., p. 154 and No. 340, paints it like our species and unites with it *P. verruculosa* Lasch. which Cooke in Illust., Plate 614, figures in such a way as to remind us strongly of *P. squarrosoides.* Either the American plant occurs in Europe also, or there is great variation in the color of *P. squarrosa,* both of cap and gills. The gills of the latter are said by all the European authors, to be pale olivaceous at first, and the spore measurements are given as 8 x 4. Maire (Soc. Myc. France Bull., Vol. 27, p. 437) says the spores are smooth. Further, the odor of *P. squarrosa* is said to be strong, disagreeable. Patouillard, Gillet and Michael describe the flesh as yellow. *P. squarrosa* may then be said to differ from *P. squarrosoides,* in the color of the young gills, the disagreeable odor, the yellow flesh, the crocus-yellow or tawny color, and the larger, smooth spores. It has been reported from the United States by various authors, and it seems desirable that the two species be more carefully studied. I have never found a plant in Michigan which could be referred to *P. squarrosa*, but Harper has illustrated collections from Frankfort, Michigan, under the latter name.

291.   Pholiota albocrenulata Pk.

N. Y. State Mus. Rep. 25, 1873.

Illustration: Harper, Wis. Acad. Sci. Trans., Vol. 17, Pl. 42 and 43.

PILEUS 3-12 cm. or more broad, firm, broadly convex or campanulate, often unbonate, *very viscid,* orange-fulvous, becoming ferruginous-tawny in age, *spotted with superficial, darker, fibrillose, scales which become whitish on drying,* margin even and at length reflexed, often appendiculate. FLESH thick, *whitish.* GILLS adnate, becoming sinuate and rounded behind, *very broad,* close, whitish at first, then grayish, at length rusty-umber, *edge crenulate and beaded with white drops.* STEM 5-15 cm. long, 5-10 mm. thick, firm, equal or tapering slightly upward, stuffed by a loose pith, soon hollow, dingy whitish or ochraceous, *covered with squarrose, brown scales* up to the fugacious ANNULUS, apex pruinose and white. SPORES ventricose-subfusiform, inequilateral, 11-14 x 5.5-6.5 micr., smooth, rusty-umber.   CYSTIDIA none.

Solitary, or two or three in a cluster. Mostly growing out of a crack or wound of living trees, towards the base of the trunk; on living sugar maple, yellow birch and hemlock. July-September. Frequent in the Northern Peninsula, rare in southern Michigan.

This fine plant prefers the sugar maple, and may yet be found to be injurious to the living trees, as it has the characteristic habit of parasitic mushrooms. Peck and Harper report it on prostrate trunks and decaying wood, but I have always found it on living trees. Morgan also reports it from Ohio on the base of standing maple trees. The white-headed edge of the gills, the peculiar scales and large spores distinguish it. The spores average longer than noted by Peck, although they vary considerably in length. The pileus may attain to quite large dimensions. Its edibility is unknown.

292. Pholiota fulvosquamosa Pk.

Torr. Bot. Club. Bull. 30, 1903.

Illustration: Harper, Wis. Acad. Sci. Trans., Vol 17, Pl. 60.

"PILEUS 6-12 cm. broad, fleshy, rather thin, convex becoming
nearly plane, *dry,* adorned with numerous, appressed, tawny scales,
concentrically cracked about the disk. FLESH white, becoming
brownish where cut. GILLS *narrow,* close, attenuated towards the
stem and attached to a narrow collar, whitish becoming pinkish-
cinnamon. STEM 5-8 cm. long, 8-10 mm. thick, equal, rigid, stuffed
or hollow, adorned below with numerous, erect, subfloccose, tawny
scales, glabrous above and below the *ample, persistent* ANNULUS,
which is white above and tawny floccose-squamulose below.
SPORES elliptical, 7-8 x 4-5 micr. ODOR and TASTE of radishes."
    About the base of oak trees. M. A. C., East Lansing. Septem-
ber. B. O. Longyear. Neebish Island, October, E. T. Harper.
    I have never collected this species. It was discovered by Long-
year, and found again by Harper. Its ample annulus, narrow gills,
and the tawny scales seem to distinguish it.

293. Pholiota curvipes Fr.

Epicrisis, 1836-38.

Illustrations: Fries, Icones, Plate 104.
        Cooke, Ill., Plate 370.

PILEUS 1-3 cm. broad, convex then expanded, innately floccose
all over when young, then minutely scaly, *tawny-yellow,* dry, not
striate, margin incurved. FLESH rather thin, firm when dry.
GILLS *adnate,* not emarginate, *broad,* close to subdistant, *whitish
at first* then yellowish to rusty-cinnamon. STEM short, 2-3 cm.
long, 2-3 mm. thick, curved or ascending, equal, stuffed then hollow,
becoming fibrillose. ANNULUS soon vanishing, at first floccose-
radiate, almost lacking. SPORES elliptical, 6-8 x 3-4 micr., smooth,
pale-yellowish under the microscope, rusty-brown in mass. CYS-
TIDIA none. ODOR none. TASTE mild.
    Solitary or gregarious. On logs of elm, etc. Ann Arbor.
June. Infrequent.
    Closely related to species of Flammula, because of its poorly de-
veloped annulus. The different color of the young gills and the

nature of the scales on the pileus, separate it from *P. muricata*. It is evident, from his description of the species (N. Y. State Mus. Bull. 122) that Peck has referred a different plant under this name, since the spores of his specimens are too large, and the gills are yellow and close. From present advices the large-spored species is probably *P. tuberculosa* Fr. On the other hand, Hard (Mushrooms, p. 264, 1908) and Moffatt (Chicago, Nat. Hist. Surv. Bull VII, p. 78) doubtless had our species. I cannot agree with those who would combine *P. muricata* Fr. with this species, although the spores are very similar.

294. Pholiota erinaceella Pk.

N. Y. State Mus. Rep. 28, 1876 (as *P. detersibilis*).

Illustration: Harper, Wis. Acad. Sci. Trans., Vol. 17, Pl. 51.

"PILEUS 1-2.5 cm. broad, hemispherical or convex, dry, *densely coated with small, erect, separable pyramidal or spine-like scales,* tawny-brown. FLESH thin. GILLS adnexed, *broad,* close, pallid becoming cinnamon-brown. STEM 1-2.5 cm. long, 2 mm. thick, equal, stuffed or hollow, *densely squamulose below the slight annulus,* often curved, colored like the pileus. SPORES boat-shaped, 7.5-9 x 4-5 micr."

On logs in woods. Frankfort. August. Rare.

Reported by Harper. The description is adapted from Peck, who says that the small, soft, crowded scales of the pileus which can be easily rubbed off, constitute a prominent character of the species. Peck changed the original name in the 30th N. Y. State Mus. Rep. because it had been preoccupied. This species may be an extreme form of *P. curvipes,* which differs in the innate floccosity of the surface of the young pileus. From *P. muricata* it seems to differ mostly in its larger spores, pallid young gills, and the superficial scales on the cap.

**Gills at first yellow, becoming ferruginous.

295. Pholiota muricata Fr.

Syst. Myc., 1821.

Illustrations: Harper, Wis. Acad. Sci. Trans., Vol. 17, Pl. 52
and 53.

PILEUS 2-4 cm. broad, convex or nearly plane, dry, obtuse or
depressed, *covered with dense, fasciculate or granular, tawny-yellow, pointed scales,* ferruginous on disk, not striate, margin when
young often adorned by remnants of the veil. FLESH thin. GILLS
adnate, seceding, moderately broad and close, *yellow* at first then
ferruginous-stained, edge concolor and minutely fimbriate from
the sterile cells. STEM 2-4 cm. long, 3-4 mm. thick, *curved,* stuffed
then hollow, tawny, *floccose-fibrillose or granular scaly* up to the
fugacious ANNULUS. SPORES short elliptical, 6-7 x 3-4 micr.,
smooth, pale ferruginous-brown. CYSTIDIA none.

Solitary or gregarious. On decaying logs, etc. Ann Arbor, Bay
View. August-September. Infrequent.

Our plants fit well the description of Fries, except that the gills
are not adnexed. They approach *P. curvipes,* but seem to me sufficiently differentiated by the pointed, fasciculate or granular scales
of the cap, which are sometimes also found on the stem, and by
the color of the gills which is yellow at first. *P. erinaceëla* Pk. is
also close, but the scales on the cap are superficial.

296. Pholiota spectabilis Fr.

Epicrisis, 1836-38.

Illustrations: Harper, Wis. Acad. Sci. Trans., Vol. 17, Pl. 44.
Fries, Icones, Plate 102.
Ricken, Blätterpilze, Pl. 55, Fig. 1, (As *Pholiota aurea*).
Cooke, Ill., Plate 352.
Gillet, Champignons de France, No. 529.
Plate LXI of this Report.

PILEUS 4-10 cm. broad, convex, then campanulate-expanded,
firm, sometimes broadly umbonate, *tawny-orange,* dry, surface
glabrous at first, then broken into minute fibrillose scales, margin
even and sometimes wavy. FLESH thick, compact, yellowish, thin

at margin. GILLS adnate becoming emarginate with decurrent tooth, *narrow, crowded,* yellow then ferruginous, edge minutely floccose-fimbriate. STEM stout, 4-10 cm. long, 7-15 mm. thick, compact, often hard, *solid, subventricose, peronate-scaly,* fibrillose in age, concolor to fuscous below the ring, pruinose and paler above. ANNULUS *near apex of stem,* membranaceous, persistent, thin, mostly entire, yellowish. SPORES broadly-elliptical, 7-9 x 5-6 micr., ferruginous, *tuberculate-rough.* CYSTIDIA none, but edge of gills are tufted with sterile cells. TASTE markedly *bitter.*

Growing from the base of yellow birch trunks. Marquette, Neebish Island. August-September. Infrequent.

A very imposing and elegant plant. Its colors, narrow gills, apical annulus, bitter taste and rough spores separate this from all others. *P. adiposa* has similar colors but differs widely in all other respects. The figures of European authors show the plant with a peronate stem in its best condition and they are excellent, but somewhat misleading after the annulus has become pendant. The spores are similar to those of many Cortinarii.

297. Pholiota adiposa Fr. (EDIBLE)

Syst. Myc., 1821.

Illustrations: Atkinson, Mushrooms, Plate 43, Fig. 144, p. 152, 1900.
> Hard, Mushrooms, Fig. 211, p. 260, 1908.
> Harper, Wis. Acad. Sci. Trans., Vol. 17, Pl. 40.
> Murrill, Mycologia, Vol. I, Pl. 7, Figs. 1 and 2.
> Marshall, Mushroom Book, Plate XI, p. 61, 1905.
> Freeman, Minnesota Plant Diseases, Fig. 129, p. 263, 1905.
> Clements, Minnesota Mushrooms, Fig. 37, p. 62, 1910.

PILEUS 3-10 cm. or more broad, compact, convex to hemispherical, obtuse, *very viscid,* covered with separable, *chrome-yellow to orange concentric scales* which are darker in age and often squarrose, margin even, appendiculate, at first incurved. FLESH thick, firm, yellowish-white. GILLS adnate, becoming emarginate, *broad,* close, thin, yellow then ferruginous, toughish, edge entire. STEM stout, 3-10 cm. long, 6-12 mm. thick, *solid,* firm, usually curved, subequal, yellow, becoming ferruginous-stained from spores, *scaly,* glabrescent. ANNULUS slight, floccose, fugacious. SPORES 7-8 x 4-5 micr., elliptical, smooth, ferruginous. CYSTIDIA none, and very short; sterile cells on edge of gills. ODOR none, TASTE mild.

Solitary or caespitose. On decaying logs, etc., and from wounds on trunks of living sugar maple and white ash. Throughout the State. June-October. Frequent, especially in the autumn. Edible.

Easily recognized by its bright color and viscid pileus. In wet weather the pileus becomes glutinous. The floccose annulus terminates the scaly part of the stem above, and is often lacking. The stem of our plant is always solid, and Fries (Hymen. Europ.) must have erroneously written "farcto," as other European authors refer to it also as solid. Massee and Ricken give spore-measurements which are too small for the American plants. Occasional specimens become larger than the size of the plant given above. The gelatinous layer of the cap should be peeled before cooking.

298. Pholiota flammans Fr.

Syst. Myc., 1821.

Illustrations: Fries, Icones, Pl. 104.
   Cooke, Ill., Pl. 368.
   Michael, Führer f. Pilzfreunde, Vol. II, No. 75 (as *Pholiota flammula* A. & S.).
   Ricken, Blätterpilze, Pl. 55, Fig. 5.
   Harper, Wis. Acad. Sci. Trans., Vol. 17, Pl. 41 C.

"PILEUS 4-7 cm. broad, convex-expanded to plane, *entirely dry,* subumbonate, *fiery-yellow* to almost orange-red, *clothed by superficial, sulphur-yellow, squarrose-fibrillose scales.* FLESH bright yellow, becoming reddish-brownish. GILLS emarginate-adnexed, *very narrow,* thin, crowded, bright yellow, becoming ferruginous. STEM 5-7 cm. long, 5-10 mm. thick, equal, mostly curved, stuffed then hollow, *bright yellow,* dry, *squarrose-scaly,* up to the torn, somewhat membranous annulus. SPORES *minute,* cylindrical-elliptical, 4 x 2 micr. ODOR almost like radish."

On decaying stumps and logs, probably only on coniferous wood. Northern Michigan. September.

Known by the paler, sulphur-yellow scales on a more deeply colored background, and by the very small spores and squarrose-scaly cap and stem. It is usually caespitose. Harper reports it from Neebish Island. The description is adapted from Ricken.

299. Pholiota lucifera (Lasch.) Bres.

Fungi Tridentini, I, 1881.

Illustrations: Ibid, Plate 85.
Ricken, Blätterpilze, Pl. 54, Fig. 1.

PILEUS 3-5 cm. broad, convex then plane, at length umbonate, *viscid*, sulphur-yellow to flavus, covered on disk by tawny or reddish-brown, appressed, fibrillose, thin scales, margin even, incurved and appendiculate. FLESH whitish, yellow under cuticle. GILLS adnate-subdecurrent, becoming sinuate, *bright yellow*, at length ferruginous, moderately *narrow*, crowded, edge crenulate from the flask-shaped sterile cells. STEM 2-5 cm. long, 5-7 mm. thick, fibrous, equal or subequal, *yellow*, paler at apex, ferruginous at base, solid, *fibrillosely peronate*. ANNULUS narrow, floccose, fugacious, rusty-yellow. SPORES obovate, 7-8 x 4-5.5 micr., smooth, ferruginous in mass.

Gregarious. On very rotten wood, in mixed woods. Marquette. August-September. Rare.

This is a well-marked plant, found but once, and apparently limited to our northern woods. Our specimens had rather short stems which were solid, and in this respect differ from Bresadola's description. *P. limonella* Pk. appears to be similar, but differs in its gills which are whitish at first and adnexed. *P. adiposa* has broad gills and the scales are large and often recurved.

300. Pholiota luteofolia Pk.

N. Y. State Mus. Rep. 27, 1875.

Illustration: Harper, Wis. Acad. Sci. Trans., Vol 17, Pl. 48.

PILEUS 2-5 cm. broad, compact, convex-expanded, dry, obtuse, *scaly, dotted on disk with fasciculate-pointed pinkish to reddish-brown scales*, elsewhere areolate-cracked and with ochraceous-brown, appressed scales. FLESH *white*. GILLS emarginate, *broad*, subdistant, *yellow* then ferruginous, edge serrate. STEM short or long, 3-6 cm. long, 4-8 mm. thick, *firm*, stuffed then hollow, curved, fibrillose, subequal, yellowish, floccose-pruinose above the slight, evanescent ANNULUS. SPORES elliptical, 7-8 x 5 micr., smooth, ferruginous in mass. CYSTIDIA none.

Subcaespitose.   On decaying log of white oak.   Ann Arbor.   September.   Rare.

Has the stature of *P. aeruginosa,* but the scales and colors differ. Our plants have pointed tuberculate scales on the disk of the pileus at first, and the stem does not remain solid.

301.   Pholiota æruginosa Pk.

N. Y. State Mus. Rep. 43, 1890, Bot. ed.

Illustration: Plate LXII of this Report.

PILEUS 3-5 cm. broad, hemispherical or convex, obtuse, *firm,* subglabrous to scaly, the scales erect, pointed and mostly on the disk, *often areolate-cracked,* dry, varying in color, *dark green, greenish or fulvous-yellow blotched with green,* the scales darker when present, margin incurved at first, often adorned with fragments of the veil.   FLESH whitish, tinged green, thin except on disk. GILLS adnate and rounded behind at first, then emarginate with decurrent tooth, *broad,* close, yellowish at first, *becoming bright orange-ferruginous,* edge entire.   STEM short, 3-4 cm. long, 4-8 mm. thick, equal or tapering at base, straight or curved, tough, cortex subcartilaginous, fibrillose, sulcate-striate at apex, *colored like pileus below* the lacerate, submembranaceous, fugacious ANNULUS whose remnants are soon colored by bright ferruginous spores. SPORES 6-8 x 3-4.5 micr., subelliptical, smooth, *copious,* bright ferruginous.   CYSTIDIA none.

Solitary or gregarious.   On old railroad ties, board-walks, old logs in woods, etc.   Throughout the State; Ann Arbor, New Richmond and Marquette.   June and September.   Infrequent.

Like *Lentinus lepideus,* this Pholiota frequents railroad ties and other wood exposed to the light.   It is a well-marked species and was found on several occasions about Ann Arbor.   The colors are sometimes very striking, since the dark green of pileus and stem contrast sharply with the bright ferruginous gills and ring, while the apex of the stem is at the same time of a rosy hue.   A study of a number of collections shows that there is considerable variation in color, as well as in the character of the surface of the pileus, so that Peck's description had to be revised considerably.   It is one of our few green mushrooms and must not be confused with *Stropharia aeruginosa.*

Section III. *Hygrophani.* Pileus hygrophanous. Cystidia present on gills.

302. Pholiota acericola Pk.

N. Y. State Mus. Rep. 25, 1873.

PILEUS 2-7 cm. broad, broadly convex then plane, sometimes depressed in age, hygrophanous, glabrous, varying *rugose-reticulated to rugulose,* yellowish cinnamon (moist) often darker on disk, paler when dry, not striate on margin. FLESH rather thin. GILLS adnate becoming sinuate, close, somewhat narrow to moderately broad, pallid, or tinged gray at first, then cinnamon. STEM 4-10 cm. long, 5-10 mm. thick, equal or tapering upward, stuffed then hollow, fibrillose-striate, whitish, fuscous at base. ANNULUS *large, membranous, flabby,* persistent, deflexed, radiately striate on upper surface, and stained cinnamon by the spores. SPORES obscurely 5-angled or obovate, *truncate at one end, pointed at basal end,* 9-10 x 5-6 micr., cinnamon and tinged rusty in mass. CYSTIDIA short, much swollen below, abruptly narrowed to a short obtuse prolongation, 18-20 micr. thick below, about 25-30 micr. long, numerous on sides of gills.

On much decayed logs of hard maple and beech in mixed woods of northern Michigan, and on debris, etc., of maple woods in the south. Common around Bay View, Negaunee, Ann Arbor. June-August.

Well characterized by the reticulate-rugose pileus, the large flabby annulus and the cystidia. Individual caps vary from rugose to almost even, the latter becoming rugose on drying, rarely is the rugosity visible except under a lens. The color of the pileus is often more ochraceous than cinnamon. It prefers to grow on sugar maple wood, often on limbs or decayed twigs or on debris. Peck says the rugosity disappears on drying while in most cases I have found it to become more prominent. White mycelial strands often connect the base of the stem with the substratum.

---

303. Pholiota confragosa Fr.

Epicrisis, 1836-38.

Illustration: Fries Icones, Pl. 105 (3).
 Harper, Wis. Acad. Sci. Trans., Vol. 17, Pl. 41, D. & E. (small plants).

PILEUS 2-6 cm. broad, convex-plane, obtuse, ground-color *almost brick-red,* or vinaceous-cinnamon when moist, dotted with a white flocculose coating easily rubbed off and which disappears with age, *hygrophanous,* pale whitish-tan when dry, margin striate when moist. FLESH thin, fragile. GILLS adnate, crowded, narrow, vinaceous-fawn color (Ridg.). STEM 3-8 cm. long, 2-4 mm. thick, equal, stuffed to hollow, flexuous, *rufous,* silky-fibrillose. ANNULUS apical, membranous, persistent, white below. SPORES 6-7 x 4-5 micr., even, brown. ODOR and TASTE mild. Northern Michigan. August-September. Infrequent.

The stem is said to be peronate in the young plant, with a fibrillose white coating which terminates in a spreading membranous ring; with age the ring collapses and the stem is merely fibrillose while the cap is denuded. The rufous color of all parts makes it easy to recognize; in dry plants the color of the cap and stem becomes cinnamon or paler, and of the gills darker.

304. Pholiota discolor Pk.

N. Y. State Mus. Rep. 25, 1873.

Illustration: Harper, Wis. Acad. Sci. Trans., Vol. 17, Pl. 61 B.

PILEUS 2-4 cm. broad, convex, then nearly plane, glabrous, *viscid,* hygrophanous, *rufous-cinnamon and striatulate* (moist), bright ochraceous-yellow and even (dry). GILLS adnate-subdecurrent, *narrow,* close, *whitish at first,* then ferruginous-cinnamon, edge minutely crenulate. STEM 4-8 cm. long, 3 mm. thick, equal, stuffed, *soon hollow,* sometimes compressed, pallid-fuscescent, fibrillose below. ANNULUS membranous, *persistent,* apical. SPORES elliptical, 7-9 x 5-6 micr., smooth. CYSTIDIA *few, fusiform,* slender, about 60 micr. long. ODOR none, TASTE mild.

Solitary or caespitose. On decaying wood, in mixed forests. New Richmond, Neebish Island, Ann Arbor. May-September. Frequent.

This species is probably more frequent than my observations so far indicate. The pileus is somewhat viscid, with a thin separable pellicle, and its color when dry is characteristic. *P. autumnalis* Pk. is said to differ in having a non-viscid pileus and a slight annulus; the colors are very similar. Some consider *P. autumnalis* identical with *P. marginata*. *P. discolor* sometimes forms scanty rhizomorphs on logs.

305. Pholiota unicolor (Fl. D.) Fr.

Epicrisis, 1836-38.

Illustrations: Cooke, Ill., Pl. 356.
   Ricken, Blätterpilze, Pl. 56, Fig. 4.
   Gillett, Champignons de France, No. 531.
   Hard, Mushrooms, Fig. 213, p. 262, 1908.

PILEUS 2-4 cm. broad, convex then almost plane, obtuse, rarely umbonate, *hygrophanous,* watery-cinnamon (moist), becoming deep *ochraceous* (dry), glabrous, even, *margin extending beyond the gills.* FLESH thin, concolor. GILLS adnate and broad behind, *subtriangular* behind, often decurrent, close, *broad,* ochre-cinnamon. STEM 2-4 cm. long, 2-3 mm. thick, *stuffed,* equal, fibrillose, concolor, darker toward base, which is often white-mycelioid. ANNULUS thin, narrow, entire, persistent, membranous, apical. SPORES 8-10 x 4-5 micr., elliptical, smooth. CYSTIDIA *few,* broadly ventricose, narrowed above and obtuse, about 45 micr. long.
   Subcaespitose. On decaying logs, etc., in woods. Spring and autumn. Ann Arbor. Probably rather frequent in places.
   Differs from *P. marginata* by its broader gills, and persistent annulus, but it is likely that intermediate forms will be found. Harper's description of *P. marginata* applies to this plant.

306. Pholiota marginata (Batsch.) Fr. (SUSPECTED)

Epicrisis, 1836-38.

Illustrations: Cooke, Ill., Pl. 372.
   Ricken, Blätterpilze, Pl. 56, Fig. 7.
   Atkinson, Mushrooms, Fig. 143, p. 151, 1900.
   Harper, Wis. Acad. Sci. Trans., Vol. 17, Pl. 54 and 55.

PILEUS 2-4 cm. broad, convex then plane, watery tan (moist), hygrophanous, *darker when dry,* glabrous, *striate on margin.* GILLS adnate, sometimes slightly subdecurrent, *narrow, crowded,* dark reddish-brown at maturity. STEM 2-8 cm. long, 3-5 mm. thick, equal, *glabrous,* stuffed then hollow, concolor, darker at base. ANNULUS distant, *fugacious.* SPORES elliptical, 7-8.5 x 4-5 micr. CYSTIDIA few or scattered, lanceolate-linear, 60-75 micr., subventricose below.

Solitary or caespitose. On decaying logs, limbs, etc., everywhere in woods. Throughout the State. Records from May 9 to November 2.

A very common little Pholiota, which appears to run into the preceding, although Fries says it is very distinct. It has appeared every month of the season in different years, but is more abundant in spring and fall. Peck has described a species under the name *P. marginella,* which he says differs from *P. marginata* by the even, fibrillose margin of the pileus, the adnexed gills and the paler, unicolorous stem. I have not seen it. *P. autumnalis* Pk. is probably the same and is said to be poisonous.

Section IV.   Muscigeni.   Growing on moss, wet ground or very decayed wood. Pileus hygrophanous. Cystidia absent, or in form of sterile cells on edge of gills.

307. Pholiota rugosa Pk.

N. Y. State Mus. Rep. 50, 1897.

PILEUS .5-3 cm. broad, (usually about 1 cm.), conical or campanulate, then expanded and *umbonate,* hygrophanous, striatulate on margin and rufous-ochraceous (moist), yellowish or pale ochraceous (dry), *becoming rugose-wrinkled on drying.* FLESH thin, concolor. GILLS *adnexed,* close to subdistant, not broad, slightly ventricose, *pallid ochraceous at first,* then rusty brownish, white-fimbriate on edge. STEM 3-5 cm. long, 1-3.5 mm. thick, slender, equal or slightly thickened at base, *hollow, fibrillose or scaly below the annulus,* white-mealy at apex, concolor or pallid. ANNULUS distant, membranous, *persistent,* beautifully striate on upper side, whitish beneath. CYSTIDIA none; club-shaped sterile cells on edge of gills. SPORES elliptical, 10-12 x 5-6 micr., smooth. ODOR and TASTE none.

Solitary or gregarious. On very decayed wood or on the ground in wet places. In mixed or frondose woods. Throughout the State.

Bay View, Marquette, New Richmond and Ann Arbor. August-October. Frequent.

This species is closely related and perhaps identical with either *P. togularis* Bull. or *P. blattaria* Fr. At the present time it seems impossible to determine its status with certainty. The figures of *P. togularis* by Fries and Ricken show the median annulus and the striations on its upper surface as in our species, and in most other respects they illustrate our plant well. Ricken also gives the spores of *P. togularis* as 10-12 x 5-6 micr. Other European authors give smaller spores. Fries changed his conception of *P. togularis* as expressed in Systema and Epicrisis so that in Hymen. Europ. he omits the hygrophanous character; Ricken, however, says it is hygrophanous, and both authors indicate that it is striatulate on the cap when moist. As to *P. blattaria*, Fries considered it a smaller plant, more ferruginous in color and with almost free gills. Ricken distinguishes it from *P. togularis* by the nature of the annulus which he says is striate also and at length falls to pieces. He also describes the plant as Galera-like, a comparison which Fries had made of *P. togularis*. Ricken assigns spores to *P. blattaria* measuring 7-8 x 3-4 micr., Massee gives them smaller yet, while Schroeter and Britzelmayr say they measure 9-11 x 5 micr. With such data not much can be decided. Harper has reported and described the two species, and gives the spore-sizes the reverse of those of Ricken. The markedly rugose surface of the pileus of the American plant described above as *P. rugosa* Pk., the expanded pileus, the colors and the spore size, would indicate that it had better be kept distinct at present.

Illustrations: of *P. togularis* Bull.
  Fries, Icones, Pl. 104, Fig. 4.
  Gillet, Champignons de France, No. 530.
  Patouillard, Tab. Analyt., No. 339.
  Ricken, Blätterpilze, Pl. 56, Fig. 5.
  Harper, Wis. Acad. Sci. Trans., Vol. 17, Pl. 59 (as *P. blattaria*).

A variety or closely related species of the same stature and appearance as *P. rugosa* was found in low, rich woods. Its PILEUS was hygrophanous, chestnut-brown (moist), pale-alutaceous (dry), never striate nor rugulose, glabrous. GILLS rounded behind, adnate, *pallid at first* (not ochraceous), then pale brown, moderately narrow, close. STEM bulbilate, hollow, innately fibrillose-striatulate, pallid or brownish, subfragile. ANNULUS apical, *subpersistent,* soft-floccose-fibrillose, white. SPORES 7-8 x 4 micr., smooth. It seemed intermediate between the genera Pholiota and Naucoria.

308. Pholiota mycenoides Fr.

Sys. Myc., 1821.

Illustration: Cooke, Ill., Plate 503.

"PILEUS 2-3 cm. broad, membranaceus, campanulate then convex, *everywhere striate,* hygrophanous, ferruginous-tawny or pale tan when dry. GILLS adnate, rather distant, narrow, ferruginous. STEM 3-4 cm. long, 2 mm. thick, glabrous, ferruginous, hollow. ANNULUS superior, membranaceous, white. SPORES 8-10 x 5-6 micr.

Among moss in swamps."

This species was reported by Longyear in 4th Rep. Mich. Acad. Sci. as having been found by Beardslee in Montmorency county. The description is adapted from Massee.

Cortinarius Fr.

(From the Latin, *Cortina, a curtain,* referring to the cobwebby threads which hide the gills of the young plants.)

Cinnamon-spored or rusty-brown-spored. Stem fleshy and continuous with the pileus. *When young provided with a cobwebby cortina* which connects the edge of the pileus with the stem; often also with a universal veil which on collapsing leaves an annulus, subannular rings, a sheath or shreds on the stem. Gills persistent, dry, adnate becoming emarginate, changing color during process of maturing, at length powdery with the clinging dark brown spores.

Putrescent, terrestrial, mostly forest mushrooms, composing a most natural group. The caps are often brightly colored and when young the gills of different species also assume various shades of color. The genus is divided into seven subgenera: Myxacium, Bulbopodium, Phlegmacium, Inoloma, Dermocybe, Telamonia and Hydrocybe. Of these the first three have a viscid pileus, and in this respect approach the genus Hebeloma. The latter is however, separable by its paler, alutaceus spores and fibrillose or absent cortina. The subgenera Inoloma and Dermocybe agree with the genus Inocybe in having innately silky or scaly dry caps, but Inocybe differs in having paler spores, a more scanty, fibrillose-cortina and often with verrucose-pointed cystidia on the gills. The genus Flammula often has rusty spores, but is lignicolous. Many of the species are known to be *edible* and while no information is at hand that any of them are poisonous, the flavor of many of them is insipid or disagreeable, and others have as yet not been reported on.

The species of the genus Cortinarius are very numerous. Peck has described 83 species from North America. Fries, in his last complete work on the Hymenomycetes of Europe, records 234 species; of these he found a large majority in Sweden, where he had exceptional opportunity to study them by reason of the astonishing number of species and individuals which occur in that moist and cool climate. To quote from his Epicrisis (1836-38), "No genus is more natural nor more sharply distinguished from others. Beginners alone would confuse them with the brown-spored genera, while experienced persons can distinguish them by their habit at the first glance. But although it is a great natural group, the species are so intimately related among themselves that to distinguish the separate ones is almost to be despaired of. The large mass and number of individuals compose at least half of the Agarics of Northern forests"; and in Systema Mycologia (1821), "I did not admit even one-half the number that I had met by diligent search, and only included those that agreed in their primary characters; very many were disregarded. In the young stage and immediately after a rain, they are quite easily distinguished. After becoming discolored and in age or dry weather even the large, well-marked species are scarcely separable."

The PILEUS may be viscid, dry, silky or scaly, or hygrophanous, and these characters are used in the separation of the subgenera. The color is often very attractive: violet, purple, red, yellow, green or shades of brown, but in most cases it fades into some shade of brown or tan in age. The size varies greatly; in the subgenera Inoloma, Bulbopodium and Phlegmacium the plants are usually of large size. In Dermocybe and Hydrocybe they are rather small. Telamonia is represented by all sizes. The GILLS are, next to the cortina, the most definite means of recognizing the genus. When young they may be whitish, yellow, green or olive, blue, violet, purple, red or shades of brown. As they mature, they become discolored from the cinnamon or rusty-brown spores which cling to the surface for some time, often producing a powdery appearance. The color of the young gills must be known in order to determine a species correctly, and in the following pages the subgenera are divided into subsections on this basis. The mature gills often show traces of the original color, especially if the spores are removed, and this makes it possible at times to determine even a fully matured plant especially when other characteristic marks are still present. The attachment of the gills varies somewhat but in nearly all species they are at length emarginate-adnate or emarginate-adnexed; a few species have the gills obscurely subdecurrent. Many species are well marked by crowded, subdistant or distant gills and frequently their width can be used to discriminate between them. The edge is scarcely ever sufficiently constant for use in diagnosis; sometimes it is very entire, sometimes much eroded or minutely serratulate, but only a few species show well developed projecting sterile cells. The trama is of the "parallel" type. The STEM is used as a means of distinguishing some of the subgenera. When it is at first covered by the glutinous veil, the plant is referable to the subgenus Myxacium. When it has a sharply defined marginate bulb, the subgenus Bulbopodium is indicated. In the larger forms of the subgenera Phlegmacium, Inoloma and Telamonia the stem is often clavate-bulbous. The veil-remnants on the stem of the subgenus Telamonia separates that hygrophanous group from Hydrocybe. Its texture is most often spongy-fleshy in the large forms, while in the smaller ones, especially of the subgenus Hydrocybe the external layer is rigid and subcartilaginous. The tissue of the stem is continuous with that of the pileus, and hence the stem is not separable from it as in Lepiota, etc.

The CORTINA is composed of loose silky hyphae, almost from the time it is discernible, and forms a "cobwebby" curtain in front of, i. e., below the gills. The threads of this curtain are inserted for some distance vertically along the stem and converge in a wedge-shaped manner toward the edge of the pileus and then coalesce with the tissue of the upper surface of the pileus. In some species it is very copious and as the pileus expands the cortina collapses on the upper portion of the stem forming a loose, fringe-like spurious ring which often becomes discolored by the falling spores. Sometimes it is more scanty and disappears early or is noticeable in the expanded plant only as a slight annular stain on the stem. In other cases, the margin of the pileus as it spreads carries with it the silky threads which remain as decorative shreds near its edge; in this case the margin is at first definitely incurved and the cortina is attached at a little distance from the incurved edge. Although the very young plant shows that the hyphae of the cortina and the surface of the pileus are continuous, as it matures the tissue along the margin of the pileus is differentiated and becomes looser so as to appear superficial along the margin.

Lying adjacent to the cortina and continuous with it on its outer side, is a thin layer of tissue, more intimately woven together—sometimes almost membranous—which is called the *Universal Veil*. It is present in a more or less well-developed form in some of the species of all the subgenera except Hydrocybe. In Myxacium it is composed of gelatinous hyphae and when moist becomes viscid or glutinous; it envelops the young button below and becomes continuous with the gelatinous layer of the pileus. In Bulbopodium and Phlegmacium it is scarcely or not at all gelatinous but fuses above with the gelatinous and similarly colored pellicle of the pileus. In the other subgenera, when present, it leaves shreds, annular zones or a sheath on the stem and is dry and silky-woven. Further descriptions of this veil are given under the subgenera.

The SPORES are of great diagnostic value in this genus, since in the various species they differ sufficiently for use as a check to distinguish forms otherwise very similar. Some authors (Ricken, Die Blätterpilze) have attempted to separate the sections of some of the subgenera on spore-characters. The marks which are useful are size, shape and the structure of the epispore. The color, although not entirely uniform, cannot be used effectively. Their size is most important. "There is no doubt that the size of the spores of a single individual varies, and that it varies when there is every evidence that the spores are mature. But that they vary within limits which are sufficiently constant, any one can determine for himself." (Kauffman, Bull. Torr. Bot. Club., Vol. 32, p. 313, 1905.) Some species have relatively large spores, 12-15 micr. or more in length, others are small, 3-5 micr. in diam. Their shape is elliptical, often almond-shaped (i. e. inequilateral), oval or spherical. The surface is usually covered with tubercular, sometimes spiny processes, which are very marked in some species but are scarcely evident in others; under the ordinary high power objective of the microscope some appear to be quite smooth, unless very highly magnified. In using this as a specific character, one must never lose sight of the fact that when young the epispore is smooth. It is, therefore, necessary to compare the spore-sizes given in the text with spores which are mature. The BASIDIA are also quite constant in size and shape for any species, and in such species as I have measured, their size is given.

The TASTE of some species marks them clearly. In *C. vibratilis*,

C. iodioides, C. elegantoides, C. infractus and *C. ochroleucus* the surface of the pileus or of its flesh has a distinctly bitter taste; a few others are sometimes slightly bitterish. Most Cortinarii have a mild or merely fungoid taste. The European *C. damascenus* is said to have an acrid taste. The ODOR is occasionally like that of radish when the plant is crushed, e. g., *C. annulatus, C. armillatus, C. evernius, C. intrusus, etc.,* but in the majority of species no special odor is noticeable.

The HABITAT is mostly the forest floor where the rich humus soil is abundant and moist. Like many other species of Agarics they thrive best on a substratum capable of retaining moisture, i. e., a forest with either a clay subsoil, or with dense masses of humus, mosses or fallen leaves. In forests of pine, hemlock and spruce, in ravines of beech, oak and maple, where the moisture is persistent or the hillside springy, one usually finds them abundantly. Many of them have a tendency to form mycorhiza on the roots of forest trees; in Michigan I have found *C. rubipes,* and *C. elegantior* var. to be thus associated with living roots. They often occur in troops of closely aggregated individuals, sometimes in arcs, pushing up the leaves in late fall like windrows; especially is this true of some of the subgenus Bulbopodium, like *C. glaucopus* and *C. aggregatus.* Others occur in tufts of several individuals or are scattered here and there in limited areas, while not a few are found solitary, especially in dry weather. The subgenera Telomonia and Hydrocybe are much more frequent in northern conifer forests, Phlegmacium and Bulbopodium in frondose woods farther south.

The following key and text of this genus includes not only Michigan species, but all the Cortinarii of the northeastern portion of the United States which have been described or which I have seen. Since I have made a more extended study of this genus than of any other, and since Dr. Peck has not monographed this group, it seemed advisable to do this with the material now at hand. Dr. Peck's type specimens have been carefully examined, and during several week's stay in Sweden, near Stockholm, some fifty species of Cortinarii were collected and studied, most of which were recognizable as Friesian species. In addition a thorough study was made of Fries' unpublished plates,—most excellent figures in color—which are deposited in the Royal Museum at Stockholm; these plates illustrate practically all the species described by Fries in his Monograph of Cortinarius and his other works. I have, therefore, included 152 species, 90 of which I have collected in Michigan, and in the latter case the description is always made from Michigan plants. Many others, doubtless definite and distinct species, have not been identified, either because of few collections or because no young stages were found. The work has been based as much as possible on the thorough foundation established for this group by Fries, with the exception that one subgenus, viz. Bulbopodium, has been segregated along lines already recognized by Fries himself. This name was proposed by Earle (N. Y. Bot. Gard. Bull., Vol. 5, p. 441) who raised the subsection *Scauri*, of Fries, to the rank of genus. For the sake of uniformity in the present report and since there is no special practical gain in breaking up such a natural genus as Cortinarius, it seemed preferable to raise the subsections of Fries only to subgeneric rank. The descriptions of the species of Peck which I have not collected are given in quotations, with such changes as adapt them to the plan of the report; in some cases additions were made from an examination of the types in order to facilitate their further study. In the key an effort has been made to avoid the use of the hygrophanous character wherever possible, so that dry weather forms may be more easily run down.

Key to the Species

(A) Pileus with a gelatinous cuticle, always more or less viscid or glutinous when moist.
  (a) Stem at base with a marginate-depressed bulb. (Bulbopodium.)
    (b) Pileus normally between 3 and 5 cm. broad.
      (c) In green-houses, mushroom beds, etc.; gills whitish to ochraceous at first; pileus pale alutaceous. 344. *C. intrusus* Pk.
      (cc) In woods.
        (d) Spores 12-14 x 6-7 micr.; pileus, gills and stem violaceous. 332. *C. caerulescens* Fr.
        (dd) Spores 8-9 x 5 micr.; pileus not blue.
          (e) Pileus ochre-yellow to citron; gills violaceous at first; bulb shallow. 320. *C. calochrous* Fr.
          (ee) Pileus olivaceous-brown; gills olivaceous at first; stem violaceous-blue. 322. *C. herpeticus* Fr.
    (bb) Pileus normally between 5 and 12 cm. broad. (See also *C. herpeticus*.)
      (c) In some part or wholly with violet blue or purple shades.
        (d) Gills white at first, never violaceous, lower part of stem yellow. 334. *C. caesius* Clements.
        (dd) Gills violaceous or purplish at first.
          (e) Pileus deep purple when young.
            (f) Flesh or gills changing to purple when cut or bruised.
              (g) Spores spherical; pileus 8-16 cm. broad. 330. *C. sphoerosperma* sp. nov.
              (gg) Spores elliptical; pileus 5-8 cm. broad.
                (h) Stem solid. 327. *C. purpurascens* Fr.
                (hh) Stem stuffed or hollow. 328. *C. subpurpurascens* Fr.
            (ff) Flesh and gills not changing to purplish when bruised; mature pileus smoky-olive-gray and streaked; young pileus blue. 329. *C. aggregatus* sp. nov.

(ee) Pileus not purple.
  (f) Whole plant pale violaceous to violaceous-white.
    (g) Spores 8-10.5 micr. long; pileus and stem tinged lilaceous. 333. *C. michiganensis* Kauff.
    (gg) Spores 10-12 micr. long; bulb with remains of a white universal veil. 324. *C. caesiocyaneus* Britz.
  (ff) Pileus not entirely violaceous.
    (g) Spores 13-16 micr. long; pileus yellow to tawny; stem violet. 319. *C. atkinsonianus* Kauff.
    (gg) Spores 10-12 micr. long.
      (h) Pileus dull tawny-red; stem pallid, scarcely lilac-violaceous. 331. *C. purpureophyllus* sp. nov.
      (hh) Pileus violet-buff to ochraceous; stem violaceous-blue; cortina copious. 321. *C. velicopia* sp. nov.
(cc) Without violet or purplish color.
  (d) Gills with green color at first. 337. *C. virentophyllus* sp. nov.
  (dd) Gills not green.
    (e) Pileus light red to vermillion at first.
      (f) Gills caesius (bluish-gray) at first; spores 15-18 micr. long. 325. *C. rubens* sp. nov.
      (ff) Gills whitish at first; spores 10-12.5 micr. long. 342. *C. sublateritius* Pk.
    (ee) Pileus not red.
      (f) Gills at first yellow; pileus yellow tawny, rusty or orange-fulvous.
        (g) Pileus coarsely corrugate; stem long, 7-12 cm. 341. *C. corrugatus* Pk.
        (gg) Pileus not corrugate; stem short, stout, with broad bulb.
          (h) Taste of flesh slowly bitter; spores 15-19 micr. long. 326. *C. elegantioides* sp. nov.
          (hh) Taste not bitter; spores smaller.
            (i) Pileus, etc., pale sulphur-yellow. 339. *C. fulmineus* var. *sulphureus* var. nov.
            (ii) Pileus tawny-yellow, orange-fulvous, etc., large.
              (k) Spores 12-14 micr. long; bulb of stem scarcely depressed. 340. *C. elegantior* Fr. var.
              (kk) Spores 9-12 micr. long, bulb broad, much depressed. 338. *C. fulgens* Fr.
      (ff) Gills not yellow at first.
        (g) Gills caesius or pallid-bluish at first; flesh of pileus at first whitish.
          (h) Pileus fulvous-streaked on a steel-gray ground-color; spores 8-9 micr. long; stem at length yellowish-stained. 336. *C. glaucopus* Fr.
          (hh) Pileus not streaked, pallid-alutaceous to russet-tan; spores 10-12 micr. long; stem whitish. 335. *C. aleuriosmus* Maire var.
        (gg) Gills at first whitish.
          (h) Pileus pale olivaceous-straw color; bulb small. 323. *C. olivaceo-stramineus* Kauff.
          (hh) Pileus without any olive tint.
            (i) Pileus hoary-canescent on an ochraceous-buff to rusty ground-color. Spores 7-9 micr. long. 343. *C. multiformis* Fr.
            (ii) Pileus and stem white; spores 9-11 micr. long. 345. *C. albidus* Pk.
(aa) Stem equal, clavate or bulbous; bulb not marginate.
  (b) Stem viscid or glutinous from the universal veil. (Myxacium.)
    (c) Stem cylindrical, 6-13 cm. long; spores large, more than 10 micr. long.

    (d)   Stem marked by floccose, concentric interrupted rings; never violaceous. 309. *C. mucifluus* Fr.

   (dd) Stem scarcely marked by thin adnate patches, or silky-fibrillose.

      (e)   Stem at first violaceous, lavender or lilac.

         (f)   Gills at first violaceous; spores 12-15 micr. long. 310. *C. cylindripes* Kauff.

        (ff) Gills at first pallid or whitish; spores 15-18 micr. long, stem 5-7 cm. long. 311. *C. splendidus* Pk. 311. *C. elatior pallidifolius* Pk.

     (ee) Stem white or pallid.

        (f)   Pileus tawny-orange; gills yellowish at first; spores 14-17 micr. long. 311. *C. muscigenus* Pk.

        (ff) Pileus yellowish-brown; gills creamy-yellow at first; spores 10-12.5 micr. long. 312. *C. submarginalis* Pk.

 (cc) Stem subequal to clavate, 3-7 cm. long; spores less than 10 micr. long (except *C. heliotropicus*).

    (d)   Taste of surface of pileus bitter.

      (e)   Pileus yellow; stem pure white. 314. *C. vibratilis* Fr.

     (ee) Pileus lavender-violet; stem white, tinged violet in spots. 317. *C. iodeoides* sp. nov.

   (dd) Taste not at all bitter.

      (e)   Pileus violet to purplish.

        (f)   Spores spherical. 316. *C. salor* Fr.

        (ff) Spores elliptical.

          (g)   Spores 8-10 micr. long, odor not of radish. 316. *C. iodes* B. & C.

         (gg) Spores 10-12.5 micr. long; odor of radish. 318. *C. heliotropicus* Pk.

     (ee) Pileus not violet nor purple; spores globose.

        (f)   Pileus pale yellow; gills violet-tinged. 313. *C. sphoerosporus* Pk. (See also *C. berlesianus* (Pk.) Sacc.

        (ff) Pileus and gills grayish to drab, stem dingy-white. 315. *C. sterilis* Kauff.

(bb) Stem not viscid (Phlegmacium).

   (c)   Stem annulate or spotted with brown or ochraceous scales.

    (d)   Pileus 5-10 cm. broad, yellow and ochraceous; stem stout, annulate. 346. *C. triumphans* Fr.

   (dd) Pileus 3-6 cm. broad, bay-red; stem spotted with brown scales. 347. *C. maculipes* Pk.

  (cc) Stem not spotted nor annulate.

    (d)   Stem very long, 10-15 cm., (8-10 mm. thick).

      (e)   Stem round-bulbous at base; on sphagnum; gills and stem at first tinged violet. 348. *C. sphagnophilus* Pk.

     (ee) Stem not bulbous, subequal.

        (f)   Spores subsphoeroid; pileus yellowish-ochraceous. 357. *C. longipes* Pk.

        (ff) Spores elliptical; pileus reddish-yellow. 361. *C. ophiopus* Pk.

   (dd) Stem not remarkably long, 4-10 cm.

      (e)   Pileus corrugated, pale ochre; gills violaceous at first; stem subequal. 352. *C. copakensis* Pk.

     (ee) Pileus not corrugated.

        (f)   Pileus reddish to tawny-orange; stem stout, clavate-bulbous; nowhere violet. 360. *C. coloratus* Pk.

        (ff) Pileus not reddish.

          (g)   Pileus olive to smoky-brownish or brownish-ochraceous.

            (h)   Spores subglobose.

               (i)   Taste of surface of pileus bitter; plant sooty-olive. 355. *C. infractus* Fr.

(ii)   Not bitter; pileus brownish-ochraceous; **gills** olivaceous. 358. *C. glutinosus* Pk.
(hh) Taste not bitter; spores elliptical.
   (i)   Gills dark olivaceous at first; stem tinged violaceous. 356. *C. olivaceus* Pk.
   (ii) Gills yellów at first; stem whitish. 359. *C. luteofuscous* Pk.
(gg) Pileus grayish to buff color or yellow.
   (h)   Pileus virgate, becoming yellowish in age; **gills** violaceous at first.
      (i)   Stem oval-bulbous at base; at first densely fibrillose. 349. *C. lanatipes* Pk.
      (ii) Stem equal; pileus dark gray. 351. *C. lapidophilus* Pk.
   (hh) Pileus not virgate, pale.
      (i)   Stem stout, clavate-bulbous.
         (k)   Pileus yellow; gills at first caesius. 350. *C. claricolor* Fr.
         (kk) Pileus buff; gills pale violaceous. 353. *C. albidipes* Pk.
      (ii) Stem 3-7 mm. thick, equal.
         (k)   Spores subglobose; gills caesius at first. 354. *C. decoloratus* Fr.
         (kk) Spores elliptical; gills whitish at first. 362. *C. communis* Pk.
(AA) Cuticle of pileus not composed of gelatinous hyphae, hence neither viscid nor glutinous.
   (a)   Pileus (and sometimes stem) distinctly scaly, usually large (except *C. flexipes*).
      (b)   Scales pink-red to cinnabar-red, present on cap and stem; **gills** whitish or pallid at first. 368. *C. bolaris* Fr.
      (bb) Without red-scales on pileus.
         (c)   Stem marked by cinnabar-red zones; pileus tawny-rufescent; gills pale brown. 422. *C. armillatus* Fr.
         (cc) Stem without red bands.
            (d)   Pileus, gills and stem persistently dark violet; stem long and stout; spores 12-16 micr. long; in conifer forests. 375. *C. violaceus* Fr.
            (dd) Pileus not violet.
               (e)   Pileus some shade of yellow.
                  (f)   Stem arising from a white mycelium; pileus and stem tawny-yellow. 369. *C. annulatus* Pk.
                  (ff) Stem arising from a yellow mycelium; pileus and stem saffron to chrome-yellow. 371. *C. croceocolor* Kauff.
               (ee) Pileus brown, umber or chocolate-color.
                  (f)   Stem provided above with a band-like annulus; whole plant soon chocolate-color. 366. *C. squamulosus* Pk.
                  (ff) Stem squarrose-scaly, brown to umber.
                     (g)   Gills at first lilaceous or purplish; spores subglobose, 5-7 micr. 365. *C. pholideus* Fr.
                     (gg) Gills at first fulvous-brown; spores elliptical, 12x6 micr. 374. *C. squarrosus* Clem.
   (aa) Pileus not distinctly scaly, rarely fibrillose or tomentose.
      (b)   Wholly or in part violet, purplish or lilaceous, at least the gills when young.
         (c)   Pileus normally large, 5-10 cm. broad.
            (d)   Gills narrow and close.
               (e)   Pileus, gills and stem unicolorus, pale violaceous; spores 8-10 micr. long. 377. *C. argentatus* Fr. var.
               (ee) Pileus brownish-lilac; stem whitish, spores 12-15 **micr.** long. 381. *C. braendlei* Pk.

(dd) Gills broad, subdistant.
  (e) Pileus, gills and stem unicolorous, lilaceous; stem clavate-bulbous. 376. *C. lilacinus* Pk.
  (ee) Pileus and gills not unicolorous.
    (f) Stem peronate or annulate from the whitish universal veil.
      (g) Gills at first dull deep purple; pileus grayish-buff at first; spores 9-10.5 micr. long. 364. *C. subpulchrifolius* sp. nov.
      (gg) Gills at first pallid, lilaceous or pale lavender.
        (h) Pileus densely · fibrillose-tomentose; gills pallid at first; stem violaceous. 412. *C. plumiger* Fr.
        (hh) Pileus subglabrous.
          (i) Pileus hygrophanous, purplish-umber, fading to pinkish-buff. 414. *C. umidicola* Kauff.
          (ii) Pileus not hygrophanous, violaceous-fulvous to rusty-fulvous, micaceous-glistening. 391. *C. caninus* Fr.
    (ff) Stem not peronate, pileus reddish-gray; gills purple. 379. *C. pulchrifolius* Pk.
(cc) Pileus medium or small in size.
  (d) Pileus 3-7 cm. broad (medium).
    (e) Stem distinctly peronate.
      (f) Pileus and stem silvery violaceous-white; stem clavate. 363. *C. alboviolaceus* Fr.
      (ff) Pileus some shade of dark purplish brown; gills smoky-purplish.
        (g) Stem clavate-bulbous, stout; spores 8-11 micr. long. 411. *C. torvus* Fr.
        (gg) Stem equal or subattenuate downwards; spores 7-8 micr. long. 415. *C. scutulatus* Fr.
    (ee) Stem not peronate.
      (f) Stem marked by reddish, subannular scales, subequal, 4-9 cm. long. 393. *C. spilomeus* Fr.
      (ff) Stem not variegated with red.
        (g) Stem long or much elongated, 8-18 cm. long, marked by remnants of veil.
          (h) Pileus grayish-tawny, dry; stem thickened toward base; universal veil violaceous. 367. *C. erraticus* Pk.
          (hh) Pileus at first violet-fuscous, hygrophanous, fading; stem intense violet at first, attenuated below; veil whitish. 413. *C. evernius* Fr.
        (gg) Stem rather short, 3-7 cm. long.
          (h) Stem rather stout, 7-12 mm. thick or more.
            (i) Bulb of stem obliquely marginate-depressed; gills at first heliotrope or deep violet. 378. *C. obliquus* Pk.
            (ii) Bulb if present not marginate; stem bulbous, clavate or tapering upward.
              (k) Pileus reddish-ashy, not hygrophanous; stem with an oval bulb. 382. *C. rubrocinereus* Pk.
              (kk) Pileus paler, without any reddish tinge; stem not round-bulbous.
                (l) Pileus hygrophanous.
                  (m) Stem marked with remnants of a universal veil. 416. *C. deceptivus* Kauff.
                  (mm) Stem silky at first, glabrescent. 441. *C. saturninus* Fr. var.
                (ll) Pileus not hygrophanous; gills and flesh at first only slightly violaceous. 392. *C. anomolus* Fr.

(hh)   Stem smaller, 4-7 mm. thick.
  (i)   Pileus, stem and gills unicolorous, pale violaceous-drab; stem abruptly bulbillate at base. 394. *C. subtabularis* sp. nov.
  (ii)   Pileus not violet; gills, flesh and apex of stem violaceous at first.
    (k)   Pileus hygrophanous.
      (1)   Pileus chestnut color when moist; stem solid. 440. *C. imbutus* Fr.
      (ll)   Pileus sooty-brown to olive-gray; in pine woods. 442. *C. livor* Fr.
    (kk)   Pileus not hygrophanous.
      (1)   Pileus pale brownish-tan; stem solid. 383. *C. clintonianus* Pk.
      (ll)   Pileus dingy-white to clay-color; stem hollow, very short. 395. *C. brevissimus* Pk.
(dd)   Pileus small, 1-3 cm. broad.
  (e)   Pileus at first conical, blackish-brown.
    (f)   Stem subannulate, slender; spores 6-7.5 x 3-4 micr. 419. *C. subflexipes* Pk.
    (ff)   Stem not annulate; spores 7-9 x 5-6 micr. 456. *C. erythrinus* Fr.
  (ee)   Pileus campanulate-convex, chestnut-color.
    (f)   Stem 4-6 mm. thick. 443. *C. castaneus* Fr.
    (ff)   Stem 1-2 mm. thick. 455. *C. fuscoviolaceus* Pk.
(bb)   No violet, purple nor lilac colors present.
  (c)   Pileus large, 5-10 cm. broad.
    (d)   Bulb of stem oval-clavate and dark brick-red; pileus hygrophanous, rufous-brown. 421. *C. rubripes* Kauff.
    (dd)   Stem not red.
      (e)   Pileus with a rufous tinge either when fresh or on drying.
        (f)   Pileus hygrophanous, very glabrous, stem pallid-whitish, subclavate. 444. *C. armeniacus* Fr. 448. *C. glabrellus* Kauff.
        (ff)   Pileus dry, reddish to brownish-orange, stem yellow or concolor, long and equal. 387. *C. whitei* Pk.
      (ee)   Pileus without reddish tinge.
        (f)   Pileus creamy-yellow, yellow, ochraceous, orange-yellow or rusty-yellow.
          (g)   Stem peronate by a close-appressed sheath.
            (h)   Sheath pale tawny-yellowish; pileus tawny-yellow, often scaly on disk. 369. *C. annulatus* Pk.
            (hh)   Sheath whitish; pileus pale.
              (i)   Pileus creamy-buff, large; spores subglobose. 370. *C. flavifolius* Pk.
              (ii)   Pileus pale ochraceous; spores elliptical. 372. *C. ochraceus* Pk.
          (gg)   Stem not sheathed.
            (h)   Pileus hygrophanous, dark ochraceous; stem almost equal, subannulate. 423. *C. morrisii* Pk.
            (hh)   Pileus not hygrophanous.
              (i)   Pileus pale yellow to buff; stem white, caespitose. 388. *C. caespitosus* Pk.
              (ii)   Pileus and stem chrome-yellow to rusty-yellow.
                (k)   Pileus streaked with rusty fibrils; stem with an oval bulb. 385. *C. autumnalis* Pk.
                (kk)   Pileus not streaked; stem clavate, streaked lengthwise. 384. *C. callisteus* Fr.
        (ff)   Pileus neither reddish nor yellow.
          (g)   Stem white or whitish.
            (h)   Pileus hygrophanous, brown when moist.

    (i) Pileus conic-campanulate; stem clavate; silky-fibrillose. 446. *C.* sp.

    (ii) Pileus convex-plane; stem tapering down, glabrous. 445. *C. duracinus* Fr. var.

  (hh) Pileus not hygrophanous, pale gray; stem clavate-bulbous.

    (i) Stem peronate by a white sheath. 373. *C. canescens* Pk.

    (ii) Stem not peronate.

      (k) Spores 7-8 micr. long; gills watery-cinnamon at first. 386. *C. catskillensis* Pk.

      (kk) Spores 10-12 micr. long; gills at first pallid. 418. *C. griseus* Pk.

 (gg) Stem brown or fuscescent.

    (h) Stem annulate by a white band; spores 10-12 micr. long. 432. *C. brunneofulvus* Fr.

    (hh) Stem annulate at times by a fuscous zone; spores 8-9 micr. long. 433. *C. brunneus* Fr.

(cc) Pileus medium size or small, between 1 and 5 cm.

 (d) Stem not very slender, more than 3 mm. thick, sometimes clavate-bulbous at first.

  (e) Gills blood-red or cinnabar-red; stem equal, not stout.

    (f) Pileus and stem tawny-yellow to cinnamon-yellow. 408. *C. semisanguineus* Fr.

    (ff) Pileus and stem blood-red to cinnabar.

      (g) Pileus rather broader than the length of the stem; spores 8-9 x 5-5.5 micr., in oak woods. 409. *C. cinnabarinus* Fr.

      (gg) Pileus narrow, stem longer; spores 6-7 x 4 micr.; on moss, conifer regions. 409b. *C. sanguineus* Fr.

  (ee) Gills not red.

    (f) Stem clavate, subclavate or at least tapering upward, often clavate-bulbous at first.

      (g) Pileus hygrophanous.

        (h) Pileus conic-campanulate at first; on mosses.

          (i) Spores 10-12 x 6 micr.; stem long, cylindrical, pallid to fuscescent. 390. *C. gracilis* Pk.

          (ii) Spores 7-8.5 x 5-6 micr.; stem subzonate from the veil; wholly fawn-brownish. 424. *C. mammosus* sp. nov.

        (hh) Pileus not conic.

          (i) Stem distinctly fuscescent, solid, pileus dark fuscous-brown. 451. *C. rubricosus* Fr. var.

          (ii) Stem not becoming dark fuscous.

            (k) Pileus white-hoary at first on a chestnut-bay-brown ground color. 450. *C. subrigens* sp. nov.

            (kk) Not markedly white-hoary at first.

              (l) Pileus grayish-umber, with rufous tinge when moist. 447. *C. erugatus* Fr.

              (ll) Pileus fuscous-brown, never rufous. 449. *C. privignus* Fr. var.

      (gg) Pileus not hygrophanous.

        (h) Gills cadmium-yellow; narrow; pileus and stem olivaceous-cinnamon. 402. *C. cinnamomeus* Fr. var.

        (hh) Gills pallid or whitish at first.

          (i) Pileus whitish, tinged pale yellowish; stem variegated with pallid-yellowish scales. 396 *C. albidifolius* Pk.

          (ii) Pileus alutaceous; stem subfibrillose, concolor. 389. *C. modestus* Pk.

(ff) Stem equal, attenuated below or subventricose; **not**
definitely thickened at the base.
 (g) Pileus watery-brown, bay-brown or chestnut color
when moist.
  (h) Gills distant or subdistant, brownish at first.
   (i) Stem rather stout, 5-12 mm. thick.
    (k) Stem normally annulate by a white zone; gills
distant. 434. *C. distans* Pk.
    (kk) Stem not annulate.
     (l) Stem subequal, gills brown, close to sub-
distant. 452. *C. uraceus* Fr.
     (ll) Stem equal; gills purplish-brown, distant.
417. *C. adustus* Pk.
   (ii) Stem 3-5 mm. thick, pallid at first. 453. *C.
juberinus* Fr. var.
  (hh) Gills close or crowded.
   (i) Stem with remnants of the veil; gills brownish-
ochre at first; spores 7 x 3.5 micr. 435. *C. nigrellus* Pk.
   (ii) Stem subsilky; gills reddish-umber at first; spores
7-10 x 6.5 micr. 454. *C. praepallens* Pk.
(gg) Pileus not dark brown.
  (h) Flesh olivaceous to green.
   (i) Pileus and stem fulvous to tawny-fulvous. 407.
C. malicorius Fr.
   (ii) Pileus and stem light olive. 410. *C. raphanoides*
Fr.
  (hh) Flesh not olivaceous-green.
   (i) Stem stout, 8-12 mm. thick.
    (k) Pileus, gills and stem yellow; spores subglobose.
404. *C. luteus* Pk.
    (kk) Pileus, gills and stem white or whitish, taste
bitterish. 397. *C. ochroleucus* Fr.
   (ii) Stem 3-6 mm. thick.
    (k) Stem peronate by a yellow sheath; gills saffron-
yellow; pileus rusty color when moist. 425.
C. paludosus Pk.
    (kk) Stem not peronate.
     (l) Stem with white annular zone; pileus yellow-
ish, fragile. 426. *C. hinnuleus* Fr. var.
     (ll) Stem not annulate.
      (m) Pileus hairy, tawny; stem short, pallid to
pale tawny. 400. *C. basalis* Pk.
      (mm) Pileus silky to appressed tomentulose;
gills yellow.
       (n) Stem rather long, 4-10 cm.
        (o) Pileus obtusely conic-campanulate, ruf-
ous-fulvous; with stem streaked with
rufous-fulvous fibrils. 403. *C. croceo-
conus* Fr.
        (oo) Pileus campanulate-convex, yellowish-
cinnamon, tawny, etc., stem chrome-
yellow. 401. *C. cinnamomeus* Fr.
       (nn) Stem short, 2-4 cm. long.
        (o) Spores 10-12.5 micr. long; pileus cinna-
mon-brown; odor of radish. 405. *C.
aureifolius* Pk.
        (oo) Spores 6-7 micr. long; pileus cinna-
mon; gills saffron-yellow to orange.
406. *C. croceofolius* Pk.

(dd) Stem slender, 1-3.5 mm. thick.
  (e) Pileus conical, then campanulate.
    (f) Pileus fibrillose-hairy, fuscous to umber.
      (g) Stem slender, with delicate white zones, fuscescent.
        (h) Spores 10-12 x 5-6.5 micr. 429. *C. iliopodlius* Fr.
        (hh) Spores 6-8 x 4-5 micr. 439. *C. paleaceus* Fr.
      (gg) Stem short annulate by single median whitish zone, fuscescent. 431. *C. impolitus* sp. nov.
    (ff) Pileus glabrous, or soon glabrous.
      (g) Pileus not hygrophanous, chestnut color; spores large, 15-16 micr. long. 398. *C. sericipes* Pk.
      (gg) Pileus hygrophanous, watery-brown, fulvous or chestnut color at first.
        (h) Stem attenuated-subrooting, soon rigid, whitish and shining when dry. 459. *C. scandens* Fr.
        (hh) Stem equal.
          (i) Stem "rubello"-tinged or yellowish at first.
            (k) Stem pallid or rufous-tinged; pileus even, with blackish umbo. 457. *C. decipiens* Fr.
            (kk) Stem yellowish at first; pileus striate when moist. 462. *C. acutus* Fr.
          (ii) Stem not yellowish.
            (k) Growing on decayed wood, gills broad; stem cingulate. 460. *C. lignarius* Pk.
            (kk) Not on decayed wood.
              (l) Gills narrow; pileus pale chestnut color when moist, spores 8-10 micr. long. 461. *C. acutoides* Pk.
              (ll) Gills rather broad; pileus watery-cinnamon when moist; spores 7-8 micr. long. 458. *C. leucopus* Fr. var.
  (ee) Pileus campanulate-convex to plane.
    (f) Pileus canescent with superficial fibrils. 438. *C. hemitrichus* Fr.
    (ff) Pileus glabrous, chestnut-brown when moist.
      (g) Pileus not hygrophanous, umbo blackish. 399. *C. castanellus* Pk.
      (gg) Pileus hygrophanous.
        (h) Spores 10-12 micr. long; stem 2-4 cm. long; gills at first yellowish, cream color or whitish. 428. *C. badius* Pk.
        (hh) Spores 6-7.5 micr. long.
          (i) Gills rufous-cinnamon; stem fuscescent, with whitish median annulus. 436. *C. rigidus* Fr.
          (ii) Gills yellowish or yellowish-cinnamon; stem pallid, spotted by subannular, white zones. 427. *C. castaneoides* Pk.

SUBGENUS MYXACIUM: Provided with a glutinous or *viscid* universal veil; pileus and stem becoming polished by the drying of the gluten.

This group corresponds to the subgenus Limacium of the genus Hygrophours. The entire plant when young is covered by a differentiated gelatinous layer which becomes glutinous in moist weather, and which breaks up on the stem so as to leave shreds, patches or rings of various degrees of definiteness. In some species the glutinous remnants on the stem are very thin and subevanescent and not easily made out; in others, e. g. *C. mucifluus,* the thick layer of the universal veil is cracked and torn crosswise, and the resultant bands or rings are rather marked and persistant, while in still other cases the stem is peronately but very thinly sheathed. Because of their great variability, especially in color, which varies with habitat, weather, age, etc., the species of this group have as yet uncertain limits and are differently interpreted by different authors.

309. Cortinarius mucifluus Fr. (Edible)

Epicrisis, 1836-38.

Illustrations: Fries, Icones, Pl. 148, Fig. 1.
    Cooke, Ill., Pl. 740 (fresh condition).
    Cooke, Ill., Pl. 738 (older stage, as *C. collinitus*).
    Gillet, Champignons de France, No. 206 (as *C. collinitus*).
    Ricken, Die Blätterpilze, Pl. 34, Fig. 1 (as *C. collinitus*).
    Michael, Führer f. Pilzfreunde, Vol. III, No. 85 (as *C. collinitus*).
    N. Y. State Mus. Rep. 48, Pl. 13, Fig. 1-6 (as *C. collinitus*).
    Plate LXIII of this Report.

PILEUS 3-8 cm. broad, at the very first subglobose, then campanulate-convex and margin incurved, finally campanulate-expanded to plane, obtuse, *glutinous when moist,* the gluten derived from the very thick gelatinous pellicle varying in color from whitish when young to *straw-yellow, orange-yellow or tawny-fulvous,* sometimes stained with rusty or sulphur hues, shining when dry. FLESH pallid or stained in age with yellow or rust color. GILLS *at first pallid or grayish-white (caesious),* then clay color to rusty-cinnamon, adnate to subemarginate, medium broad, close. STEM 6-12 cm. long, 7-12 mm. thick, *cylindrical or tapering downward,* rather stout from the first, rigid, spongy-stuffed, at the very first whitish and covered by the thick gelatinous layer of a *universal veil,* which cracks transversely, *forming scaly, thick, sometimes squarrose bands of dried gluten,* especially below, soon becoming discolored and then yellowish, rusty or tawny, terminating above with the discolored cortina in the form of a collapsed ring. SPORES 10-13 x 6-7 micr. (rarely up to 14.5 micr. long), almond-shaped, tuberculate, inequilateral-elliptic, rusty-cinnamon in mass. BASIDIA 4-spored, 36-42 x 9-10 micr. ODOR and TASTE not marked.

    Gregarious. In low, rich ground of coniferous or frondose woods, copses, swamps, etc., among mosses or on humus, or rich loam. Throughout the State. August-October. Frequent.

This species is distinguished from all others by its peculiar transversely-banded stem, although often only the lower portion shows this character distinctly. The white *cortina* extends down the stem inside the gelatinous layer as a soft, floccose layer, and when the outer glutinous layer breaks across on drying, the floccose, cortinate layer is exposed and gives the floccose effect to the bands. The young plants often arise deep in the humus, and the stout stem at this time has almost the diameter of the young cap. The gluten on the upper half of the stem; often of most of the part above the substratum, is inclined to dry or dissolve, so that the diffracted-scaly character is found only in the lower protected part. In the young stage the arrangement of the two veils can be easily made out. It is edible but should be peeled before cooking.

This is *Cortinarius collinitus* Fr. of all authors, except of Fries himself. Of this I satisfied myself by an examination of the plates of Fries which are deposited in the Royal Museum at Stockholm, Sweden, and by collections around Upsala and Stockholm. In the persistently moist climate of that region, the thick rings on the stem develop much more perfectly than with us, and this is well shown by Fries in the published plate in Icones referred to above. Furthermore, there exists in the same collection an unpublished plate by Fries, marked *C. collinitus* Fr., illustrating, in all its stages, a plant frequent in conifer forests around Stockholm. This is very similar to *C. cylindripes* Kauff., differing only in having larger spores. Fries, himself, has brought about the confusion, in his description of the two species. For example, the description accompanying Plate 148, Fig. 1, in Icones, does not apply to those figures, nor does his description of *C. collinitus* in any of his works, apply to the figures of the unpublished plate at Stockholm. Starting with his description of *C. collinitus* in "Systema," where he says the gills are "purpurascens" or "violascens," he gradually changes it in his later works, and in Hymen. Europ. describes them as at first "argillaceous" or "caesious." In Systema the scales are said to be "appressed" to the stem, and his whole diagnosis in the Systema might be interpreted—although somewhat forced— to refer to his unpublished plate. In view of these facts, I have ventured to correct what appears to have become an established error. In the case of the descriptions the matter remains debatable, but there can be no doubt about the plates.

This is a very variable species, and a number of ecological forms

might be separated. Ricken has discovered two forms with different
spore sizes, one which he calls the type has spores 13-15 x 7-8 micr.;
the other, which he calls var. *repanda* has spores 11-13 x 6-7 micr.
All collections examined by me, including two of Peck's and several
from Ithaca, N. Y., yielded the spore-size given in my description.
Two of Peck's collections, from Sand Lake and Catskill Mountains
referred to in his 23rd Report, when examined had spores measuring
15-19 x 7-8.5 micr., and in other respects showed that they did not
belong here, but are probably close to *C. muscigenus* Pk.

310.   Cortinarius cylindripes Kauff.

Bull. Torr. Bot. Club, Vol. 32, p. 321, 1905.

Illustrations: Ibid, Fig. 2, p. 306.
    Jour. of Mycology, Vol. 13, p. 36, Pl. 98, 1907.
    Mycological Bull., Vol. V, Fig. 244, p. 318, 1907.
    Plate LXIV of this Report.

PILEUS 3-7 cm. broad, *very glutinous at first* and shining, later
opaque, at the very first lavender, then yellowish with a violaceous
tinge, at length brownish-ochraceous, somewhat stained by these
colors at various stages, obtusely orbicular when young, then campanulate and expanded, rather small in comparison with the length
of the stem, margin incurved and pellucid-striate, surface smooth,
at length longitudinally wrinkled.   FLESH thick on disk, thin elsewhere, *violaceous,* soon sordid-white. GILLS rather broad, at length
5-8 mm., adnate, emarginate, not attenuate in front, *violaceous or
lavender* when *young,* becoming pale cinnamon, not crowded, thin,
edge serratulate-flocculose and paler, somewhat wrinkled at the
sides but not veined. STEM 8-10 cm. long, 5-9 mm. thick, elastic,
remarkably equal, covered by a violaceous, glutinous, universal veil,
which remains as evanescent, adnate patches and at its junction
with the partial veil as a slight annulus, smooth or fibrillose-striate
at the apex, violaceous to dingy white within, solid stuffed.
SPORES *almond-shaped,* rough-tuberculate, inequilateral-elliptic,
12-15 x 6.5-8 micr., dark brown. BASIDIA 40-45 x 10-13 micr., 4-
spored, with sterigmata, 5-7 micr. long. ODOR and TASTE not
specific.

Gregarious or subcaespitose. On low, rich ground or humus,
conifer and frondose woods. Throughout the State. From late July
to early October. Frequent.

C. cylindripes usually occurs in considerable numbers where found. Its cylindrical stem is at first a beautiful pale azure-blue, due to the thin universal veil, which fades and leaves whitish thin patches which sometimes disappear. The species corresponds to Fries' species, figured in his unpublished plates at Stockholm and named *C. collinitus.* (See notes under *C. mucifluus.*) Specimens of that species collected in Sweden are in my herbarium and have spores measuring 14-18 micr. long, much larger than in the American form. I consider that species, common around Stockholm, as Fries' original *C. collinitus.* Our species, described above, has violaceous or blue tints just like that one, and as Fries has described no other species to which the Stockholm plants could be referred, the indication is strong that he considered them *C. collinitus.* For the present the difference in the spore size will be sufficient to keep *C. cylindripes* distinct. The violaceous gills, etc., distinguish *C. cylindripes* from both Fries' and Ricken's conception of *C. mucosus,* and from the related species of Peck: *C. muscigenus* Pk., *C. splendidus* Pk., and *C. elatior pallidifolius* Pk.

311. Cortinarius muscigenus Pk.

N. Y. State Mus. Rep. 41, 1888.

"PILEUS 3-6 cm. broad, at first ovate, then convex, or concave from the recurving of the margin, subumbonate, glabrous, *viscose with a separable pellicle, tawny-orange* and widely striate on the margin when moist, tawny and shining when dry. FLESH dingy white, tinged with yellow. GILLS broad, ventricose, adnate, with a broad, shallow emargination, somewhat rugose on the sides, *yellowish,* becoming cinnamon. STEM 7-10 cm. long, 6-8 mm. thick, elongated, subequal, *viscid,* even, silky, solid, *white or whitish.*" SPORES almond-shaped, rough-tuberculate, 14-17 x 7-9 micr. (rarely up to 18.5 micr. long).

"Mossy ground under balsam trees. Wittenberg Mountains, New York. September."

This species appears to have the stature of *C. cylindripes,* but has larger spores and lacks the violaceous color entirely. The spores of the type specimens are larger than given by Peck in the original description. The color of the pileus is similar to that of *C. mucifluus* Fr.

Cortinarius splendidus Pk. (N. Y. State Mus. Rep. 29, 1878), differs from *C. muscigenus* in smaller size and *violaceous stem.* Its spores are similar, 15-18 x 6-8 micr., larger than given by Peck. The dried type specimens indicate that they are closely allied, and that one is a variety of the other.

Cortinarius elatior pallidifolius Pk. is also probably a variety of *C. muscigenus* Pk. The spores are the same, 15-17.5 x 7.5-9 micr., but the *stem is tinged with lilac.* Both varieties have a shorter stem than *C. muscigenus,* and the caps are said to be pale fuscous, although in the dried specimens they have the same shining, tawny-tan color as in that species. The last variety is described and figured in N. Y. Mus. Rep. 54, 1901.

312. Cortinarius submarginalis Pk.

N. Y. State Mus. Bull. 54, 1902.

Illustrations: Ibid, Plate L, Fig. 6-10.

"PILEUS 5-10 cm. broad, firm, convex becoming nearly plane, concave by the elevation of the margin, viscid when moist, *yellowish-brown,* generally *a little paler on the rather definite and commonly fibrillose margin.*   FLESH whitish.   GILLS thin, close, rather broad, adnate, creamy-yellow when young, soon cinnamon. STEM 7-15 cm. long, 8-12 mm. thick, elongated, equal or slightly thickened at the base, solid, silky-fibrillose, *slightly viscid,* whitish or pallid." SPORES almond-shaped, slightly rough, 10-12.5 x 5-6 micr.

"Low moist places in Woods. Bolton, New York. August. The margin is separated from the rest by a definite line, is 6-12 mm. broad and conspicuously fibrillose."   The description is adopted from that of Peck.

313. Cortinarius sphærosporus Pk.

N. Y. State Mus. Rep. 26, 1874.

Illustration : Plate LXV of this Report.

PILEUS 3-7 cm. broad, hemispherical-convex then expanded-plane, glabrous, even, *with a thick gelatinous straw-yellow pellicle,* which is glutinous when moist. FLESH thin on margin, *violaceous at first,* soon pallid. GILLS *violaceous at the very first, soon whitish* then cinnamon, adnate-submarginate, close, rather broad. STEM 5-10 cm. long, 5-8 mm. thick, subclavate or tapering upward, equal above, spongy-stuffed, *glutinous when moist from the thin universal veil, which on drying leaves thin yellowish patches on the lower portion,* apex at first pale violaceous, soon white. SPORES oval-subglobose, slightly rough-punctate, 6-7.5 x 5.5-6.5 micr.

In low, moist woods or swamps. August-September. Coniferous regions. Infrequent.

This species corresponds closely with the European *C. delibutus* Fr. which also has subglobose spores. In the American plant the spores are constantly a little smaller, as shown by two collections from Sweden. In that species the spores measure 7-8.5 x 6-7 micr. Britzelmayr reports under the name *C. delibutus,* a species with spores 14-16 x 6 micr. Such a plant, with all other characters similar to *C. delibutus* Fr., has been collected by me, but not sufficient data are at hand to describe it. It is possible that *C. berlesianus* (Pk.) Sacc. of which the spores of the type specimens measure 7-8 x 6-6.5 micr., is a form of the European *C. delibutus* Fr., but its stem has a rounded bulb.

314. Cortinarius vibratilis Fr.

Syst. Myc., 1821.

Illustrations: Cooke, Ill., Plate 744.
    Gillet, Champignons de France, No. 256.
    Ricken, Blätterpilze, Pl. 35, Fig. 2.

PILEUS 2-5 cm. broad, *surface bitter to the taste,* convex, obtuse, gibbous, *with a glutinous pellicle,* hygrophanous, *yellow, ochre-yellow to fulvous-yellow,* paler when dry, glabrous, even. FLESH soft, thin except disk, white or whitish, *bitter.* GILLS *adnate to slightly subdecurrent* or subemarginate, thin, close, rather narrow, *pallid to pale ochraceous,* then pale ochraceous-cinnamon. STEM 3-7 cm. long, variable in length, 4-10 mm. thick, subclavate or tapering either way, *soft, pure white, clothed when young by a glutinous, hyaline, universal veil* which soon dries, often viscid only at base, soft-stuffed. SPORES narrowly elliptical, almost smooth, 6-7.5 x 4-5 micr. BASIDIA 26-28 x 7 micr., 4-spored. ODOR mild or subaromatic. TASTE of *every part intensely bitter.* CORTINA white.

In conifer and frondose woods, among leaves or humus. Throughout the State. August-September. Infrequent.

The American plant, named *C. amarus* by Peck, does not differ from *C. vibratilis* Fr. as it occurs around Stockholm. The spores, bitter taste of all parts and the hyaline gluten of the universal veil are the same. *C. amarus* Pk. was originally referred to the subgenus Phlegmacium (N. Y. State Mus. Rep. 32, p. 30, 1879) but later, Dr. Peck referred it to its proper position. *C. vibratilis* is distinguished by its pure white stem, pallid gills and yellow cap; the last may take on fulvous or rufous brown hues on the disk. An occasional individual of larger dimensions occurs. The stem varies in length and shape, and in mossy wet places often becomes more elongated. The gluten often drips from the edge of the cap in moist weather and on drying the cap becomes shining. This species might be confused with *C. causticum* Fr., unreported in Michigan, in which only the viscid pellicle of the pileus is bitter. Two other European species, *C. emollitus* Fr. and *C. crystallinus* Fr. possess bitter flesh and somewhat similar colored caps, but they belong to the subgenus Phlegmacium and their stems are not pure white.

315. Cortinarius sterilis Kauff.

Torr. Bot. Club Bull., Vol. 32, 1905.

Illustrations: Ibid, Fig. 1, p. 304.
　　　Jour. of Mycol., Vol. 13, Pl. 96, p. 36, 1907.
　　　Mycol. Bull., Vol. 5, Fig. 242, p. 316, 1907.

PILEUS 1.5-4.5 cm. broad, suborbicular when young then convex-expanded, margin incurved, drab, *drab-gray to olive buff,* even, smooth, *viscid,* somewhat umbonate at times. FLESH white, soft, thin. GILLS relatively broad, 4-6 mm., drab-gray at first, then light-cinnamon, rounded behind, then emarginate, not at all ventricose, rather crowded, edge serratulate and white, later eroded, *provided with sterile cells.* STEM 4-8 cm. long, 4-6 mm. thick, at base up to 10 mm., clavate or tapering upward, solid, spongy, or tapering upward, dingy-white, tinged with light blue toward apex, clothed when fresh with the delicate patches of the *viscid,* universal veil, which is of the same color as the pileus, within pale bluish at apex, white below. SPORES subsphoeroid, almost smooth, 6-7 x 5-6.5 micr. CORTINA white or sordid.

Gregarious in swamps of cedar, etc. Bay View. August-September. Rare.

The spores and the peculiar color of cap and veil distinguish this species. It has been found only twice, in low, wet, sphagnous or mossy swamps. Its name refers to the sterile cells on the edge of the gills.

316. Cortinarius iodes B. & C.

PILEUS 2-6 cm. broad, campanulate-convex, glabrous, even, *with a tough, viscid, separable pellicle, dark violet to purplish,* at length often yellowish on the disk. FLESH thick on the disk, abruptly thin on the margin, violaceous then paler. GILLS adnate, close, moderately broad, *violaceous at first,* then gray-cinnamon. STEM 5-7 cm. long, equal or clavate-thickened or tapering to either end, 4-8 or 5-15 mm. thick, *viscid,* solid, subfibrillose. CORTINA pale violaceous. SPORES broadly-elliptical, minutely rough-punctate, 8-10 x 6-6.5 micr. TASTE *mild.* ODOR none.

Gregarious or subcaespitose.   On the ground in low, wet places in woods. August. Detroit. Infrequent.

This is very similar in color and stature to *C. iodeoides* but lacks the bitter taste of the pellicle of the cap. The color is deeper and the spores are larger than in that species. It appears to be related to the European *C. salor* Fr. which has similar colors but whose spores are truly spherical. It has been received from the eastern part of the United States where it occurs more frequently.

317. Cortinarius iodeoides sp. nov.

Illustration :   Plate LXVI of this Report.

PILEUS 2-5 cm. broad, convex then expanded, broadly umbonate to plane, *deep lavender-violet or bluish-violet when young or fresh,* fading to livid-ashy, sometimes faintly yellowish or buff-spotted, *with a bitter pellicle which is glutinous* when moist or young, glabrous, even. FLESH at first pale violaceous, soon white, thin on margin, thickish on disk. GILLS adnate then emarginate, rather narrow, close, pale violaceous, *soon whitish,* at length pale ochraceous-cinnamon. STEM 2-6.5 cm. long, clavate-thickened at base or variously thickened or subcompressed, 4-8 mm. thick, white but *covered when young by the thin, delicately violaceous, glutinous, universal veil,* stuffed, silky or glabrous. SPORES elliptical, almost smooth, 7-7.5 x 4-4.5 micr., pale ferruginous-cinnamon in mass. ODOR none or slight. TASTE of flesh mild, *of pellicle of pileus bitter.*

Subcaespitose or gregarious.   Among leaf-mold, often hidden by leaves, in frondose woods of maple, oak, etc. August-October. Ann Arbor, New Richmond.   More frequent than the preceding.

This species is easily confused with the preceding, but is clearly distinct because of the bitter surface of the cap which is quickly recognized, and the different spores. A more careful comparison shows slight differences in the colors. It is often hidden by the leaves, especially in the late fall.

318.   Cortinarius heliotropicus Pk.

N. Y. State Mus. Bull. 94, 1905.

Illustration: Ibid, Pl. P., Fig. 1-7.

"PILEUS 2.5-6.5 cm. broad, broadly campanulate, convex or nearly plane, fibrillose, *viscid, heliotrope-purple, generally spotted or variegated by yellowish-white spots.* FLESH whitish, thin. GILLS narrow, thin, close, rounded behind, adnexed, *concolorus with the pileus when young,* cinnamon when mature. STEM 3.5-7 cm. long, 4-8 mm. thick, *firm,* solid or spongy within, usually slightly thickened at base, silky-fibrillose, *viscid, whitish and spotted with purple or colored like the pileus,* white within. SPORES 10-12.5 x 5-6 micr., elliptic. TASTE mild or slightly acrid. ODOR slightly of radish.

"In woods. Smithtown, New York. August.

"This is one of the most beautiful species of Cortinarius. In some specimens the spots on the pileus are large or confluent, in others they are almost or entirely absent, but usually they are small and distinct. The purple color of the gills is persistent for some time. In large specimens the margin is sometimes adorned by fibrillose scales of the veil."

This and the two preceding are all of medium size and beautifully colored. The description and notes are adopted from Peck. This species seems to differ from *C. iodes* mainly in the larger spores and perhaps in taste and color.

SUBGENUS BULBOPODIUM: Stem dry, *at first hidden,* then usually stout, with a thick, abrupt, marginate-depressed bulb, to whose margin is attached the cortina; the universal veil is either manifest or lacking in the young stage. Pileus with a *viscid* pellicle; equally fleshy.

This is the section "Scauri" of Fries. The structure of the bulb and the development of the stem is unique among the Cortinarii, and the group deserves equal rank with the other subgenera. The "button" stage of the young plant consists only of pileus and bulb, the former smaller than and closely pressing on the bulb. The rest of the stem is invisible, since its beginnings are enclosed undeveloped under the pileus. The margin of the pileus rests on the broad bulb and produces the typical, abruptly depressed edge of that body. The cortina extends from the margin of the pileus to the bulb, to whose upper surface it is attached and, during development, is carried up on the lower part of the elongating stem. The universal veil when present envelops the bulb and extends to the surface of the pileus in the form of a thin, slightly woven membrane, which breaks away in a circumscissile manner from the margin of the pileus at an early stage and is only noticeable, after the expansion of the plant, on the exterior of the bulb or where the torn fringes of its upper portion extend above the margin of the bulb and lie against the stem; it is usually of the same color as the surface of the pileus and this shows on the bulb and on the stem immediately above it. Sometimes this veil is slightly gelatinous. Species occur which are intermediate between this and the following subgenus, where the bulb is scarcely depressed or marginate, or where the margin of the pileus almost covers the slight bulb so that the latter is margined only about its base. The stem is never peronate nor annulate by the universal veil in this subgenus. The connection of the margin of the bulb with the cap and the circumscissile manner in which the universal veil breaks across are somewhat similar to the conditions in some Amanitas.

The species of this group are numerous, and many more will probably be found in Michigan. Fries appears to apologize for including and naming so many species under the section Scauri, as witness his remarks under that section in Epicrisis: "An astonishing number of closely related forms, which, although they were all constant, I was ashamed to separate in Sys. Myc., but published them under titles which were much broader. But I am compelled to recognize them lest the limits appear to be arbitrary, since their existence in nature has been verified many times." Not a few others have already been found in the State, but their identity is not yet established.

Section I. Universal veil present.

*Gills, flesh or stem at first violaceous, bluish, or purplish, rarely olivaceous or white.

319.   Cortinarius atkinsonianus Kauff.   (Edible)

Bull. Torr. Bot. Club, Vol. 32, p. 324, 1905.

Illustrations: Ibid, Fig. 6, p. 316.
        Jour. of Mycol., Vol. 13, Plate 99, p. 36, 1907.
        Plate LXVII of this Report.

PILEUS 6-9 cm. broad, convex then expanded, *wax-yellow or flavus at first,* tinted with olivaceous, then alutaceous or reddish-tawny in places, with a *viscid separable pellicle,* glabrous, even. FLESH thick, rather soft, *at first deep violet* or lavender, slowly fading. GILLS adnate becoming slightly sinuate, rather narrow, width uniform, *deep violet or purplish at first,* edge sometimes olivaceous-yellowish, at length cinnamon. STEM 6-8 cm. long, stout, 12-18 mm. thick, *deep violet or violaceous blue,* concolor within, solid, dry, equal or tapering upward from a rather thick, marginate, broadly tur-binate *bulb* up to 3 cm. thick, and externally clothed by the *oli-vaceous-yellow universal veil,* apex of stem fibrillose, elsewhere hung with the fibrillose remains of the *olivaceous-yellow cortina.* SPORES almond-shaped, elliptical, *very tuberculate,* 13-15 (rarely 16) x 7-8.5 micr., rusty-cinnamon in mass.

Gregarious. In leaf-mould or among fallen leaves, in rich, mixed or frondose woods. Ann Arbor, Detroit, New Richmond. September-October. Infrequent.

This noble species is the prince of known American Cortinarii. Several collections in all stages of development have made it possible to emend the original description and refer it to its proper place in the genus. The colors of the fresh plants are vivid and most beau-tiful. The flesh is at first intense violet, and by peeling the pileus this color is at once exposed under the yellow pellicle. There is an olivaceous tinge in the yellow color of the pileus, cortina and uni-versal veil in the young plant, and the edge of the gills may also be laved with the olivaceous-yellow coloring. The taste and odor are mild. It seems closely related to *C. arquatus* Fr. in the sense of Ricken, from which it differs mainly in its intensely violet or pur-plish flesh. The figure of Ricken (Blätterpilze, Pl. 36, Fig. 4) however, gives a very inadequate conception of our plant. It is barely possible that this is the American form of that species.

320. Cortinarius calochrous Fr.

Syst. Myc., 1821 (segregated, Epicrisis, 1836-8).

Illustrations: Gillet, Champignons de France, No. 200.
Plate LXVIII of this Report.

PILEUS 3-6 cm. broad, *not large,* convex, soon expanded-plane, *bright ochre-yellow to citron-yellow,* fulvous on disk, *with a viscid pellicle,* glabrous, even. FLESH thickish, rather compact, whitish. GILLS emarginate-adnexed, crowded, thin, rather narrow, *rosy-violet to violaceous-purple at first,* at length pale clay-cinnamon, *edge serratulate.* STEM 3-5 cm. long, 5-9 mm. thick, solid, pale violaceous or whitish at first, soon becoming dingy yellowish, equal above the *rather small, abrupt, marginate-depressed, shallow bulb,* which is clothed at first by the *yellow universal veil.* SPORES sub-inequilateral, elliptical, 8-9 (rarely 10) x 4-5.5 micr., cinnamon in mass. BASIDIA 28-30 x 7-8 micr., 4-spored. ODOR and TASTE mild.

Solitary or scattered. In low, rich woods of maple, beech, etc. Ann Arbor. September-October. Infrequent.

A medium-sized plant, never becoming large. Known by its peculiar bulb which, in the typical condition, has the shape of a small porcelain evaporating disk with a rim, into which the stem appears inserted. Shreds of the yellow universal veil cling to the rim and the base of the stem. The plant is excellently figured by Fries in the unpublished plate in the Royal Museum at Stockholm, showing the remains of the universal veil. Gillet's figure is also accurate as to color and shape. Cooke's figure (Ill., Plate 713) cannot apply to our plant. Ricken, Saccardo and Britzelmayr give spore-measurements which indicate a related species with much larger spores.

321. Cortinarius velicopia sp. nov.

PILEUS 6-9 cm. broad, convex at first, soon broadly expanded to plane, *violet to buff at first, becoming dingy yellowish-ochraceous* as if stained, with a viscid, separable pellicle, even, glabrous, margin incurved and at first appendiculate from the copious cortina. FLESH pale blue-violaceous, *soon white,* thick, moderately compact.

GILLS narrowed behind, narrowly adnate, moderately broad, close, at length dingy yellowish or pallid, hung with the fibrillose remains then cinereous, finally rusty-cinnamon, *edge minutely fimbriate.* STEM 6-8 cm. long, 8-18 mm. thick, *violaceous-blue, fading to bluish,* at length dingy yellowish or pallid, hung with the fibrilllose remains of the cortina, dry, equal, solid, *with a marginate, subdepressed, hemispherical bulb,* which is clothed by a thin, ochraceous-buff, universal veil. CORTINA very copious, white or faintly bluish. SPORES ventricose-elliptical, *with a prominent, papillate apiculus, very tuberculate,* rather symmetrical, 9-12 x 6-7 micr. Edge of gills provided with inflated, sterile cells. ODOR and TASTE mild.

Gregarious or subcaespitose. Among fallen leaves in mixed or frondose woods. Ann Arbor, New Richmond. September-October. Infrequent.

This may be considered a segregate of *C. caerulescens,* and corresponds to Ricken's description of that species (Blätterpilze, p. 129), but is different from the conception of Maire (Bull. d. la. Soc. Myc. de France, Vol. 27, p. 426) and that shown by the Friesian unpublished plates.   The spores of our plant, as well as the very abundant cortina, are quite distinguishing. The colors of the gills and stem incline to blue. Several collections show that the pileus may be deep violet at first in some forms, but eventually the ochraceous-buff color of the universal veil pervades also the surface of the pileus. The universal veil is less manifest and less persistent than in the preceding species.

322.   Cortinarius herpeticus Fr.

Epicrisis, 1836-38.

Illustrations: Cooke, Ill., Pl. 849.
    Ricken, Die Blätterpilze, Pl. 37, Fig. 4.

PILEUS 3-10 cm. broad, convex, subexpanded, firm, smoky-olive or *olivaceous,* tinged brownish on disk, fading, *with a viscid, separable pellicle,* even, glabrous, margin at first incurved, thin. FLESH thickish, firm, abruptly thin on margin, evanescently violaceous, then whitish. GILLS rounded behind, adnexed-emarginate, close, moderately broad, smoky-violet or *olivaceous* at first, smoky-brown at length clay-color (Ridg.), then smoky-cinnamon. STEM 3-5 cm. long, 8-18 mm. thick, solid, *violaceous-blue at first,* fibrillose by the *whitish cortina,* equal above the marginate-depressed bulb, which is covered by the remains of a greenish or whitish, thin, universal veil, bulb 1-2 cm. thick. SPORES broadly elliptical, rough, 8-10 x 5-6 micr. ODOR and TASTE mild.

Gregarious. Among mosses in cedar and balsam swamps. Bay View, Michigan, and North Elba, New York. August. Rare.

This was considerd a new species in the "Key" (Jour. of Mycol. 13, p. 35, 1907) as *C. olivaceoides*. It agrees well with the Friesian species as characterized in Monographia. In the 11th Report of the Mich. Acad. Sci., p. 32, it is reported as *C. olivaceus* Pk. *C. olivaceus* Pk. has larger spores and belongs to the section Phlegmacium. *C. herpeticus* appears to be close to *C. scaurus* Fr.

323. Cortinarius olivaceo-stramineus Kauff.

Bull. Torr. Bot. Club, Vol. 32, 1905.

Illustrations: Ibid, Fig. 3, p. 309.
    Jour. of Mycol., Vol. 13, Pl. 95, 1907.
    Mycological Bull., Vol 5, Fig. 243, p. 317, 1907.

PILEUS 4-7 cm. broad, broadly convex, slightly depressed in the center when expanded, *pale straw-yellow with an olivaceous tinge,* slightly rufous-tinged in age, glabrous or silky-fibrillose, disk sometimes covered with minute scales, *viscid from a gelatinous pellicle,* margin incurved at first, shreds of the cortina attached to it on expanding. FLESH very thick, abruptly thin on margin, *white,* dingy-yellowish in age, *soon soft and spongy.* GILLS sinuate-adnexed, rather narrow, crowded, *whitish at first,* then pale cinnamon, edge serratulate and paler. STEM 6-8 cm. long, 5-18 mm. thick, spongy and soft within, sometimes becoming hollow, white and pruinate above the fibrillose remains of the cortina, *with a slight, subobsolete, submarginate* bulb from whose margin arises the copious white CORTINA; bulb when young covered by a thin universal veil of the same color as the pileus. SPORES ventricose-elliptical, with stout apiculus, almost smooth, granular within, 10-12 x 5.5-6.5 micr. BASIDIA about 38 x 9 micr. ODOR and TASTE mild.

Subcaespitose. On the ground in mixed and frondose woods. August-September. Ann Arbor. Rather rare.

It is with some hesitation placed in this section, as the universal veil is not well developed. The bulb is at first slightly marginate and the cortina is attached to it; later the bulb almost disappears

at times. The plants are sometimes deformed by a fungous para-
site, *Mycogone rosea,* causing the gills to remain sterile.   It has been
found in several states, but is apparently rare.

324. **Cortinarius cæsiocyaneus** Britz.   (EDIBLE)

Bot. Centralbl., 1895, p. 10, 1899, p. 58.
Maire, Bull. de la. Soc. Myc. de France, 26, 1910.

Illustrations: Maire, Bull. de. la. Soc. Myc. de France, Vol. 26,
Pl. 8, Fig. 1-2.

PILEUS 5-12 cm. broad, convex then expanded-plane, sometimes
depressed on the center, *bluish-violaceous-white to silvery-violaceous,*
glabrous, even, *with a viscid, separable pellicle,* silky-shining when
dry, margin becoming silky and at first incurved.   FLESH pale
violet, fading slowly, thick.   GILLS rather *narrow, adnexed,*
rounded behind then sinuate, thin, *pale violaceous, soon pale alutaceous,* then cinnamon, crowded, edge even or becoming eroded. STEM
stout, 4-7 cm. long, 1-2 cm. thick, solid, pale violaceous-white, concolor within, equal above *the large, flattened, marginate-depressed
bulb,* which is white on the surface from the *white universal veil,*
attached to white mycelium.   CORTINA *violaceous-white.*   Spores
10-12 (rarely 13) x 6-7 micr., almond-shaped, elliptical, tuberculate,
cinnamon in mass.   ODOR and TASTE mild.

Gregarious or subcaespitose.   On the ground among leaves in
frondose woods of oak, maple, etc.   Ann Arbor.   September-October.
Infrequent.

This is a segregate of *C. caerulescens* Fr.   The whole plant has a
rather uniform pale violaceous-whitish color almost exactly like
C. michiganensis.   As in that species, the gills are not at first
intensely colored nor at all purple or rosy.   It has the large size of
C. atkinsonianus with which it sometimes occurs.   The flattened
bulb is white below and on the sides, where it is clothed by the
white subgelatinous veil.   The spores are larger than in *C. michiganensis* with which it is easily confused and which belongs to
another section.   Cooke's figures of *C. caerulescens* (Ill., Pl. 721)
show the stature and color, but not the characteristic bulb and
spores; that plate is referred by Maire (Bull. de la Soc. Myc. de
France, Vol. 26, p. 18) to *C. caesiocyaneus* Britz.   Ricken places
this plant under *C. camphoratus* Fr. but without any good grounds.

325. Cortinarius rubens sp. nov.

PILEUS 3-7 cm. broad, hemispherical then convex-expanded, *vermillion-red to orange-fulvous,* unicolorous, *with a viscid, separable, toughish pellicle,* glabrous, even, shining when dry. FLESH thick, whitish. GILLS adnexed, becoming emarginate, rather broad, close, caesious or pale drab at first, then argillaceous-cinnamon, edge entire and tinged dull citron-yellowish. STEM 4-7 cm. long, 1-1.5 cm. thick, solid, dry, *pale straw-yellow to whitish,* citron-yellowish within, fimbriate from the cortina, equal above the *rounded, marginate-depressed bulb* which is clothed by the *vermillion-red universal veil* except below where it is white and attached to white mycelium. SPORES almond-shaped, very inequilateral, tuberculate, 15-18 x 7-8.5 micr. BASIDIA 45 x 13-15 micr., stout, 4-spored. CORTINA white or tinged with red. ODOR faintly aromatic. TASTE of flesh bitterish-disagreeable, slowly more intense.

Gregarious or subcaespitose. On the ground among leaves in frondose woods of oak, maple, etc., its mycelium attached to *mycorhiza* of undetermined roots. Ann Arbor. October. Rare.

The bright red color of the pileus and the universal veil is striking and is rarely seen in this subgenus. The veil is very evident on the fresh plants and shows on the margin of the bulb as a bright red to orange-red decoration, and in the button stage is continuous with the pellicle of the pileus, breaking in a circumscissile manner like the yellow veil of *C. atkinsonianus.* There is no violet or purple present in the cap although the young gills have a dull violaceous-gray tint called "caesious." The edge of the gills is citron-straw-yellow and, when seen from below, gives the impression of that color to the rest of the gills. It differs from *C. sublateritius* Pk. in its much larger spores and the distinct universal veil. It agrees closely with the description of *C. testaceus* Cke., except in details. Maire, however, says Cooke's plant is identical with *C. rufo-olivaceous* Fr. to which our plant cannot be referred, although related to it. Specimens of our species have also been received from Madison, Wisconsin.

**Gills, flesh and stem yellow at first.

326. Cortinarius elegantioides sp. nov.

Illustration: Plate LXIX of this Report.

PILEUS 4-7 cm. broad, convex then expanded-plane, *cadmium-yellow, orange-fulvous on disk,* becoming fulvous-ferruginous in age, glabrous, even, *with a glutinous separable pellicle.* FLESH thick, whitish or tinged greenish-yellow. GILLS adnate, becoming deeply emarginate and uncinate, close, *rather broad, varying pale yellowish-white, bright citron-yellow or sulphur-yellow,* at length ferruginous, thin, edge minutely crenulate. STEM 5-8.5 cm. long, rather stout, subequal, 10-18 mm. thick, dry, spongy-stuffed, yellowish-white or citron-yellow, *flesh tinged greenish-yellow,* with a marginate, subdepressed, subturbinate *bulb, which is clothed on the surface by the yellow to subferruginous, subgelatinous universal veil.* CORTINA slight, fugacious. SPORES almond-shaped, elliptical, very tuberculate, 15-18 (rarely 19-20) x 7-9 micr. BASIDIA 48 x 12-13 micr., 4-spored. TASTE of flesh tardily but distinctly *bitter.* ODOR mild.

Solitary or subcaespitose. On the ground in frondose woods of oak, maple, etc. Ann Arbor, Detroit, New Richmond. September-October. Infrequent.

Nearly always solitary or of few individuals. Known by its large spores, bitter taste of the flesh and the tinge of green in the yellow color of the flesh, etc. It has the stature of *C. multiformis* of Cooke (Ill., Pl. 708 and 709), but the spores are distinctive. The bulb is not very broad as compared with that of *C. fulgens* Fr.; it is rather soft and decays early. The stem is narrower upwards at first and colors of the stem. It is closer to *C. sulfurinus* Quel. (sense of Ricken) but differs in its spores, less abundant cortina and the colors of the stem. It is closer to *C. sulfurinus* Quel. (sense of Ricken), but neither Quelet nor Ricken mention the bitter taste nor the universal veil.

Section II. Universal veil not manifest.

**Gills, flesh or stem at first caesious, violaceous, bluish or purplish.*

327. Cortinarius purpurascens Fr. (EDIBLE)

Epicrisis, 1836-38. Obs. 2, 1818.

Illustrations: Cooke, Ill., Pl. 723.
  Gillet, Champignons de France, No. 224.
  Plate LXXI of this Report.

PILEUS 5-8 cm. broad, broadly convex to subexpanded, *dark purplish-umber or entirely violet-purple when young,* soon discolored and variegated with clay-color or brown, opaque, glabrous, even, *with a viscid, separable pellicle.* FLESH thick, compact, tinged azure or purplish, fading to whitish in age, *but changing rapidly to deep purple when bruised.* GILLS adnexed and rounded behind, then emarginate, rather narrow, close, at first azure-blue or darker, *changing to deep purple when bruised.* STEM usually short, stout, 2-5 cm. long, 10-20 mm. thick, *solid,* subequal, fibrillose from the cortina, *bulb not large, subemarginate* to distinctly marginate, scarcely ever depressed, soon oval, purplish, *flesh quickly deeper-colored when bruised.* SPORES 8-9.5 (rarely 10) x 5-5.5 micr. elliptic-ovate, rough-echinulate, dark in mass. BASIDIA 40-45 x 8-9 micr., 4-spored. ODOR and TASTE mild.

Gregarious, solitary or subcaespitose. On the ground in open woods, sometimes in bare, exposed places where soil is hard. Ann Arbor, Detroit. September-October. Infrequent.

The American plant has more purple in the pileus than shown in my collection from Sweden and as given by European authors. In all other respects it agrees with that of Europe. This is *C. subpurpurascens* in the sense of Ricken. The spore-measurements as given by Massee are too large. We have three related species which might be easily confused by not taking account of the spores: *C. aggregatus* has smaller spores and its flesh and gills do not change to purple when bruised. *C. sphaerosperma* is a much larger plant, with almost spherical spores. The common form of *C. purpurascens* is small, stout and squatty, although more luxuriant specimens occur in favorable weather.

328.   Cortinarius subpurpurascens Fr.

Epicrisis, 1836-38.

Illustrations: Cooke, Ill., Pl. 725.
  Ricken, Blätterpilze, Pl. 36, Fig. 3.   (As *C. purpurascens.*)

PILEUS 5-10 cm. broad, firm, campanulate, discoid or gibbous,
then expanded, at length depressed, *viscid, tinged* purple at first,
yellow-ochre to ochraceous tawny with smoky-brown stains, scarcely virgate, glabrous, *zoned by the decurved margin.* FLESH soon
whitish, *not changing* to purple when bruised, compact. GILLS
adnexed-emarginate, crowded, rather narrow, purplish at first then
pecan-brown (Ridg.), *becoming purplish when bruised,* edge entire.
STEM 5-7 cm. long, 10-15 mm. thick, subequal above the rather
small depressed-marginate flattened bulb, pale violaceous, *purplish
where bruised,* violaceous within, cortinate-fibrillose, *stuffed then
tubular.* SPORES elliptical-oval, 8-9 x 5-6 micr., rough. ODOR
slightly of radish after picking, somewhat pungent. TASTE mild.

Gregarious to subcaespitose. On the ground under balsam and
spruce. North Elba, Adirondack Mountains, New York. Collection Kauffman. September, 1914. Infrequent.

This species differs from *C. purpurascens* in its habit, its stuffed
to hollow stem and the almost immutable color of the flesh. The
gills and stem, however, change to purplish where bruised. It is *C.
purpurascens* in the sense of Ricken who seems to have exchanged
the Friesian names. It seems to be a species of the higher mountains, and perhaps of the northern forests.

329.   Cortinarius aggregatus sp. nov.

PILEUS 5-12 cm. broad, convex then subexpanded, obtuse and
usually irregular from crowding, at length undulate, glabrous or
white-pruinose when young, *at first bright purple-blue* to purplish-
gray, at maturity *becoming smoky olive-gray and streaked,* with a
viscid pellicle, margin at first incurved. FLESH thick, *violaceous*
then faintly olivaceous-gray to dingy white, *not turning purple when
bruised.* GILLS adnexed and rounded behind, then emarginate,
close, moderately broad, *violet-purple at first,* then gray to cinnamon. STEM 4-7 cm. long, 10-20 mm. thick, rather short, solid, dry,
purplish, darker at base, *the small bulb at the very first submarginate,* not depressed, disappearing during development. CORTINA
deep violaceous, rather copious, *attached to bulblet at first,* collaps-

ing on the stem. SPORES narrowly elliptical, 7-8 x 4-4.5 micr. ODOR and TASTE mild.

Caespitose, often in troops forming arcs of scores of individuals. In frondose woods of oak, maple, etc., in the late fall after heavy rains, half hidden by the leaves.

September-November. Ann Arbor. Infrequent, in very wet seasons.

This species is usually quite abundant in its particular woods. As the clusters or closely crowded rows of the fruit-bodies develop, they push up the thick mat of leaves in humps, an appearance which is very commonly produced in frondose woods by the late-growing mushrooms. The young clusters may be so thoroughly hidden by the leaves that they are usually not found till more or less expanded and the changes in color by that time are often extremely confusing. In that case the deep bluish-purple color of the young cap is lost and in the expanded state its surface assumes a distinct olive-gray color and is then often markedly streaked with darker shades. The bulb becomes soft, is often infested by grubs and stained yellowish. It differs from *C. purpurascens* in habit, in different shade of blue on the cap and stem, in the flesh not changing to darker purple when bruised and in the smaller spores. A vigorous cluster of young plants are intensely colored, and often silvery as if covered with hoar-frost. It is related to *C. cyanopus* Fr.

330. Cortinarius sphaerosperma sp. nov. (EDIBLE)

Illustration: Plate LXX of this Report.

PILEUS 8-16 cm. broad, *large,* broadly convex-expanded, with a *very viscid,* separable pellicle, glabrous, even, *deep violet-purple,* micaceous-shining when dry. FLESH soon whitish, *changing* to *purple when bruised,* thick, compact. GILLS adnate *then sinuate-subdecurrent,* crowded, not broad, *purple at first,* then rusty-umber. STEM 6-9 cm. long, 15-20 mm. thick, solid, stout, dry, hung with the dense, spore-stained fibrils of a very copious, purplish CORTINA, *deep purple* like the cap, *the rather small bulb subemarginate and disappearing,* at length clavate-bulbous, whitish within, becoming purple when bruised. SPORES spherical or subsphoeroid, very tuberculate-rough, 7-8.5 x 6-7.5 micr., dark ferruginous in mass. BASIDIA 30 x 9 micr., 4-spored, the slender sterigmata 3-4 micr. long. ODOR slightly of radish. TASTE mild.

Solitary or scattered. On the ground in frondose woods of oak, maple, etc. August-September. Ann Arbor, Detroit. Rather rare.

This magnificent species has only been seen thrice. It was at first passed by as *C. purpurascens* but a careful examination revealed important differences. It may be considered as a segregate of that species, although very likely it is a native of this country. No European author seems to have referred spherical spores to *C. purpurascens* or *C. subpurpurascens,* and in the European plants, both of these species entirely or partly lack the purple color of the cap. No very young specimens were found, and it needs further study. Both this species and the preceding approach the next subgenus in the scarcely marginate bulb.

331. Cortinarius purpureophyllus sp. nov.

PILEUS 5-8 cm. broad, convex-expanded, *dull tawny-red,* fading to ochraceous-fulvous, glabrous, even, *with a viscid,* separable pellicle, margin incurved. FLESH whitish, thick, compact. GILLS rounded behind and adnexed, deep *lilac-purple, color persistent,* narrow, crowded, thin, edge entire or suberoded. STEM 4-6 cm. long, 12-18 mm. thick, equal or slightly narrower upwards, *pallid or slightly tinged* lilac-violaceous at first, spongy-stuffed or solid, fibrillose from cortina, apex violaceous within, *with a marginate-depressed, flattish bulb,* which is white throughout, attached to a white mycelium. CORTINA copious, whitish (?). SPORES almond-shaped, elliptical, tuberculate, 10-12 x 6-7 micr., rusty-cinnamon in mass. BASIDIA 36-42 x 8-9 micr., 4-spored. ODOR slight or none. TASTE slowly disagreeable, somewhat bitter.

Gregarious. Among fallen leaves in frondose woods of maple, oak, etc. Ann Arbor. October-November. Infrequent.

Known by the contrasting colors of pileus, gills and stem, and the size of the spores. The flesh is scarcely tinged with violaceous except at the apex of the stem. The young gills have a deep color as in *C. purpurascens,* but the flesh has none of the characteristics of that species.

332. Cortinarius cærulescens Fr.

Epicrisis, 1836-38.

Illustrations: Cooke, Ill., Pl. 722.
    Quelet, Grevillea, Vol. VI, Pl. 105, Fig. 3.
    Maire, Bull. de la Soc. Myc. de France, Vol. 26, Pl. 8, Fig. 3-5.

"PILEUS 3-6 cm. broad, convex then convex-plane, quite thick, *with separable, viscid pellicle,* glabrous, even, *violaceous-blue, tinged ochraceous on disk,* sometimes entirely ochraceous-yellow, not hygrophanous, margin at first incurved pubescent and white, then spreading and violaceous. FLESH *pale violaceous-blue,* especially under the cuticle, then whitish, at length ochraceous-stained. GILLS arcuate, then plane or slightly ventricose, attenuate in front, rounded behind, thin, *broad,* rather broadly adnate, *violet-amethyst or violet-blue at first,* then rusty-brown, edge serratulate. STEM 3-5 cm. long, 10 mm. thick, cylindric-conic, *with a marginate bulb,* fibrous-fleshy, dry, silky-fibrillose, *violaceous-blue to amethyst-blue,* bulb white, solid. CORTINA violaceous at first. Universal veil rapidly evanescent. SPORES 12-14 x 6-7 micr., sub-amygdaliform, elliptic, tuberculate. ODOR feeble, like that of *C. purpurascens.* TASTE mild or slightly bitterish."

The description has been adopted from that of Prof. Maire (Bull. de la Soc. Myc. de France, Vol. 27, p. 424, 1911). In America I have seen specimens of this species only from Tennessee. The species stands out from the segregates of the old species as it was variously interpreted, by its large spores. In specimens from Sweden, I find the same sized spores. In size, color of the young gills and in stature it is much like *C. calochrous.* Cooke's figures (Ill., Pl. 721) and Gillet's figures (Champignons de France, No. 208) are referred by Maire to *C. caesiocyaneus,* which they illustrate fairly well. As Fries did not give spore-measurements, I prefer to follow the decision reached by Maire after he had compared the species which occurs near Stockholm, with those of France. Our American references to this plant must be considered as usually, if not always, based on collections of *C. caesiocyaneus, C. michiganensis* or perhaps *C. calochrous.* It is possible that a number of intermediate forms also occur as I have some collections which apparently support such a conclusion.

333. Cortinarius michiganensis Kauff. (EDIBLE)

Jour. of Mycology, Vol. 13, p. 35, 1907 (synopsis).

PILEUS 8-14 cm. broad, compact, firm, broadly convex then slowly expanded, *pale violaceous to lilac,* unicolor, *color persistent,* glabrous, even, *glutinous when moist or young,* then viscid, margin persistently inrolled and tomentose-silky. FLESH very thick, white or tinged with lilac, not changed by bruising. GILLS rounded behind and adnexed, or almost free, *narrow, crowded, thin,* acuminate in front, *pale violaceous-white at first,* then pale ashy, finally ochraceous-cinnamon, *edge serratulate from the first.* STEM stout, 3-6 cm. long, 18-30 mm. thick, solid, *pale violaceous-lilac* to whitish, fibrillose from cortina, *marginate-bulbous,* bulb large, up to 4 cm. broad, white beneath, flesh white except the violaceous apex. COR-TINA bluish-white, at first attached to the bulb, evanescent, not copious. SPORES narrowly elliptic-ovate, almost smooth, 8-10.5 x 4.5-5.5 micr., pale ochraceous-cinnamon in mass. ODOR and TASTE mild.

Caespitose, in small clusters of large individuals. On the ground, among grass or leaves, in low, rich, frondose woods of beech, maple, etc. Ann Arbor, Detroit, New Richmond. August-October. Infrequent.

This species is known by its large size, caespitose habit, pale gills of which the spores mature slowly, and by the lilaceous color of cap and stem. When fresh or young a clear gluten covers the pileus and sometimes the base of the young bulb, as if by a universal veil. It is very like *C. caesiocyaneus* in size and shape, but has a different habit, different color and spores and lacks the white universal veil of that species. It is doubtless in part the *C. caerulescens* of some American lists. *C. caesius* Clem. according to the description, approaches it, differing in its scarcely viscid pileus, the much thicker spores and the white gills.

334. Cortinarius cæsius Clements.

Bot. Surv. of Nebraska, IV, 1896.

"PILEUS 4-8 cm. broad, campanulate-convex, then expanded, fleshy, glabrous, *not or scarcely viscid,* obscurely *dark blue-violaceous,* finally brown-punctate, margin involute. FLESH *bluish-gray,* unchangeable. GILLS adnate, subdistant, *white then cinnamon,* not violaceous. STEM 1-5 cm. long, 10-15 mm. thick, fleshy-fibrous, solid, violaceous above, *bright yellow below,* turbinate-bulbous, subglobose-when old, bulb 3-4 cm. high and 4 cm. broad, violaceous. CORTINA bluish-gray. SPORES subelliptical or globose, 8-10 x 7-8 micr., verrucose, tawny-brown.

"Related to *C. glaucopus* Schaeff."

The description is adopted from the original. The plant was found in Nebraska and I have not seen it.

335. Cortinarius aleuriosmus Maire var.

Bull. de la Soc. Myc. de France, Vol. 26, p. 22, 1910.

Illustrations: Ibid, Pl. 7, Fig. 4-5.
Ricken, Die Blätterpilze, Pl. 39, Fig. 4.

PILEUS 5-10 cm. broad, very compact, firm, broadly convex *alutaceous-whitish at first, soon dingy ochraceous-tan to russet-tan,* sometimes sordid tawny-yellowish in age, glabrous, *with a glutinous pellicle* when moist or young, surface becoming reticulate-rivulose from the drying gluten, margin inrolled at first. FLESH thick, white or with an evanescent violaceous tinge. GILLS adnexed, *narrow,* crowded, *caesious at first* (i. e., pale livid-grayish), sometimes pallid, then rusty-cinnamon, edge erose-serratulate. STEM 4-6 cm. long, *stout, short,* 10-20 mm. thick, solid, compact, *white or scarcely violaceous-tinged,* fibrillose from the cortina, *with a thick, turbinate, marginate bulb,* bulb not depressed, white below and arising from white mycelium. SPORES elliptical-almond-shaped, minutely tuberculate, 10-12 x 5-6 micr. BASIDIA 30-35 x 7 micr., 4-spored. ODOR and TASTE mild or slight.

Subcaespitose or gregarious. On the ground in frondose woods of oak, maple, etc. Ann Arbor. August-September. Infrequent.

This is doubtless the species reported by Ricken under *C. aleuriosmus* Maire. (See Blätterpilze, p. 136, No. 428). Both Ricken's and my collections seem to be the same species, but differ from the description of the type, given by Maire, in lacking the "bitter taste" in the pellicle of the pileus, and in the slightly smaller spores. Maire's species also had a distinct farinaceous odor and no violaceous nor blue tints in the flesh and stem. The latter point, however, is a variation easily overlooked. There is evidently a series of closely related forms, differing slightly in the amount of violet present and the presence or absence of a slight odor and taste. However, I suspect the species with the bitter pellicle should be kept distinct. Some of my collections had caps which were more tawny or rusty-ochraceous than the descriptions allow. The fundamental characters are the caesious or pale gray-drab young gills, the white flesh of the stem and mostly of the cap, and the spores. This species is a segregate of *C. glaucopus* Fr. and some of my collections agree well with the color, size and shape of the Friesian plates at Stockholm, but the flesh, especially of the stem, does not turn yellowish. The European authors agree that the spores of *C. glaucopus* measure 8-9 x 5-6 micr. Forms occur which have a subaromatic odor, resembling ripe pears. As is often the case in this subgenus, when the plant develops during heavy rains, the glutinous pellicle dissolves away in part, and the pileus is later merely subviscid.

336.   Cortinarius glaucopus Fr.

Syst. Myc., 1821.

Illustration: Ricken, Die Blätterpilze, Pl. 35, Fig. 7.

PILEUS 5-12 cm. broad, convex, then expanded-plane, firm, rigid, *often wavy on the geniculate margin,* viscid or glutinous, *variegate fulvous-streaked* on a slate-gray or steel-gray ground-color, *margin greenish-gray,* at first inflexed, disk fulvous. FLESH whitish then yellowish-tinged, thick, compact. GILLS adnexed then emarginate, moderately broad, close to crowded, *at first violaceous-blue,* then clay-cinnamon. STEM 5-10 cm. long (sometimes shorter), 15-25 mm. thick, rigid, pallid with a pale violaceous-blue tinge, *becoming yellowish in age,* flesh violaceous-bluish to whitish then sordid yellowish, solid, almost equal above *the abrupt, marginate, scarcely bulbous base,* attached to a white mycelium. SPORES almond-shaped, subinequilateral, slightly rough-punctate, 8-9 x 4-5 micr. BASIDIA 28-30 x 7 micr., 4-spored. ODOR and TASTE mild.

In dense, caespitose troops. On the ground, under or among leaves, in frondose woods of oak, maple, etc. Ann Arbor. September-October. Abundant locally, but infrequent; after heavy rains.

Only the luxuriant form of this species is known to me. A squatty form is said to occur, probably in dry weather. The colors are difficult to describe and vary during development. The fresh, mature pileus usually has a steel-gray metallic lustre in wet weather, its margin is bent down forming a faint zone, and fulvous shades radiate in streaks from the fulvous center. The bulb is narrow, somewhat thicker than the stem, and scarcely depressed. Its caespitose habit is very marked. No good plate seems to exist. Cooke's figure (Ill., Pl. 712) is entirely misleading, and Gillet's figure (Champignons de France, No. 224), doubtless illustrates another species. It is not at all commmon in the regions I have visited.

**Gills, flesh or stem at first green.

337. Cortinarius virentophyllus sp. nov.

PILEUS 5-8 cm. broad, convex, expanded-plane, regular, *viscid*, glabrous, *green to olivaceous-yellowish, fading* to pale ochraceous or straw-yellow, sometimes tinged fulvous, slightly streaked by the drying gluten. FLESH thickish on disk, very thin on margin, pallid-greenish, fading, subhygrophanous, with dark watery-green border along the gills. GILLS adnexed-emarginate, thin, close, somewhat narrow, *gray-olive or green at first, becoming deep green,* edge entire. STEM 5-7 cm. long, 10-15 mm. thick, silky-fibrillose at length, *stuffed* by a fibrous pith, becoming hollow, *distinctly cyaneous or pale blue,* fading to violaceous-whitish, bluish within but fading, equal along *the subemarginate bulb,* which becomes oval or subobsolete. SPORES almond-shaped, broadly elliptical, distinctly tuberculate, 9-11 x 6-7 micr. BASIDIA 36 x 9 micr., 4-spored. ODOR mild. TASTE of flesh and pellicle of cap mild.

Subcaespitose in clusters of few individuals. On the ground, among grass in frondose woods of oak, maple, etc. Ann Arbor. October-November. Rare.

This attractive species was found only twice. The cap and gills are deep green when fresh, while the stem is pale blue. The color of the cap and flesh soon fades to pale yellowish except near the gills. The axis of the stem is composed of softer, paler, fibrous tissue which fades quickly and disappears in part leaving the stem tubular. The bulb is not truly depressed-marginate unless in the button stage which was not seen. The species is related to *C. scaurus,* but the pileus is differently colored, not "tiger-spotted," and the stem not solid. The gills and stem are also more brightly colored than in that species. It may be an American variety. The spores agree closely with the measurements given by Ricken for *C. scaurus.* It differs from *C. prasinus* in the glabrous pileus, in stature, and in the spores, which according to Ricken are 13-16 x 6-7 micr. in size. Specimens were seen from Madison, Wisconsin.

***Gills, flesh or stem yellow, fulvescent, or ferruginous.*

338.   Cortinarius fulgens Fr.

Epicrisis, 1836-38.

Illustrations: Cooke, Ill., Pl. 716 (doubtful).
    Gillet, Champignons de France, .No. 223 (doubtful).

PILEUS 6-15 cm. or more broad, firm, broadly convex to plane, bright orange to *orange-fulvous,* disk orange-ferruginous, *somewhat virgate streaked,* very viscid when moist, margin incurved at first. FLESH thick, yellowish then alutaceous. GILLS dilute yellow then *deep ferruginous-orange,* emarginate, *broad,* close, *edge entire.* STEM 4-7 cm. long, 15-25 mm. thick, firm, solid, yellow, *covered by the dense rusty-stained fibrils* of the cortina, equal or subequal above *the large, depressed-marginate bulb.* SPORES almond-shaped, abruptly apiculate, 9-12 x 6-7 micr.   ODOR and TASTE mild.
    Solitary or subgregarious.   On the ground in open beech woods. Ann Arbor.   September.   Infrequent.
    This large species is here interpreted in the sense of Fries as expressed in his unpublished plates at Stockholm.   Authors are not agreed as to its identity as shown by their plates, different spore-measurements, etc.   Fries' plates show larger plants than indicated in his description, although he says they are "showy, robust and golden."   His figures. of this and the following species show that the virgate appearance of the pileus of *C. fulgens* was to his mind one of the essential differences.   The microscope has shown that probably several species are included under the old ones.   Specimens from Bresadola with spores 15-18 x 9-10 illustrate this view. *C. phyllophilus* Pk. (N. Y. State Mus. Bull., 157,.1912), seems to approach our specimens rather closely.

339.   Cortinarius fulmineus Fr. var. sulphureus var. nov.

Epicrisis, 1836-38.

Illustration: Plate LXXI of this Report.

PILEUS 5-10 cm. broad, convex then plane, *sulphur-yellow,* scarcely changing to darker, sometimes with spot-like scales on the disk, *viscid,* even, glabrous.   FLESH thick on disk, yellow or yellowish-white, rather soft.   GILLS adnate, then emarginate, moderately broad, close, *sulphur-yellow at first,* finally ochraceous-cinnamon, edge becoming eroded. STEM *short,* 3-5 cm. long, 8-18 mm. thick, dry, *pale, sulphur-yellow,* sometimes merely yellowish-white, yellowish within, sometimes compressed, subfibrillose then glabrescent and shining, equal above *the shallow, marginate-depressed bulb* which is yellowish beneath and attached to a yellow mycelium. CORTINA scanty, whitish. SPORES almond-shaped, slightly rough, ventricose, 8-10 x 4-5.5 micr. BASIDIA 30 x 7-8 micr., 4-spored. ODOR none. TASTE mild, of pellicle not bitter.

Solitary or gregarious. On the ground among humus, in frondose or mixed woods. Ann Arbor, Bay View, New Richmond. September-October. Infrequent.

When young the whole plant is pale sulphur-yellow, sometimes paler but uniform in color. In this respect it differs markedly from *C. fulmineus* as described. The figures of the unpublished plates of Fries, however, show a much less orange or fulvous plant than is indicated by the descriptions. It is paler than *C. elegantioides* and lacks the bitterish taste of the pellicle. In the list of the 9th Mich. Acad. Rep. it was referred to *C. sulphurinus* Quel., which differs, in the sense of Ricken, in having much larger spores. Our variety agrees quite closely in the size of the spores with the European *C. fulmineus* as given by Ricken and Saccardo.

340. Cortinarius elegantior Fr. var.

Epicrisis, 1836-38.

Illustration: Ricken, Die Blätterpilze, Pl. 38, Fig. 2.

PILEUS 7-15 cm. broad, compact, firm, convex then expanded, at length wavy and depressed, *tawny-yellow to ferruginous,* glabrous, even, *with a very viscid, separable pellicle.* FLESH whitish or tinged ochraceous, thick. GILLS adnate becoming emarginate, close, rather broad, *yellowish-pallid at first, at length rusty-cinnamon,* edge serrate-eroded. STEM 4-6 cm. long, 10-25 mm. thick, solid, pallid, *becoming rusty-yellow,* fibrillose from the abundant cortina, equal above *the marginate bulb* which is scarcely depressed, *becomes rusty-yellow* and is attached to a yellowish mycelium which forms *mycorhiza.* SPORES almond-shaped, elliptical, tuberculate, 12-14 x 7-8 micr. ODOR and TASTE mild.

Subcaespitose or gregarious. On the ground, among leaves, in frondose woods. Ann Arbor. October. Rare.

This species forms mycorhiza on the red oak; the yellow mycelium was found connecting the mushrooms and the rootlets of the tree and on examination the latter were found to be ectotrophic mycorhiza. Our plants depart somewhat from the descriptions of the European *C. elegantior,* but the spores and color and other major characters are the same. It may be considered as a variety until more extensively collected. It differs from *C. fulgens* in its large spores, the pallid color of the very young gills and stem and the serrate edge of the gills. The color changes markedly to rusty or fulvous as the plant becomes mature. The bulb is not as large and depressed as in *C. fulgens.* In the European plant the color shades slightly into olive, as in our *C. elegantioides.*

341. Cortinarius corrugatus Pk.

N. Y. State Mus. Rep. 24, 1872.

Illustrations: N. Y. State Mus. Mem. 4, Pl. 58, Fig. 8-15, 1900.
      White, Conn. State Geol. & Nat. Hist. Surv., Bull. 15, Pl. 21, 1910.

PILEUS 5-10 cm. broad, broadly campanulate, obtuse, *viscid* when moist, coarsely and radiately corrugate or reticulate, *tawny or yellowish-ferruginous,* varying to yellow or ochraceous. FLESH white, thin on margin. GILLS adnate, rather broad, close, *transversely striate,* pallid or obscurely purplish-tinged at first, *soon ferruginous-cinnamon,* edge eroded at length. STEM 7-12 cm. long, 6-16 mm. thick, *long cylindrical,* often fibrillose, spongy-stuffed, often hollowed by grubs, scurfy at apex, yellowish or tawny-yellow, *with a rather small, rounded-oval bulb* which is clothed when fresh by the thin, tawny, adnate and viscid remains of a *universal veil,* pallid or concolor within. CORTINA almost lacking, evanescent. SPORES broadly elliptical, very rough-tuberculate, variable in size 10-15 x 7-10 micr. (usually 12-13 x 8-9 micr.). BASIDIA clavate, 45-48 x 12 micr., 4-spored. ODOR rather pleasant. TASTE mild.

Gregarious or subcaespitose. On mossy or moist ground in low or swampy, frondose woods. Vicinity of Detroit; but probably throughout the State. July-October. Not infrequent in appropriate habitats.

This is a curious species whose early button stage alone shows its relation to the subgenus Bulbopodium. Later there is no margin noticeable on the bulb, and no sign of the early attachment of the cortina. The cortina, in fact, disappears very early, if present at all. In the young stage, however, the cap has a much smaller width than the bulb, and appears to rest upon it in the way characteristic for this sub-genus. The species is easily known by its corrugated cap, the peculiar yellow or tawny-yellow color of the long stem and the large spores. Saccardo quotes the size of spores incorrectly. Peck has named a form with "appressed spot-light scales" on the pileus, var. *subsquamosus*.

****Gills, flesh and stem at first white, pallid or pale alutaceous.*

342. Cortinarius sublateritius Pk.

N. Y. State Mus. Rep. 54, 1901.

"PILEUS 5-7.5 cm. broad, broadly convex or nearly plane, glabrous, *viscid, light red,* margin incurved. FLESH white. GILLS adnexed, emarginate, close, thin, plane, *pallid at first,* becoming *cinnamon.* STEM short, 3-6 cm. long, 6-10 mm. thick, equal or slightly tapering upward, stuffed, silky, *whitish, abruptly bulbous.* SPORES ventricose-elliptic, abruptly-short, pointed at each end, rough-tuberculate, 10-12.5 x 5-6.5 micr.
"Woods. Westport, N. Y. October."
The description is adopted from that of Peck who says it is apparently related to *C. testaceus* Cke. which, according to Maire is *C. rufo-olivaceus* Fr., but from which it differs in its smaller size, stuffed stem and smaller even spores. It also differs from *C. rubens* in the spore character, as I satisfied myself by a study of the type specimens at Albany, N. Y.

343. Cortinarius multiformis Fr.

Epicrisis, 1836-38.

Illustrations: Cooke, Ill., Pl. 708, 709.
 Quelet, in Grevillea, VI, Pl. 104, Fig. 4.
 Ricken, Die Blätterpilze, Pl. 39, Fig. 1.
 Plate LXXII of this Report.

PILEUS 5-10 cm. broad, soon convex then expanded-plane, regular, *canescent-white-hoary when young, viscid,* soon ochraceous-buff, *becoming pale ferruginous-orange,* with a separable pellicle, at length somewhat dry and subshining, sometimes wrinkled in age from the drying gluten, margin inrolled. FLESH pallid-white at first, at length somewhat discolored, sublutescent. GILLS attenuate-adnate, then emarginate, close, not broad, *at first whitish, then alutaceous-cinnamon,* edge eroded at maturity. STEM 4-9 cm. long, 10-20 mm. thick, spongy-solid, subfibrillose, *white at first* then alutaceous, equal above the *marginate or sometimes scarcely marginate bulb,* which becomes oval at length. CORTINA *white,* scanty, *fugacious.* SPORES subfusiform-elliptical, scarcely at all rough, 7-9 x 4-5.5 micr., pale, *not becoming rusty.* BASIDIA 25-30 x 7-8 micr. ODOR and TASTE mild.

Gregarious. On the ground, in mixed woods, so far only collected in the conifer regions of the State. Bay View, New Richmond, September. Infrequent.

The button stage is white or whitish throughout, but during development it discolors more or less, assuming yellowish or rusty-ochraceous shades. Our plants never become as deep orange-rusty, so far as I have seen, as do the European plants. Specimens collected near Stockholm, showed a tendency to change from white in the button to tawny-orange in age. The species is distinct from others in the peculiar delicate hoary-white covering of the young plant, which sometimes remains on the surface of the pileus as hoary spots even after expansion. This may be considered as a form of universal veil, but is quite different in texture from the universal veil of the first section. This hoariness is best seen when plants are growing in dry weather, and reminds one of that of *Pholiota caperata.* The spores and gills are rather pale for a Cortinarius, and the species therefore approaches Hebeloma.

344. Cortinarius intrusus Pk. (Edible)

Bull. Torr. Bot. Club, Vol. 23, p. 416, 1896.

Illustration: Plate LXXIII of this Report.

PILEUS 2.5-6 cm. broad, convex-expanded, *soon plane* and sub-depressed, glabrous, *whitish to dull clay-color,* sometimes tinged tawny-ochraceous or reddish, *viscid when moist,* even or radiately wrinkled. FLESH whitish, *thin.* GILLS rounded behind, adnexed or almost free, thin, close, not broad, *whitish at the very first,* soon creamy-yellowish to tawny-ochraceous, *finally umber-brown,* edge subcrenulate. STEM 3-6 cm. long, 4-10 mm. thick, *stuffed to hollow, whitish,* at length stained by the spores, even or striate above, minutely floccose at first, glabrescent, equal or tapering, *more or less abruptly bulbous.* SPORES elliptic-oval, smooth, 6-7.5 x 4-5 micr., brownish-cinnamon in mass. BASIDIA 25-26 x 5-7 micr., 4-spored. Sterile cells on edge of gills, small, capitate, as in Galera. ODOR and TASTE slightly of radish.

Singly or in small clusters in mushroom beds, in flower beds in conservatories, plant pots, etc.

In the winter months. Received from green-houses in Michigan; reported from various points in New York, New Jersey and Massachusetts.

To quote from Dr. Peck, "Its habitat is peculiar, but it possibly finds its way into conservatories and mushroom beds through the introduction of manure or soil or of leafmould from the woods. It seems strange that it has not been detected growing in the woods or fields." McIlvaine says, "Several pints of it were collected in February—usually a famine month for the mycophagist. The crop continued well into the spring. They grew on the ground, in beds among plants, and with potted plants in a hot-house. The species is delicate, savory and a most accommodating renegade of its kind."

This species is not only unusual in its selection of a place to fruit but also departs somewhat from the usual generic characters of the genus Cortinarius. Its spores are of a peculiar color and in some respects it resembles the genus Hebeloma, and may yet be referred to that genus. Its development has not been sufficiently studied.

345. Cortinarius albidus Pk.

N. Y. State Museum, Rep. 44, 1891.

Illustration: Ibid, Pl. 3, Fig. 1-4.

PILEUS 5-10 cm. broad, convex, then expanded, *white or whitish,* even, glabrous, *with a separable, viscid pellicle,* shining when dry. FLESH thick, white. GILLS adnexed-emarginate, moderately broad, close, thin, *white at first,* then pale alutaceous to cinnamon, edge even. STEM 5-8 cm. long, 8-16 mm. thick, solid, *white,* fibrillose from the cortina, *with an oblique, marginate-depressed bulb,* attached to white mycelium. CORTINA white, copious. SPORES elliptical, scarcely rough, 9-11 x 5-6.5 micr. ODOR and TASTE mild.

Gregarious.   On the ground in low, frondose woods.   Ann Arbor.
September-October.   Infrequent.

Known by the white color of all its parts, although the pileus may
become buff in age and sometimes the bulb is discolored somewhat
by rusty hues.   It differs from pallid forms of *C. multiformis* in its
spores and larger bulb.

SUBGENUS PHLEGMACIUM: Stem dry, firm, *exposed from
the beginning,* becoming clavate-bulbous to equal, never marginate-
bulbous; cortina superior, collapsing on the upper or medium portion of the stem.   Pileus with a *viscid* pellicle.

This includes the sections "Cliduchii" and "Elastici" of Fries.
The development from the "button" stage is very different from
that of the subgenus Bulbopodium.   The stem is evident from the
first, and the cortina is necessarily attached differently, connecting
stem and margin of pileus.   A universal veil, similar in structure to
that of the preceding subgenus, may be present in the young stage
and in such cases persists under favorable conditions as delicate
shreds or as a closely adnate sheath to the lower part of the elongated stem.   Of the European species which have this veil, e. g. *C.
cumatilis* Fr., *C. varicolor* Fr., *C. triumphans* Fr., etc., only one
has been with certainty observed in this country.   Details on this
point, with respect to American species, are also not at hand, so that
I am compelled to arrange our species on a merely temporary basis.
The number of Michigan species which belong to this subgenus that
have so far been observed are relatively few, and, except for
the type specimens of Peck's species which have been examined, I
have seen few collections that can be placed here.

Section I.   Universal veil clearly manifest.

346.   Cortinarius triumphans Fr.

Epicrisis, 1836-38.

Illustrations: Fries, Icones, Pl. 141, Fig. 1.
      Gillet, Champignons de France, No. 252.
      Cooke, Ill., Pl. 692.
      Ricken, Blätterpilze, Pl. 41, Fig. 2.

PILEUS 5-10 cm. broad, convex-plane, obtuse, viscid, spotted with
superficial patches of the veil, or glabrous and appressed-subtomen-
tose on drying especially on disk, even, *apricot-yellow to ochraceous-*

orange (Ridg.), finally becoming tawny. FLESH soft, white, thick on disk. GILLS at first adnate-subdecurrent then sinuate to emarginate, close, moderately broad, *at first caesius-whitish,* then ochraceous-buff to argillaceous, edge entire. STEM 8-12 cm. long, 1-2 cm. thick above, clavate-bulbous or rounded-bulbous, solid, at first sheathed by a whitish universal veil which is *at length broken into yellowish-ochraceous annular patches terminating above in a ring.* SPORES elliptical, almond-shaped, 12-15 x 6-7.5 micr., tuberculate, rusty-yellow. ODOR and TASTE slightly of coal-tar or radish.

Gregarious to subcaespitose. On the ground in forests of balsam-fir. Adirondack Mountains, North Elba, New York. Collection Kauffman. September, 1914. Rare.

A large, northern species agreeing in all respects with specimens which I collected at Stockholm, Sweden. The collapsed cortina unites with the upper portion of the universal veil to form a band-like annulus. It was reported from New York by Peck in N. Y. State Mus. Bull. 150, 1910. Not yet found in Michigan.

347. Cortinarius maculipes Pk.

N. Y. State Mus. Rep. 54, 1901.

"Pileus 3-6 cm. broad, convex, becoming nearly plane, glabrous, but *covered with a tenacious gluten, bay-red,* becoming paler with age. FLESH whitish. GILLS thin, close, rounded behind, slightly adnexed, *whitish at first,* becoming brownish-cinnamon. STEM 5-7.5 cm. long, 6-12 mm. thick, equal or slightly tapering upward, *subradicating,* solid or stuffed, silky-fibrillose, scaly-spotted, sometimes slightly annulate. SPORES elliptical, scarcely rough, 7.5-9 x 5-6 micr."

The pileus of dried specimens is chestnut-brown and shining. Saccardo gives the spore-measurements much larger, which is clearly an error. Peck says "its prominent characters are the dark-colored pileus smeared with tenacious gluten, the pale young gills and the spotted stem. The spots are formed by the brown fibrils that at first coat the stem, and resemble those of *Armillaria megalopus* Bres." as shown in Fung. Trid., Pl. 47. These scaly spots are clearly the remains of a universal veil. The type specimens are of moderate size.

Section II.   Universal veil not manifest.

Gills at first violet, bluish, purplish or caesious.

348.   Cortinarius sphagnophilus Pk.

N. Y. State Mus. Rep. 29, 1878.

"PILEUS 5-7.5 cm. broad, convex to expanded, glabrous, *viscid, pale brown,* marked *with dark watery spots* especially on the margin. GILLS moderately broad, *subdistant,* transversely rugulose, *at first violaceous* then cinnamon.   STEM 10-15 cm. long, silky, striate, *violaceous-white,* then cinnamon, *with an oval bulb at base.* SPORES oblong-elliptical, slightly rough, 10-11.5 (rarely 12.5 micr.) x 5.5-6 micr."

Found in sphagnous marshes, New York.   The description is adapted from that of Peck and from his drawings.   The pileus is represented as pale smoky brown, the stem almost white and with an oval bulb.   "The spotted pileus is a distinctive feature."

349.   Cortinarius lanatipes Pk.

N. Y. State Mus. Rep. 42, 1889.

"PILEUS 2.5-7.5 cm. broad, broadly convex or nearly plane, *viscid, grayish,* often tinged with yellow, becoming yellowish or subfulvous and *virgate* with innate tawny fibrils when old.   FLESH whitish. Gills adnexed, narrow, close, *pale violaceous at first.*   STEM short, 3-5 cm. long, 6-10 mm. thick, *equal or tapering upward above the oval bulb,* solid, subannulate, silky above the annulus, loosely fibrillose-tomentose below, white.   CORTINA white.   SPORES elliptical, 7.8.5 x 4-5 micr."

In spruce groves, New York.   September.   The cortina is probably very copious, although it is possible that a white universal veil is also somewhat in evidence.   The virgate pileus which changes color in age and the "woolly" covering of the stem are, according to Peck, the distinguishing marks.   The type-specimens show that its place is in this group.   The plants are not large.   This approaches *C. glaucopus* Fr. in some respects.

350. Cortinarius claricolor Fr.

Epicrisis, 1836-38.

Illustrations: Fries, Icones, Pl. 142, Fig. 2.
Gillet, Champignons de France, No. 205.
Cooke, Ill., Pl. 693.
Ricken, Blätterpilze, Pl. 41, Fig. 1.
Quelet, Grevillea, Vol. VI., Pl. 102, Fig. 1.

PILEUS 5-10 cm. broad, firm, obtusely convex, at length broadly convex to plane, subdiscoid, glutinous when moist, shining when dry, even, glabrous, raw-sienna color to *orange-buff* (Ridg.), *unicolorous,* not virgate, margin incurved and cortinate. FLESH compact, *white,* thick on disk. GILLS emarginate-adnexed, *rather narrow,* close, *at first caesious to pale brownish-drab* (Ridg.), finally clay-color, *edge erose-serrate.* STEM 5-8 cm. long, round-bulbous to clavate-bulbous, 12-15 mm. thick above, bulb up to 2 cm. thick, *white,* firm, solid, fibrillose or floccose-fibrillose. SPORES almond-shaped, 8-10 x 5-6 micr., punctate-rough, pale rusty-ochraceous. ODOR and TASTE mild.

Gregarious or subcaespitose. On the ground among spruce and white pine needles. Adirondack Mountains, North Elba, N. Y. September, 1915. Collection Kauffman. Infrequent.

The cracked surface of the pileus and the densely floccose stem, said to be characteristic of the species in Europe, were not characters of the North Elba plants. The stems however, were quite silky-fibrillose with white fibrils. The universal veil is lacking. The spores agree only with the measurements of Britzelmayr. Other authors give larger spores, 10-12 x 7-8 micr., and segregation may become necessary. The bulb may be submarginate at first, but it is not depressed and the cortina is superior.

351. Cortinarius lapidophilus Pk.

N. Y. State Mus. Rep. 31, 1879.

"PILEUS 5-7.5 cm. broad, at first hemispherical, then convex-expanded, *at first cinereous,* becoming ochre-tinged, often crowded and irregular, *virgate* with appressed fibrils. FLESH whitish. GILLS crowded, *dark-violaceous at first,* then argillaceous-cinnamon. STEM 5-10 cm. long, 6-10 mm. thick, solid, *equal or slightly thick-*

ened at base, whitish." SPORES (of type specimens) broadly elliptic-oval to *subglobose,* rough-punctate, 7-8-x 6 micr.

Subcaespitose. Rocky soil in woods, New York. August.

The pileus of the dried type specimens is dark cinereous. It appears to approach *C. infractus* Fr. in some of its forms and especially as to its spores.

352. Cortinarius copakensis Pk.

N. Y. State Mus. Rep. 31, 1879.

"PILEUS 3-7.5 cm. broad, convex then expanded, often crowded and irregular, *viscid, corrugated, pale ochre* slightly tinged red. GILLS broad behind, subdistant, *violaceous at first,* the interspaces veiny, edge eroded. STEM 5-7 cm. long, rather slender, 4-8 mm. thick, *equal or tapering upwards,* stuffed, silky, whitish." SPORES broadly elliptical to *subglobose,* rough-punctate, 7-9.5 x 7 micr.

"*Subcaespitose.* On the ground in woods. New York. October."

The plants are not large, and the pileus is said to be glabrous and shining when dry. The gills are alutaceous-cinnamon in the dried type-specimens.

353. Cortinarius albidipes Pk.

N. Y. State Mus. Bull. 157, 1912.

Illustrations: Ibid, Pl. 128, Fig. 1-6.

"PILEUS 5-10 cm. broad, compact, hemispheric then broadly convex, obtuse or subumbonate, *viscid,* glabrous and shining when dry, *buff color.* Flesh white. GILLS 4-6 mm. broad, moderately close, *pale violaceous at first,* cinnamon when mature. STEM 5-8 cm. long, 10-15 mm. thick above, *clavate-bulbous and tapering upward,* firm, solid, silky-fibrillose, *white.* SPORES subglobose, 8-10 x 7-9 micr. TASTE mild.

"Among fallen leaves in woods. New York. September.

"A fine, large species, easily recognized by its buff, viscid cap, its violaceous young gills and its white stem thickened or bulbous at the base." As in most of this subgenus, the spores are said to lodge on the remains of the white webby cortina, and form a conspicuous rusty or cinnamon-colored ring near the top of the white stem.

354. Cortinarius decoloratus Fr.

Syst. Myc., 1821.

Illustrations: Cooke, Ill., Pl. 729.
Quelet, in Grevillea, Vol. 7, Pl. 107, Fig. 4.

PILEUS 3-7 cm. broad, convex then expanded, *buff or pallid clay-color*, regular, *viscid*, slightly corrugate when dry. FLESH thin, watery, *soft*, white. GILLS adnate, sometimes subdecurrent, sinuate, close, moderately broad, *caesious or pallid-gray at first* then pale cinnamon. STEM 5-7 cm. long, 3-8 mm. thick, equal or tapering upward, stuffed then hollow, *whitish*, sometimes striate above, obscurely spotted with ochraceous shreds of the veil. SPORES subglobose to oval, almost smooth, 8-9 x 6-7.5 micr.

Gregarious or scattered. In moist places in frondose woods. Ann Arbor. September. Infrequent.

A closely related form has a bitter taste according to some authors. The caesious color of the gills is soon obscure or lacking. It has not been found in quantity and the spores of our plants are slightly too large.

**Gills at first olivaceous or sooty-olivaceous.*

355. Cortinarius infractus Bres. (ex. Pers.)

Fung. Trid., Vol. 2, 1892.

Illustrations: Ibid, Pl. 163.
Cooke, Ill., Pl. 704 (Pl. 705 as *C. anfractus* Fr.).
Quelet, in Grevillea, Vol. 6, Pl. 104, Fig. 3 (as *C. anfractus*).
Ricken, Die Blätterpilze, Plate 43, Fig. 2, et. al.
Plate LXXIII of this Report.

PILEUS 5-10 cm. broad, convex then expanded, *viscid*, glabrous, even, *dark olive or sooty-olive* then tinged fulvous, *margin broadly incurved*, then spreading and often with a broad zone. FLESH whitish or slightly violaceous-tinged, firm, thick except on margin. GILLS narrowed-adnate, sometimes emarginate or spuriously subdecurrent, crowded to almost subdistant, rather narrow, sometimes broader, *dark olive or sooty-olive*, at length umber, edge crenulate-eroded. STEM 5-9 cm. long, 8-15 mm. thick, solid, clavate or with oval bulb, fibrillose, *dull violaceous above*, dingy whitish to olivaceous below. SPORES subglobose to oval, rough-punctate, 7-8 x 5-6.5 micr. BASIDIA 30 x 7 micr., 4-spored. ODOR slight. TASTE of pellicle or pileus *bitter.*

Gregarious. On the ground in mixed and frondose woods. August-October. Ann Arbor, Marquette, New Richmond. Infrequent.

This is a variable species, and was placed by Fries under two names: *C. infractus* and *C. anfractus.* Bresadola combined these and gives an excellent description. Ricken (Blätterpilze, p. 144) has again attempted to segregate them. There is no doubt that forms occur which might be kept apart on the basis of different shades of color, stature, etc. Our plants often have narrow adnate gills but luxuriant specimens occur with broad gills. In all forms which seemed to belong here, the pellicle of the pileus was bitter. According to Ricken this would be *C. subsimile* (Pers), but the colors do not agree with that. In all these forms the spores are said to be practically of the same size and shape. Further study on our plant is necessary if they represent different species.

356. Cortinarius olivaceus Pk.

N. Y. State Mus. Rep. 24, 1872.

"PILEUS 3-5 cm. broad, convex then expanded, glabrous, *viscid,* dark brown with a greenish or olivaceous tinge. FLESH *grayish.* GILLS close, rather broad, at length ventricose, *dark olivaceous at first,* then cinnamon. STEM 6-8 cm. long, 6-10 mm. thick, equal, stuffed to hollow, *white-violaceous,* thickened below *with an oval bulb.*" SPORES elliptical, very rough, tuberculate, 10-12.5 x 6-7.5 micr.

On the ground, in woods. New York. September. A study of the type-specimens and accompanying drawings show that this species is to be placed in the present subgenus. The spores differ markedly from those of *C. infractus* and *C. herpeticus,* both in size and shape. It approaches *C. luteofuscus* more closely.

357. Cortinarius longipes Pk.

N. Y. State Mus. Rep. 26, 1874.

"PILEUS 5-8 cm. broad, convex to expanded, slightly fibrillose, *viscid, yellowish or pale ochraceous.* GILLS close, plane, *brownish-olivaceous at first,* then cinnamon. STEM *elongated,* 10-15 cm.

long, 6-8 mm. thick, *tapering upward,* slightly fibrillose, whitish."
SPORES broadly elliptical to subglobose, slightly rough, 6-7.5 x 5-6
micr.

Ground in woods. New York. September.

Related to *C. anfractus* by the spore-characters, but it differs
much in the elongated stem and color of pileus. In statue it is
more like *C. ophiopus* Pk.

358. Cortinarius glutinosus Pk.

N. Y. State Mus. Rep. 43, 1890.

"PILEUS 2.5-7 cm. broad, convex, *glutinous, brownish-ochraceous,* margin narrowly involute. FLESH yellowish. GILLS adnexed, rather broad, *olivaceous.* STEM 3-7 cm. long, 6-10 mm. thick,
solid, whitish or pallid, thickened at the base, *scarcely bulbous."*
SPORES broadly elliptical to subglobose, minutely rough, 7-8 x
5.5-6.5 micr.

On mossy ground, Adirondack Mountains, New York. July.

The type-specimens show a rather medium-sized plant; the pileus
is dark, dull, rufous-brown when dried, the gills rather broad and
not crowded. "The prominent features," says Peck, are "the dull
ochraceous pileus, olivaceous gills and pallid stem. The margin of
the pileus is sometimes rimose." It seems related to *C. infractus*
by its spores and gills, but is apparently distinct because of the
change of color of the pileus on drying.

***Gills at first yellow.

359. Cortinarius luteo-fuscous Pk.

N. Y. State Cab. Rep. 23, 1872.

"PILEUS 5-6 cm. broad, broadly convex, even, glabrous, *viscid,
pale fuscous to smoky-brown.* GILLS deeply emarginate, rather
broad, rather close, *yellow at first,* at length cinnamon. STEM 9-10
cm. long, 6-8 mm. thick, equal above, *with a rounded-oval bulb* below,
solid, silky-striate, *whitish."* SPORES broadly elliptical, obtuse,
somewhat rough, 12-13 x 6-7.5 micr.

On the ground in woods. New York. October.

This species is closely related to *C. olivaceus* Pk. both in stature,
habit and spore-size. The colors differ somewhat and it needs fur-

ther study. The spores are given too large in the original description. The measurements given above were made from the type specimens.

****Gills at first white or pallid.

360. Cortinarius coloratus Pk.

N. Y. State Cab. Rep. 23, 1872.

Illustration: Plate LXXIV of this Report.

PILEUS 5-10 cm. broad, convex then broadly campanulate and discoid, *bright reddish-yellow to tawny-orange and shining,* becoming dull testaceous, glabrous, even, sometimes radially cracked on drying, *with a viscid pellicle,* margin at first incurved. FLESH whitish, thick except margin, firm, compact. GILLS adnate at first, becoming emarginate, *rather broad,* close, rigid becoming crisped on drying, thin, *whitish or pallid at first,* then pale clay-color to cinnamon-brown, *not reaching the margin of the pileus,* edge paler. STEM 5-12 cm. long, *clavate-bulbous,* 8-12 mm. thick above, 20-30 mm. thick at bulb, solid, firm, at first white and silky-fibrillose from the cortina, *white within, slightly* lutescent, marked at times by the thin remains of an evanescent, yellowish-tawny universal veil, attached at base to delicate *white* mycelioid strands. CORTINA white, cobwebby, not very copious. SPORES almond-shaped, elliptical, distinctly rough, 9-11 x 6-7 micr. BASIDIA 35-40 x 8-9 micr., 4-spored. ODOR and TASTE slight.

Gregarious. On the ground among fallen leaves in frondose woods of oak, maple, etc. Ann Arbor. September-October. Infrequent.

This is a noble species, well-marked and brightly colored when fresh. It seems closely related to *C. saginus* Fr. and may be the American form of that species. See figures of *C. saginus* (Cooke, Ill., Pl. 703, and Quelet, in Grevillea, Pl. 92), which show a much stockier plant without the reddish color which pervades the pileus of our species. The universal veil is almost obsolete and leaves only one or a few very narrow yellow-tawny marks across the stem. The bulb varies from heavy clavate to rounded-oval, depending on the amount of elongation of the stem. When crushed the flesh sometimes gives forth a slight aromatic-radishy odor. It has been collected in several states.

361. Cortinarius ophiopus Pk.

N. Y. State Mus. Rep. 30, 1878.

"PILEUS 5-10 cm. broad, convex or subcampanulate, then expanded, sometimes irregular, *viscid,* glabrou*s, reddish-yellow,* the paler margin sometimes roughened by adhering patches of the whitish veil. FLESH white. GILLS close, rather broad, *brownish-cinnamon,* edge often eroded. STEM 10-15 cm. long, 8-12 mm. thick, equal, *long* and usually much bent or variously curved, at first shaggy-scaly from the subconcentrically arranged fragments of the copious veil, *white or yellowish.* SPORES elliptical, inequilateral, 11-12 x 6-7 micr.

On the ground, among leaves in woods. Maryland. September.

The dried type-specimens have much the appearance of *C. corrugatus* in stature and colors, with a yellowish stem; the spores, however, are smaller, and the bulb seems to be lacking.

362. Cortinarius communis Pk.

N. Y. State Cab. Rep. 23, 1872.

PILEUS 2-6 cm. broad, convex-expanded, obtuse, *whitish with a gray tinge at first,* becoming yellowish or brown in age, *subviscid,* sometimes reddish, *glabrous,* margin decorated at first by white fibrils of the cortina. GILLS emarginate, at length subdecurrent by tooth, medium broad, close, *white to pallid at first,* then pale ochraceous-cinnamon. STEM 4-6 cm. long, 4-6 mm. thick, stuffed to hollow, *equal* or nearly so, curved at base, mealy at apex, subfibrillose, *white* then yellowish-stained. SPORES ventricose-elliptical, 9-10.5 x 5-6 micr. Smooth. TASTE slightly bitterish. CORTINA white.

Gregarious. On grassy ground, in frondose woods. May. Ann Arbor. Infrequent.

The spores and gills are pale brown at maturity, and in this respect depart from the characters of the genus. As Peck has pointed out (N. Y. State Mus. Rep. 30) it is much like Pholiota in these characters. The cortina, however, forms no annulus. The plants appear early with us, while Peck reports it for September-October.

SUBGENUS INOLOMA: Pileus and stem *neither viscid nor hyproghanous.* Pileus at first innately scaly, fibrillose or silky; flesh rather thick. STEM stout, the base enlarged and tapering upward, i. e., clavate-bulbous. Universal veil present or lacking.

This subgenus is composed of species which have the stature of the larger Telamoniae but in that sugbenus the pileus is hygrophanous and subglabrous and when silky or fibrillose the fibrils are superficial. A few species are included here which have a slight hygrophanous character. A few more are added which have a rather equal stem, but show their affinity by the stout habit. One group possesses a universal veil which persists on the stem in the form of an adnate sheath or annulus. In my paper (Bull. Torr. Bot. Club., Vol. 32, p. 305, 1905) this group was eliminated from the diagnosis of this subgenus as there given, but further study has convinced me that a more consistent and natural arrangement would be the recognition of the universal veil under it. The smaller Inolomas gradually approach the subgenus Dermocybe, so that the species of these two groups cannot always be readily distinguished. The stout clavate stem and scaly pileus throw a plant into the Inoloma group, while the small size, the thin flesh of the pileus and the more slender, equal stem indicate a Dermocybe.

Section I. Universal veil manifest on the stem in the form of an appressed sheath.

Gills at first violaceous, lilac or purplish.

363.   Cortinarius alboviolaceus Fr.   (EDIBLE)

Syst. Myc., 1821.

Illustrations: Fries, Icones, Pl. 151, Fig. 3.
   Cooke, Ill., Pl. 747 (faded).
   Gillet, Champignons de France, No. 191.
   Marshall, The Mushroom Book, Pl. 14 op. p. 65, 1905.
   Hard, Mushrooms, Fig. 237, p. 295, 1908.
   Ricken, Die Blätterpilze, Pl. 44, Fig. 5.

PILEUS 3-6 cm. broad, companulate at first, then convex and broadly umbonate, dry, beautifully appressed silky, *shining,* varying pale violaceous to caesious-buff, *soon silvery-white and scarcely violaceous-tinged,* even, margin persistently decurved. FLESH thin on margin, *caesious or tinged violet,* surface differentiated into a thin layer, up to 15 micr. thick, composed of narrow, horizontal hyphae about 3 micr. in diam. GILLS at first adnate, then emarginate or slightly subdecurrent, close, moderately broad, varying *pale violet to ashy-purplish at first,* soon paler, at length cinnamon-brown, edge eroded-crenulate. STEM 4-8 cm. long, *clavate-thickened at or near the base, narrowed* upwards, 5-9 mm. thick above, up to 20 mm. below, spongy-stuffed, *usually peronate by thin, white, appressed, silky-interwoven, soft universal veil,* violaceous above and beneath the veil. CORTINA white. SPORES 6.5-9 x 4-5 (rarely 10 x 5.5), elliptic-oval to narrow-elliptical, scarcely rough, *variable in size.* BASIDIA 30 x 6-7 micr., 4-spored. ODOR and TASTE mild. MYCELIUM white.

Gregarious. Among leaves or in deep humus of hemlock, mixed or frondose woods. Throughout the State. August-October. Scarcely infrequent.

It is possible that this species may be composed of an aggregation of several forms. One form has more uniform and smaller spores and the surface layer of the pileus becomes subgelatinous in wet weather. I would call this forma *pulchripes,* since the stem is beautifully marked by the violaceous color above the white sheath. Its spores measure 6-7.5 x 4-5 micr. In all other respects it shows the characteristics of *C. alboviolaceus.* All forms have the same development. In the young plant, the stem is relatively stout and clavate-subconic, with a more or less helmet-shaped young cap, scarcely broader than the stem, mounted on its apex. The mature stem is somewhat irregularly ventricose-thickened, sometimes above the base, sometimes truly clavate-bulbous. The color is typically violaceous-white but varies to deeper violaceous in the gills and flesh and the very young button is deeper violet in the interior. The color fades somewhat, but dried specimens always show the gray or violet tints. I have not been able to distinguish *C. malachius* Fr., an European plant, in this region. The nearest relative of *C. malachius* with us seems to be *C. obliquus* Pk.

364. Cortinarius subpulchrifolius sp. nov.

Illustration: Plate LXXV of this Report.

PILEUS 4-10 cm. broad, firm, subhemispherical at first, then broadly convex to expanded, often gibbous, obtuse, *not hygrophanous, innately silky-tomentose,* glabrescent, even, *grayish-buff,* becoming ochraceous or rusty stained in age, margin at first incurved, then spreading and whitened by the veil. FLESH *thick,* compact, pale caesious then whitish. GILLS adnate at first, becoming sinuate-subdecurrent, *broad,* subventricose, *subdistant, at first dull purple,* color subpersisting, at length cinnamon-umber, thickish, edge entire. STEM stout, 5-10 cm. long (often of medium length), 10-15 mm. thick, equal or slightly enlarged below, *firm,* solid, *sheathed by the distinct, appressed, dingy-white universal veil,* which terminates at or above the middle in an evanescent floccose-fibrillose ring, sometimes only marked by the thin subannular patches of this veil, apex violaceous or pale drab, whitish to drab within. CORTINA white, rather copious. SPORES broadly elliptical, distinctly rough-punctate, maturing slowly, 9-10.5 x 5-6.5 micr., rusty-umber in mass. BASIDIA 36-40 x 9, 4-spored. ODOR slightly of humus. TASTE mild.

Gregarious or subcaespitose. On the ground, among fallen leaves, in frondose and mixed woods. September-October. Ann Arbor, New Richmond. Rather frequent.

This species approaches *C. pulchrifolius* in possessing purple gills which remind one of *Clitocybe ochrapurpurea* except that they are not as bright as in that species. An examination of the type-specimens of *C. pulchrifolius* showed that our plant is distinct. The spores never come within the sizes of Peck's species, and the pileus has no reddish shades. The dried plants are also different. In spite of these things the two species are close together. Except for its lack of the hygrophanous flesh, and the character of the surface of the cap it also approaches *C. impennis* Fr. and *C. torvus nobilis* Pk. The universal veil is usually well-developed, but sometimes the remnants show only as thin patches on the mature stem. The purplish color of the gills is retained to late maturity. The spores mature slowly and the measurements must be made from mature plants. It must not be mistaken for either *C. torvus* Fr. nor *C. impennis* Fr.

365. Cortinarius pholideus Fr.

Syst. Myc., 1821.

Illustrations: Cooke, Ill., Pl. 761.
  Quelet, in Grevillea, Vol. VII, Pl. 117, Fig. 1.
  Ricken, Die Blätterpilze, Pl. 46, Fig. 4.
  Plate LXXVI of this Report.

PILEUS 4-8 cm. broad, hemispherical-campanulate at first, then expanded, broadly umbonate, *surface covered by dense, innate, erect or squarrose, dark, cinnamon-brown or blackish-pointed hairy scales,* fawn-color at first, not hygrophanous. FLESH thin, slightly violaceous, soon whitish or sordid brownish, usually infested with larvae. GILLS narrowly adnexed, medium broad, close, lilaceous at first, soon clay color to brown, edge entire. STEM 4-8 cm. long (sometimes longer), 5-12 mm. thick, spongy-stuffed and tunneled by larvae, slightly narrowed upwards, violaceous or lilac-tinged above the concentric, squarrose, brown scales which represent the sheathing universal veil. CORTINA sparse, fibrillose. SPORES oval, rough-punctate, 6-7.5 x 5-5.5 micr. BASIDIA 27 x 6 micr. ODOR and TASTE mild.

Gregarious or caespitose. In moist forests, near decaying debris or on very· rotten logs, in the conifer regions of the State. Bay View, Marquette. August-September. Infrequent.

This well-marked species is probably frequent enough in its particular localities. I have collected it a number of times on much decayed wood in wet places, a preference which authors do not appear to have noticed for it elsewhere. The color varies somewhat as to the shade of brown which the veil and the pileus possess, but the characteristic scales of the cap and stem serve for easy identification. Two European species approach it closely. *C. arenatus* Fr. differs in its entire lack of violaceous hues. This has been reported in the state list, but it is probable that it was confused with a Pholiota. *C. penicillatus* is said to lack the squarrose scales, as well as the violaceous tints of the gills and flesh. *C. asper* Pk. may be only a variety of this species.

366. Cortinarius squamulosus Pk.

N. Y. State Cab. Rep. 23, 1872.

Illustrations: · Ibid, Pl. 3, Fig. 1-3.

PILEUS 4-10 cm. broad, semiglobose at first, then convex to subexpanded and broadly umbonate, surface densely appressed-tomentose at first, *soon broken up into dense, rather large, fibrillose scales,* sometimes warty on disk, brown and purplish-tinged at first, *soon chocolate-brown.* FLESH thick on disk, abruptly thin toward margin, watery-spongy, pinkish-white to grayish-white at first. GILLS adnate then deeply emarginate, rather broad, close, *purplish at first, soon dark cinnamon to chocolate-brown,* edge minutely flocculose. STEM 8-15 cm. long, stout, *swollen near the base into a large, ventricose-clavate bulb,* tapering below the bulb, 10-20 mm.

thick at apex, bulb 2 to 3 times as thick, watery-spongy within, at first purplish, *soon chocolate-brown,* sometimes subscaly, sometimes fibrillose, *annulate above by a definite band-like collar.* CORTINA pallid to brownish, closely woven. SPORES 6.5-8.5 x 6-6.5 micr., broadly elliptical to subsphoeroid, distinctly rough, dark rusty-brown in mass. BASIDIA 33 x 6 micr., 4-spored. ODOR somewhat spicy when fresh becoming strong on drying. TASTE at first mild.

Gregarious, sometimes in troops. On the ground, in low, moist, frondose woods or swamps of maple, beech, etc. Detroit, Ann Arbor. August-September. Infrequent.

Easily known by its entirely chocolate color when mature, the ventricose, pointed bulb and the band-like annulus. It absorbs water in rainy weather and becomes watery-spongy, but on drying out it takes on a tough consistency. It can scarcely be confused with any other species. Sterile outgrowths border the edge of the gills so that they appear flocculose.

367. Cortinarius erraticus Pk.

N. Y. State Mus. Rep. 42, 1889.

"PILEUS 5-7.5 cm. broad, firm, subcampanulate or convex, obtuse, dry, silky or obscurely scaly with innate fibrils, *canescent, often becoming grayish-tawny.* FLESH dingy white. GILLS adnexed, subdistant, pale tawny, becoming darker with age. STEM 5-10 cm. long, 6-12 mm. thick, firm, solid, *thickened toward the base,* white and tomentose below, *violaceous above.* UNIVERSAL VEIL *violaceous,* often forming an imperfect annulus and sometimes remaining in fragments or floccose scales on the margin of the pileus." SPORES elliptical, scarcely rough, 7.5-10 x 5-6 micr.

On the ground in groves of balsam. New York. September.

A study of the type-specimens showed that it has a universal veil, and that the spores average larger than the size given by Peck. The color of the gills when young is not certain. It would be a rather unusual relation to find the apex of the stem violaceous while the young gills are "pale tawny." For this reason, I have included it under the present section, where it probably belongs.

**Gills without violaceous or purple tints at the first.* (Likewise pileus, flesh and stem.)

368. Cortinarius bolaris Fr,

Syst. Myc., 1821.

Illustrations: Cooke, Ill., Pl. 760.
   Gillet, Champignons de France, No. 199.
   Quelet, in Grevillea, Vol. V, Pl. 79.
   Ricken, Die Blätterpilze, Pl. 46, Fig. 2.
   Plate LXXVII of this Report.

PILEUS 3-6 cm. broad, convex-expanded, obsoletely umbonate, *variegated by appressed, pink-red, saffron-red or cinnabar red, hairy scales* on a white ground, dry, fading, the thin incurved margin surpassing the gills. FLESH white, tinged creamy-yellow, thin. GILLS adnate, close, medium broad, distinct, pallid, *soon pale cinnamon.* STEM 5-6 cm. long, 5-10 mm. thick, tapering upward and *subequal,* stuffed then hollow, *covered like the pileus by red, fibrillose-hairy, appressed scales,* sometimes subglabrescent, *flesh becoming saffron or reddish when bruised.* CORTINA white. SPORES broadly oval to subsphoeroid, scarcely rough, 6-7 x 5-5.5 micr. BASIDIA 30 x 6 micr., 4-spored. ODOR and TASTE none. MYCELIUM red.

Gregarious or subcaespitose. In the conifer regions of the State, in mixed woods of hemlock and beech. Bay View, New Richmond. August-September. Infrequent.

This Cortinarius is known by its delicate hairy-fibrillose ornamentations on the cap and stem; these are saffron-red or darker in contrast with the whitish or yellowish flesh beneath. The cap is dry, not hygrophanous, but the fibrillose scales appear as if glued thereon. This must not be confused with *C. rubripes* which is markedly different, usually very glabrous on the pileus and much larger. The figures referred to above illustrate our plant well, except that of Ricken which emphasizes the scales and shows a stem tapering downwards. The decoration on the stem apparently represents the remnants of a universal veil.

369. Cortinarius annulatus Pk.

N. Y. State Mus. Rep. 43, 1890.

Illustrations: Ibid, Pl. 2, Figs. 1-4.
Plate LXXVIII of this Report.

PILEUS 3-9 cm. broad, broadly convex at first, then sub-expanded, obtuse, dry, disk or entire surface usually *covered with innumerable, minute, pointed, erect floccose and tawny scales,* sometimes smooth, ground color, golden-tawny or tawny yellow, with a bronze lustre, margin at first incurved. FLESH thick, whitish, scarcely or not at all hygrophanous. GILLS adnate, becoming emarginate, *rather narrow,* 4-9 mm. sub-distant, distinct, *at first pallid ochraceous,* then rusty-cinnamon, rather rigid, edge paler. STEM 4-8 cm. long, apex 8-15 mm. thick, *clavate,* twice as thick below, sometimes subequal, *peronate three-fourths to apex by the thin, silky-woven,* appressed, *pale tawny or yellowish universal veil,* which terminates above in an obscure ring, solid, yellowish within, whitish and fibrillose above the veil from the *white* CORTINA, base whitish, arising from a *white mycelium.* SPORES *globose,* distinctly rough, 6-7 x 5-6 micr., dark rusty-brown in microscope. ODOR of radish. TASTE mild or slightly astringent.

Gregarious, or scattered, sometimes in troops. On the ground in frondose or mixed, rich woods. August-October, usually rather early. Ann Arbor, Detroit. Not infrequent.

This species seems to represent the American form of *C. tophaceus* Fr., but the figures of that species as given by Fries, Cooke and Quelet do not remind one at all of our species. It is not easy to bring out in a figure the metallic, somewhat glittering, luster shown by a typical pileus of this plant. Ricken's figure of *C. tophaceus* comes nearer to the exact color, but he describes that species with the edge of the gills bright yellow. *C. annulatus* differs from *C. flavifolius* in the color of the universal veil and the scaly pileus. Specimens have been seen, however, in which the color of the pileus varied to ochraceous or clay-color, with brown scales. The scales, when well-developed, radiate in a star-like or bird-foot manner connecting with one another and raised in the center to a needle-like point. In the very young plant the surface of the cap is merely densely and finely tomentose, this layer connecting with the veil on the stem. Sometimes the scales are almost entirely lacking except on the center of the disk. *C. lutescens* Pk. seems to represent the latter condition. (N. Y. State Mus. Rep. 42, 1889.)

370. Cortinarius flavifolius Pk.

N. Y. State Mus. Rep. 41, 1888.

Illustrations: Atkinson, Mushrooms, Plates 45 and 46, Figs. 152 and 153, 1900 (as *Cortinarius ochroleucus*).
Plates LXXIX, LXXX of this Report.

PILEUS 4-15 cm. broad, (usually 4-8 cm.), convex then expanded, almost plane, *creamy-buff at first,* sordid, buff to ochraceous, or pale tawny-yellowish in age, *appressed tomentose or minutely fibrillose-scaly,* sometimes only silky-tomentulose, margin at first incurved. FLESH thick, abruptly thin toward the margin, whitish, scarcely hygrophanous but moist. GILLS adnate then emarginate, *subdistant,* broad, *dull pale yellowish at first,* then *ochre-yellow,* finally yellowish-cinnamon or rusty. STEM 4-12 cm. long, *clavate or clavate-bulbous,* 6-18 mm. thick above, 15-30 mm. below, sometimes subequal, spongy-solid, *covered at first by a thin, silky-woven, appressed whitish universal veil, at length peronate* or becoming naked. CORTINA white, silky, copious, sometimes forming a rusty-stained ring above the veil. SPORES sphoeroid to oval-elliptical, minutely but distinctly rough, with an abrupt, long apiculus (as in species of Russula), 6-9 x 5-6 (incl. apiculus). BASIDIA 36-40 x 6-7 micr., 4-spored.

Gregarious. On the ground in rich humus or among fallen leaves, in frondose woods of oak, maple, etc. Throughout the State. August-October. Frequent.

A well-marked plant, often of large size and distinguished by the white universal veil which forms a very thin sheath on the stem, by the prevailing silky-tomentulose pileus and rather broad gills. It was referred by Peck to the subgenus Telamonia, but the flesh is scarcely hygrophanous, and the pileus not glabrescent. The gills are rarely "rich sulphur-yellow" as described by Peck, but the spores of the type-specimens are described above and are quite distinct. It differs from *C. annulatus* and *C. croceocolor* in the pale, delicate yellowish-white colors of cap and stem. It is apparently a native American species. *C. newfieldiensis* Ellis of the N. A. F. exsiccati No. 3052 is identical.

371. Cortinarius croceocolor Kauff.

Bull. Torr. Bot. Club, Vol. 32, 1905.

Illustrations: Ibid, Fig. 5, p. 314.
   Jour. of Mycology, Vol. 13, Pl. 93, 1907.
   Mycological Bull., Vol. 5, Fig. 240, p. 314, 1907.
   Plate LXXXI of this Report.

PILEUS 3-7 cm. broad, convex then expanded, *saffron-yellow, with dense, minute, dark-brown, erect squamules on disk,* scarcely hygrophanous, not striate. FLESH yellowish-white, thick on disk, thin toward margin, slightly hygrophanous, scissile. GILLS cadmium-yellow, scarcely subdistant, rather thick, emarginate, rather broad, width uniform. STEM 4-8 cm. long, clavate or clavate-bulbous, 9-15 mm. thick below, *peronate three-fourths of its length by the chrome-yellow to saffron-yellow universal veil,* paler at apex, solid, saffron-colored within, soon dingy, attached to strands of yellowish mycelium. SPORES subsphoeroid to short-elliptical, 6.5-8 x 5.5-6.5 micr., echinulate.

Gregarious or solitary in mixed woods, Ithaca, N. Y. Not yet found within the borders of the State. Probably to be looked for in the north. The whole surface of the pileus has a velvety appearance and feel. The entire plant is often saffron-colored. It approaches *C. callisteus* Fr. on the one side and *C. limoneus* Fr. on the other. It was originally placed under the subgenus Telamonia, but the present characterization of Inoloma admits it here. *C. croceofolius* Pk. seems to be somewhat related, but averages much smaller and its pileus is more brown and lacks the scales, and the stem is not peronate.

372. Cortinarius ochraceous Pk.

N. Y. State Cab. Report 23, 1872.

PILEUS 5-8 cm. broad, convex, *broadly subumbonate* or gibbous, glabrous, *pale ochraceous,* even or obscurely wrinkled. FLESH thick, whitish. GILLS emarginate, rather broad, subdistant, *pallid to pale ochraceous at first,* then rusty-cinnamon. STEM 5-10 cm. long, rather stout, 8-12 mm. thick at apex, *clavate or clavate-bulbous,* bulb 20-38 mm. thick, fibrillose, ochraceous above *the white, appressed, sheath of the universal veil.* SPORES broadly elliptical, slightly rough, obtuse at ends, 9-11.5 x 6-7.5 micr.

Under balsam trees. New York. October.

The original description has been completed by a study of the type specimens and of the drawings made by Dr. Peck. The sheath on the stem is white and much as in·*C. flavifolius,* but the spores are much larger.

373. Cortinarius canescens Pk.

N. Y. State Rep. 42, 1889.

"PILEUS 5-7.5 cm. broad, subcampanulate or convex, obtuse or somewhat umbonate, *silky or scaly with innate grayish fibrils, whitish gray when young,* tinged with yellow or rufous hues when old. GILLS thin, subdistant, rounded behind and adnexed, *pallid at first.* STEM 5-10 cm. long, 8-12 mm. thick, solid, *white,* equal or tapering upward from a large, soft, spongy, *clavate-thickened base, peronate and subannulate by the silky-fibrillose, white veil."* SPORES elliptical, subinequilateral, slightly rough, 10-12 x 5.5-6.5 micr. ODOR not marked. TASTE unpleasant."

Gregarious. In spruce groves. New York. September.

Peck states that it is distinct from its allies by the absence of violaceous hues in the young gills. The pileus of the dried type specimens is of a dark smoky-gray color.

374. Cortinarius squarrosus Clements

Botanical Survey of Neb., 1901.

"PILEUS 2.5-3 cm. broad, campanulate then convex, dry, sub-umbonate, *clothed on disk by dense, squarrose, umber scales,* fasciculate-fibrillose on the margin, pallid umber. GILLS slightly adnate, ventricose, sometimes uncinate, *fulvous to umber.* STEM 3-4 cm. long, 5 mm. thick, subequal, hollow, fibrous-fleshy, clothed with fulvous-umber, subsquarrose fibrils. CORTINA fibrillose, umber, fugacious. SPORES irregularly elliptical, smooth, 12 x 6 micr.

"Among vegetation on the ground in woods. Nebraska."

This species approaches *C. pholideus* and *C. squammulosus,* but the spores are larger and the gills are not described with any purplish tint when young. It is a rather small Inoloma.

Section II.   Universal veil lacking or obsolete.

Gills at first violaceous, purple, lilac or caesious.

375.   Cortinarius violaceus Fr.   (EDIBLE)

Syst. Myc., 1821.

Illustrations: Gillet, Champignons de France, No. 257.
 Fries, Sveriges ätlig. o. gift, Pl. 58.
 Peck, N. Y. State Mus. Rep. 48, Pl. 12, 1894.
 Cooke, Ill., Pl. 770 (deceptive).
 Patouillard, Tab. Analyt., No. 127.   (Immature.)
 White, Conn. State Geol. and Nat. Hist. Surv., Bull. 15, Pl. 23.
 Ricken, Die Blätterpilze, Pl. 44, Fig. 4.

PILEUS 5-12 cm. broad, convex, obtuse, subexpanded, *dry, dark violet, covered with villose, minute suberect tufts or scales,* at length metallic-shining.   FLESH rather thick, varying gray to dark violet, not becoming purple when bruised. GILLS adnate, becoming sinuate or emarginate, thick, *broad, subdistant, very dark violet,* becoming ashy-cinnamon. STEM 7-12 cm. long, *long and stout,* clavate or clavate-bulbous, 10-15 mm. thick above, *dark violet,* fibrillose, spongy in the rounded bulb, violaceous within, bulb large. SPORES *large,* rough, broadly elliptical, 12-16 x 7-9 micr. (often 16-18 micr. long, then smoother and more elongated). ODOR and TASTE mild.

Solitary or scattered. Among mosses, fallen leaves and debris of conifer woods. Found only once in Michigan; Isle Royale, Lake Superior. Frequent at North Elba, Adirondack Mountains, New York. August-October.

A striking species, not to be confused with dry specimens of the viscid-capped species, such as *C. purpurascens, C. sphaerosperma,* etc. The stem is usually long as compared with these, and the cap correspondingly smaller. The peculiar metallic luster of the dry mature pileus was observed in both our native collection and in Sweden. Both also had the characteristic fine-hairy-scaly surface not easily shown in figures but approached by Fries. No photographs exist which show this character well. The abnormally large spores were present in both our own and the Swedish plants. The whole plant is at first dark deep violet with an indigo tinge. Although nearly always mentioned in the "lists" of various **American** writers, its local or northern distribution leads me to suspect that other species have been mistaken for it.   It seems to be more frequent in the east.

376. Cortinarius lilacinus Pk. (EDIBLE)

N. Y. State Mus. Rep. 26, 1874.

Illustration: Plate LXXXII of this Report.

PILEUS 5-9 cm. broad, firm, hemispherical, then convex, *minutely silky* or glabrous, *lilac-colored,* margin at first incurved. FLESH very thick on disk, compact and firm, tinged with lilac. GILLS adnexed, rounded behind, rather broad, thick, close to subdistant, sometimes transversely rivulose, *lilac at first,* then cinnamon, edge entire. STEM *stout,* 6-12 cm. long, *with a very large clavate bulb,* 15-20 mm. thick above, bulb 2-4 cm. thick, solid, compact, bulb spongy, fibrillose, lilaceous. SPORES broadly elliptical, rather obtuse, scarcely rough, 8-10 x 4.5-6.5 micr.

Gregarious. In low, moist swampy places in mixed or frondose woods. Detroit, Marquette. August-September. Infrequent.

The lilac color persists in the dried specimens. The bulb is much broader in the young plant than the unexpanded pileus. It is quite distinct from *C. alboviolaceus* in habit and stature, as well as color. The color of the pileus is like that of the European *C. traganus* Fr., and so is the general shape of the plant, but that species is quite distinct by a strong odor and by its ochre-yellow gills at the first. More slender plants have been found which apparently belong here and these are not easily distinguished from the related species such as *C. argentatus, C. obliquus,* etc., except by the color.

377. Cortinarius argentatus Fr. var.

Syst. Myc., 1821.

Illustrations: (Fries, Icones, Pl. 152, Fig. 2 of *C. camphoratus.*)
        Cooke, Ill., Pl. 745 (771 of *C. camphoratus*).
        Gillet, Champignons de France, No. 194.

PILEUS 5-9 cm. broad, convex to almost plane, *silvery-violaceous-whitish,* sometimes with a lilac or amethystine tinge, *dry,* beautifully appressed silky, even, not umbonate. FLESH whitish or at first tinged violaceous, thick on disk, abruptly thin on margin. GILLS narrowly sinuate-adnate, narrow, *close, pale violaceous,* rarely deep violaceous at first, soon pale alutaceous-cinnamon, edge minutely eroded-crenulate. STEM 5-8 cm. long, 10-20 mm. thick, solid, subequal *above the oval-bulbous or rounded-bulbous base,* bulb sometimes subemarginate, not depressed, sometimes subobsolete, *soon silvery-violaceous-whitish,* at first somewhat deeper violet at apex, concolor within, at first subfibrillose from the *violaceous-white* CORTINA, then innately silky, not at all peronate. SPORES elliptical, slightly rough, 7-9.5 x 5-6 micr. BASIDIA 30 x 9 micr., 4-spored. ODOR mild. TASTE slight.

Solitary or scattered. On the ground in woods of white pine and beach or in low frondose woods. Detroit, New Richmond. September. Infrequent.

This seems to be intermediate between *C. argentatus* and *C. camphoratus,* and differs from both in the more abrupt bulb than is shown by the figures of those plants. On the other hand, variations occur in the same collections in which the clavate-bulbous condition is present. On several occasions single plants were found, which agreed with the others except that there was present a distinct, penetrating odor, of an earthy-radishy nature. I have here considered them all the same. The narrow gills are always close, sometimes crowded, and this distinguishes it from the preceding. The surface of the pileus is scarcely or not at all differentiated into a pellicle or other layer although a very slight viscidity develops if the plant is kept enclosed for a time in a tight receptacle. In habit, size and paler gills it differs markedly from *C. obliquus.* There is no universal veil.

378.   Cortinarius obliquus Pk.

N. Y. State Mus. Bull. 54, 1902.

Illustrations: Ibid, Pl. L, Figs. 1-5.

PILEUS 3-6 cm. broad, broadly convex, subexpanded, dry, silky-fibrillose, *violaceous-white or grayish-white,* margin at first incurved. FLESH thickish on disk, concolor. GILLS adnate, thickish, *narrow, heliotrope-purple to deep lavender at first,* at length cinnamon-brown, close, obscurely transversely rivulose, edge minutely crenulate. STEM 3-6 cm. long, short and rather stout, 6-12 mm.

thick above, solid, silky-fibrillose, *whitish,* violet-tinged within and without, *equal above the abrupt, depressed-marginate, oblique bulb.* SPORES narrowly elliptical, slightly rough, 7-9.5 x 4.5-5.5 micr., rather variable. ODOR and TASTE mild.

Gregarious. On the ground in frondose or mixed woods. August-September. Detroit, New Richmond, Marquette. Infrequent.

Well marked by the white or grayish-white pileus, the deep violet or almost amethystine or heliotrope color of the young gills and the oblique, flattened bulb of the stem. It has a dry pileus, without a viscid pellicle and must not be confused with the species of the subgenus Bulbopodium. When young, the color of the gills is in sharp contrast with that of the cap and stem. *C. brevipes* Pk. (41 st. Rep. N. Y. State Mus.) cannot be placed without further study.

379. Cortinarius pulchrifolius Pk.

N. Y. State Mus. Rep. 33, 1880.

"PILEUS 5-10 cm. broad, convex or expanded, obtuse, silky-fibrillose, *whitish or reddish-gray,* the margin whitened by the veil. GILLS emarginate, *broad, subdistant, bright purple or violet-purple,* then umber. STEM 5-10 cm. long, 6-10 mm. thick, solid, *cylindrical above the clavate or oval bulb,* silky-fibrillose, white, often tinged violet, violaceous within. CORTINA copious. SPORES elliptical, rough, 10-12.5 x 6.5-7.5 micr."

Oak woods. September. New York. Rare.

"This rare species is well-marked by the peculiar color of the young gills, which resembles that of the gills of *Clitocybe ochropurpurea.*" A study of the type showed the spores to be markedly larger than in my *C. subpulchrifolius,* and without the peronate stem. I have not collected it.

380. Cortinarius rimosus Pk.

N. Y. State Mus. Rep. 48, 1896.

"PILEUS 5-10 cm. broad, firm, convex or plane, glabrous, *at first pale grayish-violaceous,* then tinged reddish-brown, the surface cracking into appressed scales or *becoming variously rimose.* FLESH whitish. GILLS emarginate, *rather broad, distant,* sub-ventricose, *violaceous at first,* becoming brownish-ochraceous. STEM

4-8 cm. long, 8-12 mm. thick, *equal to slightly* enlarged at base, white and silky with the white veil, tinged violaceous within." SPORES elliptical, rough, obtuse at ends, 9-12 x 5.5-6.5 micr.

"Grassy ground in open places, thin woods. New York. September. A rather large and stout plant, remarkable for the tendency of the epidermis to crack in areas. The thin margin is often split." Peck considered it to be near *C. caninus* Fr. and *C. azureus* Fr., but its stout habit seems to bring it closer to this group. It must be remembered that other species often have a rimose pileus under certain weather conditions.

381. Cortinarius braendlei Pk.

Bull. Torr. Bot. Club, Vol. 32, 1905.

"PILEUS 7-12 cm. broad, firm, convex, silky, *brownish-lilac,* often varied by yellowish-brown stains, margin at first incurved and covered by the grayish-white silky cortina. FLESH lilac, especially in the young plant. GILLS adnate, slightly rounded behind, narrow, close, eroded on the edge, *grayish tinged with lilac.* STEM 5-7 cm. long, 10-15 mm. thick, stout, solid, silky-fibrillose, *bulbous,* white or whitish, bulb often pointed below. SPORES oblong-elliptic, obscurely granular, 12-15 x 7-8 micr. ODOR of radish.

"Among fallen leaves in woods. Washington, D. C. October. Sometimes the pileus loses all its lilac color and becomes wholly yellowish-brown."

383. Cortinarius rubrocinereus Pk.

N. Y. State Mus. Rep. 33, 1880.

"PILEUS 5-7 cm. broad, convex then expanded, silky-fibrillose, *reddish-cinereous.* FLESH at first violaceous. GILLS emarginate, rounded behind, subdistant, *dingy violaceous* at first, soon pale cinnamon. STEM 4-5 cm. long, 8-12 mm. thick, *short,* solid, *oval-bulbous,* silky-fibrillose, whitish tinged with violet." SPORES 8.5-11.5 (a few up to 14) x 6-7.5 micr., variable in size, broadly elliptical, obtuse at ends.

"Gregarious. On sandy soil. New York. September. Closely related to *C. pulchrifolius,* from which it is separated by its darker colored pileus and differently colored gills.   CORTINA whitish-cinereous."

383. Cortinarius clintonianus Pk.

N. Y. State Mus. Rep. 26, 1874.

"PILEUS 2-5 cm. broad, convex to expanded, with a few ap-pressed silky fibrils (*pale dingy brownish-tan*), more or less tinged with gray. GILLS close, moderately broad, *dull-violaceous at first,* then cinnamon. STEM 5-7 cm. long, *rather slender,* 4-6 mm. thick, tapering upward from a subclavate base, *violaceous above,* silky fibrillose. SPORES broadly elliptical to *subglobose,* rough-punctate, 7-8 x 6-7 micr."

Ground in woods. New York State. September-October. A re-vised description is given above, from the study of the type-specimens and the accompanying colored figures. The cap is said to be "red-dish-brown," but if so, the colors of the drawing are very pale.

***Gills at first yellow, clay-yellow, or pale cinnamon.*   (Becom-ing rusty-cinnamon or watery-cinnamon in age.)

384. Cortinarius callisteus Fr.

Syst. Myc., 1821.

Illustrations: Fries, Icones, Pl. 153, Fig. 2.
        Cooke, Ill., Pl. 774 and 864.

PILEUS 4-8 cm. broad, convex to subcampanulate, subumbonate, moist but not hygrophanous, *deep chrome-yellow to ochraceous-fulvous,* not fading, innately silky, glabrescent, margin at first in-curved and silky. FLESH thick, thin on margin, whitish or tinged yellowish. GILLS adnate, subdistant, moderately broad, *yellow at first* then argillaceous to rusty-cinnamon, edge entire. STEM 4-9 cm. long, *clavate-bulbous,* 8-10 mm. thick above, 2 to 3 times as thick below, tapering upward, firm, solid, *yellow* (luteus) within and without, *streaked longtitudinally with fulvous innate fibrils.* COR-TINA fugacious, sometimes adhering at first to the margin of the pileus, yellowish-white. SPORES elliptical-oval, 7-8.5 x 5-5.5 micr., rough. ODOR weak, subnitrous.

Gregarious. On the ground in mixed hemlock, pine and oak woods. Ithaca, New York. September. Rare.

This species differs from the yellow-gilled group of the preceding section in the obsolete or absent sheath on the stem. Ricken has described and figured a species under this name with a minutely squarrose-scaly pileus and a differently shaped stem. Our plant seems to fit the Friesian species more closely than his, and the spores agree with those of specimens from Stockholm. Its colors and shapely form make it an attractive species. It does not appear to occur often. The colors become deeper in age.

385. Cortinarius autumnalis Pk.

N. Y. State Cab. Rep. 23, 1872.

Illustration: Hard, Mushrooms, Fig. 236, p. 294, 1908.

"PILEUS 5-9 cm. broad, convex to expanded, *dull rusty-yellow,* variegated or streaked with innate ferruginous fibrils. GILLS moderately broad, close, with a wide, shallow emargination, *at length rusty-yellow.* STEM 6-10 cm. long, 10-12 mm. thick, *equal above the oval bulb,* pale rusty-yellow, solid, firm. FLESH white." SPORES elliptical, slightly rough, 7.5-9 x 4-5 micr.

"Pine woods. Bethlehem, Pennsylvania. November."

This is a somewhat confusing species. Including the type. I have seen specimens from several sources so named, but have not been able to refer any of my collections to it. The description as given by Peck is incomplete and although I have amended it so far as the type-specimens and an accompanying drawing permits, it remains uncertain as to the color of the young gills. The specimens of Peck show that it changes markedly towards rusty colors in age. The photograph of Hard represents a plant which appears familiar but as he omits a description of his own no certainty can be felt about it.

386. Cortinarius catskillensis Pk.

N. Y. State Cab. Rep. 23, 1872.

"PILEUS 5-8 cm. broad, convex or subcampanulate, then sub-expanded, even, *grayish-drab,* (pale ferruginous?) variegated with minute, scattered white fibrils. GILLS deeply emarginate, close to subdistant, rather broad, *watery cinnamon at first,* becoming darker with age. STEM 6-9 cm. long, 10-20 mm. thick,

stout, solid, fibrillose, whitish, *clavate-bulbous,* tapering upward."
SPORES narrowly elliptical, somewhat pointed at one end, 7-8 x
4-4.5 micr.

On the ground in open places. Catskill Mountains, New York.
October.

The colored drawing accompanying the type-specimens shows a
stout, clavate-bulbous plant with a grayish-drab pileus. Dr. Peck
told me the pileus never had any reddish hues and the original
description of a "pale ferruginous" pileus also is not borne out by
the appearance of the dried specimens. A plant, apparently intermediate between this and the preceding occurs in Michigan.
Cortinarius robustus Pk. belongs under this division but like that
of the preceding two species, the description is insufficient.

387. Cortinarius whitei Pk.

Bull. Torr. Bot. Club, Vol. 29, p. 560, 1902.

"PILEUS 6-12 cm. broad, hemispherical at first, then nearly
plane, with a lobed, wavy or irregular margin, dry, glabrous, *sub
pruinose, reddish or brownish-orange,* verging to tawny. GILLS
deeply and broadly emarginate, subdistant, reddish-brown (?) at
first, then brownish-cinnamon. STEM 7-12 cm. long, 15-20 mm
thick, *long, equal,* solid, fibrous, colored like the pileus, adorned
with darker, fibrous lines or striations. SPORES subglobose, 7-8 x
7 micr.

"Woods. Mt. Desert Island, Maine. August.

"A large species, intermediate between Dermocybe and Telamonia,
related to the former by its dry pileus, to the latter by its general
aspect and stout, solid stem." It is placed here for want of necessary additional data on its development. Specimens at the New
York Botanical Garden have every appearance of belonging to Telamonia.

*** *Gills at first white or whitish.*

388. Cortinarius caespitosus Pk.

N. Y. State Mus. Rep. 42, 1889.

"PILEUS 5-10 cm. broad, firm, convex, often irregular from its
crowded mode of growth, *pale yellow or buff,* a little darker on disk,

margin silky-fibrillose. FLESH *white*. GILLS adnexed, rounded
behind, thin, close, rather broad, whitish at first, then subochraceous.
STEM 3-7 cm. long, 8-12 mm. thick, subequal above, *with a clavate-
bulbous base*, silky-fibrillose, floccose-villose at apex, subannulate,
white." SPORES narrowly elliptical, *pale,* smooth, 8-9.5 x 4-4.5
micr.

"Mossy ground in open places. Catskill Mountains, New York.
The *caespitose* mode of growth, yellowish pileus, pale gills and
white flesh distinguish the species."

389. Cortinarius modestus Pk.

N. Y. State Mus. Rep. 26, 1874.

"PILEUS 2-4 cm. broad, convex to expanded, subfibrillose, even
or slightly rugulose-wrinkled, *alutaceous.* FLESH white. GILLS
close adnexed, moderately broad, nearly plane, *pallid at first,* then
cinnamon. STEM 5 cm. long, 4 mm. thick above, clavate-bulbous,
subfibrillose, hollow or stuffed with white pith, concolor." SPORES
broadly elliptical, 7-8.5 x 5-6 micr.

"Ground in woods, New York. September. Distinguished from
C. clintonianus by its paler color, more bulbous stem and entire absence of the violaceous tinge of the gills." An examination of specimens on the sheets with the type, showed that several of the larger
specimens had different spores and could not belong there. It
is sometimes caespitose. In size it approaches the Dermocybes, and
appears to be close to *C. albidifolius* Pk. In a letter, preserved at
the New York Botanical Garden, Peck states that it is near *C.
intrusus* but has different spores.

390. Cortinarius gracilis Pk.

N. Y. State Mus. Bull. 2, 1887.

PILEUS 1.5-4 cm. broad (occasionally up to 7 cm.), *conical at
first* and Roods brown (Ridg.) then campanulate and margin decurved, *with a prominent subacute umbo,* pinkish-cinnamon to *light
vinaceous-cinnamon* (Ridg.) when drying, subhygrophanous, even,
glabrescent, margin at first incurved and white-cortinate, elsewhere
silky-shining with innate white fibrils. FLESH very thin except
on center, concolor. GILLS adnate then emarginate, moderately
broad, close, pallid at first, *soon cinnamon* to cinnamon-brown
(Ridg.), edge at length crenulate-eroded. STEM 5-15 cm. long, *elon-*

gated, thickness variable, usually 4-8 mm. thick (rarely up to 15 mm.), *cylindrical,* sometimes tapering upward, at length flexuous, *solid,* white fibrillose-silky, *soon pallid* or tinged fuscous, concolor within, glabrescent. CORTINA white, persistent, rarely forming an evanescent ring. SPORES elliptical, 10-11.5 x 6 micr., smooth, pale ochraceous under the microscope. ODOR and TASTE mild.

Solitary, scattered, rarely subcaespitose, deeply imbedded at base of stem *in sphagnum and mosses* in balsam and tamarack swamps. North Elba, Adirondack Mountains, New York. Collection Kauffman. September, 1914. Frequent.

Variable in size of cap and thickness of stem but very distinct from all other Cortinarii. The pale colors, the conic-campanulate cap, the sphagnum habitat and the spores distinguish it. The type specimens in Peck's herbarium appear to have been specimens of small size. Only the young rapidly developing plants show the hygrophanous character well; they soon fade. Although the species is quite frequent in the swamps, I never saw a well-developed annulus nor definite signs of a universal veil, so that it appears to be intermediate between Telemonia and Inoloma. Occasionally the stem is subclavate below. The gills are not dark at first in good specimens and Peck may have had young, dry weather forms in which the gills sometimes become dark prematurely. It would be remarkable to find the young gills "ferruginous-brown" as described by Peck, in plants colored like this one.

SUBGENUS DERMOCYBE: Pileus and stem *neither viscid nor hygrophanous.* Pileus innately silky at first, glabrescent, flesh thin. STEM *equal* or *attenuated toward apex,* stuffed to hollow, at length slender, rather rigid or exterior. Universal veil rarely present.

Composed of medium-sized or small, rather slender-stemmed and often elegantly colored plants. The cortina is fibrillose, usually of the same color as the pileus. Fries says "easily distinct from the Inolomas by the thinness and substance of the pileus and by the stem." Several species, however, approach the subgenus Inoloma closely, especially those Dermocybes included under my first section. The stem of the species of Dermocybe is at length equal or attenuated and this character combined with the small size and the lack of distinct scales on the pileus, separates them from the subgenus Inoloma. The absence of a truly hygrophanous pileus distinguishes them from the subgenus Hydrocybe, which they simulate in size. Some of the species are quite variable and many intermediate forms occur, some of which have been given names, especially the forms near *C. cinnamomeus.*

Section I.   Universal veil more or less manifest, evanescent.

**Gills at first violaceous or purplish.*

391.   Cortinarius caninus Fr.

Syst. Myc., 1821.

Illustrations: Ricken, Die Blätterpilze, Pl. 46, Fig. 5.
    Marshall, The Mushroom Book, Pl. 31, op. p. 85, 1905.

"PILEUS 6-10 cm. broad *violaceous-fulvous, soon beautifully rusty-fulvous* to almost orange-fulvous, *micaceous-glistening,* often almost zoned on margin by the remains of the veil, sometimes scaly-cracked, campanulate-convex, obtuse, thin, compact on disk. FLESH pallid, tinged lilac. GILLS *lilac-clay color at first,* soon watery-cinnamon, at length cinnamon-fulvous, emarginate, *broad, subdistant.* STEM 7-10 cm. long, 10-20 mm. thick, *pallid,* at length rusty-fibrillose, narrowed upwards, elastic, stuffed then hollow, at first almost girdled by a pallid veil. SPORES globose, 8-9 x 7-8 micr. BASIDIA 30 x 9-10 micr. ODOR and TASTE mild."

The description is adapted from Ricken. It has been reported several times from this country but I have never recognized it. Except in size it seems to approach some of the forms of *C. anomalus* closely. Saccardo and Stevenson give slightly longer spores. Miss Marshall's plant had a disagreeable odor.

392.   Cortinarius anomalus Fr.

Syst. Myc., 1821.

Illustrations: Fries, Icones, Pl. 154, Fig. 2.
    Cooke, Ill., Pl. 776.   (Pl. 850 as *C. lepidopus* Cke.)
    Gillet, Champignons de France, No. 192 (as var. *proteus*).
    Ricken, Die Blätterpilze, Pl. 47, Fig. 1.

PILEUS 2-5 cm. broad, hemispherical-convex then sub-expanded, obtuse, even, *covered when young* by an interwoven appressed *gray silkiness, becoming pale fulvous-alutaceous when expanded,* sometimes tinged at first with a violaceous-grayish tinge, at length glistening with a micaceous sheen. FLESH thin, dark grayish-violet at first, *soon pallid,* not truly hygrophanous. GILLS adnate at first becoming sinuate-emarginate, *not broad,* close, *at first caesious, violet or grayish-purplish,* then alutaceous-brown, edge lacerate-crenulate. STEM at first clavate and 10-18 mm. thick, then elongated and slender, 5-10 mm. thick, 4-9 cm. long, *spongy-stuffed, at first violet,* soon dingy pallid, or only the apex violaceous-tinged, gray-violet within, when fresh dotted with dingy ochraceous to yellowish scales, *glabrescent* or fibrillose, soon infested with larvae, elastic on drying. SPORES almost spherical, rough-punctate, 7-9 x 67 micr. BASIDIA 34 x 7 micr., 4-spored. ODOR and TASTE mild.

Gregarious. On moist debris and humus, mosses, etc., in beech and hemlock woods. New Richmond. September. Infrequently found, probably not uncommon in the north.

This agrees exactly with the species around Stockholm, where I first saw it. It is sometimes variable especially as to shades of color and the presence or absence of the dingy yellowish remnants of an evanescent universal veil. When mature these little patches on the stem are scarcely visible. In the fully developed condition the violaceous colors have almost or entirely disappeared from the gills and stem. The flesh is moist or shot through with watery streaks when fresh but it is not truly hygrophanous. *C. deceptivus* Kauff. is very close, but is truly hygrophanous and the color is at first deeper. *C. lepidopus* Cke. is apparently also one of its forms. *Cortinarius simulans* Pk. (N. Y. State Mus. Bull. 2, 1887) is another closely allied species and perhaps identical.

393. Cortinarius spilomeus Fr.

Syst. Myc., 1821.

Illustrations: Fries, Icones, Pl. 154, Fig. 3.
Ricken, Die Blätterpilze, Pl. 47, Fig. 2.

"PILEUS 2-5 cm. broad, convex to expanded, *fuscescent, rufescent or argillaceous,* gibbous, dry, glabrescent, fading. FLESH rather thin. GILLS emarginate or adnate, crowded, thin, narrow, *caesious or violaceous at first,* at length watery cinnamon, edge very entire. STEM 4-9 cm. long, 6-12 mm. thick, subequal, stuffed to hollow, whitish, tinged lilac or violaceous at first, *variegated by reddish or fulvous, delicately appressed subconcentric scales.*

"Very elegant. The stem is colored similarly to that of *C. bolaris,* but subequal and the cortina is white." In *C. bolaris* no violet is present in the young plant. The flesh of the cap is thin.

The above is adapted from the descriptions of Fries, especially from that in the Icones, where elegant figures are to be found. Peck has reported it from New York and it is desirable to get data of its distribution in America. It seems to be very rare. The size of the spores is not agreed upon by European writers. Ricken says they are 6 x 5 micr., while Saccardo and Stevenson give them 8-9 x 7-8 micr. One collection from Sault Ste. Marie seems to belong here but the reddish color was not nearly as intense as in Fries' figure.

Section II.   Universal veil obsolete or lacking.

*Gills at first whitish or pallid, or tinged slightly with violaceous or grayish.

394.   Cortinarius subtabularis sp. nov.

PILEUS 2-6 cm. broad, campanulate-convex at first, *then plane* or obsoletely umbonate, *discoid, dry, caesious or violaceous-drab* to silvery-fuscous, *silky-shining with white silky fibrils,* even. FLESH thin, soon *pallid.* GILLS adnate then sinuate, rather broad, close but distinct, ventricose, *at first pallid with obscure violaceous tints,* at length cinnamon, never truly violet or purplish, edge entire. STEM 3-5 cm. long, 4-6 mm. thick, *equal except a slight, subabrupt, bulbillate* base, apex slightly scurfy, *pale violaceous-drab,* color persistent, silky-fibrillose and shining, sometimes marked at the base by the remnants of the *white* CORTINA, stuffed, hollowed by larvae, usually strict, later flexuous or curved. SPORES elliptical, scarcely rough, 9-10 x 5 micr. BASIDIA 30 x 7 micr. ODOR none or slight. TASTE mild.

Scattered or gregarious. On the ground among or under fallen leaves of oak and maple woods. Ann Arbor. October-November. Frequent locally.

Characterized by the peculiar, small, abrupt bulblet of the stem and the "erythrinus" or subviolaceous color when fresh. The cap often becomes a little darker or stained in age, while the color of the stem is more apt to persist. It has the stature of an Inocybe. The young gills are scarcely of the "violet" type. It seems to approach *C. tabularis* Fr. and its size and the nature of the cap are fairly well shown by Cooke (Ill., Pl. 783), differing however in the shape of the stem and in color. Old dried specimens sometimes do have the color shown by Cooke's figure. It was found frequently in the region between Ann Arbor and Detroit.

395. Cortinarius brevissimus Pk.

N. Y. State Mus. Rep. 41, 1888.

"PILEUS 1.5-2.5 cm. broad, convex, often irregular, at first minutely silky, then glabrous, *dingy-white to argillaceous.* FLESH whitish. GILLS adnexed, close, *at first pale violaceous* then whitish to cinnamon. STEM *very short,* 1-1.5 cm. long, 6-8 mm. thick equal, *hollow,* silky-fibrillose, *white,* pale violaceous within. SPORES broadly elliptical, 6-7.5 x 5-6 micr.

"Thin woods. Catskill Mountains, New York. September. Related to *C. brevipes* Pk., but smaller, with a hollow stem and shorter spores."

396. Cortinarius abidifolius Pk.

N. Y. State Mus. Rep. 41, 1888.

"PILEUS 3-5 cm. broad, convex, subglabrous, *whitish tinged with yellow or pale ochraceous,* the epidermis sometimes cracking and forming scales. FLESH thin, whitish. GILLS adnate, emarginate, subdistant, *whitish at first,* then cinnamon. STEM 5-8 cm. long, 4-8 mm. thick, equal or slightly enlarged at base, solid, *white but variegated with yellowish, floccose scales below,* silky-fibrillose above. Spores subglobose, 6-7.5 x 5-6 micr.

"Woods. Catskill Mountains, New York. September."

Closely related to this, if not the same, is a species occurring about Ann Arbor. It differs mainly in its slightly larger size and stouter stem; the shred-like appressed scales of the stem are dingy, not yellowish and the spores are slightly larger, subsphoeroid, 7-9 micr. The cuticle of the pileus is composed of differentiated, narrow, horizontal hyphae, subgelatinous, but scarcely subviscid in moist weather. Its dimensions are as follows: pileus 3-7 cm. broad, stem 5-7 cm. long, 5-12 mm. thick. Both forms differ from *C. ochroleucus* Fr. in the stem being enlarged toward the base and in the scale-like remnants of a universal veil. It should probably be included in the preceding section. It is possible that this is var. (B) of *C. ochroleucus,* mentioned in "Monographia," p. 57, which is compared with *C. sebaceoides* as to stature and shown as an almost white plant in Fries' figure at the Stockholm Museum.

397. Cortinarius ochroleucus Fr.

Syst. Myc., 1821.

Illustrations: Cooke, Ill., Pl. 775.
  Quelet, in Grevillea, Vol. V, Pl. 85, Fig. 1.

"PILEUS 4-5 cm. broad, convex, gibbous and *obtuse,* even, glabrous or minutely silky, *pallid-white.* FLESH firm, white. GILLS broader behind, adnexed, then seceding, *crowded, whitish at first* then argillaceous-ochraceous. ' STEM 5-7 cm. long, 8-12 mm. thick, solid, firm, *ventricose, white, naked,* except apex which is fibrillose from the cortina." SPORES (8 x 4-5 micr. Massee) rarely given. "ODOR none. TASTE *bitterish.*"

The description given above has been adapted from Fries' "Monographia" and "Hymen. Europ." The species is occasionally reported from this country and is not well understood, not even in Europe if we may take the meager notes into account. The figures referred to have too much of an ochraceous color to agree with descriptions. It seems to be rare as Fries has indicated, and its medium size, ventricose or downward-tapering stem and bitterish taste distinguish it from any American plants I have studied.

398. Cortinarius sericipes ⁻Pk.

N. Y. State Mus. Rep. 33, 1880.

"PILEUS 1-2.5 cm. broad, conical to subcampanulate, glabrous, *chestnut color,* often darker on umbo. GILLS ascending or ventricose, narrowed behind, *broad, close, whitish at first,* then tawny to tawny cinnamon, white on edge. STEM 2-7 cm. long, *slender,* 2-4 mm. thick, equal, hollow, silky-fibrillose, slightly mealy at apex, shining, *white."* SPORES almond-shaped, *large,* rough, 15-16 x 8-9 micr., ventricose, somewhat pointed at ends.

"Damp ground in woods. New York. October."

The type-specimens indicate a slender plant with the Inocybe habit. The spores were found to be narrower than given by Peck. The stem seems to have been subannulate by a white silky zone.

CLASSIFICATION OF AGARICS

399. Cortinarius castanellus Pk.

N. Y. State Mus. Rep. 29, 1878.

PILEUS 1-2.5 cm. broad, convex then expanded, *umbonate,* innately silky, shining, glabrous, even, *dark cinnamon to chestnut color,* umbo blackish, streaked blackish when old. FLESH thin, pallid. GILLS adnate and rounded behind, then emarginate, close, moderately broad, pallid, *soon cinnamon-brown.* STEM 4-5 cm. long, 2-4 mm. thick, *slender,* equal or attenuated downwards, *dingy white then tinged fuscous,* stuffed then hollow, glabrescent. SPORES elliptical, rough, 7-9 x 4.5-6 micr.

Gregarious or subcaespitose. On bare ground "in open fields" and borders of lakes. Ann Arbor. (Whitmore Lake.) October. Infrequent.

In color it resembles *C. nigrellus* Pk. but that species is almost twice as large, with a distinct universal veil and smaller spores. It is a slender plant, reminding one of the Hydrocybes.

400. Cortinarius basalis Pk.

N. Y. State Mus. Rep. 33, 1880.

"PILEUS 1-2 cm. broad, convex then expanded, *hairy, tawny,* FLESH thin. GILLS subventricose, *pale tawny at first,* cinnamon when old. STEM 2-2.5 cm. long, 5-6 mm. thick, short, hollow, fibrillose, pallid or pale tawny, usually with a slight, webby annulus below the middle of the stem." SPORES elliptical, smooth, 7-8.5 x 3-4 micr., pale under the microscope.

"Naked soil in woods. New York. *Caespitose,* September."

This seems to approach *C. impolitus* in its hairy pileus and in size and color, but that species has larger spores, hygrophanous pileus, shorter stem and grows in coniferous woods. The plants are small and tufted. It probably has pallid gills when very young since the change of color indicated by the description is very unusual.

****Gills at first yellowish, red or cinnamon.* (Usually elegant
plants.)

401. Cortinarius cinnamomeus Fr.

Syst. Myc., 1821.

Illustrations: Cooke, Ill., Pl. 777.
  Gillet, Champignons de France, No. 204.
  Michael, Führer f. Pilzfreunde, II, No. 70..
  Ricken, Die Blätterpilze, Pl. 47, Fig. 6.
  Hard, Mushrooms, Fig. 239, p. 298, 1908.
  Peck, N. Y. State Mus. Rep. 48, Pl. 13, Fig. 7-14.

PILEUS 2-4.5 cm. broad, campanulate-convex, obtuse or subumbonate, umbo often vanishing, *yellowish-cinnamon, yellowish-tawny,*
etc., silky or minutely and densely scaly *from the innate or appressed, yellowish fibrils, shining.* FLESH pale citron or straw-
yellow, rarely deep-yellow, thin. GILLS adnate, varying to adnexed-emarginate or scarcely subdecurrent, rather *broad,* close (not
truly crowded), *cadmium-yellow, citron-yellow or cinnamon-yellow,*
shining. STEM 3-8 cm. long, 3-6 mm. thick, *equal,* often flexuous,
chrome to citron yellow when fresh, darker when handled, fibrillose,
stuffed, *becoming tubular,* olive-cinnamon-yellow within, *attached to
a yellow mycelium.* CORTINA citron-yellow, fibrillose. SPORES
short elliptical, smooth, 6-7.5 x 4-4.5 micr. (few 8 x 5 micr.) BA-
SIDIA 24 x 6 micr., 4-spored. ODOR and TASTE mild.

Gregarious or subcaespitose. On moist rich ground, very decayed
wood or mosses, in conifer regions, in sphagnum swamps, or more
rarely in frondose woods. Throughout the State, Marquette, New
Richmond, Ann Arbor, etc. August-October. Infrequent.

This species is usually marked "common" by the writers of books
or lists; a statement which is correct enough if *C. semisanguineus*
and its forms are included. The segregated plant as described
above even with its variations is rarely common according to my
experience in Michigan and about Ithaca and North Elba, New
York. It may be more common in special localities. It is quite
variable and Fries says "innumerable forms have been set up by
authors." The colors and shape vary with the habitat, so that
sphagnum forms, e. g., have longer stems and shaded pilei deeper
colors. The spores of the American plant seem to be slightly smaller
than in those reported by Saccardo, Massee, Ricken, etc., and in

Swedish specimens collected by myself. These have spores measuring 7-8.5 x 4-5.5 micr. The following species seems closely related but differs in the spore-character.

402. Cortinarius cinnamomeus Fr. var.

Illustration: Cooke, Ill., Pl. 778 (as *C. cinamomeus* var.).

PILEUS 2-6 cm. broad, campanulate or subhemispherical, obtuse or discoid, umbonate, regular at first, then wavy-margined, *olivaceous-cinnamon-brown, tinged rufous* on disk, innately and minutely fibrillose-scaly or silky, edge incurved. FLESH yellowish-white, rather fragile. GILLS adnate, *narrow,* close to crowded, cadmium-yellow with olivaceous tint, thin, eroded-crenulate on edge. STEM 5-9 cm. long, 4-7 mm. thick, *slightly enlarged below* and tapering upward, fibrillose-striate, pale yellow, olivaceous-tinged, becoming tubular, yellowish-olivaceous within. CORTINA yellow, fibrillose. SPORES elliptical, smooth, 7-9 x 4-5 micr. ODOR and TASTE mild.

Gregarious. Among mosses in a sphagnum swamp. Bay View, Ann Arbor. August-September. Infrequent.

Differs from *C. cinnamomeus* in the rufous cast on the pileus, the narrow gills, subclavate stem and slightly longer spores. It is well represented by the figure of Cooke cited above. Variety *croceus* is smaller, gills less crowded, gills and stem *tinged olivaceous.* (See Cooke, Ill., Pl. 780.)

403. Cortinarius croceoconus Fr.

Monographia, 1851.

PILEUS 1-3 cm. broad, *obtusely conico-campanulate,* umbo persisting, firm, *rufous-fulvous to fulvous-cinnamon,* silky, *dry,* even, subshining, margin incurved. FLESH whitish, tinged red at the upper surface, yellowish toward stem, thick at umbo, thin elsewhere. GILLS adnate then somewhat seceding, ascending, rather narrow, close, *pale yellow at first, then cinnamon,* opaque, edge minutely eroded. STEM elongated, 5-12 cm. long, 3-5 mm. thick, *equal, flexuous,* fibrillose with rufous-fulvous fibrils, *yellowish within,* elastic, stuffed then tubular. CORTINA pale rufous-fulvous, becoming pallid, subfibrillose. SPORES elliptical, almost smooth, 8-9.5 x 5 micr.

Gregarious or subcaespitose. On low, mossy ground of pine, poplar, etc., near Stockholm, Sweden. September, 1907.

This species has been reported at various times in America. The figures of Cooke (Ill., Pl. 780) and of Gillet (No. 210, Champignons de France) are, however, very misleading. The above description was made from plants which I collected near Stockholm. It seems probable to me that errors have been made in referring plants to this species and that a full description at this place of what is undoubtedly the Friesian plant is desirable.

404. Cortinarius luteus Pk.

N. Y. State Mus. Rep. 43, 1890.

"PILEUS 2-5 cm. broad, conical or convex, unpolished, *yellow,* often darker on disk. FLESH yellow. GILLS adnexed, yellow, *subdistant,* moderately broad.   STEM equal, 5-10 cm. long, 10-20 mm. thick, *stout, solid* (!), silky-fibrillose, *yellow.* SPORES subglobose or broadly elliptical, 7.5 x 6-7 micr.

"Mossy woods. New York. July."

This seems to be closely related to the preceding, but the stem is stouter and the type-specimens show the gills to be subdistant and rather broad. The spores are also somewhat different.

405. Cortinarius aureifolius Pk.

N. Y. State Mus. Rep. 38, 1885.

PILEUS 1-4 cm. broad, convex-campanulate, then plane, *cinnamon-brown* or darker, dry, densely fibrillose-tomentose, sometimes scaly, especially on disk. FLESH thin, yellowish brown or pallid. GILLS adnate, subventricose, *broad,* close, thin, *yellow then ferruginous-cinnamon.* STEM 3-6 cm. long, 3-6 mm. thick, subequal, rather short, solid, fibrillose, *yellow,* brown within.   SPORES 10-12.5 x 5 micr., *oblong,* smooth, ochraceous-cinnamon in mass. ODOR of *radish.* TASTE mild.

"Sandy soil, in thin pine woods."   New York, Massachusetts. October. Specimens sent to me from Massachusetts were apparently this species except that they had more slender stems than the type. As Peck has already pointed out, the species reminds one of an Inocybe and the peculiar oblong spores are further evidence of such a position for it. It seems to be rare and needs more study.

406. Cortinarius croceofolius Pk.

N. Y. State Mus. Bull. 150, 1911.

Illustrations: Ibid, Pl. VI, Fig. 1-8.

"PILEUS 2.5-5 cm. broad, broadly convex or nearly plane, obtuse or obtusely umbonate, dry, *slightly fibrillose* especially on the margin, *brownish-cinnamon,* often paler or saffron-yellow on the margin. FLESH thin, pale yellow, grayish or dingy when dry. GILLS thin, close, *saffron-yellow verging to orange at first,* then brownish-cinnamon, often yellow, crenulate on margin. STEM 2.5-4 cm. long, equal or slightly thickened at the base, fibrillose above, *saffron-yellow,* hollow. CORTINA concolor. SPORES broadly ellipsoid, 6-7 x 4-5 micr.

"Mossy ground on the borders or in woods of spruce and balsam fir. New York. September."

This approaches *C. cinnamomeus* in some of its forms except that the gills are more deeply colored.

407. Cortinarius malicorius Fr.

Epicrisis, 1836-38.

Illustration: Fries, Icones, Pl. 155, Fig. 1.

PILEUS 2-6 cm. broad, obtusely convex to subexpanded, *fulvous or tawny-fulvous,* tinged golden yellow, *silky-tomentose,* subzonate in age. FLESH *intensely olivaceous* when fresh, scissile, thick on disk. GILLS sinuate or adnate-subdecurrent, close, not broad, *rusty-yellow then dark golden-fulvous.* STEM 5-7 cm. long, 6-12 mm. thick, equal or subequal, *becoming hollow,* fibrillose from the *orange-fulvous cortina,* tinged olivaceous, *soon yellow-fulvous,* or reddish-stained, *olivaceous within.* SPORES short elliptical, slightly rough, 6-7 x 4-4.5 micr. ODOR and TASTE mild.

Gregarious. Under hemlock and cedar in swampy woods. Sault Ste. Marie. August. Rare.

The Michigan plants had all the characters attributed to the species by Fries. The flesh of the growing plant is distinctive. In the pileus it is intensely olivaceous to greenish, bordered by a narrow zone of yellow or fulvous next to the surface; in the stem the axis soon breaks down leaving a tubular cavity, the rest of the flesh being yellowish-olivaceous, bordered by the narrow, yellow cuticular zone

which is well shown in Fries' figures.   There is a tendency for the
cap and stem to become stained dark reddish in age.   Ricken has
changed the description somewhat as to the color of the young gills.
In our plants, however, they were not olive-yellow although such
a variation is to be expected where the flesh has that color.   Ricken
also gives spore-measurements which are too large for those of my
collection.   A variety of *C. cinnamomeus* was found under white
pine and beech at New Richmond, which was fulvous on the cap
and stem and with a slight olive tinge on the gills.   A series of
intermediate forms between this and *C. cinnamomeus* seems to exist.

408.   Cortinarius semisanguineus Fr.

Syst. Myc., 1821 (as var. of *C. cinnamomeus*).

Illustrations: Cooke, Ill., Pl. 779.
       Gillet, Champignons de France, _.ɔ. 250.
       Atkinson, Mushrooms, Fig. 151, p. 162, 1900.
       White, Conn. State Geol. & Nat. Hist. Surv., Bull. 3, Plate 20,
         1905.
       Peck, N. Y. State Mus. Rep. 48, Pl. 13, Fig. 15-20, 1896.

PILEUS 2-6 cm. broad, campanulate-convex, subumbonate, (varying to conic-campanulate or broadly hemispherical, often at length
expanded and split on margin) *tawny-yellow to cinnamon-yellow,*
silky   or   delicately   fibrillose-scaly,   sometimes   shining-zoned.
FLESH dingy yellowish-white, rather firm.   GILLS adnate-subdecurrent, *narrow, crowded, cinnabar or blood-red.*   STEM 3-6 cm.
long (longer on sphagnum), 3-6 mm. thick, equal or subequal, solid-
fibrous, chrome to citron-yellow, fibrillose from the *yellow or tawny-
yellow* CORTINA, elastic.   SPORES elliptical, smooth, 5-7 x 3-4
micr.   BASIDIA 24 x 6 micr., 4-spored.   ODOR and TASTE mild.

Gregarious or subcaespitose.   In low moist swamps, sphagnum,
etc.   Throughout the State.   August-October.   Frequent.

Usually considered a variety of *C. cinnamomeus*.   There are some
forms which could be called varieties of this in turn.   This shows that
in the present group we have what is well known to exist in the
higher plants, namely, an innumerable number of very closely related
species, or varieties, or forms, or any other term which expresses
difference.   For convenience we group a larger or smaller number
of these "different" but almost like forms together and call them
species.   As details accumulate it is easier to keep the details in

mind if we make several species from an old group of one species. Hence varieties are raised to the rank of species, and forms to the rank of variety, etc. This method is not used by the theoretical biologist but is very useful for practical every day arrangements for study. The above species is easily distinguished as such in the majority of cases hence it is now kept distinct. In order to produce fundamental proof that *C. cinnamomeus* and *C. semisanguineus* are one and the same species, absolutely expressed, it would be necessary to grow one kind from spores derived from the other kind.

409. Cortinarius cinnabarinus Fr.

Epicrisis, 1836-38.

Illustrations: Fries, Icones, Pl. 154, Fig. 4.
   Gillet, Champignons de France, No. 203.
   Patouillard, Tab. Analyt., No. 647.
   Quelet, in Grevillea, Vol. VII, Pl. 110, Fig. 4.
   Ricken, Die Blätterpilze, Pl. 47, Fig. 5.

PILEUS 3-6 cm. broad, campanulate, umbonate, sometimes plane, innately *silky-shining, bright cinnabar-red,* dry, even or rimose, sometimes split on margin.   FLESH pallid-reddish, fading. GILLS adnate, then emarginate, *rather broad,* ventricose, subdistant, *cinnabar-red* then dark rusty-red, velvety-shimmering, edge entire. STEM 2-5 cm. long, 4-8 mm. thick, equal or tapering upward, *cinnabar-red,* shining, stuffed then hollow, fibrous, fibrillose.   COR-TINA concolor. SPORES elliptical, slightly rough-punctate, 7-9 x 4.5-5.5 micr. BASIDIA 36 x 7, 4-spored.

Gregarious or scattered. On the ground, in frondose woods, almost exclusively *in oak woods.* Throughout the State; Marquette, Ann Arbor, New Richmond, etc. July-August. Frequent (rare September and October).

This is one of the early Cortinarii of the season. It frequents rocky or hilly oak woods and in this respect shows a preference which is different from that of the same species in Europe where it is said by Ricken and Fries to occur almost exclusively in beech woods. As data from beech woods in this country are lacking this may also be true here but not so far as my own observation extends. This preference might seem to indicate a mycorhizal connection with the oak roots, but so far every examination showed that the reddish mycelium merely vegetates in the leaves and humus.

The species is quite distinct from the preceding ones inasmuch as every part is at first cinnabar-red. This color is dissolved out by a weak solution of caustic potash; and this is also true of *C. semisanguineus* and even of some of the preceding species in which the red color is otherwise obscured. The nearest approach to it is *C. sanguineus* Fr., which I collected near Stockholm and in the Adirondack Mountains.

409b.   Cortinarius sanguineus Fr.

Syst. Myc., 1821.

Illustrations: Cooke, Ill., Pl. 786.
Gillet, Champignons de France, No. 246.

PILEUS 2-4 cm. broad, obtuse, or umbonate, campanulate, dry, innately silky or minutely scaly, opaque, *dark blood-red.* FLESH blood-red, thin on margin. GILLS adnate, rather broad, close, dark blood-red. STEM 5-10 cm. long, 3-7 mm. thick, elongated in moss, equal or tapering, stuffed then hollow, *relatively slender,* blood-red, darker where bruised. CORTINA fibrillose, tinged red. SPORES narrow-elliptical, 7-8 x 4-5 micr., tinged red, roughish. ODOR mild; TASTE slightly like radish.

Gregarious in deep moss or sphagnum in conifer woods.

Isle Royale, Sault Ste. Marie, etc., mostly in the northern part of the State. Infrequent.

Distinguished from *C. cinnabarinus* by its habitat, its longer stem and more blood-red color. European authors do not emphasize the mossy habitat, but with us this seems to be the usual place of growth.

The color of every part of this species is dark blood-red, the pileus is silky-scaly and not as broad as that of *C. cinnabarinus*, the stem is more slender and usually longer; the spores are similar. It grows on thick moss or sphagnum under conifers. Ricken gives measurements which are too large for the Swedish plant. Peck's specimens, reported in the 23d Report, are doubtless *C. cinnabarinus*.

****Gills *at first greenish or olivaceous.*

410. Cortinarius raphanoides Fr. var.

Syst. Myc., 1821.

Illustration: Cooke, Ill., Pl. 833 (typical).

PILEUS 1.5-4 cm. broad, campanulate-convex, *obtuse,* then subexpanded and subumbonate, not striate, *densely innately fibrillose-hairy,* unicolorous, *light brownish olive* (Ridg.), scarcely shining, margin decurved. FLESH thin except disk, concolor, fading. GILLS adnate then emarginate, close, rather broad, *at first chrysolite-green* (Ridg.), then darker, thickish, edge entire. STEM 7-10 cm. long, 3-5 mm. thick, *equal,* stuffed then hollow, *olivaceous,* concolor within, fibrillose, mycelioid at base and attached to sphagnum. CORTINA olivaceous. SPORES 8-9 x 5-6 micr., oval-elliptical, slightly rough. ODOR and TASTE *mild* or slight.

Gregarious-scattered on sphagnum moss in balsam and tamarack swamps. North Elba, Adirondack Mountains, New York. Collection Kauffman. September, 1914. Rare.

The typical *C. raphanoides* is said to have a strong radish odor and acrid taste. These were lacking in our plants, and only in some respects is it very close to that species. Its sphagnum habitat in conifer woods also seems to point to a distinct species. It differs from *C. valgus* in its fibrillose hairy pileus and stature. No such plant is described from the United States. There are no violaceous hues present.

SUBGENUS TELAMONIA. Pileus *hygrophanous,* its color changing on losing moisture, not viscid, glabrous or *sprinkled on the margin with the superficial fibrils of the universal veil;* flesh relatively thin, scissile. Stem *peronate or annulate* from the remains of a universal veil.

This and the following subgenus are closely related by the hygrophanous character of the pileus, by which they are both separated from the subgenera Inoloma and Dermocybe. To quote Ricken: "By 'hygrophanous' we designate a pileus whose surface is not compact but composed of loose tissue which absorbs water readily and when soaked with moisture has quite a different color than when dried out. After several experiences this peculiarity is recognized at the first glance. If one is uncertain about it, the plants collected in dry weather are placed in a dish of water," and then allowed to dry again. The presence of a universal veil separates this subgenus from Hydrocybe. This veil is composed of a thin, woven, slightly membranous texture and extends from the base of the stem in the young plant over the marginal portion of the pileus. On its inner surface it is continuous with the *cortina,* at least part way. As the plant expands the veil collapses, sometimes adhering to the stem in the form of a sheath (peronate) sometimes leaving only remnants along the stem and often indicating its presence by delicate superficial fibrils on or toward the margin of the pileus. Since the cortina itself, when copious, may leave a slight ring on the stem of those species which belong to the subgenus Hydrocybe, one has to become familiar with the characteristics of the two veils—universal veil and cortina—in order to refer a species properly. This subgenus includes a number of large species, but many others are of medium to small size. The Michigan species of this group are not yet very well studied and a number of collections belonging here are for the present omitted. For this reason the following arrangement must be considered temporary.

Section I. Plants wholly or in part with violet, purplish or ashy hues.

411. Cortinarius torvus Fr.

Syst. Myc., 1821.

Illustrations: Fries, Icones, Pl. 157.
 Cooke, Ill., Pl. 801.
 Gillet, Champignons de France, No. 251.
 In Grevillea, Vol. VII, Pl. 117, Fig. 2.
 Ricken, Die Blätterpilze, Pl. 49, Fig. 6.
 Plate LXXXIII of this Report.

PILEUS 4-6 cm. broad (rarely broader), broadly convex to plane, obtuse or subumbonate, firm, *subhygrophanous, violaceous-fulvous, purplish-brown or copper-brown at first,* at length paler, disk rusty-fulvous, *covered with a hoary frostiness,* sometimes furfuraceous-scaly, at length glabrous, sometimes radiately wrinkled, often punctate. FLESH at first dull grayish-purple at length brownish or pallid. GILLS at first adnate, then emarginate-adnexed, *broad, subdistant,* thickish, subrigid, *dark or dull purplish at first,* then dark cinnamon-umber. STEM 4-7 cm. long (sometimes longer), 7-8 mm. thick above, *clavate-bulbous,* tapering upward, bulb 12-16 mm. thick, *peronate* to or above the middle by the whitish, universal veil, which terminates above in a flaring, membranous ring, *dull violaceous and silky above the veil, spongy-solid.* SPORES 8-11 x 4.5-6 micr., ventricose-elliptical, rough-tuberculate, *maturing slowly,* rusty-umber in mass. BASIDIA 36 x 6-7 micr. ODOR at first slight, *sweet-áromatic* after crushing the flesh. TASTE mild.

Gregarious or subcaespitose. Among humus and decayed debris in frondose or pine woods. Houghton, New Richmond, Detroit. August-September. Infrequent.

Well marked by the peculiar, though variable color, broad gills and the membranous, annular-terminated sheath of the stem. The young plants have a very bulbous stem which becomes clavate-elongated. Two forms occur as to the shape of the stem, a short-stemmed, stocky, bulbous form and a long-stemmed one in which the bulb has almost disappeared; the former seems to be more frequent and is shown by the figure in Grevillea and by our own plate. The figure in Fries' Icones represents much larger specimens than usually occur with us. Maire points out (Bull. d. 1. Soc. Myc. de France, Vol. 26, p. 27) that it is distinguished from the European *C. impennis* Fr. by its membranous annulus. The stem is often curved at the swollen base and is sometimes ventricose. Its odor reminds one of faintly aromatic substances. The spores may easily be given too small since they mature slowly. Ricken says they measure 8-9 x 5-6 micr. Peck has a variety *"nobilis,"* which may be a distinct species; it needs further study.

412. Cortinarius plumiger Fr.

Epicrisis, 1836-38.

PILEUS 5-12 cm. broad, firm, campanulate, rarely conical-campanulate, obtuse or subumbonate, expanded, *densely appressed, fibrillose-tomentose or fibrillose-hairy,* hygrophanous, fading, sepia-brown at first then light pinkish-cinnamon (Ridg.), margin often decorated by narrow shreds of the universal veil. FLESH thick on disk, thin toward margin, pallid brownish (moist) soon faded. GILLS adnate then emarginate, close, *rather broad,* pallid at first, rarely faintly tinged caesious-violaceous, then *clay color* to mikado-brown (Ridg.), edge subcrenulate or entire. STEM 5-10 cm. long, 10-18 mm. thick above, clavate-bulbous, *stout,* at length subcylindrical above, spongy within but firm, *very fibrillose, grayish-blue-violet* (Ridg.) when fresh, quickly fading, concolor within, at length

pallid or dingy. CORTINA whitish, thin. UNIVERSAL VEIL
white at first, leaving thin subannular shreds or a slight annulus
on the lower part of stem, soon sordid brownish. SPORES elliptical, slightly rough, 8-10 x 5-6 micr., pale ochraceous under microscope. ODOR and TASTE slight.

Gregarious. Bulb imbedded in wet moss and soil under spruce
and balsam trees. North Elba, Adirondack Mountains, New
York. August-September, 1914. Collection Kauffman. Frequent
locally.

Well marked by the dense tomentosity of the cap when young
and by the pallid gills. Even under the most favorable conditions
the violet-bluish tint of other parts than the stem was scarcely noticeable. It agrees well with the Friesian description, but is not the
plant of Quelet (Grevillea, Vol. 7, Pl. 112, Fig. 1), nor that of
Ricken. At times the hygrophanous character is deceptive as the
cap becomes darker with age. The universal veil is thin in small
plants and the species could be looked for under Inoloma. It differs
from *C. canesceus* by its spores and by the violaceous stem when
young. It is possible that *C. catskillensis* is a dry weather form of
this species.

413. Cortinarius evernius Fr.

Syst. Myc., 1821.

Illustrations: Cooke, Ill., Pl. 866.
    Ricken, Die Blätterpilze, Pl. 49, Fig. 2.
    Hard, Mushrooms, Fig. 246, p. 305, 1908.

PILEUS 3-10 cm. broad, *fragile, conico-campanulate,* prominently
umbonate when expanded, *hygrophanous,* sometimes irregular or gibbous, *purple-fuscous to brownish-vinaceous* (Ridg.), faded and silky
in dry weather, margin soon wavy, at first incurved and silky from
the veil, glabrescent. FLESH thin, concolor or violaceous when
moist. GILLS emarginate, adnate, thickish, *broad, rather distant,*
ventricose, *at first violaceous-purple* then cinnamon-brown, edge
whitish. STEM 10-15 cm. long (rarely 15-20 cm.), 8-20 mm. thick,
cylindrical or attenuated toward base, sometimes flexuous, *pale
lavender to deep violet,* more deeply colored at the base, *marked by
annular shreds* of the *violaceous then whitish universal veil* over
most of the surface, spongy and solid, concolor within. SPORES
elliptical, slightly rough, 8-9.5 (rarely 10) x 5-6 micr. ODOR slightly of radish. CORTINA fibrillose, whitish, evanescent.

Gregarious or subcaespitose. On moss, decayed debris and humus in coniferous woods. Bay View, Marquette and North Elba, New York. August-September. Infrequent—almost rare.

Known by its elongated stem, which is usually rather stout and tapering at the base; the young, conical pileus is scarcely wider than the stem. It differs from related species in the shape of the pileus. In dry weather the color is often pale violaceous, shading to lavender and when old the pileus is likely to be split on the margin. The violaceous universal veil collapses and forms thin and adnate annular patches above the stem, scarcely ever forming a membranous annulus as in *C. umidicola*. The description of our plants differs somewhat from the European descriptions in the differently shaped spores and stem although Fries says the stem is sometimes attenuated below. The unpublished plate of Fries at the Stockholm Museum shows a much deeper violet color than the figures of Cooke. The inconsistency of the spore-sizes and spore shapes of European authors indicates that the species is not clearly understood. Fries states that the stem has the characteristics of *C. elatior* Fr., but, except for its mode of development, this is not strikingly apparent in our plants. When deeply imbedded in moss the stems are very long.

414. Cortinarius umidicola Kauff.

Bull. Torr. Bot. Club, Vol. 22, 1905.

Illustrations: Ibid, Fig. 4, p. 312.
  Jour. of Mycology, Vol. 13, Pl. 94, 1907.
  Mycological Bull., Vol. V, Fig. 239, 1907.

PILEUS 5-10 cm. broad, (rarely up to 14 cm.), hemispherical then convex-expanded, firm, *hygrophanous, dull heliotrope-purplish at the very first,* soon umber and glabrous on disk, *fading to pinkish-buff* and covered with innate, whitish, silky fibrils, *punctate,* margin persistently incurved and decorated by narrow, whitish, transverse strips from the universal veil. FLESH lavender when young, soon faded to sordid whitish, thick on disk, abruptly thin on margin. GILLS emarginate with tooth, very broad, plane then ventricose, subdistant, thick, *at first lavender,* soon pale-tan to cinnamon, edge subserratulate, concolor. STEM 6-10 cm. long, (rarely 10-13 cm.), 10-20 mm. thick, subequal, usually thickened below, sometimes narrowed below or curved, always *stout,* solid, *lavender above the woven, sordid white universal veil* which at first covers the lower part as a sheath, but soon breaks up so as to leave a band-like annulus half-way or lower on the stem, or forming adnate patches, concolorous, lavender within and soon cavernous from grubs. CORTINA violaceous-white. SPORES elliptic-ovate, slightly rough, 7-9 x 5-6 micr. BASIDIA 40 micr. long.

Gregarious, often in troops or partial rings. In wet, swampy places, frondose or mixed woods. Marquette, Houghton, Detroit. July-September. Infrequent.

This species is probably identical with one occurring in Europe. I collected a very similar plant, with the same gregarious habit, near Stockholm, Sweden, while in company with Romell, Maire and Peltereux, who did not recognize it as a species definitely known to them. It had the same spores, and all the characters of the American plant except the less marked lavender color. I suspect it is *C. lucorum* Fr. Two other collections from Sweden brought to this country and labeled *C. impennis* Fr., the one determined by Robert Fries with spores like *C. umidicola,* the other determined by Romell, with spores measuring 11-12 x 6-7 micr., seem to show that two similar species are being confused in Europe. One of these corresponds to *C. umidicola,* and is well illustrated by Gillet (Champignons de France, No. 228), the other is the true *C. impennis* Fr. (Icones, Pl. 157, Fig. 2). If this inference is correct, then Ricken's description of *C. impennis* also applies to the former species. The taste of the plants which I collected in Sweden was like ours, not of radish. The unpublished plate of *C. lucorum* Fr. in the museum at Stockholm represents a plant very much like *C. umidicola* with several band-like rings on the stem. Cooke's figure (Pl. 1192, Ill.) seems to belong elsewhere.

415.   Cortinarius scutulatus Fr.

Syst. Myc., 1821.

Illustrations: Fries, Icones, Pl. 158.
　　　　　　 Cooke, Ill., Pl. 820.
　　　　　　 Gillet, Champignons de France, No. 249.
　　　　　　 Ricken, Die Blätterpilze, Pl. 49, Fig. 1.

PILEUS 2-4 cm. broad, at first subhemispherical and sometimes gibbous, then campanulate, firm, *brittle,* hygrophanous, *dark-purplish-chestnut or smoky-violet-umber,* unicolorous, becoming canescent with grayish-white innate fibrils, inflexed margin at first silky. FLESH concolor under cuticle, soon whitish elsewhere.

GILLS adnate then emarginate, rather broad, *subdistant,* thickish and rigid, *at first pale smoky-purple* then dark rusty-umber. STEM 3-7 cm. long, 4-10 mm. thick, *equal* or subattenuate below, *rather stout,* sometimes slender, rigid, thinly *peronate at first by the grayish-white or purple-tinged universal veil,* soon subannulate by the breaking up of the veil, at length silky-fibrillose, solid. CORTINA whitish. SPORES short elliptical, almost smooth, 7-8 x 4-4.5 micr. BASIDIA 30 x 7 micr., 4-spored. ODOR none.

Gregarious. On open sandy soil under poplar. New Richmond. September. Rare.

I have referred this collection here with some hesitation. The plants are well illustrated by the figures of Gillet and Ricken. The illustrations of Fries are apparently from selected and perfect plants such as are more common in the moist climate of Sweden than in that of our State. The description given above applies to plants entirely different from any other species of the group by their peculiar colors, the brittle flesh and the habitat. It differs most from the European descriptions in the absence of the radishy odor. It seems to have some relationship with *C. sciophyllus* Fr., but the spores of that species, according to Battaile (Bull. d. l. Soc. Myc. de France, Vol. 26, p. 336), measure 8-9 x 6-8 micr.

416. Cortinarius deceptivus Kauff.

Bull. Torr. Bot. Club, Vol. 32, 1905.

Illustrations: Ibid, Fig. 7, p. 324.
Plate LXXXIV of this Report.

PILEUS 2-7 cm. broad, suborbicular to hemispherical, becoming convex-campanulate, *subhygrophanous, fawn-colored tinged with lavender,* fading to light tan, disk alutaceous-buff, covered with minute, brownish scales when young, becoming glabrous, rugulose in age. FLESH thin except on disk, rather spongy, *lavender when young,* then pallid or sordid tan. GILLS 3-5 mm. broad, thick, moderately close, adnate, emarginate, narrowed in front, *lavender at first,* pale tan when old. STEM 3-6 cm. long, rather stout and clavate at first, then elongated and slender, solid, *at first covered by the thick, fibrillose universal veil, which is lavender,* soon fading to whitish, at length remaining as oblique, fugacious, brownish scales or partial rings, terminating above in the cortina. SPORES

7-9.5 x 6-7 micr., subsphoeroid to broadly elliptical, rough.   **ODOR** mild.

Gregarious.   On moist humus or debris in hemlock or mixed woods.   Ann Arbor, Marquette, Bay View, etc.   August-October. Frequent.

This species is close to *C. anomalus* Fr., indeed it may be considered as a hygrophanous form of that species.   The group to which it belongs is composed of a number of closely related species, unless one considers the fluctuating variation of the one species as quite extensive.   The colors of this species are much deeper violet or lavender at first than in the typical *C. anomalus* and the flesh is distinctly hygrophanous.   Nearly all these related plants (see *C. anomalus*) have a punctate pileus.

417. Cortinarius adustus Pk.

N. Y. State Mus. Rep. 42, 1889.

"PILEUS 2-3.5 cm. broad, broadly campanulate or convex, obtuse, *hygrophanous, bay-brown when moist* sometimes canescent on the margin, paler when dry, smoky-brown with age and generally rimose-scaly.   FLESH yellowish-gray.   GILLS subfree, rather thick, distant, *purplish-brown.*   STEM 2-8 cm. long, 6-10 mm. thick, *equal,* stuffed or hollow, fibrillose, brownish with a white mycelioid coating at the base, colored within like the flesh of the pileus." SPORES broadly elliptical, 8-10 x 5.5-6.5 micr.

"Subcaespitose.   In balsam groves.   New York.   September." The dried type-specimens are blackish-brown, showing a rather stout stem and small pileus.   It seems closely related to the next.

418. Cortinarius griseus Pk.

N. Y. State Mus. Rep. 41, 1888.

"PILEUS 2-7.5 cm. broad, convex, obtuse or gibbous, fibrillose-scaly with grayish hairs or fibrils, pale gray when moist.   GILLS adnexed, subdistant, *at first pallid then* brownish-ochraceous.   STEM 5-7 cm. long, 6-12 mm. thick, tapering from *a thickened or bulbous base,* silky-fibrillose, whitish."   SPORES broadly elliptical, obtuse, 10-12 x 6-7 micr.

"Mossy ground under balsam trees.   New York.   September.

"The fibrils of the pileus are similar to those of *C. paleaceus,* but the plant is much larger and stouter and the spores are larger. It is well marked by its grayish color." The color of the young gills distinguishes it from *C. adustus* and *C. scutulatus*. It seems to approach *C. canescens* in all its characters except the lack of a peronate stem.

419. Cortinarius subflexipes Pk.

N. Y. State Mus. Rep. 41, 1888.

PILEUS 1-2 cm. broad, *conical* then campanulate and subacutely umbonate, glabrous, *hygrophanous, blackish-brown* and the thin margin incurved and whitened by the veil *when moist,* subochraceous when dry. FLESH concolor, thin. GILLS adnexed, thin, close, rather broad, ventricose, *at first clay-color tinged violaceous* then cinnamon. STEM 3-6 cm. long, 2-4 mm. thick, equal, *slender,* flexuous, silky-shining, violaceous within, subannulate by the whitish universal veil, *pale violaceous when young,* especially above the annulus, pallid or reddish when old. SPORES narrow elliptical, scarcely rough, 6-7.5 x 3.5-4 micr.

Thin woods. North Elba, Adirondack Mountains and Catskill Mountains, New York. September.

Hardly related to *C. flexipes,* from which Peck separated it because of its more glabrous pileus and different gills. It has the stature of *C. fuscoviolaceus.*

420. Cortinarius flexipes Fr. minor

Syst. Myc., 1821.

Illustrations: Ricken, Blätterpilze, Pl. 49, Fig. 4.
      Quelet, Grevillea, Vol. VIII, Pl. 113, Fig. 3.

PILEUS 1-3 cm. broad, at first conical then *conic-campanulate,* hygrophanous, ground-color cinnamon-brown, *densely covered with shining grayish-white subagglutinate fibrillose scales* up to the apex of the *acute umbo,* scales small, superficial and easily rubbed off. FLESH at the very first violaceous, soon pallid or brownish. GILLS adnate-emarginate, *at first or when moist walnut-brown* (Ridg.) *with a purplish tint,* soon sudan-brown (Ridg.), broad, close to subdistant, edge entire, at first whitish. STEM 3.5-5 cm. long, 2-4 mm. thick, at first strict then flexuous, stuffed then hollow, dark violaceous at apex, soon grayish-brown, *annulate by a distinct*

white annulus above the middle, concentrically subannulate below
with white flecks, at first violet within. SPORES elliptical, pale,
7-7.5 x 4-5 micr., slightly rough, pale ochraceous. ODOR and
TASTE none.

Gregarious. In low swamps under spruce in moss. North Elba,
Adirondack Mountains, New York. Collection Kauffman. September, 1914. Infrequent.

This is a pretty plant. When fresh the general effect of the pileus
is that of a scaly-capped smoky-gray or drab-gray Inocybe. The
universal veil leaves a well-marked annulus. The species seems to
be taller and slightly larger in Sweden according to Fries. The
pileus is more densely fibrillose than that of *C. paleaceus* from which
it differs also in the dark-colored gills when young. The figure of
C. paleaceus in Icones (Pl. 160, Fig. 4) is an exact reproduction of
the size, shape and habit of our form of *C. flexipes.*

Section II. Universal veil red, tawny, cinnamon or yellow.

421. Cortinarius rubripes Kauff.

Rep. Mich. Acad. of Sci., 1906.

Illustrations: Bot. Gaz., Vol. 42, 1906.
　　Jour. of Mycol., Vol. 13, Pl. 100, 1907.

PILEUS 5-12 cm. broad, convex-campanulate then expanded, hygrophanous, *watery-cinnamon when moist, or tinged rufous,* obtuse
or subumbonate, more or less ferruginous-stained, fading to pinkish-
ochraceous, in zones from the umbo outward, at length with innate,
silky-shining fibrils, sometimes wavy and irregular, *glabrescent,*
even. FLESH thin except on disk, scissile, with a rufous tinge.
GILLS *subdistant,* distinct, rather rigid, adnate, seceding in age,
often with hoary fibrils at point of attachment to stem, *pale cin-
ereous-purple or rufous-tinged at first,* soon reddish-cinnamon, edge
entire. STEM 5-7.5 cm. long, with an oval or clavate bulb, 5-15 mm.
thick ·at apex, *bulb deep brick-red to vermillion,* paler upwards,
elastic, spongy-stuffed within, *glabrous, except for the fibrillose remains of the thin, evanescent, pale reddish, universal veil.* SPORES
elliptical, smooth, granular within, 8-9 x 4-5 micr. BASIDIA
30-35 x 7 micr., 4-spored. MYCELIUM *brick-red* and sometimes
forming mycorhiza on roots of forest trees.

Gregarious or subcaespitose. On the ground in frondose woods.
July-September. Ann Arbor. Frequent locally.

Well marked by the tinge of brick-red which pervades the whole plant on drying and shades into a deep red towards the base of the stem. The hygrophanous character is unmistakable. The universal veil is not always manifest. This species approaches the European *C. bulliardi* Fr. and *C. colus* Fr. From the former it is to be separated by the hygrophanous pileus and the spores. It is, however, uncertain what the spore-size of the Friesian plant really is. Ricken refers a plant to *C. bulliardi* whose spores measure 6-7 x 3-4 micr., "spindle-almond-shaped." Others give larger spores, and apparently deal with a different species. Boudier (Icones), gives a figure of *C. bulliardi* which resembles our plant closely. *C. colus* Fr. appears to differ in the absence of the universal veil and, according to Ricken, in the slightly larger spores, and its gills are without any purplish tint. It is similar in its "fiery-red" mycelium, and general aspect (see Pl. 50, Fig. 6, Die Blätterpilze). To add to the confusion, Peck described a species sent to him under the name *C. rubripes* Pk. (N. Y. State Mus. Bull. 105, 1906), which he says is related to *C. cinnabarinus*. It has violaceous gills when young, a grayish-ferruginous to pale alutaceous pileus, and bright red stem. The spores measure 7.5-10 x 5 micr. · It is a smaller plant than any of the others mentioned. For the present our plant must be considered a distinct species.

422. Cortinarius armillatus Fr. (EDIBLE)

Syst. Myc., 1821.

Illustrations: Fries, Icones, Pl. 158.
   Cooke, Ill., Pl. 802.
   Gillet, Champignons de France, No. 197.
   Ricken, Die Blätterpilze, Pl. 48, Fig. 5.
   Michael, Führer f. Pilzfreunde, II, No. 71.
   Marshall, Mushroom Book, Pl. 32, p. 86, 1905.
   Hard, Mushrooms, Fig. 243, p. 301, 1908.
   Plates LXXXV, LXXXVI of this Report.

PILEUS 5-12 cm. broad, campanulate with decurved margin, then expanded, not truly *hygrophanous, tawny rufescent to red-brick color,* moist when fresh, innately fibrillose or minutely scaly, with shreds of the universal veil often clinging to the margin, sometimes glabrescent. FLESH rather spongy, not very thick considering its size, dingy pallid. GILLS adnate, sometimes sinuate and uncinate, *broad,* distant, *pale cinnamon at first, then dark* rusty-brown. STEM 7-14 cm long, *clavate or elongated-bulbous,* 10-20 mm. thick at apex, up to 35 mm. thick below, solid, firm, fibrillose, brownish or pale tawny-rufescent, *encircled by several cinnabar-red zones or bands from the rather membranous red universal veil.* CORTINA at first whitish, collapsing, and forming a slight annulus colored by the spores. MYCELIUM whitish. SPORES elliptical, rough-tuberculate, 10-12 x 5-6.5 micr. BASIDIA 35 x 8 micr., with long, slender sterigmata. ODOR more or less of radish. TASTE mild.

Solitary or gregarious. On thick humus, debris, very rotten wood, etc., in the coniferous forests of northern Michigan. Isle Royale, Huron Mountains, Marquette, Bay View. July-September. Frequent.

A noble species. It is the chief of this group, as already noted by Fries. The 2-4 reddish bands, scattered along the stem, mark it conspicuously. Its large size and tawny-rufescent color help to distinguish it readily from others of the subgenus. The lack of the hygrophanous character and the rather scaly pileus at times ally it to the Inolomas with which it is more easily confused, but the texture of the pileus and its general characteristics show it to belong to the subgenus Telamonia. I have not seen it in the southern part of the State, although it probably occurs wherever hemlock trees and other conifers are native. Some consider *C. haematochelis* Fr., which has a single red zone on the stem, as identical.

423. Cortinarius morrisii Pk.

Bull. Torr. Bot. Club, Vol. 32, 1905.

PILEUS 3-10 cm. broad, convex then campanulate-expanded, *hygrophanous,* wavy or irregular on the margin, *dark ochraceous or tawny-ochraceous,* covered with minute, silky fibrils, radially rugose at times. Flesh thin except on disk, *yellowish.* GILLS adnate then emarginate-adnexed, rounded behind, *broad,* subdistant, yellow at first, then rusty-cinnamon, edge eroded. STEM 6-10 cm. long, *equal or subequal,* 8-20 mm. thick, stout, solid, fibrous-fleshy, *yellow within,* whitish or pale yellow above, *yellow to ochraceous* and becoming ferruginous to blackish-umber below, *imperfectly annulate by adnate shreds of the yellowish universal veil.* SPORES oval or broadly-elliptic, slightly rough, with an oil-globule, 7-9 x 5.5-6 micr., (rarely up to 10 x 7). ODOR weak, of radish.

"Moist shaded woods, under hemlock trees. Massachusetts. August-October."

The above description was made from specimens sent to me by G. E. Morris in whose honor Peck named it. The yellow color of the flesh, and the tendency of the cap and stem to become rusty in age is a marked characteristic. The caps of dried specimens are blackish-umber-brown. I have not seen it in Michigan.

424. Cortinarius mammosus sp. nov.

PILEUS 2-8 cm. broad (mostly 4-6 cm.), *conico-campanulate at first*, then expanded and obtusely *umbonate, hygrophanous,* fawn-color to brownish-cinnamon, scarcely tinged with olivaceous, sub-ferruginous on umbo when dry, *beautifully silky-shining,* glabres-cent. FLESH thin except on disk, concolor when moist, pallid when dry. GILLS adnate, becoming emarginate, subventricose, medium broad, close to somewhat subdistant, *at first pallid with tinge of fawn-color,* then pale cinnamon-umber, edge even. STEM 5-9 cm. long, tapering upward from a subclavate base or almost equal, 5-8 mm. thick above, pale brownish, paler above, *subannulate or with thin, concentric, fawn-colored zones from the universal veil,* some-times abruptly pointed below, stuffed. SPORES 7-8.5 x 5-6 micr., broadly elliptical, slightly rough, obtuse.

Among mosses and debris of a sphagnum swamp. Gregarious. Chelsea (near Ann Arbor), Michigan. September. Rare.

Differs from the similar species in the Dermocybe group, of which *C. cinnamomeus* is the center, in its hygrophanous flesh, lack of yellowish gills and habit, as well as by the presence of the universal veil. In this last respect it approaches *C. sublanatus* Fr. and *C. valgus* Fr. (sense of Cooke), but is much more slender. The umbo is very obtuse and well-developed from the first, and the gills are not yellow nor saffron at any stage.

425. Cortinarius paludosus Pk.

N. Y. State Mus. Rep. 43, 1890.

"PILEUS 2-4 cm. broad, conical or convex, *ferruginous when moist,* buff-yellow or pale ochraceous when dry, hygrophanous. FLESH yellowish. GILLS broad, subdistant, adnate, saffron-yel-low. STEM 5-8 cm. long, about 4 mm. thick, equal, long, flexuous, solid, *peronate and sub-annulate by the fibrillose yellow universal veil.* SPORES 7.5-9 x 5 micr.

"Mossy ground in swamps, New York. August."

Section III. Universal veil white or whitish.

*Gills at first yellowish or pallid-ochraceous.

426. Cortinarius hinnuleus Fr.

Epicrisis, 1836.

Illustrations: Cooke, Ill., Pl. 805.
  Gillet, Champignons de France, No. 227.
  Patouillard, Tab. Analyt., No. 648.
  Ricken, Die Blätterpilze, Pl. 48, Fig. 3.

PILEUS 3-6 cm. broad, campanulate at first, then expanded and recurved, subumbonate, *rusty-ochraceous or yellowish tawny,* variegated with rusty stains in age, very *hygrophanous,* paler when dry, glabrous. FLESH thin, watery-soft, fragile when fresh. GILLS adnate-emarginate, *broad,* subdistant, pale yellowish-fulvous at first, stained rusty in age, edge minutely lacerate. STEM 5-7 cm. long, 4-7 mm. thick, rather slender, unequal, *soft and fragile,* easily split longitudinally, stuffed, *curved,* yellowish-pallid becoming dingy, glabrescent, *cingulate when fresh by a white zone* about the middle. SPORES broadly elliptical, scarcely rough, 7-9.5 x 5-6 micr. BASIDIA 30 x 7 micr., 4-spored. ODOR none.

On the ground among decayed debris, in beech and pine woods. New Richmond. September. Infrequent.

This plant seems to be very close to the European one, but differs in some minor particulars. It is more yellowish on the pileus, quite fragile and the gills are less broad and distant. It is placed here provisionally. At maturity the watery-rusty stains on the cap give it a spotted appearance; its flesh is thin and at length splits radially. The stem is variously thickened or almost equal, soft and usually curved. The white band-like zone on the stem at length disappears.

427. Cortinarius castaneoides Pk.

N. Y. State Cab. Rep. 23, 1872.

Illustration: Ibid, Pl. 4, Fig. 10-15.

PILEUS 1-2 cm. broad, campanulate-convex, then expanded, *chestnut-brown to dark watery-cinnamon,* brownish-ochraceous when dry, subumbonate and usually darker on center, *hygrophanous,* scarcely silky with a few superficial fibrils, even, margin sometimes whitish from the veil. FLESH *thin,* watery-brownish then pallid. GILLS adnate then emarginate, *rather broad,* subdistant, yellowish at first, then yellowish-cinnamon to dark cinnamon, edge almost entire. STEM 2-5 cm. long, 1.5-3 mm. thick, equal, slender, stuffed then hollow, subflexuous, pallid, *annulate from the cortina and the fugacious universal veil which remains as subannular, delicate shreds on the stem below.* SPORES elliptical, smooth, 6-7.5 x 3.5-4.5 micr. ODOR and TASTE none.

Gregarious or subcaespitose. On the ground in low frondose or conifer woods or in mossy places. Ann Arbor, New Richmond, Marquette, etc. August-October. Infrequent.

This has the stature and spores of *C. subflexipes* Pk., but the pileus is more convex, and the gills and stem not at first with any violet tint. *C. badius* Pk. is also of about the same size, but its spores are almost twice as large as those of *C. castaneoides.* These three approach the slender species of the subgenus Hydrocybe, and cannot always be distinguished easily from that group, especially where the annulus or other evidence of the universal veil have disappeared. *C. decipiens* Fr. differs in its conic pileus, different spore-size and the tint of rufous present on the stem.

428. Cortinarius badius Pk.

N. Y. State Mus. Rep. 41, 1888.

Illustration: Plate LXXXVII of this Report.

"PILEUS 1-2.5 cm. broad, varying conical to campanulate-convex, umbonate, *hygrophanous, blackish-chestnut-color when moist,* bay-red or chestnut when dry, sometimes tinged gray, the umbo darker, usually whitish-silky on the margin when young. FLESH concolor when moist, thin. GILLS *broad,* subdistant, ventricose, adnexed, *at first yellowish or cream-color,* then subochraceous. STEM 2-4 cm.

long, about 2 mm. thick, slender, equal, hollow, *silky-fibrillose and subannulate by the whitish veil, concolor within and without."* SPORES large, broadly elliptical, 11-12.5 x 6.5-7.5 micr., scarcely rough.

"Mossy ground. Catskill Mountains, New York. September.

"The species is related to *C. nigrellus,* from which it differs in its broad gills which are paler in the young plant and in its larger spores." The Michigan collections formerly referred here differ somewhat and are described below, the gills are at first whitish or pallid.

**Gills at first whitish or pallid.*

429.   Cortinarius iliopodius Fr.

Syst. Myc., 1821.

Illustration: Cooke, Ill., Pl. 839 (form).

PILEUS 2-3 cm. broad, campanulate-subexpanded, mammillate, hygrophanous, *sorghum-brown* (Ridg.), *with blackish umbo when moist,* avellanus (Ridg.) when dry, and then canescent-fibrillose and silky shining, margin at first incurved and white-silky from the veil. FLESH brownish (moist), thin, scissile. GILLS *pallid at first* then cinnamon (Ridg.), adnate, rounded behind, ventricose, *rather broad,* thin, close to subdistant. STEM *slender,* elongated, 5-9 cm. long, 3-4 mm. thick, *equal,* stuffed, at length flexuous, decorated by the delicate white silky remnants of the veil, pale incarnate, *fuscescent,* fuscous-brown or ochraceous toward base within, cortex subcartilaginous. SPORES elliptical-almond shaped, slightly rough, 10-12 x 5-6.5 micr., pale yellowish-cinnamon. ODOR and TASTE mild.

Scattered-gregarious on sphagnum swamp of spruce and tamarack. North Elba, Adirondack Mountains, New York. Collection Kauffman. September, 1914. Infrequent.

It soon fades to the colors of *C. paleaceus,* with a slight drab tint. It differs from *C. paleaceus* in its scattered mode of growth, in its sphagnum habitat and especially in its large spores. In shape and size it imitates *C. decipiens,* but is usually more slender. The species as conceived by Fries is evidently very variable and the plant described above is a definite form. In Monographia, Fries speaks of the yellow flesh of the interior of the stem. In Systema, he says the stem is occasionally fuscous, lilaceous, etc. In the plates at the

Stockholm Museum there is a "rubellus" tint to the stem and gills
but otherwise the figures would represent the Adirondack specimens
well.

430.   Cortinarius badius Pk. var.

Differs from the type in the *gills becoming at first whitish,* stem
whitish, pileus watery cinnamon to bay-brown when moist, fading
to ochraceous or pale tan, obtuse. The spores measure 10-12 x 6-7
micr., elliptical, scarcely rough, cinnamon-brown in mass.

On mossy ground, frondose woods. Ann Arbor. May and October. Infrequent.

This little plant approaches *C. badius* quite closely in the size of
the spores, and by neglecting the colors, was formerly referred to it.
It needs further study. *C. punctata* Fr. (sense of Ricken) differs
in its darker-colored stem and gills.

431.   Cortinarius impolitus sp. nov.

PILEUS 8-20 mm. broad, *small,* firm, conic-campanulate then
expanded, obsoletely umbonate, obtuse, *minutely fibrillose-scaly,*
fibrils often dense at first, *hygrophanous, umber to chestnut-cinna-
mon at first,* becoming pale fawn or sometimes rufous-ochraceous,
silky on the decurved margin, even.   FLESH thin, concolor.
GILLS adnate, *relatively broad,* sub-distant, thickish, *at first whitish or pallid* then cinnamon, edge entire. STEM 2-2.5 cm. long,
1-3 mm. thick, slender, equal, stuffed, *brownish or fuscescent, annulate about the middle* by a floccose, subpersistent, whitish ring,
silky fibrillose, *cortina* dingy whitish. SPORES narrow subfusiform, subacute at ends, 9-10 x 4-4.5 micr., smooth. BASIDIA 27 x 7
micr. ODOR and TASTE none.

Gregarious or subcaespitose. On sandy soil among mosses in
low, moist places in white pine and beech woods. New Richmond.
September-October. Rather frequent locally.

A small species, marked by the median, subpersistent annulus,
the dense, minute fibrils on the pileus and by the color and the
spores. The annulus may appear below the middle or rarely be
absent altogether; in the latter case faint whitish zones mark the
stem. It seems to be partial to sandy regions.

***Gills at first brownish or fuscous.*

432. Cortinarius brunneofulvus Fr.

Epicrisis, 1836-38.

Illustration: Ricken, Die Blätterpilze, Pl. 50, Fig. 4 (as *C. brunneus* Fr.).

PILEUS 3-7 cm. broad, convex, hygrophanous, *dark watery-brown,* glabrous, even, subvirgate on drying, *margin white from the veil,* decurved. FLESH concolor when moist, thick on disk, scissile. GILLS adnate then sinuate, distinct, thickish, broad, subdistant, *soon brown to dark umber-cinnamon..* STEM 5-8 cm. long, 10-15 mm. thick, *narrower upwards* from a clavate or bulbous base, solid, brown, longitudinally streaked with paler fibrils, *annulate by a distinct whitish band at or below the middle,* from the whitish, universal veil. SPORES elliptical, distinctly tuberculate, 10-12 x 6-7 micr. ODOR and TASTE slightly of radish.

Subcaespitose. On the ground in frondose woods. Ann Arbor. September. Infrequent.

This corresponds to Ricken's notion of *C. brunneus.* But according to specimens of *C. brunneus* collected by myself and others near Stockholm, that species has spores measuring 8-9 x 5-6 micr. and the universal veil is more nearly fuscous than white. It appears as if Ricken had interchanged the two species. In order to compare the two plants I give below the description of the Stockholm *C. brunneus* which is a common plant there. Fries says *C. bruneofulvous* has the stature of *E. evernius,* which does not apply as far as the stem of the latter is concerned. No violet tints are present in our plant.

433. Cortinarius brunneus Fr.

Syst. Myc., 1821.

"PILEUS 5-8 cm. broad, campanulate or somewhat obtusely conical at first, then *campanulate-expanded and broadly umbonate,* moist, hygrophanous, glabrous on center, *umber-brown when moist,* fulvous-alutaceous when dry, margin decurved and becoming innately fibrillose. FLESH umber when moist, fading, scissile, thin on margin. GILLS adnate, rather broad, distant to subdistant, thick, *dark livid-brown at first,* sometimes with an obscure purplish tinge then cinnamon-brown, edge entire and concolor. STEM 7-10 cm. long, 5-15 mm. thick, rather stout, firm, *umber or becoming fuscous* and innately streaked with paler fibrils, spongy-stuffed, *clavate-elongated to subequal, at times cingulate above by the* remains of the fuscous universal veil which fades in such a way that the annulus may become paler than the stem. CORTINA whitish, not copious. SPORES elliptical, almost smooth, 8-9 x 5-6 micr., (rarely up to 10 micr. long).

"On the ground among mosses in moist forests of pine and spruce. Stockholm, Sweden. Collected by C. H. Kauffman and confirmed by Romell. September, 1908."

It has somewhat the general appearance of *C. distans* Pk., but is much stouter and its larger gills are less distant, spores slightly longer and universal veil different. It is evident that European authors have confused different species under this name, and hence it seemed advisable to describe the plants from the collecting grounds of Fries. Other collections from Sweden have the same spores as mine. Cooke's figure (Ill., Pl. 868) illustrates the plant well when it is fresh, but his spore-size is wrong. Britzelmayr (Bot. Centralb., Vol. 51, p. 37) reports two species under this name, one of them with the spores in the sense of Cooke. Ricken has also described a different species as shown by the spores (Blätterpilze, p. 174). Quelet's figure (Grevillea, Pl. 113, Fig. 2) does not show the plant well either as to color or veil. Saccardo and Schroeter have given the spore-size approximately correct if we may assume that the Swedish plant is the proper starting point for a revision.

434. Cortinarius distans Pk.

N. Y. State Cab. Rep. 23, 1872.

Illustration: Plate LXXXVIII of this Report.

PILEUS 2-5 cm. broad, *campanulate,* sometimes obtusely conical at first, then campanulate-expanded, *umbonate,* minutely furfuraceous-scaly, *hygrophanous, watery-cinnamon to bay-brown when moist,* tawny or subferruginous when dry, margin usually deflexed, even, often splitting radially. FLESH thin, sordid, brown then dull yellowish. GILLS adnate, then sinuate, *distant, broad,* rigid, thick, *brownish or tawny-yellow at first,* then dark cinnamon. STEM 4-8 cm. long, 5-12 mm. thick, variously thickened to equal, *often attenuated below* and curved, stuffed, fibrillose, watery-brown and unicolor when moist, the universal veil at first concolor but on breaking up leaving *a whitish, medium, somewhat persistent annular zone.* CORTINA whitish, fibrillose. SPORES oval, *rough-tuberculate,* 6-8 x 5-6 micr. ODOR sometimes slightly of radish. TASTE mild.

Gregarious or caespitose. On grassy ground in frondose woods. Houghton, Ann Arbor, Detroit, etc. July to September. Frequent.

This is one of the earliest summer Cortinarii, appearing preferably in low, grassy woods, about the time that *C. cinnabarinus* appears in the higher lying oak woods; it announces the fact that the Cortinarius season is open. It is somewhat difficult to see much difference in the formal descriptions between this and *C. brunneus* Fr., *C. brunneofulvous* Fr. and *C. glandicolor* Fr., but our plant has quite a distinct habit as compared with those. Its gills are truly distant while *C. brunneus* in spite of Fries' description, has more nearly subdistant gills, according to my use of those terms. *C. glandicolor* Fr. is a more slender-stemmed plant, according to Fries' unpublished plates, well shown also by Cooke (Ill., Pl. 789), although figured as rather stout by Ricken (Blätterpilze, Pl. 50, Fig. 3). Peck, in the original description, seems to have had specimens whose caps were "convex." All the specimens seen by me had a tendency toward the campanulate and umbonate form of pileus. The white zone at or below the middle of the stem is best seen in dry weather. The young stem is sometimes peronate. *C. furfurellus* Pk. is without doubt a synonym.

435. Cortinarius nigrellus Pk.

N. Y. State Mus. Rep. 26, 1874.

"PILEUS 2-5 cm. broad, at first conical, soon convex or expanded or subumbonate, minutely silky, hygrophanous, *blackish-chestnut when moist,* paler when dry. GILLS close, *narrow,* emarginate, *brownish-ochre at first,* then cinnamon. STEM 5-7 cm. long, 4-6 mm. thick, subequal, silky-fibrillose, pallid, often flexuous (slightly peronate by a rufous-tinged sheath in the dried type specimens). ANNULUS slight, evanescent." SPORES inequilateral, minute, smooth, 7 x 3.5 micr.

"Mossy ground in woods, New York. October. When moist the pileus has the color of boiled chestnuts, when dry of fresh chestnuts. The incurved margin of the young pileus is whitened by the veil.

The gills are darkest when young. The taste is unpleasant, resembling that of *Armillaria mellea.*"

This is very close to *C. rigida* (sense of Ricken) in stature, colors and spores. *C. rigida* is, however, not uniformly described by European authors, especially as to its spore-size.

436. Cortinarius rigidus Fr. (var.)

Epicrisis, 1836-38.

Illustrations: Cooke, Ill., Pl. 791.
      Quelet, in Grevillea, Vol. VII, Pl. 113, Fig. 4.

PILEUS 1-2.5 cm. broad, convex or conico-convex, umbonate or obtuse, *glabrous,* shining, *rufous-brown to chestnut when moist,* ochraceous to buff color when dry, hygrophanous, even and sometimes with white-silky margin, *elsewhere naked.* FLESH thin, rather firm. GILLS adnate then emarginate, rather close, moderately broad, ventricose, *rufous-cinnamon.* STEM 4-5 cm. long, 2-4 mm. thick, equal, flexuous, *fuscescent,* subfibrillose below the whitish, *median annulus,* apex pruinose. SPORES elliptical, smooth, 6-7.5 x 4 micr. ODOR somewhat fragrant, noticeable.

Gregarious or solitary. On the ground in frondose woods. Ann Arbor. September.

It is quite difficult to get any correct idea of this species from European notices. The spore-measurments per Saccardo are "6-11 x 4-6," per Ricken, "6-7 x 3" and according to others, intermediate in size. Our plants are more slender and less dark-colored than *C. nigrellus.* The species has the size of *C. paleaceus* but has a glabrous cap.

437. Cortinarius rigidus (Scop.) Ricken

Blätterpilze, 1912.

PILEUS 2-5 cm. broad, broadly campanulate-expanded, umbonate, firm and glabrous at first, hygrophanous, even, walnut-brown (Ridg.) when moist, *fawn-color on losing moisture,* soon hoary, silky-shining, margin at first incurved and white-silky. FLESH concolor, soon pallid, scissile. GILLS adnate, close, thin, moderately broad, at first pinkish-buff (Ridg.) then clay-color (Ridg.), edge paler. STEM 3-5 cm. long, 4-8 mm. thick, equal, stuffed, soon hollowed by grubs, brownish within, *white-silky-fibrillose*, some-times annulate from the white veil. SPORES *minute,* narrowly elliptical, 5-6.5 x 3-3.5 micr., smooth, pale clay-color in mass. ODOR and TASTE mild.

Gregarious or subcaespitose. On mosses under spruce, birch, etc. North Elba, Adirondack Mountains, New York. Collection Kauff-man. Infrequent.

The typical Friesian species is said to have a marked odor and specimens from Sweden have larger spores. I have included it (in the sense of Ricken) for comparison. In shape and size it imi-tates *C. hemitrichus.*

438. Cortinarius hemitrichus Fr.

Syst. Myc., 1821.

Illustrations: Fries, Icones, Pl. 160, Fig. 2.
Cooke, Ill., Pl. 825.
Gillet, Champignons de France, No. 226.
Ricken, Die Blätterpilze, Pl. 49, Fig. 5.

PILEUS 2-5 cm. broad (rarely larger), campanulate, umbonate, sometimes umbo is obsolete, umbo varying acute or obtuse, *ground color umber, watery-cinnamon or fuscous when moist,* hygro-phanous, *more or less canescent from the white, superficial, cirrate fibrils* which at first cover it, sometimes glabrescent in age, color fading to fuscous-gray or ochraceous-tan when dry, margin persist-ently white-silky. FLESH concolor, thin. GILLS adnate then emarginate, *broad,* close in front, *subdistant behind, at first brown-ish-gray* to subochraceous, at length dark cinnamon, edge erose-crenulate. STEM 3-6 cm. long, 2-5 mm. thick, equal, hollow, rigid, more or less *annulate at or below the middle* by the white, appressed ring, watery fuscous-brown within, fuscescent or brownish-fuscous without, fibrillose below the annulus. SPORES elliptical, smooth, 6-8 x 4-5 micr. (rarely 9 x 5.5). BASIDIA 30 x 7 micr., 4-spored. ODOR and TASTE mild.

Among mosses or debris in moist places or swampy woods. New Richmond. August-October. Not infrequent.

An extensive study of many specimens showed considerable varia-tion and after some experience it was possible to distinguish two forms with respect to color. Both are conical when very small and become distinctly umbonate. Form (A) had a dark fuscous cap at first, umber when mature, fading to brownish-gray with a chestnut colored umbo; the gills were fuscous at first, and the annulus less fully developed. Form (B) had a watery cinnamon-brown cap when mature, fading to ochraceous-tan; the gills were pallid, ochraceous at first, and the annulus more persistent. The pileus of both had the characteristic villose covering, the same spores and habit. The gills of our specimens are never truly crowded, and in this respect differ from the European descriptions and from specimens which I collected in Sweden. The microscopic structure of both forms was alike. The upper surface of the fresh pileus is composed of a differentiated layer of two kinds of cells, one forming erect, fasciculate fibres alternating with a layer of larger cells; these fasciculate tufts of narrow cells arise from separate points in the surface of the pileus and produce the villose effect. This upper layer is easily dissolved by rains and often disappears leaving the pileus glabrous. The stem is usually hollow, but it is not rare to find a stuffed or solid axis. Both forms are caespitose. The variation in size is such, even in the same collections, that it is very doubtful whether *C. paleaceus* should be kept separate.

439. Cortinarius paleaceus Fr.

Epicrisis, 1836-38.

Illustrations: Fries, Icones, Pl. 106, Fig. 4.
   Gillet, Champignons de France, No. 241.
   Cooke, Ill., Pl. 826.
   Plate LXXXIX of this Report.

Differing from *C. hemitrichus* Fr. in more slender habit, longer stem, the universal veil forming delicate, evanescent, subannular, white fibrillose zones along the stem, and in the pileus being more acutely conical. The colors are fuscous, paler.

In moist, mossy places in woods of oak, etc. Ann Arbor. September-October.

The spores, variability and habitat are the same as in the preceding from which it is separated with difficulty.

SUBGENUS HYDROCYBE. No universal veil. Pileus *hygrophanous,* glabrous or innately silky, changing color on losing moisture. Flesh quite thin, scissile. Stem rarely and then slightly subannulate from the remains of the cortina.

Composed of two sections: those with thicker caps whose margin

is at first incurved, and the smaller, slender species with submembranaceous pileus whose margin is at first straight on the stem
in the manner of the genus Galera. They are distinguished from
the Telamonias only by the absence of the universal veil although
several have at times a slight annulus from the collapsing of the
copious cortina and not from the outer veil. The pileus is never
viscid; it is moist when growing but the moisture disappears quickly
in sun and wind so that in our climate the dry, faded plant is
more often found than the moist plant. However, for identification of most of the species of this subgenus it is absolutely necessary to know the colors of both the moist and dry pileus since in
many of the species the pileii have a similar color when dry.
I consider this the most difficult of the subgenera of Cortinarius
both because of the great variability of the colors of most species,
and because of the unsettled condition in which the European
authors have so far left it. While at Stockholm, Sweden, I paid
special attention to this group, and found a number of Friesian
species; in many cases, however, these do not agree well with the
spore characters as given by various authors. It is clear that only
a temporary arrangement can be given of our species and it seemed
best to put on record descriptions of such species as are close to
the Friesian ones, as unnamed variations under the Friesian names.
In Michigan the Hydrocybes seem to be much more numerous in
the coniferous regions of the State than in frondose woods as appears to be also the case in Europe. I have no doubt we have quite
a number of species which are truly American.

Section I. Margin of pileus at first incurved. Pileus thickish,
of a medium or fairly large size. Stem somewhat stout.

*Stem or gills at first violaceous.

440. Cortinarius imbutus Fr.

Epicrisis, 1836-38.

Illustration: Cooke, Ill., Pl. 870.

PILEUS 2.5-7 cm. broad, *convex* then expanded, obtuse or subumbonate, even, *hygrophanous, chestnut-brown when moist,* changing color, alutaceous or rufous-tinged on disk when dry and then
becoming somewhat hoary, margin at first incurved and sometimes

decorated by whitish fibrillose scales from the cortina. FLESH thickish on disk, thin on margin, watery to pallid. GILLS adnate then subemarginate, *broad,* close, not crowded, *violaceous at first* with lavender tinge, soon cinnamon, edge concolor. STEM rather stout, 3-5 cm. long, 5-10 mm. thick, *equal* or nearly so, *solid,* at first violaceous, especially at apex, then silky-whitish and shining, violaceous within at apex, rarely subannulate from the whitish cortina. SPORES narrow, elliptical, smooth, 7-8.5 x 4-4.5 micr. BASIDIA 25-27 x 8 micr., 4-spored. ODOR none.

Gregarious or subcaespitose. On naked ground in low frondose woods. Ann Arbor. October. Infrequent.

This species is based here on the figures of Cooke and those of Fries' unpublished plate at Stockholm. The latter shows a pileus colored like ours and somewhat the same as that of Cooke's figures, but is not "gilvus" as described by Fries in his works. Cooke's figures do not show the violaceous character as do those of Fries. Other authors differ considerably in the application of this name and in the spore-size. The figure of Quelet (in Grevillea, Vol. VIII, Pl. 127, Fig. 2) is referred by Maire (Bull. d. l. Soc. Myc. de France, Vol. 26, p. 28), to *C. bicolor* Cke. and is not at all our plant. The cortina sometimes leaves a row of spot-like shreds on the margin of the pileus, sometimes it forms a slight annulus on the stem, but more often it is entirely evanescent. This species is near *C. castaneus,* from which it differs by its larger, stouter habit, its slightly smaller spores, but especially by the solid stem. Ricken considers it a variety of *C. subferruginea,* but he evidently had a plant with larger spores.

441. Cortinarius saturninus Fr. minor.

Syst. Myc., 1821.

Illustrations: Fries, Icones, Pl. 161, Fig. 2.
        Gillet, Champignons de France, No. 247.

PILEUS 3-6 cm. broad, campanulate, expanded, sometimes gibbous, glabrous, hygrophanous, pale watery brown when moist, ochraceous-gray-buff when dry, silky around margin. FLESH thin, scissile, violaceous then pallid. Gills adnate then emarginate, adnexed, *close,* moderately broad, *violaceous or tinged purplish at first* then ashy-cinnamon, thin, edge entire. STEM 4-6 cm. long, 6-12 mm. thick, subequal, slightly thicker downwards, terete or com-

pressed, *stuffed, violaceous above,* whitish below, fibrilles-
cent and shining when dry. CORTINA whitish. SPORES elliptical, slightly rough, 7-8 x 5-6 micr. ODOR and TASTE mild.

Subcaespitose. On the ground in frondose woods. Ann Arbor.
September. Rare.

This is well illustrated by the figures of Fries and of Gillet.
Ricken describes a plant with spores measuring 10-12 x 5-6 micr., and
with a much darker pileus. The pileus soon fades. It is to be
noted that although Fries describes the moist pileus as "dark bay"
color, his figures are much paler. I have not seen it dark-colored
and that character may belong to another species such as the one
described by Ricken.

442. Cortinarius livor Fr.

Epicrisis, 1836-38.

PILEUS 3-4 cm. broad, firm, campanulate, obtuse, sometimes
gibbous, *sooty-brown, obscurely olive-gray on center,* scarcely hygrophanous, *not fading,* even, innately subtomentose on disk, margin
at first incurved. FLESH thickish on disk, sooty-brown under the
center, pallid or whitish elsewhere. GILLS adnate then emarginate,
close, relatively *broad, pallid-cinnamon at first.* STEM 4-5 cm. long,
sub-equal, sometimes narrower at base, sometimes subbulbous,
slightly *violaceous above,* becoming dingy olivaceous to brownish below, *solid,* firm, at first violaceous, within. SPORES broadly elliptical, slightly rough, obtuse, 7-8 x 5 micr. BASIDIA 30 x 7 micr.,
4-spored. ODOR slight.

Solitary. On the ground in beech and pine woods. New Richmond. September. Rare.

There is an olive to sooty tinge on cap and base of stem, which
along with the violaceous apex of the stem is quite characteristic.
The plate of Fries at Stockholm, marked typical, shows a plant
with a much shorter stem, otherwise our plant is very like it.

443. Cortinarius castaneus Fr.

Syst. Myc., 1821.

Illustration: Cooke, Ill., Pl. 842.

"PILEUS 2-5 cm. broad, firm, campanulate-convex, expanded or
gibbous, even, *subumbonate,* scarcely hygrophanous, *dark chestnut*

color, shining when dry, *hardly fading,* margin at first white-silky. FLESH thin, rigid-tough, concolor to pallid. GILLS adnexed, *not broad,* ventricose, *close, violet at first,* then rusty-cinnamon, *edge whitish.* STEM 2-4 cm. long, not truly slender, 4-6 mm. thick, cartilaginous, *stuffed then hollow, violaceous or pallid-rufescent,* silky from the white cortina. SPORES elliptical, rough, 7-9 x 4-5 micr. ODOR and TASTE slight."

Gregarious. On the ground in open woods, etc.

The description is adapted from the works of Fries and his unpublished plate at Stockholm. The characteristic features, by which it is separable from *C. imbutus* and other related species with violet gills, are the *hollow stem* and smaller stature. The figures of Cooke agree with those of Fries, except that they lack the markedly violet stem and gills. Patouillard's figures (Tab. Analyt., No. 128) remind one more of *C. badius* Pk., and Gillet's figure (Champignons de France, No. 202), has aberrant colors. Peck's specimens have the correct spores. The species has been reported by various authors in this country but I have not seen any typical specimens.

***Stem at first white or pallid.*

444. Cortinarius armeniacus Fr.

Syst. Myc., 1821.

Illustrations: Cooke, Ill., Pl. 793.
Ricken, Blätterpilze, Pl. 51, Fig. 4.

PILEUS 5-7 cm. broad, firm, campanulate-subexpanded, broadly *umbonate,* obtuse, glabrous, even, hygrophanous, *sudan-brown when moist* (Ridg.), orange-buff on umbo while drying, orange-buff or tan throughout when dry, margin when dry white silky from the cortina. FLESH thin on margin, scissile, soon pallid. GILLS adnate, emarginate, *broad,* ventricose, close, thin, *at first pallid,* then mars-yellow (Ridg.) to cinnamon, edge entire. STEM 5-7 cm. long, tapering upward, 5-8 mm. thick above, twice as thick below, watery-pallid when moist, dingy whitish when dry, *silky-fibrillose,* rind cartilaginous, stuffed, spongy at base. CORTINA whitish, sparse. SPORES elliptical, slightly rough, 8-9 x 5-5.5 micr. ODOR and TASTE mild or slightly of radish.

Gregarious. Among mosses under spruce and balsam. North Elba, Adirondack Mountains, New York. Collection Kauffman. September, 1914.

Similar in stature to *C. glabrellus,* but differs in the nature of the surface of the pileus both in color and in the structure of the cuticle. As the moisture disappears the umbo fades to pale ochraceous. It agrees well with the figures of Fries at the Stockholm Museum and also with the conception of Ricken. Fries states that the plants are more robust among fallen leaves and the stem is then stout and clavate-bulbous and some of his figures show this.

445. Cortinarius duracinus Fr. var.

Epicrisis, 1836-38.

Illustrations: Cooke, Ill., Pl. 809 (not typical).
Ricken, Die Blätterpilze, Pl. 51, Fig. 2 (not typical).
Quelet, Grevillea, Vol. VII, Pl. 115, Fig. 1 (dry form).

PILEUS 4-10 cm. broad, *convex* then expanded, obtuse, sometimes gibbous, *hygrophanous, watery cinnamon-brown when moist,* tinged rufous on disk, pale ochraceous-tan to buff when dry, *glabrous,* even, margin at first incurved then geniculate and obsoletely silky. FLESH rigid-brittle, *thin,* scissile, concolor, at length pallid. GILLS adnate or slightly subdecurrent, thin, *subdistant,* moderately broad, pallid at first but *soon watery-cinnamon,* edge even or scarcely crenulate. STEM 4-12 cm. long, *tapering downwards or fusiform-subradicate,* 6-15 mm. thick, glabrous, rigid, stuffed then hollow, sometimes compressed, at length shining, *white,* at first cortinate-fibrillose. CORTINA white. SPORES elliptical-almond-shaped, scarcely rough, 7-9.5 x 5-5.5 micr. BASIDIA 32-36 x 8-9 micr. ODOR and TASTE mild.

Gregarious, often in troops or subcaespitose. On the ground, grassy places, etc., in frondose woods of southern Michigan. August to October. Frequent in very wet weather.

One of the larger Hydrocybes, usually found in quantity when it occurs. No good plates seem to exist of the plant as it occurs with us. Our specimens agree in stature, colors, spores, etc., with a collection I found at Stockholm. Ricken gives spores much larger, but Massee's spore-measurements are much smaller. It seems clear that the species of Fries is yet uncertain. A plant agreeing in the spore-character with that of Ricken and otherwise similar to the above species occurs with us in the same habitat. The rigid-brittle, convex pileus, the tapering-subradicating stem and the colors and size distinguish our *C. duracinus*. It has somewhat the appearance of *C. dolobratus* Fr. as figured by Cooke (Ill., Pl. 811) except in shape of stem and the brown color; furthermore the margin of the pileus of that species is at first incurved. Neither the pileus of our plant nor that occuring at Stockholm had a truly ferruginous or testaceous color when moist.

446. Cortinarius sp.

PILEUS 2-8 cm. broad, *conico-campanulate,* subexpanded, glabrous, even, hygrophanous, rufous-cinnamon when moist, *pale tan when dry* and subshining, margin white-silky at first. FLESH thin, scissile, at length whitish. GILLS adnate-emarginate, *broad,* broadest behind, tapering in front, medium close, ventricose, *pallid-brownish at first* then dark cinnamon, edge erose-crenulate, concolor. STEM 6-10 cm. long, 7-12 mm. thick above, *subbulbous to clavate below, stuffed,* soon cavernous, soft-spongy within, silky-fibrillose, *whitish to pallid.* CORTINA white. SPORES broadly elliptical, 8-9 x 5-6 micr., scarcely rough. ODOR and TASTE mild.

Gregarious to subcaespitose. On the ground in frondose woods, among grass, etc. Ann Arbor. September. Infrequent.

In size this species corresponds to the preceding, but differs in its somewhat cone-shaped, rather acute pileus, broad gills and bulbous to clavate stem. *C. candelaris* Fr. is half-way between the two in having a conic-campanulate pileus and a radicating stem and the spores, according to Ricken, measure 9-11 x 4-5 micr. Found in quantity, but all with clavate-bulbous stems. Specimens of *C. candelaris* from Bresadola had spores measuring 6-7.5 x 5 micr.

447. Cortinarius erugatus Fr.

Epicrisis, 1836-38.

PILEUS 3-6 cm. broad, campanulate-convex, obtuse to broadly subumbonate, *hygrophanous,* pale *umber-cinnamon to grayish-brown with rufous or fulvous umbo when moist,* on drying becoming pale reddish-gray with innate silky fibrils and *silvery sheen,* glabrous, even, margin at first incurved and entirely white-silky. FLESH thin, splitting on margin which is at length recurved. GILLS adnate-emarginate, rather broad behind, tapering in front, *close,* thin, *pallid-brownish at first,* then alutaceous to ferruginous, edge minutely erose-lacerate. STEM 4-7 cm. long (when elongated 8-10 cm.), 5-12 mm. thick, variable in length and thickness, *at first clavate-bulbous* then elongated, soft-spongy, stuffed, *pallid and streaked with silky white fibrils,* becoming sordid, not cingulate. CORTINA white. SPORES elliptical, rather narrow, smooth, variable in length, 6-8.5 (rarely 9) x 4-4.5 micr. BASIDIA 30 x 6-7 micr., 4-spored. ODOR and TASTE mild.

Gregarious or scattered in thick leaf-mould of hemlock, pine and beech ravines. New Richmond. September-October. Infrequent.

When young the pileus is firm and very silky on edge, when old it becomes soft; the stem is early affected by grubs and soon decays at the base. The color of the pileus changes markedly and hence is very variable. Sections of very young buttons show no universal veil.

448. Cortinarius glabrellus Kauff.

Jour. of Mycology, Vol. 13, p. 35, 1907 (synopsis).

Illustration: Plate XC of this Report.

PILEUS 5-10 cm. broad, hemispherical-convex at first, campanulate-expanded, obtuse or *broadly umbonate,* glabrous, *hygrophanous, with a slight pellicle,* watery cinnamon when moist, *becoming brick-color on drying,* then paler, even, margin at first incurved and white-silky. FLESH concolor then pallid, rather thin. GILLS adnate, moderately broad, broadest behind, close, *distinct,* thin, *at first brownish-pallid* then cinnamon-brown. STEM 4-8 cm. long, 8-18 mm. thick, *varying equal* to subclavate below, rather stout and firm, straight or curved at base, *pallid or whitish,* silky-fibrillose and shining when dry, stuffed. CORTINA white. SPORES elliptical, 6-8.5 x 4-5 micr., smooth. ODOR and TASTE slightly of radish.

Gregarious. On ground in moist, low, frondose woods. Ann Arbor. September-October. Infrequent.

This species was originally referred to the subgenus Phlegmacium. The pellicle of the pileus is, however, scarcely gelatinous although the surface feels somewhat slippery. This and the reddish color which appears on the pileus as it loses moisture are the most striking characters.

449. Cortinarius privignus Fr. var.

Epicrisis, 1836-38.

Illustrations: Cooke, Ill., Pl. 827 (pale, dry, small).
Ricken, Die Blatterpilze, Pl. 52, Fig. 2 (non Fr.).

PILEUS 4-6 cm. broad, gibbous, campanulate-convex, obtuse, hygrophanous, *fuscous-brown when moist, innately variegated-micaceous-silky,* paler and with tinge of drab when dry, glabrous, even, margin at first incurved at length splitting radially. FLESH thin except disk, concolor to pallid. GILLS adnate-emarginate, *rather broad,* ventricose, not crowded, *brownish at first,* then cinnamon, edge concolor. STEM 4-7 cm. long, 7-10 mm. thick, equal or subequal, sometimes *with a bulbous base, pallid with tinge of drab,* silky-shining when dry, glabrous, even, not cingulate, *stuffed then hollow.* SPORES broadly elliptical, obtuse, rough, 8-9 x 5-6 micr. ODOR and TASTE mild.

Solitary or gregarious. On the ground among humus in pine and beech woods. New Richmond. September-October. Infrequent.

The figures of this by Cooke and Ricken do not seem to apply to the same plant. Ours is intermediate between the two and fits more closely to the Friesian sense. The stem is usually clavate or even bulbous at base but equal elsewhere. The color of the pileus is soon similar to that of *C. paleaceus,* but the character of its surface is quite different and the plant is stouter.

450. Cortinarius subrigens sp. nov.

PILEUS 3-5 cm. broad, broadly *convex* from the first, then expanded-plane or subdepressed, *bay-brown* to chestnut and *variegated with white hoariness* when moist, fading quickly to cinnamon-rufous and then *hoary isabelline when dry,* hygrophanous, even, margin at first incurved and cortinate. FLESH rigid-brittle, thin, dingy pallid or brownish. GILLS sinuate-adnate, close, medium broad, *pallid to brownish* then cinnamon, edge entire and concolor. STEM 3-5 cm. long, equal or tapering downward, 5-10 mm. thick, rigid, base often curved, *stuffed then hollow,* at first cortinate-fibrillose, glabrescent and silky-shining, *pallid to white,* rarely subannulate from the white CORTINA. SPORES narrow-elliptical, subinequilateral, slightly rough, 9-10 x 4.5-5.5 micr. BASIDIA 30-32 x 6-7 micr. ODOR and TASTE mild.

Caespitose. On the ground in oak woods. Ann Arbor. October. Infrequent.

Known by its whitish stem, hoary silkiness on the pale chestnut-brown ground-color of the moist cap, the stuffed to hollow stem and its medium size. The stem and cap become firm and rather rigid when dry. When the stem tapers down it approaches *C. rigens* Fr. but the incurved margin of the convex pileus, its hoary-silkiness and more manifest cortina separate it. *C. scandeus* Fr. is distinguished by its smaller spores, conic to umbonate pileus and more slender stem. *C. leucopus* Fr. has a conic to umbonate pileus and different spores.

***Stem and gills becoming brown or fuscescent.*

451. Cortinarius rubricosus Fr. var.

Epicrisis, 1836-38.

PILEUS 3-7 cm. broad, convex-campanulate, broadly umbonate, *fuscous-bay-brown,* subhygrophanous, margin grayish, white-silky, at first incurved, elsewhere glabrous, even. FLESH thickish on disk, watery to pallid. GILLS adnexed-emarginate, *rather narrow,* close to subdistant, *soon umber-brown,* pallid-brownish at first, edge white-fimbriate. STEM 3-5 cm. long, 8-12 mm. thick above, rather stout, *clavate-bulbous,* 12-18 mm. thick toward base, firm, *solid,* grayish-pallid, *soon fuscescent,* at length dark fuscous umber below and within, at first densely white-fibrillose from cortina. SPORES broadly elliptical, rough-tuberculate, 8-10 x 6-7 micr. BASIDIA 40-45 x 9 micr., often with dark brownish content; *sterile cells* on edge of gills, slender, subclavate above.

Solitary or gregarious. On the ground among humus in hemlock woods. New Richmond. September. Infrequent.

This differs somewhat from the Friesian plants in its lack of reddish tints on the cap, and from the plant of Ricken in its larger spores. Britzelmayr gives the spores the same size as ours, and my collection from Sweden also has such spores but shows the slight rufous color when dry. It needs further study but surely belongs in its present position in the group.

452. Cortinarius uraceus Fr.

Epicrisis, 1826-38.

Illustration: Fries, Icones, Pl. 162, Fig. 3.

PILEUS 2-5 cm. broad, firm, at first ovate or campanulate then convex-subexpanded, often with a mammillate umbo, hygrophanous, *smoky chestnut brown* (Ridg.) *when moist,* even, fading to cinnamon-brown or isabelline, with blackish streaks, often *blackish on umbo,* margin persistently decurved. FLESH thin except disk, scissile, watery chestnut (moist), fragile when dry. GILLS broadly adnate, *broad,* close to subdistant, *dark watery brown at first,* then auburn to dark rusty-brown (Ridg.), edge at length black. STEM 4-9 cm. long, 4-10 mm. thick, equal or tapering slightly upward, becoming flexuous, *firm, stuffed then hollow,* pallid when fresh, soon brownish-streaked, *fuscescent, in age blackish,* rarely with narrow white evanescent annulus. CORTINA whitish, forming a silky zone on the young margin of pileus, fuscescent. SPORES broadly elliptical, 7-8 x 5-6 micr., rough. ODOR of radish when plants are crushed. TASTE mild.

Gregarious-subcaespitose.   Among moss under balsam, spruce, etc. North Elba, Adirondack Mountains, New York. Collection Kauffman. September, 1914. Frequent after heavy rains.

The species is interpreted here in the sense of the Icones of Fries. It is well marked by its spores, dark colors and broad gills. In dry weather it is scarcely recognizable; it is then often pale tan and streaked with blackish stains, quite fragile and split on the margin of the cap. There is no universal veil in the young stage, the lack of which separates it from *C. glandicolor* which is nearest to it in color and habit. As characterized by Fries, an olivaceous color is sometimes present. This form appears to be that of Ricken with very large spores. In the Monographia, Fries himself raises the question whether it is not a composite species. Cooke (Ill., Pl. 796) figures a slender plant and it is possible that this is also a separate form, as I collected such a plant in Sweden with spores 8-10 x 5-6 micr.

453. Cortinarius juberinus Fr. var.

Epicrisis, 1836-38.

Illustration: Cooke, Ill., Pl. 797.

PILEUS 2-4 cm. broad, campanulate-convex, then expanded, umbonate or umbo obsolete, *chestnut-brown to watery cinnamon* when moist, ochraceous when dry, subhygrophanous, glabrous, even, *silky-shining when dry,* margin at first incurved and white-silky from the cortina. FLESH concolor, thin. GILLS adnate then subemarginate, *subdistant,* rather broad, thin, at length ventricose, pallid-brown then cinnamon, interspaces somewhat venose, edge concolor. STEM 3-7 cm. long, 3-5 mm. thick, moderately slender, equal or subequal, even, *stuffed then hollow,* pallid at first, then brownish or fuscescent, innately silky-fibrillose. CORTINA white, fugacious. SPORES 6.5-7.5 x 4.5-5 micr., broadly elliptic-oval, scarcely rough. BASIDIA 27-30 x 6-7 micr. ODOR and TASTE slight or none.

Solitary or scattered. On the ground near wet or springy places in woods or swamps. Ann Arbor, New Richmond. September. Infrequent.

Distinguished by the spores, subdistant gills, hollow stem and colors. The pileus does not become black-stained nor black-streaked in age as do some similar species of this subgenus. The color of the pileus is variable, sometimes approaching tawny-cinnamon, and its surface is silky-shining as in *C. cinnamomeus.* Our plant agrees better with the unpublished figures of Fries and those of Cooke, than with the description of Fries; in his description, Fries states that the pileus is very bright cinnamon-fulvous, but this is not shown in his figure. The habitat is also different. The spores agree with the size given by Cooke, and doubtless we have his species here.

454. Cortinarius præpallens Pk.

N. Y. State Bull. 2, 1887.

"PILEUS 1-4 cm. broad, subconical, then convex or expanded, glabrous, *hygrophanous, brown or chestnut color when moist,* pallid-ochraceous when dry. FLESH yellowish-white, thin. GILLS rounded behind or subemarginate, *crowded,* lanceolate, *reddish-umber* then fuscous-cinnamon. STEM 2-7 cm. long, 4-8 mm. thick,

equal, subflexuous, fleshy fibrous, subsilky, *pallid or. brownish.*
SPORES subellipsoid, 7-10 x 6.5 micr.
"On bare ground in woods, New York."

Section II. Margin at first straight on the stem, Galera-like.
Slender-stemmed, with the pileus mostly conical-campanulate and
almost membranous.

*Stem or gills at first violaceous.

455. Cortinarius fuscoviolaceus Pk.

N. Y. State Mus. Rep. 27, 1875.

"PILEUS 1-2 cm. broad, convex (?) umbonate, soon expanded
and centrally depressed, *glabrous, hygrophanous, chestnut-brown
tinged with violet,* the margin whitened by silky fibrils. GILLS
rounded behind, at first plane then ventricose, rather distant, *dark
violaceous at first* becoming subcinnamon. STEM 2.5-4 cm. long,
slender, flexuous, equal, solid, silky-fibrillose, colored like pileus."
SPORES broadly elliptical, minute, smooth, 6-7 x 3-4 micr.
"Sphagnous marshes, New York."
A very similar plant occurs at Ithaca, New York., with spores
7-10 x 3-4 micr. The type-specimens, however, show the spores as
given above.

456. Cortinarius erythrinus Fr.

Epicrisis, 1836-38.

Illustrations: Cooke, Ill., Pl. 798, A.
Ricken, Blätterpilze, Pl. 53, Fig. 2.
Quelet, Grevillea, Pl. 115, Fig. 2.

PILEUS 1-2 cm. broad, rather firm, *conic-campanulate,* then subexpanded and subacutely umbonate, chestnut brown, *umbo umber
or blackish,* paler toward margin, hygrophanous, glabrous, even,
soon fading. FLESH thin on margin, scissile, watery-brown when
moist. GILLS rounded behind and adnexed, *rather broad,* ventricose, close to subdistant, pallid or pale brownish then cinnamon,
edge entire. STEM slender, 4-6 cm. long, 3-4 mm. thick, fragile,
equal, flexuous, stuffed then hollow, *apex violet at first,* pale brownish elsewhere, sometimes violet-tinged throughout, sparsely cor-

tinate, glabrescent, shining when dry. SPORES short, elliptical, 7-9 x 5-6 micr., almost smooth, pale ochraceous. ODOR and TASTE mild.

Gregarious. On bare soil in mixed woods. North Elba, Adirondack Mountains, New York. Collection Kauffman. September, 1914. Infrequent.

The slender form of the species is illustrated by Cooke. It agrees in all respects with plants found in Sweden. The stouter forms approach *C. castaneus.*

**Stem white, pallid or dingy brownish.

457.   Cortinarius decipiens Fr.

Syst. Myc., 1821.

Illustrations: Cooke, Ill., Pl. 798, B.
        Ricken, Blätterpilze, Pl. 53, Fig. 8.

PILEUS 2-4 cm. broad, at first *conico-campanulate,* then subexpanded with decurved margin, *prominently umbonate,* vinaceous-cinnamon (Ridg.), *umbo blackish while losing moisture,* hygrophanous, *glabrous,* silky-shining, margin with white-silky fibrils. FLESH thin, concolor. GILLS adnate, then emarginate-uncinate, close, *rather broad,* at first pallid or cinnamon-buff, *at length mars-yellow* (Ridg.), edge white-crenulate at first. STEM slender, 7-10 cm. long, 4-7 mm. thick, scarcely incrassate downward, stuffed then hollow, becoming flexuous, fragile, *pallid to silky-shining,* glabrous, brownish within. SPORES narrowly elliptical, 7-9 x 4-4.5 micr., scarcely rough. ODOR and TASTE slightly of radish.

Gregarious or subcaespitose. North Elba, Adirondack Mountains, New York. On mosses, sphagnum, etc., in balsam and tamarack swamp. Infrequent.

This species is placed here in the sense of Ricken. I doubt whether it is the typical Swedish species which I collected near Stockholm; the stem of that was rubello-tinged, the gills were truly cinnamon and the spores measured 9-10 x 6 micr. Britzelmayr also gives the latter size. When young and moist the cap of our plants is chestnut-brown.

Var. *minor.* PILEUS 1-2 cm. broad, stem 2-3 cm. long, 2-3 mm. thick. GILLS tawny at first then mars-orange (Ridg.), thickish, edge entire. STEM short, sub-bulbillate at base, often tinged sub-orange or reddish-orange by deposit of the spores. SPORES 7-9 x 5-5.5 micr. Under conifers, New York.

Both forms are known by the gills becoming mars-orange at maturity. Sometimes the silky fibrils on the margin of the cap are slightly rufous. No universal veil is present. The cortina is whitish.

458. Cortinarius leucopus Fr. (var.)

Syst. Myc., 1821.

Illustration: Cooke, Ill., Pl. 843.

PILEUS 1-3 cm. broad, conico-campanulate, at length 'expanded and umbonate, even, *glabrous,* roods-brown (Ridg.) when moist, *cinnamon-buff* (Ridg.) *when dry,* hygrophanous. GILLS adnate-sinuate, ventricose, not broad, subdistant, *pallid at first,* then ochraceous-tawny (Ridg.), edge entire. STEM 3-4 cm. long, 2-4 mm. thick, rather slender, *equal, silky-fibrillose or sometimes subcingulate* from the white cortina, stuffed to hollow, *white or pallid.* SPORES narrow, elliptic-oblong, scarcely rough, 7-8 x 3.5-4.5 micr. (rarely 9 micr.). ODOR none.

Gregarious or subcaespitose. On the ground or moss in pine and spruce woods. North Elba, New York, and New Richmond, Michigan. September-October. Infrequent.

This approaches *C. juberinus* Fr., but pileus is more acute, spores of a different shape and stem scarcely brownish. The spores agree with those given by Ricken and Britzelmayr, but the colors, habit and the occasionally cingulate stem are shown in Fries' unpublished plate. No form has been seen with a pure white stem as described by Fries. Cooke's figures show the faded condition. The moist young pileus is margined by the white silky remains of the cortina.

459. Cortinarius scandens Fr.

Epicrisis, 1836-38.

Illustrations: Cooke, Ill., Pl. 830 (dry condition).
  Cooke, Ill., Pl. 845 (as *C. obtusus*).
  Gillet, Champignons de France, No. 236 (as *C. obtusus*).
  Fries, Icones, Pl. 163, Fig. 3 (as *C. obtusus*).

PILEUS 1-3 cm. broad, *rigid,* conico-campanulate, *then expanded-*

umbonate, glabrous, *watery rusty-fulvous at first when moist* and striatulate on margin, *soon* honey-colored or alutaceous to paler when dry, soon even, hygrophanous. FLESH thin, concolor. GILLS adnate, sometimes emarginate, *narrow,* close to subdistant, thin, *pallid-brown then cinnamon,* edge concolor. STEM 3-8 cm. long, 2-5 mm. thick, *tapering downward,* thickened above, *attenuated at the slender curved base,* flexuous, *soon rigid,* stuffed then hollow, fulvous (moist) pallid or white and shining when dry, scarcely fibrillose at the first by remains of the scanty white COR-TINA. SPORES short-elliptical, *almost smooth,* 6-7.5 (rarely 8) x 4-5 micr. BASIDIA 25-30 x 6-7 micr. ODOR none or slight.

Solitary, scattered or subcaespitose in pairs. Among leaves and humus in frondose and conifer woods. Ann Arbor, New Richmond. September-October. Frequent in the late autumn.

It is very variable in color, and the gills are sometimes rather broad, while the spores are consistently small. The plants are often the shape and color of *C. obtusus* Fr. as illustrated by various authors, so that it seemed advisable to refer to these figures. It seems that *C. obtusus* Fr., of which I obtained several collections at Stockholm, differs mostly in its larger size, its quite broad gills and larger spores; these measure 9-10 x 5.5-6.5 micr. It is to be noted that the figures of Fries (Icones, Pl. 163, Fig. 1) of *C. scandens* can scarcely be the form referred to in his descriptions. In "Monographia" he says distinctly that the stem is "incrassate at apex, always attenuate at the base," while in the figures the stem is not attenuate. The colors of his figures also do not correspond with the descriptions. I have followed the idea of the description, as did Cooke, Ricken, Britzelmayr and others. We doubtless have forms of *C. obtusus* also, but they need further study. Fries' unpublished plate of *C. rigens* Fr. shows that species to differ from *C. scandens* in its larger, stouter habit and convex or gibbous pileus; its gills are not broad.

460. Cortinarius lignarius Pk.

N. Y. State Mus. Rep. 26, 1874.

Illustration: Plate LXXXVII of this Report.

PILEUS .5-3 cm. broad, *conico-campanulate, subacutely umbonate,* hygrophanous, glabrous, *watery-cinnamon to chestnut-fulvous when moist,* not striate, fading to pale fulvous-tan, innately silky-shining, margin at first straight and soon naked. FLESH sub-membranaceous, concolor. GILLS adnate-seceding, *broad,* close, thin, *ochraceous-pallid at first* then somewhat rusty-brown. STEM 2-5 cm. long, rather slender, 2-3 mm. thick, equal, pallid or sub-rufous toward base, often curved at base, silky-fibrillose below, *subcingulate at or above the middle by silky-white remnants of the rather copious cortina,* at length tubular, base white-mycelioid. SPORES narrow-elliptical, smooth, 6.5-7 x 4-5 micr. BASIDIA 25 x 6 micr., 4-spored. ODOR none. TASTE slight.

Subcaespitose or solitary on very rotten wood, in coniferous or mixed woods. New Richmond. September. Infrequent.

Known by the very marked subacute umbo, reddish-fulvous pileus, the cingulate stem, spores and habitat. Peck placed it under the Telamonias, but although slight colored floccules are sometimes present on the edge of the annulus, there is no other indication of a universal veil. When fresh there is sometimes a fleeting tint of violaceous at the apex of the stem. Sometimes it grows on logs when these are far advanced in decay.

461. Cortinarius acutoides Pk.

N. Y. State Mus. Bull. 139, 1909.

Illustrations: Ibid, Plate X, Fig. 4-8.

"PILEUS 8-16 mm. broad, *conic or subcampanulate,* acutely um-bonate, hygrophanous, not striate, *pale chestnut color at first,* floccose and margined by the fibrils of the cortina, *whitish and silky-fibrillose when dry.* GILLS adnexed, subdistant, ascending, *narrow,* yellowish-cinnamon. STEM 2.5-5 cm. long, 2-3 mm. thick, solid or with a small hollow tubule, *white,* then whitish. SPORES 8-10 x 6-7 micr., ellipsoid.

"Swamps. Massachusetts. October. Closely allied to *C. acutus,* from which it differs in the darker color of the young moist pileus and whiter color of the mature dry pileus, the white color of the young stem, the adnexed gills, and especially by the larger spores and absence of striae from the pileus."

*** *Stem yellowish or ochraceous.*

462. Cortinarius acutus Fr.

Syst. Myc., 1821.

Illustrations: Cooke, Ill., Pl. 845.
    Quelet, in Grevillea, Vol. VII, Pl. 112, Fig. 5.
    Engler and Prantl, Pflanzenfamilien, Part I, Sect. 1,** Fig.
    118 A.

PILEUS 5-25 mm. broad, *conical* or conic-campanulate with acute
umbo, *striate to the umbo* and watery rufous-cinnamon when moist,
pale alutaceous when dry, hygrophanous, minutely silky, margin
white-cortinate, glabrescent. FLESH submembranaceous, yellowish.
GILLS adnate seceding, close or scarcely subdistant, thin, not broad,
pale ochraceous at first then ochraceous-cinnamon, edge entire.
STEM 4-8 cm. long, *slender,* 1-2 mm. thick, equal, flexuous, tubular,
yellowish at first becoming paler, silky from the evanescent white
cortina, glabrescent. SPORES elliptical, smooth, 7-9.5 x 5-5.5 micr.
    In moist places, swamps, etc. September-October. Specimens
from Massachusetts by G. E. Morris.
    Distinguishable from the preceding two by the clearly striate
pileus and yellowish stem when fresh and moist. It is easily mistaken for a Galera.

Plate I.

NYCTALIS ASTEROPHORA.

Plate II.

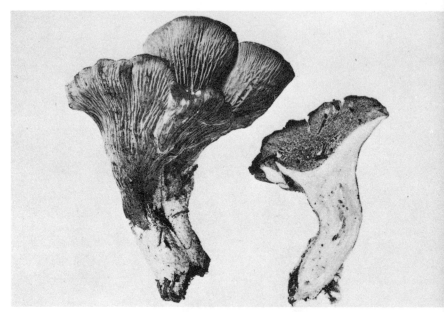

CANTHERELLUS CLAVATUS.

CANTHERELLUS CINNABARINUS.

Plate III.

CANTHERELLUS CIBARIUS.

Plate IV.

PANUS STRIGOSUS.

Plate V.

PANUS RUDIS.

Plate VI.

Plate VII.

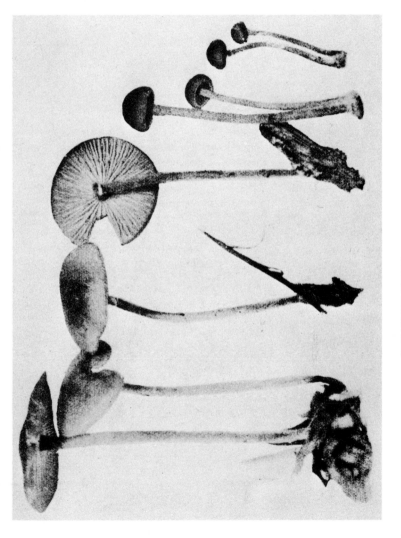

MARASMIUS URENS.

Plate VIII.

MARASMIUS CALOPUS.

Plate IX.

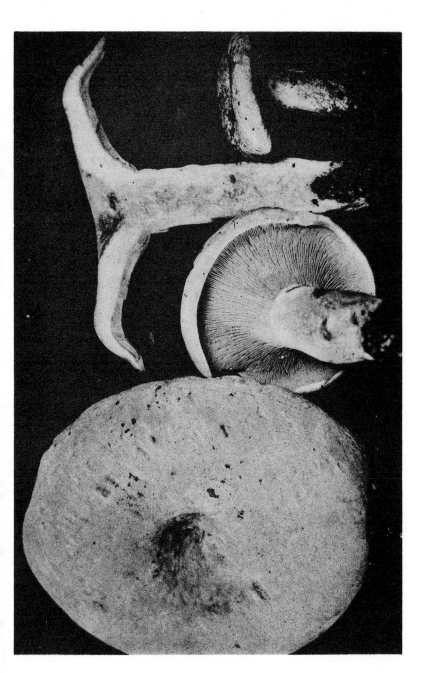

LACTARIUS PIPERATUS.

Plate X.

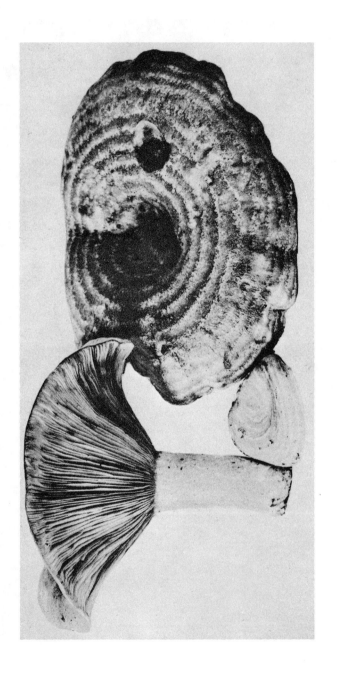

LACTARIUS INSULSUS.

Plate XI.

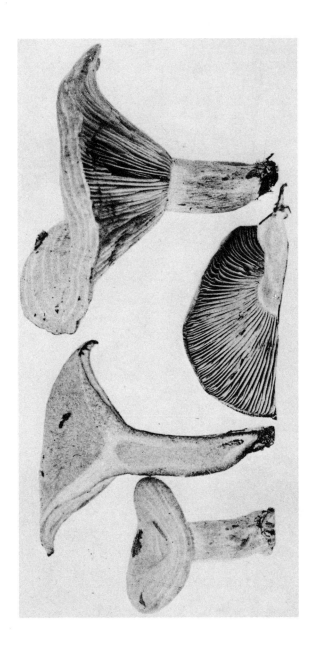

LACTARIUS DELICIOSUS.

Plate XII.

LACTARIUS VOLEMUS.

Plate XIII.

LACTARIUS CAMPHORATUS.

Plate XIV.

RUSSULA SORDIDA

Plate XV.

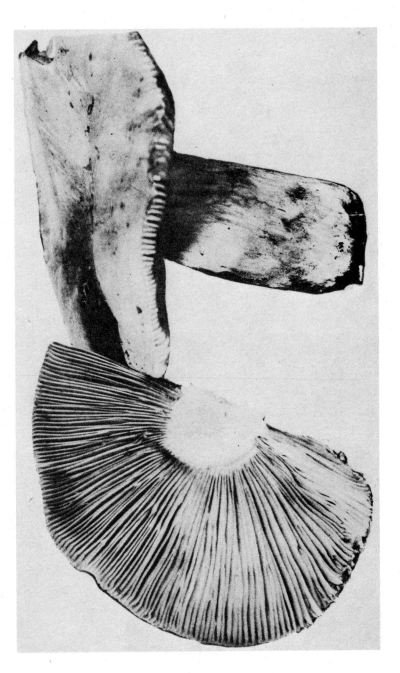

RUSSULA OCHRALEUCOIDES.

Plate XVI.

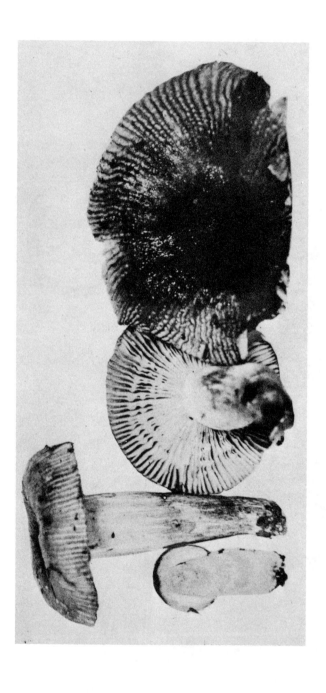

RUSSULA PULVERULENTA.

Plate XVII.

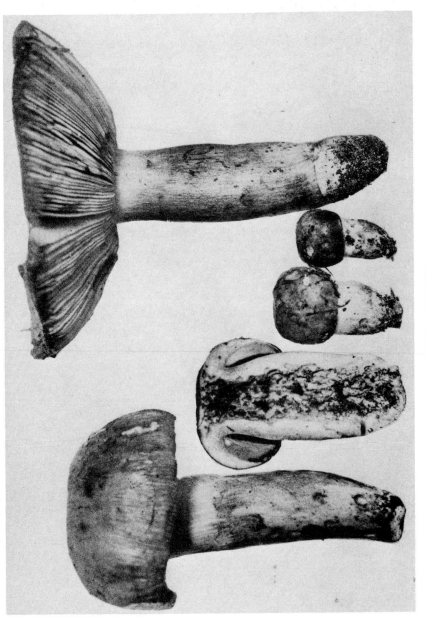

RUSSULA FOETENS.

Plate XVIII.

RUSSULA MARIAE.

Plate XIX.

RUSSULA RUBESCENS.

Plate XX.

RUSSULA TENUICEPS.

Plate XXI.

RUSSULA PURPURINA.

Plate XXII.

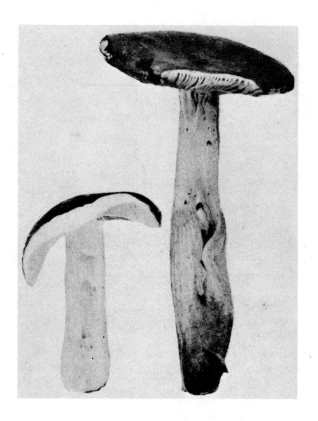

RUSSULA LUTEA.

Plate XXIII.

GOMPHIDIUS MACULATUS.

Plate XXIV.

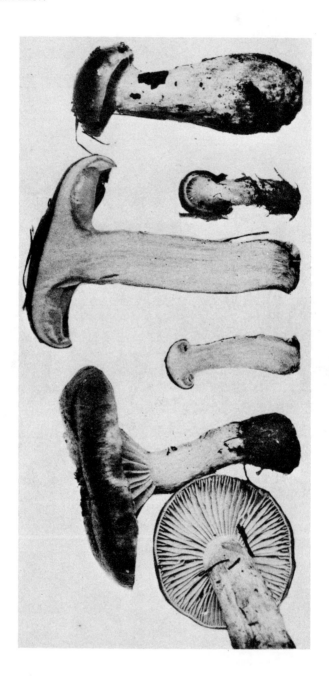

HYGROPHORUS SPECIOSUS.

Plate XXV.

HYGROPHORUS OLIVACEO-ALBUS.

Plate XXVI.

HYGROPHORUS RUSSULA.

Plate XXVII.

HYGROPHORUS SORDIDUS.

Plate XXVIII.

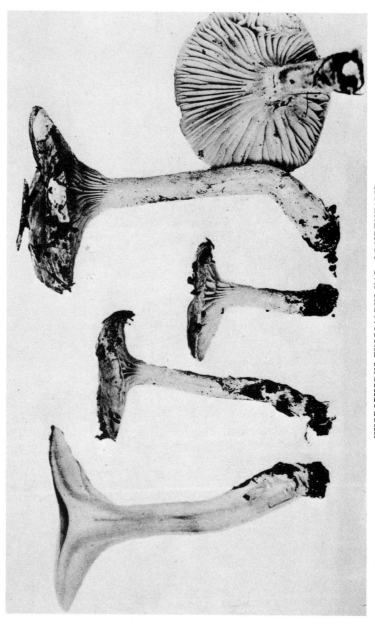

HYGROPHORUS FUSCOALBUS VAR. OCCIDENTALIS.

Plate XXIX

HYGROPHORUS PALLIDUS.

HYGROPHORUS COLEMANNIANUS.

Plate XXX.

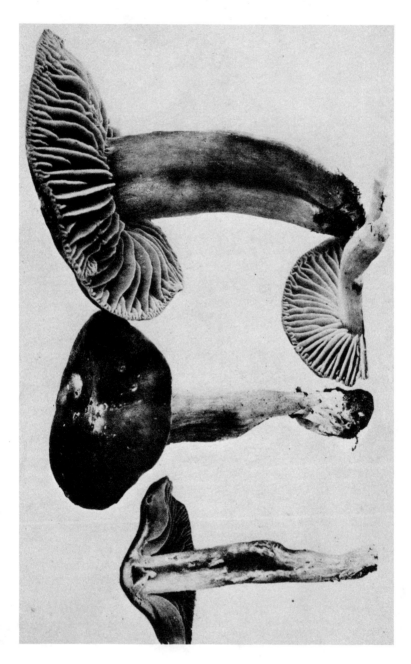

HYGROPHORUS COCCINEUS.

Plate XXXI.

HYGROPHORUS MARGINATUS.

Plate XXXII.

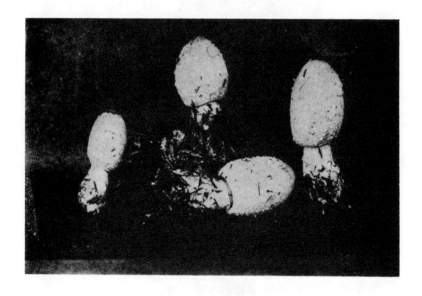

COPRINUS STERQUILINUS

Plate XXXIII.

COPRINUS INSIGNIS.

Plate XXXIV.

COPRINUS QUADRIFIDUS.

Plate XXXV.

COPRINUS EBULBOSUS.

Plate XXXVI.

COPRINUS EBULBOSUS

Plate XXXVII.

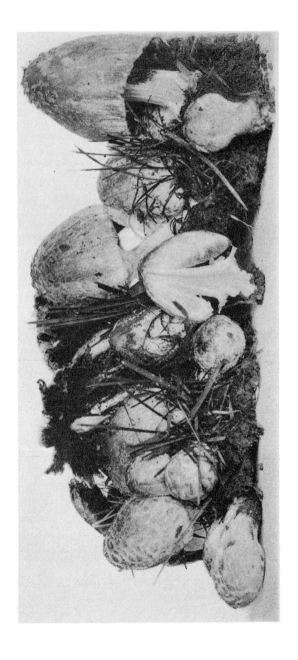

COPRINUS LANIGER.

Plate XXXVIII.

COPRINUS FIMETARIUS.

COPRINUS DOMESTICUS.

Plate XXXIX.

COPRINUS MICACEOUS.

Plate **XL**.

COPRINUS MICACEOUS.

COPRINUS BULBILOSUS.

Plate XLI.

COPRINUS SCLEROTIGENUS.

COPRINUS SCLEROTIGENUS.

COPRINUS NARCOTICUS.

Plate **XLII**.

COPRINUS EPHEMERUS.

COPRINUS PATOUILLARDI.

Plate XLIII.

COPRINUS EPHEMERUS 2-spored

COPRINUS EPHEMERUS 2-spored

Plate XLIV.

PANOEOLUS SOLIDIPES.

Plate XLV.

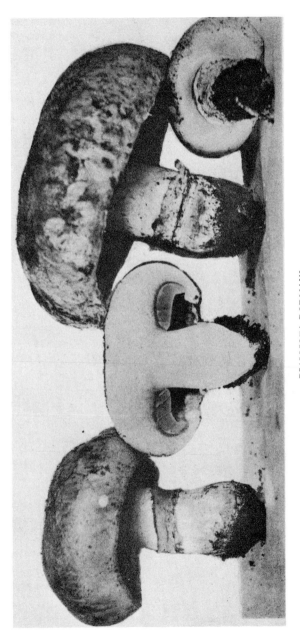

PSALLIOTA RODMANI.

Plate XLVI.

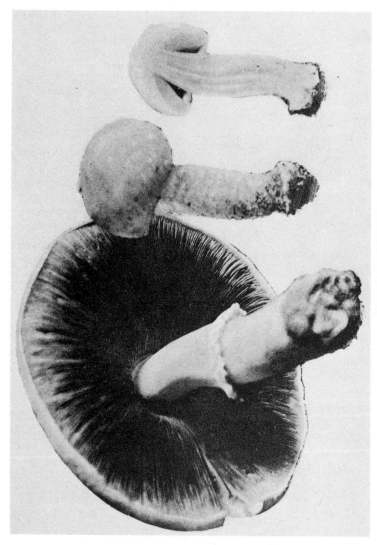

PSALLIOTA ARVENSIS.

Plate XLVII.

PSALLIOTA ABRUPTIBULBA.

Plate XLVIII.

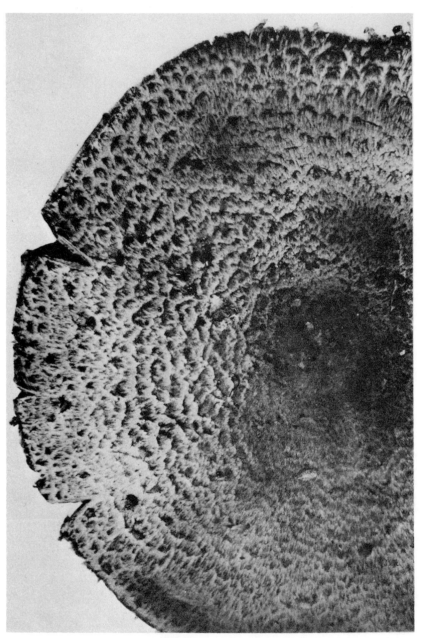

PSALLIOTA SUBRUFESCENS.

Plate XLIX.

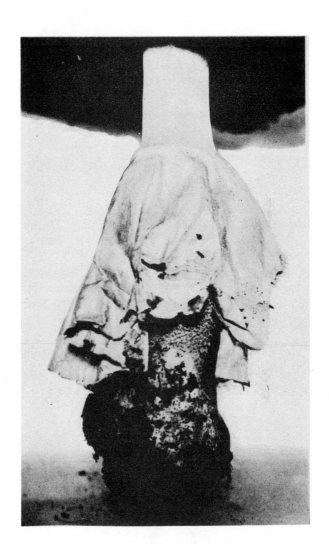

PSALLIOTA SUBRUFESCENS.

Plate L.

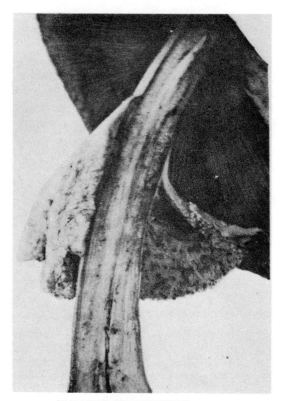

PSALLIOTA SUBRUFESCENS.

PSALLIOTA DIMINUTIVA.

Plate LI.

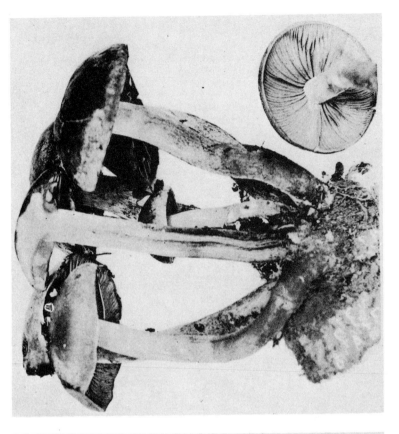

HYPHOLOMA SUBLATERITIUS.

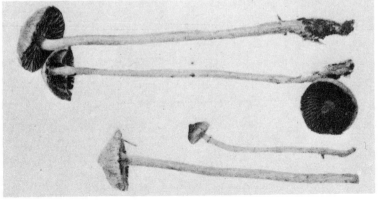

STROPHARIA UMBONATESCENS.

Plate LII.

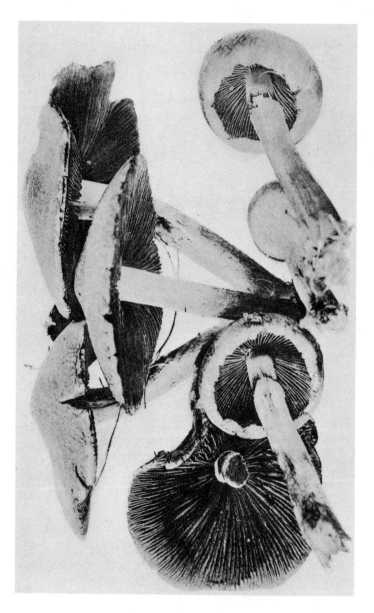

HYPHOLOMA LACHRYMABUNDUM.

Plate LIII.

HYPHOLOMA VELUTINUM.

Plate LIV.

PSILOCYBE FOENISECII.

HYPHOLOMA INCERTUM.

Plate LV.

PSILOCYBE SP., PSATHYRA SP., AND TUBARIA SP.

Plate LVI.

PSILOCYBE ATROBRUNNEA.   PSATHYRA UMBONATA.

Plate LVII.

PSILOCYBE LARGA.

Plate LVIII.

PSILOCYBE CERNUA.

Plate LIX.

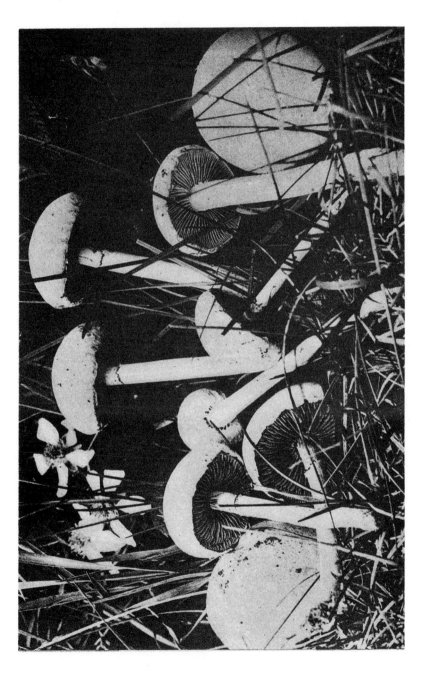

Plate LX.

PHOLIOTA DESTRUENS

Plate LXI.

PHOLIOTA SPECTABILIS.

Plate LXII.

PHOLIOTA AERUGINOSA.

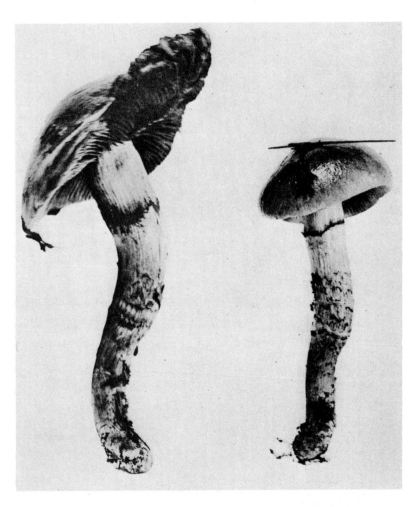

Plate LXIII.

CORTINARIUS MUCIFLUUS.

Plate LXIV.

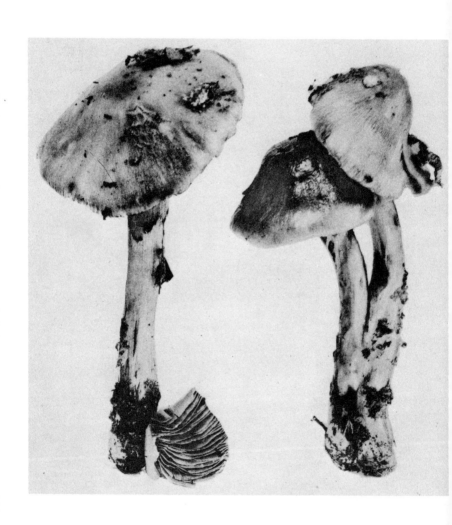

CORTINARIUS CYLINDRIPES.

Plate LXV.

CORTINARIUS SPHOEROSPORUS.

Plate LXVI.

CORTINARIUS IODEOIDES.

Plate LXVII.

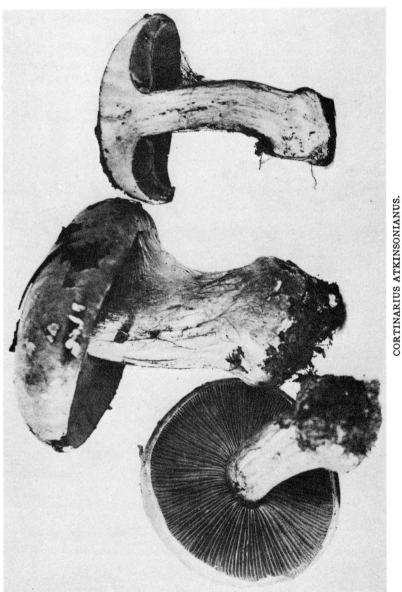

CORTINARIUS ATKINSONIANUS.

Plate LXVIII.

CORTINARIUS CALOCHROUS.

Plate LXIX.

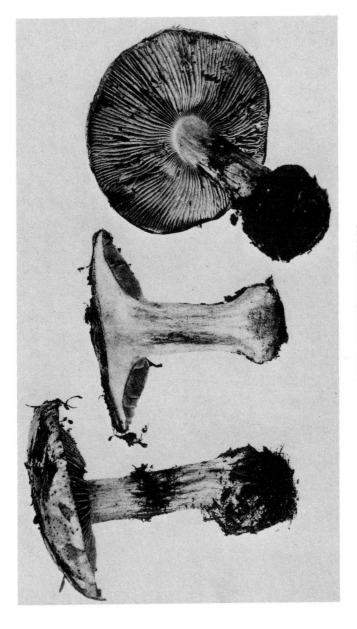

CORTINARIUS ELEGANTIOIDES.

Plate LXX.

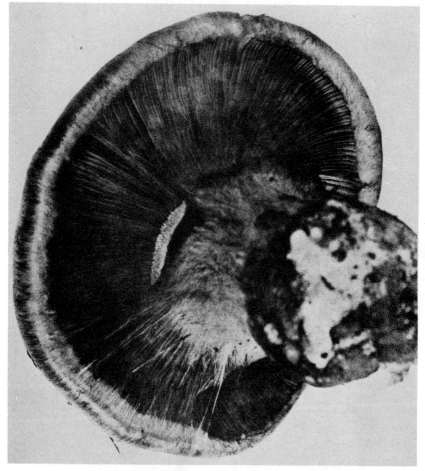

CORTINARIUS SPHOEROSPERMA.

Plate LXXI.

CORTINARIUS PURPURASCENS.

CORTINARIUS FULMINEUS VAR. SULPHUREUS.

Plate LXXII.

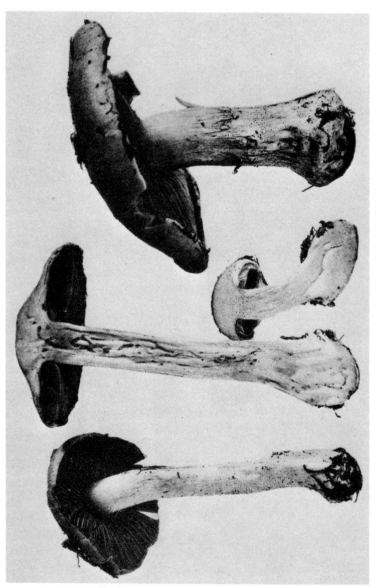

CORTINARIUS MULTIFORMIS.

Plate LXXIII.

CORTINARIUS INTRUSUS.

CORTINARIUS INFRACTUS.

Plate LXXIV.

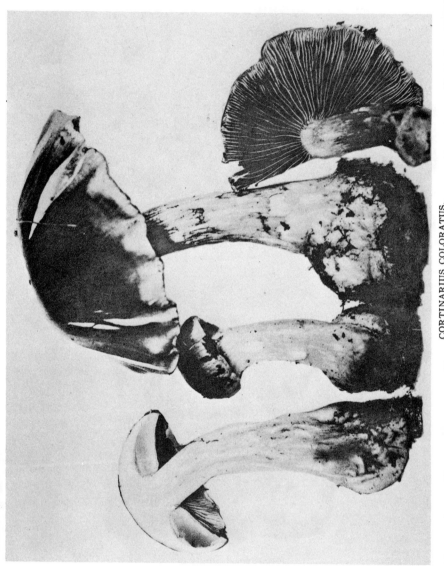

CORTINARIUS COLORATUS.

Plate LXXV.

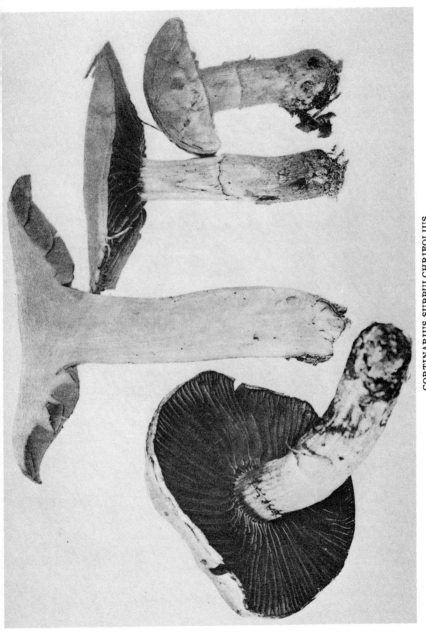

CORTINARIUS SUBPULCHRIFOLIUS.

Plate LXXVI.

CORTINARIUS PHOLIDEUS.

Plate LXXVII.

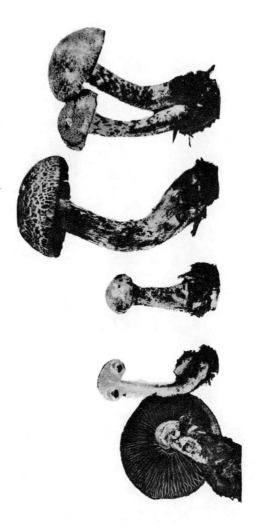

Plate LXXVIII.

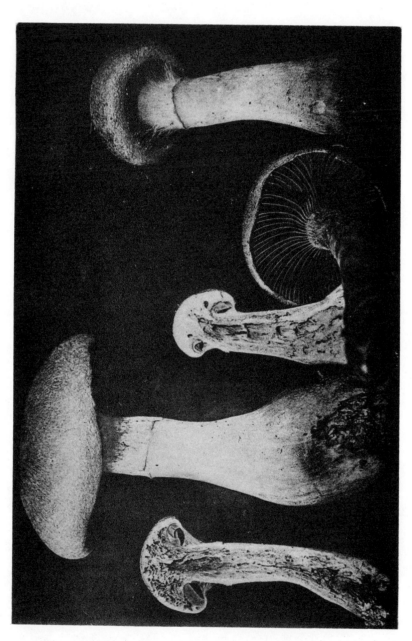

CORTINARIUS ANNULATUS.

Plate LXXIX.

CORTINARIUS FLAVIFOLIUS.

Plate LXXX.

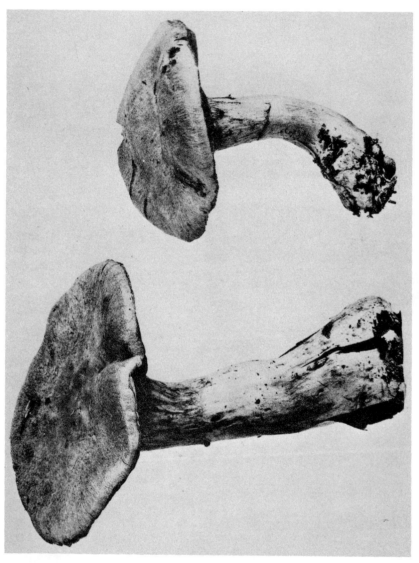

CORTINARIUS FLAVIFOLIUS.

Plate LXXXI.

CORTINARIUS CROCEOCOLOR.

Plate LXXXII.

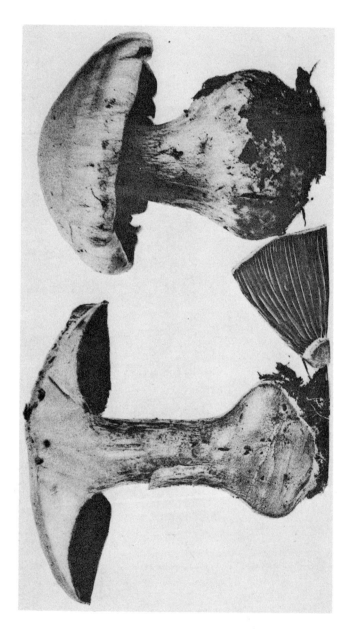

CORTINARIUS LILACINUS.

Plate LXXXIII.

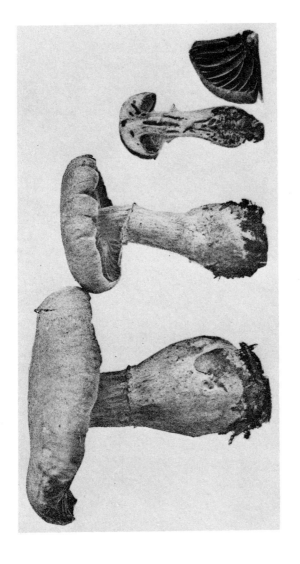

CORTINARIUS TORVUS.

Plate LXXXIV.

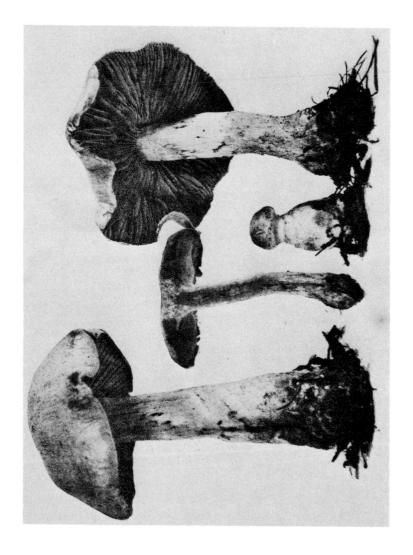

CORTINARIUS DECEPTIVUS.

Plate LXXXV.

CORTINARIUS ARMILLATUS.

Plate LXXXVI.

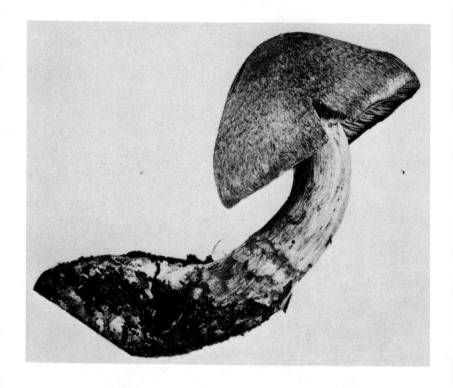

CORTINARIUS ARMILLATUS.

Plate LXXXVII.

CORTINARIUS BADIUS

CORTINARIUS LIGNARIUS

Plate LXXXVIII

CORTINARIUS DISTANS.

Plate LXXXIX.

CORTINARIUS PALEACEUS.

Plate XC.

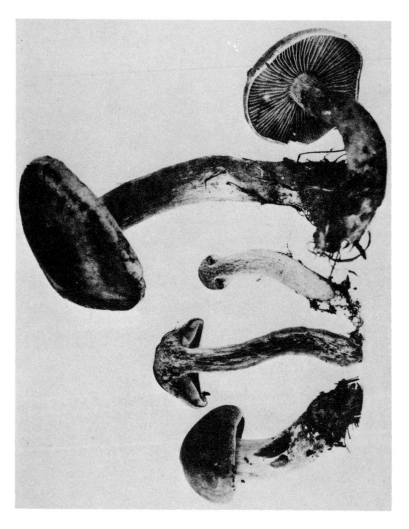

A CATALOGUE OF SELECTED DOVER BOOKS
IN ALL FIELDS OF INTEREST

A CATALOGUE OF SELECTED DOVER BOOKS
IN ALL FIELDS OF INTEREST

AMERICA'S OLD MASTERS, James T. Flexner. Four men emerged unexpectedly from provincial 18th century America to leadership in European art: Benjamin West, J. S. Copley, C. R. Peale, Gilbert Stuart. Brilliant coverage of lives and contributions. Revised, 1967 edition. 69 plates. 365pp. of text.
21806-6 Paperbound $2.75

FIRST FLOWERS OF OUR WILDERNESS: AMERICAN PAINTING, THE COLONIAL PERIOD, James T. Flexner. Painters, and regional painting traditions from earliest Colonial times up to the emergence of Copley, West and Peale Sr., Foster, Gustavus Hesselius, Feke, John Smibert and many anonymous painters in the primitive manner. Engaging presentation, with 162 illustrations. xxii + 368pp.
22180-6 Paperbound $3.50

THE LIGHT OF DISTANT SKIES: AMERICAN PAINTING, 1760-1835, James T. Flexner. The great generation of early American painters goes to Europe to learn and to teach: West, Copley, Gilbert Stuart and others. Allston, Trumbull, Morse; also contemporary American painters—primitives, derivatives, academics—who remained in America. 102 illustrations. xiii + 306pp.
22179-2 Paperbound $3.00

A HISTORY OF THE RISE AND PROGRESS OF THE ARTS OF DESIGN IN THE UNITED STATES, William Dunlap. Much the richest mine of information on early American painters, sculptors, architects, engravers, miniaturists, etc. The only source of information for scores of artists, the major primary source for many others. Unabridged reprint of rare original 1834 edition, with new introduction by James T. Flexner, and 394 new illustrations. Edited by Rita Weiss. 6⅝ x 9⅝.
21695-0, 21696-9, 21697-7 Three volumes, Paperbound $13.50

EPOCHS OF CHINESE AND JAPANESE ART, Ernest F. Fenollosa. From primitive Chinese art to the 20th century, thorough history, explanation of every important art period and form, including Japanese woodcuts; main stress on China and Japan, but Tibet, Korea also included. Still unexcelled for its detailed, rich coverage of cultural background, aesthetic elements, diffusion studies, particularly of the historical period. 2nd, 1913 edition. 242 illustrations. lii + 439pp. of text.
20364-6, 20365-4 Two volumes, Paperbound $5.00

THE GENTLE ART OF MAKING ENEMIES, James A. M. Whistler. Greatest wit of his day deflates Oscar Wilde, Ruskin, Swinburne; strikes back at inane critics, exhibitions, art journalism; aesthetics of impressionist revolution in most striking form. Highly readable classic by great painter. Reproduction of edition designed by Whistler. Introduction by Alfred Werner. xxxvi + 334pp.
21875-9 Paperbound $2.25

Two Little Savages; Being the Adventures of Two Boys Who Lived as Indians and What They Learned, Ernest Thompson Seton. Great classic of nature and boyhood provides a vast range of woodlore in most palatable form, a genuinely entertaining story. Two farm boys build a teepee in woods and live in it for a month, working out Indian solutions to living problems, star lore, birds and animals, plants, etc. 293 illustrations. vii + 286pp.
20985-7 Paperbound $1.95

Peter Piper's Practical Principles of Plain & Perfect Pronunciation. Alliterative jingles and tongue-twisters of surprising charm, that made their first appearance in America about 1830. Republished in full with the spirited woodcut illustrations from this earliest American edition. 32pp. 4½ x 6⅜.
22560-7 Paperbound $1.00

Science Experiments and Amusements for Children, Charles Vivian. 73 easy experiments, requiring only materials found at home or easily available, such as candles, coins, steel wool, etc.; illustrate basic phenomena like vacuum, simple chemical reaction, etc. All safe. Modern, well-planned. Formerly *Science Games for Children*. 102 photos, numerous drawings. 96pp. 6⅛ x 9¼.
21856-2 Paperbound $1.25

An Introduction to Chess Moves and Tactics Simply Explained, Leonard Barden. Informal intermediate introduction, quite strong in explaining reasons for moves. Covers basic material, tactics, important openings, traps, positional play in middle game, end game. Attempts to isolate patterns and recurrent configurations. Formerly *Chess*. 58 figures. 102pp.   (USO) 21210-6 Paperbound $1.25

Lasker's Manual of Chess, Dr. Emanuel Lasker. Lasker was not only one of the five great World Champions, he was also one of the ablest expositors, theorists, and analysts. In many ways, his Manual, permeated with his philosophy of battle, filled with keen insights, is one of the greatest works ever written on chess. Filled with analyzed games by the great players. A single-volume library that will profit almost any chess player, beginner or master. 308 diagrams. xli x 349pp.
20640-8 Paperbound $2.50

The Master Book of Mathematical Recreations, Fred Schuh. In opinion of many the finest work ever prepared on mathematical puzzles, stunts, recreations; exhaustively thorough explanations of mathematics involved, analysis of effects, citation of puzzles and games. Mathematics involved is elementary. Translated by F. Göbel. 194 figures. xxiv + 430pp.   22134-2 Paperbound $3.00

Mathematics, Magic and Mystery, Martin Gardner. Puzzle editor for Scientific American explains mathematics behind various mystifying tricks: card tricks, stage "mind reading," coin and match tricks, counting out games, geometric dissections, etc. Probability sets, theory of numbers clearly explained. Also provides more than 400 tricks, guaranteed to work, that you can do. 135 illustrations. xii + 176pp.
20338-2 Paperbound $1.50

THE PHILOSOPHY OF THE UPANISHADS, Paul Deussen. Clear, detailed statement of upanishadic system of thought, generally considered among best available. History of these works, full exposition of system emergent from them, parallel concepts in the West. Translated by A. S. Geden. xiv + 429pp.
21616-0 Paperbound $3.00

LANGUAGE, TRUTH AND LOGIC, Alfred J. Ayer. Famous, remarkably clear introduction to the Vienna and Cambridge schools of Logical Positivism; function of philosophy, elimination of metaphysical thought, nature of analysis, similar topics. "Wish I had written it myself," Bertrand Russell. 2nd, 1946 edition. 160pp.
20010-8 Paperbound $1.35

THE GUIDE FOR THE PERPLEXED, Moses Maimonides. Great classic of medieval Judaism, major attempt to reconcile revealed religion (Pentateuch, commentaries) and Aristotelian philosophy. Enormously important in all Western thought. Unabridged Friedländer translation. 50-page introduction. lix + 414pp.
(USO) 20351-4 Paperbound $2.50

OCCULT AND SUPERNATURAL PHENOMENA, D. H. Rawcliffe. Full, serious study of the most persistent delusions of mankind: crystal gazing, mediumistic trance, stigmata, lycanthropy, fire walking, dowsing, telepathy, ghosts, ESP, etc., and their relation to common forms of abnormal psychology. Formerly *Illusions and Delusions of the Supernatural and the Occult.* iii + 551pp.
20503-7 Paperbound $3.50

THE EGYPTIAN BOOK OF THE DEAD: THE PAPYRUS OF ANI, E. A. Wallis Budge. Full hieroglyphic text, interlinear transliteration of sounds, word for word translation, then smooth, connected translation; Theban recension. Basic work in Ancient Egyptian civilization; now even more significant than ever for historical importance, dilation of consciousness, etc. clvi + 377pp. 6½ x 9¼.
21866-X Paperbound $3.75

PSYCHOLOGY OF MUSIC, Carl E. Seashore. Basic, thorough survey of everything known about psychology of music up to 1940's; essential reading for psychologists, musicologists. Physical acoustics; auditory apparatus; relationship of physical sound to perceived sound; role of the mind in sorting, altering, suppressing, creating sound sensations; musical learning, testing for ability, absolute pitch, other topics. Records of Caruso, Menuhin analyzed. 88 figures. xix + 408pp.
21851-1 Paperbound $2.75

THE I CHING (THE BOOK OF CHANGES), translated by James Legge. Complete translated text plus appendices by Confucius, of perhaps the most penetrating divination book ever compiled. Indispensable to all study of early Oriental civilizations. 3 plates. xxiii + 448pp.
21062-6 Paperbound $2.75

THE UPANISHADS, translated by Max Müller. Twelve classical upanishads: Chandogya, Kena, Aitareya, Kaushitaki, Isa, Katha, Mundaka, Taittiriyaka, Brhadaranyaka, Svetasvatara, Prasna, Maitriyana. 160-page introduction, analysis by Prof. Müller. Total of 826pp. 20398-0, 20399-9 Two volumes, Paperbound $5.00

MATHEMATICAL PUZZLES FOR BEGINNERS AND ENTHUSIASTS, Geoffrey Mott-Smith. 189 puzzles from easy to difficult—involving arithmetic, logic, algebra, properties of digits, probability, etc.—for enjoyment and mental stimulus. Explanation of mathematical principles behind the puzzles. 135 illustrations. viii + 248pp.
20198-8 Paperbound $1.25

PAPER FOLDING FOR BEGINNERS, William D. Murray and Francis J. Rigney. Easiest book on the market, clearest instructions on making interesting, beautiful origami. Sail boats, cups, roosters, frogs that move legs, bonbon boxes, standing birds, etc. 40 projects; more than 275 diagrams and photographs. 94pp.
20713-7 Paperbound $1.00

TRICKS AND GAMES ON THE POOL TABLE, Fred Herrmann. 79 tricks and games— some solitaires, some for two or more players, some competitive games—to entertain you between formal games. Mystifying shots and throws, unusual caroms, tricks involving such props as cork, coins, a hat, etc. Formerly *Fun on the Pool Table*. 77 figures. 95pp.
21814-7 Paperbound $1.00

HAND SHADOWS TO BE THROWN UPON THE WALL: A SERIES OF NOVEL AND AMUSING FIGURES FORMED BY THE HAND, Henry Bursill. Delightful picturebook from great-grandfather's day shows how to make 18 different hand shadows: a bird that flies, duck that quacks, dog that wags his tail, camel, goose, deer, boy, turtle, etc. Only book of its sort. vi + 33pp. 6½ x 9¼. 21779-5 Paperbound $1.00

WHITTLING AND WOODCARVING, E. J. Tangerman. 18th printing of best book on market. "If you can cut a potato you can carve" toys and puzzles, chains, chessmen, caricatures, masks, frames, woodcut blocks, surface patterns, much more. Information on tools, woods, techniques. Also goes into serious wood sculpture from Middle Ages to present, East and West. 464 photos, figures. x + 293pp.
20965-2 Paperbound $2.00

HISTORY OF PHILOSOPHY, Julián Marias. Possibly the clearest, most easily followed, best planned, most useful one-volume history of philosophy on the market; neither skimpy nor overfull. Full details on system of every major philosopher and dozens of less important thinkers from pre-Socratics up to Existentialism and later. Strong on many European figures usually omitted. Has gone through dozens of editions in Europe. 1966 edition, translated by Stanley Appelbaum and Clarence Strowbridge. xviii + 505pp. 21739-6 Paperbound $2.75

YOGA: A SCIENTIFIC EVALUATION, Kovoor T. Behanan. Scientific but non-technical study of physiological results of yoga exercises; done under auspices of Yale U. Relations to Indian thought, to psychoanalysis, etc. 16 photos. xxiii + 270pp.
20505-3 Paperbound $2.50

Prices subject to change without notice.
Available at your book dealer or write for free catalogue to Dept. GI, Dover Publications, Inc., 180 Varick St., N. Y., N. Y. 10014. Dover publishes more than 150 books each year on science, elementary and advanced mathematics, biology, music, art, literary history, social sciences and other areas.